The Government of Victorian London

The Government of

VICTORIAN LONDON

1855–1889

The Metropolitan Board of Works, the Vestries,

and the City Corporation

•

DAVID OWEN

Edited by Roy MacLeod

with contributions by

David Reeder

Donald Olsen

Francis Sheppard

The Belknap Press

of Harvard University Press

Cambridge, Massachusetts

and London, England

1982

Library of Congress Cataloging in Publication Data

Owen, David Edward.
    The government of Victorian London, 1855–1889.

    Bibliography: p.
    Includes index.
    1. London (England) — Politics and government.
2. London (England) — History — 19th century. 3. Corporation of London
— History — 19th century. 4. London (England). Metropolitan Board of
Works — History — 19th century. I. MacLeod, Roy M. II. Title.

JS3571.095   352.0421   81-7173
ISBN 0-674-35885-6   AACR2

Contents

II. Vestrydom and the City Corporation

Illustrations

Editor's Preface

To several generations of Harvard students, David Owen was known as a teacher of wide vision and gentle humor; by scholars, he will be remembered for his efforts in encouraging many young American historians, including myself, to take up work on Victorian England. Unquestionably, he was better known as a teacher than as an author. Nevertheless, as John Clive recalls in his Foreword, Owen's rich service to scholarship was not limited to his one major book, *English Philanthropy,* published in 1964. In the decade preceding his death in 1968, Owen's research focused on the history of Victorian London. In 1960 and in 1964–65, he spent two long visits to England working at the British Museum Newspaper Library, Colindale, and at the Greater London Record Office in County Hall, to which he returned at least once in 1967. The present book is the result. As ever, his research nourished his teaching. His popular graduate course at Harvard — History 242 — was, in the last year of his life, especially devoted to municipal history, and several essays by his graduate students testify to his enthusiasm for the subject.

On David Owen's death, the greater part of this book existed in first draft. In many places the draft showed evident signs of haste, but it is a tribute to Owen's determination that, despite ill health, so much of the book reached this stage. Some two years following his death, by agreement with Mrs. David Owen and Mrs. Robert Shenton, I undertook to edit and correct where necessary that part of the text which was in fairly good form (chiefly chapters 2 through 9, and parts of chapters 10, 11, and 12), adding from Owen's notes and supplementary sources information which one would reasonably have expected Owen himself to have included in a finished product, but altering as little as possible his prose and presentation. Those chapters in part II that were planned but unwritten presented a different problem, which Francis Sheppard undertook to solve. This he did by writing chapters 13 and 15 and completing chapter 14. At the same time, H. J. Dyos of Leicester University, an honored figure in the field of English urban history, agreed to write an introductory essay on London, a chapter on the City, and a concluding historiographical guide to further research. When Professor Dyos's death in 1978 robbed us of a valued friend and an essential contribution, his close colleague, David Reeder, volunteered to write the conclusion and to help me prepare a comprehensive bibliography on London's Victorian history. In the meantime, Dr. Sheppard completed chapter 11 and edited chapters 10 and 12. The task of contributing a general introduction to Victorian London fell lightly upon Donald Olsen, who, despite short notice, has captured in his essay an exhilarating sense of David Owen's London which few would wish to qualify. Subsequently, a more specific introduction to the mid-Victorian "crisis" in London's government (appearing as chapter 1) was added by Francis Sheppard.

During these several years of preparation and revision, my colleagues and I have been encouraged by the kindness of John Clive, with whom we shared the privilege of completing and seeing into print the work of a distinguished teacher and friend. Many others since 1970 have joined with us in making this tribute. We would like especially to acknowledge the help of Miss Eileen Cobb of the Greater London Record Office; Miss G. Johnson, formerly Borough Librarian, London Borough of Southwark, and her colleague, Miss M. Boast; and Mr. Stanley Tongue of the library of the London Borough of Hackney, who read part of the text. By permission of Mrs. David Owen and by courtesy of the Librarian of the Greater London Council, Owen's original typescripts, together with several hundred note cards, have been deposited in the Library at County Hall, where they will provide future students with essential threads to the maze of metropolitan London. We are also grateful to Miss Anne Cosh and Miss Irene Orgill, who helped with the bibliography; Miss Elizabeth Jones and Miss Jane Matthews, who typed part I of the manuscript; and Miss K. Hill and Mrs. B. Crawford, who typed part II. My personal thanks also go to Kay MacLeod, who patiently helped me unravel the *arcana theatri* of London's administrative history.

Lewes, Sussex   Roy MacLeod
Thanksgiving 1981

Foreword
by
John Clive

I first became acquainted with David Owen when I took his graduate history seminar in the fall of 1946. The topic I proposed for my seminar paper was Disraeli's novels, a proposal he kindly but firmly rejected. "Why don't you work on something that will get you into the parliamentary papers," he asked, "say, the Poor Law Amendment Act of 1834?" The last thing I wanted to do was to plunge into what I assumed must be a dreary and depressing subject. Owen sensed my mood. "Cheer up," he said, with that slight stammer which lent his speech such special impact and authority. "You'll be reading the London *Times* as well. You'll enjoy it." Of course, he was right. I shall always be grateful to him for having steered me on to a subject that not only taught me something about the use of primary sources in what was to be my main period of interest but also introduced me to some of the major problems in nineteenth-century English social history.

The whole incident was characteristic of Owen as a teacher of graduate students. He knew what they needed to learn most; and he made them feel that learning it would be a pleasure as well as a dutifully performed task. What I did not know at the time that Owen suggested the new poor law — or, as the subject turned out, opposition to the new poor law — as a seminar topic was that he himself had completed in draft a biography of John Fielden of Todmorden, the cotton factory owner and radical M.P. who had been among the leaders of the fight against ending outdoor relief in Lancashire. I was not the only one who, some years later, tried to persuade Owen to publish his work on Fielden. But it did not meet his own highest standards; and that was that. Owen could be as hard on himself as he was on his graduate students. One of his favorite critical comments on oral seminar reports revealed his love of baseball as much as his critical acumen: "Good fielding. Few hits."

But it was as an undergraduate teacher, of the ever popular survey course on nineteenth- and twentieth-century British history, that Owen won and retained widespread renown among generations of Harvard and Radcliffe students. In his book on English philanthropy, Owen was to credit Charles Loch of the Charity Organisation Society with some of the gifts of the skillful university lecturer: "He knew the tricks of organization and emphasis that make a lecture effective, and he could put his case, even when arguable, in a fresh and arresting fashion." He himself possessed those gifts in abundance, and he added to them a talent for drama and mimicry that helped to make his course the most entertaining show in Cambridge. His "Crystal Palace" lecture, on the Great Exhibition of 1851, illustrated by appropriate slides, he himself came to regard, in his customary self-deprecating manner, as a "parlor trick." But it is still remembered by thousands as a brilliant recreation of the spirit of an age. And few who heard it will ever forget his stentorian reading of William Cobbett's letter to Henry Hunt, with its climactic "No bankers. No squeaking Wynnes. No Wilberforces. Think of that! No Wilberforces!" or his vivid impersonations of "Thimble" and "Betsy" in the same author's anti-Malthusian play.

But it would be quite wrong to convey the impression that Owen's lectures on nineteenth-century England can be adequately characterized as a series of music hall turns interspersed with the presentation of historical facts. For him wit and anecdote never existed for their own or the lecturer's sake, but solely to reinforce his principal aim in all his teaching: to bring students closer to the actual views and thoughts and habits of nineteenth-century Englishmen and women.

There is no doubt that David Owen admired the Victorians and the way in which they had managed, on the whole, to cope with the problems posed by industrialization and a rapidly expanding society. If his historical sympathies rarely remained untempered by irony, that goes to show that, as all good historians should, he possessed empathy and skepticism in more or less equal proportions. In addition, he had the rare knack of conveying infectious enthusiasm for the subjects he talked about. I know of a Radcliffe graduate who persuaded her mother to join her in a detour to Blackpool because she was haunted by a passing reference Owen had made to that luminous Lancashire resort in one of his lectures.

His lectures were never published. But those who want to savor Owen's wit at its best may do so by reading his plea "On Behalf of Scrooge," first delivered to the Signet Society at Harvard and subsequently published in the *Harvard Alumni Bulletin* (23 December 1968). Here Owen sees Ebenezer as a prophet vindicated, someone who "could detect an avalanche when it was merely a little snowslide. Christmas at the Cratchits' may have been harmless and jolly enough, but it was the beginning of the road that would lead to the Office Party." What struck Scrooge's creator as unnatural and misanthropic in his character seems to Owen merely sensible: "To Dickens, preferring to sit on the sidelines while parlor games were in progress was the sign of a perverse taste. To others it implies ordinary intelligence. Though there is no evidence that Ebenezer was acquainted with hymnology, he would probably have chosen, as his favorite Christmas Carol, the lines, 'Peace, perfect peace, with loved ones far away.' " Owen continued his defense of Scrooge in this same vein, but even in the course of his lighthearted after-dinner speech Owen the historian is never entirely obscured by Owen the raconteur. Not only does he give his listeners (and readers) a painlessly informative history of the origins and subsequent inflation of the Victorian Christmas revels. He also points out that in looking back to categorize the average Victorian one must beware of oversimplification. The Victorian-in-the-street managed, for example, to be at the same time a utilitarian and a romantic; and "the old-fashioned Christmas, an admirable symbol of that fusion, offered the prospect not merely of profits but of profits edged with tinsel and festooned with holly."

This ability to recognize complexity of motive and character, to accept the possibility of apparently contradictory qualities existing side by side, also marks Owen's treatment of the Victorians in his monumental work, *English Philanthropy, 1660–1960,* published by the Belknap Press of Harvard University Press in 1964. In that book Owen set himself as ambitious a theme as any historian of the period has ever tackled—no less than the history of transition from voluntary charitable effort in the seventeenth and eighteenth centuries to the triumph of the welfare state in the twentieth. The book is a storehouse of learning, beautifully organized and clearly and cogently presented. It still remains the standard work on the subject. And for those who are curious about David Owen's historical approach to nineteenth-century England, the chapters on the Victorians prove to be particularly illuminating.

Just as in his lectures to undergraduates, Owen's principal aim remained that of trying to see the period from the inside; of avoiding, as far as possible, the temptation to establish simple categories and distinctions; of bringing sympathy and understanding without losing critical perspective. The Victorians, Owen knew well, engaged in philanthropy for a variety of reasons: compassion for their fellows, the promptings of religion, concern for the stability of their society, social pressures, or their own special ambitions and predilections. Thus, in presenting us with seven biographical sketches, in "A Gallery of Victorian Philanthropists" (chapter 15), he tells us that a major purpose of such an excursion into the byways of biography is to illustrate some of the varieties of the philanthropic impulse — ranging from religious commitment through humanitarianism, social idealism, civic patriotism, and personal satisfaction to "an undeniable, though not necessarily ignoble, desire for self-perpetuation."

British philanthropists, whether early or late in the Victorian age, turn out to be "remarkably resistant to generalization." This does not mean, as readers of *English Philanthropy* can attest, that the historian is necessarily left with a chaotic tangle of special cases. The principal difference between nineteenth- and twentieth-century attitudes to private charity and public action is clear enough. The Victorian ethos ascribed such evils as poverty, destitution, and unemployment to individual inadequacies rather than to general failures of society. Social problems lay in the moral realm; they were personal and exceptional. The main responsibility for social welfare lay with voluntary agencies. The function of the state was largely supplementary. By the time of the First World War, an important change in outlook had occurred. Increasingly, the state was expected to intervene in the alleviation of social evils. Voluntary organizations and private charity were not enough. But the ever greater intervention of government extended rather than reversed the long tradition in Britain of voluntary effort. True, some time before 1914, the historian of philanthropy realizes that he has "been carried outside his proper sphere and has become, by imperceptible degrees, the chronicler of a public service." Yet even as late as the 1960s the welfare state "depend[ed], in an extraordinary degree, on voluntary resources, human and financial."

That, briefly stated, is the thesis of Owen's Victorian chapters. But merely to summarize them in this way does not do justice to them. It does not do justice, in particular, to Owen's tone — skeptical yet tolerant, often wryly amused, always unmistakably his own: Some Victorian hospitals "may have killed as many as they cured." Newspaper ownership "may well be regarded as a highly peripheral philanthropy." As a motive for charity, antipathy to relatives may be said to have been "an unappealing, but by no means unknown auxiliary of good works." Owen clearly believed that history should give pleasure as well as instruction.

He died in 1968. By that time he had finished the greater part of his book on the Metropolitan Board of Works, the last of his contributions to Victorian history. Its publication now will reinforce the judgment that its author's name will retain high rank for some time to come among the leading American historians of the period. Furthermore, its very existence is tangible proof of the loyalty and devotion Owen inspired. Those who gave so unstintingly of their time and labor in the course of preparing his manuscript for publication — Roy and Kay MacLeod, Francis Sheppard, David Reeder, and Donald Olsen — did so for no other reason than that of doing honor to his memory. Little did they know, when the project got under way, that their revisions and additions would in turn have to serve as a posthumous tribute to yet another fine scholar and unforgettable human being, H. J. Dyos, who, from the start, shared with Roy MacLeod, himself a former student of David Owen's, a faith in the importance of completing this unfinished work. We know that Jim Dyos would have shared our pleasure in seeing this book appear.

The Government of Victorian London

Introduction: Victorian London

by
Donald J. Olsen

It is hard to resist the temptation to reproach the past for its misdeeds and blunders. Whether we are dealing with Louis XVI or the drafters of the Treaty of Versailles or the captain of the *Titanic,* we are prone to think that we could have made a better job of it. High on the list of those who ought to have known better are the governors of Victorian London. More precisely, we vent our irritation at those who ought to have governed the Metropolis but failed, permitting it to grow into the monster it became. The worldwide phenomenon of urban decay of the late twentieth century, which might make us more charitable, in practice makes us less, since so many of the evils of our own cities seem to stem from the sins of their Victorian makers and administrators.

It is hard to resist this temptation, but of course we must, or do violence to our standing as historians. David Owen certainly did, and in scrutinizing the operations of the Metropolitan Board of Works (MBW) and its related bodies he drew on the imaginative insight that characterized all of his work. He knew that hindsight, always a dangerous guide, was especially misleading for the London historian.

While it is easy to perceive that the combination of overlapping parochial and ad hoc authorities that failed to cope with the problems of the early Victorian metropolis was the wrong answer, it is less easy to say what the right one would have been. We are still tinkering with municipal and regional bodies trying to find one that will deal ade-

1

quately with the problems of our own cities, problems that are made worse by their refusal to stand still. Thus we impose solutions appropriate to the 1950s (or even earlier) on the city of today. Our abysmal failure to stop the rot that has attacked the modern city ought to make us approach sympathetically, as Owen did, the frequently bumbling efforts of the MBW, the City, and the vestries to administer a metropolis which even then may have been not merely "ungoverned" but ungovernable.

Today we are asking the same fundamental questions that Londoners did in the 1850s. What services are to be provided for our cities? By what kind of body or bodies: private or public, centralized or local, democratically elected or appointed? How are these services to be paid for: by the beneficiaries individually, by property owners, by householders, by residents at large, by profit-making activities of the municipality, by the central government? The recent experiences of New York and Cleveland may well prefigure crises that will force other great cities—and not just in the United States—to reexamine priorities, question basic assumptions, and decide how far the functions hitherto performed by municipalities ought to be transferred to other bodies, how far they need to be performed at all.

Today the megalopolis is a worldwide phenomenon, and the spectacle of uncontrolled growth exhibited by Tokyo and Calcutta, São Paulo and Mexico City gives the New Yorker or Londoner the comfort of knowing that his miseries are widely shared. But for the Londoner of 1855, experience offered no guide, history no parallels. Victorian London was not only unique but unprecedented. If there were in the future to be many cities comparable to early Victorian London, there had been no such in the past. The Prince Regent and John Nash had thought Augustan Rome an appropriate model, and Pugin and Ruskin could (like Lewis Mumford today) hold forth an idealized vision of the Medieval City as another, but neither offered any immediately practical solutions to the challenges posed by the burgeoning Metropolis.

Victoria's London inevitably shared many of its qualities with other nineteenth-century cities, but the peculiar mixture of those qualities, together with its unmatched size, gave it then a preeminence that it has since lost, and an incomparability that was even more striking then than it is today. The frequently expressed assertion that London was different in kind, not simply a larger Manchester or Norwich, was often used to justify the perpetuation of corrupt abuses, but it was also profoundly true.

As well as being the largest, London was undeniably the wealthiest city in the world. And although that wealth was in large part based on Britain's being the first country to experience an industrial revolution,

London was itself not, in any ordinary sense, an "industrial city." It had had many of the attributes and faced many of the problems of the modern metropolis by the mid-eighteenth century, and was not to be directly affected by the Industrial Revolution to any considerable extent until the twentieth century.

London had always been an important manufacturing center, but most of its industries remained organized along essentially medieval lines throughout the nineteenth century, with the small-scale workshop employing well-organized, skilled craftsmen the norm. With some exceptions—as, for example, brewing, which had revolutionized both its technology and its scale of operations by the end of the eighteenth century—factories and mass production waited for Ford to come to Dagenham and Quaker Oats to Southall. Much of the money that flowed into the banks and insurance offices that contributed so much to the wealth and expansion of early Victorian London came from the new manufacturing centers of the north, but much came from agriculture, commerce, overseas investments, and manufacturing industry unaffected by the new technology.

Although contemporary writers were forever remarking on the sharp contrasts between the extremes of wealth and poverty to be found in London, it was in fact even more remarkable for the substantial majority of its inhabitants who were neither rich nor poor. Compared to a Sheffield or a Leeds or a Newcastle, London's population contained a disproportionately large body of *rentiers*, white-collar workers, artisans, and people in the service industries—an even larger proportion in the early Victorian than in the late Georgian period. From the skilled artisans through the growing army of clerks in the City office blocks to the business and professional men whose families occupied the terraces and squares of Bloomsbury, Bayswater, and Kensington, and the villas of Hampstead, Clapham, and the endless stretches of outer suburbia extending into Middlesex, Essex, Surrey, and Kent, most Londoners were far from destitute, yet less than affluent.

Although there were a few private palaces—such as Devonshire House, Lancaster House, and Apsley House—most even of the high aristocracy were content with a substantial terrace house in St. James's, Grosvenor, or Belgrave Square, reserving ostentatious display for their country seats. Even monarchy lived in a comparatively subdued manner. For although Buckingham Palace, in its successive reconstructions, cannot be regarded as a modest town residence, it would have been considered mean and inadequate by a Habsburg, a Romanov, or a Hohenzollern. The Queen, in any event, did not think of London as her principal residence, much preferring Windsor, Osborne, and Balmoral.

London, though dating from the Roman conquest, had the appearance of a comparatively new city. The Great Fire of 1666 had not only required the rebuilding of the greater part of the historic City within the walls, but had precipitated immense suburban developments, most notably in the fields that separated the City of London from the City of Westminster. A series of building acts, designed in particular to prevent the recurrence of a general conflagration, imposed a uniform and increasingly austere architectural style on the rebuilt City and its new suburbs alike. Neoclassical taste and the estate plans of London's great ground landlords brought to its newer extensions wide, straight streets lined with terraces of externally uniform houses. As in all other contemporary European cities, the major, imposing residential streets often concealed narrow back courts, mews, and passages containing insubstantial, badly constructed, ill-drained, severely overcrowded buildings; but outwardly London presented an appearance of newness, regularity, and, to the post-Romantic eye, intolerable dullness.

London was even larger in area than its great population would have led one to expect, for despite the many overcrowded quarters it was—by European standards—a low-density city, with the single-family house (not necessarily occupied as such) the norm. A variety of reasons, notably the abundance of cheap building land on the outskirts, lessened the density of population still further as the century progressed, and encouraged the development of neighborhoods of detached and semidetached villas, each with its private garden, in the suburbs.

Suburbanization was no new phenomenon. Bloomsbury Square offered a suburban retreat in the 1660s; Hackney, Hampstead, and Hammersmith were only three among many surrounding villages that attracted a significant commuting population in the eighteenth century. Isolated merchants' villas dotted the Essex and Middlesex countryside, and rows of terraces lined the roads linking Surrey and Kent with the Thames bridges long before 1837. The early years of the nineteenth century even saw the prototype of what was to become the nearly universal domestic environment for the English middle classes in the detached and semidetached villas of St. John's Wood. But not until the 1830s did villa suburbia change from a retreat for the eccentric or adventuresome to a ubiquitous mass-produced commodity.

Structurally, London was overwhelmingly brick, unlike the wooden cities of Scandinavia and Russia or the stone cities of France and Italy. The brick was, since the early decades of the century, more and more likely to be masked by a stucco facing. Despite the constructional requirements of the building acts, contemporaries were always pointing to the "flimsy" qualities of London buildings as compared with the substantial dwellings of Paris, designed to endure for centuries.

Flimsiness of construction was commonly, though mistakenly, attributed to another feature of London: the prevalence of leasehold as distinct from freehold tenure. Such a practice, combined with the concentration of landownership in the hands of a few ground landlords, enabled those landowners — the Marquess (later Duke) of Westminster, the Duke of Bedford, the Duke of Portland (later Lord Howard de Walden), the Crown, the Bishop of London, the Foundling Hospital, Viscount Portman, the Earl of Northampton, Lord Cadogan, among others — to exercise a degree of comprehensive, continuing, and on the whole beneficent control over their respective estates, so as to provide Stuart, Georgian, and Victorian London alike with some examples of sophisticated town planning. The degree both of sophistication and success of that planning varied from estate to estate, but in general the more attractive the district, the more likely it was to form a part of a large leasehold estate.

Just as the landed estates provided many of the services that would later be offered by political bodies, so other private organizations made up, in part, for the narrow scope and scattered nature of public agencies before the Metropolis Local Management Act of 1855. Water was supplied to the ground floors of houses in the principal streets by a number of private companies, of which the New River Company, serving much of London west of the City and north of the Thames, is perhaps the best known. Gas, both for street and domestic lighting, was also produced by a number of private companies. Education was provided by a vast if insufficient number of endowed and unendowed, charitable and fee-paying, Anglican and Nonconformist schools. These were supplemented after 1870 by the Board Schools called for by the Education Act of that year, but for the most part schooling was private and voluntary rather than uniform and comprehensive. Mass transportation was made available by the private operators of steamboats plying the River Thames, omnibuses and (from the 1870s) trams traversing the major thoroughfares, and urban and suburban railways. The trains of the Metropolitan and Metropolitan District railways offered, from the 1860s, the first underground services in the world.

The horses pulling the omnibuses and trams, the coal-burning locomotives hauling the underground and overground trains all contributed to making London even more dirty and malodorous than it would otherwise have been. For although English visitors found the stench of Napoleon III's Paris (which lacked a water-borne system of waste disposal) far worse, London, with its tens of thousands of open coal fires and its damp and overcast weather, was a smokier, grimier, and visually more dismal city than any of its Continental contemporaries. Whatever the underlying realities, London *looked* dirtier than comparable European cities. Even at the end of the century a patriotic Londoner could boast: "London is beyond comparison the dirtiest capital in the world . . . London is a sanitary place, well-drained, with a low death-rate . . . But, wholesome or not, it remains filthy — dusty, muddy, sooty, smoky, evil-smelling, sunless at noonday — filthy beyond the filthiness of the rottenest plague-spot in the East. It is the first thing that the arriving foreigner observes, the last thing that the returning Londoner forgets."[1]

London was architecturally as well as atmospherically drab. If Victorian Britain was unquestionably the greatest world power, that power found little visual expression in its capital. To the uninstructed visitor to Paris or Berlin, Vienna or St. Petersburg, each would seem to head a far more formidable state than did London. London notably lacked imposing public buildings and impressive open spaces. Trafalgar Square, under completion when Victoria came to the throne, struck Victorians as being rendered mildly ridiculous by the National Gallery along its northern side, while Whitehall only came gradually to acquire its present succession of impressive public structures. Until the new Houses of Parliament were completed in the 1850s, official London had only Inigo Jones's Banqueting Hall, Sir William Chambers's Somerset House, and William Kent's Horse Guards to symbolize the wealth and power of the Empire.

Nor at the start of Victoria's reign did London's commercial preeminence have commensurate architectural expression. True, there was Sir John Soane's Bank of England, and opposite, George Dance's Mansion House for the Lord Mayor's residence. But the present Royal Exchange was not to appear until 1844, and banks and insurance companies of world importance still operated from converted private houses along narrow City streets. By the 1850s that situation was changing rapidly, and the City would by the 1870s have achieved a collection of suitably grand commercial buildings.

The progressive improvements in public transportation during Victoria's reign were never quite able to keep up with the expanding demands for movement of goods and people from one part of the metropolis to another. Traffic congestion posed a continuous challenge, and if temporarily alleviated, was never materially lessened.

A visitor to London at the time of the coronation of the young Queen would have been struck by the paradoxical fact that whereas the quiet residential streets were broad and straight, the busy commerical streets and major thoroughfares were likely to be narrow, irregular, and crooked. And to prevent the former from losing their secluded character, they frequently were guarded by gates and gatekeepers to turn away commercial and heavy traffic. The present line of Fleet Street and the Strand connected the City with Charing Cross and Whitehall, but frequent bottlenecks, such as the one at Temple Bar near the foot of Chancery Lane, another between St. Clement Danes and St. Mary-le-Strand, and yet another at Charing Cross itself, limited its value as a through highway. Yet for all its disadvantages, it provided the only practical route westward, for Holborn Viaduct was not to be built until 1870, and Holborn Hill offered only a slow and painful ascent out of the Fleet Valley. And in any event New Oxford Street had not yet been completed as the link between Holborn and Oxford Street. The Pentonville Road–Euston Road–Marylebone Road link to the west had existed as the New Road from Paddington to Islington since its construction in the 1750s and provided the route for London's first omnibus service, connecting Paddington with the Bank, in 1829; but it lay too far to the north of centers of business and population to be a serious alternative to the Fleet Street–Strand route. Nor did any portion of the Queen Victoria Street–Victoria Embankment–Northumberland Avenue route exist. As for north-south thoroughfares, only Regent Street and Bond Street existed to the west, with Drury Lane and Chancery Lane to the east. Park Lane was literally a lane, of no importance for through traffic. Such crucial thoroughfares as Charing Cross Road, Shaftesbury Avenue, and Victoria Street lay far in the future.

South of the river the situation was more like today's, since the long straight roads extending the lines of Blackfriars, Waterloo, and Westminster bridges had been built at the time the bridges themselves were constructed in the 1750s and 1810s. But if London was better provided with broad streets than cities like pre-Haussmann Paris, in relation to its rapidly growing population and scale of economic activity, its communications were still grossly inadequate.

For whatever combination of reasons — the sublime self-confidence, bordering on arrogance, of the Victorians, a disinclination to spend money on display that might otherwise go into productive capital investment, a genuine aversion to the monumental, or a reluctance to subject individual builders to stringent architectural controls — London took a path markedly different from that of the great Continental capitals in the nineteenth century. The frequent boast that the outward disorder of London represented English freedom and individualism as effectively as the outward splendor of Vienna, Berlin, or St. Petersburg represented foreign slavery may have been somewhat glib; yet it did express a certain truth. All cities, but capital cities especially, can be seen as statements of what their rulers and owners regard as important, or at least of what they want the world to think they so regard. London, both in what it contained and what it lacked, mirrored the Victorian mind and the Victorian conscience.

The persistence of the single-family house as the standard residential unit (in outward appearance at least), the self-effacing exteriors of most of the urban dwellings of the rich and powerful, the conspicuous absence of expressions of monarchical power, the emphasis on private rather than public patronage, the preference for practical solutions to such problems as sanitation and traffic over projects of more strictly aesthetic or ideological significance, all contributed to the uniqueness of London. It did not, like Berlin, have to prove that it was a real, imperial capital; it did not, like St. Petersburg, have to prove that it was western and modern; it did not, like Vienna, have to overawe the diverse elements in a multinational empire; it did not, like Rome, have to lend legitimacy to a newly united nation; it did not, like Washington, have to demonstrate that it presided over a united and civilized people. Victorian London did not have to prove anything. Rather than a conscious statement of its rulers, it was the unconscious expression of the values and preoccupations of its inhabitants.

Yet it would be wrong to see Victorian London as having been created in a fit of absence of mind. Its unassertive character was to a great extent deliberate, the result of a decision not to proceed with pre-Victorian policies that might have made it much less unlike St. Petersburg, Vienna, or Paris than it in fact became. The failure of the Victorians to make their metropolis the outward representation of national power and imperial purpose came from their disenchantment with an earlier attempt to do just that. And that disenchantment accounts in large part for a central fact about Victorian London: that it was Victorian, different in kind from the London of the preceding generation.

That generation had hoped to transform London into a capital worthy of the victors of Waterloo. The London of the early 1820s seemed to thoughtful contemporaries to be entering a Golden Age, with George IV its Augustus. The new king, exclaimed one publication in 1823, "while he has sustained the national honour abroad . . . has done more to patronize literature, to advance the fine arts, and to improve the metropolis, than any sovereign that ever wielded the British sceptre . . . we may anticipate that England will continue to be the first country, and London the first city of the world."[2] In the same year another writer saw "the vast and magnificent improvements which the British metropolis now offers to the observation of an admiring world" as commensurate in importance with British achievements in every realm:

When I gaze on this mighty metropolis, so rapidly augmenting in size and grandeur; when I recollect the high moral and military character which your arms attained in the last war; when . . . I find that while the Duke of Wellington triumphed in the field, Dr. Jenner and Sir Humphry Davy were immortalizing both themselves and Great Britain by discoveries for which they will receive the blessings of ages yet unborn; and that Crabbe, Moore, Scott, and Byron, after raising the poetical fame of their country, still . . . promise to carry higher their own and England's reputation; and that in the fine arts . . . more may yet be expected from the pencil of Lawrence, and the chisel of Chantrey . . . I am compelled . . . to acknowledge that you are rapidly approaching the goal of national greatness; and . . . that history will dedicate one of its most interesting, and most brilliant, pages to the regency and reign of George IV.[3]

Even bearing in mind that William Cobbett, for one, was saying far less complimentary things about London during the same period, one cannot help being struck by the quantity of both literary an monumental evidence that London was in the early 1820s an object of pride and a symbol of national greatness.

Much of what even today lends London a degree of magnificence dates either in execution or conception from the time of George IV. Long before Napoleon III and Baron Haussmann imposed their vision of order and splendor on Paris, the Prince Regent and John Nash gave London its only boulevard in the form of the original Regent Street. Intended to link two royal palaces, the existing Carlton House and a new pleasure pavilion in Regent's Park, it combined the functions of a triumphal way with that of a street devoted to the luxury retail trade, where the elegant frivolities of shopping and promenading could take place against a background of architectural grandeur never equaled before or since in London. Regent's Park itself was in its original conception to have been a secluded garden suburb for the very rich, with fifty palatial villas, each screened from the others by the foliage of the park. The whole was to be dominated by the new palace and what Sir John Summerson has called a "National Valhalla,"[4] described by Nash as "a public building to receive the statues and monuments of great and distinguished men . . . the dome of such a building would rise above the houses, and form the grandest apex possible to the whole scenery."[5]

Nash planned Trafalgar Square as an integral part of the Regent Street improvements. He also prepared plans for a second grand artery to connect Trafalgar Square with the new British Museum, whose present buildings were begun in 1823.[6] There were other proposals put

forth, for such ambitious follies as an artificial island in the Thames, between Waterloo and Westminster Bridge, to support something like the
Nelson Column.[7] Private landowners great and small vied with the
Crown Commissioners of Woods and Forests in schemes of urban magnificence.

Between 1825 and 1837 all this came to an end. London experienced a
crisis of conscience, one that changed the social, aesthetic, and economic
values of those whose wishes and actions determined the ways in which it
grew. The impact of that revolution was not immediately obvious. Not
only was the London of George IV still unmistakably there in 1837, but
it continued to stand, more or less intact, for the rest of the century, an
object of shame in the eyes of aesthetes and sanitary reformers and increasingly in the eyes of ordinary Londoners as well. Cities and buildings, however flimsily built, soon outlive their brief moment of newness
and fashion, and are usually destroyed just about the time when their
virtues are being belatedly rediscovered. Even the suburban extensions
of London built in the decades following 1825 represented to a great extent the realization of the ambitious schemes set forth in the building
agreements of that year. Finally, the cautious conservatism of the building industry kept it putting up modified versions of late Georgian housing long after advanced architectural opinion had rejected the old "rule
of taste."

The new seriousness of the Gothic Revival, as expressed by Pugin and
Ruskin and the Ecclesiologists, was perhaps less remarkable than what
happened within the Classic itself: the move from Roman or Greek to
Italianate forms, and what to later eyes appeared as a willful coarsening
of detail, wrongly accounted for as representing the uneducated taste of
the nouveaux riches. Architecture adopted a more emphatic and asser-
tive quality, with window dressings, porticoes, and other structural and
ornamental features more deeply incised, more protruding, bigger,
everywhere more visible, more unmistakably themselves. Priscilla Metcalf describes what happened:

Critics who had complained that the "faint projections" of classical mouldings
"seldom produce any effect in this climate" welcomed Barry's heavily corniced
new clubs in Pall Mall [the Travellers' Club (1832) and the adjacent Reform
Club (1840)] for combining "boldness of effect with richness of detail" . . . By
1840, public taste preferred what Pooh-Bah was to call corroborative detail, if
only a set of stucco window-frames, for conferring artistic verisimilitude upon
otherwise bald and unconvincing structures.[8]

Ruskin and Pugin and Morris were only the most articulate exponents
of the new conviction that architecture was no mere arrangement of

shapes and masses, but the concrete embodiment of a system of ethics and a teacher of morality. Ruskin's proposals for a new India Office — set forth in *The Seven Lamps of Architecture* in 1849 but never put into effect — give some indication of how explicit the sermons in stone were intended to be: "Let us imagine our own India House adorned . . . by historical or symbolical sculpture . . . chased with bas-reliefs of our Indian battles, and fretted with carvings of Oriental foliage, or inlaid with Oriental stones; and the more important members of its decoration composed of groups of Indian life and landscape, and prominently expressing the phantasms of Hindoo worship in their subjection to the Cross. Would not one such work be better than a thousand histories?"[9]

Even more significant than the change in the outward appearance of buildings was the change in layout and density in the new suburbs: no longer mere expansions of existing villages or ribbon developments along main roads, but rather whole, coherent speculative estates of detached and semidetached villas.

If the physical transformation of London took decades to effect, the psychological revolution happened with remarkable suddenness. The way in which people regarded London changed completely and permanently during the decade following 1825. London turned from being an object of pride to an object of shame, from a symbol of wealth to a symbol of poverty, from a vision of health to a vision of disease, from one of light to one of darkness. Two explanations suggest themselves: the cholera epidemic of 1832 and the fall in land values that resulted from the collapse of the speculative boom in 1825.

Although London had had fluctuations in its mortality rate and although that rate had been generally high even by eighteenth-century standards, it had not experienced since 1665 any single, dramatic, killing epidemic that affected the public consciousness as strongly as the coming of the cholera in February 1832. The remarkable thing was not so much the number of deaths — 5,300 in 1832 and 1,500 the following year — as the unexpectedness of the epidemic, its unpredictability, and the swiftness with which death came to the afflicted. It is usually regarded, quite correctly, as providing the impetus for the whole movement of sanitary reform that, for all its agonizing slowness of execution, proved ultimately one of the most admirable achievements of the Victorian period. But it was equally significant as providing the shock that contributed most to the changed perception of London. Late Georgian London — rightly or wrongly — was perceived as clean and healthy; early Victorian London was at the time — and still is — *perceived* as being dirty and deadly. That its mortality rates were on the whole lower, and its sanitary standards higher, than those of most Continental cities of the period did little to alter the image. Dickens reinforced the false perception by imposing his brilliant but perverse vision of London on the consciousness both of his contemporaries and of posterity.

Leigh's New Picture of London proclaimed in 1818 that "its healthfulness is equal to that of any other metropolis in existence." It attributed the salubrity of modern London to the metropolitan improvements of the previous century, in particular the new wide streets, the "plentiful supply of water which is furnished by the different water companies," and "its system of sewers and drains," as well as to the practical application of new scientific discoveries. "These added to the natural advantages of London, in regard to soil and situation," it boasted, "wholly do away with the unhealthiness and liability to epidemic and other disorders which usually prevail among crowded populations, and which formerly characterized London itself." Even the prevalence of "coal fires, by which the temperature of the air is sensibly ameliorated," meant that London "endures little from damp."[10] Eight years later, John Britton displayed even greater complacency both as to the present and future health of the metropolis:

> With regard to the *diseases* and *proportion of salubrity* usually attaching to London, it is a satisfaction to state generally, that since the complete extinction of the *Plague* by the great fire of 1666, this metropolis has fully deserved to be considered as one of the most healthy on earth; and that, in consequence of the open mode of building that now prevails, its increase to an almost indefinite extent is not likely to be attended with additional unwholesomeness. There are now no diseases that, properly speaking, can be said to be peculiar to London, although in parts, where its buildings are still confined, there exists, as must always be the case in such circumstances, a *predisposition,* among the lower orders at least, to low fever and infectious disorders in general.[11]

Many of such exceptions to "the increase of salubrity, within the last seventy years," he attributed to "the baneful habit of dram-drinking" among "the poorer population."[12]

In *Emma,* first published in 1816, Jane Austen presents as a subject of comedy the conversations between Mr. Woodhouse and his daughter Isabella as to the supposed unhealthfulness of London. She expects her readers to take Mr. Woodhouse's assertion—"Nobody is healthy in London, nobody can be"—as simply one more instance of his valetudinarian imbecility. As for Isabella Knightly, it is very doubtful whether any Victorian novelist would regard the anxieties of a London mother about the putrid sore throats of her offspring as other than rational and laudable.

The water-borne nature of cholera was not to be demonstrated until 1884, and the prevalence of the air-borne theory of disease may have been one more factor in convincing prudent householders that the circulation of air around detached suburban dwellings made them healthier than urban terrace houses. Just as the great middle- and upper-class migration from the City to Bloomsbury, Soho, and St. James's came in part as a reaction to the Great Plague of 1665, perhaps the new middleclass migration to villa suburbia was in part a response to the fear of cholera. (This leaves unexplained, of course, the failure of Parisians, Berliners, and Viennese to respond in like manner to the impact of the disease on their cities.)

The other explanation for the sudden shift from an urban to a suburban ethos in the decade preceding Victoria's accession is the impact of the collapse of the speculative boom in 1825. It brought to an end a mania of land and building speculation that accompanied Nash's projects of urban embellishment, comparable to the speculative fever of the 1960s and early 1970s.

With the fall in the cost of money, building materials, and labor at the close of the Napoleonic Wars, London had experienced a resurgence in speculative building, but it did not become a raging epidemic until the 1820s. In the years just before 1825, and to a remarkable extent in 1825 itself, the building agreements for Belgravia, Pimlico, Tyburnia, and northern Bloomsbury were concluded, on a scale and to a degree of ambitiousness unprecedented in London building history, and never subsequently matched. So vast were the plans, and so far had Thomas Cubitt and lesser promoters overestimated the demand for luxury town houses, that as late as Cubitt's death in 1855 streets and squares he had contracted to build thirty years earlier were not yet entirely finished.

In 1824 even Eton College—the most lethargic of landowners—was contemplating dividing its 230-acre estate north of Regent's Park into no more than seventy-five building plots, of which the smallest would be more than half an acre in size, in expectation of a scale of mansion and class of resident immensely more grand than would ultimately appear on its estate. One thinks of the absurdly unrealistic real-estate developments, fragments of which still loom, the ruins of a dead civilization, from the Florida swamps, dating from the years just before the collapse of its boom in 1926. Pimlico, Bayswater, and Bloomsbury, too, had their rows of unfinished carcasses, waiting for years to be completed as town mansions.

The collapse of the credit market late in 1825 brought such ambitious schemes to an end. Bloomsbury, Tyburnia, and Belgravia were eventually completed to their original specifications, but only after agreements had been renegotiated extending the deadlines for completion and drastically lowering the ground rents to be paid. For one of the consequences of the collapse was a dramatic and permanent fall in the price of building land, not just on the estates affected but throughout England.

The price of undeveloped building land on the outskirts of English towns had roughly tripled between 1740 and 1820.[13] In London it reached a peak in 1825, fell sharply at the end of that year—by more than a third—and remained at that new low level until at least 1939.[14] There were, to be sure, fluctuations in the cost of land "ripe for building," but it was more likely, particularly after 1920, to fall below the level of 1826 than to rise above it.

Undeveloped suburban building land could be had throughout the last three-quarters of the nineteenth century at from £20 to £40 per acre per annum, or from a penny to twopence per square yard; in the case of freehold, calculating at twenty-five years' purchase, this worked out at between £500 and £1,000 per acre. This was equally true of land destined for working-class residential, middle-class residential, and industrial purposes, and applied to provincial towns as well as to London. In the years prior to 1939, land for new suburban building estates could be had for as little as £200 per acre freehold. Once it had been laid out for building, and still more once it had been covered with buildings, the value of any particular plot of ground would tend to rise, and in favored locations to rise enormously. In 1871 the architect Edward I'Anson—who was in a position to know—estimated that the value of land in the City of London had doubled over the previous half century, and in very important sites it had quadrupled.[15] But for more than a century after 1825 undeveloped land at the time it came onto the market remained either stable or falling in price.

As a proportion of the rack-rental value of a house, the original cost of land ordinarily represented something far below 10 percent. For example, villas in Adelaide Road on the Eton College estate renting in 1856 for sixty to eighty pounds per annum paid four pounds ground rent; that is, the cost of the land represented between one-fifteenth and one-twentieth the cost of the house. On the Duke of Norfolk's estate in Sheffield, perhaps a penny to threepence of the three shillings threepence weekly rent of a workingman's cottage represented ground rent. If undeveloped land in England had been free, the effect on the supply and cost of housing would have been minimal. As it was, the abundance of cheap land on the outskirts of all English towns encouraged the low-density development that came to distinguish English urban growth from that prevalent practically everywhere else in Europe.

The collapse of the boom also served as a cautionary reminder of the risks involved in projects of urban improvement. A great many people lost a great deal of money in land and building speculation in 1825. One economic explanation for the replacement of the linked terrace by the detached villa as the normal unit for middle-class housing is that it reduced the risk involved in any building scheme. The whole of a crescent or square would have to be completed before any part of it could be sold at its full value, whereas one or two villas in a semirural setting might, if anything, be more valuable before they became surrounded by similar dwellings. Slow, piecemeal development, disastrous in a neighborhood of squares and terraces, would be a prudent way of proceeding with a district of villas.

For many years after the collapse of 1825, no large-scale speculation that depended on an ever expanding market for magnificent urban residences could hope to attract investors. Private capital grew more cautious about the same time that the reformed House of Commons and the new, democratically elected vestries were showing greater interest in lower taxes and lower rates than in public splendor. And when building developers grew reckless again — as they did by the 1840s — it was from overoptimism as to the demand for suburban coziness, not urban luxury.

In this book, David Owen shows three conflicts running through the history of Victorian London: (1) between those who maintained that there was one London and those who insisted that there were many; (2) between the proponents of a policy of active public intervention and those whose principal aim was to save money; and (3) between those who argued that London could best be governed by the few and those who supported rule by the many. The three themes — the one or the many, the passion for cheapness, and the impact of democracy — lend structure to the study, and drama to the narrative. Each of the three, in addition, contains a paradox that in turn reveals a central truth about Victorian London.

Was London one or many? Did it possess sufficient common interests, a sufficiently shared character, for it to be governed and administered as a whole? Or was it merely a geographical expression, not a coherent entity in itself? Was London more than the sum of its parts, or were its parts too disparate to subject themselves to a single rule? Here is a theme central to the whole early Victorian political debate between the exponents of localism and the supporters of centralization. The paradox is that although Parliament was ultimately convinced that London was one and not many, the metropolis in fact grew more diverse, more varied, and perhaps more fundamentally ungovernable as the nineteenth century progressed.

The second paradox is that the search for cheapness, however misguided an approach to the sanitary and social needs of the metropolis, recognized an important fact about the Victorian economic achievement: that it depended on falling or at least stable prices, and did that by securing an abundant supply of everything, whether labor, raw materials, investment capital, or land; and that it was the continuing cheapness of all these that enabled the Victorians to find solutions to problems that had eluded every earlier age. The "penny-pinching," "parsimonious" vestries, stubbornly determined to keep rates down—so unlike our municipal authorities today—were at worst displaying an exaggerated concern for economy. If ratepayers and their elected representatives really preferred a lower level of public services to a rise in the cost of local government, their attitude was consistent with the universally accepted axiom that it was in everybody's best interest to keep *all* costs down, whether costs of production, distribution, or of government. In our age, in which economic growth, expanding prosperity, and a more equitable distribution of wealth have been associated with rising costs outweighed by a rising ability to meet those costs, it requires a wrenching effort of the historical imagination to sympathize with an age that sought, successfully, to improve the general quality of life not through rising wages but through falling prices. The Victorians saw the price of government, felt by the individual directly or indirectly through taxes and rates, as a burden to be reduced wherever possible, certainly not one to be increased without overwhelming reasons.

The third paradox is that although the political history of London from 1855 to 1900 saw the growing recognition of the inadequacy and inefficiency of both the vestries and the MBW, leading to the creation of the London County Council (LCC) and the new Metropolitan Boroughs, the history of the MBW throughout its brief life and of the vestries in the latter decades of the century is one of remarkable achievement. In retrospect their corruption seems petty, their delays understandable, and their accomplishments astonishing.

Both the achievements and the inadequacies of the Victorian governors of London stem in large part from their popular character. The apathetic response of the voters left vestry government by default to the few, but those few partook not at all of traditional aristocratic or even oligarchic qualities. And yet the socially inferior, ill-educated, petty-minded vestry membership, and their delegates on the MBW managed, by and large, with whatever delays and false starts, to lay the foundations for much for which the LCC and the Metropolitan Boroughs would later take credit.

Underlying the first two themes, the fact of diversity and the passion for economy, was the genuine cheapness of things in London. That Vic-

torian London itself was characterized by cheapness seems on the surface not merely paradoxical but untrue, if only because contemporaries
were continually and loudly asserting the contrary. They were doing so,
however, not because costs and prices were by any absolute standard
high or unreasonable, but because their expectations of cheapness were
even greater than the realities they saw.

Two things in particular were cheap: new housing and new building
land. The availability of apparently inexhaustible supplies of land selling
from £500 to £1,000 per acre freehold, or to be had at from £20 to £40
per acre per annum leasehold—land which improving means of transport were making increasingly accessible for residential, industrial, and
commercial uses—stimulated metropolitan growth. The extent of that
growth presented the MBW and its successors with continually increasing demands for services spread over a larger and larger area.

Whatever its effect on the cost of utilities, and whatever the social and
aesthetic impact on the surrounding countryside, suburban sprawl was
not without benign consequences. One might even attempt an adapta-
tion of the Turner thesis, with cheap land in the London suburbs playing
a role analogous to that of free land on the American frontier. Whether
or not suburbia acted in fact as a "safety-valve," it certainly relieved
many pressures that a growing population would otherwise have exerted
on the older, built-up portions of the metropolis. For although land
prices and rents in central areas inevitably rose, they rose far less than
they would have done if there had not been cheap land at the outskirts
for those who did not need to live or conduct their business in the high-
cost center.

The effects of the abundance of cheap land and of a highly competitive
building industry eager to cover that land with houses, financed by mas-
sive quantities of investment capital satisfied with a return of no more
than 4 or 5 percent, are everywhere evident in the ways in which London has disposed itself on the ground. Not just the villa suburbs but the
comparatively low density of the districts of small, two-story dwellings
with back gardens for lower-middle-class and artisan occupation reflect a
situation in which land, capital, and labor were cheap and abundant,
and one in which there was every encouragement for their utilization to
produce new rental housing.

Such cheapness and abundance helped make possible structural responses to changing circumstances, whereby buildings, streets, and
whole districts altered their social, economic, and functional characters.
The increasing specialization of neighborhoods, whether for particular
classes of residents, particular trades or industries, or particular services,
gave London a more and more intricate geography. The common notion of the rich congregating in the West End and the poor in the East

End does not begin to describe the complex ecology of Victorian London. Wealth and poverty lay often in close proximity. The new brick and terracotta mansions that sprang up on the Cadogan estate in the 1870s and 1880s were but a street away from the slums that still filled much of Chelsea. Different kinds of poverty characterized different districts, not to speak of different kinds of wealth, although Lady Bracknell's dark reference to the unfashionable side of Belgrave Square may have been an exaggeration. Shopkeepers knew to their cost that it mattered very much whether they were on the east or the west side of Regent Street, the north or the south side of Kensington High Street.

The changing character of individual streets and neighborhoods and the growing diversity of the whole metropolis could only complicate the tasks of the bodies that governed it. Not only did conditions vary from parish to parish but from street to street within any given parish. Tavistock Square and Agar Town were both in St. Pancras; yet in their appearance, social occupation, and sanitary conditions and requirements they were polar opposites. Nash's Regent's Park terraces and the slums of Lisson Grove were both in Marylebone. Along with geographical variation went temporal change, and change that took place with bewildering rapidity in unexpected directions. Meanwhile changing visions of urban virtue, changing notions as to the causes of disease, changing techniques for dealing with sanitation and communication, even changing definitions of the good and (especially) the beautiful were making obsolete or irrelevant the policies pursued by municipal authorities.

The failure of governmental bodies to provide public services did not necessarily mean that such services were not provided at all. Private bodies, both philanthropic and profit-making, in part made up for many of the inadequacies of the public authorities. The great leasehold estates, the railway, water, and gas companies, and the speculative building industry gave London a degree of supervised planning, and provided sanitation, lighting, transport, and cheap housing. Some of these were more successful than others: the railway companies were better at satisfying, even anticipating, the transport needs of London than the water companies at meeting its sanitary requirements. Often what today seems a triumph seemed at the time an evil—railway engineering works, for instance, and the proliferation of low-density districts of cheap suburban housing. The converse is also true: what at the time seemed an improvement may in retrospect appear an unconscionable destruction of London's architectural heritage. But whether judged by Victorian standards or ours, London did ultimately respond with intelligence, ingenuity, and compassion to the demands made on it by the demographic, economic, technological, social, ideological, and political revolutions of the nineteenth century.

What follows is an account of the way in which Londoners, reluctantly but overwhelmingly, became convinced that the centralizers and uni-formitarians were right and the defenders of local autonomy were wrong—that London was one and not many, that rising expenditures for social and sanitary ends were essential, and that public bodies were better suited to meet its needs than private ones. But it also shows that such decisions were not easily reached. The contemporary debate over each new project undertaken by the MBW or one of the vestries ought not to be perceived, Whiggishly, as a conflict between the far-sighted friends of humanity and the blind forces of obstructionism, but as—at least sometimes—a serious inquiry into whether the real losses that would be involved would be exceeded by the real gains the program might achieve. By his comprehensive narrative and analysis of the work-ings of London government from 1855 to 1889, David Owen has en-riched our understanding of the Victorian mind, the political and ad-ministrative process, and the nature of urban growth.

PART I

*The Evolution of
Metropolitan Government*

CHAPTER 1

The Crisis of London's Government

by

Francis Sheppard

The Act of 1855, by which the MBW was established, was a landmark of cardinal importance in the history of London's government. It was the first legislative attempt to tackle the problem of metropolitan administration as a whole, or, at any rate, almost as a whole, for the City was still virtually exempt; and however inadequate its provisions very soon came to be regarded, it was a genuine response to the crises which had recently beset London's sanitary evolution, particularly since 1848.

Of the traumatic events leading up to the establishment of the MBW probably the most crucial was the cholera epidemic of 1832. The advance of this terrible disease, as it spread from its birthplace in India, had been watched in England with increasing foreboding, but despite the long warning little preparation had been made for it. In February 1832 it finally reached London, at Rotherhithe, and during the next few months it killed over five thousand Londoners.

The chaotic state of London's administration would in any case have prevented any effective action being taken, even if the Government itself had given a more vigorous lead. At the center of the whole vast built-up area, the ancient City Corporation reigned supreme over its sacred six hundred acres, its existence and countless privileges confirmed by innumerable royal charters extending over seven centuries. Its time-honored and complicated hierarchy of Lord Mayor, Sheriffs, Court of Aldermen, Court of Common Council, and Court of Common Hall, plus the asso-

23

ciated City Companies or Guilds and the City's four members of Parliament, all conferred immense prestige and influence upon the City Corporation. But ever since the end of the great constitutional struggles of the seventeenth century this prestige and influence had almost invariably been successfully used to defend the status quo, and "no interference from outside" had been the perennial watchword of the Corporation and its allies. Thus, when Sir Robert Peel was planning the establishment of the Metropolitan Police, he had privately confessed that he would "be afraid to meddle" with the City, which was duly exempted from his act of 1829. Similarly, at the time of the Municipal Corporations Act of 1835, by which the government of all the other large cities and boroughs was remodeled, the City Corporation was not included, and although a Royal Commission reported on its workings in 1837, the promised bill to rectify this omission did not materialize.

But the City had also steadfastly refused to enlarge its boundaries and accept responsibility for the new suburbs which had grown up all around it. Here in 1831 lived some one and a half million people (over nine-tenths of the whole population of London), whose local affairs were variously managed or mismanaged by the vestries of over ninety parishes or precincts situated in the three counties of Middlesex, Surrey, and Kent. These vestries or parish assemblies presided over districts of every conceivable size, ranging from the tiny Liberty of the Old Artillery Ground near Bishopsgate, with a population of under fifteen hundred in 1801, to the great parish of St. George's, Hanover Square, inhabited by over sixty thousand people. But they all discharged substantially the same functions, the chief of which were the paving, lighting, and cleaning of the streets, the relief of the poor, and the maintenance of the peace. Apart from the largely nominal oversight exercised by the justices of the peace, the vestries operated unsupervised, and this absence of supervision was reflected in their diverse constitutions. Many of the parish vestries, particularly in the still largely rural areas, were of the "open" variety, where all male ratepayers were entitled to attend the often disorderly meetings. But in the great new suburbs "close" or "select" vestries were more common, and here membership and power were restricted to a group of from thirty to a hundred of the "principal inhabitants," who had usually been originally nominated in a local act of Parliament, and who filled vacancies by making further nominations as they pleased. Many of these select vestries were in the more fashionable western parts of London, such as St. Marylebone or St. George's, Hanover Square; and sometimes the disorderly open assembly of a parish with a rapidly growing population was converted, by an act engineered by the leading inhabitants, into a select vestry. (St. Pancras in 1819 provides a case in point.)

But in the late 1820s select vestries in their turn came under sustained attack, chiefly for their exclusiveness and extravagance, and in 1831 John Cam Hobhouse, one of the radical M.P.'s for Westminster, successfully promoted an act giving all ratepayers in parishes with select vestries a vote in the election of their vestrymen. The act only applied in parishes where a majority of the ratepayers had decided, by a poll, to adopt it; but in London it was duly adopted in five of the largest parishes with select vestries (including St. Pancras), and there a radical reign of the most vigorous and repulsive economy was at once inaugurated.

Most of the labors of the vestries, whether open or select, were performed under powers conferred by their own individual local acts of Parliament. There were also innumerable autonomous paving trusts and commissions, all established by yet more local acts, and responsible (to the exclusion of the local vestry) for paving, cleaning, lighting, and sometimes (prior to 1829) watching the streets of a particular district — an estate, perhaps, or a hamlet, or a single street or even part of a street. And lastly there were the seven independent Commissions of Sewers, whose members were nominated by the Crown; an eighth, responsible for the City, was an offshoot of the Corporation. Until the early nineteenth century, when it acquired its malodorous significance, the word sewer meant a channel for the removal of surface water; and the maintenance of these channels, all of which flowed into the Thames, was the sole function of the various Sewer Commissions. Household sewage was disposed of into cesspools, and in Westminster until 1815, and in some other parts of London until later still, it was a penal offense to discharge such sewage into the Commissioners' channels.

Such, in brief, was the state of London's government at the time of the cholera epidemic of 1832. Outside the City there was, prior to 1855, no administrative authority concerned with the whole area,* and it is therefore not surprising that such great metropolitan improvements as the formation of Regent Street and Trafalgar Square were executed not by any municipal authority but by the Crown, under the auspices of the Commissioners of Woods and Forests, who administered the estates of the Crown and whose First Commissioner was a member of the Government. And this tradition of Crown responsibility for metropolitan improvements — the direct result of the lack of any adequate system of metropolitan government — continued long after the great days of Nash and George IV right into the 1840s, when, as a result of the inquiries of successive parliamentary Select Committees into the mounting conges-

---

*Except, after 1829, that of the Metropolitan Police, and after 1844 of the Office of Metropolitan Buildings, a short-lived and somewhat ineffective body set up in a recodification of the eighteenth-century acts for the control through district surveyors of the construction of buildings.

tion of many parts of London, such thoroughfares as New Oxford Street and Victoria Street, and even Victoria Park, Hackney, were all formed by the Crown acting through the Commissioners of Woods and Forests.

Apart from such improvements as these to the physical fabric of London no other significant legislative measures were taken during at least the two decades prior to 1848 to advance conditions of living in the capital. And these conditions were in fact steadily deteriorating. Between 1831 and 1851 the population rose from 1.6 million to 2.3 million, with a consequent increase of nearly one-third in its overall density, and in the years 1840–1849 the death rate stood at 25.2 per thousand compared with 22.5 for the whole of England. Moreover these general figures concealed the far more terrible incidence of death in poor districts, such as the slums of Church Lane, St. Giles in the Fields, where in the 1840s 310 out of every thousand children died before reaching the age of one, and of every thousand aged one, 457 died before reaching the age of two.

But despite the legislative neglect of the condition of the capital in the 1830s and most of the 1840s, the passing of the Poor Law Amendment Act of 1834 had inaugurated a new era in the history of the public administration of the whole country, although London had to wait for many years for statutory provision to be made for its unique circumstances. The act of 1834 had superseded the haphazard methods of poor relief hitherto practiced by the parish authorities by a central Poor Law Commission, from whose offices at Somerset House in the Strand all the activities of the new local Boards of Guardians of the Poor were to be controlled. The architect of this revolutionary measure was Edwin Chadwick (1800–1890), the friend and disciple of the aged philosopher, Jeremy Bentham. As the salaried secretary of the new central Commission, he largely controlled this formidable new administrative engine in its early years, and soon he became one of the most unpopular men in the whole country, detested alike by the poor and by the vestrymen and local Boards of Guardians for the detailed central direction to which he ruthlessly subjected them.

In 1837–38, during an epidemic of typhus in East London, Chadwick's attention was drawn to expenditure by the local Board of Guardians in prosecuting landlords for neglecting to remove the decaying refuse and stinking pools of sewage in which the disease was thought to breed. The inquiry which he instigated suggested that many of the "Causes of Fever in the Metropolis . . . might be removed by proper sanatory [sic] Measures," the chief of which were to be the construction of drains or sewers to all houses and the provision of a plentiful supply of water to carry away the sewage.

This report provided the blueprint for the mid-nineteenth-century sanitary movement. It was followed by the famous *Inquiry into the Sanitary Condition of the Labouring Population of Great Britain,* published in 1842, and in 1844–45 by the reports of a Royal Commission on *The State of Large Towns and Populous Districts,* all produced under Chadwick's aegis. Although concerned with the whole country, all of these reports contained vast quantities of information about the terrible sanitary state of London; and their evidence challenged every vested interest — landlords, vestries, paving boards, Commissioners of Sewers, and above all, the water companies.

Water was, indeed, a key element in the arterial system of drainage now being promoted everywhere by Chadwick. A plentiful and constantly available water supply piped into all houses would provide the motive power for the removal of domestic sewage by the natural flows within a properly constructed network of sewers; and the resultant liquids would, it was thought, be capable of profitable use as agricultural manure. But the trouble was that London's water supply was grossly deficient in both quantity and quality. The poor obtained their water from the companies' communal cocks in the alleys where they lived, and both here and in houses to which water was piped the supply was only available intermittently, not continuously. Most of the companies drew their water from the Thames between Chelsea and London Bridge, from those very reaches of the river into which the Commissioners of Sewers discharged their drainage. So long as the Commissioners had only been concerned with surface water drainage, and house sewage reposed in cesspools, this arrangement had not been challenged. But when, with the growing use of water closets, both house drains and the overflow pipes from the cesspools were increasingly connected to the common sewers, which discharged into the same stretches of the river as those from which the water companies drew their supplies, widespread pollution became inevitable.

Chadwick proposed to supplement his system in London by a single Crown-appointed Commission which would provide and administer drainage, paving, street cleaning, and of course water. By the mid 1840s there was widespread public concern about sanitary matters, and several bodies, such as the Health of Towns Association (founded in 1844), existed for the diffusion of information on the whole subject. But Chadwick's centralizing ideas were too much for the Government, which in September 1847 established yet another Royal Commission, to inquire "what special means may be requisite for the Health of the Metropolis."

By this time cholera was again known to be advancing from the Orient, and under this terrifying threat the first recommendation of this Royal Commission — that all the seven Crown Commissions of Sewers should be replaced by a single Metropolitan Commission for the whole London area except the City—was at once acted upon; and the City Sewers Commission only survived because it was not a Crown appointment. In 1848 a Public Health Act at last established a three-man General Board of Health, presided over by the First Commissioner of Woods and Forests and equipped with extensive sanitary powers over all the country. The act was only to last for (in effect) six years and did not apply to London; but there was a promise that a similar measure for the capital would follow shortly.

This prospect, which might perhaps have led to a Crown-appointed commission on Chadwickian lines, responsible for the whole gamut of London's drainage, paving, cleansing, and water supply, evoked passionate hostility from the vestries and paving commissioners, from the water companies, and above all from the City Corporation. A violent pamphlet war ensued between the anticentralizers, led by Joshua Toulmin Smith and the champions of local elective sanitary administration on the one hand, and the Health of Towns Association and the supporters of Chadwick's theories of centralized management on the lines of the Poor Law Board on the other. The City Corporation was indeed so alarmed that in order to forestall the Government it hastily promoted a bill of its own for enlarging the powers of its Sewers Commission; and embedded in this act was a clause permitting it, if it so desired, to appoint a Medical Officer of Health.

So by the end of 1848 the lines of battle for the crucial struggles of the ensuing seven years on the field of metropolitan sanitary evolution had been drawn; and the battle itself began in earnest in June 1849, when cholera appeared in the City. By this time the City Commissioners of Sewers (who consisted of the Lord Mayor, Aldermen, and one Common Councilman from each ward), equipped with extensive new powers by its recent new act, had appointed a part-time Medical Officer of Health. This was Dr. (later Sir) John Simon (1816–1904), who was to become the leading figure in the second generation of sanitary reformers. During the eight months between his appointment and the outbreak of cholera in the City he built the framework of an entirely new local medico-sanitary administration. He organized weekly returns of all deaths; and the City police were required to provide him with reports of street nuisances, on the basis of which the four City Inspectors of Nuisances (acting under the Nuisance Removal Acts) enforced the cleansing of privies, the suppression of cesspools, and the removal of dung and excrement. He persuaded the New River Company to supply water twice a day instead of only once; his office became the hub of sanitary action, and he battled with his masters, the City Commissioners of Sewers, many of whom regarded his activities with deep hostility.

Between June and October 1849, when the epidemic was over, more than eight hundred people died of cholera in the City alone. But this terrible fact enabled Simon, in his first annual report to the Corporation (published in November), to expose the full extent of the sanitary problem there. He won the support of a few of the City Sewers Commissioners, and his opponents — known as the "dirty party" — fell back on the defensive. He and the City Medical Officership of Health became famous all over the country.

Meanwhile, Chadwick's new Metropolitan Commission of Sewers had failed abysmally. Chadwick had insisted — probably rightly — that the building of a new system of main drainage could not start until the Ordnance Survey had made detailed maps. In the whole of London some fourteen thousand people died of cholera, and in September 1849 Chadwick was removed from the now discredited Metropolitan Commission.

But he was still a member of the General Board of Health, and he now turned his attention to the metropolitan water supply, the investigation of which had devolved upon the Board from the now defunct Royal Commission of 1847 on the Health of the Metropolis. In May 1850 his report demanded that the use of Thames water should cease in favor of new pure sources to be piped from Farnham in Surrey, the eight existing companies should be amalgamated, and "the whole works for the supply of water, and for the drainage of the metropolis" should be consolidated "under one and the same management."

As on previous occasions, this stirred up all the anticentralizers in the vestries, the water companies, and the City Corporation; and (as previously) Chadwick's ideas were too much for the Government of the day So the Metropolitan Water Act of 1852 contained no provision for the unified administration of water and drains, or even for the amalgamation of the water companies; but the latter were, however, required to cease, by 1855–56, drawing any supplies from the Thames below Teddington.

So ended the last chance to establish a single authority for the management of metropolitan water and drainage. The Metropolitan Commission of Sewers proceeded on its ineffective course, now dominated by the civil engineers of Great George Street. But in the City, in the very citadel of the anticentralizers, Simon was now building up permanent administrative machinery for the prevention and eventual elimination of insanitary conditions; and so when, in the summer of 1854, cholera visited London again, the City produced only 211 of the 10,738 victims in the whole of the capital.

Chadwick and his centralizing ideas were thus totally discredited, and, with the City's sanitary successes plain for all to see, the anticentralizers and defenders of local self-government were correspondingly cock-a-hoop. Just at this moment — in the summer of 1854 — the limited statutory span of life of the General Board of Health established in 1848 was coming to an end; and such was now the power of the anticentralization lobby that even the enforced resignation of Chadwick (at once followed by those of his two colleagues on the Board) did not prevent the House of Commons from rejecting the Government's bill for the temporary continuation of the Board's existence. With cholera raging in London, another bill to reconstruct the Board in more acceptable form was hastily passed; and with the need for the reconstruction of the whole field of London's government now too urgent to be postponed any longer, Chadwick passed into limbo to the jeers of the triumphant anticentralizers.

CHAPTER 2

The Creation of the Metropolitan Board of Works

When the Board of Health was dismantled in 1854, Edwin Chadwick had not yet experienced the final humiliation. That came when one of his most virulent enemies in Parliament, Sir Benjamin Hall, became president of the reconstructed Board. Hall had been regarded as an ardent champion of the "local self-government" school of thought and the spokesman for the London vestries. As the Member for Marylebone, he had carried the anticentralization torch in the House, and had repeatedly attacked Chadwick—partly, one suspects, because he disliked Chadwick's principles and partly because he simply disliked Chadwick. But Hall was a man who, though ruthless and unsparing in opposition, in office carried out policies essentially similar to those that he had condemned. In a word, though Hall still represented the hopes of the anticentralizing party, in some degree legitimately, his principles failed to stand up against the crisis he encountered in the summer of 1854 during the outbreak of cholera. The epidemic forced him to reconsider some of the implications of his previous position, and converted him into an extraordinarily vigorous and able president of the new Board of Health.[1] When he went to the slums to see for himself, he discovered that a laissez-faire policy simply would not answer, and that the central government must act positively—a bitter cup for Toulmin Smith and the anticentralization hosts.

What should be the nature and machinery of this positive policy? It was out of the question to reappoint the Metropolitan Commission of Sewers. Not only had they accomplished nothing but a bad sewer in Victoria Street, but they had run up the debt from £64,000 (November 1847) to over £587,000, with, moreover, a punitively high cost of management.[2] Whatever one may think of their railway building talents, the engineers clearly had not performed with distinction in sewer construction, though here one must emphasize the insufficient rating powers with which they had been armed. But if not the Commission of Sewers, what would be Hall's prescription? "I was determined," he recalled, "on the merciful abatement of the epidemic that ravaged the Metropolis, to turn my attention to the state of this vast city. I knew that, unless great and speedy radical changes in the constitution of its local affairs were effected, it was utterly hopeless to expect those affairs to be well conducted."[3] Actually the skeleton of the organization which he outlined to the House on 16 March 1855 had been suggested the previous year by a Royal Commission on the London Corporation, presided over by Henry Labouchere.[4] Hall ignored, however, the primary recommendation of the Commission, which proposed the creation of a series of municipal organizations throughout the metropolis, one for each of the seven Parliamentary boroughs. Instead, he chose to accept an alternative recommendation that a Board of Works be created for the entire metropolitan area.

But what was that area? There were several possibilities, all different and each with something to be said for it. He might have taken the immense district covered by the old coal tax, or the somewhat smaller area of the Metropolitan Police District, or the smallest of the three, the Registrar-General District, comprising about 117 square miles. The reasons for this choice are not clear, save that that was the area taken by the Royal Commission of the previous year.

In bringing in his Metropolis Local Management Bill in 1855,[5] Hall reviewed the existing London government, its inconsistencies and anomalies.[6] He pointed to the different qualifications for the local franchise and for vestryman, showing that in St. Giles and St. George's, Bloomsbury, no one could attend or vote in the election of vestrymen unless he was rated for the poor at twenty-five pounds and no one could serve as a vestryman whatever his rating, if he let part of his premises. In St. John's, Hackney, the qualification for voting was a rating of forty pounds; in St. Mary's, Stratford-le-Bow, it was fifteen pounds, and in Mile End Old Town twelve pounds. Along the Strand, Hall noted, in about three-quarters of a mile one would encounter the empires of nine different paving boards, each, no doubt, with different tastes as to types and grade of pavement. He went, in some detail, into the incredible confusion of jurisdictions in the Strand–St. Martin's area, where, for example, at one point (Wellington Street) within a distance of one hundred yards there were four separate authorities. London, he might have indicated, contained "a greater number of governments than even Aristotle might have studied with advantage."[7]

It was this profusion of local authorities that made the reform of metropolitan services seem so infinitely complicated. Something like 250 local acts applied to the metropolis, which was administered by 300 different bodies. These probably comprised in all about 10,550 commissioners—at least, the 137 that answered Hall's questionnaire included over 4,700 commissioners. The plethora of paving boards was best illustrated by St. Pancras, frequently cited by contemporaries and subsequent writers on London affairs. The population of the parish had grown five times over—along with Kensington, Islington, Poplar, Lambeth, and other areas—since 1801; and indeed, since 1841 its population had risen from 72,000 to 170,000. The public services of this gigantic parish, with its large estates (such as the Bedford, the Southampton, and the Foundling estates) were administered by nineteen boards—sixteen for lighting and paving, and three for lighting only. They represented all degrees of administrative efficiency, and the differences in cost among them were staggeringly unrelated to the quality of their services. These boards comprised some 427 commissioners, 255 of them self-elected. The worst of it was that, with all its army of functionaries, nominal and genuine, parts of the parish were wholly neglected.[8] There was no answer, Hall concluded, but to make a clean sweep of such bodies.

He might wipe out the special commissions for paving and lighting, but he rejected the notion of turning the metropolis into one great municipality, as a generation of municipal reformers following him were to do, on the ground that it was too huge—that Hampstead and Chelsea, Fulham and Whitechapel had little in common. No doubt, also, the specter of City opposition loomed up as a formidable deterrent to such a daring idea. Nor would he have anything to do with the more modest approach taken by the Royal Commission, which recommended a number of smaller governments. Some of the individual Parliamentary boroughs, he argued, were too large for municipal institutions to be successfully introduced—Tower Hamlets with 550,000 inhabitants and Marylebone with 400,000, for example. Five months before, the *Observer* had reflected that, however much centralization terrified half the metropolis, in practice the only good turns that had been done to London government had come through it. "Local self-government, has not answered; centralization will not be listened to; and local government, under control, in the metropolis has as yet proved inoperative."[9]

In 1855 Hall proposed to divide the metropolis into municipal districts

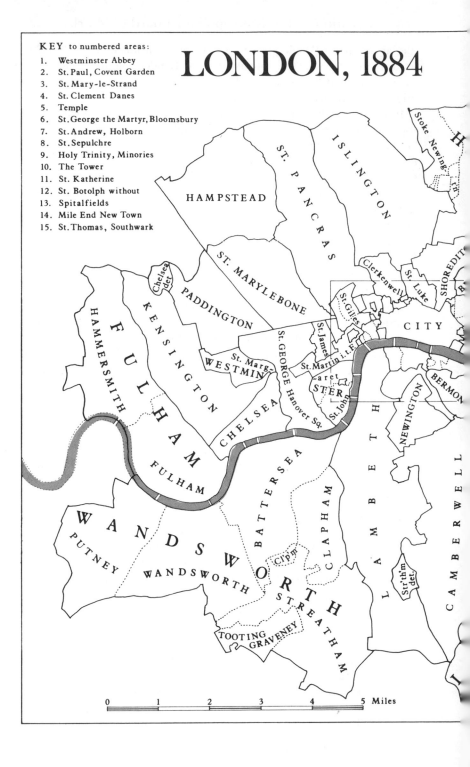

LONDON, 1884

KEY to numbered areas:

1. Westminster Abbey
2. St. Paul, Covent Garden
3. St. Mary-le-Strand
4. St. Clement Danes
5. Temple
6. St. George the Martyr, Bloomsbury
7. St. Andrew, Holborn
8. St. Sepulchre
9. Holy Trinity, Minories
10. The Tower
11. St. Katherine
12. St. Botolph without
13. Spitalfields
14. Mile End New Town
15. St. Thomas, Southwark

HAMPSTEAD

ST. PANCRAS

ISLINGTON

Stoke Newing'n

ST. MARYLEBONE

Clerkenwell

St. Luke

SHOREDIT

Chelsea det.

KENSINGTON

PADDINGTON

St. Giles

CITY

HAMMERSMITH

FULHAM

ST. GEORGE Hanover Sq.

St. Marg-

WESTMIN

St. James

St. Martin i.t.F.

St. John

BERMON

CHELSEA

CHELSEA

aret

STER

FULHAM

BATTERSEA

L   A   M   B   E   T   H

NEWINGTON

CLAPHAM

PUTNEY

W   A   N   D   S   W   O   R   T   H

Cl'm

Str'th'm det.

C   A   M   B   E   R   W   E   L   L

WANDSWORTH

STREATHAM

TOOTING

GRAVENEY

| 0 | 1 | 2 | 3 | 4 | 5 Miles |

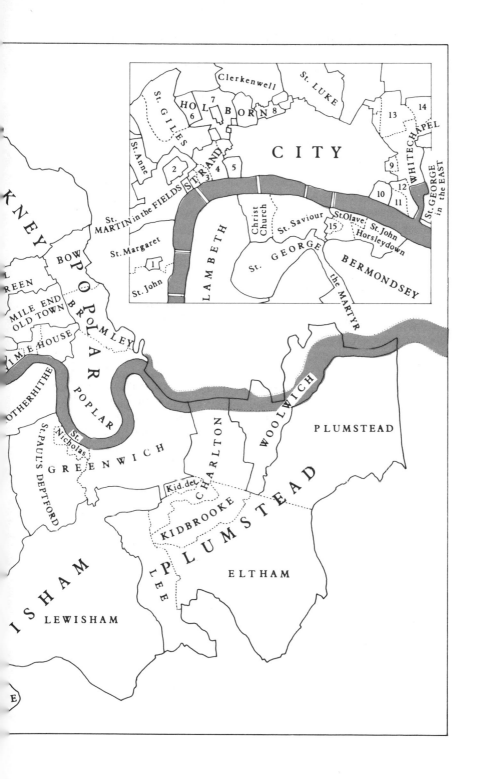

without creating municipal corporations — that is, to continue vestry organization in a modified form and to set up a central body (the MBW) to handle certain public services for the entire metropolis. The larger parishes were to continue with vestries of their own, similar (though by no means uniform) in powers and procedure. The smaller ones would, for purposes of representation on the central body, be associated together to form district boards. Each of the parishes and district boards would send one or two members to the MBW, which would not, therefore, be a popularly elected body, but, as was promptly pointed out and over the years was increasingly urged, rather a "super-vestry," with many of the defects of its components.[10] Still, whatever Hall's private views, it would have been suicidal to think of superseding the vestries. Nor is there any reason to believe that Hall wished to get rid of them. His experience as Member for Marylebone had convinced him that, if vestries were properly safeguarded and given explicit terms of reference, they could be made to work.[11] All that he wished to do was, in some degree, to regularize them, while leaving their powers of "local self-government" substantially intact. Meanwhile, the paving boards could be swept away, to nobody's sorrow but their own.

The opposition aroused by Hall's bill, to say the least, was pallid. Henry Fitzroy criticized the proposal,[12] but it was suspected that his views might have been affected by his interest in the Southampton Paving Commissioners. Viscount Ebrington[13] voiced the curious apprehension that the local parliament of forty-six members would discuss politics instead of sewerage questions and so would threaten to overshadow the authority of the Speaker and that of the Imperial Parliament.[14] The City complained that its representation was small as measured by its prestige and dignity, while at least one city member contemplated regretfully the failure to go ahead with incorporation. But the bill passed the second reading without a division.

Nor, with one exception, were significant changes made at the committee stage. To be sure, one Tory charged that the bill was but another step in the sinister progress of centralization, which was "depriving the parishioners and ratepayers over the expenditure of their money."[15] The one significant change made in committee had to do with the method of electing to the vestries. Hall had provided for an all-parish election, the plan followed in Marylebone and St. Pancras, with its obvious dangers. This scheme was altered to an election by wards, as was followed by the Common Council of the City.[16] Beyond this no changes of consequence were registered, and, in fact, at the committee stage the clauses of the bill were discussed in an atmosphere of overpowering indifference, with, at one time, only twenty-five members present.[17]

The Metropolis Local Management Act of 1855, which formed the initial charter of the MBW, was a long and rather complicated statute. It not only set up the metropolitan governing and sanitary authorities, but it laid down a code, quite explicit in some respects, for their behavior. In spite of its detail — perhaps because of it — the act had not foreseen the new demands that would be laid on the Board during its tenure; it even, in some respects, proved unsatisfactory for the immediate needs of the Board. In 1860 it was amended and supplemented. It had to be amended in minor ways in 1856 and 1858 and in a more sweeping fashion in 1862. Here only the main features of the metropolitan structure created by the act of 1855 can be outlined.

At the outset, some order would be introduced into the composition of the vestries and their method of election. Hall chose to reconstruct them by making Hobhouse's act compulsory[18] — that is, by making them all select vestries to be elected by the ratepayers. To vote, one must be rated at forty pounds (save in certain circumstances), and the number of members composing the vestries was adjusted roughly according to population. A large and populous parish would have a vestry of considerable size — as in the case of St. Pancras — while a thinly populated parish would have a proportionately smaller vestry. Each vestry would have its own panoply of officials, including, of course, a vestry clerk. On the clerk, and on his skill at conciliating opposing points of view, his sense of when and how to intervene, and his orderliness in transacting business, depended, in a large degree, the welfare of the parish. An able clerk could do much to control, or at least to reduce the damage done by, a riotous or irresponsible vestry. Vestries were given charge of local services — including (except for the main sewers, which were vested in the MBW) minor street improvements. Here was sufficient authority to justify the exultant cries of satisfaction which rose from the vestries at this apparent triumph of local self-government.[19] Only later did they realize that their self-congratulations were not wholly warranted.

The new MBW would be composed of forty-five members, who were elected by the various vestries and district boards. Six of the larger vestries returned two members each,[20] and sixteen, one each. Fourteen members came from the district boards, and three from the City. From the start the City had been a far from eager champion of the new measure, and its representatives in Parliament demanded three members as the price for withholding active opposition. Service on the Board was to be unpaid, save for the chairman, who was to receive something between £1,500 and £2,000 a year. Did Sir Benjamin Hall, one is tempted to ask, regard this body of forty-five purely as a means of getting the metropolitan sewage question handled by a representative body, or did he conceive it as a government *in posse* for the metropolis? Clearly some of the early Board members, the strict constructionists of the group, thought of themselves purely as members of a sewer-building enterprise and held that the Board should be extinguished when the sewers had been constructed. Clearly, also, sewers were the primary assignment of the Board: it was intended as a successor to the Metropolitan Commission of Sewers. But, on the other hand, Hall seems not to have imagined himself creating an ephemeral body, which would disappear, except for an administrative skeleton, as soon as the sewers had been built. Two additional duties which were specifically laid on the Board would suggest that he intended to create a semipermanent body: the Board was to assume responsibility for the naming of streets and the numbering of houses, and, more important, it was to have charge of street improvements — including initial building, widening, and straightening — which were of a metropolitan character. It was given oversight of the building act passed at the same time.[21] In short, although it would be too much to maintain that Hall was consciously establishing an urban government in the MBW, he was creating, more or less deliberately, a body which would take on many of the duties of the modern municipal government, simply because a more suitable agency did not exist. But neither Hall nor anyone else could have had any notion either of the variety of demands that would be made upon the Board or of the number of responsibilities that it would be tempted (not unwillingly, it must be admitted) to discharge.

But who was to pay for all this and how? The Victorians, one does not need to be reminded, were deeply committed to the principle of economy in government. Some of it, no doubt, was principle — at least their intellectuals tended to rationalize it as principle[22] — but much of it was a simple reluctance to contribute money for public purposes. In an era of light (but spotty and uneven) taxation, even moderate demands from a municipal authority seemed arbitrary and oppressive, and they were the occasion for howls of protest and growls of defiance. The London system of rating contributed to this resistance, for rates, by and large, were not concealed in the rent and paid by the landlord but were paid directly by the householder, who was, of course, quite aware of what he was doing and the amount he was paying at any given time. From the tradesman class that dominated London vestries as a whole, opposition was strong and continuous. This group, like French peasants, regarded spending money for public services as wasteful and unnecessary, and their philosophy was mean and penny-pinching. Their apostles of economy were ready to cry out against each new penny on the rate, and the greatest triumph that a new vestry could record was a reduction in the rates.

In some degree, the central government shared these attitudes. As a result, Hall's provision in the act of 1855 for financing the improvements the Board was to introduce turned out to be quite inadequate. Although the Board, like the Metropolitan Commission of Sewers, could impose rates on the metropolis, its borrowing powers were also gravely circumscribed. It could raise money only through the expedient of borrowing a sum to be secured by a mortgage on the rates. The Commissioners of Sewers had already discovered that this was impracticable, indeed impossible. Insurance companies, the principal source of large sums, were not inclined to accept such security, nor was money readily available from them in the amounts required. A workable scheme would require a further act of Parliament, which would provide for the issue of bonds secured by a Treasury guarantee. This came in two years, assisted by a hot summer which made the river, with its load of sewage, intolerable. The financial problems of the Board were by no means solved in 1857-58, for intercepting sewers cost more than expected and vestry resistance to increases in rates was constant, but at least these problems were defined in rational terms.

During the autumn of 1855, elections to the new vestries were taking place throughout the metropolis. Hall's act had been hailed as a victory for the principle of local self-government, and the elections excited a good deal of interest. In the vestries, already organized under Hobhouse's act, there was no marked change in the type or caliber of men returned. Indeed, the new act made remarkably little difference to local routines. In parishes that still had open vestries, of course, the change was more striking, but the make-up of the new vestries and district boards seems to have been about what one would expect, dominated, as they were, by tradesmen, publicans, builders, and solicitors. An exception was St. George's, Hanover Square, which continued to show a quasi-aristocratic complexion.

More important were the elections from the vestries to the Board. Here, in general, what had been predicted occurred. Vestries tended to return men who had been prominent in vestry affairs, not necessarily men of large or statesmanlike abilities but men who were determined to defend local interests against all comers. From the City came Alderman William Cubitt, Deputy Harrison, and Henry Lowman Taylor. The first was Sheriff of London in 1847, a distinguished builder and a former consultant to the late Commission of Sewers. Harrison, a wholesale stationer and a person of some intelligence, was a candidate for chairman who defended the interests of the City consistently but with a degree of tact. Henry Lowman Taylor, a member of the Board during most of its history, exemplified the popular stereotype of City leadership. A wholesale ironmonger, Lowman Taylor's perspectives were limited by the boundaries of the City.[23] According to his lights, he was honest enough, but with a testiness and a capacity for obstruction that made him extremely difficult to handle. He had been a leader of the "dirty" party in the City—the antisanitarians—but he had been won over, in part, by the effectiveness of Dr. John Simon's work.[24] These three men, of course, formed the nucleus of the City bloc on the Board, and they strove, if not for actual control, at least to protect the autonomy of the sacred square mile.

Marylebone sent as one of its members J. A. Nicholay, an Oxford Street furrier who had been active in parish affairs, and an extreme representative of the local self-government school. J. J. Moreland, the promoter of the Greater London Drainage Company, was returned for St. Luke's, and A. H. Bristow, a university man and a large conveyancer, appeared for Greenwich. Bristow turned out to be level-headed and fair-minded and, indeed, became one of the balance wheels of a body that often gave signs of running away.[25] And, to assure chaos on the new Board, St. George's, Hanover Square sent John Leslie.[26] Leslie had acquired neither knowledge nor wisdom since the days of the Sewers Commission. He was the same pig-headed, opinionated, ignorant character who had turned Chadwick's Commission into a shambles and had harried the Board of Health,[27] and as long as he remained a member of the new Board, its procedure would be disrupted by his apparently random attacks.

Among the forty-five members returned—or rather forty-four, since one, John Thwaites, was returned from both Southwark and Greenwich—Thwaites's election was by far the most momentous. For, as chairman until his death in 1870, he guided the Board with sound sense and extraordinary patience. Though he was a Westmoreland man, a contemporary newpaper could still describe him as "a type of the time we live in . . . the natural product of London matter-of-factism."[28] Determined rather than imaginative, he was solid and dependable, an excellent moderator and a sound judge among opposing points of view. He had been a person of some consequence in Southwark, and a leader in such enterprises on the south side of the river as the Surrey Gas Consumers Company, which had been formed to break the hold of the profiteering commercial companies, and which had reduced rates markedly.[29] As one of the elected members of the final Commission of Sewers, he had kept his eyes and ears open and had turned out a pamphlet which still remains a useful introduction to the sewerage dilemma of the metropolis.[30] When in the chair at the Board, the expression of his eyes was heavy with gloom; his face reflected no emotion. Neither praise nor blame seemed to affect him, and his somber smile could never develop into a laugh. Yet nothing seemed to escape him. In that often rowdy "Senate of Sewers" he used the gavel when it was needed, sometimes rising in his seat to command silence. As chairman he often had to take the blame for actions of which he himself disapproved, and, indeed, for inaction which he had done his best to avoid. Conceivably his qualities were not unconnected with his faith, that of an "old-fashioned Calvinist" of the Strict and Particular Baptist persuasion.[31] In any case, Thwaites's fifteen-year chairmanship was the Board's outstanding period of achievement. Clearly its success cannot be ascribed entirely to his diligence and judgment. But, for whatever reason, one feels that after his death in 1870 the Board lost much of its momentum. Its two major achievements — main drainage and the embankment — were behind it, and no such obvious tasks loomed up for the future. Still, while Thwaites was in command, the Board seemed to be in diligent, firm hands. Lord John Manners, at his death, referred to his "determined spirit, great energy, capacities of no common order, together with a rare patience and power of reconciling conflicting views and interests."[32] The record of the Board, in a large degree, was to depend on the drive and the tactical skill of its chairman.

It would be excessive to imply that the Board got off to an auspicious start. Once the huzzahs over the triumph of local self-government subsided, it became obvious that the "Parliament of the Parishes" had much to learn about the transaction of business. The first meeting took place in Burlington House, in December 1855, with Nicholay of Marylebone as temporary chairman and Josiah Wilkinson, a barrister sitting for St. Pancras, as honorary secretary. There was no shortage of candidates for permanent chairman, for, aside from the prestige and the opportunity to write one's name large in the history of modern London, the salary, £1,500, was a sound enough inducement. Hall's candidate had apparently been Sir John Shelley,[33] the Liberal Member for Westminster, who, however, withdrew from the competition. J. A. Roebuck, Lord Ebrington, Lord Robert Grosvenor, Richard Jebb (the former chairman of the Commission of Sewers), and a half dozen others were in the running. Harrison put himself forward as the candidate of the City group. Among the speeches of the candidates, Roebuck's was the longest and Thwaites' one of the shortest. But when it came to voting, Thwaites led all the way, followed by Roebuck and Harrison; he was elected, no doubt, by the solid local vestrymen who saw him as one of themselves.[34]

The Board took over the old headquarters of the Sewers Commissioners at 1 Greek Street and transacted its business from there. Meetings, however, were held at Guildhall, which had been offered by the City members. This was a dubious benefaction, for the hall was large and equipped with galleries where the constituents and partisans of the various members could assemble to hear the debates. The prospect — indeed, the certainty — of an audience aroused the baser instincts of members, who used the meetings of the Board as a platform from which to impress their constituents. Long and vaporous speeches marked the earlier meetings, with three of four hours spent on discussions of trivialities, which left the agenda papers untouched.[35] Sometimes there was frank obstruction by Lowman Taylor, whose attack on Sir Benjamin Hall required a call to order from the chairman, or there were the reckless forays of John Leslie, "alone in the fellowship of his crotchets."[36] Comparisons were even drawn between the behavior of the Board and the noisy vestries of Marylebone and St. Pancras, not wholly to the disadvantage of the latter.[37] It was a field day for the irresponsible oratory of the "unruly member." The *Observer,* at the end of the first year, spoke of the Board "as a perverse little assembly" possessed by a fatal lust for talk.[38] The current London sobriquent, "the Metropolitan Board of Words," seemed, unhappily, to be all too accurate.

One of the difficulties — which, to some extent, persisted throughout the Board's history — was the reluctance of the members to confine the Board's business to committees. Their jealousy of committees, in fact, approached the pathological, so little did they realize the dimensions of their problem. The consequence was that the Board's main committee, the Works and General Purposes Committee (though called by different names at different times) was not, properly speaking, a committee at all. It was simply a committee of the whole, the entire Board sitting as a committee, with debate as unbridled as that in the regular sessions, or perhaps more so — though it is hard to say, since the public (and reporters) were excluded from these "committee" meetings. In fact, it was urged with some justice that the advantage of such committees was not greater efficiency but simply the exclusion of reporters. This decision did not ingratiate the Board with the metropolitan press, but, indeed, accounted in part for the readiness of editors to attack it.[39] Certainly the Board did not begin its labors in a shower of favorable publicity.

Decisions as to the selection of the "expert" officers of the Board — specifically, the clerk, architect, and engineer — in some degree turned on the power struggle between the vestries and the City group and its allies, and on the degree to which the Board would endeavor to continue the traditions and personnel of the Commission of Sewers.

The clerk's office was contested by twenty-two candidates, but the decision presently was seen to lie between two — E. H. Woolrych, a barrister who had been secretary to the extinct Commissioners, and Josiah

Wilkinson of St. Pancras. Woolrych, who won by a narrow margin, was regarded in some quarters as a City man,[40] but whatever his affiliations he proved, during the time he served, a clerk of signal ability, who read his minutes with dispatch and paid close attention to the debate. But the newspaper which suspected that the post with the Board would offer him insufficient scope was correct. In four years he applied to be relieved of his duties as clerk and suggested that he be appointed Legal Adviser and Standing Counsel. This proposal, and his subsequent appointment at £800 a year, brought a shower of protests from economy-minded vestries and the City Commissioners of Sewers, which thanked the City representatives for "their manly and determined opposition to this noxious measure."[41] Still, Woolrych had a point. The legal questions which the Board had to decide, as its main drainage and street improvement plans developed, were mounting in number and complexity, and professional advice was plainly required.[42] When, in March 1861, Woolrych resigned to accept a better appointment, the Works and General Purposes Committee wisely decided against another counsel and proposed, instead, that the Board handle the business in its own office through a legal department headed by its solicitor, who, in this instance, was William Wyke Smith.[43]

The appointment of architect went smoothly enough, and resulted in the election of Frederick Marrable. Marrable, no great architect, was apparently a prosy person; one gathers this from the *Elector,* which speaks of a dull meeting of the Board, as when you "have the dull business of that dull man, Mr. Marrable, on the carpet."[44] He remained with the Board five years, until February 1861, when he resigned, complaining not without justice that he had been grossly underpaid. During the five years, he claimed, he had written no less than five thousand reports—for which the Board offered to raise his salary from £800 to £1,000, an increase which Marrable thought contemptible.[45] The Board selected his successor, George Vulliamy, a former pupil of Charles Barry's and an architect of some distinction, from twenty-three applicants. The son of a well-known watch and clock maker of Pall Mall, Vulliamy was an architect of sound training and wide travel, and until old age and ill health partly incapacitated him and left him prey to the scandals which disfigured the closing years of the Board's history, he was an official of distinction.[46]

The critical appointment was, however, that of engineer. By his success in carrying out the assigned enterprises the Board itself would be judged. J. W. Bazalgette, because of his association with the Metropolitan Comissioners of Sewers, was the obvious candidate, unless the notorious failures of that body were to be held against him. Furthermore, he had been identified with a particular plan of sewerage and with "the Great George Street clique of engineers,"[47] who were thought to be using his candidacy as a means of getting themselves into the saddle. But whatever his former loyalties, the fact is that in Bazalgette the Board was getting a great engineer, better than it realized. The son of a commander in the Navy, at seventeen Bazalgette had begun to work with Sir John McNeil. He had been engaged on canal and dock works, and, more recently, had been in charge of the 166 miles of main sewers and twenty-seven contracts for new sewers in the metropolis.[48] His principal competitor was Robert Rawlinson, a thoroughly competent engineer, who had just returned, wounded, from the Crimea. In presenting his claims, Bazalgette admitted that he had indeed, like every other engineer, formed an opinion on the drainage question, but denied his complete commitment. He would, he insisted, come at the question as a fresh issue. Aside from Rawlinson his opposition was feeble, and Bazalgette was elected by a substantial majority.[49] In this appointment, the Board did rather better than it deserved, for, although Bazalgette was not infallible, the main structure of his work has stood up over the years. And he was not only a gifted engineer, but, what was equally important, a skillful administrator, who brought to completion a series of undertakings of enormous complexity, after a highly discouraging and messy start.

It is hard to estimate the influence of the City during the early years of the Board's existence. Newspapers published outside the walls, where there was jealousy of the City and resentment over what was regarded as its narrow parochial attitudes, naturally ascribed a sinister power to the City's three members and their allies. These were estimated by the *Observer* as about a dozen in number, along with twenty belonging to the metropolitan group and ten falling in between.[50] Certainly the City group was clear about what it wanted and did not want and, in Harrison and particularly Lowman Taylor, had two tacticians skilled in assault and obstruction. Both Woolrych and Bazalgette were regarded as City appointments,[51] though whether correctly or not it is impossible to judge. But at least the City men opposed the appointment of an assistant engineer known to be hostile to Bazalgette and in favor of small-pipe sewers.[52] Certainly, if Bazalgette was the candidate of the City, he was equally the candidate of the Great George Street engineers, who were committed to tunnel sewers.

The MBW started off with an establishment of about fifty, in addition to numerous other functionaries—draftsmen, chainmen, and the like—and an annual wage bill of about £25,000 plus nearly £1,000 for retiring allowances.[53] This, it soon appeared, was a minimal complement, and through the years, as the work of the Board increased in volume and complexity, the establishment was constantly augmented. Included in the fifty were a clerk, six assistants, and eight district clerks to oversee the collection of rates. This was to be one of the most troublesome of the Board's duties, particularly at the outset, when rates had to be collected to discharge the debts accumulated by the Metropolitan Sewer Commissioners. The total of rates owed to the Commissioners in several districts of the metropolis totaled nearly a quarter of a million pounds, virtually none of which had been collected.[54] The Board thus faced the unpleasant necessity of issuing thousands of summonses and warrants, for it could not afford to let the precepts which it forwarded to the vestries and district boards be ignored. Collecting for the deficit accumulated by the Commissioners of Sewers, however, was an especially painful operation. Yet in only one case did reluctance to pay these reach open resistance. This was in St. George's, Hanover Square — certainly not a straitened district — where the parish refused to collect the rates and some individuals defied the Board by refusing to pay. Under these circumstances the Board had no alternative but to deploy its own collectors in the parish and collect the rates for itself. It was a disagreeable business, but the resistance, which was perhaps a reflection of John Leslie's influence, soon subsided. Vestries continued to howl about precepts and a considerable number of summonses were still issued against individuals, but a collective stand against the Board's rating procedures was no longer a practical policy.

Within three years, it became obvious that the Board's Greek Street offices were not suitable for its business. Not only was there no meeting room for the whole Board, which was still holding its sessions at Guildhall, but, as the business of the Board expanded, there would not even be the necessary office accommodation. In the early summer of 1858, a committee recommended the purchase of Berkeley House in Spring Gardens, just off Trafalgar Square. The terms were thought to be reasonable, and the committee was authorized to go ahead. But it had reckoned without the Board's constituency. Vestry after vestry launched its protest, and Board members were forced to take a grilling in local vestries and to explain their conduct. "Can such things be?" the *Observer* exclaimed apropos what it called a lavish and ridiculous misuse of ratepayers' money; and in Marylebone the vestry kept at it all the following spring, roundly attacking Nicholay, the robust defender of local self-government, for his alleged part in the business.[55] A few years later the vestries, of course, looked pretty silly. For Spring Gardens proved a good buy: the total cost of the new buildings, fittings and all, was about £19,000, and the return on the sale of 1 Greek Street amounted to nearly £6,500.[56] In the new building was a board room, together with a committee room and a members' room equipped with a table, ten chairs, and writing equipment.[57] This was no luxury, for meetings of the Board and its committees were frequent and they could be unconscionably long. The Board held regular weekly meetings, often two or three, together with such committee meetings as the members were expected to attend. When one recalls the hours of windy, profitless debate to which they were subjected, it is surprising that attendance kept up as well as it did. What is not so astonishing, however, is the number of retired or semiretired men who accepted membership. In 1861, for example, the roll included at least eight who had retired, as well as some others who were well along in years and had cut down a good deal on their business commitments.[58] Thwaites might point out that the average speech in the Board covered only four minutes, but some members professedly had left the Board because of the amount of gabble-gabble to which they were subjected.[59] In any case, a conscientious member found himself heavily burdened. Some took it seriously and attended faithfully; others were more casual. But bodies of abler men have accomplished much less in their time than did this group of London citizens.

CHAPTER 3

The Problem of Main Drainage

The MBW owed its immediate existence to a crisis in metropolitan drainage. The cholera outbreak of 1854 added an element of urgency, which the inaction of successive Commissions of Sewers did nothing to allay. Sir Benjamin Hall, therefore, had fallen back on the expedient of a semirepresentative body armed with more extensive powers and with the primary assignment of solving the sewerage riddle of the metropolis. And notwithstanding the barrage of pointless oratory to which it was constantly subjected, and the time-wasting tactics its members indulged in so freely, the Board promptly got down to the business of planning a system of main drainage.

Originally the drainage of the Thames basin had occurred through the several streams which flowed into the river, and which were by 1855 largely covered over and serving as sewers. In the past their sewerage function had been to carry away surface water from houses and buildings as efficiently as possible. Household waste either was taken care of in cesspools or, in the poorer sections of the city, was simply allowed to lie in the street or court. During the first half of the century the situation perceptibly worsened. For one thing, the London population more than doubled, and the amount of water used increased proportionately. The growing popularity of Bramah's beneficent invention, the water closet, made essential an improved method for disposing of liquid household waste.[1] The Building Act of 1844 required new houses to have drains

47

connected with the public sewers,[2] and Chadwick's first Metropolitan Commission (1848–49), spurred on by the cholera epidemic of the same year, set about abolishing cesspools. Houses were not required, but were encouraged, to drain into the sewers.[3]

The result was a grave deterioration in the state of the river. At certain points, notably between Westminster and Waterloo bridges, the banks, at low tide, displayed horrible accumulations of mud and filth, which tainted the atmosphere with a revolting aroma. In 1858 *The Builder* pointed out that Thames water had not been impossible fifteen or sixteen years before and persons living close by had not hesitated to drink it, but that to do such a thing now would be insane. Meanwhile, the vestries debated "whether it was wholesome or not to pass the sewage of a population of about three millions of people to a river in the very center of it!"[4] The ultimate discomfort was reached in that year in the "Great Stink," but there had been ample warnings against shilly-shallying. As long as London dumped its sewage in the river, the river would inevitably become more noxious. The difficulty that substances disgorged at ebb tide would return on the flood was compounded by the fact that the low level of many London sewers made it impossible for sewage to escape except at the flood.[5]

When J. W. Bazalgette had been elected engineer-in-chief, any controversy as to size and type of sewer was in fact settled. On the one hand, Chadwick's expedient of converting the river into a cesspool did not ingratiate him with metropolitan opinion, even though, in his view, it was only a temporary measure and would be succeeded by a system of sewage utilization for fertilizer purposes. This notion, misguided as it was, Chadwick thought essential to his schemes.[6] London sewage was a valuable asset and must be made to yield a profit. Moreover, although Bazalgette might profess an open mind on the matter, there was never any likelihood that the Board would go back to Chadwick's pipe sewers. If the metropolis were to divert the sewage from the river by means of intercepting sewers, these could not be the small pipes urged by Chadwick but must be substantial tunnels. Not only that, but they must be large enough to carry off a reasonable fraction of rainfall. Pipes would do well enough as house drains; they might even be used for some street drains. But the building of intercepting sewers was a major undertaking, and one did not send a boy to do a man's job.

On 8 February 1856 the Board got down to business sufficiently to request Bazalgette to submit plans for a system of intercepting sewers.[7] On his basic plans he had to do little further work, for they were, in essentials, those that he had prepared for the Commissioners of Sewers in 1853. Moreover, Bazalgette and William Haywood, the City engineer, had in 1854 prepared a report on northern drainage. These plans rested, in turn, on Frank Forster's earlier work and on a sheaf of plans and suggestions (including some submitted to the Commission of Sewers) which had become the common property of the engineering profession. The plans produced by Bazalgette were frankly made up of ingredients from various sources, "so often repeated in some shape or other, that it would be difficult to determine who were the first authors."[8] But if Bazalgette could not claim original authorship, he did what was probably just as difficult: he took the useful elements out of the different plans, blended them into a workable whole, and applied their special features to the peculiar needs of individual districts. His report on drainage south of the Thames was finished first, on 3 April; the northern bank had to wait until 22 May.

The essential problem of the southern bank was the large amount of reclaimed marshland. This body of land along the river was generally below high water, in some places as much as six feet below, so that sewers beneath the basements of houses could discharge for only about four hours in each tide. The sewers accordingly became stagnant reservoirs for some sixteen hours a day. Rainfall from the high levels descended into the low districts and flooded the cellars of houses there. Bazalgette therefore proposed to intercept the waters from the upper district to prevent their flooding lower down and eventually swelling the river. The high-level sewer would thus begin at Clapham Common and would pass along, intercepting various main sewers, until it joined the low-level sewer at Deptford Creek. Thence it would flow by gravitation through Woolwich and across the Plumstead Marshes to a point opposite Barking Creek—a total distance of nearly twelve miles. The low-level sewer would take off at Putney and would join the upper level at Deptford Creek, thence proceeding to Plumstead Marshes. This, with the addition of two smaller branch sewers, would make up the southern intercepting system. At two points in the complex, some special pumping equipment would be required. The first would be at Deptford Creek, where the low-level sewage would have to be pumped to join that of the upper level so that it could flow by gravitation to the outfall; for this, engines and pumps of about 520 horsepower would be needed. The second would be at Plumstead Marshes, where sewage could be discharged for only two to four hours a tide; and this would have to be stored in huge reservoirs above the main outfall. For this lift of twenty-one feet an engine yielding over 650 horsepower would be required; with duplicate engines, over 2,340 horsepower would be needed for the two lifts.

The north side presented substantially the same problems, and for this, also, Bazalgette built on previous plans. Interception was to be managed by three principal lines of sewers, together with a fourth to handle the growing western area. The high-level sewer would take care of the northern suburban area, receiving at Kentish Town the contribution from Hampstead and Highgate and then proceeding through Stoke Newington and Hackney to Old Ford, where it would join the middle level, which had started at Kensal Green and reached Old Ford by way of Oxford Street, Old Street, and Bethnal Green Road. And so on to the outfall at Barking Creek. Low-level drainage was a more complex problem. For one thing, the area could not be drained by gravitation, and if the intercepting sewer ran, say, along the Strand and Fleet Street, that would involve rebuilding and reversing the direction of the branch sewers south of the line, in order to purify the Thames. It was possible to build a sewer independently of an embankment, but that would cause great inconvenience to the Strand, Fleet Street, and the East End. Much of the cost and difficulty, Bazalgette pointed out, would be obviated if a decision in favor of an embankment could be made at once. As it was, he included in his figures and estimate for building a low-level sewer which would begin in Grosvenor Row, Chelsea, would pass along to the Strand, and then go eastward to the pumping station near Abbey Mills where its contents would be lifted some thirty-six feet to the high level. Finally, there was the sewage from the western districts, where Bazalgette correctly foresaw that there was certain to be a staggering increase in population. Here he proposed to begin a sewer on the extreme western fringe of the metropolitan area and (in order to bypass the objections raised against a previous proposal to build deodorizing works for the area) to carry the sewerage to Barking through the low-level sewer.

Bazalgette's system assumed a future population of 2.3 million north of the river and 1.13 million to the south — a total of just under 3.5 million. This allowed for an increase of 1.25 million residents over the 2.25 million population of 1851, or an increase of more than 40 percent. Although this estimate would seem generous enough under any conditions other than the staggering growth of urban complexes in the nineteenth century, it proved, of course, inadequate: by 1889 the population of London (which included five more square miles than the 1855 figure) had reached 4.5 million. For Bazalgette's 3.5 million he provided sewers which would handle nearly 400 million gallons of sewage and rain water. For the total system his estimates came to £2,135,196, or, if the western sewage were carried to Barking, £2,413,376.[9]

So far, in spite of much talk, clashing views, and sheer obstruction, the Board had made fair progress with its main drainage plans. Even before Bazalgette made his report on drainage north of the river, however, a caution light had been hung out of Sir Benjamin Hall's office. The First

Commissioner, who had to approve the plans of the Board, wanted assurances, other than the Board's, that the outfalls were far enough down
the river so that the sewage would not return.[10] The problem, of course,
was the powerful tides in the Thames. (Even now, standing on Westminster Bridge when the tide is coming in, one is fascinated by the speed
at which large pieces of wood and other floating waste are making their
way upstream.) Bazalgette argued that, if the sewage were released at
ebb tide, his outfalls at Barking Creek and Plumstead Marshes would
give the necessary margin of security. Others disagreed. The War Department, for example, was uneasy about the proximity of the southern
outfall to Woolwich Arsenal, and there was some sentiment among the
Board members for considering a new scheme, presented by two engineers, which called for no sewage to enter the river above Gallion's
Reach.[11]

The issue was drawn when Hall, after careful consideration, rejected
Bazalgette's plans for the southern outfall. Bazalgette's scheme, he insisted, was flatly contrary to the Metropolis Local Management Act,
which provided that sewage should flow into the river only outside the
metropolitan limits. Bazalgette agreed to move the outfall downstream
as far as the Erith Marshes, and then the Board passed a proposal to
carry the sewage to a point in Long Reach below Erith. But this did not
end the matter: on the contrary. And yet it is hardly worthwhile to recall
the dreary sparring that went on all summer and fall between the Board
and the Office of the First Commissioner. The Board's attitude was simple and understandable. As a group of vestry representatives, their object was to get a satisfactory sewerage system at as low a cost as possible.
That meant that the outfall must be as close to the metropolis as was
legal.[12] No allowance could be made for a margin for safety, however
pleasant it might have been to carry the sewage farther down the river.
On the other side, Sir Benjamin, indifferent to the cost of the sewerage
system, was determined to get the outfalls as far downstream as possible.
But it was a moot question where the optimum point—that is, where the
outfall could be far enough away to be safe and no farther—really was.

In September, Bazalgette at the request of the Board took another
look at his problem. He laid out four more expensive possibilities, of
which the second (Plan B), raising the cost of construction to Barking to
£2,734,000, was the one favored. It called for a discharge of sewage into
the river at Halfway Reach, at Erith, at or near high water so that it
would not flow up river save during heavy storms, when, in any case,
the sewage would be so highly diluted as to cause no nuisance.[13]

The Board wrestled with Bazalgette's suggestions. Thwaites attempted to persuade the First Commissioner that Government money

was necessary, especially when the extension was needed to meet the requirements of parties outside the metropolis; and the metropolis became half convinced that nothing was going to happen. Ultimately the Board, after two or three weeks of debate, reached a consensus of sorts for Bazalgette's Plan B, amid suggestions that plans were being contemplated to discharge the sewage below Gravesend if the Government would find the additional resources.[14]

The truth of it was that the Board was wholly at sea on the drainage question. What was decided one day was undone the next amid waves of defiant but empty oratory. Plans had repeatedly been proposed and withdrawn, either rejected by Sir Benjamin Hall or abandoned on Thwaites's assurance that Hall would certainly reject them. And now the members were solemnly proposing, said the *Observer*, to locate the outfall at Erith Marshes only three-quarters of a mile by water from the metropolitan boundary, from which sewage would certainly flow into the metropolis at least once a fortnight.[15] Two deputations to Hall had obtained no satisfaction; one of them, in fact, which stayed for over two hours, had been upbraided severely by Hall.

Hall rejected Plan B decisively, announcing that until the outfall question was settled further talk was pointless. Upon this decision, the Board abandoned Plan B and agreed to substitute the outfalls suggested by Captain Burstal, at the upper part of Erith Reach, which would require an additional mile.[16] Meanwhile, metropolitan opinion seems to have been almost unanimous in blaming the Board for these delays.[17] The Board had got off to a bad start; it had done little to propitiate the press, and in the long-drawn-out feud with the First Commissioner, it had shown little ability to reach a consensus. A correspondent to the *Illustrated London News* spoke of the "sullen Pistol-like compliance with Sir Benjamin Hall's desire" with which "they have—a fraction at a time—amended their plan for Thames Purification," and suggested that the situation called for greater aptitude than Thwaites and Company appeared to possess.[18]

Hall now insisted that he could make no decision without referring the outfall question to a Government Commission of Engineers. Its members—Captain Douglas Galton, R.E., and Messrs. Simpson and Blackwell—were appointed at the end of December 1856, and seven months later submitted their report. This proved to be a remarkably thorough study, over five hundred pages in length, full of detail on the past and present of metropolitan drainage, but offering little reasonable guidance to those who had to plan a drainage system. As the *Elector* (not an impartial critic) put it, "They had taken enough time to bring their united wisdom to ripeness. They had invited suggestions from all . . .

Yet after all it [their report] is found to have some of the worst faults as a drainage scheme that were ever presented to human thought."[19] Their rejection of Erith Reach for the outfalls was, of course, arguable; their proposal that sewage be intercepted from a much larger area, at a considerably higher estimated cost, was perhaps desirable, but was barred to the Board both by the terms of its appointment and by its financial resources. But what brought down the wrath of critics was the Commission's recommendation of large open outfall sewers, two channels of "black cholera-producing muck . . . on both sides of the river."[20] The referees might claim that the Board's plan was unimaginative, that it had predicted too small a population increase. But it was not difficult for the engineers retained by the Board—Messrs. Bidder, Hawksley, and Bazalgette—to shoot the Commission's plans full of holes. The proposals were either financially impractical, illegal, or technically unsound.[21]

It was now the summer of 1858, and still no action had been taken. The Board and Hall were still deadlocked when two things intervened. First, the Whig government fell and Hall was replaced by Lord John Manners as First Commissioner. Perhaps more important, the summer turned out to be hot and dry, and in early July when the thermometer rose to 94 degrees in the shade, the condition of the river became unbearable. "Gentility of speech," observed the *City Press,* "is at an end—it stinks; and whoso once inhales the stink can never forget it, and may count himself lucky if he live to remember it."[22] This situation was new only in degree, for, as the *Observer* reported, the condition of the river had been worsening for years.[23] During the previous summer the Lord Chamberlain had complained to Sir Benjamin Hall of "the pestilential state of the atmosphere at times in and about the New Houses of Parliament [which] has on several occasions compelled me to leave the terrace and I am frequently obliged to close the windows of my office."[24] The summer of 1858, however, saw the scourge more intolerable than ever, and members of Parliament opened fire on the Government. "It was a notorious fact," urged one, "that Hon. Gentlemen sitting in the Committee Rooms and in the Library were utterly unable to remain there in consequence of the stench which arose from the river."[25]

Hard as the situation may have been on luckless members of Parliament, for the Board members it offered a strategic opportunity. Now, it appeared, they could get from Parliament whatever powers they thought necessary to do the job, with virtually no questions asked. Thwaites was not the man to let such an opportunity slip, and he determined to take advantage of the crisis and the support which he could enlist in the metropolis to get the Government's consent. "This is an occasion," remarked *The Times,* when the fool's argument that "something must be

PUNCH, OR THE LONDON CHARIVARI.—July 3, 1858.

DIPHTHERIA.   SCROFULA.   CHOLERA.

FATHER THAMES INTRODUCING HIS OFFSPRING TO THE FAIR CITY OF LONDON.
(A Design for a Fresco in the New Houses of Parliament.)

1. Father Thames Introducing His Offspring—Diphtheria, Scrofula, and
Cholera—to the Fair City of London.

done" was really true, and Parliament at last recognized the fact.[26] In
just over two weeks, the Government rushed into Parliament a bill
which not only set the Board up as a body independent of the Office of
Works, but which also gave it powers to raise the necessary funds
through borrowing-powers the Board had been seeking for the past two
years.[27] Is the problem of the Thames, Disraeli asked, a local or a national problem? The noble river, now a "a Stygian pool, reeking with in-
effable and intolerable horrors," would be a municipal problem if London were like other cities. But since London was different, the river
could not be handled locally. Admittedly, the MBW had given a disappointing performance during its first two years. But that fact he ascribed
to the inadequate powers it possessed. The solution was to give the
Board both responsibility and power: to make it "a real corporation; to
invest it with sufficient funds—to endow it with sufficient power, and to
give it not only power, but responsibility."[28] This meant, primarily, two
things. First, the Board henceforth would have the power to borrow up
to £3 million with interest at no more than 4 percent guaranteed by the

Government, the interest to be carried and the principal repaid through a sewer rate of threepence. Second, the Board should now make its own decisions without the sanction of the First Commissioner of Works.

Comment and criticism tended toward the perfunctory, for all realized—and probably hoped—that the bill would pass. Several members (correctly) doubted whether £3 million would be sufficient, others voiced doubts about the MBW and its unrepresentative character, and still others commented on the Government's almost indecent haste to get its bill through Parliament. Robert Lowe criticized the Board's intercepting system as resting on too low an estimate of population growth, preferring the referees' plan of a canal to Sea Reach, while Robert Stephenson, in reply, found Lowe's speech nonsense, for the intercepting system was the only one that was capable of expansion without disrupting the rest of the system. There was difference of opinion as to whether Barking Creek, the Board's terminus, was far enough downstream to secure the metropolis, an uncertainty which, apparently, even Stephenson shared. But, as he pointed out, the decision was not irrevocable. If Barking Creek did not work out well, the outfall could still be carried to Sea Reach.[29]

The bill passed on 2 August 1858, without overcoming all criticism. But how would the Board respond to what seemed a grudging vote of confidence? One member probably spoke for the House—and indeed for the metropolis—when he "hoped they would talk less and do a great deal more than they had hitherto done."[30] There was some apprehension over the blank check that Parliament had so hastily given the MBW. *The Builder* was indignant over the whole business, particularly the casual course of the debate in Parliament and the decision to spend £3 million on an experiment, despite "all defective *data* for it, and all plausible reasoning to the contrary."[31] But one ought perhaps not to lay too great stress on the opinions of Victorian leader writers. They might vary week by week, the writer oblivious—or indifferent—to what he had proclaimed the previous fortnight or month, and blandly contradicting his, or at least his paper's, former judgment. To nobody's surprise, on 11 August the Board voted to accept the plans of Messrs. Bidder, Hawksley, and Bazalgette—in substance, Bazalgette's schedule of the order in which the various sections of the work ought to be carried out.

The decision was in favor of beginning with the northern high level from Hampstead to Old Ford, to be built at a cost of approximately £150,000.[32] Sixteen tenders were received, ranging in an astonishing spread from £152,430 to £270,000.[33] Not altogether wisely, as it turned out, but in the orthodox fashion, the Board awarded the contract to the lowest bidder, Moxon of Cannon Street and Dover.[34] It did not always do to select the lowest tender, as the Board was to discover, but to do otherwise would have raised cries of jobbery.

Moxon's contract was not the smoothest operation in the Board's history. Work began on Hackney Common in January 1859. In the spring, John Leslie, correct for once, discovered that the bills presented by Robert and Gotto, subcontractors in charge of excavating for the new sewer, claimed much more material removed than had been the case. Leslie was right, but his haranguing of the Board was termed by the chairman "injurious and disorderly," and, when he refused to withdraw, the Board, not reluctantly, voted to censure him. The Board then referred the case to an outside engineer, who concluded that the bills showed an excess of 22,000 cubic yards over the amount called for by the specifications.[35] In June 1860 it became clear that Moxon was in trouble. Creditors had attached his property, and he assigned to the London & County Banking Company the sums he owed to the Board. Work had been suspended on the sewer, and, if it was to be resumed, a new arrangement would have to be made. The reasonable solution seemed to be for the Bank to take over as nominal contractor, after receiving a payment from the Board on account of the sums due.[36] Trouble with low-bidding contractors was a constant feature of the Board's history, and was no doubt one of the reasons why its members came to rely on well-known, reliable contractors, in spite of the criticism which this brought down on their heads. Some Victorian contractors were sailing remarkably close to the wind. Sometimes their tenders were simply too low; sometimes an unforeseen pressure would topple them. But for many, contracting was precarious business.

There was trouble, too, with the northern middle-level sewer, for which W. H. Rowe had contracted at £264,553. He was found by the engineer to be using inferior materials—soft facing bricks—and otherwise violating the terms of his contract. At first Rowe announced his intention not to proceed; however, the Board replied that he must continue unless he wished to be held liable for loss and damage. But when, after repeated warnings, he continued to make use of inferior, soft bricks, the engineer ordered him to stop the works. Obviously, Rowe was approaching insolvency and could not get the money or credit to provide the bricks called for in the contract. He did, in fact, go bankrupt shortly afterwards, and Thomas Brassey took over the middle-level contract.[37]

The tenders for the southern high level did not cover so wide a range as those for the northern high level, varying from £217,000 to £242,700. But, again, the contract first went to the lowest tender, Messrs. Helling and Company. When another contractor was appointed, Helling soon complained that payments made by the Board—80 percent of the value of the works executed—were inadequate. Bazalgette retorted that, after nine months out of twenty on the job, only a sixth of the work had been completed. Helling, like Rowe, had obviously put in his bid without sufficient cash reserve to carry him through. Presently, he had to make arrangements with his creditors and turn the completion of the contract over to his sureties.[38] For the low-level southern sewer from Deptford Creek to Crossness, Helling's bid was so low as to terrify his potential sureties and he had to give up the contract.[39]

Meanwhile, the contractors for the short Acton branch of the northern middle level also joined the growing club of bankrupts, while the one who was building the sewer viaduct at Deptford Creek across the property of the Surrey Gas Consumers' Company was making a mess of the job and demanded further advances. Again, the contract had to be withdrawn and given to the solid firm of Aird & Webster.[40] Such experiences would be worth remembering when cries of "jobbery" and "favoritism" were later raised. But as for the present, the summer of 1860, one gathers, was a difficult one for contractors and an anxious one for the Board. Even before this epidemic of bankruptcies, *The Times,* complaining of the lack of visible progress, had reflected, "The Great Metropolitan Drainage question really beats all questions ever known. There is no end to its complications, embarrassments and difficulties."[41] And, when a mistake was discovered in one of the contracts which might have cost the metropolis a substantial sum, *The Times,* oracular as ever, proclaimed, "A flood of twaddle and chatter passed over the town, pompous little great men and loud little foolish men, and ill-natured little idle men—turned the columns of every paper into a bad imitation of the *Frogs* of Aristophanes . . . Alas! everybody has been chattering, and nobody has been attending to the real work of the Board."[42] *The Times* was only partly correct. However much chattering there may have been in the meetings of the Board—and there was an enormous volume of bad oratory sprayed around in this Parliament of the Parishes—at least two essential officers, the chairman and the engineer-in-chief, were diligent and alert. To their indefatigable labors, London, in large measure, owes its intercepting sewers.

Notwithstanding casualties among the contractors, by mid-1861 the entire system seemed in a fair way to being completed within a reasonable time. The northern high-level sewer, nine miles from Hampstead to the River Lea, had been completed, and the southern high level, where a change of contractors had been necessary, was now going well enough. The southern outfall sewer, seven and a half miles from Deptford Creek to Crossness, was progressing well, in spite of some rather complicated engineering problems, including a tunnel under Woolwich a mile long and forty-five to seventy-five feet deep. On this spur, the contractor marshaled twelve steam engines, a steam hoist, a tramway across the marshes from the outfall to Woolwich Arsenal, and a locomotive for the conveyance of material.[43] This southern outfall was a huge tunnel, eleven feet in diameter. With the letting of the contract for the northern outfall, the five and a half miles from the River Lea to Barking Creek, the system (with the exception of one important line and some of the pumping stations) would be substantially complete. This northern outfall was the largest single contract (£625,000), with its two and three lines of nine-foot sewers.[44] The missing spur was, of course, the northern low level, which was held up in the hope of a decision about an embankment.

As the sewerage system moved from the drawing board into reality, metropolitan opinion perceptibly sweetened. Papers which had damned the Board for flagrantly wasting time and money two years before, now turned to praise. Both the *Observer* and the *City Press,* no friend of the Board in the past, praised the work extravagantly.[45] In the interests of better public relations, the Board in 1861 staged a specially conducted tour for fifteen hundred members of vestries and district boards — an expedient which converted the *Marylebone Mercury* into an enthusiast for the new sewerage system. The day apparently went off beautifully, with everybody profiting from Bazalgette's detailed explanation of the various features of his plans, and was marred by only two casualties. A vestryman slipped off a plank and was precipitated into the ooziest mud; and the party's food was lost when its boat collided with another on its way down river.[46] In the following summer, members of Parliament and peers took a similar tour, with similar huzzahs for Bazalgette and main drainage.[47] There were no casualties then.

Even in its incomplete state, the main drainage system was an impressive sight. When it was completed it would cover between eighty-two and eighty-three miles. The object was, of course, to get out of the Thames the baneful influence of 52 million gallons of sewage that had daily been poured into it and to divert this mass to the lower river, some fourteen miles below London Bridge. At Barking Creek and Crossness, the sewage would be cast into the river during the first two hours of ebb tide, which would, according to Bazalgette's computations, carry it to twelve miles below the outfalls, or twenty-six miles below London Bridge. Further, the system was designed to give improved drainage to the entire metropolitan area, even to carrying away all but heavy rainfalls.[48] The system was capable of intercepting some 400 million gallons of sewage. It is difficult for a nontechnical hand to give a fair picture.

Certainly by this time Chadwick's notion of main drainage by small pipes seemed preposterous. Bazalgette's tunnels, huge as they were, did not appear excessive. Except for the western sewers, which were smaller, these ran in diameter from four by three and a half feet to twelve feet. The whole system was built in twenty-six contracts.[49] Perhaps the best evidence in justification of Bazalgette's plan is that it forms the basis of London's twentieth-century system.

To get an idea of the process of construction, one can turn to the *Illustrated London News*. The drawings give an impression of the variety of construction demanded of the contractors and the extraordinary solidity of the result. Here, for example, instead of sinking the sewers, the contractor has carried them as an aqueduct across low, swampy country; there, he has had to build culverts to drain the land before he could even get to the business of the sewer. For the northern outfall the contractor had to have sixty acres of gravel land for ballast; and for the various pumping stations, which could contain engines of nearly 2,500 horsepower, he had to become a builder.[50] Small wonder that the newspapers' boos and hisses of a few months before suddenly turned into crows of triumph as they discovered that the metropolis was acquiring an asset of permanent value.

It was, however, a costly asset, and when it appeared that the cost would exceed the estimate by a substantial figure, questions were raised, on and off the Board. In the autumn of 1861 Bazalgette still anticipated completing the system for not too much more than the £2,800,000 estimated.[51] But by the spring of 1863, this hope had faded. The explanation apparently lay in precisely the kinds of emergencies that seem to overtake such enterprises. The price of bricks went up by between 12 and 20 percent, and a strike of London workmen affected the contractors disastrously.[52] Then too, the failure of Rowe, contractor for the northern middle-level sewer, and the readvertising for tenders, added another £78,000 to the bill. Over £225,000 was accounted for in changes required by act of Parliament after the estimates had been made. In any case, the sad truth was that London's main drainage was to cost not the £2,800,000 that had been contemplated but an estimated £4,115,000.[53] Bazalgette argued strenuously in defense, citing the authority of Robert Stephenson and Sir William Cubitt for the soundness of his original estimate. He pointed out also how closely recent contracts had been following his own estimates. In any event, whether or not the estimates had been legitimate, the Board now had no alternative. It had spent £2,200,000 and had only £800,000 left to meet future demands. And that sum was running out at the rate of about £85,000 a month.[54] Nothing remained but to ask Parliament for an act to increase the Board's borrowing powers by some £1,200,000.

Bazalgette had followed the policy of opening each branch of the drainage system as it was completed. But by the summer of 1864 he was predicting that, except for the low-level sewer and the pumping stations, the whole assignment would be finished within a year. About sixty-six miles of intercepting sewers, together with pumping stations and reservoirs, had been constructed. Could not the formal opening be set for the spring of 1865? The Main Drainage Committee invited the Prince of Wales to preside over the opening, and named 4 April as the day. Invitations were sent to a distinguished party, including a number of royal personages, archbishops, cabinet ministers, Members of Parliament, the Lord Mayors of London and Dublin, and the presidents of learned societies. There were nearly five hundred acceptances.

On the appointed day the royal party landed at the Barking outfall, inspected it, and passed on to the southern outfall at Crossness. Then the Prince of Wales set in motion four pumping engines, and the main drainage system was formally in operation.[55] In its enthusiasm the Main Drainage Committee proposed to shower the sum of £10,000 on the chief engineer and his assistants in recognition of the successful project, "which is universally pronounced to be one of the greatest works of this or any other age."[56] The result, predictable enough, was a blast of protests from the vestries.[57] Main drainage or none, the emotions of vestrymen remained as soundly committed to economy as ever.

Despite the formal opening, one important link in the chain remained incomplete. This was the northern low-level sewer, inextricably bound up with the building of an embankment, and the Abbey Mills Pumping Station, where engines were to lift the low-level sewage to the outfall sewer. The sewer was held up by special factors, notably delays in the Metropolitan Railway construction, but the pumping station was pushed through to completion and, in 1868, began to handle sewage from the sections of the line already completed. This Abbey Mills Station—the building and some of the equipment still have a place in the system—was regarded as the crowning glory of Bazalgette's scheme, partly because it was the largest plant of its kind in the world. The structure was built in cruciform shape, with the longer dimension over 142 feet, and with an ornamental cupola 110 feet high rising at the crossing. It was designed, in the Victorian fashion, to blend utility with aesthetic pleasure, but some objected to its great cost and to its nonfunctional character, complaining that it "might be taken for a mosque or Chinese temple . . . For embellishments no music-hall in London could be compared with it, and the cost of the roof alone [would] be sufficient to erect a building suitable for the purposes for which the pumping station is required."[58] Though to the twentieth-century eye the building appears to

2. Construction of Abbey Mills Pumping Station, West Ham

be a good enough example of Victorian Romanesque, Bazalgette could not ascribe it to any specific style, finding it to be "mixed, and the decoration consist[ing] of coloured bricks, encaustic tiles, and stone dressings, carved work being introduced at the caps of piers and columns."[59] Today the structure seems a delightful monument to the Victorian passion for giving even the most utilitarian of buildings, standing in a swamp, an aesthetic hallmark. It looks like anything but a pumping house. It should, by all means, be preserved as a capital example of that impulse.

Whatever one's judgment of the pumping station as a structure, the contents were imposing. The station was equipped with eight engines, each of 142 horsepower, capable of lifting 15,000 cubic feet of sewage per minute to the required height of thirty-six feet. Two engines were in each of the four wings of the building. Each engine had two boilers, eight feet in diameter and thirty feet long, each in turn working two great pumps. When, in June 1868, Thwaites opened the pumping station, the

main drainage scheme was practically complete, and the units still un-
completed would be filled in presently. It was obviously a success, and
those who, in the early years of the Board's career, had prophesied the
prompt extinction of the Board and had published leaders under such
titles as "The Uselessness of the Board of Works" now had to eat their
words.[60] Apparently the MBW had arrived.

With the intercepting sewers under control, the Board could turn its
attention to its other drainage responsibilities. By the Metropolis Local
Management Act of 1855, all main lines of sewer, some 165 miles of
them, had been turned over to the Board, which was made responsible
for their upkeep. These sewers, most of them old watercourses north of
the river, as a whole emptied into the Thames. They represented all degrees of decrepitude. When cesspools were abolished, the old watercourses came into service as sewers, but before they could be used effectively they required deepening, straightening, and covering. In fact, at
the time they came under the Board's control, something like one-fifth of
them were still open. In 1864 the Board voted to make about £390,000
worth of repairs on the metropolitan main sewers, and to make them
within four years.[61] The Board knew that this would not be enough. In
the end, these repairs and renovations cost nearly £750,000.[62]

During the years in which the intercepting sewers were being laid, the
British public was bewitched by the fantasy of profits to be made from
the use of the sewage as fertilizer. With Chadwick this prospect had been
an obsession; and with newspaper editors, members of Parliament, and
public men generally, hopes of profitable utilization ran high. Though
the Board at first entered with some cordiality into the enterprise, its
leaders came to recognize, sooner than the public, that the use of sewage
as fertilizer on a large scale involved so many practical difficulties as to
be, for the foreseeable future, impossible. In 1860, as a beginning was
made on the main drainage works, the Board advertised for tenders and
ultimately received a half-dozen, of which only one included details. The
committee was still considering these when a Select Committee of the
House of Commons returned a report which on the whole endorsed the
use of sewage, not unduly diluted, as fertilizer.[63] This report, it was suspected, might stimulate tenders, and the Board advertised again, in July
1863. While these latest tenders were being considered, another Select
Committee of the House, under the chairmanship of Lord Robert Montague, launched another inquiry.[64]

This was by no means a model committee, nor was Montague a
model chairman. Throughout he was governed by an *idée fixe* that metropolitan sewage was a valuable asset which the MBW was going to
squander, and by the notion that the Board was not only inefficient but

corrupt. He tried to show that very few tenders had been received because of the heavy costs involved, and implied that the Board had been hasty in selecting the scheme that they chose.[65] He thought that he sniffed corruption in the granting of the Embankment contract, in a discrepancy in the size of the northern reservoir, and in the Board's choice of engines. *The Builder* was understating the case when it observed, "it does not seem clear to us that the [Montague] committee are not going out of their province."[66] It was unquestionably true that the Committee, in addition to its terms of reference, was staging a fishing expedition into several transactions of the Board. It had before it a contractor who thought himself wronged, and it sought to convict Bazalgette of a tainted past. But the Committee did summon a number of agriculturists and engineers who had successfully used sewage on land and concluded that it was "not only possible to utilize the sewage of towns, by conveying it, in a liquid state, through mains and pipes to the country, but that such an undertaking may be made to result in pecuniary benefit to the ratepayers of the towns whose sewage is thus utilized."[67]

The question now came down to whether Messrs. Napier and Hope, the most persistent applicants, should be awarded the concession. The Board's suspicions should have been more thoroughly aroused than was the case, for Napier was the author of an extraordinarily silly report on the Bagshot Sands written for the old Board of Health.[68] Napier and Hope proposed to construct a huge culvert to carry sewage the forty-four miles from Barking to the Foulness Sands on the Essex shore. The fifteen to twenty thousand acres of this desert would blossom as a rose through the application of the sewage of the metropolis. Before accepting the Napier Hope tender, the Board looked over the field. The Main Drainage Committee visited Rugby, Croydon, Carlisle, and Edinburgh, all of which used sewage as fertilizer, and at three of them found the smell offensive. But their report was somewhat qualified, for the members were simply unable to appraise the results with any confidence.[69]

Meanwhile, trouble was blowing up with the City Corporation, which had sensed the possibility of profit and which now put in its claim for the future contents of the reservoirs at Barking Creek. Between the two parties there was disagreement on principle, for the City took a dim view of the attempt to reclaim 15,000 acres of "quicksand on the shores of the German Ocean."[70] There were, in fact, two approaches—neither, as it turned out, of any profit. Napier and Hope intended to apply the whole mass of sewage to one area, the assumption being that sewage had within itself everything necessary to grow crops. The City Corporation took the position that London sewage ought to fertilize a much larger area than the Foulness Sands, and had fortified itself with the magisterial opinion of Justus von Liebig. "There is not the slightest doubt," said the Baron, "that every penny expended in that frivolous undertaking will be irretrievably lost."[71] His prophecy was infallibly correct, but the City was being just as absurd as the Board when it contended that London sewage ought not to go for less than £2 million a year!

In spite of all the talk, the Board got only two reasonably firm tenders, from Napier and Hope and from one Thomas Ellis, former Irish solicitor and promoter by nature, who intended to put up a reservoir on Hampstead Heath. However much the enthusiasts for sewage fertilizer might argue that this disappointing response was all the Board's fault, the fact is that advertisements did not bring a host of adventurers. There was literally no practical alternative to accepting the offer of Messrs. Napier and Hope, and the Board decided to take it by a vote of 26 to 9, the two City members present voting against it.[72] A Select Committee of the House in 1865 agreed that the scheme would be a useful and profitable way of using sewage, despite the reservations of scientific experts. Augustus Voelcker, a distinguished agricultural chemist, for example, doubted whether manure could be applied to sand successfully, and was certain that towns would not profit much from its sale.[73]

The agreement with Messrs. Napier and Hope was fair enough. They were to construct along the whole line a nine-foot six-inch culvert and to take as much sewage as would pass through a culvert of this size. The provisions all reflected the dogged optimism of promoters. The concession was to last for fifty years, and the two parties were to share the net profits on a fifty-fifty basis, which were thought likely to rise as high as 20 percent on a capital of £2 million. Finally, the promoters were to deposit as security, to be forfeited if the culvert was not completed, the sum of £25,000 — the only profit the MBW ever made from metropolitan sewage!

For a time the work of the promoters went well enough. But presently capital came in more slowly, investors grew cautious (the financial panic of 1866, of course, did not improve the company's prospects), and in 1868 the work came to a standstill.[74] By the summer of 1870 it was clear that the company had no future, and the Board voted that the £25,000 deposit was forfeited. Despite its supporters claiming that the company was the innocent victim of a grandiloquent plan which was impossible of fulfillment,[75] the company was liquidated. Its remaining capital was shown to be a little less than £500,000, of which it salvaged only about £2,600. It was a costly venture for promoters and investors alike.

Meanwhile, the Board was still receiving plans for the sewage from south of the river, among them one by Thomas Ellis, the unsuccessful competitor for the northern concession. His scheme seemed to offer some attractive features, and the Board began negotiations, though its engineer estimated the cost of Ellis's works at nearly £1 million more than Ellis's estimates. Perhaps fortunately for the promoter, the money market was tight after the crisis of 1866, and the Ellis project expired in infancy, with no great damage to the participants.[76]

Though these earlier attempts had failed dismally, hope was not dead in the breasts of those who professed to see a fortune in sewage. Experiments were still going on in the early seventies, the best publicized being those of an enterprise felicitously named the Native Guano Company, which was carrying on tests at Crossness. Here the sewage was treated with alum, blood, and clay — the ABC process, it was called — to make a more complete manurial product.[77] What had occurred here was precisely what had been suspected by some well-informed persons. It was entirely possible to make fertilizer from sewage. The question was whether the resulting product could be sold at a profit. The experiments of the Native Guano Company seemed to show that the cost of making the product was five to six times its sales value. As the company itself, it spent all of its capital on futile experiments and in the end was ordered by the Board to remove its equipment from the Crossness pumping station where the tests had taken place.[78]

With the completion of the main drainage system, the initial task of the MBW was finished. It was an unquestioned triumph, and, though it had eventually cost about £4.6 million, London opinion adjudged it worth the price. "London," *The Times* could exult in 1873, having conveniently forgotten its indignant leaders of five years before, "has been transformed in a comparatively brief period, if not into a clean, at least into a healthy city . . . The Board of Works has done itself credit, and its constitution and methods have been far more than justified . . . It has done its work effectually, expeditiously and cheaply."[79] Even the vestries had become reconciled to the sewerage rates they were charged. There had been no criticism, on or off the Board, when in 1865 Thwaites received a knighthood from Her Majesty.[80]

Though the intercepting system was clearly justifying itself, details of its operation were inevitably going to raise questions. One of its arguable features still was the placement of the outfalls; they were as close to the metropolis as could be managed without allowing the sewage to return within its limits. This was the result of a nice calculation, which of course was not universally accepted and whose conclusions were, as it turned out, not for eternity. It was predicted that questions would be raised and that charges of relieving London at the expense of settlements downstream would be made.

The Thames Conservancy Board, consisting largely of representatives of the City, the Admiralty, the Board of Trade, and Trinity House, was first in the field. The Thames Conservators were responsible for maintaining the river in a navigable condition, avoiding excessive charges for dredging and for preventing pollution. Though the MBW tried repeatedly, it was never able to get a seat on the Conservancy, a fact which led to remarks about everybody being represented but the people of London. Communication between the two bodies was always formal and uneasy. In January 1868 the Conservators complained that deposits at Crossness and Barking Creek were interfering with navigation, and in March, Lord Eustace Cecil raised a question about mud at the outfalls. The Home Secretary advised arbitration to see who should clear it away, but neither side responded cordially. The Conservators said that they had no money, and the Board reminded the Conservators that the outfalls had been located where they were with the permission of Parliament.[81] The Conservators then promoted the Thames Navigation Act of 1870, which in two of its clauses required the Board to keep the river free from banks or obstructions to navigation resulting from the flow of sewage. And here the matter rested for a decade.

Meanwhile, in January 1869, the inhabitants of Barking, led by their vicar, had entered the controversy with a memorial complaining of obstruction and pollution of Barking Creek by the discharge of sewage. Robert Rawlinson, and engineer of distinction, was instructed to hold an inquiry. The investigation took six days, with the Board sending up some twenty-five witnesses. Although Rawlinson's report queried whether the outfalls were not, in fact, too close to Central London, it did not accept the Barking remonstrations, which, Rawlinson held, were either untrue and irresponsible or unproved. Barking, he recalled, was an unhealthy spot, outfalls or no outfalls, and was innocent alike of sewerage of its own and of municipal government.[82]

The drainage front remained relatively quiet for the better part of a decade. There were, of course, details that gave trouble. Bazalgette, for example, had difficulty with the ventilation of the sewers, and a committee to whom the question was referred could find no answer other than local palliatives.[83] But toward the end of the 1870s it became clear that the question was entering a new phase. Bazalgette had built the system for a population of 3.5 million, which had given a margin of roughly a million. By 1871, the population had reached this figure,[84] and was continuing to soar. By 1889 it exceeded 4.5 million. Furthermore, communities farther up the river were adding their offensive contributions to the total. This was, indeed, the situation which had been foreseen by a number of critics at the time the main drainage system was built. But it had been politically impossible to carry the outfalls farther downstream at the cost of higher rates; and, anyway, the engineers had pointed out, this could be done at a later date.

London began to realize that, well-designed and well-constructed as the main drainage system might be, there were still changes which might be required. The heavy storms and high tides which occurred in the mid-1870s produced grave floods and some loss of life. Did the Board's improvements have something to do with these disaster? It was suggested (and denied) that the embankments, by narrowing the channel at some points, must have tended to throw a greater quantity of water on the unprotected parts of the river, and that the removal of the old London and Westminster bridges had increased the volume of tides.[85] For the low-lying south bank, some of which was normally below the river level at high tide, these storms were a disaster. Early January 1877 saw storms, a high tide, and a flood of unexampled severity. Within a few days the Lord Mayor's relief fund had reached £4,500, and a meeting of delegates from the affected parishes was demanding remedial measures.[86]

Whose fault was it and what was to be done? Here the Board and the affected parishes did not see eye to eye. The Board's formula was simple. It proposed, with Parliament's permission, to carry the necessary works into effect and levy rates on the areas involved. Here, of course, it met with opposition from the riverside vestries, which demanded that the cost be taken out of general metropolitan funds. In any event, individual owners could do something. The Board had found numbers of wharfingers entirely cooperative in raising their frontage, and of about 800 riparian owners and occupiers, 200 complied fully and 150 partly. But 450 still held out.[87] Much would have to be left to a higher authority, presumably the vestries and district boards.

These appeared in force, with batteries of expensive counsel, to oppose a bill which would charge them with the costs of flood protection. It was, of course, a nice problem to distinguish between improvements which were properly metropolitan and those which were local. Vestries naturally sought to show that their improvements were properly metropolitan and to shove the expense off on the metropolis. There was much discussion along familiar lines — for example, why should Fulham pay for protection for the Southwark river front? And even the Board had been far from unanimous on the question, twenty members having voted for throwing the taxation on the vestries with frontages on the river, fifteen for making the cost a metropolitan charge.[88]

When the Select Committee on the Prevention of Floods Bill voted in 1877 to make the cost a metropolitan charge, the Board decided to drop the bill. But the following year it returned to the fray with a new bill which proposed to make flood protection the responsibility of the owners of front property.[89] In other words, the persons primarily affected by river floods would have the obligation for keeping them out, and would be compelled to pay the cost. But whereas, in the bill of 1877, vestries and district boards would have been the enforcing agent, that power would now be exercised by the Board itself.[90] Actually, the hostile parishes were few—only Fulham on the north and Wandsworth and St. Saviour's, Southwark on the south—but a covey of railways, wharfingers, and gas companies appeared with counsel.[91] Bazalgette was quite justified in pointing out that certain firms spent more in opposing the bill than their compliance with the Board's request would have cost them.[92]

By this time over twenty-seven miles out of the total of forty-six and a half miles had been protected (that is, nearly three-fifths), and the question was losing some of its power to excite emotion.[93] In spite of an attempt by Chamberlain and Dilke, who were members of the Select Committee, to have the cost considered a metropolitan charge, the Board's argument was accepted and its bill—now presented as a private act—passed in 1879.[94] Owners of property, therefore, would be obliged to execute the necessary flood protection works at their own expense or to repay the Board the cost of those executed by the Board. Similarly, vestries and district boards would be responsible for public property in their control.[95] It may be that the Board in this new act was taking the easy—and illogical—way out of a dilemma, arguing in effect that since "the Thames is the common property of Londoners," they should share in both the benefits it brought and the occasional losses it inflicted.[96] That was, no doubt, a fair criticism, though one should not be unduly sympathetic toward wharfingers and other waterside businesses; as Bazalgette put it, "if they enjoy the advantage of being up on the river, and derive great wealth from the river, it is not an unreasonable obligation to expect them to construct their wharves so as to keep the water from overflowing."[97] Still, the shift in principle from the bill of 1877 to the new bill appeared to be one purely of expediency, and one on which the Board itself was sharply divided. It does not do to look to the MBW for the enunciation of progressive social principles. This was out of the question, given its make-up and the parochial outlook of many of its members.

Apart from river flooding, there was also, and more commonly, floodingfrom heavy rainfall. Should the main drainage system have prevented the flooded cellars that were more or less endemic on the south bank? Perhaps, answered the newspapers, but after all, London had grown unimaginably in twenty years. Our fathers "boldly grappled with the outlay of millions; they made London the healthiest Metropolis in the world; and if they declined to face the outlay of an extra million or two in anticipation of wants not then ascertained, let us be ready to complete the work they began."[98] Actually, Bazalgette's main drainage system had not been designed to cope with storms of this volume, and the strain on it grew greater year by year as more land was settled and more roads paved. Districts which had formerly escaped now suffered from overflow. As the *City Press* observed, not quite fairly, "In plain words, the main drainage system was designed for London as it was, not for London as it is."[99]

The intercepting sewers, to repeat, were intended to carry off only as much rainfall as could be *reasonably* managed. To handle exceptional falls, overflow weirs had been constructed at the junctions of the intercepting sewers and the main lines following the valleys. When the intercepting sewers were full, the water flowed over the weirs and down its original channels into the river. In a heavy rainfall the contents of the sewer would, of course, be extremely diluted, and no great harm would result from its discharge into the river. As time passed, however, and London grew, the margins in this scheme narrowed, and even lesser rains caused serious difficulties. The Board had the question under consideration for some years but could not bring itself to a decision. By 1879, however, protests grew and, in fact, reached the point where a deputation from two parishes, Lambeth and Wandsworth, went to the Board to complain about the recurring floods.[100] The Board now took the inevitable step and decided on a series of storm sewers, which were begun in 1880 and completed in 1886 at a cost of about £700,000.[101]

Still, the most troublesome perennial question connected with main drainage had to do with the location of the outfalls at Barking and Crossness, eleven and thirteen miles respectively down river from London Bridge. In the late seventies, this again became an active issue, emerging initially as a by-product of the old feud between the Thames Conservancy and the Board. In December 1877 Captain Calver, for the Conservators, issued a report on the change in the river bed, a report which Bazalgette promptly termed nonsense.[102] In September 1878 a tragic accident added kindling to the smoldering blaze. The *Princess Alice*, an excursion steamer, collided with another boat and dumped its passengers into the river at the time and place where the outflows were spewing forth their noxious contents. A large number were drowned, and of the 130 survivors 14 died subsequently. Although there were some wild newspaper charges that those in the water had been choked by sewage and the death toll vastly increased by the existence of the outfalls, such statements were not widely credited. What did seem possible — indeed likely — was that persons who were saved from drowning but died afterwards had been poisoned by the sewage in the river.[103]

Some of the more thoughtful members of the press pointed out that in the past quarter-century much new engineering knowledge had been acquired. To a generation that had been accustomed to dumping its sewage into the river, it seemed an incomparable benefaction to get it taken away as far as Barking. The river at Barking Creek seemed almost wide enough to be an estuary of the sea. That view, however, had sounded more convincing in 1855 than it did in 1878. As London's population increased and the mass of sewage mounted, one could not accept so readily the Board's argument that the sewage was practically all carried away on the ebb tide and that, anyway, it was so thoroughly diluted by the river as to make no difference.[104]

Unfortunately, in meeting this criticism, the Board chose to adopt a stiff-necked stance, as it had increasingly tended to do during the late 1870s. The Board's activities had diversified and had become more complex. But its resources for carrying them out had not expanded, and clearly it suffered from lack of energetic, imaginative leadership. To answer the attacks in the metropolitan press, the Board determined to see for itself, and it organized two expeditions to Gravesend, to convince "the public" as *The Builder* ironically put it, "that the discharge of the sewage of a city of four millions of inhabitants into the river is not detrimental to that river, or only to a very small extent."[105] The two safaris were carried out, apparently, with exemplary conscientiousness — albeit the conscientiousness of semiamateurs — and the members came away with the predictable conclusion that neither had the polluting of the water gone to dangerous limits nor had the silting of the river amounted to anything serious. Whatever the technical competence of the tests that were made, at least the Board showed its goodwill by spending two bitter winter days on the deck of a steamboat on the river — even if, announced *The Times*, the facts might have been determined just as ably by a laborer at a pound a week.[106]

The Conservators were not, however, chiefly concerned with pollution, and still less with the Board's do-it-yourself demonstration. What they demanded was that the Board undertake dredging, which was prescribed by the Thames Navigation Act of 1870 if the formation of shoals or banks resulting from the discharge of sewage should prove an impediment to navigation. The Board denied that it was an impediment, but the Conservators insisted on action. The way out, according to the act, was an arbitration, with three arbitrators, one appointed by each of the contesting parties and a third by the Board of Trade. The inquiry was long — twenty-five days and some 1,170 pages of evidence — and technical, with batteries of expert witnesses who seemed to cancel one another out. Still, the arbitrators' conclusions appeared, in general, to bear out the MBW's contention that the banks had not arisen, within the meaning of the act of 1870, from the flow of sewage at the outfalls.[107] What had created the banks, they concluded, was the precipitation of matter suspended in the water, of which metropolitan sewage formed only a small fraction. Incidentally, the arbitrators noted that in the four years 1875–1878, all of which had had virtually a uniform amount of rainfall, the sewage flow had increased by about 14 percent. The shoals, to the arbitrators, were natural formations, the inevitable result of dredging in a stream charged with solid matter, and were no responsibility of the Board.

This cheering verdict soothed the Board, but not for long. Complaints over the condition of the river continued and grew in volume. In 1881 one deputation with petitions signed by 13,500 waited on the president of the Local Government Board to protest, and *The Times* agreed that from Richmond to Gravesend the state of the river had been deteriorating.[108] The City Corporation, as the Port Sanitary Authority, joined in the chorus, together with the Plumstead vestry, and pressure mounted on Sir William Harcourt, the Home Secretary, to appoint a Royal Commission to examine the matter.[109] When Harcourt announced his Commission — with Lord Bramwell, an eminent judge and brother to the engineer appointed by the Board on the 1879–80 arbitration, as chairman — the Board was not reassured, for two of the six members, it was charged, were on record as opposing the position of the outfalls.[110]

The Bramwell Commission carried on an exhaustive and fair-minded inquiry, and emerged in 1884 with conclusions which were by no means unfavorable to the Board, however the Board might have regarded them. Its historical survey sketched the background lucidly, and its analysis of the current problem seemed objective enough. But the conclusion that a serious nuisance existed was inescapable. The daily discharge of sewage was immense, and the idea that this could be effectively diluted by the water of the river was a fallacy. The Board could not refute this judgment effectively; it could only insist that the evidence was exaggerated — as, indeed, some of it was — and that the worst of the odor was the result of exceptional conditions, for the summer of 1884 had been notoriously dry.[111] At any rate, when the Commission's First Report appeared with its conclusion that the outfalls were an indubitable nuisance,[112] the Board decided on partial noncooperation. Having disagreed with the First Report, it said it was not prepared to propose any scheme for the treatment of sewage — the topic of the Commission's further inquiries.[113]

That the Board took this attitude was regrettable, especially since much of its main drainage work had been highly creditable. If it had admitted that the times had changed, that the volume of sewage now carried by the system exceeded the original estimates, and that the system would have to be altered, as it could be without revolutionary changes—in short, if it had shown a reasonable flexibility—it would have received praise throughout the metropolis. But instead, the Home Secretary had to apply pressure to get action from the Board. In July in a tough letter, Harcourt quoted from Lord Bramwell's report of an expedition taken by the Commissioners to examine the condition of the river: "The River," he reported, "was in such a state as to be a disgrace and a scandal to the Metropolis and civilisation . . . We proceeded up the River, and traced the Sewage nearly to Limehouse. Up to Greenwich it appeared unmixed sewage, then patches of natural water appeared, which increased till the sewage ended. The Tide had then two hours to flow, and I cannot see why some sewage should not reach London Bridge, or nearly."[114] Harcourt also quoted from police reports that reached similar conclusions, and demanded a report from the Board. The reply of Sir James McGarel-Hogg, the Board's chairman, was no doubt true enough, but it could hardly have been reassuring. The crisis, one gathered, was the result of exceptional heat and drought, combined with the Board's inability to get a deodorizing agent in sufficient quantities. London opinion did not embrace the Board's view. "The Metropolitan Board," exclaimed *The Times,* "has nostrils constituted on peculiar principles and perceived nothing until this year but a slight scent of violets in the neighborhood of its sewage outfalls." In spite of the Board's position, it continued, "The freeing of the Thames from pollution must be undertaken as a work to be done and paid for, whatever the cost may be."[115]

Despite frequent prods through 1885 the Board apparently took no action. A conference of vestries and district boards was eager for action, but experiments which the Board carried on proceeded with disappointing calm.[116] It was not until the end of 1885 that the Board decided to accept part of the Bramwell Commission's report and made plans to precipitate the solid matter and to carry the sludge out to sea.[117] This was the beginning of a long and deliberate series of developments which resulted, in January 1887, in the expenditure of £406,000 for the building of works at Barking, and in May 1888, of £259,816 for works at Crossness. Similarly, the Board, finding that farmers were not drawn irresistibly to the use of sewage as manure, even when offered it free of charge, contracted for the building of first one boat and then, when that appeared to work well, of another to carry the sludge out to sea.[118]

The Board certainly had not been eager to follow the recommendations of the Bramwell Commission. In some degree, perhaps, this reluctance reflected the attitude of Bazalgette, the designer and superintendent of the original system, now an old and tired man. He did not, of course, relish seeing his main drainage, on which so much praise had been lavished, called into question. Moreover, he had been with the Board for so long that he had, perhaps, gained an excessive influence over its decisions. But whatever the Board's attitude, Londoners were delighted that at last a decision seemed to have been made, or at least to be in the making. Perhaps the era was passing when one could say, with *The Times,* "Anybody who has frequented the Thames would, though he had been years away and returned blind, recognize its stream by the dull brooding atmosphere of odours the Metropolitan Board of Works brews from its London sewage."[119]

The Board, in its twilight hours, had thus reached the solution the Bramwell Commission had recommended. This solution is the one, in substance, that is still being followed by the Greater London Council. The Board can be criticized, but not for having built badly in the first place. It may have been short-sighted to stop at Barking and Crossness, but, in fact, it had no practical alternative, in view of the hostility of the Treasury. Given the attitudes of the 1850s, it was hardly an obligation of a London agency to carry London sewage to the sea at the cost of a million or so additional pounds to the London ratepayer. Where the Board was more blameworthy was in its obstinate refusal to recognize that something had finally gone wrong with the outfalls. No impartial witness, observed *The Builder,* could doubt that the river was full of London sewage.[120] The time had clearly come to revise the location of the outfalls and to consider the recommendation that the sewage be deodorized, as, in fact, the plans had originally specified. That the Board took so long to reach this decision constituted another black mark against it when it entered upon its days of adversity.

CHAPTER 4

The Embankment

When the Thames Embankment Act became law in 1862, there was nothing novel about the notion of embanking the Thames. A history of small embankments, largely for commercial purposes, lay in the background, and seemed to suggest the desirability of a larger and more splendid venture. The removal of the old London Bridge in 1832 had brought about a marked change in the character of the river, an increase in the height of the tides and a general, though not uniform, lowering of the river bed. Furthermore, as Londoners contemplated the changes in the metropolis which had taken place since the turn of the century, the extension of the residential areas to the north and east and of docks and warehouses to the east, they saw a river front that was clearly unworthy of the growing magnificence of London. At least from the middle 1840s, an embankment was a realistic possibility, favored by an increasing number of influential Londoners. But the problems of how it would be built and by whom seemed far from solution.

In 1844 a Royal Commission, following the Select Committees on Metropolitan Improvements of the thirties, looked into the question and examined some plans that had been submitted. The Commission, in an interesting essay on the difficulty of improving London, noted the existence of "classes of interests — municipal, commercial and professional — associated and represented in various ways (in accordance with our popular institutions) [which] necessarily exercise, in their several spheres, an extensive influence on public opinion." As the Commission went on to say, these pressures are "infinitely various, and often conflicting in their tendencies," and they would represent a major handicap to anybody that had to make the decisions and supervise the work.[1] In any case, it was a task beyond the resources of private individuals. Plainly it awaited the intervention of the State. The Commission concluded that an embankment ought to be built between Westminster and Blackfriars bridges on the Middlesex side, estimating that about £215,000 would be required.[2]

Throughout the 1850s the opposition of the wharfingers was so virulent that no progress was made.[3] During the decade, however, the question took on new importance, partly because of the creation of the MBW. To build or not to build an embankment might greatly influence the Board's plans for its intercepting drainage system. All the plans of private firms of engineers put forward throughout the 1840s and 1850s had one weakness in common: they were designed to be commercially profitable, that is, to offer wharfage facilities for business houses on the river. To its credit, the Board would have no truck with this notion. A committee of the Board dismissed two early plans with the comment that their promoters had prejudiced their "schemes by attempting to make them commercially remunerative." The committee considered "that a work of such magnitude and of so peculiar a character . . . ought not to be left to commercial enterprise, but should be carried out by a public body and by means of public funds, and conducted solely with a view to the public advantage."[4] Whether or not the Board was primarily concerned in maintaining its own role as builder of the Embankment makes no difference. On this issue its position was indubitably correct.

What gave special urgency was the construction of the intercepting sewers. Obviously, if there was to be an embankment, the northern low-level sewer should be built as a part of it. Otherwise there would be the messy prospect of laying the sewer under the Strand, with the certainty of months of confusion and interference with business activities. Indeed, such a course would require a reversal of the flow of sewage for a considerable distance between the Strand and the river.

In 1860 a Select Committee of the House, with Sir Joseph Paxton in the chair and with such members as Sir Morton Peto, William Cubitt (Lord Mayor at the time), and William Tite (architect and member of the Board), examined a number of plans that had been submitted.[5] All of them involved either facilities for wharfingers or substantial amounts of land to be left for building purposes to recoup some of the cost. John Thwaites, chairman of the MBW, put up a strong case for regarding the Embankment as, at least in part, an imperial charge, and also argued for an extension of the coal and wine dues,[6] which were usually applied to improvements within the City. And Bazalgette spoke convincingly of the superiority of an embankment to the Strand route for his low-level sewer.

The Select Committee's recommendation was satisfactory to the MBW insofar as the Board was to do the job, financed by an extension of the coal and wine duties. But the Select Committee could not make up its mind whether the Embankment was to be simply a public amenity or whether it would be constructed, at least in part, for commercial purposes. Having heard from a number of wharfingers, the Committee members merely soothed their uneasy spirits by remarking that they and other businesses would also have improved facilities on the new Embankment.

The recommendations of the Select Committee were reasonably clear-cut, but they did not deal with all of the issues involved. For example, they made no attempt, beyond some general observations, to specify the character of the Embankment that was to be built. What was needed, they held, was a more searching, technical examination of the problem by a Royal Commission, taking advice from engineers, surveyors, and builders. This was set in motion in February 1861 when the Government appointed a Royal Commission under the chairmanship of William Cubitt.[7] The Cubitt Commission numbered among its members a reluctant John Thwaites, who regarded the exercise as both unnecessary and as an expedient on the part of the Government to postpone decisive action.

In spite of Thwaites's skepticism, however, the new Commission examined over fifty sets of plans and many witnesses, and it came out with clearer guidelines than had any of the previous bodies.[8] It pointed out how absurd it would be to try to save the coal wharves between Westminster Bridge and Temple Gardens,[9] for they were no longer essential for the distribution of coal to the metropolis. Railways had made such wharves obsolete, or at least superfluous. The obvious course was to wipe out all docks and wharves and to make the Embankment west of Blackfriars Bridge a means of beautifying the river. The Commission went on to propose a spacious roadway along the shore and a new street from Blackfriars Bridge to the Mansion House. If the wharves were disposed of, the construction of the Embankment would be simplified, as Bazalgette noted.[10] There was, however, an augury of trouble ahead — Daniel Norton and Sir James Pennethorne for the Crown, as well as the Crown lessees, objected to the proposal for a roadway between the Crown estates (which were leased by wealthy aristocrats) and the river.[11] In the end, this matter of the lessees turned out to be a vexing problem.

Neither the Crown nor its lessees, who included such figures as the Duke of Buccleuch and Lord Clifton, behaved in a conspicuously magnanimous fashion.

One feature of the final report outraged Thwaites. This was the Commission's recommendation that the Embankment's construction be vested not in the MBW but in a special commission. Cubitt and his colleagues had reached this conclusion largely as a result of the evidence of G. P. Bidder, a prominent engineer, who suggested that the machinery of the MBW was cumbersome and not suited to carrying out such works "either expeditiously or economically."[12] Thwaites recalled the history of the Embankment idea and noted the bodies that had agreed on the Board as a proper agency for building it. Had Thwaites been present when the issue was discussed in the Commission? He said no—and he was a devout Baptist local preacher. He explained also, in a protest attached to the report, that he could not have been present when it was discussed and decided. Cubitt, Lord Mayor of the City of London and a highly respected builder, replied acidly that Thwaites's memory had failed him and that he had, indeed, been present when the critical decisions were taken.[13] The record of the Commission affords no further enlightenment.

Whether or not he had taken part in the Commission's decision, Thwaites had no intention of accepting it without a fight. Although he could hardly have worked for the aggrandizement of the MBW, as the *City Press* charged, Thwaites was never reluctant to accept further duties for the Board, nor complaisant when it was suggested that it be shorn of its power or functions.[14] In August and September 1861 he negotiated with William Cowper, First Commissioner of Works, in an effort to persuade the Government to disregard this recommendation of the Cubitt Commission and to leave the work under the unfettered control of the Board. Indeed, with the knowledge that the continuation of the coal and wine dues had been assured, the Board had already instructed its engineer to prepare plans for carrying out the proposed Embankment in connection with the low-level sewer.[15] Thwaites soon discovered that Cowper had no intention of creating a special commission, but that he was equally unwilling to give the Board the kind of free hand it desired. Cowper reminded Thwaites of the questions that would require legislation and of the difficulties which would arise if the Board attempted to handle them by private members' bills. What the Government proposed, therefore, was to carry a bill authorizing the plan recommended by the Royal Commission and empowering the Board to carry out the work. In other words, the Board was to execute plans, formulated by the Commission, to build a kind of street from Blackfriars Bridge to the Mansion

House, the cost of which would be defrayed by the coal dues. The Board would also build the Embankment, but under a more restricted warrant than it had in building the sewers.[16]

The bill which Cowper introduced in March 1862 called for the plan of embankment recommended by the Royal Commission.[17] Its great advantage, he pointed out, was that it meant that the coal wharves would be superseded by a solid Embankment, and the beautification of the river would be assured.[18] The plan, *The Times* held, was a good one, in spite of Sir John Shelley's fears for his wharf-owning Westminster constituents.[19] From the beginning the problem of what to do about the wharves had been the toughest issue, frustrating a long line of architects and engineers. "These coal-heavers are as unnecessary in the side streets of the Strand as so many Ethiopian serenaders,"[20] *The Times* pronounced; this new plan was the inevitable one, combining the best features of its predecessors and differing from them only in the absence of ingenious singularities which the metropolis could well do without.

The Select Committee on the bill, chaired by Cowper, met in May 1862 and brought out both the interested parties and the champions of the obstructive elements. William Cubitt expressed surprise that anyone even thought of having the new street from Blackfriars Bridge to the Mansion House executed under any auspices other than those of the City, and assured the Select Committee that his Royal Commission had never entertained such a fantastic idea.[21] Shelley harried all witnesses who spoke in favor of the plan, though whether with any hope of getting a stay of execution for the wharfingers or merely to raise their probable compensation is not clear. The Embankment was now, however, to end at Blackfriars Bridge rather than continuing to Queenhithe, as had been originally contemplated, because the many wharves below the bridge were economically important and could not be disposed of except at great cost.

But the most disturbing witnesses who came before Cowper's Select Committee were representatives of the wealthy and aristocratic Crown lessees. Their residences were on land owned by the Crown and administered by the Office of Woods and Forests; but their opposition to a roadway along the Embankment was warmly opposed by the Office of Works. On one level, in fact, this became a battle between the Office of Works, which correctly thought it absurd to mutilate a great plan for public improvement in the interests of a few Crown lessees, and the Office of Woods and Forests, which fought valiantly, if myopically, on the lessees' behalf.[22] Charles Gore, the Commissioner of Woods and Forests, summoned a meeting of the lessees, whose unanimous opinion, to nobody's surprise, was that a roadway between their houses and the river would injure the residential value of their property. Cowper was not interested. He pointed out that these houses were not guaranteed an unrestricted view of the river and that their owners must give way before the needs of an important improvement. He announced his intention of going ahead with the plan proposed by the Royal Commission, and the Treasury supported him.[23]

Perhaps, if the First Commissioner of Works was immovable in his decision, the Select Committee could be delayed. Gore accordingly had Sir James Pennethorne draw up a plan which would avoid the roadway from Whitehall Stairs to Westminster Bridge. This was duly presented to the Select Committee as a plan shorter and cheaper — in a word, superior to the Embankment road.[24] The plan, supported by Gore and Edward Horsman before the Select Committee,[25] proposed that the road should leave the Embankment at Whitehall Stairs and pass through Parliament Street.[26] Obviously this was no real alternative. It would have amounted to shutting traffic in front of the residences of Crown lessees and concentrating all traffic in Parliament Street. And nothing could have been more absurd than compelling the traffic to go by Parliament Street just for the sake of the gardens of the Crown lessees.

The Select Committee came up with the recommendation, obviously a compromise, for a footway, not a roadway, from Whitehall Stairs to Westminster Bridge. The aristocratic residents had objected to having their private gardens skirted by a public roadway; therefore the public was to be permitted to walk but not to drive along this section of the Embankment. The Committee's report, *The Times* asserted, was a trivial contribution and a gigantic *suppressio veri*. What a preposterous situation, when the Commissioner of Woods and Forests could take the initiative in organizing the opposition to the public interest, calling a meeting of the Crown lessees, commissioning Sir James Pennethorne, and setting on foot resistance in Parliament![27]

A lively debate followed in the House. Cowper had no intention of accepting the recommendations of his Select Committee. There were charges that, in rejecting them, he had undercut his own Committee, and countercharges that the Committee had been subservient to the Duke of Buccleuch and the other lessees. To nobody's surprise, all charges were roundly denied. Horsman, in a long and rather adroit speech, characterized the whole fuss as a civil war between two Government offices, and noted that the Duke of Buccleuch had been singled out as a symbol of aristocratic usurpation. (Buccleuch had prudently not appeared before the Select Committee.) In a blunt speech, Lord Palmerston, then Prime Minister, refused to tolerate any more nonsense. He pointed out that the question at issue was really a simple one —

whether to stop the Embankment roadway at Whitehall Stairs or to go on to Westminster Bridge. From that elementary issue the House had been led down all sorts of absurd by-paths — onto questions of the make-up of Commissions, the integrity of Select Committees, and the like. Every irrelevancy, he suggested, had been introduced to divert the House from the real topic of debate "and to involve it, like one of Homer's heroes, in a cloud for the purpose of defending their darling object."[28] It was obvious that, if the river was to be embanked at the expense of Londoners, Londoners, rather than a few Crown lessees, should have the benefit of it. Led by John Locke, M.P. for Southwark, the House, as *The Times* reported, was persuaded that the absurdity was too great to be "concealed even by the mass of rubbish with which the Blue-book enveloped it"; "and the common sense of the House triumphed over the 'alternative' of Sir James Pennethorne, the sophistry of Lord R. Cecil, and the indecision of the Government."[29] During these years *The Times* was inclined to state its position with excessive emphasis. But apparently at least one scheme of urban improvement was to impose hardships not solely on the lower classes!

The Government thus agreed that the Board was the proper agency to build the Embankment. The convenient coal and wine duties, which had been renewed for ten years in 1861, were to bear the cost. The Coal and Wine Duties Continuance Act of 1861 had provided for fourpence of the total coal dues of thirteen pence per ton to be allotted to the City Corporation for improvements in or near the City, while the wine dues and the remaining ninepence of the coal dues were to be paid into a new account called the Thames Embankment and Metropolitan Improvement Fund. The Embankment Act of 1862 now allowed the Board to use this fund to pay for the project. This decision did not delight all hands because the tax was inherently objectionable, but the act was probably as fair as was politically possible in the 1860s.[30]

When it came to estimating its resources for the Embankment, the Board, on the authority of the First Commissioner of Works, put the annual yield of the coal and wine duties at £160,000. Since a total extension of twenty years of House dues had been granted in 1863, the Board felt entitled to borrow £2 million to cover the cost of the northern embankment and the new street (now Queen Victoria Street) from Blackfriars Bridge to the Mansion House. Concerning the new street, there was to be a sharp dispute with the City Corporation, which did not warm to what it regarded as an invasion by a foreign power. The £2 million loan, it was estimated, would cover the £1 million that the northern embankment was expected to cost, and £625,000 for the street, leaving a surplus of £375,000. But this would leave most of the southern embankment unpaid for. The Board therefore included in its bill for the southern embankment a clause permitting it to pledge the security of its general rates.[31]

In spite of *The Times'* indignation over what it professed to regard as intolerable delay,[32] Bazalgette got the project under way with reasonable speed. His plans for the first section (from Westminster to Waterloo Bridge) were ready by mid-July 1863, and a printed copy of the specifications — some fifty-six pages of them — was circulated to potential contractors.[33] The specifications included thirty-four sets of drawings of the Embankment and works associated with it. It is unnecessary to go into great detail about them, for architecturally the Embankment was relatively uncomplicated. The first section was to be about 3,740 feet long and to include the low-level sewer, which would intercept the sewers of Victoria Street and Regent Street and other sewers discharging into the Thames. The Embankment would also have built into it a subway to accommodate gas mains, water pipes, and other facilities, whose repair would otherwise involve a good deal of digging up of streets. The river wall was to be remarkably sound in its construction. Built within iron caissons or cofferdams, its foundations were to be carried down at least twenty feet below Ordnance datum — lower if the engineer thought necessary. At the base would be twelve and a half feet of concrete, surmounted by about eight feet of brick wall. Subway, sewer, and river wall were to be tied into one another at intervals of six feet by means of cross walls eighteen inches thick. On Bazalgette's recommendation, the river wall was to be faced with granite down to generally eight feet below datum. Bazalgette wisely preferred granite in place of the less expensive iron facing, although, as it turned out, contractors were to have some difficulty getting in sufficient quantities of granite of the high quality specified.[34]

These were the Embankment's essential features. In addition, however, specifications were provided for a series of landing stairs and steamboat piers. The landing at the foot of Buckingham Street (York Stairs) was to be equipped with a large and elaborate basement in which water for flushing purposes would be stored. There was some sniping comment: if the structural aspects seemed sound and deserving praise, as much could not be said (according to *The Builder*) for the decorative features. Drawings for the lamp pedestals, which Bazalgette exhibited at the 1863 Royal Academy show, were condemned as dismal, "neither monumental nor according to the true principles of decorative art."[35] Some revised drawings a year later drew less disapproving comment, but these, too, were regarded as sadly deficient.[36] But in general the plans seemed wellfounded and were welcomed as such.[37]

One final specification needs to be noted, if only because of the trouble it caused later. For fill, the contractor was (under clause 16 of the Thames Embankment Act, 1862) to rely on the Conservators of the Thames, who would thus gain a market of sorts for the results of their regular dredging operations. If, however, the contractor should fail to receive a supply that was sufficient in both quality and quantity, he was authorized to obtain it where he could. In other words, the contractor was obligated to get his fill from the Conservators as long as they could supply it efficiently. This was a provision that could well lead to difficulties between the Conservators and the Board, for it was easy to imagine a difference of opinion between them as to whether the material was being supplied in sufficient quantities or was of a sufficiently high quality.[38] Finally, construction was to occupy two years and a half, though there were certain loopholes available to the Board's engineer which would save the contractor from the official penalty of 1 percent a week on the amount of his tender. In order to manage the business of the Embankment, the MBW resolved itself into a committee of the whole Board—nine being the quorum.[39]

If the plans for the Embankment were relatively simple, negotiations for the necessary land were infinitely complicated. These fell largely on the Board's architect and its solicitor. The first step was to decide what land was required for the Embankment and what land would be sufficiently affected to be entitled to compensation. The committee inspected a number of maps supplied by the engineer and architect, with sections colored blue to indicate necessary land, red to indicate affected land, and yellow to show land that the Board need not worry about. An early estimate of the cost, made by a pair of distinguished valuers, had been £419,500, but the amount was expected to run higher than this because they had taken no account of necessary compensation payments to the Duke of Buccleuch, Sir Robert Peel, and the other Crown lessees.[40] At the end of 1863, the Board thought it prudent to engage a well-known valuer, George Pownall, whose reports ran remarkably close to those of the Board's architect, George Vulliamy, although both of them were, of course, well below the amount claimed. On Whitehall Wharf, for example, the original claim amounted to £16,300, Vulliamy's valuation to £14,800, and Pownall's to £14,639; and on Cannon Row, where the original claim was for £22,550, Vulliamy's estimate was £17,523 and Pownall's £17,600.[41]

Much dickering was necessary before the Board could reach a settlement in the case of the more important properties. For Whitehall Wharf, for example, the Board's offer of £14,500 was refused by the lessees' solicitor with the statement that the estate in question had been valued for Chancery at £16,300 on a compulsory sale. But, continued the solicitor, "to close the matter and to put an end to further discussion, it was determined with great reluctance on the part of my Clients that, subject to the approbation of the Court an Offer should be made to accept £15,000 for the property."[42] The Board replied with an offer of £14,639, which, the Board's solicitor suggested, was so close to the demand for £15,000 that there ought to be no further trouble. When this, too, was rejected, the Board raised its offer to £14,670. Eventually, retreating inch by inch, it agreed to pay the £15,000.

Other examples are instructive. Beck, Henderson & Child, wholesale and retail seed merchants, who moved from Adelphi Wharf to Upper Thames Street, claimed compensation of £6,754 5d. in a bill made up of eleven separate items "submitted with much cleverness and ingenuity."[43] The Board solicitor thought that £2,514 would be sufficient, largely because the firm had bettered its position by moving. The firm replied that the important consideration was water transportation, which was essential to the conduct of its business. Pownall agreed that the issue lay in the question of how vital the access to water was, since in other respects the firm's situation was better than before. In the end, after an examination of its books, he was instructed to negotiate on the basis of £4,000.

A more difficult case — and the first one that went to court — was the claim of one Gwynne, a hydraulic and mechanical engineer, who asked for £40,000 and demanded a special jury. Gwynne had taken new premises in Battersea at a cost of £7,000, but he contended that waterside premises were essential to him. Counsel employed by both sides argued the case for five days in the Sheriff's Court, Red Lion Square. What Gwynne got was not his claim for £40,000 but £14,000, a verdict that must have annoyed him for, under instruction, his solicitors wrote to demand immediate payment of the amount of the verdict, with a threat to charge interest unless it was paid "tomorrow."[44] The solicitors actually threatened to start proceedings unless the entire amount was received the next day. In reply, the committee solemnly voted that the Board solicitor acknowledge the letter "in such terms as he may deem proper."[45]

Altogether the committee, in spite of its cautious and frugal policies of compensation, accumulated a substantial bill.[46] Practically nobody got the full extent of his claim: the average cut seems to have been somewhere between 25 and 50 percent. In the two years between November 1863 and December 1865 the Board paid forty-four separate claims totaling £200,977 out of the £297,765 originally demanded.[47] This, of course, did not exhaust the claims the Embankment caused. The new street still had to be provided for, and there were correlative demands for compensation, such as that of the Duke of Buccleuch. For damage done to Montague House by the Embankment an umpire had awarded £8,325. When the Board refused to pay it, the Duke brought suit; the Board fought him through the various stages until in 1872 he finally won in the House of Lords. It was of little use that the *Metropolitan* — not an unbiased source — thought it strange that the Duke should receive compensation for the loss of a privacy that no longer had any substantial existence.[48]

For the first contract (Westminster to Waterloo Bridge) the Board received thirteen tenders, and for the second (Waterloo Bridge to the eastern end of Temple Gardens) fourteen. The second segment was shorter and awarding it produced no particular complications. A. W. Ritson & Company, with a bid of £229,000 (the highest of the fourteen was £264,000), was named without argument. The first contract, however, was another story. The difficulties over it formed the basis of charges of corruption which figured whenever a critic wished to work up a case against the Board, from Lord Robert Montague's committee in 1864 to the *Financial News* writers of the 1880s. Ironically in this affair of the Embankment contract, however, the Board and its engineer appear to have been beyond criticism.

The original decision of the Board was to award the first contract to Samuel Ridley, whose tender was the lowest of the thirteen, which ranged from £495,000 to £520,000. Three weeks later, however, the Board reversed itself and bestowed the contract on Furness, who was third on the list. The reasons for this change of heart seem to have been twofold. First, there was real doubt about Ridley's ability to complete the job: although his solicitor enclosed a list of railway, dock, and harbor contracts, mostly in Canada, this seemed not convincing, and the letters about his experience were conspicuously vague. Second, there was uneasiness about Ridley's integrity. Doubts emerged from a story brought back by Bazalgette from Waring Brothers, who had once employed Ridley as a navvy ganger. Waring reported to Bazalgette in strict confidence that Ridley had disappeared with £100 intended to be paid as wages to his men.[49] Both objections to Ridley as an Embankment contractor were well taken, but the second could not be brought into the open without committing a breach of confidence. Aside from that question, however, Bazalgette had looked rather thoroughly into Ridley's competence and experience as a contractor and had concluded, probably correctly, that he had done little to equip him for such a job.

Ridley was, of course, outraged. He at once scurried around and obtained as partner a respected contractor, whose original tender was, however, much above Ridley's and who, although honest, was a remarkably poor financier.[50] That arrangement the Board wisely refused to countenance. At this juncture, evidence came to light of an arrangement among Bazalgette, Furness, and Sir John Rennie, which seemed to suggest that Bazalgette might be under obligation to Furness. The question had to do with the agency for a concession for works in Odessa, which Rennie and Bazalgette had obtained. They had seen that Furness received the concession from the Russian government — with a commission to the two agents.[51] Although this, as Bazalgette insisted, had no connection with the Embankment contract, since in the Russian affair he was under no obligation to Furness, the Board regarded his apparent involvement with a contractor (or potential contractor) of the Board as indiscreet. Superficially the Odessa contract did look suspicious, but it is clear that it had little to do with the Embankment. When the contract was taken away from Ridley, Bazalgette had not favored Furness, whose tender was third lowest,[52] but rather had recommended Baker & Son, the second on the list. Unfortunately, Baker disliked certain features of the Board contract and declined to accept it. Bazalgette then urged readvertising for tenders, though this had proved an expensive routine in the case of one of the main drainage contracts. But the Board chose to award the contract to Furness, who was regarded as a reliable contractor.

The Board had by no means heard the last of the Ridley-Furness affair. Lord Robert Montague's Select Committee on Metropolitan Sewage in 1864 wandered far from its terms of reference and went on a fishing expedition for material derogatory to the Board. The Montague Committee heard evidence from Samuel Cokes, Ridley, Thwaites, Bazalgette, and others. Bazalgette found Ridley's statements so outrageous that he tried to get Waring Brothers to release him from his pledge of confidence — which they refused to do — and Thwaites said enough before the committee to indicate, at least to Ridley, the source of the trouble. That led to an unpleasant correspondence between Waring and the Board, in which Waring asserted that he had been misrepresented by Bazalgette and otherwise tried to escape from an embarrassing position. The airing of Ridley's irresponsible charges before Montague's committee served no useful purpose. It was not an able, objective committee, and, as *The Builder* put it, "members of the . . . committee are making publicly such injurious assertions with reference to the contracts" that the Board ought to come out with a clear and precise statement "setting themselves and their engineer right with the public."[53] It would be difficult to fault the Board for throwing out the Ridley tender in the first place, and equally difficult to show that Bazalgette had favored Furness's tender. Both Thwaites and Bazalgette were under considerable pressure in the Montague Committee to give Waring's story as refutation of Ridley's charges. Thwaites, unhappily, yielded to the temptation and got the

Board into an embroglio with Waring Brothers, who apparently changed their story. Clearly there were no corrupt motives in the Board's decision; but, just as clearly, once the notion had been planted that this had been a peculiar transaction, it was hard to uproot. Actually, the Odessa connection, innocent as it was, supplied opponents of the Board with another weapon of attack, and it was used indiscriminately by pamphleteers, reformers, and political opponents. It was another stick with which to beat an unpopular dog.

Bazalgette's uneasiness about Furness's ability to complete his contract satisfactorily proved to be justified. There was some trouble at the outset over the size of his working force and some complaint from Furness over Bazalgette's restrictions as to the type of granite he could use.[54] The contractor also encountered some delay in getting the necessary wharves and in experimenting to determine the best form of iron caissons. Nevertheless, the work appeared to be under way, and Bazalgette's report in July 1864 was encouraging. By the end of the year, however, Bazalgette's apprehensions were aroused, both because of certain engineering blunders and because of the slow progress of the work.[55] In January 1865 the Embankment committee made a visit to the contractor, and found good progress in the preliminary operations.[56] But granite was a problem. Both contractors, Ritson and Furness, had constant difficulty in getting granite in sufficient quantities and of the type specified, and their work was substantially delayed.[57] Dalbeattie (Kirkconnel) granite from Scotland was specified for the top courses of the Embankment, but this was delivered so sporadically that both contractors had to look around for supplementary supplies. They canvassed quarries in Jersey, Guernsey, Devonshire, Cornwall, and Sweden, picking up small quantities in each of them.

The second contract was, of course, simpler than the first and produced much less fuss. Ritson's contract was only about half the size of Furness's — his segment of the Embankment was only about half as long — and it was carried out with no more than a normal amount of friction. In October 1865, in fact, Ritson had accomplished work to nearly the same value as had Furness, and, except for the failure in granite deliveries, would in all likelihood have completed it on schedule. But by the winter of 1865–66, the MBW was getting nervous about both contracts. Henry Lowman Taylor called for a report (and prognosis) from the engineer, who estimated that Ritson had completed roughly £145,000 of his £229,000 contract, that he had averaged only slightly over £8,048 a week but that to finish on schedule he would have to average over £14,000 — an unlikely prospect.[58]

Meanwhile, neither contractor found his relations with the Thames

Conservators—from whom they were both condemned, by clause 16 of the Embankment Act, to acquire fill—an agreeable experience. Bazalgette had sensed with remarkable accuracy that the clause would be a troublemaker,[59] and he had sought to persuade the Conservancy to agree to a modification. But the Conservators would have none of it, professing themselves entirely satisfied. Trouble broke out early in 1864 when it became known that the contractors were getting most of their ballast not from the Conservators but at lower prices from private sources. This was not an edifying controversy, and at this distance it is impossible to separate right from wrong, to decide between charge and countercharge. The contractors alleged that deliveries from the Conservators were slow, uncertain, and of poor quality; the Conservators countered with the assurance that their material was good and was available in adequate quantities. The Board commissioned two engineers, who reported that a good deal of the fill supplied by the Conservators was only soft mud; the Conservators countered with two of their own who vouched for its excellent quality.[60]

There was, one suspects, some merit on both sides. No doubt Conservancy delivery, especially in the beginning, was slow and erratic, and, no doubt also, the charge was higher than that at which contractors could get alternative fill. This was exasperating to Furness, who was skating on thin ice and also could probably have got fill for nothing from the City and West End excavations. Anyway, the contractors were bound by clause 16 and therefore had no redress.[61]

In February 1865 the Conservators appealed to the Board of Trade to compel the MBW (which was caught in the middle) to see that its contractor adhered to his contract. The Board of Trade suggested independent engineers as arbitrators. In the end the engineers who were appointed, Messrs. Rawlinson and Coode, supported the case of the Conservators. But, they conceded, the Conservators were charging too high a price. The MBW wriggled and stalled; Bazalgette fought, apparently on honest ground, for at least a fraction of land ballast. But the Board of Trade threatened decisive action unless the MBW complied with the views of the arbitrators. It was not until the summer of 1865 that the Board and its contractors finally gave up the battle and agreed to take river material exclusively.[62]

By early 1866 the MBW was getting nervous over the slow progress being made on Furness's contract. With less than eight months to run, he had completed less than half his work. Ritson's contract, too, was behind schedule, though not so seriously. Bazalgette could think of a number of explanations, some of them legitimate, which made the contractors seem less delinquent, but the committee was not to be readily satisfied.[63] Furness was called to account, once in January 1866 and again in April. The fact was that Furness was going bankrupt. He had taken up the contract with insufficient resources, and those on whom he relied for finance proved unable in the financial crisis of that year to make the necessary arrangements. Happily, as far as the Embankment was concerned, the bankruptcy posed no insuperable difficulties. In the end Thomas Brassey agreed to join with Furness, and work proceeded, though only after most of the summer had passed with negligible progress.[64]

The Furness affair, which was later aired in the Court of Bankruptcy, would be irrelevant were it not that it reveals a good deal about the background of at least one Board contract. It is hard to discover the facts, for Furness's testimony before the Court was so confused and vague as to be almost unintelligible. It came out, however, that a member of the Board, William H. Doulton, had been influential in arranging sureties for Furness. Counsel tried to imply that Doulton's activity might have assisted Furness in winning the contract — a charge that both denied stoutly. Within the Board the attack on Furness was largely the work of Ridley's aggrieved partisans, who once more resurrected the old Odessa contract. In addition, another member of the Board, Charles Mills-Roche, a solicitor, seemed to be involved in Furness's dealings, and was suspected of undue eagerness in persuading Furness to take granite from the Lundy Granite Company. It was suggested that if Furness had agreed to take granite from that source, he would have got Mills-Roche's vote for him as contractor. The Board had some difficulty in resolving the situation, though both members were cleared, or at least it was voted by a substantial majority that the charges had not been proved; but the affair left a bad taste. Doulton resigned from the MBW, having found the Board's conclusions unsatisfactory and not a clear-cut vindication. Mills-Roche was not censured directly by the Board, but it was emphasized (by a vote of 19 to 7) that any connection of a business or professional character between a member of the Board and one of its contractors — or potential contractors — was highly objectionable. Nothing, they said, could be more "calculated to shake the confidence of the public in the integrity of [the Board's] proceedings."[65]

This affair as a whole nicely illustrates some of the many problems in the contracting business and shows that some of the contractors, even substantial ones, were operating on a perilously narrow margin. It also indicates that even with such important and honorable businessmen as William Doulton, the notion of conflict of interest, of the sharp distinction between public and private business, was only meagerly developed. Doulton apparently had received no personal profit from his services to

3. The Embankment at Charing Cross, showing the Metropolitan Railway
   and Low-Level Sewer

Furness, though apparently money had passed through his hands on the
way to the sureties. Yet he was involved with Furness in a way no member of the Board should have been.

In spite of all the difficulties, the two contracts progressed, though
considerably behind schedule.[66] The 1867–68 report of the Board noted
that Furness had finished the low-level sewer, the subway, the connections of the Victoria and Regent Street sewers with the low-level sewer,
and the Westminster steamboat pier; that he had completed also nearly
1,800 feet of the river wall; and that, in short, he had finished £450,000
of his £520,000 contract.[67]

The third segment of the Embankment, however, from Temple
Gardens to Blackfriars Bridge, was held up by factors for which neither
the Board nor the contractor could be blamed. In the fall of 1866 the
Board called for tenders, but difficulties emerged with the Metropolitan
District Railway. The District had intended to build under the Embankment, but it had run into trouble. It had spent the whole of its paid-up
capital on the Kensington-Westminster section of the line, and, given
the bleak economic circumstances of 1866, there seemed to be little pros-

pect of selling the rest of its shares. Indeed, in May 1866 Overend, Gurney and Company expired, and shortly afterwards the great engineering firm of Peto and Betts, the principal backers of the District, failed with debts of £4 million.[68] The District asked to delay building under the Embankment until its Kensington-Westminster line began to return a profit. The Board, however, was eager to move ahead.

The special problem the Board and the railway faced was the continuous line of wharves existing along the river and around Whitefriars Dock. These included, most conspicuously, those belonging to the City of London Gas, Light, and Coke Company. The Board had specified in its Embankment Act of 1862 that the railway would be carried on a viaduct supported on arches. But the District Railway's act, which passed through Parliament after the Board's act, provided that its tracks were to be carried in the space between the viaduct and the water. This would have the effect of shutting off the gas company's communication with the river, a change that would obviously require compensation to the company.

There followed a long and frustrating series of negotiations. The District was in no great hurry to reach an agreement, and, in fact, gave every evidence of stalling. Finally, the Board had again to invoke the aid of a Board of Trade arbitrator, whose decision led finally to an agreement.[69] In the long run, the controversy proved beneficial, for it got the City Gas Company off the Embankment and permitted the Board to build a solid embankment rather than a viaduct, a cheaper and more attractive solution. With this settlement, the Board called for another set of tenders. William Webster, who was already busy on the southern embankment, was the lowest bidder at £126,500.[70]

Meanwhile, the Board was laying plans for an embankment on the Surrey side of the river. The southern bank, low lying and vulnerable, presented problems somewhat different from those of the northern bank, in that the need for flood control was necessarily more prominent. The Royal Commission on the Thames Embankment in 1861 — of which Thwaites was a member, though he could not attend because of illness — recommended that the MBW go ahead with plans for the southern bank. The Board wished to build an embankment from London Bridge to Vauxhall, to protect property from floods. But the First Commissioner of Works refused to countenance the plan. The wharf owners, he pointed out, objected strongly to any embankment, and the bargemen appeared to be satisfied with the current state of things.[71] On this point, however, the Board foresaw the future much more accurately, and, when the floods of the mid-1870s came, there were regrets that nothing more decisive had been done.

The Board did receive a green light from the First Commissioner, however, on embanking the south bank from Westminster to Vauxhall, where the need for protection from flooding was also grave. There had been the usual modifications in the plans before the act was finally passed, some suggested by firms with property on the river, others by the Lambeth vestry, and others by the Board itself in the interests of economy. The upshot was that there would be a river wall of 4,300 feet, together with a paved roadway and footway.

When the MBW received tenders in July 1865, it appeared that more trouble with Ridley might be in store, for his bid was the lowest of the eight submitted. The Board, having failed to discover that he had added to his stock of experience since the unpleasantness over the northern embankment, gave the contract to William Webster, whose bid was, in fact, £11,000 below Bazalgette's estimate.[72]

In the course of preparing to construct the southern embankment, the Board paid for its land some £771,600.[73] Its most notable coup was the sale of eight and a half acres between Westminster and Lambeth bridges to St. Thomas's Hospital, which had been forced by railway works to leave its old site near London Bridge. The Board determined not to sell for less than £100,000; the hospital wished to get the land for £80,000, but gradually raised its offer from £80,000 to £90,000 to £95,000. The Board closed with the hospital for £95,000.[74] The arrangement was a sound one for both sides. For the Board it took a substantial bite out of the expense of the Embankment, which as a result amounted to £1,014,525 net.[75]

Meanwhile, plans for the new street along the Embankment from Blackfriars Bridge to the Mansion House (Queen Victoria Street) had aroused the resistance of the City. Assuming that this particular street was necessary, which was open to question, why should the MBW be allowed to invade the City to build it? Indignation was strong within the Corporation's Court of Common Council, and was curbed only by the fear that if the City howled too loudly Parliament might remove the fourpenny coal tax. Those who urged caution were denounced for their apparent willingness to give up City privileges to save City cash.[76]

By this time the bill for the new street had been approved by a Select Committee, notwithstanding the opposition of the Corporation. Benjamin Scott, the City Chamberlain, had failed to get anywhere with his claim that the City could build the street more readily than the Board.[77] The Corporation had labored to convince William Cowper, the First Commissioner of Works, that the new street was its responsibility, with the implication that the ninepenny coal duty (or some part of it) should revert to the Corporation. But Cowper gave this notion short shrift, for the street had already been assigned to the MBW.

The City's opposition, however, did not end with the Select Committee. City leaders now mounted an attempt to persuade the House of Commons to reverse the Select Committee's decision. One of the members for the City resubmitted the proposal which the City had already presented to the Committee, to the effect that the Corporation would build the street at a cost of £300,000 to the ratepayers, taking an additional £350,000 from its own funds.[78] But there seemed, indeed, grave doubts that the Corporation had that much available money. It was fine, Cowper suggested, to hear that the City was so well fixed, but there would be enough other uses for such resources in improving the City.[79] The Corporation had little chance of getting what it wished; but its chances were not improved by Alderman Thomas Sidney's speech, in which, at least to his confreres, he managed to let the side down. Sidney, in fact, charged the City with having acted unwisely: this was not a question of principle, but of expediency, and in any case, the MBW was not a foreign power. Clearly the street was more metropolitan than local, and it had been preposterous of the Corporation to offer £350,000 simply to keep the Board out of the City.[80]

The City was defeated in the Commons, but there were still stirrings in the Court of Common Council, where a group of patriots aligned themselves against the moderates. The former, who felt that the old Improvement Committee had not been sufficiently aggressive in defending the position of the City, had persuaded the Court to appoint a special committee. But this body had been unable to do more than the Improvement Committee. When the City's claim to the ninepenny coal duty came up, Cowper told them flatly that this was not a City but a parliamentary fund, and that it had already been committed to the MBW. The insurgents continued the battle and passed a vote to carry the fight to the House of Lords.[81] In the end, the internal struggles brought about the resignation of one of the City members of the MBW,[82] but the insurgents failed to change the Board's plans. Nor did the City obtain the right to manage the railway which was to be built under the street. As Bazalgette pointed out, this was part of a general system of railways and must remain under central management.[83] The matter was now settled: the MBW was to build Queen Victoria Street and was to control the construction underground.

The problem with the street, as with other new streets, was not its construction, which was a relatively simple matter. What delayed and complicated the whole procedure was the difficulty of acquiring the necessary property. Over 550 separate properties—freeholds, leaseholds, and yearly tenancies—had to be acquired, and this took both time and patience. In the end, some £1,990,378 was paid out in claims (out of the

1. Site Clearance for Building Queen Victoria Street and the District Railway, about 1869

£2,612,106 asked), though some of this amount, of course, was recovered in land sold or let for building lots.[84] Nine hundred feet of the roadway on the eastern end were opened for traffic in October 1869. The other 2,550 feet were held up by the Metropolitan District Railway, which showed little haste in completing its construction.[85] As late as December 1868 the railway had not yet begun its works below Mansion House Street.[86] But the District line was finally completed and opened to traffic in November 1871. The net cost was £1,076,287 — considerably over the original estimate — and it should, perhaps, have been greater. For the MBW had been exceedingly stiff-necked in the case of at least one property which might well have been kept as an open space but which the Board had insisted on selling for building purposes. This was the triangular plot just to the west of the Mansion House, which a succession of memorials from City notables and a deputation from the Royal Institute of British Architects had urged the MBW to keep as an open space. Here the Board, whose rudimentary sense of City planning was always likely to be conquered by its feeling for pounds, shillings, and pence, refused to budge. And it was cold comfort to those who wished an agreeable amenity next to the Mansion House that on the first attempt to sell the plot at auction, the only offers were well below the price set by the Board.[87]

Meanwhile, the Embankment as a whole was nearing completion. In July 1870 Bazalgette reported that the third contract (from Temple Gardens to Blackfriars Bridge) was well along and the Board could make plans for the formal opening. The original plan called for the Queen to attend the ceremony, but in the end it was the Prince of Wales who opened the Embankment on 13 July 1870. The contractor had to work up to the last minute, including the Sabbath, only to receive a motion of censure (which was, however, unseconded) from a Sabbatarian member of the Board.[88] None could complain that the ceremony was lacking in dignitaries. Members of the Royal Family, a number of Household representatives, leaders of Parliament, archbishops, ambassadors, assorted dukes, and other noblemen brought tone to the occasion; and the Embankment was formally opened in a fashion that gave satisfaction to the metropolis. Only the *City Press* deplored what it called "the shabby ceremonial."[89] (Only the City, one gathers, could stage a suitable ceremonial.) Otherwise the event was unquestionably a success. *The Times,* which had blown hot and cold toward the Board, now paid "a tribute of approbation to the Metropolitan Board of Works and their Engineer, for the manner in which this work has been planned and executed."[90] The net cost was £1,156,981; and the following amounts of materials were used:[91]

Granite	650,000 cubic feet
Brickwork	80,000 cubic yards
Concrete	140,000 cubic yards
Timber (for coffer dams, etc.)	500,000 cubic feet
Earth fill	1,000,000 cubic yards

The Board had indeed gone from rags to riches, and with the opening of the Embankment reached the zenith of its popular esteem. The Embankment had transformed an unappetizing, smelly waterfront into an attractive promenade which in some degree relieved the growing traffic congestion of the metropolis. If not so significant an amenity nor so great an engineering feat as the main drainage system, it was nevertheless

5. The Completed Embankment, about 1900

more striking to the eye. It marked London, to even the casual visitor, as a metropolis which in spite of its decentralized political regime was looking to the future. Later, as its prestige declined, the Board could at least look back with pride on a major assignment well done.

The Times leader already quoted went on to recall that the Board had also "succeeded in reclaiming from the river more than thirty acres of ground, which the Ratepayers are not likely to surrender without a struggle." This referred to an unsavory controversy that was developing between the Office of Woods and Forests (then under the Treasury) and the Board (with the backing, for once, of public opinion throughout the metropolis) over what was to be done with the land reclaimed from the river by the building of the Embankment. It was a complicated issue in which, it appears, law was on one side and justice on the other.

In 1862, in its zeal to get the cooperation of the Office of Woods and Forests—and, perhaps, as *The Times* said, being "young and modest" and incapable of "effectual resistance"[92]—the MBW had agreed that the land reclaimed in front of Crown property between Westminster Bridge and Whitehall Stairs should be handed over to the Crown as its absolute property. The remainder of the reclaimed land, given over to the charge of the Board, was to be used for public amusement and recreation; and it seems to have been assumed that the land claimed by the Crown would be kept for similar purposes. It came, therefore, as a shock when it appeared that the Office of Woods and Forests had every intention of putting up buildings on two and a half acres of its waterfront. The Board, in short, was supposed to keep its section of the river front for public recreation, while the government was proceeding to turn a part of the Crown land into income-producing property. It was all typical of the chronic, cheese-paring, tax-cutting compulsion of Victorian Liberals. The Treasury was unyielding in its application of the law, and its charge, the Office of Woods and Forests, never acutely alert to broader social values (as it had demonstrated in the controversy over the Crown tenants) was equally stubborn.

On 8 July 1870 W. H. Smith challenged the Treasury's intentions on the floor of the House, implying ungenerous behavior on the part of Gladstone's Government. He was answered by the Chancellor of the Exchequer, Robert Lowe, and by Gladstone in hard, legalistic speeches. Lowe suggested that if the metropolis was so eager to have the land for recreational purposes, the Crown would be willing to sell it; and Gladstone noted that Smith was really inviting the Government to make a gift of £150,000 to the metropolis.[93] In spite of resistance from the Liberal side, Smith carried by fifty votes his address to the Queen. This was not a question, *The Times* noted, which could be dealt with in legalistic terms. After all, it had been the contribution of metropolitan ratepayers that had converted the river bank from a mud flat and a burial ground for dead cats and dogs into an attractive plaza, thus increasing the value of adjacent property. Whatever its legal rights, the Crown had no moral right to the property, nor had it the right to do with the property as it wished.[94]

In the meantime, some voices in the metropolis were heard in protest. The Kensington vestry petitioned Parliament, and a "large and influential meeting" of Westminster electors gathered in St. James's, Piccadilly, to consider the behavior of the Government.[95] Through it all, W. H. Smith, a friend of the Embankment, who was to equip it with twenty benches for the public, seems to have organized the resistance effectively. In the summer of 1871 the Government retreated sufficiently for Gladstone to move the appointment of a Select Committee on the question[96] — specifically, on whether the land reclaimed from the river between Whitehall Gardens and Whitehall Place should be appropriated in whole or in part to the advantage of the inhabitants of the metropolis.[97] The Committee's recommendation was a compromise. The Board should have its public garden but it should transfer some land to the Crown. The Commissioner of Woods and Forests could not have been happy about the Committee's recommendation, manifest in his vigorous defense of the Crown's interests and his odd argument that a public garden in front of the Crown tenants would depreciate the value of the houses.[98]

Indeed, the Government's attitude was unaltered by the report of the Select Committee. "We are not," announced Gladstone, "prepared to bring in an Act for the purpose of parting with the property of the Crown for a value altogether inadequate."[99] To emphasize how far removed a satisfactory solution still was, Charles Gore (Commissioner of Woods and Forests) wrote to the MBW on 29 February 1872, reminding the members that it was nonsense to think of giving property to London without pay. "It seems scarcely worthwhile to compromise so many sound principles, forego so large a sum of money, and rip up so many settlements and agreements merely to give the inhabitants of London the privilege of recreation on Land which is not theirs."[100] He proposed a handsome building for the site; the Board, in reply, took its stand on the report of the Select Committee.

It would be wearisome to follow the course of the offers and counteroffers during 1872. Robert Lowe introduced a bill providing that the Board should pay £40,000 for the property, or a sum to be set by arbitration.[101] The Board held fast on the Select Committee's recommendation of an annual rent of about £170. *The Times* meanwhile was hammering away, demanding that the land be turned over to the public and arguing that the question ought not to be decided on the assumption that Crown land was the Monarch's private land.[102] Another Government bill and another Select Committee, which reached a decision more in harmony with the Government's wishes, followed in 1872.[103] Public opinion, however, was having its effect — even on Robert Lowe — and the Government made concessions. It was not until early 1873 that the two parties got together and the Board received, in substance, what it had been demanding. The Board was to turn over to the Office of Woods and Forests a piece of its land on the south side of Whitehall Place, in return for the plot of land desired for its public garden. For the land that it received in excess of the land that it relinquished, the Board was to pay to the Office of Woods and Forests a sum calculated on the basis of rent paid by the Crown lessees.[104] Not, perhaps, a generous arrangement but, as compared with the Government's earlier proposals, a satisfactory one, and one which must be credited largely to W. H. Smith, backed by metropolitan public opinion that was remarkably united and firm.

Two more questions remained to be settled before the Embankment could be regarded as finished: what agency was to control and maintain the roadway, and how to approach the Embankment from the north.

It had been the practice of the Board, when it had completed a street, to turn it over to the appropriate local authorities for maintenance. Although the original Embankment bill had provided for similar treatment, the MBW had prudent second thoughts. Was not the Embankment a national work which it would be absurd to hand over to local authorities? The Embankment (North) Bill proposed to reverse the earlier judgment and to vest the roadway in the Board. The bill produced a chorus of dissent, with protests from the Middle Temple and Inner Temple, the City Corporation (which, however, did not gain a *locus standi* before the committee), the City Commissioners of Sewers, the vestries of St. George's, Hanover Square, of Lambeth, and of Westminster, and the Marquis of Salisbury. The most determined opponent was, of course, the City, one of whose M.P.'s intoned the familiar litany, "The Metropolitan Board of Works were attempting to establish for themselves a jurisdiction as regarded their part of the Embankment within the City."[105] Despite the opposition of the City Sewers Commissioners, the bill went through, and the Embankment became a permanent ward of the MBW and its successors.

The other issue, the approach to the Embankment from the north, had to do specifically with what is now Northumberland Avenue. The question dragged on for nearly a decade before the Board finally made arrangements to buy Northumberland House, the last of the fine old houses which members of the aristocracy had erected between the river and the Strand in the sixteenth and seventeenth centuries. It was, to say the least, unfortunate that the house had to go; and the Board, with its customary insensitiveness to aesthetic values, perhaps did not make as great efforts as it might have done to devise alternative plans. Still, a direct route from Charing Cross to the Embankment was essential, the straighter the better, and this became more apparent after the Embankment was opened to traffic. The scholarly fourth Duke of Northumberland, who died in 1865, had apparently been willing, indeed eager, to sell; but his cousin and successor, who was eighty-six at his accession, was not inclined to mar his few years as Duke by selling the house which he had inherited.

The question remained unresolved until 1872, when the Board, observing the traffic flow on the Embankment, concluded that a direct route must be opened to Charing Cross. The sixth Duke was agreeable to negotiations, and he finally consented to sell for £500,000. When the Board applied to Parliament for powers, a last-ditch campaign to save Northumberland House developed, led by Lord Elcho, Baillie Cochrane, and others; and in the Private Bills Committee they advocated a curvilinear approach, which would lengthen the street but save Northumberland House. However, if any part of his garden was taken, the Duke said he would insist on selling the house, with the result that the Board would have a monument on its hands.[106] At this distance it is hard to judge the Board's proposal. Was the house worth all the fuss? Perhaps. But the curvilinear street was more practicable and more attractive than the Board liked to think, though, of course, more costly to lay. The Private Bills Committee approved the bill, though with a condition — which was much resented by the Board — that elevations for the buildings on the new street must be approved by the Council of the Royal Institute of British Architects. The Board felt its sense of responsibility offended and refused to accept the Committee's recommendation unless this clause was modified. The Committee agreed to change "approved" to "submitted," and the Board accepted the modification, though under protest. As it turned out, one ought not to censure the Committee for its precautions. Northumberland Avenue emerged as a thoroughly commonplace street, and the two architects on the Board, on whom the members relied for counsel, were the two members involved in the scandal which disfigured the last years of the Board's life. Even after the agreement to buy the house had been reached, there was still a faint hope of saving it. Lord Elcho called a "public meeting" in Willis's Rooms — on Boat Race Day — and as late as August 1874 William Butterfield, the architect, wrote to *The Times* pleading that the plan for a curved street be followed and some public use be found for Northumberland House.[107] The Board, however, had no intention of giving up its advantage now. The only concession it made was to open the house to the public for two weeks before it was demolished.[108]

The final stage of the Board's embankment-building projects was relatively uneventful, once the contract was awarded. This was to embank the river from the Royal Military Hospital to Battersea Bridge, the stretch from Millbank to the hospital having been done by the Government some thirty-five years before. The act authorizing the Embankment was passed in 1868 and tenders were submitted in early 1871. The contractors bidding on the Chelsea Embankment, at least the low bidders, seem to have been amateurish and marginal. The winner of the contract, hastily going over his figures, discovered serious errors and begged leave to bow out. The second lowest bidder complained about the Board's plan of payments (the contractor got nothing until he had completed 7.5 percent of his work) and relinquished his contract. The Board readvertised for tenders and again the lowest bidder discovered a grave error in his calculations. The upshot was that the Board again fell back on William Webster, the fourth lowest, who was at least a reliable contractor.[109] From this point on, the construction of the Chelsea Embankment, which included the low-level sewer, went smoothly enough, and when its roadway was three-quarters of a mile in length it was formally opened by the Duke and Duchess of Edinburgh, on 9 May 1874. In honor of the completion of the embankments, Sir James McGarel-Hogg, now chairman of the Board, was awarded a KCB, and Bazalgette received an amply merited knighthood.

With the embankments safely in place, the Board might have assumed that its problems with the river banks were permanently solved. The Chelsea Embankment, however, had not yet been formally opened when there was trouble on the south bank, particularly in the Bankside area, to the west in Lambeth, and higher up the river in Battersea—in short, wherever the shore was low and there was no embankment to repel the floods. In the spring of 1874 and the fall of 1875 excessively high tides occurred and the river overflowed, causing great distress to the poor residents and considerable loss to businessmen. Measures had to be taken to prevent a recurrence, but whose responsibility was it? The Board pointed out that it did not have the powers: the Metropolis Management Act had imposed such duties on the vestries and district boards, which were to have the necessary work done and divide the cost with the parties affected. All the Board could do in these circumstances was to exhort the local authorities, some of which reported resistance on the part of property owners and occupiers and complained that their own powers were inadequate. The Board decided to apply to Parliament to strengthen the hands of the local bodies. Here the hitch was the familiar one: who was to pay the bill? The vestries naturally disagreed among themselves. The Select Committee to which the bill was referred on 23 April 1877 ultimately recommended that the charge be laid on the metropolis as a whole, a decision which the Board resented and which led it to abandon its bill for the 1876–77 session.[110]

Meanwhile, in the month of January 1877, there was another disastrously high tide. This time the Board, though lacking statutory authority, moved in to apply what pressure it could (short of compulsion) upon property owners to raise their frontages in the danger zone along the river. Board engineers surveyed the river banks and reported to owners what changes would be necessary to make their river fronts safe. A surprising number of them complied with the Board's recommendations. Still, the essential question regarding responsibility remained unsettled. The Board pointed repeatedly to its own lack of authority, and its position was legally secure. Whether it had moral responsibility is less easy to decide. In a word, had embanking the river on the north made the southern bank more vulnerable to floods? Certainly the low, marshy banks, some of which had been reclaimed from the river by artificial embankments, were liable to flooding, and it was hardly worthwhile to speculate whether the MBW's embankments had increased the danger. But the Board was in no great haste to bring in a new bill, and it had to be nudged on several occasions by the Home Office.[111] Not until 1879 was the bill submitted, substantial agreement having been reached among the contending parties. The Metropolis Management (Thames River Prevention of Floods) Act of 1879 empowered the Board to require wharf walls and river banks to be raised to sufficient height to prevent another overflow, but this was still to be done at the expense of the owners. The Board thus was able to make good the principle of individual responsibility for which it had been arguing. It had been dilatory about submitting its bill, but it showed vigor in executing the new act. Engineers prepared a plan for every property owner showing what was required. There were, of course, some complaints; some owners wished to build walls according to their own designs rather than the Board's, and toward these the Board's policy was decently liberal.[112] This was an enormous task, since in all about forty-one miles of frontage were involved. But at least, when it was complete, the river was securely fenced in and the danger of another ruinous flood had been enormously reduced, if not wholly averted.

With the building of the Embankment the MBW completed the second of its two major tasks and achieved a good measure of prestige. During the next fifteen years, however, as Londoners took the main drainage system, the embankments, and certain new streets increasingly for granted, they tended to forget the body that had been responsible for them. At the same time, the Board itself seemed to lose its sense of direction, no longer having any large jobs on which to concentrate. Owing in part to its new chairman, in part to the multiplicity of little tasks imposed upon it in the late 1870s, and in part to the inherent defects in its constitution, which only became more glaring as the years wore on, the last fifteen years of the Board's life showed a steadily weakening grasp on reality and a steadily growing inability to follow a consistent policy.

CHAPTER 5

Thoroughfares and Buildings

Building the Embankment and supplying main drainage raised engineering problems of greater or less consequence. Of quite another order of difficulty was the assignment of street improvements imposed on the MBW by the Metropolis Local Management Act. The laying out of new streets, though this required some skill, was a relatively simple matter compared with the negotiations necessary to acquire property and finance.

The problem confronting the Board was simply, once again, the congestion caused by the astonishing growth of the metropolis, which had doubled in population in the forty years between 1811 and 1851. The railways, of course, had contributed to this urban elephantiasis, with nearly a million and a half passengers arriving each year at Paddington and over 700,000 at King's Cross, to cite only two examples. Some 200,000 entered the City each day on foot.[1] A Select Committee in 1854–55 called for new routes to relieve streets packed with traffic and for the abolition of tolls on roads and bridges. But there was little prospect of satisfactory action until some central body with overall authority was set up, and the Committee therefore expressed satisfaction over the imminent establishment of the MBW, which would possess power "to carry out those changes which the existing state of London renders it impossible much longer to postpone."[2]

The Committee was overoptimistic. Though the Board had sufficient formal power to carry out extensive street improvements, its range of activity was severely circumscribed. At the top of the list, both because it was desperately needed and persistently lobbied for, was a new street in Southwark, to carry traffic from Borough High Street to Blackfriars (Goods) Station, and connecting with Stamford Street to the west. The arguments for such a thoroughfare were obvious, and the Board at once got an act authorizing such a street. A second much needed thoroughfare was designed to improve access to Covent Garden. Garrick Street — it was to be named after the Garrick Club, which moved to the new street from King Street — would connect Cranbourne Street and St. Martin's Lane with King Street and thence with the market. This would be a short street, only 140 yards in length. One would hesitate to say that this street was more urgent than any of several other possibilities, but the Board was perhaps drawn to it by the offer of the Duke of Bedford, the owner of the market, to contribute £15,000. The third street improvement to be undertaken — the act for this was passed in 1858 — was a new approach to Victoria Park, northeast of Bethnal Green, from Limehouse. This approach called for a new street, Burdett Road, from East India Dock Road to Bow Road.

These were the street improvements to which the Board, for one reason or another, was definitely committed, but they by no means exhausted its hopeful intentions. The Works and General Purposes Committee, indeed, made a careful study of the requirements of the metropolis, trying to see its needs as a whole, and came out with a list of forty possible improvements, some of them substantial and costly, totaling (including Finsbury Park) £16 million or £17 million.[3] Some of these were little more than pipe dreams or were listed simply to conciliate clamorous local interests; but some of them, such as the removing of Middle Row, Holborn, to facilitate the flow of east-west traffic, and the extension of Commercial Road, Whitechapel, were surely needed. And in the course of its thirty-five years, the Board could list about forty improvements (to a few of which the local authorities contributed), varying in expense from Queen Victoria Street (which cost over a million pounds) and Shaftesbury Avenue (over £775,000) to comparatively inexpensive improvements in Newington and South Lambeth.

According to the terms of the Metropolis Local Management Act, the MBW was to make street improvements of a "metropolitan" character, while those regarded as "local" were to be handled by the vestries and district boards. Obviously this was not a clear-cut distinction, and the Board was under some pressure to construe local improvements as "metropolitan" and then to listen to the ingenious arguments of vestries and their solicitors. With local improvements, however, the Board was authorized to assist, usually to the extent of one-third the cost. Such a provision, of course, seemed to give an advantage to the more affluent local authorities, notably the City, which had cash available for street improvements. Indeed, the amount of money the Board poured into the City caused an outcry from more necessitous vestries which were not inclined to accept the "to him that hath shall be given" principle, and who charged the Board with favoritism toward the City. In fact, however, the City profited not because of favoritism but simply because it had sufficient resources to provide the required two-thirds.

The three streets with which the Board inaugurated its program seemed, to impatient local interests, to make desperately slow progress. The reason is not obscure. Even after the route was determined — and that in the case of Southwark Street produced some discussion[4] — there was the trying business of acquiring the necessary property. In 1859–60 the Board reported that it had disposed of claims amounting to over £306,000 for about £222,000; these included 102 freeholds and copyholds and 71 leaseholds and goodwills.[5] But it was impossible to hurry this process; in some cases as many as six or seven claims were made on behalf of a single piece of property. In all, the Board paid out £454,000 on claims totaling over £700,000.[6] In a few instances, cases had to be taken to court. Garrick Street and Burdett Road were less troublesome, though the first was held up for some time by a single stubborn leaseholder whose claims, the Board thought, were excessive, especially when his lease was about to expire. In the end, the Board decided to wait until his lease ran out. To build this street, only 140 yards long, it had eventually to deal with about ninety claims for which it paid out £103,000.

Gross costs for two of the street improvements were heavy. For Southwark Street, 1,124 yards in length and 70 feet wide, the total cost exceeded £610,000, and even when partly offset by returns from the disposal of building lots, it remained high — over £366,000.[7] Garrick Street also was fairly expensive. The gross cost ran to about £121,500, but this was largely met by the sale of lots, by the Duke of Bedford's contribution, and by allocations from the London Bridge Approaches Fund, as provided for in the act passed some five years before for disposing of the surplus from that curious fund.[8] The Victoria Park approach (Burdett Road), on the other hand, was relatively inexpensive, amounting to only £38,000.

Frequently, as in the case of Garrick Street, the cost to metropolitan ratepayers for improvements was negligible. But each individual case required a separate solution, which the Board found only through experience. For the Southwark and Covent Garden improvements, for example, the Bank of England lent £400,000 at 4.5 percent — no great bargain; yet for Burdett Road the Board did better, getting £42,000 at 3.5 percent from an insurance company.[9] But a satisfactory technique of financing such projects on a regular basis was still some years off.

It would be of doubtful value to run through the street improvements made during the Board's lifetime. A full list, with net costs, was given in its final annual report in 1888.[10] One may, however, review a few of these improvements because they involved special features of one kind or another.

There was, for example, the Board's attempt to relieve the congestion in Park Lane, in the course of which, in 1865, it ran head-on into the Crown lessees who were established in Hamilton Place and defended by the Office of Woods and Forests. Clearly some relief was necessary for Park Lane, which, with the building up of Pimlico and Belgravia and with the railway termini in Pimlico, had turned into a major north-south artery. To the Board, the obvious way to relieve pressure at the Piccadilly end was to convert Hamilton Place into a public thoroughfare, and a bill was introduced for that purpose.[11] The Crown tenants took fright and managed to get the bill turned down by a Select Committee.[12] With the prospects apparently bleak for an approach through Hamilton Place, the Board adopted another strategy and brought in a bill for widening Park Lane by encroaching on Hyde Park. This proposal, introduced in two sessions, was thrown out by another Select Committee, which, however, made reference to Hamilton Place as the most suitable solution.[13] Once more, the Board moved forward to attack Hamilton Place. How firmly would the Office of Woods and Forests and the Treasury continue to support their lessees? In the end, the Office notified the Board that it would not oppose directly, provided that clauses were inserted guaranteeing compensation to the Crown and its lessees, not only for the property actually taken, but also for the loss in value suffered by all the houses in Hamilton Place that were affected by its becoming a thoroughfare.

Recalling the recommendation of the Select Committee the year before, the Board members were inclined to hold firm. There was no reason, they felt, why Crown tenants should be regarded as being in a special position. Unmoved by petitions against the bill from such notables as Lord Eldon,[14] the Marquis of Coningham, and the Duke of Buccleuch, the Board persisted and the bill passed. After the act had gone through Parliament, the MBW was offered £50,000 by a "lady resident in the immediate vicinity of Park-Lane" to throw overboard its idea of opening up Hamilton Place and to bring in instead another bill for widening Park Lane. The lady (who turned out to be a Mrs. Brown of Hertford Street) professed no direct interest in the residents of Hamilton

Place, but she had been a frequenter of the gardens "for the last thirty years." The Board, in reply, sympathized with Mrs. Brown's difficulty, but, under the circumstances, declined to reopen the question.[15]

Thus far the Board's decisions on street improvements had been largely of an ad hoc character, gravely needed but not part of an overall plan. Many, if not all, had been inherited from the Select Committee on Improvements in the 1840s.[16] The only comprehensive statement formulated by the Board was that drafted by the Works Committee in 1859, but this was not a plan so much as an exhaustive list of improvements assigned several degrees of urgency. Some voices protested the Board's policy, or lack of it. In 1866 *The Builder* deplored the absence of a coherent plan and looked wistfully across the Channel to Paris where Baron Haussmann was working his miracles.[17]

In the early 1870s the Board blocked out a new artery of east-west communication. This plan resulted ultimately in the Metropolitan (Shoreditch and Minor Street Changes) Street Improvement Act, 1872, but not before controversy had exhausted the players. The battling began when Shoreditch and Hackney requested a widening of High Street, Shoreditch, to eighty feet. On investigating, the Board members discovered that the need was urgent, for the existing street was on the average only twenty feet wide. They resolved to widen it to seventy feet and brought in a bill, which was referred to a Select Committee.[18] As usual, vestry opposition arose, but, more important, the Committee criticized the Board for not making this improvement part of a general plan. McGarel-Hogg's answer could not have been convincing: he admitted that the Board had no general plan, but excused this on the ground that "the demands come upon us so fast and so heavy that really it is as much as we can do to consider the claims and demands that are made upon us."[19] Although the Committee was justified in criticizing the Board, it failed to acknowledge that the Board was simply reacting to local pressure from the districts that would be directly benefited.[20]

Again, one must feel a measure of sympathy for the Board, hemmed in as it was by economy-minded vestries, and with the bulk of its income allocated for years ahead to the main drainage system. The sewer rates, the Board felt, together with other minor additions, had created a load of taxation that was as high as ratepayers should be asked to bear. In the mid-sixties, the Board had made gestures toward reforming local taxation in London and instituting an improvement rate which would be assessed on the landlord as well as the occupier. Before the Select Committee on Local Taxation in 1866, Thwaites had argued that the metropolis would be wealthy enough to handle the expense that a program of improvement would require, if the incidence of the system were not unfair.[21] But the Ratepayers' Defence Association had risen in righteous indignation, and petitions had poured in from the vestries.[22] Though convinced of the inadequacy of its own taxing powers and also of "the absolute physical necessity" of more extensive improvements in the metropolis, the Board had had to abandon its efforts to create such a rate.

Under these circumstances, the Board protested that the metropolis could not be improved according to any general blueprint. Plans, it argued, had to be carried out according to the requirements of the individual parts. There was, thus, an overwhelming argument for a new line of east-west communication to the north of the Oxford Street–Holborn–Cheapside line. A new street, taking off from New Oxford Street at the corner of Hart Street (now Bloomsbury Way) would proceed via Theobald's Road and Old Street to the High Street, Shoreditch, and thence in a southerly direction by Commercial Street to Whitechapel and the Docks or eastward to Bethnal Green. A number of gaps in this line would have to be filled in, the most conspicuous one being a connection between Theobald's Road and Old Street (the connection which was to become Clerkenwell Road). On the face of it, this seemed like an obvious measure to cope with the increasing traffic to and from the railway stations.

Against this plan and the several other improvements coupled with it, a number of vestries objected in the familiar way and for familiar reasons. The Board must have been surprised when Hampstead came out with an expression of its "hearty approval of the projected measures," and with an exhortation to other metropolitan authorities to take a "broad and liberal view . . . instead of seeking merely to secure local and isolated interests."[23] This appeal to the vestries to look beyond their own boundaries to the welfare of the metropolis, seconded by *The Times,*[24] of course, had little effect on such vestries as St. Pancras, Islington, and the more remote Fulham, which persisted in their complaints. Although there was room for differences of opinion about the Board's plan, the basis of the vestries' objections did not lie in disagreement over the precise route or the traffic volume. Their case, pure and simple, rested on their conception of London as a collection of parts, which had few, if any, responsibilities for the whole. Their argument, specifically, was that the proposed improvements in Shoreditch and Clerkenwell would be of no value to Camberwell and Deptford and that therefore the latter should not be charged with a share of the bill. To add strength to the opposition, William Haywood, the engineer of the City Commissioners of Sewers, came out with a pamphlet criticizing the scheme and submitting traffic statistics (which, the Board contended, were based on false premises).[25]

Again and again, spokesmen for the MBW sought to show that its plan was not simply a surrender to a series of local pressures. When the dissident vestries, having failed to convince the Board, carried the fight to the House of Commons, they won support from such metropolitan M.P.'s as William Torrens, John Locke, and William Gladstone, who represented boroughs that were hostile to the scheme. In the House, the vestries were finally defeated,[26] but the battle over the Shoreditch Improvement Bill drove the Board to accept the fact that the idea of London as a community was still remote.

In the meantime, the Board moved on to new projects. Of these the most important were two West End streets, one from Tottenham Court Road to Charing Cross (Charing Cross Road), and the other from New Oxford Street near its junction with Hart Street (now Bloomsbury Way) to Piccadilly Circus (Shaftesbury Avenue). In time, the corrupt exploits of those in the office of the Board's architect who dealt with the Shaftesbury Avenue leases would remain uppermost in posterity's memory.[27] In 1872, however, the plans attracted a different kind of notoriety. The original report presented to the Board which included these two streets and a number of street-widening projects estimated that the whole would cost something like £4,200,000. Viewing the prospect, *The Times* remarked that the conventional criticism of the Board as only an oversized vestry was now likely to veer toward the other extreme.[28] And admirable as were the Board's intentions with regard to new thoroughfares, it showed at the outset its usual insensitiveness to aesthetic and historical considerations. An early plan, for instance, proposed to remove the steps in front of St. Martin's-in-the-Fields and make the approach to the church from the north and south ends of the portico, a plan which at once produced a vigorous protest from the church, which pointed out, correctly enough, that if the steps were removed the portico would have no meaning.[29]

This question was settled by amending the plan. But before the bill could pass through Parliament, another obstacle had to be disposed of. This was an amendment put by Lord Salisbury (who owned property along the line of the proposed Charing Cross Road) that would limit the Board to taking only the property needed for its new street and would bar it from taking any further property, in accordance with the usual procedure, that might be needed to give frontages to the street after it had been built. Henry Fawcett led the attack on Salisbury's amendment, which had been introduced into the bill during its passage through the Lords, charging that it did violence to sound practice in denying the Board valuable frontages which could later be sold.[30] In supporting Salisbury, John Gorst, the future "fourth party" man, articulated what was a common attitude toward the Board, and one which, regrettably, was not without some substance: "The Board," he charged, "was an overgrown vestry, supported by architects, surveyors, and solicitors, and represented no one but themselves [and that] from first to last the land jobbing which had been indulged in by the Metropolitan Board had saddled the ratepayers with enormous expense, and that considerable improvements could have been effected much more economically if the Board had not existed, or if they had ceased the land jobbing in which they had indulged."[31]

Was the Board's policy of attempting to sell frontages a misguided one? Certainly not in principle. There might be a difference of opinion about the prices which the Board tried to get and about the volume of frontages that it attempted to market. In 1879, for example, there were still lots on Northumberland Avenue standing vacant because, as a churchwarden of St. Martin's argued, the period of leases was too short and the prices too high.[32] (He was, of course, bothered by the loss to the parish in rates.) In the main, however, it is difficult to show that the Board lost money for London ratepayers by its leasing policy — save perhaps by the culpable exertions of functionaries in the architect's office.

In the meantime, the Board's critics charged, the cutting through of Charing Cross Road was proceeding at a snail's pace. It would, indeed, be hard to argue that the project was completed with conspicuous dispatch. There were a number of reasons for the delay, but the principal explanation lies in the anomalous responsibilities which were vested in the Board with regard to working-class housing. In the years 1859–1867 some 37,000 people, according to H. J. Dyos's estimates, were forced to move as a result of railway construction in the center of London.[33] The Midland Railway had to raze a whole slum — Agar Town — to get to St. Pancras Station.[34] In addition, houses, a considerable number of them, were taken for street improvements and to provide sites for new business blocks. What had happened to the displaced population was a question no one could answer with certainty. There was no reason to believe, however, that these communities had gone far or that their removal had done more than increase the already grave congestion in nearby working-class districts. It was this worsening of the plight of London's working classes, and the increasing difficulty of obtaining accommodation reasonably close to the center, that underscored the growing agitation for Government action on housing.

All the housing measures passed by the Government involved the MBW, with the exception of the first one, the Torrens Act of 1868, which turned out to be virtually inoperative. Even the Metropolitan

Street Improvement Act of 1872 obliged the Board to reserve for housing certain plots in the new thoroughfare that would connect New Oxford Street with Shoreditch, although it did not give the Board power to construct dwellings for working people. The metropolis, however, was getting increasingly agitated over the problem, and Disraeli's new Conservative Government of 1874 was committed to taking action. The newspapers were not enchanted by the prospect of the Board and the City Corporation becoming local housing authorities, but there seemed no alternative.[36]

The Artisans' and Labourers' Dwelling Act of 1875 ("Cross's Act," after its author, Richard Cross, Home Secretary, 1874–1880 and 1885) has been generously praised by historians, and, indeed, its intentions were admirable.[37] In practice, it resulted in the building of a certain number of working-class blocks, but it totally failed to take account of the realities of the problem in the metropolis. (Later, under section 33 of the Metropolitan Streets Improvement Act of 1877 — the act authorizing the cutting through of Charing Cross Road and Shaftesbury Avenue — the Board was required to provide land suitable for housing the evicted members of the laboring class, in this case over ten thousand of them; but this provision turned out to be a considerable trial.)[38] The Cross Act of 1875 also authorized the Board to buy up and clear sites that had been declared by local medical officers, and established to the Board's satisfaction, to be "unfit for human habitation." The Board was further obligated — and here was the catch — to sell or let the cleared ground for the housing of approximately as many people as had been evicted.

In retrospect, the act of 1875 oversimplified matters gravely when it assumed that either commercial builders or semiphilanthropic housing bodies would rush to buy or lease land at figures which would enable the MBW to balance its books. The old owners and leaseholders got full commercial value, or better, for their property. But when the Board attempted to dispose of it, there was little response. The result was that London ratepayers, as sensitive as ever to increased burdens, were presented with a tremendous bill. Working-class housing in London by the 1880s had got itself into a terrible muddle.

When Cross's Act was passed, applications for clearance came from several sections of London. The two which received the greatest attention during the first year were from Whitechapel and Limehouse and from Holborn. The second bore upon the area between Gray's Inn Road and Leather Lane; in that case, the scheme which the Board devised ran into trouble in the Home Office and failed to win approval. But the Whitechapel-Limehouse scheme, having to do with the section to the east of the Royal Mint, an area with few business premises and many houses definitely unfit for human habitation, fared better. Mortality in this district was nearly two and a half times that of the metropolis as a whole. As approved by Parliament, the Whitechapel scheme displaced 3,669 people, but provided space for housing some 3,870 in blocks four or five stories high. With this improvement was to come a widening of several neighboring streets.[39]

So far so good. By March 1876, some fourteen vestries and district boards had officially applied, and by October, the total had risen to twenty-two, of which the Board recommended action in eleven instances. These involved the removal of nearly 15,000 persons and over 5,750 rooms.[40] But presently the Board began to run into trouble. The procedure set up by Cross's Act for taking land turned out to be cumbersome and slow. The Home Office appointed in each case a special arbitrator to assess the compensation to be paid, which, in the absence of guidelines, often turned out to be excessive; that is, the arbitrator sometimes would set compensation at about the level that would have been paid had the house been sound. Moreover, in the first few instances at least, the process was inordinately deliberate. In the case of the Whitechapel-Limehouse scheme, not until nineteen months after the arbitrator, Sir Henry Hunt, had been appointed could the Board send out the thirteen-week notice of eviction.[41] In other words, twenty-two months elapsed before the Board could get to work. Nevertheless, whatever justice there may have been in later charges, at this early stage the delay was not the Board's responsibility alone.

An equally grave fault of Cross's Act was its failure to provide for new dwellings. It could authorize the Board to take land and clear sites, but there was a serious discrepancy between what the Board, with some reason, thought its sites were worth and what housing associations were willing to pay. In August 1877 the Works and General Purposes Committee reported that, for the land reserved under the Metropolitan Street Improvements Act of 1872, the Improved Industrial Dwellings Company (Sir Sydney Waterlow's venture) had offered on average only about half of what had been estimated.[42] For the land taken under Cross's Act the report was equally dismal. Waterlow's Company made no move at all to bid on the land taken for the Whitechapel-Limehouse scheme, finding some of the conditions objectionable. A change in conditions still did not bring potential buyers, who managed to resist even the lure of the public auction which the Board organized.[43] In fact, by June 1879, not a square yard of land had been sold, and cleared sites simply lay idle—with no bids whatever or bids that were so low as to be wholly unacceptable.[44]

Newspaper editors were beginning to raise angry voices — to ask what had gone wrong.[45] The root of the trouble, the *Daily News* pointed out, was that the Board, always mindful of its duty to the ratepayers, was reckoning the value of the land on a commercial basis, while those who supplied working-class housing required a much lower figure.[46] This, of course, is the rock on which plans for working-class housing have traditionally foundered; the value of land in the center of a metropolis always places it well beyond the reach of the planners. The MBW and its critics were both, in a sense, right, given the different premises from which they were arguing. The Board did not feel justified in penalizing its ratepaying constituency by selling land for working-class housing at bargain prices, even though its critics were suggesting, either literally or by implication, that it ought to do so.

One may ask, however, whether the Board took the most expedient way out of the impasse.[47] By the summer of 1879 the situation was becoming critical. No land had been sold and no advance had been made toward providing working-class dwellings.[48] At this juncture, following oral negotiations, the Board received from the Peabody Trustees an offer for six sites. The Trustees agreed to pay £10,000 for the Whitechapel plot as well as certain amounts per foot on the other sites that would bring the total well below the calculations of the Board.[49] The Board's first impulse was to refuse the offer. But the failure of a public auction to arouse any interest convinced the members that their predicament would have to be viewed realistically. Their recommendation, over some opposition, was to accept the offer, even though it might, as one member charged, mean a loss of £70,000 an acre.[50]

The vestries, of course, were livid, and protests poured in. It was clear that the metropolitan ratepayer was going to take a terrible drubbing — a loss on the six sites variously estimated at between a quarter and a half a million pounds.[51] The Bermondsey vestrymen, smarting over the loss, came up with some sensible proposals to which it attempted to gain the adherence of other vestries. The chief stumbling block, they suggested, was the high-level of compensation which arbitrators were awarding to owners of run-down property. Their solution was to authorize the MBW to provide working-class housing in the same neighborhood, though not necessarily on the same street, since street fronts could sometimes be used more profitably for commercial enterprises.[52] But those whose primary interest was working-class housing saw this as a sellout. It certainly smacked of gross favoritism to the Peabody Trust, which in any case, because of its shrewd management of considerable resources and its policy of choosing tenants well above the lowest class, was no favorite with the other housing organizations. Indeed, in the Select Committee on the Artisans' Dwellings Improvement Acts in 1881–82, Sir Sydney Waterlow complained that the MBW had acted unfairly to bodies (such as his own Improved Industrial Dwellings Company) that were trying to provide working-class housing without the resources of the Peabody Trust.[53]

In actuality, the Board no more fancied the arrangement with the Peabody Trustees than did the vestries and the other housing organizations. But it felt hamstrung by the provisions of the act of 1875, and it sought an amendment which would reduce the compensation to be paid to owners of unhealthy houses and would at the same time relieve the Board of providing new housing in the same area for displaced tenants. The Artisans' Dwellings Amending Act of 1879 lessened, but, in the Board's view, by no means remedied the faults of the earlier statute. The action of the Select Committee of 1881–82, followed by the Artisans' Dwellings Act of 1882, made further improvements in the procedure. But there was little that could be done to clear up the confusion, in view of the differing premises from which the parties were acting. It was, of course, a conflict of claims and interests, most of them legitimate, a conflict that has continued to baffle urban authorities from that day to this.

The MBW spent much time on these questions. Yet, even though during its lifetime its job seemed too big, its record in housing was not discreditable. It carried out twenty-two improvement schemes in areas containing nearly fifty-nine acres. In the course of these operations over 7,400 tenements (exclusive of registered lodging houses) were removed, and in their place were erected 263 blocks of improved dwellings. The total amount spent by the Board in carrying out the Housing Acts came to more than £1.5 million. How much of this was recovered by the metropolitan ratepayer does not appear. Nor is there evidence — and in its absence such a thing is improbable — that these new dwellings were, to any great degree, occupied by those who had been evicted, or even by tenants of the same class. Almost inevitably (and this was admittedly true in the case of the Peabody blocks) an improvement in housing accommodation is reflected in a higher class of tenant, and the last plight of the poorest tenant is worse than his first.

The Board encountered the same problem in the administration of the street improvement acts. It was not given authority to build laborers' dwellings, and again, building societies "evinced no alacrity to take lands for such a purpose."[54] Although these acts required that the evicted working-class tenants be provided for, they gave the Board no power to take positive steps to see that it was done. Beyond doubt — even allowing for inefficiency and bureaucratic delays — this was the paramount obstacle to the building of Shaftesbury Avenue and Charing Cross Road, for both of which a substantial removal of dense and fetid slums was necessary.[55] In vain the Board tried to get the Home Secretary to moderate the requirements imposed by the Streets Improvement Act of 1877. It got for its pains a letter of sympathy, but little else. It was essential, as Richard Cross urged, first to house the displaced tenants and only then to carry out street improvements.[56]

The consequence was that the cutting through of these new streets dragged on almost interminably. When the Liberal Government took over in 1880, the Board members appealed to the new Home Secretary, Sir William Harcourt, who again gave them little more than sympathy—though he recognized the difficulties which they confronted. Faced with the impossibility of getting administrative action, the Board concluded that it had no alternative but to press for an amendment to the act.[57] Both the delay and the threatened removal of numbers of tenants gave an occasion for reformers to needle the Board. In the House of Commons, J. F. B. Firth, the leader of the municipal reform movement in London, in a question designed to embarrass the Board's chairman, Sir James McGarel-Hogg, asked why the Board had spent five years on the improvement between Tottenham Court Road and Charing Cross. Obviously Firth's primary interest was neither in the poor nor in getting the new streets completed, but in the creation of a new and representative governing body for the metropolis.[58]

With the Artisans' Dwellings Act of 1882, the Board made modest gains in administrative policy. What it proposed to do next was to get the Streets Improvement Act of 1877 liberalized to at least the degree that the housing acts had been changed. The Home Office, however, refused to go beyond the provisions of the new dwelling acts, which required the clearing authority to provide housing for at least half of those displaced and also simplified the arbitration procedure. The Board was somewhat annoyed by the refusal of Harcourt to follow the recommendations of the Select Committee of 1882 and his insistence that a new bill must not go beyond the terms of the new housing acts.[59] But there he stuck and the Board had to comply.

It is not clear how much of the housing muddle can be charged to the MBW. The procedure prescribed was slow and complicated, and the provisions for compensation discouraged both builders and building societies. Yet until new housing was provided, no decisive step could be taken. This fact was denied by some of the more dedicated reformers, however. A letter to *The Times* charged that the difficulty was not with the law but with local administration, and that where some individual interest was involved, as in the case of a public house, matters would move rapidly enough. In 1884, again, the Board tried to gain support from Parliament for a further liberalization of the Streets Improvement Act. This proposed modification, which had the backing of Sir Charles Dilke, would have authorized the Board to appropriate land elsewhere when it was impossible to house the displaced on the land at the original site. Sir Sydney Waterlow charged that this would reverse the policy of the last twenty years. But Dilke, surely no enemy of the poor, denied that this would be a reversal and reminded the House that the Select Committees of 1881 and 1882 had recommended relaxing the law.[60] By this time, however, Harcourt's bill for reforming metropolitan government was on the horizon, and although it was withdrawn, there could be no doubt in anyone's mind that the days of the Board, at least in its current form, were numbered.

In all, during the less than thirty-five years of its existence, the MBW's operations had resulted in providing improved working-class dwellings for more than 38,000 persons.[61] A list of the Board's street improvements is even more impressive. Exclusive of the grants made to vestries and district boards for local street improvements (which aggregated over a million pounds in addition to the half million for certain works carried out in connection with the completion of the Inner Circle underground railway), the total net cost of the Board's street improvements amounted to nearly £7.5 million. Yet, limited by its fear of ratepayer's revenge and its own uncertain taste, the Board failed, aside from the Embankment, to beautify the metropolis as it might have done. One study speaks of the characteristic MBW streets as lined with commercial premises of a uniform height, broken by tenement blocks intended to house the displaced slum dwellers.[62] No critic placed the Board's accomplishments on a level with Haussmann's rebuilding of Paris. Neither Shaftesbury Avenue nor Charing Cross Road was a distinguished street, while Northumberland Avenue was condemned by an architect as "one of the saddest of thoroughfares, and to its hope-abandoned wayfarer there is a temptation in its proximity to the River."[63] Even so, the MBW's achievements were notable. None of it was simple business—even without the knavery in the architect's office.

Like any public body, especially one that was accustomed to listening to outside voices, the Board had trouble in naming its new streets. *The Builder* thought Charing Cross Road "unimaginative," but itself had suggested Shaftesbury Avenue; and *The Times*, having rejected the name Shaftesbury as overused, reflected that soon the Board would provide the new street "with one of the weary commonplaces which seem to make up its birthday book."[64] Actually, the Board was in frequent hot water with neighborhoods in attempting to impose some rational order on the naming of streets and on the numbering of houses, which also fell within its supervision. There was alarm lest the Board descend with a requirement for a sweeping change in names and numbers. Yet its decision to give the New Road the three names of Marylebone, Euston, and Pentonville was surely not terrifying, nor were its efforts to keep control over the naming of new streets in order to avoid an additional batch of King, Queen, Waterloo, and Wellington streets.[65] Formerly two or three men building a number of houses had each been able to give his name to a part of the street. Now the MWB, acting on the request of the local vestry, moved in to prevent the use of subsidiary names. The Board, commented *The Builder,* had been relatively tactful and cautious and had usually accepted the local recommendation unless the name suggested would duplicate one already in use; but the judgment of vestries, the editor concluded, was far from impeccable, as when the Clerkenwell vestry wanted to change the name of Bagnigge Wells Road to Coppice Road.[66] The Board made some progress in clearing up eccentric numbering and duplicating street names, to the slight improvement of the lot of postmen. In its first eighteen years, it renumbered 120,000 houses, renamed 1,500 streets, and named over 2,400 new ones.[67] But those who know twentieth-century London will not be inclined to exaggerate the Board's triumphs.

The MBW's connection with the administration of the building acts was even more peripheral than with street improvements. It is not necessary to recall the earlier acts, or the corps of surveyors who supervised them. In 1855, in his speech introducing the Metropolis Local Management Act, Sir Benjamin Hall took occasion to include a severe criticism of the District Surveyors, which those officials duly resented. They were alarmed lest what they regarded as their vested rights be interfered with by the new legislation, and were also disturbed that henceforth they were to receive their appointments from an elected body (the MBW) rather than from the magistrates and the Lord Mayor and aldermen. In any event, the Building Act of 1855 improved the status of the District Surveyor substantially and did not subordinate him completely to the MBW — certainly not as much as the Board would have wished. New buildings and alterations were supposed to clear through the District Surveyors: builders had to give two days' notice of impending changes and supply particulars about them; and then building operations would be carried on under the direction of the surveyor, who collected his fee from the builder.

The powers of the Board, in short, were not only limited by statute but were shared with the District Surveyors — by 1874, with some fifty-nine of them. But the Board spent a good deal of time on building act questions, through its Building Act Committee of fifteen members and a special department in the office of the supervising architect. Each Friday, the architect laid before the Board forty to fifty reports on building act matters, most of them noncontroversial. But three or four of them would have to be referred to the Building Act Committee, generally because of a difference of opinion between the architect's office and the vestries. The Board of itself had no power to correct an infraction if the vestry declined to act. In Fulham, a brewery built beyond the line, but since the vestry was not disposed to intervene, the brewery continued its illegal occupancy.[68] Over the years, however, the Board managed to increase its power. In 1869 responsibility for "dangerous structures" was taken from the Fire Brigade and lodged in the Board; and in 1878 it got further powers with respect to the width of new streets, the construction of theatres, and the foundations of buildings. Yet four years earlier, an attempt to pass an amendment act had failed largely because of the opposition of builders. Once again, the Board found itself hamstrung by the feebleness of its powers. Victorian London did not willingly submit to regulation, especially if there were genuine doubts, as in this case, about the efficiency of the regulating agent. The Board gained a little more power by legislation in the early 1880s,[69] but never as much as it wanted and never enough to enforce an effective building code. As in its other activities, the MBW represented a transitional stage of metropolitan government, pointing the way to a regime of broader functions and more businesslike administration, a move away from the extreme localism of the early nineteenth century and (hesitantly and against much opposition) toward the considerable degree of centralization that was to prove essential in the twentieth century.

In 1877 a Select Committee on the Metropolitan Fire Brigade investigated, among other topics, the danger of fire in theatres and music halls and the lack of supervision of these structures. The Lord Chamberlain, as the time-honored regulator of theatres, testified that he could do nothing but suspend a theatre's license—a penalty that he thought too stiff for a minor infraction.[70] It seemed an obvious expedient to vest the responsibility for checking on the safety of theatres in the always available and usually willing MBW, and the Select Committee recommended that no new theatre or music hall should be licensed until the Board had certified that it had satisfied the requirements against fire. This was what might have been expected; but the Committee's further recommendation—that the Board should have power to require owners to remedy dangerous structural defects, insofar as this was possible at a "moderate expenditure"—presaged trouble.

In the following year these recommendations were embodied in an act of Parliament. No exceptional difficulties arose about new theatres and music halls. But old structures presented a complicated task of inspection, judgment, and negotiation, for there were more than four hundred London theatres and music halls of all ages and degrees of soundness. To inspect them thoroughly, to decide what changes were necessary and whether these could be interpreted as requiring a "moderate expenditure," was a major task. Whether the Board acted as expeditiously as it might have done is a debatable question, and will call forth varying answers. In any case, the Board had just got well into its work when English opinion was appalled by the fire at the Ring Theatre in Vienna, where in December 1881 some hundreds of lives were lost. There were, of course, resounding demands in the House of Commons for action—especially for the MBW to display greater energy in its inspection activities.[71]

What made the Board's position more difficult was a seeming disagreement with Captain E. M. Shaw of the Fire Brigade.[72] Captain Shaw was requested, pursuant to a letter from the Home Secretary requiring a report on the actual condition of London theatres and the changes necessary to prevent loss of life, to inspect all theatres. Shaw, the MBW was at pains to point out, was not limited by the terms of the act which bound the Board, and his report was formulated without reference to cost. By mid-April 1882, he had completed his inspection of forty-one theatres (eight of them still unbuilt) and called for sweeping alterations and structural changes. The Board, alas, restricted by the terms of the act of 1878, could not demand changes as freely as Shaw had.

The work of the Board was not made easier by the rumors of corruption circulating through the metropolis, rumors which were later confirmed in substance and which focused on the London Pavilion in Piccadilly Circus. In August 1882 *Punch* referred as follows to the theatre, which the Board owned "as sole proprietor": "The London Pavilion is not a model of solidity in construction—in fact, one newspaper has irreverently called it a 'Tinder-box'—and it is curious that no fussy Provincial Member has drawn the willing Press to this probably unsurveyed and highly-rented building."[73] Yet at this first stage of their labors, the Board members seem to have worked with reasonable speed and efficiency. The *Daily Chronicle* could assert that the public had "no reason to complain of the laxity of the Metropolitan Board of Works in the performance of their duties in respect to the examination of theatres."[74] Of the forty-one theatres inspected by Shaw, two closed voluntarily and two were closed by the Lord Chamberlain because of representations made to him by the Board. The others all received certificates after completing structural changes of greater or less consequence.[75] Theatre owners demanded arbitration in only a few cases, and in most of these they lost.

What transformed the suspicion and resistance of the theatre owners into active opposition was a request from the Lord Chamberlain in 1885 that the Board inspect and grant a certificate to theatres and music halls before he licensed them. The Lord Chamberlain wanted to fortify himself with an MBW certificate, a reasonable enough desire.[76] But this, the Board pointed out, was impossible under its current powers. Then, replied the Lord Chamberlain, why not ask Parliament for the necessary powers? When in October 1885 the Board decided to promote a bill — or rather asked the Government to introduce one — to increase its authority, it was inviting trouble.[77] The bill failed to pass in 1886 and was reintroduced in 1887, but in neither year did it get beyond the early stages. Among the factors, no doubt, were time and the pressure of business. But there was also a mobilization of theatre owners, who protested against the notion of giving any more power to the Board. A deputation of owners, including Henry Irving, D'Oyly Carte, and Augustus Harris, called on Henry Mathews, the Home Secretary.[78] They were smarting, no doubt, from the expense caused by the Board's required alterations, and they had complaints about the delays in getting decisions from the Board.[79] But there are also hints that the owners resented the actions of an official in the architect's office who had taken to demanding free passes, presumably for members of the Board and their parties:

> So pity Augustus Harris. What wonder he turns "a reb,"
> 'Gainst the pitiless applications of the stall-devouring Hebb.[80]

By this time the MBW was nearing the end of its life, and scandals had been specifically charged against it by the *Financial News*. There was little that any champion of the Board could do but point to what it had accomplished in making London theatres reasonably safe from fire.

The question of the toll bridges over the Thames was a well-worn subject even before the MBW was created. House of Commons committees had reported on the issue several times since 1835, and the Select Committee of 1854, disturbed by the mounting volume of traffic and its diversion from natural routes by the existence of tolls, had come out flatly in favor of freeing the bridges and improving communications across the Thames.[81] Of the bridges across the river, only London, Blackfriars, and Westminster (the first two built by the City Corporation and under its management) did not require the payment of tolls, with the result that they — especially London Bridge — got the lion's share of the traffic. London Bridge, the Select Committee was told, handled as many pedestrians and vehicles as Southwark, Waterloo, Blackfriars, and Westminster together.[82] Waterloo Bridge (built by Sir John Rennie in 1817) had clearly been a disaster from its opening; the shareholders had lost their investment, and the bondholders had received nothing.[83] The managers of the bridges would have been delighted to sell out to a public authority, but not for a nominal figure. And prices would certainly rise when it seemed likely that a serious attempt would be made to acquire them for the public.

Shortly after its creation the MBW considered making such an attempt. In 1857, it tried to get the City to cooperate in taking over Southwark Bridge, recalling that at one time the Corporation had bargained with the bridge company. The Corporation, still resenting the Board's actions, would have none of it: this was now the Board's business, the Corporation replied stiffly.[84] The Board concluded, however, that in carrying out its main drainage commission it had a more urgent use for its money. A bill introduced in the spring of 1865, which would have involved a small addition to the rates, was opposed by the Board.[85] Evidence given before the Select Committee on that occasion emphasized the eagerness of the bridge companies to get rid of what were proving costly embarrassments. But regrettably, there were no resources that could be tapped.

The first significant step was taken outside the heart of the metropolis. Certain suburban districts were demanding, not unreasonably, some immediate and specific benefit from the coal duties which they were paying. In the Coal and Wine Duties Continuance Act of 1868, which continued these duties to 1889, provisions were incorporated which looked toward the liberation of a series of up-river bridges by permitting those responsible to borrow on the security of the duties for 1889. The following year legislation was more specific. By the Kew and Other Bridges Act of 1869 a committee of twelve was set up, with six members each from the Board and the City, to free certain bridges beyond the limits of the metropolis but within the area from which the coal duties were collected. The freeing of these western bridges turned out to be more complicated than had been expected, with the exception of Kingston, which was simple and cheap. Staines was a public trust with a bonded indebtedness and large arrears of interest, but the committee managed to cope with this and the bridge was opened in February 1871. Kew caused much more trouble because of what the committee regarded as an excessive claim. Although in March 1872 its owners were reported as asking £60,000, a few weeks later the demand had risen to more than £68,000. The committee finally called in an arbitrator, who fixed the sum at

£57,300. The greatest embarrassment was presented by the Hampton
Court Bridge, for which the managers asked £123,000 even though the
committee suspected that it was worth £40,000. Again arbitration was
required, with the result that the bridge company's demands were pared
down from £123,000 to £48,000.[86] Clearly the owners of the bridges did
well on these transactions; at least, the sums they received were far better than they would have obtained commercially. When it was apparent
that a sale might be in prospect, the asking price went up. The company
owning Kew Bridge, for example, had failed to dispose of it for £33,000,
but they finally sold it to the Committee for £57,000.[87]

By the late 1860s and early 1870s public opinion was moving toward a
freeing of all the bridges. In 1868–69 there was talk of an association to
attack the general problem of tolls, and in February 1870 the Metropolitan Free Bridges Association was organized.[88] There were also rumblings from districts where tolls were considered a special handicap. Sir
Henry Peek and W. H. Smith, for example, attempted to get tolls removed from the Government bridge at Chelsea; these tolls, which had
never been sufficient to pay the charges, were thought to have prevented
an increase in population around Battersea Park. But as Gladstone told
the House of Commons, his Government refused to have commerce
with such hearsay—not that it believed in bridge tolls—and refused to do
more than communicate with the MBW, "in case the Board think fit to
make a proposal to put the saddle on the right horse, and cause the
charge to fall on the inhabitants of London on whom it ought to fall."[89]

By the autumn of 1872 the Board decided that the time had come to
act on the metropolitan bridges as a group. Population was continuing
to mount, and traffic was steadily becoming more dense. The sweets of
free transit had been tasted by those who used the Southwark Bridge,
which the City Corporation had recently purchased for £200,000 (it had
cost £700,000 originally).[90] As a result, the traffic over this bridge was
said to have increased tenfold.[91] But, again, in the Board's newest attempt there was the familiar question of who was to pay and how. The
Government, though all eagerness to get rid of the tolls, found it difficult
to swallow the Board's proposal of extending the coal dues some years
beyond 1889.[92] By the time the bill was prepared, Government opposition had become firmer, since new sources of supply which the Government had hoped to open up had failed to materialize.[93] In the face of
Government opposition there was no possibility that the bill would make
any progress, and it was withdrawn.

When the Gladstone Government fell in January 1874, the Board immediately set to work on the Conservatives. But no method of financing
the project presented itself, other than that of extending the coal and

wine duties. Stafford Northcote, the new Chancellor, dashed the rising hopes of the Board when he declined to go along with that suggestion. Of the bills that were introduced and withdrawn, one had been framed by the Free Bridges Association, with Francis Hayman Fowler, the Lambeth representative on the MBW, as chairman. The propaganda of the Association dramatized the cause effectively. It showed, for example, that the ratio of pedestrians crossing Blackfriars Bridge to those crossing Waterloo Bridge, with its toll charges, was about five to one, and that it was over four to one in the case of Westminster Bridge as against Waterloo. It also emphasized the obvious inconvenience tolls created for the poor laborer—the necessity for taking the long way around to avoid the toll (even if it was only a halfpenny), and the clusters of wives and children at one end of the bridge at noon waiting for someone to carry the bag containing the laborer's dinner across the bridge.[94]

The bill introduced in October 1876 encountered technical difficulties, but the following year it was reintroduced and passed. The operation it specified was to be financed by borrowing on the part of the Board to the limit of £1.5 million, and it included all the bridges within the metropolis as well as an additional one over Deptford Creek. The act of 1877 was, of course, the decisive step in proceedings against bridge tolls in the metropolis; armed with this authority, the Board was able to start work. Some of the bridge shares shot upward when it appeared that the public was about to step in. Shares in the Waterloo Bridge Company, whose property was perhaps the most conspicuous white elephant of the lot, had risen from two or three pounds apiece to twelve or thirteen pounds on the strength of this new interest.[95] There were, of course, differences in the financial states of the various bridges. Some, such as Hammersmith, Fulham, and Battersea, seemed to be doing well enough. Others—most conspicuously Waterloo—had been financial failures from the start. Virtually none of the bridge owners objected in principle to selling out—if the compensation was satisfactory.

The total demanded by the bridge companies was approximately £2,338,000—so much more than the Board had intended to pay that all but three (the Chelsea Suspension Bridge, Putney, and Hammersmith) had to be submitted to arbitration. The negotiations and arbitration proceedings went with reasonable speed, chiefly because the Board had been bargaining for certain of the bridges for some time. The most difficult, and the most expensive, was Waterloo Bridge, which required nearly £475,000. Troublesome as it was, the reason Waterloo did not cause even greater difficulty was probably that the Board had begun its negotiations several months before the act had been passed and that, as these proceeded, engineers offered evidence that the bridge was structurally precarious. The tidal river had sapped the foundations of the piers, and the bridge company could not raise the capital to make them secure. In the end, Rennie's old bridge was sold for less than half its original cost.[96] For the freeing of Waterloo Bridge the great day was 5 October 1878. The tollkeepers wearing their white aprons, with big pockets for coppers, continued to collect tolls up to the last minute. Traffic was brisk, for there were many who wanted to boast of having been among the last to pay a toll. Then two omnibuses drove up with a deputation from the MBW, and the gates at both ends were swung shut during a speech from Dresser Rogers, member for Camberwell, after which the gates were opened and a crowd of people rushed across.[97] As for the cost of the other bridges, Vauxhall required £255,000 from the public, Albert and Battersea (owned by the same company), £170,000, and Hammersmith £112,000; the remaining six were all under £100,000. Thus the total paid for bridges under the act of 1877 was about £1,377,000, or a little more than half of what had been demanded.[98]

But the Board's troubles were not over. Costly repairs were needed on at least five bridges. Putney and Battersea, which were both made of timber and dated from the eighteenth century, were the most desperate cases; there seemed no alternative to total rebuilding. This was done at a cost of £300,000 and £143,000 respectively. Waterloo and Hammersmith required about £63,000 and £83,000 respectively, and other bridges called for smaller amounts.[99] There were the usual troubles with local areas—complaints over methods of detouring, plans for approaches, and the rest—but on the whole, the Board carried its plan through efficiently and with reasonable expedition. There remained one crying need for Londoners having to cross the river. a bridge to the east of London Bridge. Such a bridge had been discussed for several years, and in the spring of 1878 the Board had its engineer draw up plans for one to cost £1.25 million.[100] A struggle with the City Corporation was avoided when the Common Council decided to cooperate rather than fight the Board's proposal, and the two applied jointly for authorization. But who was to pay? Again there seemed no source of funds except future coal and wine dues. Memorials from vestries, for and against, showered in, but the fatal blow came when the Treasury refused to go along with the extension of the coal duties.[101] Then, after the Board in an excess of optimism had decided to go ahead with its bill, it was thrown out by a Select Committee. Obviously, although such a bridge was needed, it raised more problems than the Board had expected. There was, for example, the choice between a high-level and a low-level bridge; there were particular questions about Bazalgette's plans; and there were a number of powerful interests, such as the City Corporation, wharfingers and shipowners, and the Thames Conservators, who opposed the bridge for reasons of their own.[102]

The MBW's bill was killed, but the question was still very much alive. And the Board, well aware of the desperate need for improved communication across the river, retired to consider the next step. There was little difference of opinion in the press that, of all the possible new improvements to the metropolis, Thames communications were primary; the other proposals could wait.[103] When Bazalgette came up with an ideal scheme for a bridge across the river near the Tower, and for two tunnels, one at Shadwell, the other at Blackwall, the Board took a hard look at the probable cost and then retreated hastily, concluding that for the present a single tunnel — between Nightingale Lane and Bermondsey — would have to do. Again, there was an outcry. Some demanded a bridge; others wanted a tunnel located at a different point. Indeed, at this juncture it seemed doubtful whether anything would be done. The Corporation, too, was making little progress with its plans. As the *City Press*, not a hostile critic, observed, the Corporation seemed "at wit's end" about the matter; there was little to choose between the Corporation's absurd idea of a steam ferry and the Board's plan of one miserable tunnel. From either point of view, the *Press* thought, this was sheer farce.[104] When the Board's bill for a tunnel was brought in early in 1884, it was referred to a Select Committee which, under the chairmanship of Sir Hussey Vivian, investigated the whole problem. It liked neither the Board's proposal for a subway between Nightingale Lane and Bermondsey — it was not far enough down the river — nor a scheme received from a private company for a duplex bridge below the Tower. But it learned that there was a substantial sum accumulated in the City's Bridge House Estate and suggested that the Corporation take responsibility for the bridge. Thus the Corporation obtained statutory power to construct Tower Bridge in 1885. For the Board, however, the matter of cross-river communication descended into utter chaos. There was little enthusiasm for the tunnel at Shadwell, as the Select Committee had suggested, but something had to be done. Again, there was maneuvering and pressuring among the East End vestries to get the tunnel conveniently located for their parishes.

The expedient hit upon by the MBW was that of two steam ferries, one between Poplar and Greenwich and the other crossing the river at Woolwich. Unfortunately, its bill gave both those who disliked the ferry proposal and those who disliked the Board an opportunity for censure. C. T. Ritchie, one of the M.P.'s for Stepney, condemned the Board for having disregarded the Select Committee's recommendation; and James Bryce, another of the Stepney M.P.'s, thought that the Board had acted with little regard for the people of London and that "the case for a reform of London government which the feebleness or wilfulness of that Board disclosed was very strong indeed."[105] Sir Hussey Vivian pointed to the weakness in the Board's proposal for a tunnel from Nightingale Lane to Bermondsey and suggested that its investigation had been perfunctory. The proposed location of the tunnel had been a compromise decision that satisfied nobody; it had been opposed, Sir Hussey intimated, by nearly every public body in London.[106]

Despite the opposition, not only in Parliament but among commercial ferryboat owners, the Board persisted in its purpose and let contracts for the construction of two ferries, each to provide accommodation for a thousand foot passengers and ten horse-drawn vehicles. And in 1887, as the clouds were gathering around its head, the Board got through Parliament a bill for a tunnel at Blackwall, thus going back to one of the features of Bazalgette's original plan. The tunnel was to cost about £1.5 million. All this was fair enough. What created an unpleasant odor around the affair was the Board's incredible pigheadedness — or malice — as it approached its own extinction. Obviously an agency about to be replaced ought to make no large commitments that would bind its successors. Nevertheless this is what the Board proceeded to do, apparently with all deliberation. Two weeks before it was to be superseded by the London County Council, it resolved to receive tenders and to accept the most favorable — and this under protest from both the Local Government Board and the London County Council. As one member put it somewhat imaginatively, the Board refused to be "intimidated."[107] What he was thinking of is impossible to divine, but the Board's action left a taste in the public mouth that was scarcely less bitter than that caused by the scandals in the architect's office.

CHAPTER 6

The Miscellaneous Duties of a Municipal Government

Critics freely charged the MBW with empire building, with an inability or unwillingness to say no if it was asked by the Government to assume new responsibilities. This charge was understandable enough when it came from those who, like J. A. Nicholay,[1] held that the Board had been created as a sewer-building agency and should confine its activities within narrow limits. Although he and others never suggested that the MBW should disband after the main drainage system had been completed, they opposed adding fresh obligations to its range of duties, to vesting in it the responsibility for managing those services which have since become the commonplaces of municipal government. As for the vestries, they were not particularly interested in good government (above a certain minimum), and they were still less interested in any new services that would add to the rates. How real was the fear of centralization and how much a smoke screen behind which the vestries could carry on their jobbery may be argued. But certainly only a few eager reformers saw London as a community which, sooner or later, would require an active central government. When, therefore, the Board, either at the request of the Government or on its own initiative, entered new spheres, there was little enthusiasm among its constituents.

Yet, inevitably, new duties came to the Board. It had been made partly responsible for enforcing the building code, and for the safety of theatres, and it was the agency that acquired and repaired the bridges. It

126

was also to be given responsibility for fire protection; and it was to make a valiant, if indiscreet, attempt to assure Londoners of adequate supplies of water and gas at reasonable prices. The Board was expected, too, to acquire and manage open spaces for the metropolis, as indeed it did. Nor was it to be above assuming odd jobs as they came up. Among these were such community chores as inspection of cattle for rinderpest or other diseases, the supervision of dairies, cowsheds, and milk supply, and the regulation of slaughterhouses and "offensive businesses." When it was necessary to control the storage of petroleum and explosives, the Board was there to undertake the work. Finally, it was asked to supervise metropolitan baby farming by carrying out the Infant Life Protection Act 1872, a statute that in practice proved faulty and accomplished little. What all this meant was clear enough to those who had eyes to see: the growing complexities of urban living, the rising standards of public health, and the lack of suitable agencies made it inevitable that the MBW should develop into a quasi-municipal administration. Obviously, the Board was not properly constituted for such a variety of activities, it lacked coercive power over the vestries and its liaison with Parliament was far from perfect. But from Parliament's point of view the Board was a convenient device. When a matter arose that needed to be handled centrally, there—the Home Office was aware—was the Board; and the Board was in no position to refuse such commissions, and, indeed, had no inclination to do so. The consequence was, *faute de mieux*, that the MBW was saddled with a multitude of miscellaneous chores.

First of all, there was the Fire Brigade, which, typically enough, was put under the management of the Board with a degree of financial support that proved to be quite inadequate. It was the Great Fire in Tooley Street, Southwark, in June 1861 that started the hue and cry for better fire protection.[2] The fire, which raged for two days in the warehouses and wharves to the south of London Bridge, consumed huge quantities of tar, tallow, and other inflammable substances and even spread to schooners in the river. Nothing like it had been seen in London since the Great Fire two centuries before, and it cost the life of the first superintendent of the London Fire Engine Establishment, James Braidwood. The Establishment was a curious organization. Traditionally, protection from fire in London had been a private responsibility. Some vestries had volunteer groups with a few paid officers, and many fire insurance companies maintained their own small brigades. In 1832 a number of these had been amalgamated into a single London Fire Engine Establishment, with eighty full-time firemen and nineteen fire stations.[3] Within limits this seems to have been an efficient, well-run organization.

The limits, however, were obvious. The Brigade was more interested in saving property than in saving life — the Royal Society for the Protection of Life from Fire, an eighteenth-century charitable enterprise, was supposed to handle that side of the business — and logically it was obliged to notice only insured property. The protection given outlying districts was reported to be negligible, and the resources of the Establishment were concentrated at the center where costly fires might be expected to occur. The Tooley Street fire, which presented the insurance companies with claims for over £2 million, provoked further reflection from both claimants and companies. The companies, in a panic, threatened a prodigious increase in rates, and merchants and warehouse owners reacted violently. But beyond that, the companies saw the absurdity of their position. There was no more reason why they should assume the burden of protecting London against fire than that the police service should be in the hands of a private agency, as one of their officers argued before the Select Committee of 1862. And they wondered by what chain of developments they had been maneuvered into accepting responsibility for the fire protection of London. Their expenditures had steadily risen, owing to the growing number of fires, and they still received no assistance from public funds. It was, they were prepared to argue, grossly unfair.

The consequence of their protest was the House Select Committee of 1862.[4] The hearing before the Committee was notable for the unveiling of a scheme, championed by the Metropolitan Police and destined to reappear intermittently during the next fifteen years, to make the Fire Brigade a branch of the police force, under the direction of the Police Commissioners.[5] Captain Eyre Massey Shaw,[6] who had come over from Belfast to succeed Braidwood as superintendent, argued that no one could make skilled firemen out of London police constables.[7] But the Select Committee accepted Commissioner Sir Richard Mayne's argument and recommended that a fire brigade for the metropolis be formed as a branch of the Metropolitan Police.[8] Captain Shaw was asked to work out a scheme for the vast area covered by the MBW. His plan, however, appalled Sir George Grey, the Home Secretary, because of its estimated cost of £70,000. As a result Shaw came down to £52,000, and then to £50,000 — a purely arbitrary figure representing a halfpenny rate plus £10,000 from the Government plus a contribution from the insurance companies.[9] This Grey accepted. Nevertheless, the Committee's intention of consigning the new Fire Brigade to the management of the Police Commissioners failed owing to complications introduced by the City. Since the undertaking was to be presided over by the Commissioners, the City demanded that its own brigade be supervised by its own police. With such a solution out of the question, the only other eligible supervisory agency was, of course, the MBW, always available and reasonably willing.

The Board agreed to add the Fire Brigade to its empire, though not all of its constituents were enthusiastic about the development. The *Marylebone Mercury* was indignant at the increase in rates that would occur and at the shifting of responsibilities from the insurance companies, and also because the new arrangement would be a grave infraction of the sacred principle of local self-government. Furthermore, the paper computed, Marylebone would pay a thirteenth of the cost, while presenting only a fiftieth of the risk. The vestries of both Marylebone and St. Pancras passed motions asking the metropolitan members of Parliament to oppose the bill at every stage.[10] When the Board agreed to take over the Brigade it was with the understanding that the insurance companies and the Government (for the protection of government property) should carry their fair share, with the companies, according to the agreement, paying in a percentage of their policies not to exceed £10,000 a year.[11]

The Government and the insurance companies consented to this arrangement, and the Metropolitan Fire Brigade came into being, with Captain Shaw as director. Shaw, only thirty-five at the time, was an able, strict administrator and a student of the art of fire fighting. Throughout the years he acquired a reputation as an authority on the subject.[12] He was also, it appeared, something of a bon vivant and a ladies' man, who in 1886 was cited as corespondent in a divorce suit, though he escaped without censure. One suspects that W. S. Gilbert's reference to him in the Fairy Queen's song in *Iolanthe* — "Type of true love kept under" — was inspired by his tastes as well as his occupation. The arrangement made with the Government and the companies called for an annual payment of £10,000 by the former and a contribution from the latter at the rate of £35 for every million pounds of their policies, which on the basis of the year 1863 would amount to £10,156. The Board would raise its share of the budget by a rate not exceeding a half-penny in the pound, and it might borrow up to £40,000 to carry out the Metropolitan Fire Brigade Act of 1865.

There were some administrative changes, necessitated in part by the obligation to cover much more territory; but, substantially, the Brigade operated as had the old Establishment. When the Board took over, the force consisted of 130 officers and men, 17 fire engine stations, 2 river stations with floating engines, 9 land steam fire engines, and 27 hand-power engines.[13] By the time the MBW was superseded (1888), the force had grown to 674 officers and men, 55 fire engine stations, 27 street stations, with hose carts and other facilities proportionately increased.[14] Some 29 temporary stations were set up, and the parishes were asked to maintain them until the Brigade could take permanent measures.[15] Meanwhile, Shaw was canvassing the equipment problem, inspecting parish engines and recommending that some of them be purchased, pointing to the superiority of steam over the old manual engines, and urging the purchase of additional floating engines for the protection of the waterfront. Although it was plainly too early to draw sweeping conclusions, the first year showed encouraging results in that the proportion of serious fires had been reduced from 34 to 25 percent (512 serious and 990 slight fires in 1865, 326 serious and 1012 slight in 1866). Through the 1870s and 1880s the trend continued—from 25 percent serious in 1866 to 10 or 11 percent during the 1870s, and in the 1880s never rising above 9 percent.[16] And in 1888 the percentage of "slight" fires reached the all-time high of 94.

One of the Brigade's early problems was its relation to the Royal Society for the Protection of Life from Fire, a private charity. Obviously the sharp distinction between the force responsible for the protection of property and those who were to protect life could not be continued. The Society, moreover, was quite willing to go out of business, providing it was paid enough to assure pensions to its servants and to establish a fund to reward those who protected life from fire. The Board was happy to take over the Society's work on such reasonable terms, paying £2,500 for equipment valued at £9,000 and absorbing sixty-seven of the Society's force into the Brigade.[17]

During its career under the Board, the Fire Brigade had two major problems beyond routine administrative matters. One was the perpetual shortage of funds that afflicted most of the Board's activities, and the other—an issue in its own right—was water supply. During the first year of the Brigade's existence its three sources of revenue returned about £52,000, actually a bit over Sir George Grey's hopeful estimate. Yet, though the income on the halfpenny rate rose with the expansion of London's population, and the contribution from the insurance offices rose with the increase of business, funds were gravely short of the legitimate needs of the Brigade. It was especially preposterous to think of meeting the capital expenditure necessary for new fire stations and equipment from the £40,000 which the Board was entitled to borrow under the act of 1865. By the Metropolitan Board of Works (Loans) Act of 1869—an important development in public finance—the Board was freed from some of the limitations on its borrowing powers and could acquire resources for plant construction. But these loans did not help with running expenses, and there were constant complaints from the men concerning low pay and the lack of what would now be termed fringe benefits.

Captain Shaw admittedly was a strict disciplinarian, who knew his business thoroughly and did not seek advice on the affairs of the Brigade. He was, said the chairman of the Board's committee, "an absolute minded man and he does not like any interference of that sort [in disciplinary matters]. I do not want to say anything upon that head, but we leave Captain Shaw to discipline his own army."[18] Was it because of this that recruiting for the Brigade was getting more difficult and men were leaving it? That trend seems to have been clear. During the past ten years, Shaw told a Select Committee in 1876, 640 men had left, and there was no longer a waiting list. In fact, it was now hard to get young seamen — the Brigade hired only seamen[19] — whereas a few years earlier a thousand applicants had wanted jobs.[20] Shaw would have insisted that the shortage was due not to strict discipline but to other factors, most of them traceable to low pay: the men were overworked, and the whole system was understaffed; in consequence, no reserve was left to deal with extreme emergencies.

Rumors of insufficient staff and niggardly compensation had brought about the appointment of the Select Committee of 1876.[21] C. T. Ritchie, who had moved for the Committee, pointed to the low numerical level of the Brigade's personnel (the more serious when London's population was growing so rapidly), to the apparent indifference of the Board toward requests for a pension plan, and to its paltry compensation for serious injury from accidents in the line of duty.[22] The firemen, Ritchie insisted, were not so well treated as either the Metropolitan police or the City police.

The Select Committee took evidence during two sessions and came out with a report that was a curious combination of the sensible and the eccentric. It pointed out that, although the fire service was clearly underfinanced, the Board had made no serious effort to persuade Parliament to enlarge its revenue. Admittedly Sir George Grey's emphatic opinion and a sense of the heavy demands that were being made on ratepayers were deterrents. The Select Committee, at the same time, found the efficiency of the Brigade exemplary, given its resources. These, they were informed, had increased during the decade, but not enough. The halfpenny rate had risen from about £32,000 in 1866 to about £43,000 in 1875, and the contribution of the insurance offices from £11,000 to £18,000.[23] Could the insurance companies raise their rate of contribution? No compelling arguments for such a move were adduced by the Board, though obviously a higher rate would have been desirable. The companies, on the contrary, maintained that their contribution was purely voluntary and should be reduced. They argued with emphasis, if sometimes for the wrong reason, that a large part of the funds had now been diverted to an effort "in which the fire insurance offices have no interest whatever"—the saving of life.[24] They pointed out, correctly enough, that their original contribution had been made to limit the spread of fire in areas where it might be enormously destructive, and they regarded the protection that the Brigade was giving to the suburbs as a waste of money.[25] At the least, it was tolerably clear that no higher rate was to be forthcoming from the companies.

Not uncommonly, when a Committee sought to deal with Board problems that were largely financial, its suggestions were not helpful. This instance was no exception. Two years before, the firemen had presented a memorial calling attention to their limited superannuation arrangements and to the absence of regular provision for the incapacitated. This petition had not been pigeonholed, as some unkindly suspected it might be, and the Board made plans to introduce a superannuation scheme, though the men objected to some features of it.[26] But, as the Select Committee asserted, the Board had taken far too long to meet the men's legitimate grievances. No doubt this reflected a certain insensitivity and inertia on the part of the Board—as when a fireman, injured and discharged for physical infirmity, was presented with fifteen pounds[27]—but even more it indicated that the Board had no alternative but to pursue a cheeseparing policy, given the temper of Parliament and, still more, that of the metropolitan ratepayer. There should be, the Committee proclaimed, more stations, more engines, more fire escapes, better telegraphic communications (between fire stations), and an increase in the force.[28] This was admirable advice, but, as always, who was to pay?

The Select Committee's solution was neither original nor helpful. Again, without pressure from any particularly reputable witnesses, save for Edwin Chadwick, now seventy-seven years old and still harping on his *idées fixes*, the Committee emerged with the old recommendation of making the Fire Brigade a branch of the police force.[29] There was some testimony from provincial centers—from Liverpool, for example—of the successful unification of the two services. But the Metropolitan Police Force itself was not clear that it wanted to take over the Fire Brigade. One of the Commissioners testified strongly against amalgamation, though an assistant commissioner angled his evidence just as strongly in favor.[30] The former pointed out that the change would be a purely technical transfer of management and would save no money. The latter produced the familiar argument: a ready-made reserve force was at hand in several thousand Bobbies, who could also be trained to act as turncocks, and all at little additional expense. Betraying a staggering ignorance of (or indifference to) City emotions, he advocated placing the City Brigade under the Metropolitan Police.[31] The Committee was swayed, apparently, by the vision of an available reserve of Police Constables at little additional expense, by the prospect of a disciplined force of 10,000 men patroling the streets from stations located at close intervals. It was another Victorian vision of efficiency and economy; but unfortunately it ignored some of the realities of firefighting.

The MBW was, of course, indignant over the Select Committee's recommendation.[32] After all, the Metropolitan Fire Brigade was an efficient organization, which had reduced the percentage of serious fires substantially and without further impositions on the ratepayer.[33] Yet occasionally there were moves, not especially purposeful, to carry out the Committee's recommendation. In 1879, after a serious fire in his house, Lord Granville proposed turning the whole business of fire protection over to the police, and, as late as 1883, Selwin Ibbetson was urging that the recommendation be put into effect.[34] The fact was, however, that the problems of the Fire Brigade were not organizational (save in its relations with the water companies) but financial, and during the 1880s its situation became graver. The Brigade ran annual deficits, the Government auditor regularly disallowed the working account, and the Board, just as regularly, introduced an indemnity bill. The revenue from rates was rising, as was that from the fire insurance offices, but more slowly than the demands of the metropolis for fire protection. Obviously the solution would lie not with the Government but with the ratepayers and the insurance companies. But would the insurance companies increase their contribution? A committee of the Board pointed out that the insurance contribution, after rising in 1869 to 42 percent of revenue from rates, had steadily declined until in 1883 the proportion was running at no more than 27 percent.[35] The fire insurance offices, however, showed no inclination to increase their contributions and, indeed, threatened to open the whole question of their taxation for the benefit of the Brigade.[36]

And so it went on. There was no difference of opinion in London as to the Brigade's desperate need for more money.[37] The revenue in 1888 was a little more than double what it had been in 1866 — £113,600 (plus another £22,500 for the service of the debt) as compared with £52,000[38] — but this was far too little to take care of the needs of the mushrooming metropolis with its increasing demands for adequate protection. Almost annually in the middle 1880s, the Board prepared bills calling for an increase in the rate and in the contributions of the insurance companies, but for various reasons (among them the strenuous opposition of the companies and their friends in the House), none of these went far. In 1888 as the Board approached its extinction the question was still unsettled: the insurance companies were adamant in their refusal to raise their contribution from £35 to £40 per million of policies although the ratepayers were to have their liability doubled (from a half-penny to a penny). In its final annual report the Board observed that the difficulty was wholly due to the stiff-necked opposition of the companies and their sympathizers in the House. These had "hitherto always blocked the Board's bills, and thus prevented their being brought forward for discussion at the only hours available for the purpose."[39]

On one question the Select Committee of 1876–77 elicited huzzahs from the Board. Aware that the Brigade had two major problems, not only finance but water supply, the Committee condemned the anarchy of London's water system, which rested in the hands of a series of private companies, and recommended that control be consolidated in the hands of a single authority. Both the necessities of fire fighting and the demands of the vestries, which were revolting against the intermittent supply of impure water at excessive rates, forced the Board to give consideration again to the problem of water supply. The differences among the various companies were, of course, considerable, but the system, as a whole, was an absurdity and, by the middle of the nineteenth century, an anachronism.

The issues surrounding the metropolitan water supply question are complex, and they cannot be explored here with any degree of thoroughness. The MBW had first been drawn into the picture by the report of a Select Committee in 1867 on the East London water supply,[40] and then a year later by a Royal Commission on the Metropolitan Water Supply, presided over by the Duke of Richmond. Before this, however, there had been rumblings in the vestries, including demands for a constant (as opposed to an intermittent) supply and criticisms of the quantity supplied. The Select Committee,[41] with A. S. Ayrton as chairman,[42] came out in support of a constant supply and proposed the MBW as the supervisory agency. The Royal Commission, after an exhaustive inquiry, responded with a flat demand for public ownership, holding that "a sufficiency of water supply is too important a matter to all classes of the community to be made dependent on the profits of an association."[43] Both bodies were firm in the opinion that a constant supply of water was essential to modern living; both agreed that the act of 1852, which required a constant supply only on written application of the owners or occupiers of four-fifths of the houses, had failed dismally.

The times were not particularly opportune for such action as the Royal Commission had recommended (public ownership), especially in relation to enterprises so thoroughly entrenched as the eight water companies that supplied the metropolis. As it turned out, the Government attempted to play it both ways and on 25 May 1871 introduced a bill calling for a constant supply at high pressure and placing the companies under the control of the MBW as the regulating agency. But the bill went on to give the Board power to purchase the companies, by compulsion or agreement, and then to assume responsibility for supplying London with water. Obviously this was destined to cause trouble, and the Government did not press it. Still, there was too much feeling in the metropolis to let the matter drop. In the House, Lyon Playfair launched an attack on the water companies' monopoly, arguing that water should certainly be supplied by a public agency; but he was suspicious of the effectiveness of the MBW, which was "easily influenced by the clamant demands of particular vestries," and believed its lack of firmness might nullify any new policy.[44] Playfair's views were not shared by other more rate-conscious metropolitan members and still less by the water companies, which at once registered their disapproval. Alderman Lawrence charged the Board with having a large staff and not enough work after the Embankment had been finished, and Sir James Lawrence announced that the project would involve taxing the metropolis to the extent of £10 or £15 million.[45] The Government gave up, omitted the purchase clauses, and on 1 June 1871 reintroduced a more modest bill. This now provided chiefly for a constant supply and specified the methods by which it could be attained. Thus was the major recommendation of the Duke of Richmond's Commission nullified.

The new bill was opposed both by the companies and the Board—the one, of course, arguing that it went too far, and the other that it did not go far enough—from which the Select Committee inferred that it had a fair enough bill. To provide a satisfactory constant supply was more complicated than might at first appear, because this would require different and better fittings than did the old intermittent supply. Moreover, since the water was not metered but was billed in proportion to the rates paid, fittings that were leaky and inefficient could easily cause a considerable loss to the company. The companies fought throughout to emasculate the bill and to displace the Board as the supervising authority. For a while it looked as though they might succeed; their suspicion of the Board was profound, especially since it was the agency that had professed the ambition of taking them over. Nor was there much enthusiasm in Spring Gardens for the bill as it was passed by the House of Commons.

The Metropolis Water Act of 1871 did not provide directly for a constant supply but rather laid down the conditions under which one could be obtained. The MBW objected to the fact that the act set up the Board of Trade as a regulatory authority between itself and the companies, and the Board of Trade did not seem conspicuously zealous. No company was required to provide a constant supply until it had drawn up the regulations under which the supply was to be given and these had been approved by the Board of Trade, and no company was at pains to make its regulations simple or inexpensive. The MBW, finding the regulations originally laid down by the companies to be highly objectionable, appealed to the Board of Trade and got a commission appointed.[46]

In the meantime, the provision of a constant supply was left to the initiative of the companies, whose action, to say the least, was not precipitate. In March 1873 the first step was taken by the East London Company, and gradually most of the others followed. Fifteen years later about 53 percent of all the houses served were on constant supply. But, as is often the case, this average served to blur the facts: for the East London Company, 85 percent of houses had the new service; for the Grand Junction, 78 percent; but for the Chelsea Company, which had hardly begun the changeover, only 19 percent.[47]

One of the Board's main interests in a constant supply, it should not be forgotten, was the efficiency of its Fire Brigade. When the supply was intermittent and the pressure low, the work of the fire fighters was seriously handicapped. During the previous decade, Captain Shaw told the Select Committee in 1876, there had been 586 cases "in which the water supply was not satisfactory."[48] And there were 79 cases of "short supply." With a constant supply at high pressure, firemen answering a call could obtain water immediately; but with intermittent pressure, delay was inevitable. If there was no water in the pipes, the Brigade would have to wait for the appearance of a company turncock to turn the water on to the point of delivery, and this could be a long and uncertain process.[49] There would be no really effective fire service until the water companies gave a constant supply. Yet the MBW, because of the stringency of the regulations proposed by the companies and agreed to (with modifications) by the Board of Trade, hesitated to require constant supply of the companies, as it had been authorized to do by the Metropolis Water Act of 1871. These regulations, the MBW felt, with their requirements of unnecessarily costly fittings, would impose undue burdens on the occupiers. Perhaps the Board accepted defeat too readily in this instance. Rather than cooperating with the unsatisfactory act, it chose, with the support of a number of the vestries, to press for its amendment. At the same time, there was suspicion that the companies had framed their regulations in order to avoid, for as long as possible, the necessity of giving a constant supply.

The companies and the Fire Brigade were also at loggerheads over the use of hydrants in place of the wooden plugs which at most points gave the fire fighters access to water. Plugs were, of course, notably inefficient. They could be pulled easily enough, but the water then had to be collected into a tank or pool before it could be used. Moreover, the plug could not be replaced by the firemen but had to be turned off by a turn-cock. To men battling fires, a hydrant with its mechanism for attaching the hose directly to the water supply had clear advantages. After a company announced that it was providing a constant supply of water, the Board was obliged to specify what plugs or hydrants were required; the company would then furnish and install them at the Board's expense.[50] By the mid-1870s so little progress had been made in getting a constant supply and there was so much uncertainty about the cost and type of hydrants to be used that few steps had been taken by the Board, to the annoyance of the two companies that had already instituted a constant supply over a fraction of their territory.[51] Even so, within the next fifteen years the work spread: the Board had ordered and accepted nearly nine thousand hydrants by the time it was disbanded.[52]

The water companies and their bad service had, of course, been a public issue for many years. No one concerned with the public health of London could ignore the problems presented by an intermittent supply and (it was urged) by excessive rates. Chadwick's fight in the early 1850s against the conditions under which bad water was — or was not — supplied to the metropolis, and against the standpipes or the wretched tubs in which it was collected for slum courts and in which it became foul under the intermittent system, had got nowhere. The water companies, with their parliamentary allies, were strong enough to defeat a mild Government bill in a House of Commons in which cross-purposes dominated.[53] With its defeat and the fall of Chadwick shortly afterwards, the water question receded from the public consciousness until the parliamentary inquiries of the late sixties.

The issue was brought up again in 1876–77 by the Select Committee on the Fire Brigade, which once again noted the absurdity of a metropolis supplied by eight companies. These, the Committee concluded, should be consolidated in the hands of a single authority which should administer the service not for private profit but for public convenience. The MBW could not be indifferent to such encouragement as this, and it made plans to present a bill to Parliament.[54] Unfortunately, Sir James McGarel-Hogg, the Board's chairman, presented two bills, which, although reasonable enough from the Board's point of view and decided upon in consultation with responsible engineers, seemed preposterous to the House. One bill provided for the purchase of the property of the old water companies; the other provided for a new supply, for there were strong opinions that the current supply, mostly river water in origin, was both impure in quality and inadequate in quantity. *The Times* found occasion to congratulate the Board on its decision, but correctly predicted that "a terrible row" would ensue. The water companies, *The Times* recalled, represented powerful vested interests, and these did not lack spokesmen on the Board itself. Moreover, there were few signs that the Board was acting with any more energy and determination than usual—if anything, it was split by differences of opinion.[55]

The prediction was sound. McGarel-Hogg's motion in favor of the first bill, supported by Henry Fawcett, was opposed by two metropolitan members. One of them, Alderman Cotton, a professional City man, charged the Board with being a "very ambitious body, constantly endeavouring to assume to itself all kind of functions and move its neighbours' landmarks."[56] What prevented even a full debate on the question, however, was the Government's refusal to make parliamentary time available. Neither bill went a measurable distance toward passage. The vestries, many of which were willing to support the purchase of the old companies, wanted no part, as they put it, of a dual supply; all were opposed to starting an independent water system.

The failure left the Board in an embarrassment. The expense of preparing evidence and professional charges in connection with the two bills had amounted to nearly £16,000. There were rumblings in the vestries and on the Board itself. James Watkins, a St. Pancras demagogue representing that vestry on the Board, sent a circular letter to the members protesting against its reluctance to prepare a detailed return of the expenditure.[57] And when the Government auditor held his hearing, a number of ratepayers appeared before him to argue that the Board had exceeded its powers. The auditor agreed and disallowed more than £6,600.[58] There was no way to relieve the Board members of that obligation except through a bill of indemnity, which the chairman agreed to introduce. McGarel-Hogg presented his bill briefly and penitently,[59] with a commitment never to introduce another bill without some consultation with the Government. Indignation was exhibited chiefly by those who apparently had little connection with either London or the question at issue, but Sir Charles Dilke came to the Board's support: "And if the House think well to go straight to the question and ask why these Bills were introduced last year, I may say it was because the people of London are poisoned by the water supplied by the Water Companies and wronged by their charges."[60] The indemnity bill passed at 3:00 A.M. in a House of only forty-nine—both features typical of the attention given by the House to London bills.

The Board's fingers had been badly burned, and there would be no more initiatives in that quarter. But others found London's water situation intolerable. The following month a debate was set off in Parliament by a speech from Fawcett in which he reviewed the entire situation, reminding the House of the number of committees which had urged the formation of a single central authority over the metropolitan water supply. But who should administer the new system? Probably not the MBW, though it had done good work; better to have a public water commission. The speakers, even to Cross, the Home Secretary, agreed that the public was excited over the water question and that something would have to be done, but all were puzzled about what action ought to be taken.[61]

The Home Secretary's answer was a bill providing for purchase of the water companies and their administration by a public body constituted for the purpose. How expensive would the operation turn out to be? The figures were those provisionally agreed upon by E. J. Smith, a surveyor acting on behalf of the Home Office and the water companies, and, if accepted, they would make this an expensive transaction for the ratepayers. Vernon Harcourt, who took over the Home Office from Cross, moved for a Select Committee on the question. This Committee, too, agreed that the companies should be under the control of a public body and should be purchased if satisfactory terms could be worked out.[62] But there was grave doubt whether Smith's terms offered an admissible basis for purchase, and the MBW, the City Corporation, and the public shared the Select Committee's doubts. The price indubitably was stiff; the metropolis, the Committee estimated, would let itself in for an addition to its debt of some £33 million.[63] But was this an unreasonable figure? Smith insisted that the amount, high as it was, would turn out to be a moderate price. The Committee disagreed, and the Government took no action. Harcourt intimated that solving the water tangle would have to await the creation of a municipal government for the metropolis.

Before long, there was some reason to think that it had been a mistake not to buy the companies on the basis worked out by Smith. Their price was rising daily, and, if London waited until it had a municipal government, the amount might go completely out of sight.[64] And when it appeared that Harcourt's Government Bill of 1884 would be withdrawn,[65] the MBW again entered the fray against the water companies. On three different occasions the Board asked Parliament for power to prepare and submit a scheme for taking over the companies, and three times it was refused. All that could be done now, the Board members concluded, was to protect the public as best they could. In 1885, for example, the Board's counsel appeared before a Select Committee of the Lords to make sure that a bill to increase the statutory powers of two water companies would not open the way for a claim for increased compensation. But again, although neither bill was passed, the Board found itself in

difficulty with the Government auditor, who disallowed expenses incurred while fighting the bills.[66] There was little prospect that the Board
would escape from the straitjacket in which it was confined. It could take
neither offensive nor defensive action, and its bills, classified by Parliament as public, had no chance of passing without government support.
Wiser heads were now convinced that the action of the House in rejecting Smith's arrangements had been sheer folly. Indeed, Smith's
arguments put forward in 1880 now appeared quite correct, and the
public would have done well to have accepted them. The profits of the
companies, it turned out, would have been quite sufficient to meet
the interest charges.[67] By 1888 the Board, in fine, had not succeeded in
coming to grips with the companies. But its failure was not for want of
trying.

London's gas companies offered a challenge no less insistent than that
of their brethren who purveyed water. At the beginning of the Board's
regimen, the metropolis was supplied by no fewer than twenty companies, which, to say the least, did not provide a notably efficient service. The companies competed among themselves in expensive chaos,
though in the course of it their rivalry assured the consumer of prices
that were not outrageous. In 1857, however, the gas companies determined to have done with this ruinous competition; they divided the metropolis into thirteen districts, each of which was monopolized by one of
the principal companies. The consequence was a sharp increase in gas
prices, and as a result, in at least one district a group of consumers mobilized to form their own company. The Surrey Consumers Gas Company, in which John Thwaites and Dresser Rogers were active, imposed
something of a check on the old-line companies, but it seems to have had
no permanent effect.[68] The local authorities were still indignant when
the gas companies, in 1860, got an act of Parliament validating the division of the metropolis and specifying the standard of gas that was to be
supplied.[69]

This act solved nothing save some of the problems of the gas companies, which proceeded, it was charged, to raise prices and reduce quality. There was feeling against the companies in many quarters of the metropolis, but nowhere was it better organized than in the City. In the
early 1860s there was debate about what steps to take: whether to try to
get the City exempt from the act of 1860 or to otherwise browbeat the
companies (three of which served the City) into reducing their rates.
This was all rather difficult because the companies had their representatives in the City itself. One was Alderman Dakin, chairman of the Great
Central Gas Company, which, curiously enough, had started out as a

model, consumer-controlled company but had left the path of rectitude and become grossly overcapitalized.[70] In order to pay the 10 percent dividends to which the companies were entitled, it had had to charge exceptionally high rates for the gas it supplied.

By 1865 the City Corporation, having decided to be done with compromise measures, applied to Parliament for exemption from the act of 1860 and for the right to purchase the City companies' plants. The gas companies took fright and offered to reduce the price by sixpence, but these fruits meet for repentance came too late.[71] The passage of the City Gas Bill through Parliament must have been accompanied by an entertaining clash of rival interests, for neither the City nor the gas companies lacked influence. J. A. Roebuck charged that members had been importuned and buttonholed to death, the victim being "pulled by one tail of his coat by one, and the other tail of his coat by the other."[72] The Select Committee on the bill noted that the effect of the act of 1860 had been to raise the market value of company shares and to make it possible for every gas company to pay dividends of 10 percent, as well as to pay back dividends and put away reserve funds.[73] Higher prices and poorer quality seemed to have been the gas record since 1860. The Committee finally recommended more complete supervision of the gas companies.

The MBW was brought into the gas imbroglio at the end of 1866 when it received an inquiry from the Board of Trade. The Government, it was stated, intended to introduce a bill in the following session and wished to get the views of the Board. It appeared that the Government was contemplating vesting in the Board either regulatory power or the right to purchase the companies. Under what terms should these be arranged? The Board, taking first a regulatory stance, urged a maximum price of three shillings and sixpence per thousand cubic feet, a lighting power of eighteen candles, and a quality superior to that called for by the act of 1860. The Board also demanded constant testing of the gas by appointees of its own and inspection of the accounts of the companies by the Government auditor. If, on the other hand, the companies were to be purchased, they should receive, the Board argued, no more than 6 percent on the paid-up capital.[74]

The Government bill was introduced in the House by Sir Stafford Northcote and was referred to a Select Committee under the chairmanship of Edward Cardwell.[75] The Committee's assignment was exceedingly complicated, for, in addition to passing judgment on Northcote's bill, it had also to consider counter proposals made by gas companies and private bills from other sources. The hearings of the Cardwell Committee soon became bogged down in confusion. The Board of Trade amended its original draft in a way that the MBW thought conceded too much to the companies, and the companies thought conceded too little. Controversy centered on the price and quality to be required, a disagreement which the Select Committee was unable to resolve. Indeed, the Committee found the gas companies anything but cooperative, and recommended that unless they could agree during the recess on terms satisfactory to the consumers, the local authorities of the metropolis should be given every facility to provide an independent supply. Ultimately the Committee recommended against passing the bill.

This, of course, was no solution, and in the following year (1868), the City moved to get its own independent supply. Another private member's bill, providing for stricter regulation, was submitted at the same time, and both were referred to a Select Committee from whose deliberations emerged the City of London Gas Act of 1868. This act did not authorize the City Corporation to suppply gas, but it subjected the companies to closer scrutiny and obliged them to provide gas of sixteen candles for three shillings and sixpence. The act also provided, however, for three commissioners to be appointed by the Board of Trade to make revisions in case the companies objected to the specifications.

The City Gas Act, although it did not apply to MBW territory, marked enough of an advance to arouse the envy of the Board. The Board of Trade agreed that provisions similar to those in the City might be extended to the rest of the metropolis, especially since three more companies had applied for bills permitting them to raise more capital. The Board was not reconciled to the terms proposed in some of these company applications. It demanded, for example, that the Imperial Gas Company reduce its proposed price to three shillings and ninepence and raise the candlepower to sixteen.[76] In opposing the Imperial Company's bill, the Board urged strongly that future bills should conform to the terms laid down by the City Gas Act; there was, counsel pointed out, sound reason for making that act the model for other enactments, with the Board as the supervisory agency.[77] The Board then proceeded to mobilize such metropolitan sentiment as it could, circularizing vestries, M.P.'s, and newspapers with a statement describing its efforts to get the act of 1860 amended. No efforts, the statement intimated, had been spared to see that a new bill was passed: the Board members had seen to it that counsel represented them before the Cardwell Committee, yet they had achieved not the passage of the bill but only a special report maintaining that the act of 1860 was not sufficiently favorable to consumers and leaving the companies with no inducement to keep their expenses low. In 1868, the statement continued, the City of London Gas Act had given the City better gas at lower prices, together with daily tests and the auditing of the companies' accounts. And now in the present session (1869) the Board had again moved in with counsel to oppose the companies' acts. But despite this pressure, the Select Committee declared the preamble proved, though with an alteration favoring a reduction in the price of gas and lowering the dividend to 7 percent. The Board, its parliamentary committee held, had no option but to petition the House of Lords.[78]

The bills promoted by the three gas companies passed through Parliament, but no one could say that the result was satisfactory. To begin with, five of the companies were still operating under the act of 1860, while the other three had come under new enactments. Shaw-Lefevre,[79] at the Board of Trade, after intimating that the Government was interested in promoting amalgamation of the companies, explored with the MBW the possibility of the Board's introducing a bill. When the deputation from the Board pointed out that it was not an especially strong initiator of legislation and suggested that the bill ought to come from the Government, he indicated that the Board of Trade might stand behind any effort that the MBW could make. Although the MBW issued notices of a bill, in the end it was the Board of Trade that made noises about amalgamations, but with no decisive legislative result.[80] Nevertheless, there were continued gestures at amalgamation among the gas companies.

In 1872–73 the issue of regulation was sharpened when the largest of the companies, the Gas Light and Coke Company ("the Chartered"), which had been most active in absorbing other companies, applied to the Board of Trade for permission to increase its rate from three shillings and ninepence to four shillings and ninepence. The reason given was the rise in the price of coal, which the company proposed to pass on entirely to the consumer. Commissioners appointed by the Board of Trade denied the company its full claim, but they did establish four shillings and fourpence as the price for 1873, an increase of sevenpence. In January 1874 the same company appeared to apply for an increase to five shillings and twopence and succeeded in getting five shillings. The Imperial Gas Company joined in the appeal and for 1874 got an advance of elevenpence. These were the two biggest companies, which accounted for more than twice as much of the invested capital as all the rest put together.

This orgy of rateraising was too much for the Board, which thought of itself as the guardian of consumer interests, and there were also signs of rebellion in the vestries. It was, in truth, a curious situation when, as the *Weekly Times* pointed out, the rate on one side of Chiswell Street, served by the Gas Light and Coke Company, was five shillings, and on the other side, where the Independent Company reigned, it was three shillings and fourpence. Indeed, the rates charged by gas companies in the metropolis ranged from three shillings to five shillings.[81] A motion in the MBW charged that "practically, to obtain a fixed rate of income, the companies are permitted to tax the consumer to an unlimited extent."[82] In response, the Board's Works and General Purposes Committee submitted three alternative proposals: (1) to establish new gas works which would enable the Board to supply gas on a competitive basis; (2) to acquire the property of the companies; (3) to tighten the regulatory procedures then being applied to the companies. Unable to choose among the plans—or perhaps unaware of the absurdity of bringing in three bills—the Board agreed to submit bills in the order named for dealing with the gas companies.[83]

The press, in general, thought the Board's first proposal preposterous and unnecessary. Meanwhile, James Beal and his Metropolitan Municipal Association sent a deputation to Sir Charles Adderley, the new president of the Board of Trade, who took the occasion to read the gas companies a lesson. He commented on "the absurd extravagance of the present system" and advised them to get together with the MBW and the City Corporation to work out a solution rather than treating the remonstrances of these bodies as sheer impertinence. The last statement from the chairmen of the gas company boards, he added, had amounted to a simple defiance of the public complaint, for it had given only vague assurances that some time, when the companies were good and ready, they might reduce the price of gas.[84]

The three bills were duly laid before Parliament early in 1875. Of these, the most interesting was the third, the Metropolitan Gas Companies Bill, which was debated at length after the others had been withdrawn. It was designed to apply the same standard of regulation to all the companies, thus doing away with the tremendous variations in the quality of gas required of them, the prices they were permitted to charge, and the rate of return they were permitted (or as they interpreted it, entitled) to earn. For example, candlepower ranged from twelve to sixteen, while the maximum interest permitted ran from 7 percent to 10.

The Board's bill followed the usual course. McGarel-Hogg got it through the second reading, against an articulate and well-disciplined group of spokesmen for the companies, and it went to a Select Committee.[85] All the metropolitan gas companies appeared before the Committee to oppose the bill, though it became clear that they were not unanimous in their views. The principle of the bill was novel but sound: if prices were raised, dividends would have to be reduced. The Select Committee insisted that if the relationship was to work in that direction it ought also to operate in reverse, and suggested to the MBW that, if prices went down, dividends might properly go up. This seemed to offer a desirable inducement to economy and careful administration on the part of the companies, which was one of the chief objects of the bill. But when the Select Committee declared the preamble proved, intimating that there should be a uniform power of sixteen candles and an initial price of three shillings and ninepence, all but one company declined to have further commerce with the proceedings. By this time, 5 August, it was too late in the session for the bill to be brought to the floor; and so the Board had to withdraw it.[86]

By the next year (1876) the situation had changed. Three of the largest companies — the Chartered, the Imperial, and the Independent, controlling nearly £9,000,000 out of a total capitalization of roughly £10,675,000 — arranged a plan of amalgamation, accepting the terms of the previous year's bill. The South Metropolitan also agreed to accept these provisions, with three shillings and sixpence instead of three shillings and ninepence as its initial rate, and began to absorb other companies south of the river. Clearly, both the pressure of public opinion and the progress of the industry itself, with its greater efficiency in the sale of residual products, had accomplished significant results; and low coal prices also offered an obvious advantage. But the sliding-scale device, suggested by the Board and incorporated in acts of Parliament, had something to do with the improved service. In 1877 *The Builder* canvassed the whole problem again and emerged with the conclusion that "3s.9d. per thousand is not the lowest price at which the inhabitants of the metropolis should expect to be supplied with gas."[87]

Included in the Board's miscellaneous duties was the responsibility for daily testing of the gas supplied. This began under the provisions of the Gas Light and Coke Company's Act of 1868, which conferred upon the MBW the same powers as the Corporation enjoyed within the City. An examiner was at once appointed for that section of the company's operations that fell outside the City. By 1871 the Board was testing gas supplied by the three major companies — not without some friction and occasional complaint as to quality — and by 1888 it had nearly twenty stations where gas was tested to see that it conformed to candlepower regulations laid down in the acts and to the degree of purity specified by the gas referees appointed by the Board of Trade.

Another branch of the Board's activities which, in spite of some just criticism, was of permanent value, was its work in acquiring certain parks and open spaces and having them set aside for the use of the public. More than that, the Board, because it was the only permanent all-metropolitan body, was also given custody of many open spaces, so that by the end of its tenure it was managing more than 2,600 acres of public parks and commons. Although it was agreed that the Board performed efficiently enough as custodian, not everybody approved of its policy in acquiring the commons for public use. There was a strong feeling on the part of Shaw-Lefevre and other members of the Commons Preservation Society that the Board was far too indulgent toward lords of manors and that it lacked aggressiveness in pressing the public interest.[88] The Board, these men charged, bought the lords' rights over various commons (thus encouraging avarice on the part of others) rather than proceeding according to the Metropolitan Commons Act of 1866, which would have enabled the Board to bypass the lords and their rights at little expense.

With the parks, too, the Board came in for criticism, chiefly because of its shortsighted theory of financing such acquisitions—which was that the way to purchase a new open space was by selling a small part of the land for building lots. In the case of Finsbury Park, the area where it gave principal offense, the Board proposed to sell twenty acres on Seven Sisters Road for building. This plan aroused a howl of protest, and a deputation called on the Commissioner of Works bearing a petition with 14,000 signatures.[89] The objectors pointed out that the act had originally authorized the MBW to buy 250 acres, which in the course of negotiations had been cut down to about 120, and that now the Board was proposing to hack 20 more acres from the already shrunken plot.

Beyond doubt, the Board was taking a penny-pinching view of its obligations, but it was under a good deal of pressure from both the vestries and its own members. The St. Pancras vestry, for example, urged the Board to stand firm and not to be shaken by the demanding Islingtonians, and the Marylebone vestry took the same position.[90] Even within the Board the original vote to buy the Finsbury property had not been overwhelming—evidence of the familiar localism of those who spoke for the vestries. There was always great enthusiasm for an improvement which would directly affect the local area but indifference or hostility toward one which would benefit other areas. As William Newton told a Select Committee of the House, the Board had to contend with local jealousies, especially the hostility of suburban vestries toward improvements in Central London. "We have the greatest difficulty in the world to get the representatives of outlying districts to vote for internal improvements. Those suburban districts which have parks really do not see the necessity of carrying out improvements in the centre."[91]

It was not only the remote districts that were motivated by local interests. Those at the center could find no justification for parks that would benefit other districts. Thus both St. Pancras and Marylebone had opposed the original acquisition of Finsbury Park, though one member of the Marylebone vestry had had the grace to wonder whether this showed good taste since Marylebone was comfortably surrounded by government-provided parks.[92] And earlier, Kensington had besought the cooperation of St. Pancras at a meeting that was being organized to protest against the levying of taxes to provide parks for densely populated districts. In this instance one of the more broad-minded of St. Pancras's politicians had resisted, pointing out that Kensington, after all, had been well supplied with parks by the government, and St. Pancras had withheld its cooperation.[93]

The matter of parks had been well up on the Board's agenda from its earliest days. The Parks Committee received deputations from interested vestries, including one from Hampstead with the suggestion that some two hundred acres of the Heath might be had for £50,000; and in early 1857 the Board voted for two parks, one north of the river and the other to the southeast. The problem of Hampstead Heath occupied the committee and the Board for some time. Obviously if purchase was delayed the cost would rise, and the committee thought the argument for early purchase was overwhelming; but it also thought that some of the cost should be met from government funds.[94] Of the two parks on which the Board did decide to move, the one north of the river — the Finsbury project — was nothing new. But even after the Board had voted to go ahead, it was in no great haste, being still hung up on the matter of finance. The bill for Finsbury Park went through Parliament in the summer of 1857, and only in 1863, shortly before the act expired, was the decision taken to buy the land — though the amount had been reduced from the 250 acres authorized by parliament until only 116 could be purchased. The Board got the property for about £57,000; and the total cost, including planting, draining, and park buildings, amounted to about £95,000 by 1868-69.[95]

Except for the outcry caused by the Board's perverse idea of selling twenty acres for building purposes, Finsbury Park affairs went smoothly enough. But on the matter of the proposed building lots the Board was stubbornly determined, relying in part upon a clause in the act of 1857 which authorized it. A good deal of pressure was required to persuade the Board to abandon its views, but finally in 1872 the Parks Committee, "looking to the change of public opinion," recommended that building be prohibited.

Southwark Park, consisting of sixty-three acres in the parish of Rotherhithe, southeast of the river, was the Board's other initial benefaction to metropolitan areas without large open spaces. The plot, bought in 1864 for £55,160, cost in all (by 1868-69) £99,740, and was opened as a park in 1869.[96] Southwark Park was, in fact, an excellent example of somebody's foresight — or perhaps good luck. When purchased, the land was surrounded by market gardens and was far more expensive than the Finsbury Park land; but during the next two decades, as the working population moved in and working-class housing enclosed it, the park each year increasingly justified the money that had been spent on it. Of course, as in the case of Finsbury Park, the Board was determined to compensate the ratepayers in part by selling building lots. But as with the plans for the Finsbury lots the Board, after obstinate resistance, finally yielded to public outcry.

The Board also took action in regard to an open space in central London — Leicester Square — which in the 1850s was one of the most objectionable eyesores in the entire metropolis. It could have existed only in a country with a complicated and partly customary land system, and in one that was feeling its way toward a local authority with the power and inclination to override private rights where necessary. Residents of the area had been complaining for some time, and in 1863 the Board responded by taking measures for dealing with the square under the Gardens in Towns Protection Act. The square seemed to have no owners, and the Board had not anticipated trouble.[97] But owners suddenly appeared with an action for trespass, in which the Court of Queen's Bench sustained them, and the Board was unable to get the decision reversed on appeal. It then resolved to apply to Parliament directly. As its Annual Report for 1871 pointed out, the matter of acquiring title was immensely complicated and no one could estimate precisely what it would cost. To be on the safe side, the Board set £50,000 as the limit of its borrowing power for the purpose, which, predictably, set off a fuss in the vestries. The result was that the Board had to withdraw its bill and look for help elsewhere.

In the end it was private philanthropy that pointed a way out of the muddle: Albert Grant, a City financier, came forward with a proposal to acquire the various interests in the land. He had already been negotiating with those who professed to hold title. This was clearly a handsome gesture, and the Board gratefully accepted his offer. Plans were launched at once to convert the horrid area into a useful open space.[98]

In the course of its career the MBW acquired a good many — its final report says "all" — of the commons and open spaces within its jurisdiction. During the second half of the nineteenth century (the lifetime of the Board), Londoners were becoming increasingly aware of the importance of open spaces in their metropolis, which was expanding at an alarming rate. The Commons Preservation Society was founded in 1865, on the heels of a report of the Select Committee on Open Spaces, which recommended the repeal of the Statute of Merton and the prohibition of further enclosures within the metropolitan area.[99] The commons, admittedly, were deteriorating—becoming dumping grounds for refuse, reservoirs of gravel, and haunts for tramps and gypsies—and in the face of an expanding population, the idea of enclosure had begun to appeal to certain lords of the manor.

The question of the lords' rights was, of course, extremely complicated. Were they, as was contended before the Select Committee, practically absolute because the rights of the commoners were so meager that they could be safely disregarded? Or were the commoners' and residents' rights sufficient to prevent enclosure? The Board's solution, as proposed by its chairman, John Thwaites, before the Committee, was to buy up the interests of both the lords and the commoners on behalf of the public, an undertaking that, he agreed, might cost some £6 million. To raise such a fund a part of the land would have to be sold: to this solution Thwaites stubbornly adhered.[100] It proved to be the main point at issue between the Board and the Commons Preservation Society, and the Select Committee's report showed little sympathy for Thwaites's plan—or any plan which would cut down the amount of open space in London.

It was therefore difficult for the Board and the Commons Preservation Society to cooperate, for the Society was determined to fight the claims of the lords in the courts. Since these were by no means open-and-shut cases, it was necessary for the Society to pick carefully the case and the court. Had Parliament elected to follow the Select Committee's recommendation and to repeal the Statute of Merton, the task would have been easier.[101] But certainly the Society did excellent work, through the courts, to preserve the London commons. As for the Board, its own formula sometimes worked well, but sometimes it was carried through only at punitive cost. The 267 acres of Blackheath came to the Board at no expense, since the Earl of Dartmouth made no claim with regard to manorial rights and, in fact, assisted in settling a scheme for the common. The commons at Hackney, however, amounting in all to about 150 acres, cost a total of £90,000. Between these two extremes were such open spaces as the 144 acres of Tooting Bec Common, which the Board got for £10,200, and the 220 acres of Clapham Common, for which the Board paid £18,000.[102] These figures, reasonable enough if one assumes that the lords' interests had any substance, were excessive if the lords' rights were valueless. The Commons Preservation Society charged that the Board had proceeded recklessly, "often giving large sums for them [the rights], wholly regardless of the fact that every such purchase tended to raise the hopes and demands of other lords, and to encourage them in the view that they had a valuable property to dispose of."[103]

One of the most complicated cases in the London area was the negotiations surrounding Hampstead Heath. Scarcely had the Board been elected when pressure began to be applied for the purchase of the Heath.

Deputations from vestries favoring the scheme and opposing it appeared before the Board members, who thought, for a time, that its owner, Sir Thomas Maryon Wilson,[104] might be reasonable in his demands. That hope proved illusory; he turned out to be exceedingly stuffy and his claims preposterous, based as they were on the premise that he was virtual owner in fee simple of the common.[105] But his successor, Sir Spencer Maryon Wilson, seemed inclined to negotiate on reasonable terms, and the Works and General Purposes Committee suspected that all of his rights in the 240 acres could be got for between £45,000 and £50,000.[106] The eventual purchase price was £295,500, but £100,000 was contributed either by the charity committees or by subscription. The Commons Preservation Society, however, was unhappy over the Board's decision to buy the Heath, arguing the importance of fighting through in court the early cases against lords of the manor. (A suit instituted on behalf of the commoners had been brought against Sir Thomas but had not been resolved because of his death.) The Board, claimed the Society, had paid excessively for Sir Spencer's dubious rights (though no doubt the deal would have been seen as a bargain if a verdict had been given in favor of the lord's right to enclose), and the transaction would, no doubt, tend to rouse the avarice of other suburban lords.[107] But whatever regrets there might be, the Heath, at least from 1870 on, was the property of the public.

In the early 1880s Hampstead Heath again became an issue. As the London population flowed northward—to Hampstead, Golders Green, and beyond—pressure for housing in the area increased and the use of the Heath for recreation grew apace. Adjoining the Heath were two considerable open spaces which, the Commons Preservation Society correctly argued, were necessary to make the Heath of maximum utility and to protect it from being encircled by building lots. These were the estates of Kenwood and Parliament Hill, owned by Lord Mansfield, and a smaller property owned by Sir Spencer Maryon Wilson. Apparently Lord Mansfield had no intention of turning his land into building lots, though his heir did not appear to share his public spirit, but Sir Spencer had already advertised his property for building leases. There was every reason to act before these plots, totaling over 400 acres, were permanently lost.[108]

A committee was formed exclusively for this purpose, and in July 1885 a deputation, along with allies from the Kyrle Society and from the St. Pancras and Hampstead vestries, visited the MBW.[109] (Previously the owners had been persuaded to postpone any action they might have planned.) The Board, however, declined to purchase, on the ground that considerable expense would be visited on the ratepayers, and the committee got little encouragement. But the Society (backed by the St.

Pancras vestry, which now found itself in the unusual position of urging a large expenditure on the Board) pointed out that only a small rate would be required to raise the £200,000 which it wished the Board to provide. As it transpired, the Hampstead and St. Pancras vestries had already agreed to put up £50,000 and the City of London Charities a like sum,[110] and the sanction of Parliament had been obtained. Finally, therefore, the Works and General Purposes Committee voted by a narrow margin that the Board should provide half the sum necessary (not to exceed £152,500). Predictably, this solution satisfied neither party. Shaw-Lefevre and the Commons Preservation Society were aggrieved that the amount was not larger, and the Board laid itself open to a flood of memorials from the more remote vestries, protesting (in the words of one from Newington) against "an unnecessary and scandalous waste of the Ratepayers' money."[111] During the most critical days the Commons Preservation Society planted letters in the newspapers from such writers as Octavia Hill, George Lewes, Baroness Burdett-Coutts, and Shaw-Lefevre himself,[112] and the editors responded with exhortations to the Board to go ahead. Admittedly, the Board was slow and uncertain in arriving at what now looks like an obvious decision, and apparently it acted only because it found public and newspaper opinion more formidable than the protests of a number of vestries.

In the other complicated and long-drawn-out case, that of Epping Forest, the Board took an unheroic part. The issue was extremely confused, as disputes over English land rights can be. The lords of the nineteen manors in Epping Forest, who regarded each manor as a separate entity, held that the commoners had rights of common only in their particular manor, not over the entire forest; and these lords were moving gradually to enclose the whole area. Only when the solicitor of the Commons Preservation Society discovered that the commoners of all nineteen manors had historically had the right of pasturing their cattle on the entire forest waste could action be taken. The City Corporation, which held property in a manor at Ilford, then proceeded to bring suit against the majority of the lords of manors who had carried on enclosures.[113]

The Government had not proved helpful. A bill introduced by the First Commissioner of Works in 1870, which assured the public of only 600 acres, was regarded as such a sellout that it was opposed by both the Commmons Preservation Society and the Board, and the House of Commons rejected it by a majority of over two to one. At this juncture the City Corporation brought in two bills: one to enable it to purchase the rights of the lords of manors, and the other to empower it to levy a small duty on grain (the metage on grain) brought into the port of London. Both of these bills enraged the Board, which was indignant at what it regarded as sharp practice on the part of the Corporation. In the first instance the Board was offended by the implied criticism of its initiative and by the aggressiveness of the City Corporation in trying to take the management of the forest into its own hands, so as "to exclude this Board who have been specially entrusted by Parliament with the duty of providing and preserving open spaces for the recreation of the people."[114] In the second case the Board was rightly bothered by the proposed metage on grain, although the Commons Preservation Society and the newspapers had accepted the imposition of the duty without blinking. This, the Board pointed out, was entirely contrary to current tendencies toward the removal of restrictions and freedom of trade, and had been ventured on by the Corporation in the hope "that the object to which it is proposed to apply the money would reconcile the public to the impost," as indeed it had. Nevertheless, the Board had little support. Two or three vestries at once sent memorials urging it to stop opposing the City bill, while *The Times* found its attitude very unconciliatory.[115]

Meanwhile, the inquiry of a Royal Commission set up by the Government in 1871 and the three-year-old suit started by the City Corporation were proceeding independently of each other, but the results turned out to be similar. Sir George Jessel's decision, as Master of the Rolls, was a complete vindication of the Commons Preservation Society's position. He not only ordered enclosure to cease but required the lords to disgorge some three thousand acres that had been unlawfully enclosed during the past twenty years. The Royal Commissioners agreed with Sir George's findings but proposed a more indulgent policy toward the land already enclosed. In the end, the Government ignored the recommendations of its Commission, and the City Corporation bought out the lords at an average of about twenty pounds an acre. The managing body for Epping Forest, as laid down in an act of Parliament, was to consist of twelve members of the City Corporation plus four representatives of the commoners. An attempt of the MBW, through an amendment proposed by Henry Fawcett, to gain the right to nominate four members was overwhelmingly defeated — and the London press as a whole thought that the Board should have no complaint. Several newspapers recalled its supineness and its inclination to think of difficulties, legal and practical, when it should have been taking action.[116] There seemed to be no regrets over the metage duty that had been required to assure the purchase of Epping Forest, though on its opening in May 1882 the corn trade of London demanded a special part in the ceremonies, and a year later *The Echo* recalled that, after all, the people and not the City had provided the necessary funds, and that the Corporation was taking undue credit for what it had accomplished with other people's money.[117]

Whatever the MBW's lack of initiative in fighting for the public's rights with regard to open spaces, there were few complaints about its management of the plots already acquired. Yet in the early 1880s the Board fell foul of the new, small but aggressive socialist movement. The principal issue was that of public meetings on Peckham Rye Common, which were forbidden under a bylaw prohibiting such gatherings. Something of a furor was aroused; Joseph Firth wanted to know, also, about prohibiting cricket, football, and athletic sports on the commons of greater London. The London Trades Council added its voice in protest, no doubt inspired by the Board's action in having a number of offenders brought to court. In this case the Board, as on so many other occasions during its final years, acted stuffily and without understanding, though admittedly it was caught in the middle between working-class demands and the petitions of local residents. In the House of Commons, the Peckham Rye question provided an admirable stick for the municipal reformers, and they used it to good advantage. It was not until February 1884 that the Board members got around to formulating a code for public meetings on certain commons, and not until July of that year did they reach a decision as to which open spaces were suitable for public meetings and which were not.[118]

In addition to fire protection, water and gas supply, and open spaces, it was also the MBW's fate to be put in charge of a number of miscellaneous services which are today the routine responsibilities of municipal governments. Among these were the Board's obligations to administer the regulations against contagious diseases of animals, to inspect and license dairies and cowsheds, to regulate slaughterhouses, to control the manufacture and sale of petroleum and other explosive substances in London, and to supervise the administration of the Infant Life Protection Act of 1872.

The fight against the cattle plague, which first struck in 1865, was carried on with vigor and considerable skill. Though the Board obviously was not organized to cope with such an emergency, it moved quickly to set up the necessary local committee and to arrange for the destruction of infected animals. This action was greeted by cries of "Centralization!" from certain vestries and by charges from newspaper editors that the rinderpest was not all that serious and was being handled improperly.[119] As further scares occurred—and there were several during the Board's tenure, which produced a succession of acts of Parliament—the preventive service became better organized and more competent. The Board also had a certain supervisory power, not well defined, over dairies and cowsheds. But by improvising a set of standards and turning them over to the licensing justices they were able to exert some control. Finally, the duty of inspecting slaughterhouses and supervising some of the offensive trades (such as glue making, tripe boiling and blood drying) was imposed upon the Board by an act of 1874. At that time there were approximately 1,500 private slaughterhouses in the metropolis. In fourteen years the number had been reduced to 732, which were brought under regulation and occasionally visited by an inspector. Many, if not most, of the surviving undertakings were still unsuitable for urban location, but the division of licensing authority among seventeen tribunals made it difficult for the Board to deal with them more rigorously. On the other hand, the Board's power to approve of new slaughterhouses was sparingly exercised, less than half the applications being sanctioned.[120] Similarly, with the offensive trades the Board's powers were too limited to accomplish anything very drastic. The Act of 1874 divided such businesses into two groups: some could not be reestablished after they had been shut down, but others, with the Board's sanction, could be started anew. The reduction of these businesses, all of which were the results of animal slaughter, was sketched in a table included in the Board's final Annual Report. The number had been diminished but not so drastically as the Board had hoped, for it had not been given the power to abolish such premises. Unless the owner gave up his business or committed an extraordinary breach of the bylaws, there was little the Board could do.[121]

The furor over explosive substances was set off by a dangerous explosion in Regent's Park. A canal boat loaded with benzine blew up, causing some loss of life and ghastly destruction in the area. Here again the Board was assigned the responsibility for enforcing the Explosives Act of 1875 — for searching out places of surreptitious manufacture and supervising transit through the metropolis. By 1888 some 3,300 premises were being registered annually for the storage and sale of explosives, and these were regularly inspected by officials of the Board. In regard to petroleum, which had been omitted from the act of 1875, there was less certainty because much of it did not fall under the various petroleum acts of the 1870s and 1880s. To be liable under these acts, the petroleum had to give off an inflammable vapor at seventy-three degrees Fahrenheit, which was obviously a difficult standard to apply. The Board required all persons having petroleum to keep it on licensed premises, and attempted to supervise the wharves and dealers' premises most carefully. In 1888 (the last year of the Board's tenure), for example, it granted nearly 1,450 licenses under the petroleum acts and received over 4,700 reports from its inspectors.[122]

Finally, the Board labored earnestly to make effective the Infant Life Protection Act. The loopholes were too great, however, because the majority of infants farmed out for care did not come within the terms of the act. Only infants under one year of age who were taken care of in houses of more than one child were protected. Still, ineffective though the supervision may have been, it was at least helpful to have an inspector who was concerned with and called attention to abuses in baby farming.

Such wide-ranging issues were the Board's daily concern. They may appear small and excruciatingly complex. But such a list does at least demonstrate how the MBW, which had started out chiefly as a sewer-building agency, found its functions expanding and its establishment mushrooming. These services were all desperately needed by a metropolis that was increasingly subjected to the hazards of urban living and that had no other agency to deal with them. Parish hierarchies were plainly out of the question, and complaints about the dangers of centralization were becoming more feeble. Thus the MBW, with all its weaknesses, found itself carrying on many of the functions of a municipal government even though in many cases it had been given the responsibility but not the authority to do so.

CHAPTER 7

The Routine of Administration

When the MBW set up shop in 1856, it was composed of men whose experience in public affairs had been limited. The members, by and large, had served in local vestries (some prominently), and some had had contact with the work of the old Commissioners of Sewers. Consequently, as a group they tended to see metropolitan problems through parochial eyes, and to adhere to the illusion that the Board marked the triumph of local self-government, which to them meant parochial autonomy. Their early behavior—the intemperate and interminable oratory, the reluctance to transact the mass of their business through committees, the boisterous tone of their deliberations—suggests inexperience and an inflated notion of their own importance. In the early 1860s the majority of the Board were tradesmen (fourteen) and men retired from business (eight). Beyond these, there were six magistrates, three engineers, two builders, and an architect; five solicitors and three barristers; six booksellers and three stationers; and two civil servants, a broker, a wharfinger, a surgeon, and a manufacturer.[1]

By the mid-seventies the Board's personnel had not changed drastically for the better. The *Observer*, in a highly critical analysis, charged this "group of singularly obscure individuals" with "failure to rise above the most commonplace level."[2] The vestries, on the whole, were more representative, argued the editor, because men elected by the vote of the parish must be known to their neighbors, while those elected to the Board had to be known only to the vestry. A few members were reason-

156

ably well known, such as William Newton (Amalgamated Society of Engineers), General William Codrington, and Alfred Lawrence.[3] By 1875 the number of builders, architects, and surveyors had increased to seven, the six booksellers and stationers were holding their own, and the solicitors had been reduced to three. A fair occupational sample, taken from the 1875 list, runs as follows: conveyancer, retired tradesman, owner of houses in Spitalfields, publican, tailor, soap manufacturer, builder, retired bookseller, coach builder. Throughout the Board's history, the number of members who had retired from business was conspicuous. The reason is obvious: the demands made by the Board upon its conscientious members were such as to make membership almost a career in itself. It is hard to imagine that men would have joined the Board unless they had had leisure time to spend or had hoped to benefit, financially or otherwise, from their affiliation.

Yet one should not be unduly critical of the Board's membership, however faulty its method of election may have been. Thumbing through the early list one finds such names as Alfred Rhodes Bristow (Greenwich), a graduate of King's College, London, and a solicitor with a large conveyancing practice; F. Chalmer (Chelsea), a barrister and magistrate who had a wide connection with public institutions in his neighborhood; and Alderman Cubitt, the retired head of William Cubitt and Company, the great firm of builders. Also on the list are W. Dennis, the Islington builder and an old parochial reformer; T. D. d'Iffanger from Marylebone, principal of a grammar school in Maida Vale; and W. H. Doulton, a spiny character and member of the Lambeth pottery firm as well as a lecturer on Shakespeare at Mechanics' Institutions. Alderman Humphrey, owner of large docks in Southwark and a former M.P., "almost alone in the fellowship of his crotchets,"[4] appeared on the Board too; and, regrettably, the egregious John Leslie was returned from St. George's, Hanover Square. Islington sent John Savage, a wealthy man whose profession was really public affairs; and Hampstead elected Thomas Turner, a barrister, who was Treasurer of Guy's Hospital. It is clear that the Board, during most of its history, could draw upon a measure of ability and dedication far beyond that implied by the frequent denunciations of its membership. One cannot accept without qualification the standard epitaph for the Board: "It did some excellent things, but it was a terrible body."

Until 1870 the MBW sat under the chairmanship of John Thwaites, and during this period its most signal achievements—main drainage and the Embankment—came about. Though not a man of vigorous or lively imagination, Thwaites had good judgment, a passion for hard work, an equable, judicial temperament, and indomitable persistence. In 1862 he worked himself into a dangerous illness, so that his physician ordered him to take at least two months off; in 1870 he was stricken with "English cholera" and died at the age of fifty-five. The vacant chairmanship created a problem, not only for the Board but for the Government. It was rumored that the Government, wishing to get rid of Acton Smee Ayrton, member for Tower Hamlets and the First Commissioner of Works, had offered certain inducements to the Board to accept him as chairman.[5] In any event, the Government talked at the time as though the appointment would only be temporary because decisive action would soon be taken on the question of London's government. There were several candidates for the chairmanship both inside and outside the Board, among them Lord Robert Montague, who had not commended himself to Board opinion by his performance as chairman of the Select Committee of 1864. But it was inconceivable, most observers thought, that the Board should go outside its own membership for a chairman. The honor and profit of the chairmanship, *The Hornet* observed cynically, were too tempting to men of the vestry class, who might, through the position, ascend a notch or two socially.[6] This, no doubt, was true, even though some could see an advantage in electing a peer or a politician from outside the Board.

The solution hit upon was a compromise, but one that seemed to embody some of these motives. The man chosen (from a slate of five) was Colonel James McGarel-Hogg, who had been a member of the Board for three years, representing St. George's, Hanover Square.[7] Before the election, it had been agreed that the chairman's burden had been too heavy and that henceforth each of the Board's committees (other than committees of the whole) should have its own chairman and deputy chairman — that, in short, there should be a degree of devolution of authority in the Board's affairs.[8] At the instance of the Home Office, McGarel-Hogg's election was for a single year, the implication being that action on London government was imminent. Whether because of his performance or simply because the major tasks set up for the Board had been completed, during McGarel-Hogg's chairmanship the Board substantially lost its momentum. McGarel-Hogg's background was the conventional one of a man of the upper classes: Eton and Christ Church Oxford ("he was generally voted a very good boy, if not a particularly brilliant scholar") and sixteen years in the Life Guards, during which he rose to the rank of lieutenant colonel. In 1859 he resigned his commission, having married the daughter of a peer, to devote himself to politics; he sat first as Conservative member for Bath (1865–1868), and then for Truro and Hornsey. There is evidence that McGarel-Hogg was a reasonably diligent and interested member of the Board, but his election probably owed much to his social standing and his membership in Parliament, where, admittedly, the MBW needed someone to speak for

6. Offices of the Metropolitan Board of Works in Spring Gardens, Exterior

it. As chairman he took his post seriously, attending daily at the Spring Gardens office, and he presided at the meetings with urbanity. But there seems not to have been the dedication and drive that his Primitive Baptist predecessor had embodied. McGarel-Hogg was made a KCB on the completion of the Chelsea Embankment, and in 1887 was created Lord Magheramorne, having inherited from Charles McGarel the estate in County Antrim known by that name. McGarel-Hogg seems to have been an estimable person and a courtly figure, a "fine-looking, soldierly man, with clear-cut features, and snow-white hair."[9] But he was an unlikely candidate for vigorous municipal leadership.

Some of the Board's difficulties in undertaking new activities have been described in earlier chapters. Members of the Board, devoted to the myth of local self-government and innocent of the dimensions of their problems, objected to the use of committees to transact Board business except in emergencies. The City members, notably Henry Lowman Taylor, were set on obstruction, and the "Senate of Sewers" seemed given over to senseless and factious talk, so that the *Observer* termed it a "perverse little assembly."[10] Particularly distressing to the press, and a source of complaint throughout the Board's entire tenure, was its penchant for going into a committee of the whole and excluding reporters. Some of the more important committees — especially the Works and General Purposes Committee (under different names) — were commit-

tees of the whole, which enjoyed the right to debate in private. The press
was justified in its complaint. There was little excuse for such secretive-
ness, the more so because it needlessly aroused suspicions. The lack of
enthusiasm with which the Board was often viewed by reporters was, in
part, the result of its apparent fear of newsmen. Certainly the Board had
accumulated no margin of goodwill which would inspire newspapers to
give it the benefit of the doubt when questions arose.

For conscientious members, the MBW involved a heavy commitment. It sat normally at twelve on Friday, and might continue in session throughout the afternoon. The average attendance at these plenary
sessions was more than thirty out of the Board's forty-six members for
the 48 meetings.[11] These were the figures given by Thwaites in 1861 to
the Select Committee on Local Taxation, as reflecting the early years of
the Board's history. Five years later, the average attendance at plenary sessions was thirty-six, in addition to 166 committee meetings,[12]
which included 66 meetings of committees of the whole.[13] After the
membership had been increased to sixty in 1885, the average attendance
ran between forty and forty-five. The Board's final report, indeed, lists
369 separate committee meetings, including 52 meetings of committees

7. Offices of the Metropolitan Board of Works in Spring Gardens, Council
Chamber

of the whole. The other committees, which were usually composed of seventeen members, normally met once a fortnight.[14] Of the standing committees, such as the Finance Committee, the Parliamentary Committee, and the Fire Brigade Committee, all seem to have been reasonably hardworking, their number of meetings running from 20 to 31. In addition to the standing committees, there were some 125 special committees and subcommittees which held meetings. All members of the Board had two main meetings a week, the Works and General Purposes Committee on Mondays and the Board on Friday, each of which was likely to take up half a day, as well as an indefinite number of special committee and subcommittee meetings each week.

The increase in the number of committees and meetings shows how much the MBW's business grew over the years. Its functions multiplied, and with them its establishment. A fair measure is the increase in wages and salaries in the Board's accounts, although this is difficult to isolate because of the numbers of temporary employees appointed by the Board at various times. According to a return in 1861, the Board's total wage bill was under £24,000, a figure that included nearly 60 temporary employees (chiefly clerks of the works on the main drainage operations and draughtsmen).[15] About 136 in all were on the payroll. By 1867–68 this number had swelled to about 300, exclusive of the Fire Brigade, which was always considered a quasi-autonomous enterprise. The difference was partly accounted for by the crews necessary to man the pumping stations and other installations in connection with main drainage. But, in addition to the engineer's department, which was the largest of the various branches, there were thirteen in the architect's department, eight in the solicitor's, twelve in accounting, and nineteen in the clerk's department.[16] By 1878, in fact, it was necessary to add another story to the Spring Gardens building to create more office and storage space. By 1880, to take a later date at random, the staff had increased further, reflecting the number of new tasks that the Board had assumed as well as the normal expansion of the central staff.[17] In that year the salary bill of the central office had risen to nearly £44,000.[18]

In spite of the criticism which its work frequently encountered, the MBW's financial management was one of its more successful activities. This was true notwithstanding the whisperings of corruption and jobbery that pursued it (with some justice, as appeared later), and notwithstanding its chronic penury. On the whole, the Board was not only careful but at times imaginative in its financial decisions. There was difficulty at the start, for the unpaid debts accumulated by the former Commissioners of Sewers amounted to £288,222. However much ratepayers might object to paying for facilities from which they would benefit, there was no doubt that they would object to paying for a dead horse, for such it seemed, although some sewers had actually been laid.

The Board's procedure for raising its own poor rates was to issue its precepts, or "rate-demands," in January to the overseers of the poor. These were returnable in June, after which noncompliance would leave the parish in default. But the Board soon encountered resistance. In 1857 and 1858 Lambeth, Camberwell, Woolwich, Greenwich, and St. George's, Hanover Square, declined to pay up. Camberwell held that the charge made (according to the terms of the Metropolis Management Act) for works carried out by the Commissioners of Sewers was unfair, since they would benefit the parish only slightly: the charge was £8,000 while the benefit, it was urged, came closer to £500.[19] And, indeed, a bill was brought in on behalf of the parish to authorize the Board to reapportion the charges.[20] As for Greenwich, the Board summoned about five-hundred ratepayers to the parish police court, to show cause why distress warrants should not be issued against them, a case that was appealed to Queen's Bench. The Board made good its claims and the Greenwich District Board was judged in default by something over £9,000.[21]

More serious was the controversy between the Board and St. George's, Hanover Square, which flatly refused to collect the rates. The Board's response was to send its officers to the parish to make the collection, which cost the parish more than if it had used its own collectors.[22] Even then some members of the parish threatened defiance, and the Board responded by threatening distraint. This episode was one chapter in the story of strained relations between St. George's and the Board during its earlier years, a feud fomented at least in part by the tactics of Leslie and his friends.[23]

It was as well for the Board that its own sewerage plans were still incomplete while it was having to collect the debts left by the Commissioners of Sewers, for some of its earlier precepts were fairly substantial, especially since they were issued to pay for unsatisfactory work. In 1858, for example, the City was billed for nearly £16,000, Marylebone for over £12,000, and St. George's for almost £12,000.[24] The parishes gave up their poor rates grudgingly and late: in the fall of 1859, only £11,000 had been received of the £55,000 due a fortnight after the June deadline.[25] The Board foresaw worse trouble when the full pressure of main drainage cost should be applied, and began to cast about for sources of revenue other than rates, preferably taxes whose incidence was not too obvious. The Finance Committee canvassed the sources of revenue open to other corporations, domestic and foreign, for improvements, besides determining the total amount of local taxation collected annually from the metropolitan area and the value of imports and exports in the port of London. The committee discovered that the metropolis was much less fortunate than other corporate towns, in that these had corporation estates, market and ferry tolls, and port dues to supplement what could be raised from the rates. Against its meager resources — its ceiling on loans had been set at £3 million by the act of 1858 on main drainage — the Board had already made commitments that exceeded the £3 million and was considering over £1 million more. In short, the Board, the committee concluded, was in a difficult position, since it was expected to finance works of an extensive character "whilst the sole provision made by law for meeting their cost, viz. a direct tax on houses and other property rateable to the relief of the poor, was wholly inadequate for its object."[26] There was a possibility, the committee believed, that the Board might get either a share of the duties on cabs and omnibuses in the metropolis or a fraction of the coal duty.

The MBW also had doubts whether the machinery set up for collecting its rate was adequate. Would it not be more efficient to have its own collectors working directly for the Board? The Finance Committee thought that an appropriate amendment might be introduced, along with others that the Board was considering, to the Metropolis Management Act.[27] It was a reasonable suggestion, but the vestries and district boards to whom it was referred quickly disposed of the notion and the Board dropped it.

Still, it was questionable whether rates in the metropolis were higher than in other cities. Figures collected by the Finance Committee showed Manchester, Liverpool, Birmingham, Leeds, and Edinburgh paying more rates exclusive of the poor rate.[28] Had the metropolis reached the limit of what could be raised by direct taxation? This question could not be readily answered. Thwaites told the Select Committee on Metropolitan Local Government in 1866 that, rather paradoxically, such taxation had indeed reached the limit, but that the metropolis had sufficient property to pay for its improvements.[29] What he meant, of course, was that the burden of direct taxation was inequitably distributed — that some areas, inhabited largely by working-class residents and struggling tradesmen, were paying seven and eight shillings in the pound, while parishes like St. George's, Hanover Square, were well below what they could comfortably afford. Not only were there enormous variations in the rates, but these were imposed on property valuations which might either approach market values or be gravely below them.[30] St. George's, Hanover Square, was said to be underrated by £400,000, with a poor rate on this low assessment of only fivepence, while Bethnal Green, assessed at a high figure, had to pay a rate of one shilling and tenpence halfpenny.[31] Clearly, there was something to be said for a uniform valuation throughout the metropolis.

The main obstacle to achieving uniform valuation was the fact that the Board based its rates on the county rates,[32] and these were revised infrequently and irregularly. The Surrey rate had not been revised for five years and the Middlesex rate for three, although the poor rate valuation was being continuously revised.[33] In the rapidly growing London of the 1860s, this inevitably led to gross inequalities. In Paddington, for example, the poor rate valuation ran £97,000 above the county rate, and in Kensington, £84,000 above. In other parishes the discrepancy, though less striking, was large enough to be disturbing. In any case, the Board lost the equivalent of the difference between the poor rate and the county rate valuation, and some injustice was done to parishes where the property assessments had been more recently revised.

By the mid-1860s the Board's financial situation was desperate. Obviously no help was to be gained from the national purse, nor were such expedients as the Metropolitan Horse and Carriage Duties any more promising: an application to the Treasury met with a stern refusal to consider granting an imperial subsidy or to make available the carriage (hackney) duties. Government buildings and the royal parks, the Board was reminded, conferred some advantage on the metropolis, and that was enough.[34] This encounter, in fact, ended all serious talk of the hackney duties revenue, although in the following year, when Thwaites testified before the Select Committee, he was still fuming over the Government's rejection. Throughout the 1860s the Board's rate ran between 5.00 and 6.99 pence, though such figures, of course, mean little unless one knows how the property was valued.[35] Meanwhile, the metropolitan ratepayer's unhappiness remained unassuaged:

> There's a rate for the Thames highway,
>   And another for cleansing the river,
> But the Board have doubled their pay,
>   While the river's as muddy as ever.
> There's a rate for the large new street,
>   Which is empty the whole of the day,
> But the Board in a conclave meet,
>   And compel the ratepayers to pay.
> There's a rate for each grand new scheme —
>   *Pro communi* (hem!) *boni* they vote it —
> A "bonum" too often, 'twould seem
>   For the jobbers alone who promote it.

Chorus: Charges and rates and charges,

>   Oh, how the list enlarges!
> Rates and taxes and rates
>   Are doubled by Sir John Thwaites.[36]

Some of the Board's financial complaints were supported by George Goschen, president of the Poor Law Board, in a speech delivered in early

1868. The whole basis of municipal taxation was so erratic, he stated, that a well-to-do resident of the West End might contribute 1 percent of his income to municipal purposes while the poor person in the East End might pay 6 percent. Goschen favored rating the owners of property and lease-holding occupiers as a measure of relief to the occupiers. In any case, he conceded, the MBW had come to the end of its resources: it could not raise the rates on the current basis, despite the fact that it was only beginning to make improvements which were absolutely necessary.[37] *The Times* joined in the chorus of alarm and sympathy for the Board. There was no evidence that its debts had been accumulated recklessly or extravagantly, or that its rates were excessive in proportion to the obligations that the Board had assumed. But still the Board's difficulties were extreme, the more so because, although it had exhausted its resources, its work was only half done. And it could not possibly refuse to assume obligations for new improvements. Here was an odd case. "Usually, when people cannot see how to get money, they have at least the option of not spending it, but the Metropolitan Board of Works, while it is utterly at a loss for fresh income, can put no effectual stop to fresh outgoings."[38]

By the following year, 1869, action was desperately needed to resolve the MBW's financial problems. A variety of expedients had been tried since 1858. Then, for the purpose of constructing main drainage, the Board had received the right to borrow under a Government guarantee the sum of £3,000,000, which had been raised in 1863 to £4,200,000. In return, the Board had been required to collect each year a sum equal to a rate of threepence. The proceeds of this rate had been mortgaged to the Bank of England as security for the loan. As for the Embankment, it had been financed through the ninepenny coal and wine dues. All this, which was hardly adequate to guarantee the schemes already set in motion, left no margin for further improvements. Nor did various proposals for a change in the rating system get far enough to take any pressure off the Board. Finally in 1869, led by A. S. Ayrton, Parliament acknowledged the desperate character of the Board's plight and set up machinery to alleviate it.[39] The source of the original idea cannot be identified. It seems obvious enough today, but at the time it marked something of an innovation in municipal financing.[40]

The heart of the problem, Ayrton explained to the House, was the difficulty faced by the Board in long-range borrowing. It had no option but to borrow on a hand-to-mouth basis and therefore to pay high interest rates. Under this procedure, the Board had accumulated a debt of about £8 million, chiefly the result of such unexpected demands as the construction of fire engine houses and the heavy cost of the Embankment. What was now proposed, in a word, was to consolidate all the existing loans into a single debt, as with the national debt, to be called the metropolitan consolidated stock. The stock would be redeemable in sixty years, and for this purpose, as well as for paying the interest on the debt, a fund would be established called the consolidated loans fund. In future, instead of raising three rates (for general expenses, main drainage, and the fire brigade) the Board would raise a single consolidated rate. In short, the procedures of national finance were to be applied to the problems of municipal development.

Following the passage of the Loans Act of 1869, the Board's issues of stock were bought up with avidity by investors; indeed, the security seemed so impeccable that after 1871 trustees were empowered to invest in metropolitan stock. For the Board, the great advantage was the low rate of interest at which it could now get money. Formerly, its loans for purposes other than main drainage had come largely from insurance companies, generally at 4.5 percent. Now that figure was cut to 3.5 percent and was reduced in 1881 to 3 percent. The average price of a £100 share, which never went below £94 10s., rose as high as £102 2s. 7d. just before the interest rate was reduced.[41] The Board, for its part, exceeded its commitment under the act. Each year it paid off one-sixtieth or more of the principal on the debt, together with the interest on the balance that remained unpaid.

The Board's easier circumstances were promptly reflected by a decline in the rates that had to be raised. In 1871 the rate fell from 5.10 pence in the pound to 3.31 pence and in the following year to 2.68 pence.[42] It remained at an unusually low level until 1879, but from that point climbed upward again because of the Board's more extensive improvement policies. Yet in spite of the relief given in rates some vestries still seemed vaguely alarmed. The Clerkenwell vestry, in December 1871, passed a resolution looking toward the time "when the Hackney Carriage and the Coal and Wine Dues should be applied and continued for the purpose of Metropolitan Improvements . . . and requesting the Board to take the necessary steps for carrying out such resolution." The Board reminded Clerkenwell that the coal and wine duties had been anticipated for many years to come and that hackney carriage duties in their old form had been abolished.[43] And William Newton carefully explained to his Mile End constituents how much better off they and the Board were as a result of the Loans Act.

In addition to the effect of the new procedures on the Board's solvency, its income grew naturally as the ratable value of the metropolis increased. From £11 million in 1856 this value rose to £14.5 million in 1866, £23 million in 1876, and to over £30 million in 1886, nearly trebling in thirty years.[44] W. H. Smith, in an exchange of letters between the Treasury and the Board, urged caution, arguing that it was the

Treasury's duty to see that the Board's borrowing was kept within safe limits. It would be imprudent to expect the value of ratable property to increase indefinitely! The Board replied that borrowing limits had been established by Parliament and that the Treasury's functions were limited to the terms and conditions on which the borrowing could take place.[45] This was not an unfriendly exchange, even if the Treasury did argue for a go-slow policy just when the Board wished to "completely repair the previous neglect of centuries." There was, however, no reason for the Treasury to anticipate that the Board's easier financial condition would induce recklessness.

Among the issues arising in the MBW's correspondence with the Treasury was the question of increasing the Board's borrowing powers sufficiently to allow it to make loans to certain metropolitan boards. Already the Board was acting as banker for vestries and district boards, for the Metropolitan Asylums Board, and for the London School Board. Now it was proposed that the privilege be extended to Poor Law Guardians or any other metropolitan local boards on the same terms. This, in fact, was one of the signal, if unpublicized, services of the Board, and in the process the Loans Act of 1869 made a substantial difference. Formerly local boards, with the Board's sanction, had had to borrow from an insurance company or other lending agency at rates of interest from 4 to 5 percent. It would clearly be an economy to have the Board borrow such money as the other boards required and then lend it to them. The Loans Act of 1869 had, indeed, made provision for raising the £500,000 required by the managers of the Metropolitan Asylums District, and in 1871 the Board was authorized to lend money for improvements to vestries and district boards. The London School Board also was empowered by the elementary education acts of 1870 and 1872 to borrow money from the Board for the erection of school buildings. And by a new Loans Act, passed in 1875, all other metropolitan boards obtained similar privileges. In short, the Loans Act of 1875 converted the MBW into something like a banker for the permanent improvements of metropolitan agencies.

The Board used this privilege freely. Vestries and district boards borrowed £182,000; Boards of Guardians, £101,000; and other public bodies, some £377,000. Except for large loans to the School Board and the Metropolitan Asylums Board, this was mostly disbursed in small amounts, and it covered a wide range of facilities — paving, sewerage works, recreation grounds, buildings, public baths, and assistance in library construction.[46]

The Loans Act of 1875, although it increased the lending range of the Board, limited its borrowing power. At the insistence of the Treasury (which, of course, held the upper hand), the Board was to bring its finance bills to Parliament annually and to enumerate specific purposes. This was agreed to with reluctance: a year, the Board insisted, was too short a time for which to plan effectively; the amount required for three years would not be excessive. It looked for a while as though a compromise of two years might be agreed upon, but in the end the Treasury won its point and each year the Board had to bring in its bill.[47] Each year, therefore, the Board submitted for Treasury approval its schedule of borrowing for the year and also awaited the approval of Parliament.

The Board's reluctance to submit its bills annually may have sprung from its perennial difficulties with Parliament. As an orphan agency with no ministry to speak for it, the Board inevitably had trouble. During question time, questions were frequently addressed to McGarel-Hogg, whom the Speaker permitted to answer even though he lacked ministerial status. Apparently he was the only official in the House who could speak authoritatively on metropolitan matters. It was, one member pointed out in 1887, preposterous that a body which annually presented a budget of about £3 million had never had an officially recognized representative in the House.[48] Relations between the Board and the Commons were always anomalous and inconvenient, and when McGarel-Hogg moved to the Lords they became almost intolerable, especially as the unpopularity of the Board increased. Bills emanating from the Board usually received casual treatment, with little or no debating time assigned, and often they were brought in at the tag end of session. In 1881, for example, the Board's money bill was introduced at 2:30 A.M. on 18 July, having been in the hands of the Treasury for two months; it was passed on 22 July at 2:45 A.M.[49]

Yet the financial record of the Board was an excellent one. After Arthur Gunn took over accounting, that office was admirably handled; it "would compare most favourably with the largest Departments of Government," the Government auditor said in 1876.[50] The financial work was by this time a huge operation. The board was the largest rating authority in the kingdom. Each year it raised large sums, both for its own work and for other municipal bodies, and it contributed substantially to the local improvements of vestries and district boards. Most of these amounts were fairly small, though in 1888, for example, the Board contributed £10,707 to Poplar, over £30,000 to the City, and £4,300 to Kensington.[51] Though it might seem another example of "to him that hath shall be given," beyond a doubt these contributions helped to stimulate the activities of local authorities. It is difficult to disagree with the opinion of Henry Harben, resident director of the Prudential Assurance Company and one of the ablest of the Board's new members in the 1880s, that the financial policy of the Board was one of its strongest achievements.[52]

CHAPTER 8

The Odor of Corruption

It was one of the MBW's misfortunes that it never enjoyed sufficient public esteem to carry it over rough places in the road. It got off to a bad start, and despite an initial period of public euphoria the public impression of the Board rapidly deteriorated. As early as 1859 *The Times* noted the "flood of twaddle and chatter [which] passed over the town, pompous little great men and loud foolish little men, and ill-natured little idle men — small vanities and pomposities of every size and form — [which] turned the columns of every newspaper into a bad imitation of the chorus in the *Frogs* of Aristophanes." The writer went on to condemn the double election system, which "has never produced anything but cliques and jobbing."[1] Only the principle of popular election would improve the quality of members.

One ought not to set too much store by the views of a *Times* leader writer. These were subject to change by the week. Nearly every annual report was hailed with enthusiasm by *The Times*. In 1862, concerning the new report, *The Times* remarked that "the Metropolitan Board of Works has discharged very difficult tasks with as much success as could reasonably be expected . . . [and] we doubt whether they could have been advanced more effectively under any other hands."[2] This was well before the completion of the main drainage system sent everybody into a dither of congratulation. But a month later came a sour leader, which concluded that if the Board "were ever to become popular, it would be an insufferable tyranny to the whole country."[3]

169

In short, the metropolitan press sang a changeable tune. It could see little merit in the Board's constitution. The system of double election, instead of protecting the metropolis from irresponsible demagogues, had populated the Board with vestry types, worthy enough, no doubt, for vestry purposes but not of the caliber to deal with the problems of a city of three million. Occasionally, especially when the Board had executed a feat of particular distinction — completing the main drainage of the Embankment, for example — the press would burst forth in an anthem of praise. Generally, however, any failing, however slight, brought a flaying from the newspapers, and any achievement brought leading articles emphasizing that "in spite of the Board's second-rate character, it did a reasonably good job here." Some of the criticism reflected the natural and reasonable demands of municipal reformers for a popularly elected governing body, and, as the number of reform advocates rose, the criticisms of the MBW became more bitter. Some of them, obviously, were justified. Many of them, on the other hand, were simply convenient sticks with which to beat the dog of unreformed London government.

The Board had remarkably little success in dealing with public criticisms, and just as little in presenting itself as an interesting, lively institution. To resort to a current cliché, its public image was distinctly bad. This it was never able to correct, nor did it seriously try. The men of Spring Gardens handled their public relations abominably. Their practice of going into committees of the whole — especially the Works and General Purposes Committee — outraged the press (which was, of course, excluded), and their open debates were often windy, long drawn out, and trivial. In any case, because of its own lackluster image and the weaknesses in its constitution and, perhaps even more, because of the zeal of municipal reformers, the Board was sprayed by a constant stream of criticism. What this meant, perhaps, was that the Board had wholly failed to arouse any sense of civic patriotism among Londoners or to appeal to the imagination of the metropolis.

From the 1860s onward, press and public could always picture Spring Gardens as at best the center of discreet jobbery, or, often, as a cave of outright corruption. The direct evidence for such a view was astonishingly slight, but, given the pallid character of the Board and the ambitions of the reformers, it is not surprising that every peccadillo — or the faintest suspicion of one — was exploited. The odd thing was that so little came to light: one can only conclude that until the 1880s there was remarkably little substance in all the charges that were freely bandied about. In the middle 1860s there was, of course, the business of the contracts for the northern outfall and the Embankment, with the implication of a conflict of interest on the part of the Board's chief engineer. Whatever one may think of the ways of engineering contractors at mid-century, Bazalgette's involvement in the Odessa contract clearly had no connection with the rejection of Ridley's tender and the acceptance of Furness's. Ridley was shown to be relatively inexperienced, irresponsible, and (though this was not brought out before the Montague Committee) near the edge of bankruptcy. The charges against Bazalgette were spread before the preposterous Montague Committee in 1864 and shown to be without substance. With Montague's encouragement, an absurd series of charges was also made by Ridley and his friends, which, in due course, proved groundless. Montague emerged with as little credit as his witnesses. Either he was utterly naive or he hoped to make political capital out of the attack on the Board, a not too difficult achievement.

Yet Bazalgette's involvement with Furness in the Odessa contract (and thus presumably his guilty bias in Furness's favor in connection with MBW contracts) was the principal count against the Board until the roof fell in during the 1880s. Time after time in the next quarter-century, amid vague charges and innuendos, the Odessa myth was given a ritual disinterment, regardless of the fact that it had been decisively buried. This necessity for resorting to a myth to find charges against the Board suggests that the Board's behavior during most of its career was relatively innocent. Surely if the municipal reformers could have found any less flimsy charges, they would have used them. But J. F. B. Firth in his book *Municipal London* (1876) — some seven-hundred pages of analysis and arguments for reform — could find no specific charges of corruption to prefer, save the tired old Odessa myth. This does not mean, of course, that he intended to be easy on the Board. His book contains dark hints of the possibility of graft, as well as criticism of the irresponsibility and secrecy in whch the Board carried on its work. But of specific charges the book is relatively innocent, and those that Firth elected to bring are the sins of which the Board had been proved guiltless years before. Yet it was these that the reformers, both Firth and the wilder and more reckless James Beal, were obliged to fall back on when they looked for concrete charges to level against the integrity of the Board.

In 1864, shortly after the Montague Committee completed its sittings, James Beal, who was in 1870 to become Honorary Secretary of the newly created Municipal Reform Association,[4] exploded a series of fourteen charges against the Board in the vestry of St. James's, Westminster. The animus behind his attack was clear. Most of the charges were sheer nonsense, the result of misinterpreting a statement, of his unfamiliarity with technical questions, or of the semiwillful misconstruction of material to which the dedicated zealot is often addicted. Beal charged that the foundations of the northern outfall had not been carried as deep as they were supposed to have been (actually they were carried deeper), and that a cofferdam for the northern outfall, estimated to cost £16,000, had never been built. In fact, the dam had been duly built and had "been traversed by several thousand people including Members of both Houses of the Legislature as well as the several Vestries and District Boards of the Metropolis."[5] The Board regarded these charges as wildly irresponsible—as it did much of the evidence before the Montague Committee—but, aware that when mud is thrown freely, some is going to stick, it took pains to refute these charges in detail. A pamphlet consisting of twenty-three pages plus fifty-four pages of documents dealt with the allegations systematically and conclusively.[6] But, hollow though they were, the weary old charges would continue to be dusted off and used again by those determined to discredit the Board.

Undiscriminating as was Beal's barrage, he came close with one shot. In 1865 in a petition presented to Parliament by Lord Elcho, Beal added a supplementary item to the Odessa scandal.[7] His charge was that three members of Parliament—Frederick Doulton, Sir William Jackson, and Meaburn Staniland[8]—had been involved in the Furness-Bazalgette dealings for profit. Beal's accusations fell fairly flat at the time, but two years later Furness's bankruptcy proceedings showed that they were not without substance, though distorted and exaggerated as Beal's charges usually were. From Furness's confused testimony it is difficult to get a lucid notion of what had happened. Doulton, certainly an honorable and high-minded man, had in fact been involved as no member of the Board should have been. Other things aside, section 54 of the Metropolis Local Management Act of 1855 specifically prohibited such involvement. When a committee of the Board failed to give him the complete clearance that he desired, Doulton resigned. One of the other two members of the House who had been charged by Beal was shown to have had nothing to do with the affair, and the other was a case of mistaken identity.[9]

Rumors of corruption continued to circulate in the metropolis for the next two decades, though with remarkably little specific evidence. It did not help when, in late 1868, the Board's accountant was shown to be in default for over £2,000 and was of course discharged. He obtained acquittal on a technicality, but there was no question that he had appropriated a considerable sum from money entrusted to him for the payment of weekly wages and from the petty cash fund.[10] This was an embarrassing episode, for it seemed to suggest not only knavery among the paid officials but careless administration on the part of the Board itself.

In the latter 1870s a special committee of the Board examined the real estate operations of a member of the Board and reached the conclusion that he ought to resign. The member was Joseph Storey, recently returned by the St. Luke's, Clerkenwell, vestry and a fairly crude and insensitive man. The episode belongs to vestry politics more than to the affairs of the MBW, but it is cited here in order to show that the Board could act with decision and firmness when one of its members fell under suspicion of corruption. The case had to do with claims for compensation in connection with the Board's Whitecross Street improvement scheme, in which there appeared an item for over £47,000 signed by Storey and two other persons. Rumors had reached the Board that Storey was one of three adventurers who had been interested in property to be purchased for the Whitecross Street scheme and the Golden Lane improvement, to which the Board had agreed to contribute nearly £40,000.[11] Letters appeared in the London press (some of which seem to have been the work of James Beal) charging the Board with dilatoriness and with being concerned only with appearances.[12] The Board in fact acted with admirable promptness. A special committee was at once appointed to investigate the affair; then the Works and General Purposes Committee (a committee of the whole) formulated its report. In the Golden Lane affair (the simpler case to explain), it emerged that three vestrymen had engaged in a triple sale of property along the route of the intended thoroughfare; this was followed by the final purchase of the property by the parish of St. Luke's, Clerkenwell (where Storey was chairman of the improvements committee), for £4,000 more than the sum paid by the last owner. The land had been sold originally for £4,000, had been bought back by the original owner for £8,000, and had been unloaded on the parish for £12,300.

The Works and General Purposes Committee was firm with Storey. In its own words, it "used every endeavour to convince [him] of the incompatibility of his position as a Member of the Board with his transactions in connection with the properties in question."[13] The committee members felt only regret when Storey failed to "admit the force of their representations" and refused to resign, for they did not doubt the existence of a sharp conflict of interest between his duties on the Board and his private concerns. There, however, the Board exhausted its direct power, although it did apply pressure through the parish by withdrawing the contribution it had promised for the two improvement schemes.[14]

Through the summer and fall of 1878, the uproar in Clerkenwell continued, with memorials, turbulent vestry meetings, and ratepayers' meetings. What finally curbed the vestry, which seems to have been in a deplorable condition, was the report of the surveyor for the MBW, who concluded that the parish had given £4,270 beyond its proper value for the Golden Lane improvement. When the Board withdrew its promised contribution, the vestrymen's days were numbered. They could howl about the unfairness of the Board's decision and could brace themselves against the ratepayers' demands, but there was little else they could do. Repeatedly, the Board refused to help unless the vestry faced reality and resigned.[15] The vestrymen protested and finally decided to pay 5 percent interest on the property that they had agreed to buy but could not pay for.[16] When the vestry finally gave up the battle and resigned, the parish showed its disapproval of the old policies by not reelecting most of those who had been most intimately concerned with them, including Storey and a number of his friends. Storey, lacking a vestry base, finally resigned from the MBW.[17] In this case no one could charge the Board with failure to act vigorously on a conflict-of-interest issue. On the other hand, the very fact that such a man as Joseph Storey had won a seat on the Board suggests a weakness in its constitution.

Certain other episodes, which were later to take on a special significance, suggested that architects on the Board were not as sensitive as they should have been to conflicts of interest. In 1875 when plans were being made for a national opera house on the Embankment, it was charged in the Commons that the Board had forced the owner of the property to accept both the architect and the contractor. The architect was Francis Fowler, a member of the Board, and the builder was William Webster. Although the charge was refuted by both McGarel-Hogg and W. H. Smith, apparently on solid grounds, it seems to have had some substance.[18] Again, in 1883 a member of Parliament asked, with regard to the Hotel Metropole site on Northumberland Avenue, whether one of the architects was not a member of the Board and whether he did not have a share in the property. Hogg answered both questions in the affirmative.[19] The questioner did not press his point, but he had laid a finger on the other Board architect who was to figure later in the Royal Commission's inquiry.

There had been still other indications that all might not be well in the architect's office. In July 1875 Thomas James Robertson, at the time an assistant clerk, was charged with having shown certain confidential books of the Board to a firm of solicitors concerned with compensation claims. For his cooperative attitude he received an honorarium of two guineas, as evidenced by a cheque which he had endorsed "Robinson." Robertson convinced the committee of his innocence, at least they forgave him because of his youth and poverty and because the firm of solicitors would not appear to support the charge.[20] Again, in October 1883 a subcommittee of the Board discovered that one Scott, who had been discharged for attempting to extort money from the owners of theatre buildings which it was his duty to visit, had been reemployed in another branch of the architect's office. It was Robertson—one of the two principals in the scandal that was to break in 1886—who had rehired Scott and who, when summoned before the subcommittee, professed ignorance of Scott's previous dismissal.[21] Robertson's explanation was again accepted, and on his promise that Scott would not be employed in the future the committee simply filed away the incident. Nobody at the Board seemed inclined to dig too deep into matters in the architect's office. After all, the chief architect, George Vulliamy, a man of unquestioned integrity, had had a long and successful career with the Board, and although by the 1880s he was elderly and in frail health, it did not seem to occur to the members that he had lost control of his subordinates. Still less did they perceive that these men, and not Vulliamy, were running the office.

By the 1880s the climate of opinion in London was changing. Centralization no longer seemed the ominous bogey it had been in the 1850s. Instead, there loomed the more practical question of how huge urban agglomerations were to survive without a great measure of centralized direction. Sentiment was rising in favor of a solution of the problem of metropolitan government, though no one could say that it had yet reached the dimensions of a tidal wave. The London Municipal Reform League, in which J. F. B. Firth was a leading figure, was founded in 1881, and the pitch and effectiveness of its agitation gradually increased through the eighties. It was understood that the Gladstone Government that came to power in 1880 would introduce a bill for the reform of London government. In this new atmosphere, there was a livelier interest in questions of metropolitan administration and a greater disposition to criticize existing forms. Yet the reformers could not charge the Board with serious corruption. There was no evidence up to this time of anything gravely amiss in the Board's administration; the old charges which echoed in the Odessa-Ridley-Furness imbroglio were badly shopworn. It was probably a fortunate circumstance for the reformers that corrupt transactions of some consequence were about to be brought to light. Obviously—though it was denied at the time—they strengthened the demands of the reformers and aided C. T. Ritchie with the London section of his Local Government Bill in 1888. For though the reformers were not ultimately responsible for liquidating the MBW, their criticisms increased the head of public steam over London government and made it seem quite impossible that the Board should continue, even if its constitution were altered.

The final furor was set off by a series of articles in the *Financial News*, the first of which appeared on 25 October 1886. Subsequent stories appeared throughout the following year.[22] The authors were Harry Marks, editor of the *News* and the son of Professor Marks of the Marylebone vestry, and W. R. Lawson, who did skillful and effective legwork for the series. Within the limits of the genre, this was a brilliant piece of muckraking journalism. Some claims were trivial and overstated, some were false, and some rehearsed the shopworn charges made thirty years before. But in their main emphasis the allegations were correct. They not only provided evidence of the corrupt practices of underlings in the office but also implicated responsible officials of the Board (or those thought to be responsible), as well as two members of the Board itself. The authors must have felt a good deal of satisfaction when their principal allegations were later documented by the Royal Commission on the Board of Works in 1888.

The *Financial News* articles were released in an atmosphere full of sympathy, and other London papers took up the cry. The reform movement hailed the disclosures. Moreover, public antagonism mounted against the coal and wine duties, on which the Board had relied to finance the Embankment and to free the Thames bridges of toll. Extensions of the duties for these purposes had already been accepted, but when the Board asked for a further extension the Gladstone Government received the request with conspicuous reserve. Better things were expected from a Conservative government, less strongly committed to Gladstonian financial principles. Yet Lord Randolph Churchill, sensing the new spirit and aware of the political dynamite being planted by the *News*, not only denied the request of the Board but did it in substantially the same terms used a few years before by the Gladstonian Leonard Courtney, then Financial Secretary. The bulk of the London press hailed Churchill's "chilling response."[23] The radical *Echo* suggested that the duties be extended for two years only and that the revenue be used to provide parks.[24] But this suggestion only reflected the dilemma of the radicals who desperately wanted something done to improve living in London, but who were perfectly aware that if the matter was left to the decision of the ratepayers not much would be accomplished.

When the *Financial News* attack began, the Board had only a meager reservoir of public goodwill to draw on, and this was exhausted as the series developed. *Punch* was only reflecting the opinion of Londoners when it repeatedly characterized the Board of Works as the "Board of Perks."[25] The *Financial News* directed its primary attack against the management of the Estate Office of the Board. Several articles that were intended to deal with other "scandals," some of them thoroughly stale, proved less convincing. But the detective work done on Thomas James Robertson (Assistant Surveyor), on F. W. Goddard (Chief Valuer to the Board from 1877), and, with less reason, on John Hebb (Assistant Architect), was skillful. Suspicions were also raised (justifiably, it turned out) toward J. E. Saunders, an architect and one of the City's representatives on the Board since 1863. The *News*'s chief attack was aimed at the Board's method of disposing of surplus land, specifically the intricate transactions surrounding the leasing in 1884–85 of the Pavilion Music Hall site in Piccadilly Circus, an extraordinarily complicated story that can be told here only in part.[26]

What the *Financial News* account described in essentials and the Royal Commission later established was a chronicle of corruption which seemed to confirm the worst suspicions of the Board's enemies. The Piccadilly Circus site was acquired by the Board in 1879 with an eye to the future cutting through of Shaftesbury Avenue, though the Board had no immediate use for the land. In the summer of 1879 R. E. Villiers, a music hall proprietor, leased the ground, paying the Board a rental of £7,000 a year, in addition to £50 a quarter which he paid to F. W. Goddard. He continued to be a tenant of the Old Pavilion, for the Board was not able to proceed with the improvement until 1884. But in 1883, when it looked as though the Old Pavilion was about to be demolished, Villiers met with Goddard and Robertson, who agreed to help him gain a building lease of the site. In return for this, one W. W. Grey (Robertson's brother) was to have the west corner for a public house. The profit, estimated at £10,000, from the selling of Grey's public house on Tichborn Street was to be divided between Goddard and Robertson. With this much settled, it was full steam ahead to make certain that Villiers got the site for his new Pavilion.[27]

In November 1884 the time had come for action, and Robertson told Villiers that he must apply to the MBW for permission to make an offer. The Board's superintending architect and its solicitor were instructed to report on the request. The former put the value of the site at £3,000 ground rent plus £15,000 as the value of the licenses. This report, it appears, was much more the work of Vulliamy's subordinates than of the architect himself. The draft was in Goddard's handwriting, and after it had been turned over to Robertson to be copied, Vulliamy signed it. Clearly, Vulliamy had little to do with the document. He was old, tired, and sick, and he left much of the office work to his subordinates. Villiers's testimony before the Royal Commission was not inaccurate: Vulliamy was "a very charming old gentleman, but very peculiar and erratic; you could not pin him down to any decided course, you could not get a decided answer out of Mr. Vulliamy on any subject."[28] Although Villiers's initial offer had been £2,700 for the ground rent, he at once agreed to meet the Board's figure. Favorable action on his tender was hurried through the Board, in spite of another bid of £4,000. Oddly enough, the man who made the motion to accept was Henry Harben, managing director of the Prudential Assurance Company, who was regarded as one of the abler and more forward-looking Board members. Apparently he felt, unlike William Selway and some other members, that the Board had gone far enough in its negotiations with Villiers to have made a moral commitment.

The Board therefore granted two leases to Villiers, one for £2,650 for the Pavilion and the other for £350 for the west corner of the site, on which the Piccadilly Restaurant was to be built. Some of the most mysterious of all the Villiers-Robertson-Goddard transactions concerned this latter plot, which was made over to Robertson's brother, W. W. Grey, a licensed victualler, and to a company in which Robertson's family connections were prominent, "a very nicely arranged family party."[29] This company, capitalized at £40,000, proved a resounding failure, and Robertson lost a considerable sum of money. Goddard, however, continued to collect his £50 a quarter, and in December 1886 when Villiers sold the Pavilion, Goddard received £5,000 in the debentures of the new company, later modified to £4,000 in debentures and £1,000 in cash.[30]

This was the most sensational charge against the Board's administration and the only one that the *Financial News* could describe in detail. There were also intimations, however, that all had not been well with leases on Northumberland Avenue: a hotel syndicate had turned up with leases for the sites on which were erected the Grand Hotel and the Hotel Metropole. But the investigators for the *News* could unearth no positive evidence of corruption in the Board's dealings there. When the Royal Commission investigated the affair, it appeared that Saunders was heavily implicated, that he had been appointed architect and had apparently done remarkably little in return. Still, it was on the Pavilion affair that the *News* struck its most telling blows.

The Robertson-Goddard corruption in the Pavilion affair was brilliantly exposed, but perhaps the *News*'s finest hour came in its reporting of the Board's laughably inept attempt to deal with the charges. There had been complaints from one or two local vestries almost as soon as the agreement with Villiers was made, and several metropolitan dailies took up the cry after the lead had been given by a public protest meeting.[31] But it required the revelations in the *Financial News* to force the Board into action. Through 1885, in fact, business at Spring Gardens proceeded as usual. Robertson was cutting a wide swath, ostentatiously driving around town in his own carriage with a liveried servant,[32] and Goddard, on whom suspicion had not yet fallen, was continuing to prosper. The Board's initial investigation was undertaken by a special subcommittee of six, with Lord Magheramorne as chairman. In its long report, presented in mid-July, the subcommittee betrayed almost unbelievable naiveté. It managed to elicit all the facts except the essential ones; it had Robertson and other officials on the carpet. But the witness whose evidence was vital, namely Villiers, was out of town, and the Board attempted to close the case without his evidence. Thus, although the subcommittee could find Robertson "injudicious in allowing relatives to become tenants of the Board without informing the Board," it failed to discover "anything worthy of more severe censure."[33]

This bland verdict may have satisfied the subcommittee, but certain other members, as well as the press, found it alarming. The *Pall Mall Gazette*, in a leader captioned "Mr Robertson Must Go — and Twenty More," suspected that the debate on Robertson confirmed the ugly rumors about "certain rings" in the MBW. People declared that the members of these rings were in alliance, offensive and defensive, with one another. Contractors and builders and architects grumbled that there was no getting through the Board unless such and such architects were employed [presumably Saunders or Fowler], or such and such a manufacturer's goods were purchased.[34] This charge was not novel, and anyone with the record of municipal politics before him would be inclined to suspect an element of truth. But the Royal Commission, although it sought earnestly to run down the charge, and though it was told that there were rings within the Board, was not able to pinpoint their existence in a satisfying fashion. *Lloyds,* two days after the publication of the subcommittee's report, found it impossible to believe that Robertson alone was involved, and recalled other problems in the Board's behavior which had never been cleared up: for example, the suspicions relating to the Northumberland Avenue leases when important tenants had to call in a member of the Board (Saunders) as well as their own architect.[35] Here, the editor thought, a commission of inquiry was clearly needed.

In fact, the subcommittee's report did not pass the Board without a struggle. A number of more drastic amendments were made from the floor, the sharpest one to the effect that "it is inexpedient that Mr. Robertson should remain in the service of the Board." This amendment produced a long and violent debate and lost by only six votes, 25 to 19. But the debate on the report continued week after week. Robertson himself reopened it by asking for a public hearing and then submitting a long written statement.[36] Finally the Board decided to appoint a special committee to investigate the charges made in certain newspapers and in one vestry (St. James's) with regard to the sale of lands by other than public auction. This referred to statements made by one F. C. Keevil, who had been annoyed by his failure to get a Shaftesbury Avenue site.[37] But the committee, sitting in public during the recess, was unable to get either Keevil, who showed himself to be an irresponsible windbag, or James Beal to give evidence. Beal, in a pompous note, declined on the grounds that this was a mere whitewashing ritual. The *Financial News* also bowed out on the grounds that the tribunal was not a proper one. Only Mark Judge of Paddington, a dedicated reformer, appeared as a witness.[38] Judge maintained, correctly enough, that the circumstances of the Pavilion deal called for an inquiry by some independent authority, and though he declined to level a charge of corruption at individuals, he condemned the selling and letting of public land by private treaty. Apart from his testimony, the committee had the greatest difficulty in collecting evidence. Although the widest publicity was given to its sittings, no one came forward to substantiate charges. Whether this was because of doubts about the tribunal, or because there was relatively little substance to the broader charges against the Board, or because such suspicions were difficult to document was not clear. But certainly, in sitting and waiting for witnesses to make charges, the committee offered only the caricature of an investigation, and it could find little to report. It was no wonder that the metropolitan press regarded the whole business as eminently unsatisfactory. The *Daily News* reported that the "Metropolitan Board of Works enacted an entertaining farce yesterday, the spirit and success of which will surprise even those best acquainted with the most incompetent body in London. The Board has unanimously acquitted itself of improper conduct, and congratulated itself upon the fact that no one has come forward to accuse it."[39] And the *Standard* asserted that the inquiry came to an end "in a manner which simply serves to show the inefficiency and unsuitability of the tribunal which undertook the investigation."[40] *The Times*, too, with heavy irony, called it "an excellent investigation . . . everything [being] present for a successful investigation with the single exception of the other side." As it is, *The Times* concluded, "the whole must appear a farce and a rather audacious farce."[41] Having failed to discover further evidence of corruption, in mid-November the Board came to an astonishing verdict with regard to Robertson. Unable to decide whether to discharge him or to let the old censure stand, the Board determined to remove him from the architect's office but to find him another niche in the organization, where presumably his activities would be closely supervised. The Works and General Purposes Committee canvassed the various departments, none of which appeared eager for Robertson's services. Finally at the end of March the committee decided that he would have to go. In spite of amendments proposed by various of his friends, the committee was able to push its decision through the Board. To quote the *Financial News*, "after fifteen months of stirring up, Spring-gardens had at last found its conscience."[42]

Beyond doubt the Board had made an exceedingly bad showing in its handling of the Pavilion inquiry. How much responsibility can be laid at the door of the Board's chairman, Lord Magheramorne? Certainly a more vigorous leader would have considered the Board's procedure inappropriate. For one thing, he had been away on holiday in August and September when the situation was going from bad to worse. In November the issue of Robertson came to a vote, first in subcommittee and then before the Works and General Purposes Committee. In both instances the committee vote was a tie, and Lord Magheramorne then voted with the Robertson party in a gesture, said the *Financial News*, of "eccentric amiability."[43] Magheramorne had been elected in the first place to what the Home Secretary had assured the Board was to be only a temporary post, and he had been chosen partly because he was a member of Parliament and by far the most socially elevated member of the Board. He had performed in a reasonably conscientious fashion, but administrative leadership of a municipal body was quite foreign to his instincts and education. One would not naturally look to Eton, Christ Church, and the Army as a training ground for the management of such agencies as the MBW. Magheramorne's increasing age and his accession to a peerage, not to mention his frequent absences in Ireland, served further to relax his administration and tended to make him seem ignorant of—or indifferent to—the gossip about the Board current in London.

The discharge of Robertson came too late to save what was left of the Board's shaky reputation, In fact, it seems doubtful whether even this decision would have been taken without the votes of the new members who had recently been elected to the Board in the expansion of its membership from forty-five to sixty, following the act of 1885. This increase had, in the words of *Lloyds,* "destroyed the peace of the Metropolitan paradise [and] a whiff of more healthy atmosphere has been introduced."[44] Meanwhile, there were fresh demands from the vestries for a Royal Commission to investigate the Board's affairs. In mid-October T. G. Fardell,[45] the new member for Paddington, an old Etonian and Cambridge man, reported to *The Times* that sixteen vestries and district boards had urged such an inquiry.[46] The Board's own attitude toward such an investigation was not encouraging. A motion by Fardell in early October had lost by one vote, and it was not until mid-November that the Board decided to inform the Home Secretary that it would give every assistance to a public investigation if one was instituted. In short, the Board was not going to ask for an inquiry, but it was not going to resist one.[47]

In February 1888 when Lord Randolph Churchill moved in the House for a Royal Commission, London opinion (outside the MBW) was unanimous in thinking such an investigation overdue. T. G. Fardell, backed by a group of Paddington reformers, has been credited with having persuaded Churchill, then Chancellor of the Exchequer, to make an assault.[48] Most of Churchill's charges were drawn from the *Financial News,* the irresponsible and trivial ones as well as the accurate; he also cited the opinions of minority members of the Board in favor of a government inquiry.[49] R. G. Webster, a member for St. George's, Hanover Square, and by no means an old Spring Gardens hand,[50] attempted some defense of the Board. Indeed, he pointed out that it had greatly changed in personnel since 1885 (the year Webster had entered), and that most of the charges antedated that year. Few members of Parliament could realize the amount of work that the Board had to get through in order to make decisions on something like 300,000 questions a year, with a staff of about 1,250. Each week the Board held over 350 meetings (full Board, committees, subcommittees), and it had to cope with an immense amount of excess work that Parliament had cheerfully handed over. Henry Broadhurst (Liberal M.P. for Nottingham West) wished to extend the investigation to the vestries and district boards, but the Home Secretary thought, quite reasonably, that the House should hesitate to pass such judgments at 2:30 in the morning.[51]

The small body that was constituted under Churchill's motion was a Royal Commission, not a Select Committee of the House. In consequence it lacked the political overtones and the pulling and hauling of partisan forces often characteristic of Select Committees, conspicuously of Lord Robert Montague's investigation in the 1860s. This was, instead, to be a quasi-judicial inquiry, and the chairman was to be T. H. Farrer, Baron Herschell, a distinguished judge who had been Lord Chancellor in Gladstone's ephemeral 1886 Government and was to take the same office again in 1893. His colleagues were F. A. Bosanquet and H. R. Grenfell. The inquiry was conducted in an impeccable fashion. Herschell proved an admirable chairman, soft-spoken and scrupulously fair but in complete command of the proceedings. A local London newspaper characterized his manner as "bland and conciliatory. Izaak Walton was wont to bait his hook as though he loved the work; and the same remark applies to Lord Herschell."[52] Herschell's hook was so skillfully baited that it pulled in some substantial and unanticipated fish. Occasionally, when witnesses displayed memories so porous as to verge on the pathological, he would become annoyed and would instruct them, with some firmness, to wake up and tell the truth. The Commission called every person whose evidence could conceivably be of value — as well as some, such as Keevil and James Beal, whose windy and unsupported charges were received by Herschell with obvious annoyance. All of those with stories to tell on the special questions that the Commission was investigating were, of course, summoned, and every member of the Board was called in the attempt to run down some of the vaguer charges that had been made. Lord Magheramorne, in explaining the work and policies of the Board, did not emerge as a witness who was in command of his job. On several occasions he had to be prompted by the Board's counsel, Meadows White. The result of the twenty-four sessions, which lasted from May through August, was an interim report of 40 pages, accompanying over 500 pages of evidence.

It was a devastating document, yet it could have satisfied neither the prosecution nor the defense. For although it exonerated the Board from the charges of general corruption which had been so freely brought, on the Pavilion site it substantiated and, indeed, enlarged on the allegations of the *Financial News*. The Commission deliberately limited the range of its inquiry; it was not going to scrutinize the whole range of the Board's activities or pass judgment on how well it had done its work. Yet neither was it going to don blinkers when it found evidence of misconduct, regardless of whom it involved or when it had taken place. The report constituted a fascinating guidebook through some of the shadier avenues of the Board's operations. It documented some of the charges of the *Financial News,* rejected others, and established a case against certain officers and members of the Board who had not figured significantly in the attacks of the *News*. But having pilloried this group, the Commission went on to acquit the Board of wholesale corruption, to the annoyance of certain municipal reformers who had made loose and vague charges. "There are other departments of that body," confidently asserted Stead's *Pall Mall Gazette,* "which reek with corruption quite as much as those which have already been exposed."[53] Nor could the Board have been elated by the Herschell verdict, which not only confirmed suspicions about two of its servants but implicated two of its most senior members. In any case, the fate of the Board was already sealed. Ritchie had brought in his Local Government Bill before the Commission began its sittings, and it got through Parliament while they were still in progress. To quote the *Pall Mall Gazette* again, "So the Metropolitan Board of Works is to be tried as well as hanged — but to be hanged first and tried afterwards."[54]

On the Pavilion scandal, the Herschell Commission's report implicated Goddard far more heavily than the *News* had done, and it also showed the architect Saunders to have been an integral member of the corrupt circle at Spring Gardens. Goddard and Robertson were in strategic positions to do well for themselves under the system by which the Board disposed of its surplus lands — especially when supervised only by an old, sick chief. When a new street was to be cut through, it was the duty of the superintending architect to arrange for the purchase of the necessary land, and freeholders and leaseholders were instructed to put in their claims. These having been settled by the solicitor (on the average for about half the amount demanded) and the building line having been established by the architect, the architect then fixed a reserve price for each lot (in confidence) and a day was appointed for receiving tenders. Tenders that exceeded the reserve price, of course, raised few problems, but unlet sites were left for a few days of private negotiation. Theoretically, the *Financial News* noted, tenders were the only way of disposing of sites, but in practice the Board might, if tenders were unsuccessful, rely on private negotiation and, more rarely, on auction. The ultimate power of decision lay in the hands of the Works and General Purposes Committee, which of course met without benefit of press or public.[55]

In this procedure, corrupt but influential underlings had an excellent chance to line their pockets. And both Robertson and Goddard had attained to positions of influence. Goddard had been with the Board almost from the beginning, having been employed first as a temporary assistant in the architect's office in December 1862. He climbed the ladder steadily and in 1873 was made chief assistant surveyor and valuer at a salary of £600 a year. He was now an important official, in immediate control of the Board's dealings in land, and his influence over Vulliamy was considerable. Though he was regarded by Vulliamy and everyone else in the Board's administration as above suspicion, the Commission showed beyond a doubt his heavy involvement in corrupt practices. Robertson likewise had spent years in the service of the Board, having received his first appointment as assistant clerk in the accountant's department in 1866 when he was sixteen. In 1868 he was transferred to the architect's department, with an increase in salary from £60 to £90 a year. From then on, his rise was steady until he was able to control the estates office of the Board in (to him) an exceedingly profitable fashion. There seems to have been a question whether, in title, he was simply a clerk in the office or "deputy surveyor;"[56] but whatever his title his influence over land operations was significant. It was his luck to have a number of brothers, who under different names collaborated with him. The flashy streak in Robertson's character—his love of display, his liveried footman, and his fast, plausible speech—aroused suspicions among certain of his more alert superiors. But until the Pavilion affair he had always managed to talk his way out of serious trouble, as he had in 1875. Now the Commission not only confirmed the Pavilion charges of the *Financial News,* but showed beyond question that he had been implicated in the disposal of sites, especially public house sites, in various parts of the metropolis.[57] Yet both Goddard and Robertson had shown a certain restraint in their demands. The *Pall Mall Gazette* estimated (with how much truth it is difficult to judge, but the total probably does not err on the side of understatement) that they had each made nearly £11,500 from their dishonest activities.[58] Though a grave matter, such a sum does suggest a certain element of caution in the behavior of the two buccaneers.

Both men tended to specialize in public house sites, of which the Board had a fair number to dispose. Here, Goddard's position as chief valuer was especially strategic, and those with tenders to submit soon found that it was wise to have a special friend at the Board. For more than a decade, he and Robertson had been getting "gifts" from applicants for Board sites or from current tenants who planned to buy after the Board had made improvements. In fact, the story of the depredations of this precious pair was far more complicated and their operations were far more extensive than even the *Financial News* had dared to imagine, or at least had been able to describe. Goddard showed a good deal of versatility in the types of toll that he managed to levy. He established relations with brokers who handled Board sites and with surveyors acting in compensation cases. One of the brokers testified that during the past fifteen years his firm had paid Goddard a third of all its commissions with the Board, and another broker set his payments at 15 percent.[59] Moreover, with Frederick Marrable, the Board's former superintending architect,[60] Goddard for some years effected a profitable cooperation in compensation cases.[61] (All along, Marrable had revealed himself as a man whose sense of honor was a bit elastic.)

The Herschell Commission continued by confirming the suspicions of the *Financial News* with regard to Robertson's dealings and, in fact, amplified them considerably. More even than Goddard, Robertson had been interested in public house sites all over London. It was easy to suggest to the owner selling to the Board that the purchase price should be shared with the official who had handled the business and who, by implication, had brought the Board to a favorable decision. In one instance Goddard received as much as one-third of the purchase price.[62] Then there was the case of the Yorkshire Grey, taken in the widening of Theobald's Road. The owner, one Thomas Whorlow, bought a new site from the Board for £2,500 but thought it enough of a bargain to give Robertson and Goddard, indirectly through their agents, £2,000 in addition.[63] Besides the Yorkshire Grey, Robertson had dealings with Thomas Legge for two sites in Tite Street, Chelsea. It was a rather complicated affair, but it resulted in Robertson getting leases to the property for a straw; and he sold them, in turn, to the Prudential Assurance Company.[64] Through his brother John Grey, Robertson acquired the lease for the Old Swan in Shoreditch Road, Bethnal Green; and he showed skill, too, in milking builders who were seeking Board land.

Robertson's relations with Statham Hobson, something of a speculator in London real estate, also drew the attention of the Commission. Hobson, who was the lessee of the site on which the Colonial Institute was built, had wished to buy in on favorable terms — twenty-five years' purchase. He had had some trouble completing the deal with the Board but, apparently thanks to Robertson, it had gone through. Robertson had profited by £350. Hobson, the Commission pointed out, had had every reason to be delighted with his purchase, and the Board had been singularly foolish to have sold out at that figure. Hobson had also made a handsome profit from sites in Clerkenwell and in Shaftesbury Avenue and had paid Robertson several hundred pounds for them.[65]

Several minor officials were also involved. Goddard's son Matthew had made a modest but useful take, and Walter Bradly, who was the official next in line to Goddard in the valuing department, had engaged in land operations in Battersea and Deptford. This was land which the Board was apparently going to take and on which Bradly did well for himself. Finally, among the paid officials of the Board, there was the case of John Hebb, the assistant architect, who was charged with the inspection of theatres. That he was a competent architect with some standing in the profession is implied by the shock *The Builder* professed when he was exposed.[66] Hebb's offense had been the writing of requests for tickets to a number of theatre managers, who, one suspects, would not have been so incensed at the practice had it not been for the Board's attempts to make them conform to safety standards. Admittedly Hebb's actions were highly improper, especially for an official who had to sit in judgment on the managers, but if this was graft it was so minor and so amateurish as to be ridiculous. Certainly it was not worth the emotional lather into which *The Times* worked itself.[67] And, as it happened, some of the theatre managers retaliated by sending Hebb seats located behind pillars or in other impossible parts of the house.

Unhappily, the Herschell Commission was not able to hear Vulliamy's explanation of the behavior of his trusted assistants, though he probably would not have had much to contribute. It had been apparent for some years that he was no longer up to his duties. As the deputy chairman of the Board observed, for at least the past four or five years "Mr. Goddard and Mr. Robertson were Mr. Vulliamy."[68] It had been a point of discussion in the Board whether he ought to be asked to retire, a step that he was reluctant to take because he was hard pressed financially. His resignation, which took place in the spring of 1886, was not the result of a voluntary decision.[69] But, having shed Vulliamy, the Board had trouble finding a satisfactory successor, and he was allowed to return briefly. Then, just as the *Financial News* unleashed its first charges, Vulliamy died.[70] It was a sad end to what, in some respects, had been a distinguished and highly honorable career.

There was little that Robertson and Goddard could do by way of defense before the Commission. Robertson made a dismal impression. His lies were elaborate and transparent, and before he was due to appear a second time he absconded, unwilling to face another encounter. He returned later and, in a maneuver to gain immunity from prosecution, offered to give further evidence, but the Commission declined to call him again.[71] The two Greys took off for the Continent before they could be summoned and therefore did not appear before the Commission. As for Goddard, he was medically unable to give evidence — apparently his illness was legitimate — and was showing symptoms of mental instability. Villiers introduced a number of letters from Goddard, some of which showed a strong animus against Robertson, from whom he seems to have feared blackmail. Other letters clearly indicated a man who was coming apart. Goddard announced that he was taking up spiritualism, and reported that he was suffering the agonies of hell. "If you knew the pains of the damned," he wrote Villiers, "they could be something like mine."[72]

Painful as was the exposure of paid officials of the Board, even more shocking were the revelations about two of its longtime members. Certainly, Francis Hayman Fowler had been a pillar of the Board since he had been returned for Lambeth in 1868. He had been active in its affairs at Spring Gardens, and outside he had pushed for good causes. As chairman of the movement for freeing the bridges of tolls, he had done important and useful work. About J. E. Saunders there had been whispers, suggestions that some of his commissions as architect were not unrelated to his membership on the Board. The *Financial News* had hinted that his appointment as architect (or collaborator) on the Pavilion and on the Grand and Metropole hotels (Northumberland Avenue) had come simply because of his position at Spring Gardens. The "facts are no secret to Mr. Saunders' brother architects. They have, we are assured, frequently formed a subject of discussion in professional circles, both public and private. They have been the occasion of comment by officials of the Royal Institute of British Architects. Doubtless the Metropolitan Board takes a less squeamish view of them."[73] As early as 1879 and again in 1881 and 1883, successive presidents of the Institute in their inaugural addresses had attacked specifically the misdeeds of which Saunders and Fowler were later found guilty and had mentioned the MBW by name.[74] Rumors, perhaps more than rumors, had circulated about the two men, but it took the Royal Commission to bring in a bill of particulars against them.

Both men were members of the Building Acts Committee, and, more significantly, were on its five-member subcommittee on theatres. That position, combined with their technical knowledge as architects, enabled them to extract a toll for advice and services, largely nominal, from those who had (or wished to have) dealings in Board property or those with building problems over which the Board might have some jurisdiction. As the Herschell Commission put it, "their official position led people to seek out their professional services."[75] Both were specialists in theatre construction, and both were members of the Royal Institute of British Architects (RIBA). Both men, and especially Fowler, had such solid reputations that the Commission was genuinely surprised, in spite of the allegations already published about Saunders in the *Financial News,* to find how deeply implicated they had been. What shocked the Commission most was the refusal of either man to admit that he had behaved reprehensibly. Fowler, for example, made himself out to be unbelievably naive in his refusal to see a connection between payments made to him and services he was expected to render with the Board.

Q. 7452   "We know now that it [£100] was paid to you as a bribe. Did that never occur to you at all?   —I should think not."

Q. 7454   "Your position never seemed an equivocal one even to you?   —It did not."

Such answers seemed preposterous to Herschell, who in the Commission's report registered no doubt about "our duty to express emphatically our condemnation of their conduct, and the more so inasmuch as they have . . . sought to justify their proceedings and assert even now that they see no impropriety in them."[76]

Fowler and Saunders acted sometimes together, sometimes separately, and sometimes in cooperation with Goddard or Robertson. One case was that of the Albany Road estate in Camberwell, for which, on Fowler's motion, the Board had turned down the plans. When the builder appealed to Spring Gardens, he was put into contact first with Fowler, who made a number of suggestions, and then with Saunders, who made some more. For these services Saunders received fifty guineas and Fowler fifty pounds.[77] The affair of the Criterion Theatre offers another interesting example of their collusion. The Criterion, the underground theatre at Piccadilly Circus, had simply been declared unfit by the subcommittee on theatres, and the Lord Chamberlain was therefore expected not to renew its license, which was to expire shortly. The surveyor engaged by the proprietors was unable to get any information from the Board as to what could be done, and ultimately sought the advice of Goddard, who suggested a consultation with Fowler and Saunders. They agreed to advise, which they did with such success that the Board reversed its previous ruling and informed the Lord Chamberlain that it was not necessary to close the theatre. The new decision was pushed through the Board with the aid of speeches by Fowler and Saunders, who pointed out that the proprietors were willing to make structural alterations. For their efforts on behalf of the owners, Fowler and Saunders each received 100 guineas and Goddard 50 guineas.[78]

Saunders's misdemeanors were admittedly more flagrant than Fowler's. He had managed to get himself employed profitably as architect of the Grand Hotel and the Hotel Metropole in Northumberland Avenue. He had suggested to Frederick Gordon that he tender for the Northumberland Avenue sites, and that he be associated with the operation as joint architect. Gordon labored hard before the Commission to prove that Saunders had done something for his substantial fee — more than £3,500 — but with little success. Lord Herschell implied that

Saunders's major service, as Gordon must have known, was to oil the wheels at Spring Gardens.[79] Saunders had also been helpful in cases where advice was useful on the purchasing or leasing of land held by the Board. Statham Hobson, for example, had consulted him on his (Hobson's) bid for the land on which the Colonial Institute was later built, and had paid him £100 for his advice.

As the *Financial News* had suggested, Saunders had also been deeply involved in the Pavilion scandal, where he had solicited a commission in a singularly bald fashion. Aware, no doubt, that employment as Pavilion architect would be exceedingly profitable, Saunders had intimated through an intermediary that he would like the appointment. He had managed to displace the firm to which Villiers had been tentatively committed, and in the end had become the official architect of the music hall — though his drawings of the elevation proved so unsatisfactory that another architect had been commissioned to design that. Obviously, Villiers had not particularly wanted Saunders as his architect, but had concluded that it would be imprudent to reject him after he had offered himself so brazenly.

There was no evidence, the Commission conceded, that either Fowler or Saunders had thrown unnecessary difficulties in the way of architects applying to the Board. But there was considerable dissatisfaction with the way applications had been treated, and with the Board's practice of not giving reasons when applications were rejected. Obviously a disappointed applicant could not expect the Board to provide him with substitute building plans. But the Board's policy left the way open for an agency within the Board which could smooth out such matters, and the two architects filled this need. Clearly, the Commission observed, both Robertson and Goddard had thought that Saunders and Fowler could ease the path of an application, and they had had good opportunities for knowing.

One is puzzled by Saunders and Fowler's insistence on their innocence. It seemed, in part at least, a sincere emotion, felt by men who appeared to think all the fuss rather absurd. This issue is probably related to the rise of the professions in the Victorian age and their battles to establish standards of ethics to which their members would be obliged to conform.[80] The behavior of the architectural profession, one gathers, had never been worse than in the years 1830–1850, but after 1850 it improved, partly because of pressure exerted by the RIBA. Yet commissions obtained through special and unfair influence had by no means disappeared. Early in the century it had been standard practice to use every device, fair or foul, to get a commission, and certainly the vestiges of that habit had not wholly disappeared. Can Fowler and Saunders be considered holdovers from earlier days, unhabituated to the new ethos? Whatever the explanation, their sense of the distinction between public responsibility and private profit was, to say the least, badly blurred.

This fuzzy delineation of the spheres of public and private interest was clearly a factor contributing to the odor of corruption in Spring Gardens. The Board consisted, in the main, of small business and professional men, not of civil servants or even of politicians. Membership was part-time and officially nonremunerative, and the perspective that members brought to their duties at Spring Gardens was often that of their own trade. A hazy distinction between private interest and public responsibility was almost inevitable. Indeed, the position was complicated by the fact that it was perfectly possible for a member to be involved in legitimate business dealings with the Board. Membership was not intended to injure a man in the practice of his trade or profession. The Herschell Commission, which thoroughly deplored the activities of Fowler and Saunders, recognized Fowler's point when he argued: "Because I go to the Board I am not going to cut my throat if a man comes for an opinion. It would be impossible for a professional man to join the Board, particularly an architect, if he were precluded from earning a fee for giving a professional opinion."[81] The point was a good one, even if it had little relevance to the cases of Fowler and Saunders.

Although the Commission did not find Spring Gardens a slough of corruption, it saw in some of the Board's procedures an encouragement to misconduct. One of these procedures concerned the handling of land transactions, which was done by the Works and General Purposes Committee. A large and unwieldy body, the committee was unable to make intelligent decisions on technical problems and therefore had to depend to an excessive degree on the advice of its paid officials. Thus Robertson and Goddard, with only feeble supervision from the infirm Vulliamy, could play fast and loose with the Board's interests, and Fowler and Saunders, the sole architects on the Board for some time after Sir William Tite's death in 1875, were also able to turn their position to profit.

But aside from the activities of this group of four the Commission was able to find little that was discreditable. In fact, the other charges of the *Financial News* fell pretty flat. Some notice was paid to the allegation that George Brown, a member of the Board, had used his position to prevent the tearing down of a house of his because it was a safety hazard. The Commission thought the claim justified but, since it seemed to be only an isolated case, attributed little significance to it. Moreover, there proved to be little substance to charges that the Board had placed its advertising in favored newspapers such as the *Metropolitan*. And James Beal and E. C. Keevil emerged clearly as irresponsible rumormongers. Beal had been writing to the newspapers, implying that he had a quantity of fresh, damaging evidence when he literally had nothing new.[82] Keevil, too, had shown his inability to distinguish between fact and rumor. His charge of corruption was documented by such observations as, "hundreds of people will tell you that the Metropolitan Board is corrupt."[83] Such charges recalled the weary old questions of corruption in the engineering department, of the Odessa affair, and of the contract with Furness. It was all exceedingly tiresome and, the Commission concluded, largely without foundation. Indeed, the engineering and finance departments were given a clean bill. The Commission commended especially Arthur Gunn, the chief accountant, who had his facts at his fingertips and obviously ran a highly efficient office. More than that, the Commission went out of its way to praise the financial policies and administration of the Board.

All of the members of the Board were invited to appear before the Commission in its search for sharp dealing. Most of them had little to contribute, but some evidence emerged of control, though not dishonesty, by a small ring or inner cabinet. It is exceedingly difficult to identify the members of this inner ring. George Edwards, deputy chairman in the years 1886–1888, thought that Colonel Munro, William Selway, John Runtz, and two or three others (including Fowler) were members,[84] a charge that was promptly denied by Runtz.[85] Another member denied that either Fowler or Saunders was a member.[86] Plainly Selway and Runtz were men of great influence at Spring Gardens. They spent an enormous amount of time in the work, and their colleagues had confidence in their judgment. One suspects that this inner group, which no doubt existed, was in reality a shifting, informal body, composed of those who seemed most committed to the Board and who had impressed their fellow members as men of wisdom and integrity. Among this group, the Commission could find no evidence of corruption.

In short, there were plenty of grounds on which the MBW could have legitimately been attacked, but wholesale corruption was not one of them. Its vision was narrow: in its debates and some of its activities it revealed a tradesman's mentality. Its procedures were overly secretive, so that questionable decisions got little airing and such men as Goddard and Robertson had the opportunity to carry on their corrupt activities without exposure. Clearly, more work had been thrust upon the Board than its constitution and procedures permitted it to handle properly. But only a relatively small amount of graft was uncovered, and that was localized in one department.

The Commission concluded that "against the vast majority of [its members] not even a suspicion of corruption or misconduct has been breathed. We believe that many members of the Board have cheerfully given for the public good much valuable time, and have rendered most important public services."[87] This verdict was so encouraging to many members of the expiring MBW that it revived their hopes for the future. The Commission did not agree with the extreme charges of the municipal government enthusiasts, some of whom continued to howl after the report had been submitted. Mark Judge for one, the architect from Paddington, recently elected to the Board, was audibly dissatisfied with the Commission's conclusions. His Inquiry Committee, which had been formed to press the charges against the Board and its officials, had been represented at the hearings by its own counsel, and to this he had not hesitated to leak presumably confidential material from the Works and General Purposes Committee's proceedings.[88]

In actuality the motives behind the campaign against the MBW were largely political. Accusations of corruption, graft, and jobbery were useful weapons with which to attack a body that was regarded as an obstacle to the attainment of a municipal government for the metropolis. The charges against the Board as a "den of thieves" were the fulminations of men who wanted it out of existence for reasons that had little to do with its procedural probity. Although there had been some corruption, and it had been going on for too long, the level of the Board's performance on the whole was high. The deputy chairman, E. R. Cook, in addressing Lord Herschell reminded him that "there are a good many old members of the Board who have been deeply pained and hurt by the comments which they see in the public prints, and which they hear around, in which we are all classed together as if the whole of the members of the Board were dishonest. We are called thieves and bandits; we are spoken of as corrupt in every sense of the word."[89] One cannot help feeling some sympathy for its members, but the fate of the Board as an institution was already settled. Was there, however, the hope of a blessed resurrection for its members as members of the new London County Council? Alas, it did not work out that way. When the returns came in, they showed that only a few Board members had been able to make the grade, and these were chiefly the reformers who had been elected to the Board during its dying days. There could be no doubt that the metropolis wanted to have done with the MBW and its membership—wanted to move ahead with a municipal organization which would contain few reminders of the past.

CHAPTER 9

The Twilight of the Metropolitan Board of Works

Throughout its life the MBW was doomed to carry on its operations in an atmosphere of impermanence. Sir Benjamin Hall recognized that his Metropolis Local Management Act of 1855, which created the Board, was a compromise solution to the problem of London government; then, however, it was the strongest medicine that metropolitan opinion would accept. Later Hall himself was quoted as saying, "I have never considered my measure as at all complete, but I was very glad to get anything passed at that time."[1] No doubt he was interested primarily in solving the metropolitan drainage problem. But in 1855 he also spoke of the Board as an institution which, under favorable conditions, might develop into the kind of central administration that London so badly needed. "I knew that, unless great and speedy radical changes in the constitution of its local affairs were effected, it was utterly hopeless to expect those affairs to be conducted."[2]

Year after year, the Government piled added burdens on the Board—bridges, parks, theatres, baby farming, and other duties— responsibilities which it could not readily refuse and indeed showed no reluctance to accept. By the 1880s, toward the end of its life, the Board was carrying on many of the activities of a municipal government but without either the organization or the power to sustain them. This Board, John Stuart Mill had told the House of Commons as early as 1868, "was created for a limited and temporary purpose, and it had gradually become a central municipality."[3] To that *The Times* added its

193

epilogue: The Board "shows the craving that exists for central administration, and yet it is not the kind of institution required . . . It is not
really a representative and popular body, but it is a 'body,' and that
seems to be enough . . . It was pressed into one service after another,
until it became a powerful, permanent, busy, and not ineffective corporation. It may not represent the metropolis, but it has drained London."[4]

From the beginning there had been doubts about the Board's composition and the scope of its activities. Certainly it looked like a feeble instrument to use in dealing with a metropolis that in 1854 "contained more
people, more wealth, more power, more moral worth, more of everything good and everything bad, than all the states of Greece put together
and . . . a greater number of governments than even Aristotle might
have studied with advantage."[5] Before long, objections were raised both
to its composition and to the double election process by which its members were selected.[6] The result, it was argued, would be a set of "vestrymen on pedestals"[7] (as *The Times* later termed them), men chosen by
each vestry from its more active members; and the indifference with
which the public regarded the vestries would be transferred to the
MBW. Given this electoral process, it was unlikely (wrote Mill in 1861)
that any of "the very best minds" of the locality would find their way onto
the Board.[8] A constant stream of criticism was directed against its
method of election, and there was widespread dissatisfaction among concerned citizens. One suspects that perhaps the chairman of the Board
himself sympathized with this concern, though naturally he refused to be
drawn into the debate.[9] Some Londoners thought that direct election
was the only way in which interest could be enlisted in local affairs. But
the critics never made any real progress in changing the method of election, and at the end of its life the Board had substantially the same form
as it had had at the beginning.

As one looks back, it seems almost incredible that London had to wait
until almost the end of the century before it received a rational government. Other British cities had achieved this decades before. While the
industrial cities of the north were battling against vicious odds to lay the
foundations of a civic polity, London was still in 1880 "a confused and
anomalous wilderness of parochial jurisdictions and extraparochial liberties, whimsically unequal in their scope and tenour, and frequently irre-
concilable in their pretensions and powers."[10] One is almost tempted to
concede something to those who argued that a sense of community was
wholly lacking in this vast metropolitan agglomeration of many governing bodies. Perhaps the "many" were so strongly entrenched, so aware of
their history and their privileges, as to preclude any attempt to settle the
problem of London government on less particularistic lines.

Could the many be persuaded to give way to the one—or at least to the few? The metropolitan reformers were not only painfully weak in number, but they could not agree on a program. They seemed quite unable to choose between the one and the few—between one centralized government for the entire metropolis and a few smaller, self-governing municipalities that would correspond, presumably, to the parliamentary boroughs. Both points of view were urged before the second Ayrton Committee in 1866, with W. E. Hickson, Edwin Chadwick, and one or two others taking a firm centralizing position (as might be expected), and James Beal and several witnesses, chiefly from the City, advocating a group of metropolitan municipalities.[11] In its final report of 1867 the Ayrton Committee made certain recommendations that Parliament could have regarded as radical. First, let the metropolis be removed from the three counties in which it was situated and be set up as a county in itself. Second, let the Board itself be altered: let most of its members be chosen directly by the ratepayers, its name be changed to the Municipal Council of London, its procedure be somewhat reformed, and its powers be increased.[12] These proposals would not have created a full-dress municipal government in the metropolis, but they would have brought about a substantial change, shocking to some quarters.

The recommendations of the Ayrton Committee got nowhere, and the champions of the few had the field left largely to themselves. As late as 1880 the idea of the few was put forward in an earnest article by McCullagh Torrens[13] published in the *Nineteenth Century,* and it was championed by the City for obvious reasons. Throughout the century, although the problem of London government was not primarily theoretical, those who opposed change went forward under the banner of "local self-government" to battle against the forces of "centralization." Fear of intrusion by the central administration was, of course, deeply rooted in English history, and the designs of the monarchy had been frustrated more than once by London's resolute opposition. The habits of local self-government were deeply entrenched, and Bumbledom could always think of fresh justifications for a scheme of things that had long since outlived its usefulness. It is unnecessary to do more than recall the views of Joshua Toulmin Smith, a barrister and antiquary with an almost obsessive concern for local institutions. A leader of the anticentralization movement and perhaps its most extreme spokesman, Toulmin Smith wrote a shelf of books championing parish government and decrying attempts to cover the ways of Old England with a layer of bureaucracy.[14]

Toulmin Smith was a zealot, and his deification of the parish, especially the urban parish, was plainly absurd. But he was haranguing an immensely sympathetic audience when he talked to London vestrymen. Their commitment to local self-government savored perhaps of some principle, of more tradition, and of a great deal of "anxiety to win a clear field for small jobs, petty authority, and the unchecked rule of number one."[15] In some respects, it was unfortunate that the metropolis had not expanded into open country but had grown through the absorption of villages, many of which had well-established parish governments and resented any idea of incorporation into a larger polity. In some cases, the opinions of the vestrymen were too narrow even for the local parish newspapers, themselves not conspicuous for the broadness of their views. The *Shoreditch Observer*, for example, noted, "Centralisation must be a terrible thing — a monstrous evil — if all the parochial authorities say . . . be true . . . In fact, every improvement which threatened to disturb the crude ideas, and to change the antiquated habits of parochial people is centralisation — a thing to be feared like a pestilence and suppressed like a vice."[16]

During the latter half of the century, as urban living became more complex, opposition to centralization moderated. It seemed increasingly absurd to stress the uniqueness of boroughs such as Islington, Paddington, Chelsea, and Bethnal Green. The Metropolis Local Management Act of 1855, though it disappointed some of the more avid reformers and was widely hailed in the parishes as a victory for local self-government, actually took an important step toward unified government. On the surface the vestries seemed to have had their powers increased because they took over those of the special commissions for paving and lighting that were dissolved; the MBW, too, was not given the power to coerce the vestries. But the act did attempt to deal with the metropolis as a single problem, and it pointed the way inevitably toward a single directive authority over the metropolis. Almost as soon as the MBW was established, there were proposals to make it more representative of the metropolis as a whole, to convert it into an institution that looked less like "a vestry vestrified to the nth power."[17] As early as 1861, the first Ayrton Committee reported in favor of a Board elected directly by the ratepayers, a recommendation which aroused opposition in the vestries and little enthusiasm in the House.[18]

Indeed, throughout the 1860s and 1870s proposals for reform were largely viewed with apathy and indifference. All of them followed the principle invoked by the Royal Commission of 1854 and adopted by the Metropolitan Municipal Reform Association created by James Beal in 1865.[19] Mill's *Representative Government* (1861) had already attacked the low caliber of the Board members and, by implication at least, had called for change.[20] Beal's organization had remarkably little influence, except that it had something to do with inspiring a series of debates in Parliament. The question was first raised in 1865 by Sir William Fraser and again in 1866 by Lord Robert Montague, who deplored the local self-government mystique which had resulted in the metropolis being "martyred for a sentiment, and inconvenienced for a social principle of Anglo-Saxon times."[21] The most significant legislative attempt of these early days, however, came with Mill's two bills, introduced in 1867 and 1868, chiefly for the education of the House and without hope that they would get anywhere. The bills were not well considered, but they called attention to some of the facts of life in the metropolis—that the local "government of the metropolis was a parish government" and that the MBW was unintentionally developing into "a central municipality."[22] Mill's prescription, which accorded both with his own fear of bigness and with the ideas of the Metropolitan Municipal Reform Association, was to set up nine municipalities—one of which was to be the City—corresponding largely to the parliamentary boroughs.[23] Mill's enthusiasm for the City, as might be expected, was not extravagant. In *Representative Government* he had referred to "that union of modern jobbing and antiquated foppery, the Corporation of the City of London."[24] His plan would have rendered the City as respectable and harmless as was practicable; a direct assault on it was obviously out of the question. To nobody's surprise, his final bill (1868) died quickly. It was quite impossible, without Government support, for any such proposal to make progress, and Government support was not even considered. What was curious, as *The Times* pointed out, was the fury with which the bill was assaulted from all sides, especially when everyone had assumed that it would expire naturally.[25]

In 1869 and 1870 Charles Buxton, supported by Tom Hughes, introduced variants of Mill's bills. Here he encountered opposition not only from those who wished to do nothing but also from the champions of a somewhat more centralized government, who had appeared on the scene after the Ayrton Committee of 1867 had come up with its rather radical proposals for strengthening the Board.[26] The details were at the time of little consequence. In the 1870 bills, a central corporation of London was to be set up in addition to the individual municipalities, with a substantial representation of aldermen and councillors from the City. Naturally, the MBW inclined toward the Ayrton plan, which would have transformed the Board into the Municipal Council of London, rather than toward the Buxton-Hughes bills, which would have submerged it in a new body. The Board, indeed, sent a committee to talk to the Home Secretary, reminding him that although the need to strengthen London government was obvious, it was quite impossible to act given "the position of the City Corporation, and its antagonism (instances of which were cited by Sir John [Thwaites]) to all legislative improvements originating with the Board."[27]

Among the reformers the balance was shifting away from those who advocated a series of municipal governments (the few) toward those who favored a unified administration (the one). A deputation with a number of distinguished members called on the Home Secretary, Cross, in May 1873 to plead the cause of a unified municipality,[28] and in both 1875 and 1876 Lord Elcho presented material that further disturbed the complacency of Cross and the other members of the Disraeli Government. Much of it came from J. F. B. Firth's *Municipal London*, which had just appeared. Elcho's argument was effective — partly because it was less specific than the proposals of the 1860s — and it provoked some interesting remarks from Robert Lowe (Home Secretary, 1873–1874). Elcho was ready to get rid of the MBW, despite the "considerable public work and service" it had performed, and he appealed to the City Corporation to broaden its scope and place itself at the head of the municipal movement. Cross, as a loyal member of a City Company, replied without fervor, turning his speech into a defense of the Corporation.[29]

Another resolution, presented by Sir Ughtred Kay-Shuttleworth in 1878, was stronger than Elcho's, and it produced a long and interesting debate. Kay-Shuttleworth's attack was marked by ill will toward the Board. Parodying Milton, he painted an alarming picture of metropolitan London:

> With district upon district, board on board,
> Confusion worse confounded.

His solution, too, was to reform the City Corporation and elevate it into a municipal government.[30] Perhaps the Board did deserve criticism for its shortcomings, but it found some surprising figures among its defenders. The theme running through most of their replies was simply, as Pandeli Ralli (Liberal MP for Bridport) put it, the piling "upon the Metropolitan Board of Works duties of a most incongruous character, from supervising baby farming to demolition of unwholesome dwellings, and from main drainage — its original function — to the storage of petroleum and the care of bridges."[31] Sir Sydney Waterlow, who shortly before had finished a term as Lord Mayor of the City, echoed the same theme; and Charles Dilke, in a speech that in sophistication and knowledge contrasted strikingly with some of the others, came out for a strong central administration, as opposed to the older schemes of decentralization.[32] He correctly ascribed the difficulties experienced by the Board in carrying its bills through Parliament, not to mismanagement on the part of the Board, but to the fault of the House itself, which insisted on considering them as public bills. It was virtually impossible, another speaker noted, for private members to get opposed bills through the House because of the accumulation of Government business. Kay-Shuttleworth won a rather hollow victory. His motion passed the House 116 to 73, but the City had not bothered to oppose it, apparently convinced that Disraeli would not act on the resolution anyway.

In the election of 1880, J. F. B. Firth was returned to Parliament from Chelsea. With this indefatigable and knowledgeable reformer in the House, parliamentary waters became more troubled. Almost immediately Firth brought in another private member's bill, reinforced by a group of Radicals—J. E. Thorold Rogers, T. B. Potter, W. H. James, and H. R. Brand[33]—a bill proposing a strong central authority. More solid and much wiser than Beal, Firth had never accepted the decentralization position of the Municipal Reform Association, and this bill contemplated a central body formed by enlarging the MBW, which would be elected directly by the ratepayers. The *Marylebone Mercury,* finally persuaded that reform was bound to come, agreed that some such plan as Firth's could work well enough: "By general consent the Board has done its work well hitherto, and there is no reason to think it would suddenly become inefficient if it were reorganised on a broader basis"[34] But Firth's bill was squeezed out by Government business and failed to reach a second reading. It was more than ever apparent that a private member's bill would stand no chance of success.

In the following year, the reformers decided that a public organization was needed to agitate for the reform of London's government. The initial impulse had a singularly obscure source. In 1877 a middle-aged Welshman, John Lloyd, who had served as a J.P. in Wales, had come to London to read for the bar. Like many countrymen in the metropolis, Lloyd was shocked by the random character of local administration, and three years later he ventured to put an advertisement in 1880 suggesting an organization dedicated to agitating for a municipal government. The advertisement was seen by James Beal, whose own organization had accomplished little and was by then foundering badly. The two of them aroused the interest of other reformers, notably Firth, and the result was the formation in 1881 of the London Municipal Reform League with Firth as chairman. The League started modestly enough, but sensing a renewed interest in metropolitan reform, it pushed its campaign with vigor and rapidly enlisted a group of able recruits, among whom were Sir Charles Dilke and Sir Arthur (later Lord) Hobhouse. The League launched a series of Muncipal Reform pamphlets, which included one piece of effective propaganda by Hobhouse, *Some Reasons for a Single Government of London,*[35] largely a reprint of his earlier article in the *Contemporary Review.*[36] This was an admirably clear statement of the case for a unified government in the metropolis. The League quickly gained strength. A comparison of its sixth annual report (1887) with its first puny report reveals its rapid growth. In 1887 Lord Ripon was president, and some other distinguished men were vice-presidents. A group of members of Parliament appeared on the general council, together with nine peers and a number of metropolitan vestrymen. From the point of view of public interest, municipal reform had become a live issue, though, as the League admitted, it had made little progress legislatively.

This was disillusioning because in 1880, when a Liberal Government had been installed, the prospects had seemed favorable. Yet it had soon become apparent that reform would not be an easy matter; indeed, the years 1880–1885 saw Parliament in a singularly distracted state. There was the Irish question (and Irish members who would not allow the House to forget it); there was trouble in Egypt and South Africa; and there was pressure from Radical Liberals for an extension of the country franchise to bring it into parity with the borough franchise. The League applied all possible pressure on the Government, and, indeed, was encouraged when the Queen's speech in 1882 seemed to promise action. In neither 1882 nor 1883, however, were the expected measures introduced by the Home Secretary, and it was not until April 1884 that Sir William Harcourt brought in a bill for a municipal government in London.

Harcourt's bill was widely regarded as presaging the disappearance of the MBW. During the previous year the press had become divided on that issue, largely along partisan lines. Some papers, including the *Daily Telegraph,* thought it a great pity to liquidate such an efficient agency.[37] Others dismissed the Board with a "the-sooner-the-better" leader. The *Telegraph* recalled some of the difficulties with which the Board had had to contend. It found "the powers of this body . . . so restricted, it has to deal with so many conflicting interests, and is hampered by the interference of so many discordant authorities, that it fails, in the main, to compensate for the lack of a strongly centralised and independent municipality. It has no kind of traditions, state, or prestige; it is a big vestry, with a limited sphere of action, and that is all. It is snubbed by her Majesty's First Commissioner of Works one day, taken to task by Parliament the next, and ridden rough shod over by a railway company the third." In January 1884, a speech given by Bazalgette before the Institution of Civil Engineers drew enthusiastic leaders from half-a-dozen London papers. The Board, all admitted, had accomplished an enormous amount for the metropolis during the past thirty years. But the Board had also done so well, the *Daily Chronicle* pointed out, that ratepayers wished to go on in the same direction. They were demanding a common municipality for the whole metropolis, which would be directly responsible to themselves and would have full control of the gas and water supply, as well as of the other important concerns with which the variety of local authorities and private speculators were then attempting to deal.[38]

The cardinal principle of Harcourt's bill was the reform of the City Corporation and its transformation into a central governing body for the metropolis.[39] He pointed to the absurdity, then widely recognized, of trying to set up in metropolitan London a series of municipalities, a practice as reasonable, he suggested, as reviving the Heptarchy.[40] The

City Corporation, Harcourt suggested, had never lost the instincts and habits of municipal government, and it had behind it, of course, a great tradition. His bill specified that below a central council of 240 elected members would be district councils, but these would have no independent authority. Finally, the whole of the metropolis would form the County of the City of London. Harcourt's initial speech was an able one, and its reception, except by the institutions due for liquidation or drastic change, was not hostile. *The Times* termed the bill an "able piece of constructive legislation," and latter-day students are inclined to agree.[41]

During the Easter recess, however, opposition crystallized, and the City Corporation contested the bill. The MBW reiterated its commitment to the idea of a central municipal government, but resented the degradation of the vestries into district councils which would be only committees of the central council. The Board was raising the old "local self-government" cry on behalf of the vestries, and the vestries themselves of course reported almost unanimous opposition.[42] The *Metropolitan* published a long list, covering a column and a half, of organizations and meetings that had passed resolutions against the bill—though without listing the bill's supporters.[43] But the supporters were also active. The Reform League was indefatigable in its agitation, holding meetings all over London at which the City Corporation was roundly attacked for its privileges and for its stubborn opposition to the Harcourt bill. Thus the City, MBW, and the vestries all saw eye to eye in opposing the bill, and were determined if necessary to make a bitter fight of it.

Actually this was not necessary, for the Government, beset on every hand by urgent problems, handled the bill with a conspicuous lack of enthusiasm. Not until July did it get around to a second reading, when time was short and the bill already looked old. Harcourt, however, opened with a vigorous speech. He began by summarizing the sources of opposition, observing that the Mayor and Corporation had done all they could in and out of Guildhall "to carry on the war very much as Mr. Pitt carried on war . . . not only with his own forces but with forces which received such other assistance from the British Treasury as might be necessary to support his own warlike efforts."[44] The MBW, the Home Secretary continued, was not averse to a single government in the metropolis but disliked the one contemplated in the bill. The vestries naturally were little impressed by his scheme, for a basic principle of the bill was that there must be a central control of the vestries to insure uniformity of action for the entire community. In addition, Harcourt recalled, the Middlesex magistrates had come out in opposition "in a series of resolutions so eulogistic of themselves . . . that even Lord Salisbury has stated that he thought them a little strong."[45] The magistrates, obviously, did not look forward to losing their administrative functions. Harcourt defended solidly the principle of a central body, observing that "each succeeding want has been met by giving further authority to a single body—the Metropolitan Board of Works—and not to the Local Authorities."[46]

C. T. Ritchie (who four years later was to bring in the bill that set up the London County Council) raised the bogey of centralization once more,[47] although Firth in a long and wearisome speech clearly established the need for a central authority and detailed the maneuvers made by the City in attempts to defeat the bill. Speaking for the City, a former Lord Mayor proclaimed: "The Corporation of London was now the most perfect Municipal Government which existed in the world",[48] but the current Lord Mayor, R. N. Fowler, elected to aim his fire chiefly at such technicalities as the inconsistencies and contradictions in the bill. Another former Lord Mayor, Sir Sydney Waterlow, who always provided relief from the conventional City responses, came out strongly for the notion of a single central body, though he objected to certain provisions of Harcourt's bill. Gladstone, speaking on the final day of the debate, was curiously ineffective. His words seemed to be those of a leader preparing to withdraw the bill. Questions of local government had never interested the Grand Old Man, and the project of establishing a municipal government for the metropolis lacked those elements of moral appeal that were needed to arouse his most aggressive fighting instincts. In any case, London was far from being the most urgent problem of 1884; his reforming eye was focused way across the Irish Channel. Presently it became clear not only that the Government had given up any idea of getting the bill through but that the interest of the House was minimal. As one Irish member put it, he had no desire to spend a warm July night "in discussing the second reading of a Bill intended to perish."[49] Finally on 10 July, to the indignation of the reformers, the Government did withdraw the bill. All along, the Government had shown little sense of urgency. Harcourt had introduced the bill at a time when it could hardly hope to pass, and any remaining possibility had disappeared in the three months that had elapsed between the first and second readings.

Why, nearly half a century after the report of the Municipal Commissioners on London (1837), was the metropolis without a rational local government? Some of the obstacles have already been hinted at. First, there were still divisions among the reformers, even though by the 1880s the overwhelming majority had accepted the notion of a single body in command and, with the exception of McCullagh Torrens, had abandoned the thesis of the few as opposed to the one. Second, during the 1880s, although the Municipal Reform League had held meetings throughout London and recruited to its banner some prestigious figures, the League was not yet a formidable engine of agitation and its opportunities for bringing pressure to bear on Parliament were limited. Third, the reforming groups had attracted considerable public interest, but it was not yet clear how keen the public really was to have a rational metropolitan government.

These obstacles, of course, were not alleviated by the attitudes of members of Parliament, whose responses varied from fear to indifference. Absurd as it seems today, fear was a factor of some importance, possibly of decisive importance. There was a pervasive reluctance to create an *imperium in imperio*, set up in London, that could intimidate the central government as Paris had repeatedly intimidated France. Parliament had no intention of establishing new local units which might develop into a formidable counterforce. Conceivably, that argument threw dust in the eyes of members who feared an imminent decline in the prestige of Parliament. And in 1884, when opponents abstained from using the argument, Gladstone could point to at least one bogey that had died a well-deserved death,[50] even though his remarks brought forth cries of "No, no!" from the members.

The truth is that the House as a whole had little interest in London's government and its problems. Debates on metropolitan questions were treated with monumental indifference. Even Harcourt's important speech on the bill's second reading, as Ritchie pointed out, drew only between fifteen and fifty members.[51] This was typical. A debate on London government could empty the House with amazing speed, and unless the Government was prepared to crack the whip there was not much chance of getting such a bill through. Most members of Parliament, and especially those from the provinces whose constituencies were even less concerned with the problem, were not interested enough to listen to the debates, still less to take an active part in the battle.

Although the reformers had gone beyond the earlier notion of dividing the metropolis into a series of municipal governments, Ritchie once again brought forth the well-worn anticentralization thesis during the 1884 debate on the Harcourt bill,[52] and the Conservatives proceeded to adopt it as their prescription for the metropolis. No doubt their espousal of this plan reflected their connections with the City, which was finally beginning to feel its way toward a method of dividing the metropolis. Throughout the century, the face of the Corporation had been stubbornly set against reform. "Do what you want with the metropolis but leave the City alone," had been its cry. The government under which the City functioned had been both wasteful and full of legalized graft — jobbery, sinecures, and lavish expenditures on unnecessary luxuries. The Corporation was indeed an anachronism, but like many other anachronisms — especially those well protected by financial resources — it had successfully resisted all efforts at liquidation. The City was fabulously rich, and its semi-independent government, guaranteed (so the Corporation argued) by a series of charters extending back to the early Middle Ages, gave it a powerful voice in metropolitan questions. In Parliament, its interests were safeguarded not only by its own four members but also by many other members who happened to be liverymen of the City Companies or who otherwise enjoyed close relations with City interests.

Nonetheless, it had come to a point, the *City Press* reflected in 1885, when change was not only desirable but necessary.[53] And the Corporation's committee on municipal government was slowly mulling over a proposed bill.[54] To have come this far was a distinct mark of progress, for the Corporation was intensely jealous of its position and authority, bristling whenever another governmental agency wished to enter the City. The Corporation had proposed originally that it and not the MBW should build the section of the intercepting sewers that passed through the City, and it had resented the idea that the Board should lay down Queen Victoria Street in the City. Against this kind of resistance the head-on attacks of reformers were bound to fail. Inevitably they aroused the bitterest opposition, not only from the Corporation but also from those who had a nostalgic attachment to the City and regarded it as a bastion of English liberty. During the latter half of the century, however, the reform movement began to make slow inroads on the traditional practices of the Corporation. The City's well-financed public services became the most efficient in the metropolis, and it spent large sums on such public improvements as the Holborn Viaduct and on amenities like Epping Forest and Burnham Beeches. The Corporation thus sought, and quite successfully, to justify its existence and the retention of its privileges.

Although implied threats from parliamentary sources had been sufficient to start the City on its way to reform, before the 1880s its traditional status had not been seriously menaced. On a few occasions, the Corporation had had to exert itself to prevent change, but ordinarily little effort had been required. The bills brought in by reformers in the 1860s and 1870s had had so little support in the House that the City had viewed them with unruffled calm. But Harcourt's bill of 1884 raised cries of alarm.[55] It seemed to be aimed directly at the City: the expansion of the City Corporation, which it proposed, would have changed the Corporation's character so completely as to mean its virtual abolition. Such, at least, was the argument advanced by leaders in the City, and they took extreme measures to defeat the bill. As was revealed before a Select Committee appointed later on the motion of Charles Bradlaugh and George Howell,[56] the Corporation, or its agents acting on the authority of a special committee of that body, had gone to desperate lengths to prevent the enactment of the bill. Though malversation in a legal sense was not established — it would have been difficult to do this other than before a court of law — the Select Committee elicited the fact that in one year (1884) over £14,000 of the Corporation's money had been spent in fomenting militant opposition to reform among the London populace.[57] A nauseous story emerged: reform meetings had been disrupted by paid bullyboys; forged tickets to meetings of the Reform League had been printed and circulated in order to pack its meetings with opponents; and a bogus antireform body, the Metropolitan Ratepayers' Protection Association, had been created and generously subsidized. The Corporation's expenditure had been so excessive and the exploits of its committee (or the committee's agents) so disreputable that responsible opinion in the City was shocked. Even the *City Press* conceded that tighter control should have been maintained.[58]

It became very apparent that the City presented the most formidable opposition to the hope of making London into a municipality, far more so than that of the vestries. Since the head-on attacks of the reformers had been ineffective, a different approach — a flanking movement, which might in time neutralize the City Corporation — was attempted by C. T. Ritchie, president of the Local Government Board in Salisbury's Ministry. Often the British dealt with cumbersome relics of the past in this manner rather than by trying to destroy them.

Ritchie's local government bill of 1888 had to do with county government in the country at large. But certain clauses, which were almost concealed in the text, proposed to separate London from the three counties in which it was located and to establish it as a new county with its own council — the London County Council (LCC). Ritchie had obviously undergone a change of heart during the previous four years, for while in 1884 he had opposed Harcourt's bill in the name of local self-government, he now asserted that London lacked "any authority which has the weight and power which an authority proposing to speak in the name of so great a centre ought to have."[59] Ritchie was careful to deny any connection between his bill and the scandals surrounding the MBW. The bill, he insisted, had been in first draft some eighteen months earlier, before the *Financial News* had unloosed its charges against the Board.

The reformers, if Firth is any guide to their reaction, greeted Ritchie's bill with general approval, apparently because it seemed to treat both the MBW and the City more roughly than Harcourt's bill had done. "The general position," Firth concluded, "is that the Metropolitan Board of Works dies at once — like a man who is beheaded — but the City of London is only to die gradually."[60] Surrounded by a free municipality, it would be only a matter of time before the Corporation expired. But Firth was wrong. Ritchie's bill was really less radical than Harcourt's: by disturbing the City so little the bill gave it what it wanted. Indeed, the City itself could find only a few points of contention. It resented, for example, the denial of its right to elect its own judges as well as the Sheriffs of Middlesex County, and on these points the *City Press* burst forth with a threatening leader: "Hitherto, no Government, however strong, has been able successfully to attack the City. The Corporation's arm is long, and its reprisals heretofore have been unfailing."[61] Whether these objections were as serious as the City liked to think is doubtful. On further reflection, in fact, the City was rather relieved, not only that it had not been annihilated but also that its power had not been extended over the whole of London, the latter alternative nearly as dire a prospect as the former.[62]

Despite their general approval of the bill of 1888 the reformers raised certain objections, but none of them were substantial. They found the idea of selected members (aldermen) of the LCC, who were to be chosen by the elected members, offensive to their democratic views, and they resented Ritchie's intention of keeping the control of the police and of the Asylums Board out of the Council's hands. Yet when they failed to convince him of their case, they accepted these provisions, which fell somewhat short of their ideal of the complete municipality. The *Metropolitan*, which traditionally had spoken for the MBW and for the vestries, liked the bill because it set up a frankly transitional scheme, wisely leaving local bodies alone for the present but "promising, if Providence and the Opposition permit, to deal with them in good time."[63]

Students of municipal affairs have since deplored the fact that Ritchie did not grasp the nettle more firmly. He had not interfered with the vestries, which were, after all, the institutions that had given the MBW its particular character. These continued unchanged for another ten years. He also left untouched the bewildering chaos of authorities and districts in the metropolis. A decade before, one student had calculated that a map of London showing the various districts set up for the purposes of education, of justice, of the police, and of the metropolis management acts would contain some three hundred colored patches running into and intersecting one another in a crazy fashion, divided by lines that might run down the middle of a street or might even bisect a house.[64] This was true enough. It might have been better if metropolitan government had been reconstructed according to some rational plan, but English reformers have rarely proceeded in that fashion. To preserve an anachronism, but to alter it gradually so that it can meet the new situation with reasonable success, has been, for better or worse, the more characteristic English approach. Ritchie's bill was not an heroic document, and it went through Parliament with comparatively little fuss. Actually, those in the House of Lords who objected to the reorganization of London government did so only on the grounds that the measure was not sweeping enough. Yet, cautious as the Local Government Act of 1888 was, it sup-

plied the metropolis with a popularly elected council, and in a large degree it altered the tone of metropolitan government.

The quality of the new LCC contrasted dramatically with the medioc-
rity of the old MBW. Oddly enough, the members of the Board had
gravely underestimated the obloquy they had attracted, and a considerable number (most of them, in Magheramorne's view) had confidently
expected to be elected to the new body. But this was not to be. The scandals unveiled by the Herschell Commission had obviously had an effect
on the electorate, even though it might not quite have agreed with the
harsh judgment of Stead's *Pall Mall Gazette* that the Board seemed to be
"divided into two classes: clever knaves who jobbed and virtuous nobod-
ies who winked."[65] But beyond all this, London was simply tired of the
MBW. As *The Times* put it, "We want to get out of the groove, once and
for all, of vestries and Boards of Works, metropolitan or district . . .
Probably every vestryman and every member of the Metropolitan Board
of Works thinks himself quite good enough for election to the County
Council. We trust the Londoners will think very differently."[66] They
did. When the returns came in, only five members of the Board were
among the successful candidates and most of these belonged to the new
wing. There is little reason to disagree with the judgment of the *City Press*
that the feeling against the Board and everything connected with it was a
potent factor in many constituencies. The new Council was to be pre-
ponderantly composed of "local government reformers."[67]

As for the Board, its twilight was not its finest hour. It seemed determined to compound its felonies by making matters as difficult as possible
for the body that was to succeed it. Its closing meetings were more riotous than ever. Mark Judge, who had obtained a seat on the Board only
to poison its last hours, was a constant source of trouble. He argued persistently that the report of the Herschell Commission had stopped short
of what might have been found out, and he contributed in other ways to
a reign of disorder.[68] As if determined to drink the cup of perversity to
its depths, the Board voted a series of heavy expenditures with which the
new Council would have to contend. The salaries and pensions of its
officers were raised in lighthearted fashion. Then, against appeals to
leave such matters to the new Council, it sanctioned the encroachment
of the Samaritan Free Hospital onto Marylebone Road. When urged in
the Lords, to leave decisions of this kind to their successors, Magheramorne struck a superior attitude, proclaiming that the Board did not intend to be intimidated in the execution of its duty. "This is truly delightful," observed *The Builder*, "as coming from a man who is known to be a
mere ornamental chairman."[69]

The Board's gravest offense in its last days concerned the Blackwall
Tunnel, which it had obtained the power to build at a cost of over

£1,500,000. Etiquette, if not normal procedure, would have led the MBW to abstain from further action and to leave the placing of the contract to the Council. But the Board was determined to make one last assertion of its authority. Speeches were made to the effect that the Board was not to be threatened by a "licentious press." Two deputations, moreover, appeared from the East End parishes to urge the Board to keep its memory green by going ahead with the tenders, deaf to protests from the LCC and the Local Government Board. This sort of thing was clearly intolerable: the Council could not be asked to take over when its hands had been completely tied by such heavy commitments. Consequently, Ritchie announced that he was prepared to receive an application to advance the appointed day for the takeover (1 April). Given this hint, the Council acted and the doom of the Board was pronounced. It came to an inglorious end on 21 March 1889, before it had had time to do irretrievable damage, and the new County Council promptly moved into Spring Gardens.

The Board's sorry performance during its final weeks, one suspects, confirmed the views of its worst critics. As *The Times* put it on 20 March, London felt that it was well rid of a "body which was so blind to its own dignity, of the plainest precepts of public duty, indeed, to the ordinary restraints of public decency" as the Board had shown itself to be.[70] Indeed, Londoners were soon to look back on the era of the MBW as a bad dream. Historians, including Sir Laurence Gomme, could speak of the imposition on London of "the ugly and useless machinery of the Board of Works," a description which, Sir Gwilym Gibbon and R. N. Bell correctly pointed out in the next century, was "a travesty of the fact."[71] After the passage of fifty years, historians could point to the period of the Board as an age of enormous and unappreciated labor. Even *The Times* of 2 February 1889 (six weeks before the leader just quoted), reflected more sympathetically on the work of the Board. The student, it observed, would probably conclude that before the era of the MBW London had been the worst-governed capital in the world, whereas, during the Board's thirty-three years of existence as chronicled in its final report, it had dealt with some of the worst aspects of metropolitan life and had made London, if not an Elysium, at least not intolerable. But *The Times* also cautioned, and fairly enough, that more than once in its career the Board had missed the opportunity for becoming the nucleus of something greater.[72] "To its good deeds," the paper concluded on 20 March, "justice will some day be done. On its bad deeds, now that it is virtually dead and gone, the most merciful verdict is silence."[73]

8. Peace to Its Hashes (opposite)

PEACE
TO ITS
HASHES

Obiit, March 21, 1889.

TO THE MELANCHOLY MEMORY OF
THE METROPOLITAN BOARD OF WORKS.
IT WAS AN UNFORTUNATE INSTITUTION.
FLUSHED, IN THE EARLIER YEARS OF ITS EXISTENCE,
WITH A LAUDABLE AMBITION
TO COMMAND THE RESPECT AND ADMIRATION OF THE RATEPAYERS.
IT GAVE AN EMBANKMENT TO THE THAMES,
DRAINED LONDON,
AND SUDDENLY SHOWED THE WORLD
HOW JOBBERY COULD BE ELEVATED TO THE LEVEL OF THE
FINE ARTS;
THEN FIGHTING TO THE END, IT WAS MORE ANXIOUS
TO LEAVE AN INHERITANCE OF SPITE TO ITS SUCCESSOR,
THAN TO RETIRE FROM THE SCENE OF ITS LATE LABOURS WITH
DIGNITY TO ITSELF.
UNWEPT, UNREPENTANT, YET UNHUNG,
IT HAS PASSED FOR GOOD AND AYE TO THAT OBLIVION
FROM WHICH IT IS POSSIBLE THE MORE THOUGHTFUL AND
PHILOSOPHICAL RATEPAYER
MAY THINK IT WOULD HAVE BEEN AS WELL,
FOR THE INTERESTS OF MUNICIPAL HONESTY,
THAT IT HAD NEVER EMERGED.

PART II

Vestrydom and the City Corporation

CHAPTER 10

A Bird's-Eye View of Vestrydom

Metropolitan vestries in the age of the MBW were a motley lot. Their most conspicuous characteristic was their almost infinite variety—in area, population, resources, and organization. The Metropolis Local Management Act of 1855 had served to rationalize in some degree the chaos of parish government, but it had by no means established a uniform policy throughout London. The act recognized as district authorities the elected vestries of twenty-two parishes, and to cover the other fifty-six parishes it set up fifteen district boards of works, each acting for a group of parishes and elected by their vestries. There were, in short, some thirty-eight local authorities in the metropolis, in addition to the City Corporation and a number of extraparochial units, such as the Inns of Court and the Charter House. The act also wiped out the old mass of paving and lighting boards which had carried on their business quite independently of the parish vestries, and after 1855 their duties became the responsibility of the vestries and district boards.

The act, however, made no attempt to interfere with parish boundaries, so that even the twenty-two large parishes in each of which the vestry served as the local authority showed enormous variations in size. North of the river, Islington (3,107 acres) had the greatest area; to the south, Camberwell (4,332 acres), though in mid-century still sparsely settled, was the largest. At the other extreme, St. James's, Westminster, the smallest of the twenty-two parishes, accounted for only 162 acres. In some sections, especially in the older quarters, the parish boundary lines

213

were totally irrational. St. Martin's-in-the-Fields, for example, surrounded St. Paul's, Covent Garden, so that it was impossible to get from
St. Paul's to any other parish without crossing St. Martin's.[1] St. Margaret's Westminster, and St. George's, Hanover Square, intermingled in a
most confusing way; while Chelsea had a detached portion at
Willesden.[2] Parish populations varied almost as much as their areas. In
1861 St. Pancras had a population of nearly 200,000, while at the other
extreme St. John's, Hampstead, in the suburbs had 20,000 and St. Martin's-in-the-Fields at the center had fewer than 23,000. As the century
progressed, the parishes of Central London tended, of course, to stabil-
ize or to decline, while those on the periphery grew, and minor alterations had to be made in the arrangement of vestries and district boards.
A number of vestries were allowed to withdraw from district boards and
establish themselves as separate local authorities.

The size of the vestry bodies reflected these differences in population — or rather, the differences in the number of rated householders — in
the parishes. Where there were fewer than a thousand rated householders the vestry would have only eighteen members. Vestry size increased
at the rate of twelve new members for every additional thousand rated
householders,[3] until the maximum of 120 was attained — a figure
reached in half a dozen parishes. It is not surprising that vestries of this
size hailed themselves, at least at the outset, as parish parliaments. If a
parish had over two thousand householders, it was divided into wards,
and voting took place on a ward basis. The method of voting prescribed
by the act indicates that reforming impulses in London were still under
close control. Voting was by show of hands, though a poll could be called
for by five ratepayers.

Another curious provision of the Metropolis Local Management Act
was the attempt to graft on to what had become a purely civil body a reminder of its ecclesiastical origin. The churchwardens and the incumbent were to be ex officio members of the vestry, though things often
worked the other way around and the churchwardens were usually
chosen from the elected vestry members. Indeed, the act appears to have
acknowledged that in some places the incumbent as well as the senior
churchwarden had an automatic right to act as chairman of the vestry,
for only "in the absence of the Persons authorized by Law or Custom to
take the chair" could the vestry choose its own chairman for each particular meeting.[4] One suspects that Sir Benjamin Hall did not realize how
difficult the post of presiding officer would turn out to be for certain gentlemen of the cloth. In most parishes the incumbent abandoned his post
for reasons of prudence, and in others, apparently, from sheer boredom
and a conviction that presiding at the vestry had no special relation to
the cure of souls.

According to the *South London Advertiser,* vestries throughout the metropolis welcomed the new act, along with Hobhouse's Act (which in 1831 had given ratepayers in some parishes the right to vote for vestrymen) as a "Magna Carta of parochial liberties . . . Lambeth is to have a House of Commons of its own . . . Every parish, on either side of the Thames, is to have, like Marylebone [which already enjoyed the freedoms of Hobhouse's Act], its little Senate, and its great debates."[5] The larger parishes were duly divided into wards, as the act directed, and the new vestries were elected. During the early days of the act observers professed to see a marked improvement in the behavior of vestry meetings. To a degree, this was wishful thinking. It is true that in some vestries a number of men of a better social position than those who had traditionally sat there stood for election. Some of these had hitherto taken little part in parish affairs, and their election had an astringent influence on the conduct of vestry business. In St. Pancras, for instance, the first election brought out a number of candidates of higher-than-average status who hoped to accomplish something under the new act.[6] Some of them were elected and did useful things. But gradually they retired—or were defeated—and left the field to inferior men, in whose hands the vestry inevitably deteriorated.

One editor, not unbiased, discovered a great improvement in vestry meetings throughout the metropolis. The old riotous scenes, he confidently prophesied, would be things of the past: the tumultuous uproar; the hired ruffians primed with beer to make a disturbance at the behest of their fugleman; the rabble-rousing speeches. South of the river, he continued, where the vestries had fallen into a deplorable state, the improvement was most striking. In Lambeth, where parochial partisans had gone to meetings as if marching to battle, there could now be found a number of "well-educated and respectable gentlemen going through the agenda in a quiet and orderly manner." The cliques within the Newington vestry had been addicted to jumping on tables, upsetting inkstands, and generally behaving in a boisterous and outrageous fashion. Such exhibitions, the editor concluded with a burst of optimism, were now matters of history.[7]

Alas, this was a pleasant enough pipe dream, but it bore little relation to reality. When the mists rolled away, the same old faces were seen in the vestries and, to a great extent, the same men were in control. It is true that vestry performance was somewhat better and vestry discipline somewhat improved, but this was not a universal development and should not, in any case, be exaggerated. Vestry meetings in the four parishes that are to be examined in detail could be raucous and riotous, full of sound and fury. Even St. George's, Hanover Square, where "the superior class" formed "a good proportion of the whole vestry,"[8] and which was regarded by other vestries as the embodiment of good breeding, was thought exceedingly untidy and informal. St. George's was, indeed, an exception to the general run of vestries. The average vestry, metropolitan opinion held, was simply "composed of men who seek to relieve the pressure of trade or the *ennui* of retirement by the discussion of gas-pipes and paving stones."[9] Such a view was perhaps unfair to numbers of hardworking, conscientious vestrymen, but it was not out of line with the impression given to the Ayrton Committee in 1866 by a number of witnesses.

It was clear by that year that, save in exceptional cases, interest in vestry elections had almost vanished. A succession of witnesses reported that a poll was rarely demanded and that the election might be carried out by a small group gathered in a public house. Immediately after the passing of the Metropolis Local Management Act, these witnesses conceded, there had been renewed interest in the elections and contests in many wards. But later on this interest had evaporated. Chelsea and Newington, for example, reported meager attendances at election meetings, and contests were rare. At St. Martin's-in-the-Fields not a single poll had been demanded during the previous five years.[10] The classic case, cited by J. F. B. Firth, was that of the vestry which issued three thousand notices to ratepayers, but when the appointed day came round only the vestry clerk, a churchwarden, a rate collector, and three vestrymen were present to elect the vestry.[11] The only report to the Ayrton Committee that was slightly encouraging with respect to popular interest was that from William Newton, representing Mile End Old Town. At the last election, he pointed out, the lowest number of votes polled in any ward by a winning candidate had been fifty[12] — not a staggering total admittedly, but enough to make the election more than a hole-and-corner affair. Nevertheless, parish elections in general failed to raise much of a head of steam; in 1885, for instance, less than one in thirty of the electors throughout the whole of London took any part in the vestry elections.[13]

Nor were the issues which occasionally aroused the parish electorate likely to be of much consequence. In 1877 the parishes of Mile End and Paddington, the *Metropolitan* reported, were much agitated over the "refreshment question"—that is, the vestry's (or its committees') habit of eating and drinking at parish expense—and the election focused mainly on that issue.[14] The liveliest issues, however, were financial; it was easy to touch off a drive against rates that were felt to be too high or that were expected to rise. Parochial electoral associations figured in a good many local elections. In a series of satirical articles entitled "Our Vestry," the *Metropolitan* found two associations in its imaginary parish, "The Ratepayers' League" and "The Defence League." The former, with branches in several other parishes, consisted of one clever man and five devoted followers. The latter, a purely local organization, had only three members—president, secretary, and treasurer. The objects of both were laudable, but the public, "which grumbled at 'parochial mismanagement' and 'oppressive rates,' held aloof from either."[15] Though a caricature, this picture is not so distorted as one might think. Usually a parish ratepayers' organization was small, and its life was likely to be "nasty, brutish, and short."

Ordinarily such organizations were called into being by a specific issue in the parish, which aroused in a fraction of the ratepayers a sense of parochial injury. They formed an organization of sorts and rushed to duly convened ward meetings to vote for their candidates. Perhaps they failed. But by the following year these candidates, being men of some ambition, entered into a compromise with the sitting candidates, some of whom retired to make way for the "new blood—a favorite expression which is supposed to include all the virtues,"[16] as the *Metropolitan* put it. To repeat, ratepayers' associations, with their practically interchangeable names, usually represented purely local issues and had no affiliation with national parties, although later in the century local Liberal and Conservative clubs occasionally put forth lists of candidates. Some of the local associations effected useful reforms in the parish and survived for a few years. But it was here today and in liquidation tomorrow, or in rivalry with a still newer group, for most of these organizations.

To more recent observers the typical vice of the Victorian vestries was not corruption or jobbery but the cheeseparing economy that they tried to practice. It is not easy to see—when looking down from a twentieth-century mountain of high taxation—just how hard pressed the London householder really was. In parishes with large numbers of indigent inhabitants, the poor rate could reach staggering figures, especially before the Common Poor Fund was established in the 1860s to equalize in part the burden of the poor. But given the differences in rating practice from parish to parish, one can hardly draw general conclusions about the situation of London ratepayers as a whole. Certainly they thought they were badly used and that rates had reached impossible heights, and such men as Sir John Thwaites were inclined to agree with them. Thwaites, in fact, told the Ayrton Committee in 1866 that, paradoxically, the metropolis would have had sufficient resources to meet the demands that were made upon it, had it not been that a faulty rating principle placed the heaviest burden on those least able to bear it.[17]

Whether justified in its attitude or not, vestrydom was firmly committed to economy as a principle of local government. The "Economical Member" was always a fair target for ironic treatment by the press. Especially contemptible was his attitude toward the paid officials of the parish, particularly when they had the temerity to ask for an increase in salary. The mere mention of the words "increase of salary" sent him into a state of frenzy. "If he is not satisfied with his salary, we can find plenty of men to do the work at half the price," he would announce. This stock argument of all economic vestrymen may have been true enough, but it was, to say the least, shortsighted economy. "Character, long service, extended usefulness, enlarged experience, the wisdom and honour of old age, are nothing worth,"[18] moaned the *Metropolitan*. Vestrydom, as a whole, was not a generous employer. The impression seemed to be, as Firth suggested, that two pounds a week was reasonable pay for an inspector of nuisances, while some vestries thought twenty-five shillings sufficient.[19] Throughout the history of the vestries, economy was a primary consideration, sometimes almost the sole consideration, in decision making.

In some degree, this reflected the composition of the vestries. They were made up predominantly of tradesmen, with a sprinkling of lawyers, physicians, surveyors, and retired businessmen. Parish clerks giving evidence before the Ayrton Committee were at pains to make their vestries appear to be of as high social standing as possible, but it is clear that a large proportion of the members were tradesmen. In the West End, members of the upper and upper-middle classes bulked somewhat larger than in the constituencies to the east and south of the river, though it is less apparent what part they actually took in vestry proceedings. Chelsea counterbalanced a majority of tradesmen with an earl, an M.P., assorted colonels, and some solicitors.[20] St. James's, Westminster, according to its clerk, boasted a superior class of men in the vestry, including Lord Elcho and the Honorable Frederick ("Poodle") Byng. Another witness, however, corrected the impression conveyed by the clerk, pointing out that three of the four wards sent small tradesmen to the vestry and that the five or six men of greater distinction all came from a single ward.[21] St. George's, Hanover Square, with its large population drawn from the leisured class, necessarily included a heavy proportion of gentlemen, "but when they leave town at the end of the [parliamentary] Session for the remaining six months of the year, the vestry is left to a minor class of men."[22] The Kensington vestry was divided almost exactly between forty-three tradesmen and forty-four others, who included twenty-nine gentlemen, three clergymen, three solicitors, three architects, two barristers, two surgeons, one parliamentary agent, and one physician.[23]

In other sections of the metropolis the predominance of small tradesmen was even more conspicuous. A spokesman from St. Martin's-in-the-Fields complained that, though some superior tradesmen sat on the vestry, the highest social classes were unrepresented. Lord Overstone, the banker, had been a member but had not appeared often because meetings set for seven o'clock were "against the attendance of the class of persons to which he belonged."[24] Islington reported a great many publicans on the vestry, as well as a number of city men, but the latter were little concerned with vestry business and rarely attended. As elsewhere, however, the bulk consisted of small tradesmen.[25] A witness from St. George's-in-the-East, too, said that most of the thirty-nine vestrymen in his parish were tradesmen, but insisted that they were in a large way of business. They included a brewer, two engineers, two contractors, two carriers (one of whom used 150 horses in his business), and a wholesale druggist.[26] Finally, Mile End Old Town, through William Newton, reported a vestry consisting of about 20 percent retired men, eight or so professional men, but the overwhelming majority tradesmen.[27] It is clear that the vast bulk of metropolitan vestrymen were in trade on a small or moderate scale, and thus the response of the vestries tended to represent the small tradesman class.

Nobody would deny, of course, that economy is a legitimate consideration in government. But the London vestries seem to have been guided by a penny-pinching, pound-foolish philosophy. The first and often the sole question raised about a suggested improvement was its cost, and such issues as superannuation allowances for officers about to retire produced pitched battles, in which the outlook of the small tradesmen was at its most myopic. To some of them, apparently, nothing mattered but the rates, and the surest way to get elected was to make resounding attacks on the extravagance of the old members and resounding promises to cut the rates. Sometimes, inevitably, they overdid it and got the parish into a position in which even the electors became aware that rates must go up if the parish was to escape bankruptcy. The fiscal notions of the average vestryman would not have been reassuring to anyone who doubted that economy and efficiency were synonymous.

One of the critical problems of the vestry system had to do with the number of vestrymen who attended meetings consistently. It was of little consequence to have landed gentlemen and professional men as members if they rarely appeared. There are, of course, no figures on such matters, but there are occasional hints that often such men were members of the vestry only in a formal sense.[28] Generally speaking, their interest was negligible and their attendance infrequent, for they could not or would not spare the time from their other commitments to go to vestry meetings, especially when these were scheduled at awkward hours. For the vestries as a whole the figures of attendance were not encouraging. Most of the parish clerks who appeared before the Ayrton Committee put the average at about 50 percent. Beal thought that St. James's, Westminster, got only fifteen or eighteen members out of sixty to attend (a probable understatement); and William Newton put the attendance at Mile End at fifty or sixty men out of eighty-four.[29] But for the entire metropolis 50 percent would probably be a fair enough average.

The essential officer of the vestry was the clerk, often though not necessarily a solicitor and, in the larger parishes, usually a full-time administrator. It was the clerk who kept the machinery running while the vestry argued and debated and while reform movements, honest or politically inspired, rose and fell. The prospect of an election to the clerkship was certain to get a huge turnout of vestrymen, most of them committed to one or another candidate. For these posts were regarded as highly desirable as well as virtually permanent for the one elected. But as with every other phase of parish administration, there were wide differences between parishes. As regards salaries, for example, in 1872 Shoreditch paid its clerk only £250 as compared with £520 in St. George the Martyr, Southwark, £470 in Clerkenwell, and £650 in Islington. The clerk of St. Luke's, Old Street, received £800 but had to pay his staff from this, as did the clerks of Bethnal Green (£750) and St. George's in the East (£500).[30] No doubt there were sound reasons for some of the variations in the pay of parish clerks, but it is hard to explain such large discrepancies. In one parish, perhaps, the customary salary was simply continued, while in another a clerk with drive and a solid party of friends might get his pay raised to what he considered a reasonable amount. Whatever he was paid, the clerk was an indispensable figure in the parish hierarchy. Without efficient clerks, certain parishes might have collapsed.

The procedures followed by individual vestries had their distinguishing marks, and the routines differed one from another. The Marylebone vestry met weekly. Others, including Paddington, St. Pancras, and St. George's Southwark, met every fortnight. But Marylebone took a two-month holiday in August and September, a luxury not enjoyed by any of the others. Policies toward admitting the press also varied. Representatives of the local newspapers that were launched in the 1850s were, on the whole, welcomed by the vestries, though with exceptions. Whereas most of the Central London vestries admitted the press, the East End was less unanimous. St. George's in the East and Mile End Old Town received reporters cordially, but Poplar and Limehouse excluded them — to the indignation of the publishers.[31] The handling of meetings varied, too. In some vestries an action did not become final until the minutes were confirmed at the following meeting, where debate might therefore be as lively as it had been on the original motion. There were also differences in the method of choosing the churchwardens each year and in the relation between the vestry and the guardians of the poor.

Not all metropolitan vestries had bent the knee to the Poor Law Board, and as in the case of St. Pancras there might be constant feuding between the local directors or guardians and the central board. In parishes where a local act was still in force in addition to the Metropolis Local Management Act, the chaos could be considerable. In Whitechapel, for example, four bodies were concerned in the government: the vestry, the board of works of the district of which Whitechapel formed a part, the guardians of the poor (who acted as the poor law union, in which Whitechapel had the dominant voice), and a body of sixty-eight members called the trustees (who had been brought into existence by the Whitechapel Improvement Act of 1853). The 1853 act had empowered the trustees to set the rates, but two years later Hall's act had transferred this duty to the vestry. The trustees were, however, still an active element, for they were all assistant overseers and thus saw to the collection of the rates.[32] In parishes which themselves composed poor law unions, relations between the vestry and the guardians were far from clear. The guardians (sometimes called by another name in accordance with a local act) estimated their own financial needs; the vestry voted the rate, increasing or perhaps reducing it; and the parish collectors made their rounds. This procedure, of course, opened the way for bickering and active dissension between the two bodies, and this would have been even more bitter but for some overlapping of membership between the two bodies. The position of the guardians, however, was anomalous in that they might be elected by the vestry but were not responsible to it. In some parishes, to be sure, guardians were elected by vote of the ratepayers, but in others the vestry put them into office. Once elected, however, the guardians were not responsible to the vestry but only to the Poor Law Board. Relations were especially difficult between the two bodies when the guardians wished to launch a forward policy and the vestry wanted to stand pat (or vice versa). It was not, to say the least, an ideal administrative structure.

By the 1880s the enthusiasts for vestry government had declined noticeably in numbers and vociferousness. A parish newspaper in 1884 doubted whether "the Vestry system was the most perfect embodiment of the sacred principle of local government so openly claimed for it."[33] Enthusiasts still howled against the supervision of the Local Government Board and its auditors, and they were visibly pained by the great increase in expenditure caused by the Metropolitan Asylums Board. Denunciation of the Whitehall bureaucrats, the "erratic and tyrannical action of the Local Government Board," would still get a response from vestries and boards of guardians, but the buoyant enthusiasm for local self-government was not what it had been in earlier decades.[34] Indeed, a good many "respectable" Londoners agreed that vestries were a failure, a view which was underscored in the mid-eighties by the inquiry of the Royal Commission on the Housing of the Working Classes. The Commission, which took Clerkenwell as a case study, discovered a shocking state of affairs in the relationship which existed between the vestry and the owners of marginal house property. Twelve or fourteen members of the vestry were themselves house farmers, renting out one-room tenements in old single-family houses. With an average attendance at vestry meetings of only between twenty and twenty-five, this group could form a powerful obstacle to remedial action, especially when they could place a disproportionate fraction of their number on the vestry committees. And there were also ten publicans who held vestry seats and played along with the landlords.[35] Altogether it is not surprising that observers took a pessimistic view. One could only read with amazement, Lord William Compton told the Commission, of what took place at the vestry meetings: "The violence of the language is something extraordinary." And, he implied, the vestrymen in their election of officials, were careful to avoid damaging their own interests.[36] Nor was Clerkenwell unique. From other parts of London came similar evidence, suggesting that parish rule had reached a nearly decadent state.

Yet with all the criticisms that can be lodged against the vestries, they did much for the metropolis. London was a more civilized place in which to live in 1888 — still more so in 1900 — than it had been in 1855, and some of the improvement must be credited to the vestries, assisted and sometimes stimulated by the MBW and the LCC. By Hall's act of 1855 the vestries had been made responsible for certain local duties, the most important of which were paving and care of the streets, constructing and maintaining local sewers, holding house owners to certain standards with regard to drainage, and enforcing a sanitary code of sorts. Of course, as with nearly everything else connected with the Victorian metropolis, there were tremendous disparities between parishes and between local boards. One measure of this is given by the replies turned in by metropolitan vestries to a comprehensive questionnaire addressed to them in 1870 by the MBW. Not only the state of affairs reported but the tone of the replies differed enormously. Since the MBW inquiry had been undertaken in part to defend the vestries and the Board from attack and to show that they were accomplishing important work in the metropolis, the apparent indifference of some respondents must have resulted from either stupidity or unconcern.

In the area of sewer building the record of the vestries was impressive. Lambeth, for example, had laid down fifty-three miles at a cost of nearly £200,000, and Camberwell had spent over £100,000 on fifty miles. Naturally the newer areas, in general, had had more extensive programs, but some of the older parishes also had added creditable lengths of sewers. In paving, the vestries as a whole had made fair progress — some of them remarkable progress. Indeed, the totals spent in the fifteen years 1855–1870 on sewerage, paving, and other improvements were substantial, though, again, they varied tremendously (and in some cases apparently inexcusably) from parish to parish. St. Pancras had spent nearly £885,000, Lambeth over £700,000, Camberwell over £500,000 — all of these were large parishes — while St. George's-in-the-East, Mile End Old Town, Clerkenwell, Chelsea, and others, had all fallen below £100,000, and some of them well below.[37]

The vestries had also made more or less effective provision for watering a high proportion of the streets under their control. (On this topic, some returned answers that are difficult to interpret.) Again, striking differences existed in the cost of watering operations from parish to parish. The cost of carting water varied from a high of £70 a mile in St. Martin's and £67 in Paddington to a low of £19 in Mile End, and the cost of the water itself ranged from £9 to £5, with the average of the larger parishes running between £20 and £40.[38] There was good reason for variations in such charges, but hardly to the degree that was reported.

All in all, Firth concluded, London's greatest advance during these years was in local drainage. In 1856 no more than a tenth of the houses had drained into a main sewer, but by 1876 there were probably fewer than a tenth which did not.[39] Even so, in the mid-eighties the Royal Commission on the Housing of the Working Classes did not find the situation above criticism, largely as a result of inadequate local supervision.[40] This inadequacy was due to the reluctance of many vestries to appoint and pay enough inspectors of nuisances. As late as 1885, there was only one inspector for each 56,000 people in Islington, for each 86,000 in Bermondsey, and for each 105,000 in Mile End, while St. George's-in-the-East had one for each 15,000 people, St. Olave's one for each 11,000, and St. Giles one for each 9,000.[41] The situation would have been dangerous enough if all the inspectors had shown an enthusiastic devotion to duty, but many did not exert themselves sufficiently. Sometimes they found good reasons for not displaying greater energy, for they were not unaware of the strength of the small-landlord group in some vestries, an interest that was concerned to avoid a rigorous inspection. Moreover, inspectors were generally paid very meager salaries, no more than two pounds a week at the most and perhaps as little as twenty-five shillings.[42] Sometimes their appointment had been a purely formal one by the vestry in order to comply with the letter of the law; in any case, the inspectors of nuisances had no technical training but were perhaps ex-sailors or ex-policemen.

The vestries had done their sewerage job with some success. Thousands of cesspools had been filled and the houses connected with the main sewers. Much less can be said of their work in nuisance abatement: in the cleaning of houses; in removing pigsties and slaughterhouses; and in preventing overcrowding in tenements and seeing that they were equipped with proper sanitary appliances. These duties belonged partly to the inspectors of nuisances and partly to the medical officers of health. Unlike the inspectors, the medical officers left a creditable record in the history of the metropolis. They were not particularly well trained, and not all wrote effective reports. Some feared their employers in the vestry too much to take effective action, and others simply lacked drive. But numbers of them stood up to their employers and in some cases (as in St. George's, Southwark) put their jobs on the line, threatened to resign, and in some cases did, rather than join the parish's conspiracy of silence about hazards to public health. Again, vestries showed the greatest diversity in their attitudes toward the medical officers. Some of these officers, encouraged by their vestry, were responsible for strategic advances. Others, frustrated and defeated, could do no more then lay the foundation for future progress.

By the 1880s — indeed, before that — Londoners were taking a dim view of vestry rule. The quality of individual elected and the indifference of the electorate were disheartening to progressives. The narrow views of the function of government held by vestrymen as a whole, their inclination to measure every proposal by a financial yardstick, and the lack of a central agency which could apply pressure — all of these assured that the metropolis would have governing bodies that lacked both vigor and imagination. Yet with all these failings, the metropolis improved almost spectacularly during the rule of the vestries and the MBW. Certainly J. F. B. Firth was no enthusiast for either, but he concluded in 1876 that "with all their faults and defects — and they are many — the Vestries have done much for London. Any comparison drawn between our condition to-day and our condition twenty years ago in any single matter, under vestry control, abundantly proves this. But the benefits have been very unequal."[43]

The five local authorities to be examined in the following chapters — The City Corporation and the vestries of St. Marylebone, St. Pancras, St. George the Martyr, and St. Leonard, Shoreditch — were not necessarily "typical." It is, indeed, hard to imagine any group of vestries that could be regarded as typical, for diversity was the most distinctive characteristic of local government in the metropolis. Perhaps a more representative set could have been chosen. But the range of selection depended on the existence of local newspapers, which are far more revealing of events and attitudes than are the official vestry minutes. The City was, of course, an inevitable choice. The next two, St. Marylebone and St. Pancras, were selected in spite of the fact that they have some similarities, for St. Marylebone was supposed to be one of the best-governed parishes and St. Pancras was at some stages one of the worst and was always one of the most raucously governed. Moreover, it was possible at certain points to study both from the same newspapers. The last two parishes, St. George the Martyr, Southwark, and St. Leonard, Shoreditch, were chosen partly at random and partly because of the existence of a file of useful local newspapers.

CHAPTER 11

The City Corporation

The character of the parishes in the metropolis, with their intertwined confusion and their stubborn localism, greatly hindered the development of a rational form of municipal government in nineteenth-century London. But the difficulty was infinitely increased by the existence of the City of London, that ancient and affluent square mile at the heart of the metropolis which had had its own municipal corporation for centuries and expected its special status to remain undisturbed forever. The City Corporation — protected by over a hundred charters, some dating from the early Middle Ages, and strengthened by a record of courageous opposition to the intrusion of royal authority — was clearly the greatest single obstacle to a unified government for the metropolis. The world had not changed basically for the City, and it was therefore content to perpetuate a scheme of things that had become largely outmoded. The City government, in consequence, had come to resemble an enclave of traditional and chaotic institutions, well-paid sinecures, and customary practices that had lost all relevance to the real world of the nineteenth century. And City spokesmen proclaimed these things to be the historic liberties of Englishmen. "Are the citizens of London — are the people of Great Britain — prepared to resign without a struggle the last of the glorious rights and privileges bequeathed to them by their Saxon ancestors?" asked a Sheriff of the City and a future Lord Mayor in 1858.[1] Throughout the century the City remained the major obstacle to municipal change, jealously clinging to its privileges and resisting any attempt on the part of other metropolitan agencies to compromise what the Corporation regarded as its local sovereignty.

By the mid-nineteenth century the City was, indeed, a curious organism. It had managed to escape the reforms imposed on all the other large old corporations by the Municipal Corporations Act of 1835, though the Government had professed the intention of taking the City's affairs in hand, and the second report (1837) of the Commissioners on Municipal Corporations had concentrated entirely upon London's affairs.[2] For a number of reasons, however, the Whig administration had failed to act. In the late 1830s the Government was already running down hill and was not anxious to challenge the power of the City, which had been loyal to the Whig standard. In addition, however, the City already seemed to be similar to the model that the Municipal Corporations Act was setting up elsewhere. That act had been directed primarily against the close corporations. But the City was one of the few open corporations in which the medieval tradition of free election to the Common Council and the Court of Aldermen still survived in some form. In short, the City Corporation gave the appearance of being a popularly elected body, and its claim of providing local self-government of a semipopular sort seemed plausible.

But the reality was otherwise. Although the Corporation did give representation to the freemen of the City (and after 1867 to all ten-pound ratepayers), it was desperately in need of reform. The assemblies and departments of the Corporation had descended, substantially unrevised, from past centuries; some of the duties of the officers seemed to have little connection with the demands of the mid-nineteenth century; and the whole structure was ill coordinated and chaotic. To reformers the Corporation seemed like some prehistoric monster which had mysteriously survived into the modern world.

To make matters worse, in the middle of the century the population of the City began to decline: although the Corporation's officers, with their "day censuses," were at some pains to prove that the government census, which noted only the "sleeping population," misrepresented the real state of affairs, the number of residents was clearly decreasing. By the end of the century the peak figure of 130,000 reached in 1851 had collapsed to 27,000. Nevertheless, the City was becoming more than ever the commercial and financial center of the vast metropolis of London, and the source of considerable revenue for the Government. In fact, the old residential areas were gradually being taken over by business enterprises, and the City was turning into a gigantic countinghouse-cum-warehouse. The City government began to be needed more to provide facilities for businessmen than to administer a residential district.

Throughout its history the Corporation had received from the Government numerous rights and privileges with regard to trade and commerce. There was, for example, the monopoly enjoyed by the Fellowship of Porters, established in the seventeenth century, to carry corn and other measurable goods within the Port of London. It is not clear how burdensome to consumers this monopoly was, but it raised the question of another privilege which undoubtedly was oppressive. This was the right of metage — the right to levy charges for the measurement of corn and certain other goods imported by sea — which at one time had been a valuable service to the London community but by the nineteenth century had become pure fiscalism. In 1872, therefore, the metage dues on grain were commuted into a fixed duty to be charged for thirty years, and the proceeds were applied to the preservation of open spaces near the metropolis.[3] Then there were the coal dues, payable on all coal brought into greater London (the metropolis extending over a twenty-mile radius). In 1861 ninepence of the total of thirteen pence levied on each chaldron was allotted to build the Embankment, and the remaining fourpence was allocated to the City Corporation for such uses as Parliament should thereafter sanction.[4] This was obviously a highly anomalous impost and was increasingly so recognized. Had both the ninepence and the fourpence not been used for important public services, they would probably have been abolished much earlier. The Corporation had also been granted rights over markets. Under charters from Edward III and Charles I, it claimed rights over the establishment of markets within a radius of seven miles of the City. Other markets (notably those of Covent Garden and Spitalfields) had, however, been established by more recent charters granted by Charles II to private individuals, but the City still maintained firm control over those for cattle, meat, and fish. As a shipping center, too, the City had for centuries exercised conservancy functions over the River Thames, and when in 1857 the Government insisted on a more broadly based controlling body, the Corporation was able to keep its position as the most important single voice on the new Board. It was also able, year after year, to frustrate the efforts of the MBW to gain representation.

The assemblies by which the City was governed, three in number, were the Court of Common Hall, the Court of Aldermen, and the Court of Common Council. The first one, consisting of liverymen of the City Companies, met in the nineteenth century only to select two senior aldermen to be submitted to the Court of Aldermen as candidates for the Office of Lord Mayor, and to elect certain other officers. The Court of Aldermen also had declined in importance from earlier days, though the office of alderman was still sufficiently honorific. Aldermen were elected, one from each ward, for life. The Court, sitting with the Lord Mayor, designated men to hold certain important and profitable offices, and it was in charge of the City's police force. Aldermen were ex officio justices of the peace, presiding as magistrates at Guildhall while the Lord Mayor sat at the Mansion House.

During the nineteenth century the decisive voice in City affairs was the Common Council, which consisted of 206 members in addition to the Lord Mayor and the aldermen. It was in this body that City "stand-pattism" was most deeply entrenched and in which City myopia was native. Nevertheless, a reform group would occasionally appear within the Council and demand a change in some of the Corporation's most dubious practices. Outright corruption in the Common Council was, however, apparently rare, though the legal perquisites were by no means negligible. By his membership a Common Councilman could participate in the "Worship of Gammon" (enjoyment of the perquisites of office)[5] for which the City was noted throughout the metropolis; he would come into contact with men of the highest rank in every department of the public service, and have a voice in the distribution of "a patronage which in extent and value has rarely been equalled by a public body."[6] As a member of one of the committees, the councilman might get numerous free dinners "which would make a Shoreditch 'feeding committee' turn green with envy," and enjoy excursions up and down the river — even, perhaps, a trip to Ireland. "He has a pocket book every year," Firth charges, "which costs more than £1 per head to print . . . he has his pocket full of public gloves; wands to carry on public occasion; heavy medals to transmit as heirlooms to generations unborn . . . schools at which to educate his own children, and rights of presentation at the City of London and other schools for the children of his friends; surely he is a man to be envied!"[7]

Councilmen were elected from the twenty-five wards, roughly according to population. The maximum number of councillors from any one ward was sixteen and the minimum was four. Some of the wards, however, were absurdly small both in population and in the number of inhabited houses. In 1871 Cornhill, for example, with 69 inhabited houses and a population of 309, returned six councilmen, as did Cordwainer, with 62 houses and 382 inhabitants; Bread Street, with 61 houses and 517 inhabitants, returned eight councilmen; and so on up to Farringdon Without, which with over 2,000 houses and a population of nearly 20,000, sent only sixteen members. Overall, in the 1870s the Common Council was returned by the electors of a population of about 75,000 inhabiting 9,305 houses.[8]

The franchise was not exercised, of course, by the total male population or even by the resident ratepayers. The right to participate in the election of aldermen and councilmen belonged only to those who enjoyed the freedom of the City. But to become a freeman, even after 1835 when the requirement was somewhat liberalized, was an expensive process for small tradesmen, and many of them evaded and resisted when the Corporation sought to increase its revenue by increasing the number of freemen. In the early 1850s the Corporation had issued some four thousand summonses to City businessmen of all kinds to compel them to take up their freedom.[9] This the Corporation was clearly entitled to do in the case of retailers, since only a freeman could legally operate a retail business within the City. It was bad enough for retailers when the Corporation compelled them to take out their freedom; but it was worse still when, as one of its victims claimed, the Corporation charged six or seven hundred wholesalers with being retailers in order "to convict us of trading by retail, and thereby oblige us to become free of the City, the object being to get the money."[10] Some of the great merchants and financiers simply regarded the whole business as tedious nonsense and took no steps to become freemen.[11] These men the Corporation was powerless to coerce.

It is not entirely clear today to what social classes the Common Councilmen belonged. In evidence given to the Royal Commission of 1854 on the state of the City Corporation, reformers freely charged that both the Court of Aldermen and the Court of Common Council were composed primarily of small-minded tradesmen. James Acland, secretary of the City of London Municipal Reform Association, "entertaining the conviction, as I do, that counter transactions in small coins have no tendency to give a man an enlarged view," thought that such men were ill qualified for the offices they filled.[12] Acland's evidence about the composition of both courts was, indeed, hardly reassuring. Among the aldermen, for example, in addition to a banker, a solicitor, and two stockbrokers, there were two auctioneers, two wharfingers, two builders, an ironmaster, a retired saddler, a bookseller, a corn factor, a wine merchant, a tea dealer, an upholsterer, a grocer, and a clockmaker.[13] And the Common Council, a much larger body, had a similar composition. Here the largest single professional group contained twenty-one lawyers (who were there, the same witness thought, because of lush opportunities for commissions and jobbery). They were followed by: fourteen stationers and papermakers; thirteen spice, lead glass, and other merchants; ten woollen drapers; eight carpenters, builders, and architects; eight butchers and provision dealers; seven bakers; seven oilmen; seven auctioneers; six publicans; six grocers; six ironmongers; six printers and booksellers; five wharfingers and coal factors; five corn factors; and so on, amounting in all to a very wide variety of trades.[14]

Other witnesses confirmed Acland's case against the City government. One of them reported it to be "notorious that the higher class of merchants in London keep aloof altogether almost from the corporation affairs," leaving them to the smaller shopkeepers who enjoyed having the control of large funds in their own hands.[15] Another, a former governor of the Bank of England, repeated this complaint, adding that as long as the two courts were full of those in inferior branches of trade, the larger financiers and merchants would have nothing to do with them.[16] A director of the Bank, with nearly fifty years' experience of the City, thought that the Corporation had slumped much in general esteem during his lifetime. In his early life, he asserted, the corporation had to a considerable extent represented the principal bankers and merchants of the City.[17] Samuel Morley, the great hosiery merchant and philanthropist, admitted that he had never taken an active part in City government, though he had frequently been urged to become a member of the Common Council. He had neither the time nor the inclination to indulge in some of the rituals expected of Common Councilmen, notably the frequent eating and drinking. Able men, he said, had no leisure for the external show and pageantry in which councilmen were expected to participate.[18]

These views expressed by reformers and critics to the Royal Commission in 1854 were not surprising. The previous Royal Commission had reached much the same conclusion in 1837, when its report had stated that the abstention of the highest classes of commercial men from Corporation affairs was "very undesirable."[19] As for the Corporation witnesses who appeared before the Commission in 1854, they gave a different picture, though by implication they conceded that the reformers' charge had some substance. Perhaps the fairest judgment was that of Thomas Dakin, a chemist and druggist, a councilman and future Lord Mayor. Dakin, while admitting that the civic leaders seldom belonged to the princely commercial houses, nevertheless denied that the Common Council was in the hands of small shopkeepers. For instance, of the eight members from Bridge Ward, six were wholesalers; in Dowgate all six were wholesalers, and this was also the case in Walbrook. Yet it was true, Dakin conceded, that the Corporation did not consist of City men of the greatest eminence. These, as well as some of their less distinguished colleagues, had other and more demanding concerns.[20] Similarly, Charles Pearson, the City Solicitor, took Acland to task for his analysis of the Court of Aldermen. He attempted (with reasonable success) to show that Acland's analysis, while literally true, was wholly misleading; he pointed out that sixteen of the aldermen were county magistrates and eight were or had been members of Parliament.[21]

Ten years later more reliable evidence was at hand when A. S. Ayrton, Liberal M.P. for the Tower Hamlets and an old enemy of the City, called in the Commons for a return showing the occupations and residences of the aldermen and councilmen.[22] He also asked for the number of electors in each ward. The total of these for the whole of the City proved to be 7,163, the numbers varying from 103 in Lime Street Ward to 1,020 in Farringdon Without. On occupations and social standing, the return tended to confirm Dakin's view. The personnel of the two bodies seemed to represent a fair cross section of the upper- and lower-middle classes of the City's daytime population, including only a few members of the business aristocracy. Of the 206 Common Councilmen, eight returned themselves as "gentlemen," ten as "of no occupation," and three as having "retired from business." Twenty-three termed themselves "merchants," and there were a number of professional men—twenty-one solicitors and accountants, six physicians and surgeons, two barristers, and one actuary. Then followed the auctioneers (nine), booksellers (eight), oilmen (eight), wine merchants, builders, warehousemen, tailors, and woollen merchants (six each). The rest of the list recorded the widest variety of trades and occupations, over fifty in all.[23] The councilmen were certainly not of the highest commercial and financial classes, but neither were they solely a group of small tradesmen, although such men did appear among their number.

Ayrton's return also called for the place of residence of the Corporation members, and this was perhaps more significant in determining social standing than was occupation. In 1854 not one of the aldermen and not more than twenty-five of the councilmen lived in the City.[24] Ayrton's return showed that still in 1865 only a small minority of aldermen and councilmen maintained residences in or near the City. No alderman, again, and only twenty-eight councilmen had a private address in the City. But the most impressive point about the return—the point that serves to qualify one's impression of the Common Council as an assembly of small tradesmen—concerns the addresses they gave. These were mostly in the West End or in the suburbs—by no means mainly the lower-middle-class suburbs. To take a ward at random, the alderman and eight commoners from Broad Street gave as their addresses Tunbridge Wells, Upper Clapton, Lower Tulse Hill, St. John's Wood, Highbury Park, Hackney, Finsbury Square, Clapham, and Russell Square. Such addresses are reasonably typical of the entire list, and at the least they suggest deliberative assemblies whose members' private interests had to a large extent shifted away from the City. It is difficult to imagine that a councilman who lived, say, in Wimbledon, in Farnborough, or in Ewell, Surrey, could have given his best thought to City problems or, indeed, could even have attended Council meetings regularly.

In addition, Firth found in 1875 that the twelve great Livery Companies no longer took any special interest in the government of the City. With the exception of twenty-four aldermen and councilmen, all the members of the two courts were liverymen; but of these only about thirty represented the twelve great Companies, two of the richest of which, the Mercers and Ironmongers, had no members at all in the Corporation. Instead, the minor Companies had taken over the membership, with a list headed by thirty-seven Spectacle-makers, twenty-three Loriners, and ten Stationers.[25] This, indeed, was an ironic situation: the great Companies had virtually turned the City Corporation over to the minor Companies. Here, perhaps, is further support for the contention that, as a whole, the members of the Corporation were no longer figures of first-rate importance in the City.

Why, with members whose interests had ceased to be concentrated exclusively in the City, were aldermen, councillors, and other City leaders so bitterly opposed to any change in the status of the square mile? That attitude on the part of the officials — the Chamberlain (finance), the Remembrancer (bills in Parliament and protocol), the City Solicitor, and the others — was natural enough. Their posts were immensely profitable and had been won through long years of waiting, sometimes at considerable cost to themselves. The election in 1853 to the office of Chamberlain, for example, had cost the winning candidate about £5,000. Not only did the candidates have to maintain an electoral establishment of substantial size but they had to pay off a notoriously corrupt electorate.[26] But in addition to those with a well-defined vested interest in the old regime in the City, any intimation of change would also excite indignant cries of protest from ordinary members of the Common Council. Admittedly their perquisites, as Firth pointed out, were agreeable enough. No doubt, too, City tradition and the pageantry of City rituals — indeed, the long history of City polity, in which merchants and tradesmen had spoken for British liberties — also had a deep appeal to those who liked to regard themselves as legitimate successors of the earlier defenders of freedom. But there was also a widely held feeling that the City was the acropolis of the trading classes, the place where they were supreme and where the aristocracy should have little influence. This justification was given in 1867 to the Select Committee on Metropolitan Local Government (headed by Ayrton) by a City watchmaker, who suggested that the "Lord Mayor has a particular political authority, which I consider to be very beneficial for middle-class people; and I think that if you abolish the Lord Mayor of London, you very much abolish the authority of the trading classes, as opposed to what may be called the aristocratic classes." The City of London, he continued, "does give an authority and a position to men in trading communities, which otherwise they would lose, and . . . the chasm would be very large between the aristocracy and the trading classes if such a body did not continue to exist."[27]

The City was, however, generally able to evade without too much difficulty the attempts made to reform its polity. Many Londoners had thought it peculiar that nothing was done to put into effect the recommendations of the Commissioners on Municipal Corporations in 1837. But in the early 1840s there had been more urgent matters than the anachronistic polity of London to deal with, and the Corporation had itself made some minor reforms, none of them of great significance. In 1848, however, the Government was about to promote a public health bill for the whole of London, and in face of this threat to its independence the Corporation had pushed a bill of its own through Parliament. The Corporation had certainly not intended at the time to make the City the scene of an advanced experiment in public health administration; in fact, the City fathers, who argued in and out of season that the condition of the City was excellent, were full of self-congratulation whenever questions were raised. But under the terms of its act, and apprehensive over the approach of another cholera epidemic, the Corporation — or rather the Court of Sewers — chose as its first Medical Officer of Health the young and imaginative John Simon. This story falls outside our period and has been admirably told by Dr. Royston Lambert,[28] but, briefly, the Court of Sewers, goaded by Simon and gradually responding to his flattery and his vision of a City with a high reputation in public health administration, at last acted. Gradually the "dirty" party gave way. Aldermen Thomas Sidney and Henry Lowman Taylor — derisively called by *The Times* "the Defender of the Filth"[29] — abandoned their previous opposition and were, in part at least, converted to sanitary reform. Led by its young Medical Officer, the City rode out the next cholera epidemic, of 1854, with conspicuous success and "emerged as a shining example to the rest of the nation."[30] Whatever valid criticisms could be made of the Corporation's rule, it could no longer be attacked as incompetent in its public health administration.

But criticized it was — and with justice. Back in 1843 the *Westminster Review* had led off with a seventy-five page article, based largely on the revelations of the Commissioners' Report of 1837 and on other less significant documents.[31] *The Times* took up the attack, supporting Simon in his running fight with his City employers, assaulting the Corporation's management, and charging it with widespread corruption and waste. The result of *The Times*'s offensive was the Royal Commission of 1854 on the State of the City Corporation, which gave the City administration a careful scrutiny, though its final recommendations were by no means satisfying to municipal reformers. At least one of the Commissioners had expected the results to be more decisive. Sir George Cornewall Lewis thought "that the City have continued their old system just a little too long, that public opinion among the great body of the community has got ahead of them, and that when the exposure has arrived they find themselves with scarcely a friend out of their own ranks. They are like Louis Philippe when the day of adversity and trial is come: they have nothing to look back upon but a long course of selfish and sordid conduct and there are no acts which enlist any public sympathy in their favour."[32]

The Royal Commission of 1854 heard in some detail from both sides (prosecution and defense), and the inquiry proceeded along familiar lines. What emerged was that the City, institutionally and spiritually, was at variance with the new Victorian zeitgeist. The world no longer held with monopolies, special privileges, and ancient and prescriptive rights. Free trade had become an article of faith among Englishmen, and the City was a prime field in which to apply this gospel. Moreover, since other municipal corporations had been reformed twenty years earlier, the City seemed to be the sole survivor from the bad old days; and its archaic institutions, its financial confusion, and its smug professions of virtue were all out of place in the mid-century world. Much of the evidence given to the Royal Commission attacked the Corporation because of its exclusiveness and because it was a crowd of small tradesmen glorying in their attainment of sham distinctions. The Corporation was rapped for its secrecy and its coziness with its charters, which it refused to divulge to hostile litigants.[33] Witnesses criticized the ill-advised attempts of the Corporation to force tradesmen to take out their freedom at a cost of several pounds each, as well as the old rights which the Corporation still enforced, such as porterage and metage. There were charges, mostly justified, of an extravagant, overcomplicated administration, with an abundance of sinecures and needless duplication of officials. Critics also attacked the Corporation for the incredible complexity of its finances. Money which passed through its hands, W. E. Hickson noted, was deposited in as many as sixty different accounts and was never brought together in a single balance sheet. It was, therefore, almost impossible to reach a fair judgment on the Corporation's real financial situation—a frequent complaint both before and after 1854. Hickson was inclined to acquit members of the Corporation of personal corruption, though he found the finances of the establishment a nightmare and thought that the divided management from which the Corporation suffered throughout its structure was an administrative horror.[34]

There was also the question of secret "slush funds," which were supposed to exist in considerable amounts. It appeared, indeed, that there were such funds, although they were nothing, a City representative insisted, like the secret-service funds of eighteenth-century governments. Still, certain expenditures had been entered vaguely on the Chamberlain's books, such as money spent in opposing bills in Parliament. To defeat, for instance, the Government's bill for removing Smithfield Market from the City, the Remembrancer admitted that £2,750 had been spent on "private modes" of opposition, in addition to the £3,170 used for normal legal charges.[35] His principle, simple and clear, was to oppose every bill which would interfere with the rights and privileges enjoyed by the Corporation.[36]

Against these attacks the City mounted what, on its own terms, was a persuasive enough defense. The Corporation never had difficulty in employing and paying for competent talent, legal and otherwise. The Town Clerk, Serjeant Merewether, provided over seventy pages of useful and somewhat technical evidence on the City's polity and practices; and Charles Pearson, the City Solicitor, entirely at home before the Commissioners, refuted a number of points made by the prosecution. He also tabulated the recent achievements of the Corporation, which appeared to have been always on the side of virtue.[37] Finally, the Corporation placed in evidence a formal fourteen-page reply to the hostile witnesses. This, at least for debating purposes, was an effective document. The Corporation charged misrepresentation of the City's financial management and of the character of the personnel of the two assemblies. The reply also insisted that some of the charges were based on ignorance of current procedures—that, in short, the critics were assuming that eighteenth-century practices still obtained at Guildhall.[38]

The Commission was not, however, convinced, and its detailed recommendations, though less sweeping than the reformers had hoped, would have met some of the most persistent complaints. The Commissioners proposed, among other things, to abolish compulsory metage and the Fellowship of Porters, to cease to require the freedom of the City as a prerequisite for the practice of trade, and to incorporate the City police into the metropolitan force. They recommended, also, that the Corporation's accounts be consolidated as a step toward making them more intelligible, and that the conservancy of the Thames be taken away from the City and vested in a board. The coal dues (which the Commission thought could hardly be expected to continue permanently) were likewise to be placed under the control of a board.[39]

It would be an exaggeration to say that the Government hastened to put the Commission's recommendations into effect. Trouble was looming in the East, and the Crimean War was about to absorb the country's interest and effort. Over the years, however, most of the Commission's detailed proposals were adopted, sometimes through action by the Government, more often by a voluntary decision on the part of the City. At the least, the inquiry put the Corporation on notice that the Government was to apply a closer scrutiny to its behavior and that it had better move, however prudently, toward less exclusivism and more efficiency.

The Commission's more general proposals did, however, include the establishment of a Board of Works (the MBW) for the whole metropolis. The implementation of this measure in 1855 would have provoked more of an outcry from the City Corporation had it not been assumed that the Board would expire once its primary function of sewer building had been completed.[40] To the Corporation the creation of the MBW appeared as something of a threat, though how great was not clear at the outset. The City protested only mildly against what it later professed to regard as its painfully small representation — three members — on the Board. But it made an early attempt to exert control over Board procedures, sometimes indulging in outright obstruction, chiefly through Aldermen Cubitt, Henry Lowman Taylor, and Deputy Harrison. How important the City's influence was in the Board's early days is not easy to decide. The City "group," estimated by the *Observer* as about a dozen,[41] had a good deal of influence in the election of the first clerk (Woolrych) and the first engineer (Bazalgette). Deputy Harrison, in fact, had made a creditable run for the chairmanship, coming in third after Thwaites and Roebuck. Throughout the early days of the Board, the City's aim was clear: to manipulate the Board for the benefit of the City and to fight any diminution of the Corporation's authority.

The fact is that, once adjusted to the new relationship, the Corporation got along well enough with the MBW save when an issue of jurisdiction arose. City ratepayers, of course, howled about Board precepts as vociferously as did other sections of the metropolis, especially those precepts designed to pay for some of the projects of the defunct Metropolitan Commission of Sewers. Although the vestries in other areas were indignant that the City got so much from the Board (largely because the Corporation had the resources to contribute the share the Board required), the Corporation was resentful over what it saw as the small amounts spent by the Board in the City. In June 1859, for instance, when the Board declined to contribute to widening Shoe Lane, the Common Council regarded it as an exhibition of shameful niggardliness, one member pointing out that though the Board had got about £83,000 out of the City, it had returned only £6,450.[42]

The feuding became sharp when in 1862 the Board proposed to invade the City in order to make improvements that the Corporation regarded as falling within its own jurisdiction. Such an instance was Queen Victoria Street, which was to be built in continuation of the Victoria Embankment and was to extend from Blackfriars Bridge to the Mansion House. A deputation from the City got little sympathy from the Government, which professed great willingness to allow the City to go ahead with the new street, but out of its own funds. What the Corporation wanted, apparently, was for the Government (or the MBW) to put up the money with which the City could build the street.[43] But the trouble by no means ended there. The Corporation's Bridge House Estates Committee and its Improvement Committee both filed petitions against the bill being promoted by the Board, and 120 inhabitants of the Ward of Cheap wished to do likewise. Two questions, the *City Press* reflected editorially, were involved: the broad objection to the board's undertaking improvements in the City, a principle which, if it was once admitted, might be carried to horrendous limits; and the more specific question whether this street was really needed. The Corporation, the *Press* urged, had no alternative but to oppose on principle all bills authorizing other authorities to make improvements in the City.[44] The Queen Victoria Street question, indeed, was a crucial test of the City's ability to resist outside interference.[45]

Within the Corporation the issue resolved itself into a tug-of-war between the older, more responsible members and a group of insurgents led by William Lawley, a pawnbroker and silversmith and a die-hard champion of local self-government in the strict City sense. In a fine frenzy, Lawley denounced both the Corporation's Parliamentary Committee for recommending that no further opposition be offered to the plans of the MBW and everyone else who would save City cash by surrendering City principles and privileges. He professed the greatest dismay at any step which would bring the MBW into the City. Thomas Dakin, more realistic, pointed out that a Select Committee of the House of Commons had already voted favorably on the preamble of the bill, and that nobody in his senses could expect that decision to be reversed.[46] Even before the Select Committee had come into being, the City had attempted and failed to make its case for building the new street itself (presumably with the aid of the ninepenny coal tax). In fact, City witnesses had been given short shrift by William Cowper, the First Commissioner

of Works, who had dismissed as nonsense the claim that the building of
the proposed street would invade City rights. The City then tried other
expedients, such as offering £350,000 as a contribution toward the new
street, apparently on the assumption that it would be given the right to
collect the ninepenny coal dues. But Cowper again refused to yield, noting that the City could not possibly handle the work with only the fourpenny tax and that the Government proposed to make no further
grants.[47]

The Young Turks within the Corporation had managed the appointment of a special committee under Lawley's chairmanship, but in May
1863 the members had to report that the bill for Queen Victoria Street
had gone through the House of Commons. They put the best possible
face on the matter, blaming the defeat in part on the abdication of the
City's supporters in the House, who had talked bravely of nailing their
colors to the mast but at the moment of crisis had hauled them down
with embarrassing speed. Other councilmen were quick to attack Lawley and his new committee, suggesting that they had done nothing except damage the character of the Corporation. This debate, in fact,
showed an admirable prudence on the part of the more solid members of
the Common Council, even though they could not muster enough votes
to defeat Lawley. Alderman Sidney, for example, an M.P. and a magistrate, thought that the Corporation had taken an absurd line. Why, he
asked, was it worse for the MBW to build a street than for a railway
company to build a railway—especially since, when the Board's street
was finished, it would become the property of the Corporation?[48]

The Corporation's internal battle over Queen Victoria Street had one
curious repercussion. Apparently in an attempt to find credible excuses
for the failure of his committee, Lawley precipitated a bitter debate in
the Common Council in which he alleged that a City member of the
Board (Deputy Harrison) had divulged information about the funds that
the Corporation might have used for the building of Queen Victoria
Street. Instead of denying the charge directly, Harrison resorted to hem-
ming and hawing. Others defended him vigorously, deploring that he
should be spoken of so offensively "by the small mushroom members of
the Court."[49] Although Harrison finally denied Lawley's allegation, he
nevertheless resigned his seat on the Board. Lawley, after professing
the utmost respect for Harrison, denounced him again, asserting that
the City had lost much through the behavior of its representative on the
Board and that Queen Victoria Street had been handed over to the
Board through "want of judgment and right feeling" on the part of those
who had arrogated to themselves leadership of the Court of Common
Council.[50]

This was a curious revolt, and its origin is not clear. Was it simply an uprising of new men in the Court, assaulting the entrenched older men; or was it perhaps a demonstration of the outer, populous, underrepresented wards (Lawley sat for Farringdon Without) against the dominance of the small central wards? In any case, in spite of the credit assigned to Harrison for his work on the Board—among other achievements, he had been partly responsible for saving the fourpenny duty for the City—he had behaved either stupidly or guiltily. He could have solved the problem easily by a straightforward denial rather than by resigning and implying that he would come back if invited. Instead, the Court accepted his resignation with appropriate regrets and elected someone else to take his place.[51]

Partly because of the activity of such people as A. S. Ayrton and partly because of pressure from within the Corporation, the early 1860s witnessed a number of attacks on the City's unreformed institutions. Each session of Parliament, the *City Press* observed in 1864, saw a new gesture of hostility against the Corporation, which had (it thought) exhibited a lamentable want of firmness. The Government had given up trying to reform the Corporation outright, and instead had fallen back on a policy of trying to isolate it from the rest of the metropolis. The chief opponents of reform had been in the Livery, which had invariably risen in protest against any proposal for the redress of abuses. Fundamental to any scheme of reform (the *City Press* continued) was the abolition of the silly distinction between freemen and "foreigners," and the extension of the City franchise to all who paid scot and lot.[52] This step would be opposed by the Livery, ever determined to maintain its sway over the Corporation. The right of the Livery to elect the Chamberlain and other officials was a perversion of common sense.[53]

The reformers agreed with the *Press*'s judgment that the Common Council was too big and with its attack on the grave disproportion in representation between the larger outer wards and the smaller central wards, whose members virtually controlled the Council. As a first step the *Press* proposed that the Corporation should get rid of half its antiquated trappings and move forward with more vigor.[54] Such disparities in representation as that between Farringdon Without, where sixty-four voters were required to elect a councillor, and Lime Street, where only twenty-four were necessary, were preposterous.[55] Thomas Rudkin, a portly victualler who sat for Farringdon Within, carried on the attack of the outer wards with a demand for a committee on Corporation reform which would investigate a whole range of questions including the balance of representation. Another councillor, half in fun, correctly called the Corporation "an antiquated, lumbering, obstructive and extravagant institution, quite unsuited to the present habits and wants of the public."[56] There was, in short, considerable disaffection within the City community in the 1860s, and proposals for internal self-reform, spear-headed by the *City Press* and the councillors from outlying wards, were frequently discussed; but the Corporation could not bring itself to do more than glance at this alarming prospect.

A City agency that drew the special fire of the group from the outer parishes (led by Lawley, Rudkin, and James Medwin, a leather dealer) was the Court of Sewers. Although appointed by the Common Council, the Commissioners of Sewers were really not accountable to the Corporation, for the Council had no power to interfere with their activities. Moreover, the amount of money that the Court of Sewers spent each year constituted a powerful instrument of patronage and, indeed, of corruption. The Commissioners of Sewers had operated in the City for many centuries, but their powers had been greatly extended by the City of London Sewers Act of 1848, supplemented three years later by another similar act. In addition to sewers, the Commissioners were concerned with such varied services as lighting and paving, sanitation, gas, and street improvements. The Corporation decided broad questions of policy; the Commissioners worked out the details. In the mid-1860s the Commissioners were spending over £150,000 a year.[57]

If the Sewer Commissioners made a creditable record and avoided serious trouble, that was largely due to the energy and competence of its engineer, William Haywood, who had been appointed as a young man of twenty-four back in 1846. Haywood had cooperated with John Simon, the Medical Officer — indeed, had complemented him — in his projects to improve sanitary conditions in the City. The reorganization of the Commissioners of Sewers by the 1848 act, which had specified their powers in some detail, gave them, Haywood asserted, "control, directly or indirectly, over nearly every one of the physical conditions of the City which are likely to affect the health and comfort of the inhabitants."[58] After Simon had been translated to the national scene, Haywood continued to work, methodically and patiently, for the improvement of the City.

The Commissioners of Sewers were, in fact, a rather anomalous board, the creation of the Corporation but not responsible to it, and they were therefore fair game for the dissatisfied. A move to change the constitution of the Commission by admitting to it all the eligible Common Councillors, thus making it virtually identical with the Corporation, was started in 1864 by the group representing the outer parishes. Not surprisingly, this attempt aroused the opposition of most of the aldermen and their deputies (those Common Councilmen appointed by the aldermen to assist in the government of each ward), who summoned enough support to defeat the motion; and they were able to do the same thing again on a similar motion a fortnight later.[59] After all, out of ninety-six members of the Court of Sewers, some fifty-four were aldermen or deputies. Throughout 1865 and 1866 the question was brought up again, with appeals to the "Young members," but by this time the Council was thoroughly bored with the subject and Medwin was upbraided for raising the question for a fifth time.[60] The protesters, it may be admitted, had a point. Here was a body, appointed each year by the Common Council, which had achieved a position of independent statutory authority and performed most of the duties for which, in other cities, the local municipal council would have been responsible.[61] But the volume of criticism was not great enough to affect the position of the City establishment, which was well entrenched in the Sewers Commission. Not until 1897 were the Commission's powers transferred to the Corporation and exercised through the Common Council.

The Commissioners, with their able engineer, did an efficient job for the City, far better than that done by most of the metropolitan vestries. And they spent a great deal of time on their assignment. In 1862, for example, they held meetings on 43 days, and their three committees held 111 meetings. Their inspectors visited nearly 8,000 houses, and on the strength of their reports the Commissioners issued over 1,600 notices ordering improvements of various kinds.[62] In succeeding decades the Commissioners continued their work of cleaning up and improving the City until, by common consent, its services were regarded as the most efficient in the metropolis. The sewerage system worked admirably, the streets were washed and cleaned frequently and regularly, and the death rate was extremely low.[63] Admittedly the Commissioners' problems of finance were less acute than those of comparable authorities elsewhere, but the quality of the City's public services was viewed with respect even by those living in less fortunate areas.

There would be little point in detailing all the nineteenth-century improvements made in the City either under the direction of the Commissioners of Sewers or of other agencies of the Corporation, but a few are of special interest. The new Cannon Street, costing about £540,000 (net) was completed in 1854, and in the following year the cattle market in Islington, moved from Smithfield and built at a cost of over £400,000, opened its gates for business.[64] Three years before, Holloway Prison, costing nearly £100,000, had been built. In the 1860s came Blackfriars Bridge (nearly £400,000); and the City's monumental improvement, the Holborn Viaduct, which carried the roadway over the Holborn Valley,

9. Building Holborn Viaduct, 1869

was constructed between 1864 and 1869 with an expenditure of over £2,400,000, much of which was drawn from the fourpenny coal duties.[65]

This useful tax was always most adroitly defended by City men. When a Select Committee of the House of Commons asked the City Solicitor about the propriety of taxing people twenty miles away for improvements in the City, he replied "that the improvements in the City of London should be subjected to a different treatment, and should be judged by a different rule from the improvements in other localities, for this reason: it is the centre of the great national monetary and public establishments, to which the whole world have [*sic*] resort."[66] The City, in fact, wanted to have it both ways, claiming the right to make its own improvements as it pleased but with money provided by the whole metropolis.

The City also did its part in freeing the Thames bridges. Of the crossings within the City, London Bridge and Blackfriars were free, but at Southwark Bridge, the property of a private company, tolls were still being collected. The issue was precipitated in 1864 when a bill for buying the Southwark and Waterloo bridges was introduced for the MBW by — what treachery! — Alderman David Salomons. To finance this transaction, the Bridge House Estates Fund, derived from property held by the Corporation almost from time immemorial and used for the building and maintenance of bridges, was to provide some £50,000. The Common Council was in a dither over the prospect of such an invasion of the Corporation's domain, but it finally decided to discuss the matter with the Southwark Bridge proprietors. The ensuing parleys produced an offer from the proprietors either to sell the bridge for £200,000, or to free it of tolls for a trial period of six months for a fee of £1,834. Against the warnings of Henry Lowman Taylor (who was substantially correct, as it turned out) that once the tolls were abolished it would be impossible to impose them again, the Council accepted the six months' arrangement.[67] Salomons kept up the pressure, citing at the end of the six months the enormously increased use to which the free bridge had been put: almost ten times as many persons and over six times as many vehicles had crossed in the six months' period. Again Taylor urged caution, contending that this was a metropolitan improvement, and the most that Salomons could extract from the Common Council was an assurance that the bridge would be kept open free of charge for another six months.[68] In the following year, however, after another debate in which the same sharp differences of opinion were revealed in the same old speeches, the council finally agreed to negotiate for the bridge, and at the end of the year (1866), it decided to buy the bridge for £200,000, taken from the Bridge House Estates Fund.[69]

This marked the principal connection of the City with the business of freeing the Thames bridges. In 1873, to be sure, there was the unpopular question of collaborating with the MBW in freeing three small bridges at a cost of £60,000, of which £20,000 was to be contributed by the Corporation.[70] Three years later the Corporation was also incensed at the terms of a toll bridge bill, which, as it emerged from the Select Committee of the House of Commons, provided for the management of the bridges not by a joint committee but by the MBW itself. The Lord Mayor urged the Corporation to consolidate its strength in Parliament, cultivating the members favorable to its cause and getting them to act in concert.[71] Obviously, observed one councilman, the Select Committee had been exceedingly eager to hand over power to the Board.[72] The agitation of the Corporation was, however, unnecessary, for the bill was finally withdrawn. But the Corporation, which obviously wished to get its finger into the pie, now proposed to return to the plan of joint action with the Board.[73]

A historic monopoly which the City was eager to preserve was its control over markets within seven miles of the City limits. The Corporation was acutely aware that, in a metropolis whose population was rapidly increasing, adequate market facilities constituted both a legitimate popular demand and a valuable source of revenue. Indeed, without such facilities, the Corporation would lay itself open to vigorous and merited criticism. The second half of the century, therefore, saw most of the old markets replaced, expanded, or otherwise altered.

The opening of the live cattle market at Copenhagen Fields, Islington, in 1855 prepared the way for building a new "dead meat" market on the site vacated at Smithfield. The Markets Committee, with Henry Lowman Taylor as chairman, proceeded with deliberation—too slowly, some critics thought[74]—and the new Smithfield Market was not opened until the fall of 1868. It was, however, regarded as admirably adapted for its purpose: a great block of stone and brick and glass, warm in color, the *City Press* commented, and chastely finished.[75]

In later years other new markets were built and existing ones altered. The furor over contagious diseases brought in by foreign cattle resulted in the building of the Deptford Cattle Market (1871), at a cost (including the site) of about £380,000. Billingsgate Market, "the college of bad language," also came in for enlargement and rebuilding at a cost of over

10. Smithfield Dead Meat Market, about 1895

£270,000 (1877). *The Hornet,* accustomed to turning a critical eye on City financial management, had thought the original estimate by the Markets Committee of £150,000 preposterous, and did not regard the talk of shortage of money in the City treasury as more than an engaging nursery tale. This, it continued, ought not to be treated as other than a fable until "the Court alters the system of finance, which would disgrace an East-End vestry." The Corporation, it prophesied, would obviously continue to pull money "out of the empty and yet inexhaustible City purse," as, indeed, the expenditure of nearly £250,000 to rebuild Leadenhall Market (including the approaches) in 1881 was soon to prove.[76]

One market decision made by the Corporation was virtually forced upon it. In 1871, after some debate and much hesitation, the City accepted from Angela Burdett-Coutts the gift of her neo-Gothic Columbia Market in Bethnal Green, which was already failing in its primary object of providing cheap food supplies in the East End. Some councillors suspected that the City was acquiring an imposing white elephant, as in fact it was. It operated the market for only three years before returning it to its founder.[77]

But these steps did not satisfy the mounting metropolitan clamor against a provisioning system controlled by the Corporation, and attacks on its domination became staple items in the case of the reformers against the City. When in 1881 Firth introduced into an MBW money bill a clause authorizing the Board to make itself a market authority in opposition to the City, the Corporation became uneasy, but it was uncertain about what steps to take. Some councillors could even see merit in the popular objections to the limited market facilities available in London. The particular issue was the alleged continuing inadequacy of Billingsgate Market and the demand for an improved system of distribution of fish. The clamor in the metropolis, even the *City Press* conceded, was not without substance. The question could not simply be settled on the basis of vested interests, with every other consideration left in the background. Furthermore, the members of the MBW, "with the alacrity which they usually display when an opportunity is given them against the Corporation," was now thinking of trying to take over the Corporation's traditional market functions, at any rate outside the City itself.[78] As it happened, the Board failed to reach a decision about a site for a new fish market in north London, and the issue was returned to "the only properly constituted market authority" — which then decided to maintain Billingsgate but to establish a small "inland" fish market at Farringdon, where dealers could get their fish, now mostly brought into London by railway, without facing the Billingsgate monopoly. This experiment did not prove a success,[79] but in general the Corporation's administration of its markets during the latter part of the nineteenth century was businesslike enough; and a very large amount of capital was invested in improving them.

Among the contributions made by the City Corporation to the public welfare perhaps the most memorable has been the preservation of a number of open spaces, large and small. Of these the most important are Epping Forest in Essex and Burnham Beeches in Buckinghamshire, both of them acquired during the second half of the nineteenth century but neither of them bought with money provided by the ratepayers of the City — a fact which was frequently emphasized by the Corporation's less fortunate metropolitan rivals, notably the MBW. The Epping Forest affair, which gave the metropolis over 5,700 acres of common land and forest on its northeast border, is a long and complicated story. By the first half of the nineteenth century the enclosures made by the lords of the numerous manors in the locality had reduced the area of the forest from around 9,000 to 6,000 acres. And in the 1850s and 1860s the rush to enclose was still going on, topped by the enclosure in the mid-sixties of 1,300 acres in the Manor of Loughton by the lord of the manor, who was also rector of the parish.[80] Although the Commons Preservation Society had recently been formed to organize resistance to the threatened enclosure of commons everywhere, it lacked a person or corporation with undoubted common rights in the area and with the will and resources needed to stand up to the manorial lords.

In 1854 the City Corporation bought an estate in Ilford (near Epping Forest) for use as a cemetery, and therefore it did possess such common rights. And when the Commons Preservation Society appealed to the Corporation to take up the cause for the metropolis and to enter upon legal proceedings, the Corporation after earnest consideration and much prodding by Benjamin Scott, the Chamberlain, finally agreed to do so. But this was not simply a disinterested gesture on the part of the Corporation. As George Shaw-Lefevre, the founder and chairman of the Commons Preservation Society, pointed out in an account that, on the whole, is enthusiastic about the City's behavior, the Corporation "with a keen eye, to their advantage, perceived that great popularity might be achieved by fighting for the interest of the public in a case of such importance and magnitude, and were the more inclined to embark on it, at a time when the separate exclusive rights of the Corporation were threatened by the general demand for a single Municipal Government of London." In 1871 the Corporation therefore decided to bring a suit in the name of the City's Commissioners of Sewers, in whom the Ilford estate was vested, against sixteen of the nineteen lords of manors who had made recent enclosures.[81]

How were this suit and the other expenses that might come in its train to be financed? There was no intention, apparently, of dipping into the Corporation's capital for the amount. Instead, here was a chance to prolong (in suitably modified form) the ancient dues on grain, which, surely, no reasonable man could object to if the proceeds were to be used for such an estimable object as saving Epping Forest. The bill successfully promoted by the Corporation for this purpose in 1872 therefore provided for the commutation of the metage dues into a fixed duty to be charged for thirty years, the proceeds being applied to the preservation of open spaces near London.

This ingenious measure seemed to raise few objections, even among those who had been inveighing against the analogous coal duties. But an exception was the MBW, which had been badly outmaneuvered by the Corporation. In 1864 the Board had been invited by a perplexed Treasury to ask Parliament for powers to enclose Epping Forest as a place of recreation. For reasons that are intelligible, if not admirable, the Board had declined this invitation as tactfully as possible, pointing out that the Forest was outside the area of its jurisdiction. Surely, the Board had insisted, it was the duty of the Government to preserve open spaces near the metropolis, and perhaps a Select Committee of the House of Commons would provide the correct prescription.[82] In 1870, however, the Board was more farsighted than the Government in its attitude toward a bill introduced by A. S. Ayrton (then First Commissioner of Works), which proposed to salvage only 600 acres of the forest as a public open space. The public, the Board's parliamentary committee concluded, would be badly dealt with if this proposal went through.[83] And since the Government of Mr. Gladstone — and Robert Lowe — would inevitably take a too limited view of its responsibilities, little was to be hoped for from that quarter. Nor, thought the Commons Preservation Society, could anything be expected from the Royal Commission which was appointed by the Government in 1871 to unscramble the respective rights involved and to formulate a scheme for the preservation of the open land in the forest.

It was rather on the City's involvement in the matter that the Commons Preservation Society was now pinning its hopes. But the Corporation's bill of 1872 to use the corn dues for the preservation of open spaces put the MBW in an awkward situation in which it had to work hard to justify itself. Its Works and General Purposes Committee argued that the Board had not been neglectful in dealing with the forest, and it pointed a suspicious finger at the methods by which the Corporation was proposing to finance its public-spirited gesture: the Corporation had seen that the days of the corn metage were numbered, and here was an excellent chance to exchange these old rights for the right to levy a statutory duty on grain. Perhaps, the Board's committee suggested, "the object to which it is proposed to apply the money would reconcile the public to the impost."[84] But whatever the Corporation's motives may have been, its tactics proved brilliantly successful, for in July 1874 the Master of the Rolls gave judgment in favor of the Corporation in all essentials, prohibiting any more enclosures and requiring the removal of all fences erected since 1851.

In 1878 Parliament passed a bill for the final settlement of Epping Forest. The Corporation had meanwhile simplified matters by buying up the lords' rights over more than 3,000 acres at about £20 an acre. The scheme placed the control and management of the forest in the Corporation, and rejected the claim of the MBW to have a share in it. The Board, in fact, would have been wiser to keep silent, since it had missed its chance at an earlier stage. The London press was practically unanimous in opposing the Board's claim even though it was supported by an amendment to the Government bill proposed by Henry Fawcett. The total cost to the Corporation was about £240,000, which of course was provided by the commutation of the metage dues on grain — a notable example of how an ancient and long unjustifiable impost could be refurbished to produce constructive results. The Corporation emerged from the long and tiresome business with added prestige, and when in the spring of 1882 the forest was formally opened, newspaper editors sang the City's praises. The London corn trade, too, requested a special part in the festivities. *The Times,* however, recalled correctly that neither the Corporation nor the corn trade was ultimately responsible, but the people of London. "Londoners pay, and Londoners derive the benefit."[05]

The extent of the general benefit which Londoners received from the Corporation's rule was, however, impossible to measure, for, as contemporaries repeatedly asserted, it was (and is) exceedingly difficult to discover reality behind the obscurities of the Corporation's financial statements. A comprehensive balance sheet was never issued, and the particulars of the City's financial position were often carefully concealed. But in spite of the City's wealth, its inhabitants did not escape rates and taxes. In 1855 William Tite (later Sir William), architect of the new Royal Exchange and later an important member of the MBW, said in evidence before a Select Committee of the Commons that, although the poor rate was light, other rates and taxes in the City were high, a fact which he attributed chiefly to the heavy tithe and to costly public improvements. The Corporation's property, one of its major sources of income, he thought, was well though expensively administered;[86] in elaboration of that point Francis Bennoch, a former member of the Common Council who had become a City reformer, offered a statement "designed to show that what was done by the Manchester Corporation for £12,000 cost the City £112,000."[87] The Corporation was, in fact, constantly and justifiably criticized for the costliness, waste, and antiquated practices prevalent in its financial affairs.

So confused were the City's finances that they were often criticized even by those who ordinarily could find little wrong in the Corporation's behavior. In 1859 the *City Press* thought that the Corporation's financial policy had produced a situation which no member of its various courts would have tolerated in his private affairs. The root of the trouble, according to the editor, was that the Corporation's resources consisted of a variety of separate funds which were intertwined like the strands of an exceedingly complex spider's web, but which were never displayed in a single statement.[88] Attempts to do so yielded unsatisfactory results; but for the decade 1856–1865 the Corporation's total receipts, according to the *City Press,* amounted to £3,183,528, of which £1,067,722 was in rents, £169,110 in market tolls and market rents, and £576,684 in coal and corn dues.[89]

In the late 1860s and early 1870s there was some concern about the financial impact of the extensive program of improvements on which the City had embarked. One of the problems was the amount of unoccupied land which was being acquired in connection with the Holborn Viaduct project and with market improvements, and which had not yet been sold. Such apprehensions, it presently appeared, were absurd. The total ratable value of the City was skyrocketing—indeed, during the decade 1860 to 1870 it nearly doubled—and it was clearly preposterous to talk about City bankruptcy. In 1871, *The Hornet* reflected, the City would finish the year with a surplus, a situation which had been reached without the sacrifice of a single dinner or junket. It was cheering, the editor added ironically, to know that the coal dues, "that little tax the fat City levies on the pinched-up fireplaces of poor, shivering starvelings all over London, are increasing and that the yield will give increased facilities for little extravagances. Some wretches may die of exposure this winter, but they will have the opportunity of witnessing the Lord Mayor's Show."[90] By 1874, in fact, the Corporation's total annual receipts from all sources had gone up to nearly £2 million.[91]

In the late 1870s there were indeed signs of a change of heart within the Corporation, with some pressure for a more rational policy. When a motion was made in Common Council in 1878 for a committee to prepare a Corporation balance sheet, it was only narrowly defeated. One member asserted: "No more remarkable proof of the peculiarity of opinion and tradition in this Court can be offered than that a simple statement of this kind astonishes and frightens a great many members . . . The nation, the Metropolitan Board of Works, and the School Board expose their affairs, and every corporation in the kingdom, and why should this Corporation be an exception?" And Councillor Rudkin pointed out that keeping the Corporation's financial affairs like a sealed book would make a bad impression outside the City, but he was unable to get a favorable vote from the Court, though he came closer than would have been thought possible twenty years earlier.[92]

Despite the arcane ways in which it conducted its financial business, the Corporation's expenditure for the general benefit of Londoners was not trivial. One may write off the money that went into pageantry, elaborate dinners ("the cult of turtledom"), and hospitality to visiting dignitaries. On a more serious level, between 1849 and 1882 the Corporation spent nearly £3,000,000 on its markets, nearly £500,000 (since 1835) on the City of London School and the Freemen's Orphan School, £75,000 for the Guildhall Library and Museum, and nearly £310,000 for open spaces (including Epping Forest and Burnham Beeches).[93] Admittedly the money for some of these expenditures was extracted from the rest of the metropolis, and in other cases there was income to offset expenditure, but in general the City had an impressive record in public improvements. Firth puts the total expenditure for the 115 years from 1757 to 1872 at nearly £10,000,000, and of this amount over £5,000,000 was spent after 1850. The list of improvements, which was formidable, included a fair number of items that would have been difficult to finance from the rates alone.[94]

But although the Corporation might (and often did) make expenditures out of its own bounty for the general good, it always resisted any attempt by an outside authority to impose a new tax on the sacred square mile, however desirable the object might be. Thus the MBW's parliamentary bill for a fourpenny improvement rate, sponsored in 1867 by Ayrton and Tite, produced a tremendous hubbub in the City. How about spending some money, the *City Press* suggested, on the improvement of Ayrton?[95] The paper discovered a wave of protests throughout the metropolis at this gross invasion of local rights:

> Come, ratepayers, rally round to the fight,
> And let our old London put forth its full might,
> And tell those good gentlemen, Ayrton and Tite,
> We'll look after our own IMPROVEMENT!

At Guildhall the usual group of City leaders gathered to mount the usual attacks on the MBW: the City was underrepresented on the Board, and an improvement rate would reduce the City to the status of an ordinary vestry and enthrone a group of ambitious men on the Board as its overlords. The Board had opposed the City's own improvement rate bill and helped to defeat it, and now it was attempting to pass one of its own to cover the whole metropolis.[96] In addition, indignant ratepayers' meetings took place all over the metropolitan area, for few things were more terrifying to the average ratepayer than the specter of a new rate.[97] To the City the bill was especially unattractive because it was sponsored by an old enemy, A. S. Ayrton, whose activities in the House of Commons had frequently put the Corporation on the defensive. When the bill was finally quashed, the Corporation gave itself credit for the victory. Certainly the City's Local Government Committee had been indefatigable not only in stirring up opposition in the metropolis but in obtaining expressions of opinion from the country at large.[98]

From the beginning, of course, the Corporation had regarded the MBW as a threat to its own autonomy, as an instrument through which Government ministers could control the entire metropolis, including the City. City voices charged the Government with having perverted the recommendations of the Royal Commission of 1854 by instituting a plan which would enable the Board to assume many powers beyond those for which it was originally established, and thus "to weaken the authority of the only municipal body in the metropolis."[99] Corporation and citizens alike were urged to stand fast and to maintain in the great metropolis one spot where local self-government could be seen to work effectively.

As for the future government of the metropolis, the Corporation had few doubts about how it ought to go—but not to the point of taking any aggressive action. Although the City Remembrancer, testifying before Ayrton's Select Committee in 1867, would have been satisfied if things had reverted to their pre-MBW status—"I object to any authority that comes and interferes with us"[100]—other City witnesses were convinced of the need for some central authority, or rather, authorities. For obvious reasons, the notion of a single supreme government in the metropolis, whether new or created by the extension of a reformed City Corporation, had little appeal within the square mile. Plainly, if an all-metropolitan government was to be built, the proper scheme would be a series of municipalities, perhaps the six parliamentary boroughs and the City, each of which would be a separate corporation. On one occasion, William Lawley moved in the Common Council to offer £5,000 to each parliamentary borough that obtained a charter of incorporation under the Municipal Corporations Act. He contended that an important principle was involved. If municipal institutions had been more widely diffused, the notion of centralization would not have gained ground in such a shocking way. This was a gesture of the "new men"—Lawley, Rudkin, and Medwin—and it did not succeed. How insane, others protested, to give away £30,000 in this fashion![101]

In the late 1860s the issue of municipal government gathered new energy, stimulated by James Beal's Municipal Reform Association, and most of the talk followed a pattern favored in the City. On the one hand, it was hard to defend the existing system of metropolitan administration; it was "a deformity and an absurdity conjoined," with overlapping districts, superfluous agencies and boards, and many other defects invidious to the reformers.[102] But on the other hand, the creation of a centralized metropolitan government would lead to "the entire destruction of everything . . . believed to be valuable in the history of the municipal government of the country." What made the *City Press* and City leaders furious was the proposal of the members of Ayrton's Select Committee of 1867 to exalt a reconstituted MBW into a Municipal Council for the whole metropolis. Were they, these leaders asked, determined to sacrifice the City Corporation, that splendid demonstration of successful local democracy, to the ambitions of a mere Board of Works?[103]

During the spring of 1868, when bills on metropolitan government were again pending in Parliament, the Common Council was busy on the question of what to do about the whole troublesome business. Five motions on municipal government were made at one meeting, all of them proposing in one way or another to establish a number of boroughs in the metropolis. Councillor Fry, admitting that the MBW might have to be continued while these new boroughs were being set up, thought that in the meantime the Corporation, which "has for many centuries existed as a distinct and independent municipality, exercising all its appropriate functions, and having been entrusted with the execution of great and important public works," should dissolve its connection with the Board.[104] A month later he returned to the fray, again roundly criticizing the Board and professing mystification as to why the City had ever accepted membership in a body which would treat it on a par with Hampstead or Bethnal Green.[105] It was an oratorical effort that won a cheer from his fellow councillors, though it contained nothing new. Throughout the debate, however, as in the evidence given in the previous year to Ayrton's Select Committee by City witnesses, there was grave uneasiness about the growing power of the Board, which showed no apparent inclination to expire even though its main drainage projects had been completed.

Presently the opposition went into action. Henry Lowman Taylor emerged as the defender of the Board, pointing out that the City had done remarkably well from improvements made with its aid.[106] The debate lasted for some six hours and was exhausting and inconclusive. At the next Council meeting the question got tangled up in a procedural feud between, on the one side, Lawley and his Local Government and Taxation Committee, and, on the other, certain members who demanded the appointment of a special committee to reexamine the whole matter. Lawley held firm, made it a question of confidence, and won his point.[107]

Yet there were others in the City, though few of them were members of the Corporation, who were prepared to look for a more radical solution to the problem of metropolitan government. In 1870 *The Hornet* forecast in all essentials the plan that Sir William Harcourt was to submit to the House of Commons in 1884: that of reforming the Corporation and extending its rule to the whole metropolis. But in such a scheme the City could obviously not hope to enjoy greater representation on the new body than it was entitled to by area and property valuation (the matter of population was prudently left unmentioned). To *The Hornet* the report of Lawley's committee meant only disappointment and a missed opportunity because it suggested nothing beyond the old plan of setting up municipalities in the different parliamentary boroughs, making no reference to the unreformed Corporation. One daring councilman did actually move that the powers of the Corporation, properly reformed, be extended to the entire metropolitan area; but in reply Alderman Thomas Sidney treated the Court to a dose of his infallible "rest and be thankful" doctrine, dwelling on the ancient glories, rights, and privileges of the Corporation, much as a doting mother would speak of her favorite child, "with blind adoration."[108]

Even the *City Press,* usually unquestioningly loyal to the Corporation, could find little merit in Lawley's report, which, it thought, had simply skirted the problem. It was silly to think of molding the metropolis into municipal form without interfering with the Corporation, "whether for its annihilation or rejuvenation." The Corporation now had a chance, the *Press* argued, to stretch out its arms to the farthest limits of the metropolis and to do for "Greater London" what it had done in times past for "Little London"—"that is, unite all the interests and sympathies of citizenship in a common bond, and in the necessary relationship to a common centre." But this view clearly was much too imaginative for the Corporation. It was quite willing to draw revenue from the whole metropolis in the shape of coal dues and other imposts, but it would not act creatively to give unity and common purpose to the new municipalities. Precisely what the *Press* wanted is not clear, but it was evidently calling on the Corporation to take some initiative in reorganizing London.[109]

By this time, however, the immediate danger seemed to have passed. The 1870s were not fruitful years for metropolitan municipal reform, and the City fathers could relax in the confidence that no threats to their basic position were in sight. Instead, they became more genuinely concerned with public improvements and, indeed, pushed through an impressive program on that front.

In the 1880s it was a different story. The general election of 1880 was marked by a shift in the political allegiance of the City, which after fifty years of Liberal loyalty returned only one Liberal and three Conservatives, an outcome partly due, apparently, to the suspicion that another Government headed by Gladstone would bring another assault on cherished City institutions. It was terrible, the *City Press* reflected, to be perpetually threatened with extinction "when we are so well governed."[110] At this stage, however, the City was less bothered by the possibility of extinction than by the prospect of having its boundaries extended so that the old square mile would lose its own unique identity. Meanwhile, the stir made by Firth's Municipal Reform League was becoming more insistent, and the League was adding prestigious names to its list of vice-presidents. In 1882 the Queen's Speech from the Throne seemed to promise prompt action, and in the House of Commons Sir William Harcourt, the Liberal Home Secretary, flayed the City for its filibustering tactics against a bill recently brought in by the MBW. "It appeared," he charged, "that the City of London were prepared to object to any Bill brought in by the Metropolitan Board of Works which in any way affected the City of London." The City, he added, spoke for only 50,000 people: what about the four million for whom this was a good bill?[111]

The City's attitude was to oppose any bill proposing centralized government of the kind the Reform League was championing. The *City Press* suggested that the whole agitation had been churned up by a few cranks such as Firth and Beal, aided by Ayrton: the only people "who denounce existing institutions are a few busy, noisy, insignificant individuals, who hope, in the general scramble that would ensue upon the breaking up of a grand and wealthy institution, to find something that would exactly suit them." Beneath this opposition there was an obvious fear of democracy and what the democratic voter might do if City property were laid open to him. "Outsider" predicted in the *Press* that if after seven hundred years of active life the Corporation were to be abolished, the Church and the House of Lords would be next in line for extinction — and they would not survive for long.[112]

The rumors about Harcourt's pending bill on municipal government had been disturbing to the City, and the reality, when it was unveiled in 1884, was no less alarming. The *Press* at once saw it as presaging the doom of local self-government (in spite of the smooth compliments with which Harcourt had sought to assuage City feeling). Here was a Government bill proposing a single centralized administration for the whole metropolis — an aberration against which the *Press* quoted the sentiments of John Stuart Mill (now dead), Samuel Morley, McCullagh Torrens, and W. H. Smith. The Court of Common Council held a special meeting on the bill to consider a report from a special committee which gave an alarming (though familiar) verdict — the bill would clearly destroy local self-government everywhere! The only dissentient voice seems to have been that of the eccentric and disreputable Sir John Bennett, grandfather of Sir Sydney Cockerell, who professed to disapprove of the Corporation's privileges. Shortly afterwards the City wards also held indignation meetings, all of which voted heavily against the bill.[113]

Harcourt's bill had to wait nearly three months to be debated, and ultimately it was abandoned due to lack of parliamentary time. (It could not be brought in again the following year because by then the Liberal Government had been replaced by Lord Salisbury's Conservative administration.)[114] Shortage of time had been the immediate cause of its demise, but during the long period between the first and second readings of the bill the City had regrettably resorted to dubious and even sinister techniques of opposition. These did not come to light until three years later (1887), when two Radical members of the House of Commons, George Howell and Charles Bradlaugh, obtained the appointment of a Select Committee to inquire into charges of "improper use and Malversation of Public Funds of the Corporation of London."[115] There had been gossip about the behavior of some of the organizations that had opposed the bill, which could only have been supported by City money; but the City members of the House had scoffed at the charges as "anonymous tittle-tattle" and had not seriously opposed the appointment of a committee to look into the matter.[116] What emerged was an unappetizing story of the resources of the City being freely used to defeat a bill in Parliament. The behavior of certain Corporation officials on this occasion was objectionable enough, but what really piques one's curiosity is the question (unanswerable, of course) of how often this kind of maneuver had taken place in the past. Probably it had not happened often on such a scale, but we have already noted the expenditure of substantial sums to defeat other bills in the House.

The Select Committee found that between 1882 and 1884 a special committee of the Corporation had issued five reports purporting to show that the local authorities of the metropolis, with almost entire unanimity, regarded the notion of a single municipality as costly and ineffective. As an alternative the special committee had sketched a plan for ten metropolitan municipalities, and it had sought money with which to oppose Harcourt's centralization scheme. G. P. Goldney, the City Remembrancer, had employed a Mr. Palmer, the Conservative agent for Finsbury, to carry on the campaign. Palmer, in turn, had employed men to break up meetings of Firth's Municipal Reform League — or at least to add a hostile element to the audience. Were these men bullyboys and toughs? Goldney insisted that they were mainly clerks hired for a shilling a meeting. A number of other agents under his control had also conducted meetings, chiefly in north and east London; and the Select Committee found that the Anti-One-Municipality League and the Metropolitan Ratepayers' Protection Association (both opposed to Harcourt's bill) were largely spurious organizations subsidized out of Corporation funds.[117]

As for the charge that men had been hired to break up reform meetings, the Select Committee concluded that both sides had packed their meetings, and that each had attended the meetings of the other. Some of these rallies, notably one in Kensington Town Hall organized by the Municipal Reform League and held on 24 May 1884, had gone to dangerous lengths, with three hundred "trusted" men surrounding the platform to confront "nearly as many" others who were in Palmer's pay.[118] Another device, apparently also the brainchild of Palmer, had been to have a large number of forged tickets printed for the reform meeting in St. James's Hall on 5 June 1883. Precise evidence is lacking as to where these tickets came from, but a goodly number had found their way into the office of the City Chamberlain, who, no doubt, had made effective use of them.[119]

Two main questions, the Select Committee reported, had confronted it. First was the question whether the special committee of the Corporation had had the legal right to spend City money for the purpose of resisting the reform or abolition of the Corporation. On this question City witnesses put up a strong case, noting that from time immemorial the Corporation had spent its money without parliamentary control. The Select Committee concluded that the City had, if not the legal right, a prescriptive right (which had been exercised for centuries) to keep its expenditures free of outside control. The second question, which was easier to assess, was whether these expenditures had been proper for such a body as the City Corporation to make. Here the answer was clearly in the negative. The expenditure on advertising had been excessive, and the subsidizing of so-called political organisations like the Metropolitan Ratepayers' Protection Association was clearly out of bounds for a public body. To place corporate funds in the hands of irresponsible and unknown persons for the purpose of creating the appearance of an active, but in reality nonexistent, public opinion had been calculated to mislead Parliament. The Corporation's committee had kept no supervision over the agents employed, so that much of the money had been used for improper and indefensible purposes. The committee's total expenditure, had, indeed, been heavy — some £19,000 out of Corporation resources — and the more responsible members of the Corporation were gravely embarrassed.[120]

Even the *City Press* could not deny the fact that the Select Committee had unearthed an unattractive state of affairs, though it argued that the report would be disappointing to enemies of the City because the evidence heard by the Select Committee had not sustained the charge of malversation of public funds. The *Press* did, however, admit that the Corporation's special committee had failed to maintain adequate control over its agents, "either as regards the amount expended or the manner of its expenditure." But it had all been in a good cause, that of saving both the Corporation and the entire metropolis from a horrid fate.[121]

The Corporation itself was quite unrepentant, and when in February 1888 its special committee issued its report on the findings of the Commons Select Committee it professed the most virtuous of motives for having sought to protect not only the Corporation but the whole metropolis "from the greatest calamity that could well befall it, namely the handing over of its government and its enormous assessment to a body of impecunious professional men, whose sole object would in all probability be their own self-aggrandizement."[122] Perhaps the expenditure on advertising and literature had been a trifle heavy, but, after all, an enormous population had had to be instructed! Yet, though the Corporation's committee put the best possible face on past events, there was no denying that City assumptions of superiority had suffered a body blow.

Meanwhile the *City Press* had continued to preach the virtues of a plan of separate municipalities, and in July 1884 it had welcomed the withdrawal of Harcourt's bill, which would now give the corporation "time to mature a scheme that, founded as it will be on their successful experience, will strengthen, not destroy, local self-government."[123] Imagine its shock and surprise when only a fortnight later the Corporation decided to break up for the summer holiday! Still, there seemed to be no immediate danger, and by January 1885 the Municipal Reform League was in partial, "if not total, collapse" — only a shell of its former self and almost bankrupt.[124] All through 1885 the *Press* continued to sing a gleeful dirge for the League, which it pictured as a small ring of agitators with little or no public backing. In the meantime, despite the exhortations of the *Press*, the Corporation continued to do nothing; and when, in the general election of 1886, the metropolis returned forty-six Conservatives, the immediate danger seemed to have passed.[125] They would certainly oppose the notion of one great municipality, which Lord Salisbury himself had denounced. Almost up to the introduction of Ritchie's Local Government Bill in 1888 the *Press* continued to babble about the Corporation's intention of using the opportunity presented by the Government's rumored consideration of local government reform to introduce a bill of its own for a series of municipalities.[126]

Ritchie's bill dealt gingerly with the City, and the Corporation had good reason to feel relieved. Naturally there was indignation over the threat of being degraded to the position of an ordinary petty sessional borough, "when Birmingham and Manchester, even Bradford and Newcastle, will have more unfettered scope and freer local self-government than the City, which is the centre of our national and commercial life."[127] But the City was not destroyed. In large measure, Ritchie had accepted the advice so frequently given by Guildhall and had left City institutions substantially untouched, choosing instead to build around them. Indeed, if the City had not begun to look on Ritchie's bill with a favorable eye it would have been abysmally stupid, even suicidal. Whether, since then, the City Corporation has responded acceptably to the lease of life which the Local Government Act of 1888 gave it may be open to argument. But clearly its sense of public responsibility and public obligation has expanded so much that the present Corporation hardly seems the lineal descendant of the body that so bitterly resisted change in the 1880s.

CHAPTER 12

St. Marylebone

Writing in the mid-1870s, J. F. B. Firth described St. Marylebone as "probably the best-managed Vestry in the Metropolis."[1] It would not do to dispute the judgment of this competent, on-the-spot observer. Yet his statement should not be accepted without qualification. Certainly most members of the vestry, who were fond of speaking of "the grand old parish" and of praising its government and traditions (and by implication themselves), would not have been tempted to disagree with it — except, perhaps, in the years when the rates rose sharply. As compared with St. Pancras, its neighbor to the east, Marylebone's record during the second half of the nineteenth century was relatively uneventful, although dissident minorities or aspiring demagogues could at various times turn a vestry meeting into a bear garden. Marylebone's vestry showed the same inability as other vestries to get along with the guardians of the poor, and the guardians, in turn, had their difficulties in staffing and administering the institutions for which they were responsible. The vestry also displayed the same cheeseparing economy in dealing with parish officers, and the same tendency to measure every proposal by its effect on the rates. Still, when all reservations have been made, Marylebone stands as a reasonably well administered community, certainly one of the best in the metropolis.

The parish of Marylebone, one of the largest in London, stretched from Oxford Street on the south to Hampstead on the north and from

Edgware Road on the west to Tottenham Court Road and the parish of
St. Pancras on the east. Altogether it contained some 1,500 acres and a
population that had risen from 96,000 in 1821 to 160,000 in 1861. From
then on, like other central urban areas, Marylebone slowly declined until in 1901 its population numbered only 133,000. By the middle of the
nineteenth century any distinction between town and country had been
wiped out. An equally important force in establishing the modern character of the parish was the London and Birmingham Railway, which in
the late 1830s cut through to its terminus in Euston Station, dividing the
prosperous residential areas of Marylebone from the squalor of St. Pancras, Somers Town, Agar Town (now entirely obliterated), Camden
Town, and other wretched districts. From that time on, there was to be
a sharp contrast between the two parishes. Nowhere in London, Hugh
Prince tells us, was the contrast between two sides of a railway track
more sharply drawn than between the terraces of Regent's Park and
those of Camden Town.[2]

That is not, of course, to say that either parish housed only one class,
as did certain East End and Surrey parishes. In Marylebone, Regent's
Park and the fashionable squares — Cavendish, Portman, and Manchester, for example — were lined with the houses of the aristocracy, with
their phalanxes of servants; the main streets were filled with handsome
shops catering for a predominantly wealthy clientele; and farther out,
St. John's Wood would presently be built up by well-to-do men from the
City and elsewhere in London. But there was another Marylebone, a
world of mean streets and closed courts, where — as in Church Street
ward, in the streets behind Lisson Grove — prostitutes, thieves, and Irish
laborers made their headquarters. But this was the only one of the eight
wards into which the parish was divided in 1855 (when Sir Benjamin
Hall's act came into operation) that housed a population on the edge of
destitution. On the diagonally opposite border of the parish, southeast of
Regent's Park, there was, however, another not much less disreputable
section. Every house, Michael Sadleir asserts, in Bolsover, Carburton,
Clipstone, and Charlton (now Hanson) streets, as well as in the upper
part of Great Titchfield Street, was a brothel, a rooming house, a common lodging house, or a tavern with access to the upper floors.[3] A verita-
ble parade of prostitutes patrolled Portland Place, and in 1857 it was said
that some thousand abandoned women had collected in the area to the
west of Fitzroy Square.[4] Farther south, off Oxford Street, were districts
which caused no trouble — Berners Street and Rathbone Place, for example — although it was well known that many of the houses there were
occupied by ladies who plied their illicit trade. There were a few dis-
creetly managed bagnios, and most of the ladies had a limited and re-

spectable clientele.[5] But the vestry, though it tried repeatedly, was never able to take effective action against the prostitution that flourished in some corners of its domain.

Marylebone was one of the small number of London parishes which in the early 1830s had reorganized their affairs in accordance with Hobhouse's act. In the spring of 1832, when the air was heavily charged with the reform spirit, over 6,700 Marylebone ratepayers (out of an electorate of about 8,500) had voted to adopt the act, with only twenty opposing.[6] Henceforth, in place of the select vestry, which had been in power since 1768, a new open vestry, freely elected by all the ratepayers, would govern the parish.[7] For a time the Radicals, directed by the Parochial, or Barlow Street Committee, which had been responsible for the adoption of Hobhouse's act, had things their own way, and they embarked on a program of drastic and reckless costcutting. But by the late 1830s the dictation of the Radicals and the fever for penny-pinching economy had run their course, and the parish returned to more normal behavior. The Parochial Committee lost much of its dictatorial power, though it continued as the dominant local political organization until the late 1840s and conducted the affairs of the parish to the general satisfaction of the ratepayers. But a realignment was about to take place.

The first new organization, the Ratepayers' Protection Association, came into being in 1849 as the result of a clash between the venerable Radical M.P., Joseph Hume, and some leaders of the old Parochial Committee. The Ratepayers' Protection Association was regarded, in some quarters at least, as an unnatural alliance of dedicated Tories with Whigs and Radicals. In 1850 and 1851 the Association succeeded in defeating the Parochial Committee and found itself with two-thirds of the vestry seats. Thereupon the Parochial Committee expired and the Association was left in command, but not for long. It attempted to hold the reins too tightly, and an insurgent movement developed within its ranks which attacked the association as arbitrary and as tending to send to the vestry men who were mere delegates. The consequence was a secession of some twenty vestrymen who formed another organization called simply the Ratepayers' Association, and who collected among their adherents the remnants of the original Parochial Committee.[8] This new body, usually known as "the Orientals" because its meetings took place at the Oriental Hotel, resented the charge of its opponents that it was a Parson and Church and State crowd and that it had been formed under Tory inspiration.[9] But in any case it gathered strength rapidly, and in the election of May 1852 was able to defeat the Ratepayers' Protection Association — or "Alligators", as they were generally known because of the inability of one of their number to spell "alleged" in the charges made by

the group against the old Parochial Committee.[10] For the time being at
least, the Orientals had control of the vestry, and they were to maintain
their position for several years. Whether they were, in fact, a Church-
King-Tory party may be questioned, but clearly they were heavy with
solid respectability. Most of the loud and sometimes irresponsible radicalism was left to the other side.

With the collapse of its electoral position, the Ratepayers' Protection
Association retired to regroup its forces. Officially, the Association dissolved itself, but profiting from a move sponsored by the Orientals to re-
assess the parish on the basis of the house tax (thus raising the rental, the
opposition argued, by some £150,000), it reemerged in 1855 as the Independent Association, having effected an alliance with some of its late opponents.[11] Actually the new body contained elements of three older parties. It is, of course, impossible to identify a conflict of principle in such
shifting parish cliques. In this case, controversy seems to have revolved
primarily around the rating reassessment, during which several prosperous Oxford Street tradesmen (such as Clement George, an upholsterer,
Richard Michell, a dealer in French flowers and feathers, and J. A.
Nicholay, a prominent furrier) were accused of having enjoyed unduly
low assessments. In any case, the Independent Association was at pains
to present a varied list of candidates, salted with some members of the
aristocracy from Portman Square and Cavendish Square, a number of
wealthy residents of Portland Place and Harley Street, and several professional men, as well as the customary group of tradesmen.[12] As not infrequently happened in parish elections, a good many of the same names
appeared on both the Oriental and Independent lists. The election of
1855, the last before Hall's act, was a close one, but the Orientals again
came out on top, though by only 87 votes in a poll of nearly 3,500 (out of
16,000 eligible ratepayers).[13]

The vestry viewed Hall's bill with general satisfaction, interpreting it
as a triumph for the local self-government that the parish championed.
Only the year before, the vestry had sent an enthusiastic resolution to
Toulmin Smith approving his Anti-Centralisation Union and emphasizing its own enthusiasm for extending the principles of local self-government.[14] Moreover, because Sir Benjamin Hall sat in Parliament for
Marylebone, the vestry naturally felt an exceptional interest in his proposals for the metropolis. Yet for some members Hall's Metropolis Local
Management Act stopped somewhat short of perfection, and there was
regret that the Government had not seized the occasion to extend to the
whole of the metropolis the "municipal institutions which are at once the
depositories and safeguards of public liberty".[15]

In Marylebone the transition to the new regime established by the act

went smoothly enough, especially since there was no thought of changing parish clerks. W. E. Greenwell, a solicitor, had held the office since
1851 and was to continue in it until his retirement in 1886.[16] The parish
was divided into eight wards, none of which contained fewer than 500
householders, with quotas of vestrymen varying from 9 to 18. The total
membership of the vestry was set at the maximum, 120. As compared
with some later contests, this first one under the new act produced a
good deal of excitement. The chief issue, again, was the reassessment of
rates on the basis of the house tax, which was opposed by the Independent Association. The curious thing, the *Observer* noted, was that the
aristocratic parish of Marylebone returned, with one or two exceptions,
the extreme Radical party, while "the noted radical parish of St. Pancras, as it is termed," tended to move in the opposite direction. Yet all
the interest was not sufficient to produce a poll in three of the Marylebone wards, while in some of the others the contention was over only a
few names, the bulk of the list being accepted without dispute.[17] Two
years later the electors had settled down to their normal apathy, and only
two wards had a contest. Even these were merely attempts by one or two
individuals to get a place on the successful list.[18]

The first meeting, in 1855, of the new vestry (called the "Municipal
Council" by the *Observer*) drew about a hundred members, and the
gallery was crowded.[19] This vestry, in fact, was reasonably conscientious
in its attendance, never, during the first fifteen weeks of its existence,
falling below seventy-four and with an average attendance at regular
meetings of slightly over eighty-five.[20] The pot was still boiling over the
reassessment, and indignation ran high, with large numbers of appeals
against particular assessments. But the vestry got down to business and,
among other things, elected its representatives to the new MBW. The
contest was active, with eight candidates being nominated. To no one's
surprise, J. A. Nicholay, the Oxford Street furrier, led the poll, followed
by the younger Thomas D'Iffanger, who had kept a school in Maida
Vale and who, in spite of a bland manner, had aroused both enthusiasm
and opposition in Marylebone.[21] In March 1856 Nicholay was also
elected churchwarden by a large majority. For years he had been a
leader in parish affairs. A man of strong, if narrow, views, he was almost
the archetype of the metropolitan radical, thoroughly committed to
economy and local self-government and snorting furiously at any centralizing gestures from the Government.

Even if the Marylebone vestry did not have the pronounced aristocratic coloring of that of St. George's, Hanover Square, in social standing it
was considerably above the average for the metropolis. In 1857 a letter
in the *Marylebone Mercury* pointed out that the vestrymen included nine-

teen doctors and surgeons, eleven civil engineers and builders, and seven service officers.[22] Granted that some stretch of the imagination would be necessary to accept all of the names as belonging in the category to which the writer assigned them (Nicholay, for example, as one of the officers), and granted also that for a builder to be on the vestry was no mark of distinction either for the individual or for the parish, this was still a rather impressive list. Social standing did not, of course, assure responsible behavior: only two or three members, bent on gaining influence for themselves, could have a disastrous effect on the vestry meetings. In the early years of the new vestry probably the most disturbing force was Edward Hodges from the Portland Place ward (which included the shady Bolsover Street district), whose gift of extreme utterance, combined with political shrewdness, made him a force to be reckoned with. He had organized the Independent Association out of the ruins of the old Alligator party, and he continued to speak for the small shopkeepers against the ratepayers of higher social standing. Another disruptive member was Charles Freeth, a builder, who, however, had little of Hodges' influence or political sense. His speeches were windy and incredibly silly, but they took time and had a ruinous effect on vestry proceedings.

Sometimes these meetings became almost riotous. In the fall of 1858 the vestry debated a proposal to raise the clerk's salary above £400. One speaker pictured the Marylebone post as the most poorly paid of all the metropolitan parishes, which was certainly not true. Deputations of ratepayers were brought to the meeting to protest against the proposal, and the debate was raucous and rancorous. Hodges took a leading part in the proceedings. As the ratepayers moved onto the floor to get into the argument, the clerks and beadles rushed in to retrieve their books and papers. A week later the debate was resumed, with ratepayers' deputations again appearing and crowds in the galleries doing their best to intimidate the vestrymen. After an excessive volume of oratory and many disturbances from the gallery, the vestry settled the matter by voting a modest increase.[23]

Four years later Hodges and Freeth were still causing trouble, and the *Mercury* concluded that the behavior of the vestry had become even worse than that in St. Pancras. The paper was referring to a row over the confirmation of the minutes of the previous meeting, in which Hodges had delivered a speech that would have been unrivaled in the annals of vestry abuse had Freeth not outdone him. Civilization, the *Mercury* concluded, was a stage that the vestry had left far behind.[24] It spoke of the dreadful results produced by a few turbulent and factious members who behaved "by the outrage of every rule that should guide the proceedings of a public body."[25] In the elections of May 1862, however, there was some evidence that contests had been encouraged in the hope of getting a better type of vestryman. The *Mercury*'s feeling that the vestry was losing its last shreds of respectability seemed to be shared by the parish, but little was accomplished.[26]

And so the vestry went on, raucous or well behaved, depending on the personnel and the issues and also, one suspects, on the attitude of the local paper reporting its proceedings. In the fall of 1866, some of the radical group (a number of whose leaders had been defeated in the spring) proposed to form a new central association to curb the extravagance of the current vestry and to resist the encroachment of the central Government on local liberty. This body proposed to work against the division of the parish into wards, which, it argued, had destroyed the unity of parish organization.[27] Nothing is known of the later history of this enterprise, but by the early middle seventies the parish seemed to be moving with almost suspicious smoothness. There were no issues of consequence and few disputes. Not even an increase in rates caused more than a murmur or two. The *Mercury* judged Marylebone to be a splendid parish, with able officials, excellent sanitary arrangements, and a model workhouse, a judgment which agrees with that of Firth, quoted at the beginning of this chapter.[28] In fact, the parish was criticized for having no crying needs or flagrant abuses, which left the local press with little to attack!

The reforms which the vestry made were minor in character and were introduced without much fanfare. For example, in 1876 it proposed to scrap the examination of weights and measures by the leet jury and to appoint instead a paid inspector to perform this work. The leet jury consisted of a dozen persons selected by the vestry whose duty it was to tour the parish in groups of four to test the accuracy of all tradesmens' scales and measures. This was an agreeable arrangement for the tradesmen, who were generally forewarned of the jury's arrival by the loafers who accompanied the four. Moreover, the jury could only act until sundown; after that the shopkeeper could be as dishonest as he wished. The apparently innocent proposal to abandon the leet jury produced an outcry in the parish, evidently for two reasons: paying an inspector would add to the cost of government; and tradesmen had good reason for opposing a professional inspection. There was, in fact, an active debate in the vestry, and ultimately the proposal was passed by a majority of only seven votes.[29] Similarly, the ceremony of perambulating the boundaries of the parish, observed in Marylebone every seven years, persisted until 1880. This was a happy enough ritual — sometimes excessively so, as when, in the late fifties, a clerical vestryman from St. Pancras deplored (in the press) having seen two Marylebone vestrymen publicly drunk.[30]

When the observance was at its height in that decade, a lunch might be served to very large numbers of parishioners, including nearly three hundred children. It was all jolly good fun, but it was not until 1880 that the vestry decided that perambulating the bounds could be more efficiently done by a committee.[31]

One characteristic feature of Marylebone policy was the form taken by the ratepayers' associations. At least by the late 1870s and early 1880s — and perhaps earlier — these were organized on a ward rather than an all-parish basis. Although most of them were pretty meager bodies, they arrogated to themselves the right to nominate lists of vestrymen, and, given the apathy of the mass of ratepayers, they were usually successful in electing their slate. Some of them had fewer than fifty members, who paid one or two shillings each in membership dues. The only active association was that in the Bryanston Square ward, a ward close to Edgeware Road that had a socially mixed population, which sometimes got a hundred people to attend its meetings, in contrast to the ten or twelve who might appear at meetings of the Portman Square Ward Association.[32] Yet, if this picture seems excessively bleak, the *Mercury* concluded in 1881 that the ward associations, often with a membership of one to two hundred, were not unrepresentative. In any case, without these agencies to nominate and practically elect candidates to vacancies, there would have been real difficulty in maintaining a supply of vestrymen.[33] The apathy of ratepayers, save when some scandalous proceeding emerged, was an ever present fact. Apparently they were perfectly content to let the vestrymen be nominated by a pitifully small group.

It took some time for the vestry to acclimatize itself to the notion that the Metropolis Local Management Act was something more than just a charter of local self-government. As it became more and more evident that the MBW fancied itself as the government of the metropolis, the hostility of the vestry toward the Board became more marked. Throughout the life of the Board the vestry's attitude was remorselessly parochial, and members whose outlook was less circumscribed were regarded as traitorous or soft-headed. The most objectionable proposals of the Board, of course, were those that had to do with raising the rates or that threatened to do so, for Marylebone vestrymen, like others in the metropolis, felt it was their major responsibility to keep the rates down. A Local Management Association held meetings in which radicals inveighed against the coal tax, against the number of improvements which were planned for the City (but none for Marylebone), and against the main drainage scheme, for which, one speaker maintained, there was no real demand. It was the duty of the Government, one meeting concluded, to abolish the MBW forthwith.[34]

In the early years there was trouble over the expedients by which the Board sought to collect money for the sewers built by the superseded Metropolitan Commissioners of Sewers, including the ill-starred Victoria Street sewer. The first precept went only to those parishes that were thought to have benefited from the sewer, and for the time being Marylebone resisted successfully. It was a hard problem for the MBW, which shifted its policy more than once—at one time proposing to tax the entire metropolitan area, at another proposing to strike only the parishes that had benefited. In the end the parish found the Board's solution acceptable, since the decision, embodied in the Local Management Amendment Act of 1862 was to make the charge a metropolitan one.[35] But in the meantime radicals in the vestry attacked the Board, charging that it took money out of the parish's pocket and did nothing in return, and demanding that the parish wash its hands of the Board.[36]

There were other controversies, all of them with fiscal overtones. Some vestrymen attempted to unseat Nicholay for having favored the moving of the Board's headquarters to Spring Gardens, an unexpected posture for this economy-minded member which suggested that even the most committed champions of local rights and "small government" could be changed by a period of service on the Board.[37] The vestry joined in the hue and cry raised against the Board's proposal to increase the salary of its architect, Frederick Marrable, from £800 to £1,200, and then by degrees to £1,500. Nicholay declared that this would be an act of suicide for the Board, and, when Marrable's resignation was reported, Nicholay's colleague D'Iffanger called the change beneficial because the Board could get an equally good architect for £800.[38] On the other questions of the early 1860s the Marylebone vestrymen behaved in a predictable fashion. They did not like the prospect of the Board's taking over the fire insurance companies' Fire Engine Establishment: Dr. G. H. Bachhoffner, a founder of the London Polytechnic Institute and a lecturer on popular science, thought that the fire companies ought to pay the total cost of fire fighting, and another member denounced the scheme as rank centralization since it would also take the control of the parochial fire engines out of the hands of the vestry.[39] On sewage utilization, the vestry took the popular London attitude that money could be made out of it, though one member, the Reverend Professor D. W. Marks of University College, was sensible enough to say that the discussion would have no practical result. Freeth, the builder, asserted that the sewage was of "inestimable value," and Bachhoffner added that the solid sewage might be worth £3,600 a day, though, he noted cautiously, no plan had yet been proposed to make effective use of this mass. The vestry's way out was a vague resolution of encouragement.[40]

As was the case in the other metropolitan parishes, the Board's difficulties with Ridley and the Embankment contract had their repercussions in Marylebone. Here again, it was Hodges and the radical group that led the charge against the Board in the vestry. Bachhoffner, with a better understanding of engineering realities than his fellow vestrymen, undertook the defense. Obviously he had little use for Ridley and his pretensions, and he was able to prevent the vestry from petitioning the House of Commons to take action.[41] In the following year (1865) a vestry committee chaired by Bachhoffner looked into the contracts once more. Its report produced a long, tiresome, and riotous debate, but in the end the vote seems to have gone favorably for the Board.[42]

By the mid-1860s the vestry was beginning to realize that the existence of the MBW by no means meant an extension of parish self-government. The conduct of the vestry's representatives on the Board did not particularly commend itself, and there was some talk of replacing them. But that would have amounted to one of those revolutions that vestries indulged in only rarely. D'Iffanger, who died suddenly in 1865, was too good-natured (the *Mercury* thought), allowing his constituents to be deprived of what was rightfully theirs by less scrupulous colleagues representing other parishes. And Nicholay, who carried on till 1873 (nearly twenty years) had shown himself too narrow for the post: before the Montague committee in 1864 he had made a bad impression, with his absurd intemperance of speech and bigoted ideas.[43] On top of the parish's discontent with its representatives came the Board's Improvement Rate Bill calling for the rate to be divided between the owner and the occupier. The vestry was opposed both in general and in detail — in general because this was another centralizing device and was therefore bad by definition, and in detail because the maximum figure proposed (fourpence in the pound) was too high, even though it included the old sewer rate of threepence. One member pointed out that those who opposed the rate obviously had little hope of getting the improvements contemplated for Marylebone, and still less of acquiring Hampstead for the metropolis.[44] Throughout the wrangling the Marylebone vestry was much less convinced in its opposition than was St. Pancras. Some members even favored the principle because it would get at the landlords. Finally the vestry, in spite of a public meeting in which feelings apparently ran high, decided not to oppose the bill actively.

Marylebone attitudes were revealed even more unmistakably in the violent hostility aroused by McCullagh Torrens' bill for working-class housing. Here the principal ground of opposition, as always, seems to have been financial, for the bill, it was argued, would certainly raise the rates. Public meetings were held, and at one of them a letter was read from the Marylebone members of Parliament showing how virtuously correct had been their behavior in opposing the bill. At an invitation from Marylebone, indignant deputations gathered from a number of London parishes, all furious at the proposal. Such a measure, they argued, was not at all necessary with so many voluntary housing societies already at work, but if there was to be a housing act the local vestries and not the MBW should be given the job of implementing it. Throughout the affair, Marylebone's attitude remained highly parochial, exalting parsimony into a principle of political action.[45]

Yet myopic as the views of the vestry may seem today and riotous as some of its debates were, the parish in 1888 was very different from what it had been in 1848. In fact halfway through this period Marylebone may have deserved the accolade given it by Firth. To be sure, some anachronisms remained. The parish did not have a large Dissenting population, and it continued to pay Church rates long after most metropolitan parishes had stopped doing so. There were occasional attempts to get rid of them, but even as late as the 1880s ratepayers in Marylebone were being taxed to pay for the half-dozen churches built in the days of the old select vestry, though by then there were nearly thirty churches in the parish.[46]

By the Metropolis Local Management Act of 1855 all vestries and district boards were required to appoint a Medical Officer of Health. In Marylebone this new post was established with reasonable smoothness, and successive officers worked conscientiously at their tasks, some of them exceptionally so. Initially the vestry, wisely declining the proposal of three physicians that they be jointly appointed to the office, elected R. D. Thomson in spite of the rumor that he was the candidate of Dr. Farr, the Registrar-General, and would be a channel through which Government influence entered the parish.[47] His first responsibility was to get accurate weekly figures of the number of deaths in the parish, figures which the vestry had at first tried, unsuccessfully, to get directly from the Registrar-General because the district registrars demanded an additional fee of threepence per death. When the attempt to get the fee down to a penny failed, the vestry accepted threepence with as good a grace as possible.[48] A proposal made in 1862 to raise Thomson's salary from £400 to £450 in order to compensate him for extra work in the analysis of gas and adulterated food was refused by the vestry, one vestryman observing that the country was "on a free trade basis" and that members of the public, knowing that some food was adulterated—that both good and evil were put before them—could get the good if they were willing to pay for it.[49] The post of Medical Officer was considered quite a plum. Even as Thomson lay on his deathbed, maneuvering was taking place on behalf of various candidates. Dr. Whitmore, a member of the vestry and the unsuccessful candidate in 1856 when Thomson had been elected, already had enough votes promised to be elected. He did at least have the decency to resign his seat, so that he would not be elected while a vestry member. When, in an acrid debate over the question, someone pointed out that the vestrymen's performance looked bad, they decided to go through the motions of advertising for candidates, knowing of course that they were going to elect Whitmore. And this they did by a huge majority.[50]

In the field of health the parish made a showing that was creditable — neither the best nor the worst in the metropolis. Between 1861 and 1870 (a decade of epidemics) annual deaths ran at twenty-five per thousand, higher than in Kensington and slightly higher, curiously enough, than in St. Pancras, but distinctly lower than in such parishes as Stepney and Whitechapel where the rate was thirty per thousand.[51] Conditions in the parish, however, were not as salubrious as the vestry liked to believe. In 1873 a bad outbreak of typhoid fever that centered in Marylebone was traced to milk supplied, ironically, by the Dairy Reform Company in Orchard Street just off Portman Square.[52] Two years later the parish was in the throes of a smallpox epidemic, which crowded all the available hospital space and inspired the vestry (in desperation) to appeal to the Metropolitan Asylums Board to provide additional accommodation. One vestryman, more consistent than his fellows, expressed astonishment that the local-self-government convictions of the vestry had broken down so readily that they would attempt to evade their responsibilities by appealing to a central body.[53] The vestry and its sanitary committee, a not very active body which met infrequently, sometimes found their self-congratulation on the good health of the parish sadly misplaced, or at least mistimed. In the fall of 1881, for example, they were boasting that all was well in the parish just at the moment when typhus was raging in Charles Street, a short street (now obliterated) which connected Mortimer Street with Goodge Street. The situation was so grave in fact, that the *Mercury* demanded that a house-to-house visitation be carried on by an augmented sanitary staff.[54]

Marylebone's third Medical Officer, Dr. Wynter Blyth, who was appointed in 1880, was well qualified and industrious, but he often found the vestry a dead weight with which he had to deal gently and tactfully. He wrote long and illuminating annual reports — the one for 1883 covers 160 pages — examining the community in detail, pointing to the bad districts with their dreadful housing, their high death rates, and their proneness to epidemics. He singled out the worst of the pestholes, drawing attention to their overcrowding and to the condition of their drainage. By the end of the 1880s, however, it was obvious that sanitary conditions had improved enormously. The report for 1886, for instance, pointed to the vast improvement in house drainage. During that year Dr. Blyth's five sanitary inspectors, each of whom was responsible for a particular part of the parish, had examined and reported on twelve hundred drains, and they were constantly looking for nuisances and threats to the health of the parish. To check food adulteration, nearly six hundred samples had been analyzed. Milk was the most heavily adulterated, but in 1886 only 8 percent of the sample gave evidence of foreign matter.[55]

In the area of public improvements, the vestry's record though not up to twentieth-century standards, was nevertheless impressive. At the time of the Metropolis Local Management Act a considerable number of Marylebone streets were still without sewers. Some of those that did exist were so choked with sewage as to be quite impassable, while others were so filled with noisome fumes that several accidents had occurred to workmen. Sometimes the sewers were constructed higher than the basements of the houses which they were expected to drain, "and it was therefore necessary for the sewage to be lifted into the sewers by pumping or otherwise."[56] Parts of the parish were still supplied with water from public wells, some forty-four of them, which provided water "for the most part offensive to taste and smell."[57] Goaded into action by new legislation, notably the Sanitary Act of 1866, the vestry set about the business of improving parish services. When in 1870 the MBW (at the instigation of the House of Commons) called on the vestries to report their achievements, Marylebone's record was highly creditable. Though the vestries generally were at no pains to understate their achievements, it is impossible to doubt that Marylebone had made real progress. Measured by cost, it was well up on the list, exceeded by only three or four parishes. The vestry reported that during the fifteen years since Hall's act it had laid down twelve miles of new sewers and seven and a half miles of drains under the public way to connect with the sewers. Old and dilapidated sewers had been reconstructed, and all sewers (the vestry reported, probably with some exaggeration) were then clean, well ventilated, and sufficiently deep to fulfill their purpose. Under the Nuisance Removal Act the vestry had required some forty-five and a half miles of drainpipes to be laid at the expense of owners and occupiers. Over 4,000 cesspools had been emptied, disinfected, and filled up; water had been piped to over 8,000 closets, in many of which there had been no previous supply; and over 5,600 houses had been cleansed, ventilated, and otherwise improved. The vestry's outlay on opening new streets and repaving old streets was impressive, especially since most of the cost had been taken from the rates. Nearly £350,000 had been spent on paving, repaving, and repairing streets (the bulk of this work having been done by the parish's own workmen), and nearly £55,000 on opening up new streets. The total amount spent on improvements during the fifteen years was nearly £460,000, of which close to £350,000 had been drawn from the rates.[58]

Such developments, the vestry argued, had already changed the parish for the better. In the Lisson Grove district, for example, the annual death rate, which from 1861 to 1865 had been thirty per thousand, had declined by 1870 to an average of twenty-six. Yet Marylebone's sanitary arrangements should not be described in overly idyllic terms. Six years later the sanitary committee was proposing to raise, partly by rates, partly by loan, a large sum to carry out a vast program of sewer reconstruction.[59] And the parish was still opposed to public amenities which might add to the rates. During the winter and spring of 1888, Thomas Reed and Frank Debenham (of Debenham and Freebody) agitated indefatigably to get a public library for the parish under Ewart's act of 1850. Admittedly London parishes had not rushed to take advantage of this act; only two (Westminster and Wandsworth) had reached favorable decisions by the end of 1884. But in 1886–87 a dozen parishes changed their minds, and Marylebone might have been expected to be one of that group. Throughout the spring of 1888 Reed and Debenham pushed the library idea by holding two meetings a week in different parts of the parish, but to no avail. In a plebiscite the ratepayers voted heavily in the negative, though the voting proces, the *Mercury* reported, had been suspicious, with instructions to vote no being handed out by young men dressed as policemen.[60]

Indeed, in the vestry the sovereign test of a new proposal was likely to be its probable effect on the rates. One obvious way to ingratiate oneself with the ratepayers was to reduce (or at least to promise to reduce) the rates. A new group, wishing to gain seats on the vestry and then move into a commanding position, would inevitably charge its predecessors with gross extravagance and would pledge to lower the rate level. This might last over one or two rating periods, but then the rate would bounce back and rise even higher than before. The rates in Marylebone showed a tendency to fluctuate not merely because of varying demands but also because of the vestry's bad judgment, some of it deliberately bad. In 1864, for example, the parish found itself in financial hot water. The previous year had ended with a surplus of £3,000, and the vestry had reduced the rates. But in 1864 the surplus was spent and a debt of more than £3,000 contracted, for which even the increased rates were inadequate. Apparently the £3,000 surplus had not, in fact, been a surplus at all but merely money allocated for paving Oxford Street and building certain new sewers, which had not been used because neither project was accomplished. It was no economy, the *Mercury* cautioned, to levy utterly inadequate rates. Low rates did not mark a parish as well administered but probably the contrary. The proper test was what work had been done and how well.[61]

In Marylebone, the collection of rates seems to have been managed with reasonable efficiency — sasve for the occasional collector who defaulted. As was customary, the collectors were paid poundage for their services, and losses through noncollection were fairly small. In 1859, for example, only about £400 was lost out of a total amount of about £35,000.[62] But the collection of rates sometimes did give trouble. It was often difficult to change the rate collectors' districts to coincide with the boundaries of the wards, and it was even more difficult to decide whether the same collectors should handle both the poor rate and the main drainage rate.[63] Toward defaulting collectors and their sureties the vestry could behave with great firmness, even toughness. In 1867 two veteran collectors were found to be in default, one for £678 and the other for £1,262. The vestry at once discharged both of them, as well as Henry Watts, the old senior clerk whose duty it was to check on the performance of the collectors. When Watts tried to resign instead, the vestry refused to accept his offer and insisted on his discharge. The *Mercury* found the behavior of the vestry disgraceful, claiming that it had been so slow in getting warrants against the defaulting collectors that they had been able to disappear, and that then it had victimized a helpless old man. The vestry held firm, too, against the sureties for the collectors (by a vote of 25–23), one of whom was certain to be ruined.[64] There were other cases of dishonesty among parish officials, but defalcation (embezzlement) never became as much of a habit in Marylebone as in St. Pancras, where within a few months five officials were shown to be about £5,000 short in their accounts.

In the late seventies a band of "Irreconcilables" in the vestry regularly slashed the clerk's recommended rates. A proposed rate of four shillings and fourpence would be promptly cut to four shillings, and one of four shillings and sevenpence to four shillings and a penny halfpenny.[65] The result was that the parish found itself running a heavy deficit of some £19,000 in 1881, while St. Pancras, for whose financial administration Marylebone had traditionally felt contempt, had a surplus of £3,500.[66] By 1882 the situation had become worse, partly due to expensive poor-law enterprises; so in February 1883 the clerk asked for a rate of four shillings and elevenpence, which was cut by the economizers to four shillings and ninepence halfpenny.[67] The clerk had obviously learned that in making his initial estimates he had to allow for the onslaughts of the economizers. Therefore for 1884 (Marylebone being one of the parishes that set its rates for the year rather than either quarter by quarter or semiannually) he asked the vestry for five shillings and twopence to allow for an increase in the School Board rate and for new paving. This, the editor of the *Mercury* asserted, was the highest rate ever levied in the parish.[68]

It is true that the vestries had control over only a small fraction of the rates they had to impose. The poor rate, the police rate, the county rate, the school rate, and the MBW precepts were not assessed by the vestry. In Marylebone, as in other London vestries, precepts from the School Board were received with indignation and sometimes they produced threats against the local members of that Board. In the 1885 election two economizers led the poll, followed by the Reverend Joseph Diggle, the unadventurous and economically minded chairman of the School Board.[69] In 1887, however, the vestry even denounced Diggle for extravagance because he had championed an increase in the salary of the Board's clerk.[70] Earlier the vestry had opposed not only the attempt to force the water companies to provide a constant water supply but also the proposal that the MBW take over the water companies.[71] This opposition, again, came from the economizers, as well as from those who continued to fear that the Board threatened local self-government. The same attitudes were reflected in the vestry's resolution that the Board should not have responsibility for administering the Artisans' Dwellings Act. Still less creditable was the attitude of the strong minority which voted against the proposal to transfer the care of the fish markets from the City to the Board. The *Mercury* could find no explanation other than sheer perversity for this unaccountable preference for the City.[72]

By the early 1880s, in fact, Marylebone suspected that the days of local self-government might be numbered, and the parish establishment mobilized to resist. In 1884 the vestry elections hinged on the candidates' attitudes toward Harcourt's bill, with ratepayers' associations passing resolutions condemning it and attempting to unseat candidates known to favor it. The *Mercury* thought it absurd that a few men calling themselves a ratepayers' association should overthrow a great Government measure.[73] The vestry itself staged a ratepayers' meeting, and although it was held at three o'clock in the afternoon in a smallish hall a fair number of ratepayers appeared. The vestry majority appeared to have matters under control when Thomas Reed and William Debenham, Liberal insurgents, brought in an amendment. They offered the argument, solidly realistic, that local self-government had already disappeared from the vestries. When the vestry controlled only a shilling and a penny halfpenny out of a rate of four shillings and tenpence, it was a waste of time to defend local self-government. In any case, the MBW and the London School Board, not the vestries, had done the really valuable work. This made sound sense, but it was received with reservations by the Marylebone ratepayers even though some insisted that the Reed-Debenham case had won the support of a majority of the meeting.[74]

Many of the parish's most difficult problems, financial and otherwise, were connected with its responsibilities for the poor. By twentieth-century standards, the parish workhouse looked after an enormous number of inmates. In a typical week in April 1873, for example, the house had nearly 2,000 inmates, in addition to 450 in the pauper school and 214 lunatics, and in October 1880 the number was nearly 2,200.[75] The poor rate was the largest single item in the rate bill during the late fifties—larger than all the other items put together. Clearly an establishment of some size was necessary to administer this enterprise, which handled both outdoor (home) and institutional relief.

Until 1868 poor relief in St. Marylebone was the sole responsibility of the directors and guardians of the poor, who, under the provisions of a local act, were appointed by the vestry; in fact, about half of them generally were vestrymen. In 1868, however, the Poor Law Board directed that the guardians of St. Marylebone (and of ten other large London parishes where local acts had hitherto applied) should be elected by the ratepayers in accordance with the provisions of the general poor law acts. The vestry had no direct control over the policies of the guardians, either before or after 1868. Vestrymen might argue about the amount to be collected in the poor rate and might dispute some of the policies pursued by the guardians, but in the last analysis the guardians were their own masters, subject only to the Poor Law Board and later to the Local Government Board.

In the mid 1850s, however, the Marylebone directors and guardians were still holding the Poor Law Board at arm's length. But a scandal in the workhouse in 1856 concerning the flogging of women by the master, Ryan, allowed the Board to move in and begin an investigation. Apparently the directors had had some notion of hushing the matter up, but unfortunately for them it had come out in the open when proceedings were being taken before a magistrate. Ratepayers and vestry were indignant at the apathy of the directors, for the flogging had evidently been premeditated and severe, and more decisive action by them might have prevented the Board's intervention. As it was, this intervention could have been the thin edge of the wedge, bringing poor relief in Marylebone under the control of the central authority.[76] But the directors dug in and did little save defy the orders of the Poor Law Board to dismiss the offending master. Even a reminder from the Board that it was itself entitled by law to remove the master of the workhouse failed to impel them to action.[77]

There were three parties involved in this issue—the vestry, the directors, and the Poor Law Board—none of which agreed fully with either of the others. The vestry's principal objective was to keep the Poor Law Board out of the parish. The vestrymen were uneasy about the directors' promotion of Ryan (previously a storekeeper in the workhouse) to be master of the house, and also about the policies which had brought in the Poor Law Board. The vestry shilly-shallied from meeting to meeting but ultimately shifted away from its earlier position of placing confidence in the directors and leaving everything in their hands. The directors, for their part, at first breathed defiance, virtually daring the Board to come and get them. Later, however, Ryan resigned (though there was some doubt in the vestry whether this action had really been taken), and the directors, under pressure from the vestry, accepted the resignation.[78] And finally, the Poor Law Board, seeing its chance to extend control over this obstinate parish, served notice that an inspector would attend the next meeting of the directors. In defiance the vestry invoked Marylebone's local act, which, it argued, took precedence over the Poor Law Act of 1834. The Board continued to apply pressure, and the parish to resist. The vestry then discussed a motion that Parliament be asked to exempt Marylebone from the jurisdiction of the Poor Law Board, and that Sir Benjamin Hall be requested to assist in the passage of such an act and to "otherwise actively oppose the Government in its attack on the independence this Parish has hitherto enjoyed in the management of its poor."[79]

This was a forlorn hope. Hall was not the man to give his sympathy and aid in such a bad case. The deputation from the directors that visited him—it was said for three hours—got a wholesome lecture. He reminded them of the correspondence between the Board and the directors, which had recently been presented to the House of Commons,[80] and he recapitulated the facts of the case from the beginning. If the picture given in the papers presented to the House was correct, the Poor Law Board, he argued, had no alternative but to intervene. When Hodges, the leader of the deputation, insolently declared that he and his colleagues did not want Hall's opinions but only his support, Hall told them that they would get his opinions whether they liked them or not.[81] Later, when he thought that the vestry had received a biased account of the deputation's visit, Hall continued his assault by sending every vestryman a copy of a recent adverse report of the Lunacy Commissioners on the treatment of the insane in the Marylebone workhouse. The fact was, one vestryman observed, "that the deputation had a fair stand-up fight with Sir B. Hall, and Hodges and Co. had got a great licking (roars of laughter, and hear, hear)."[82] After all, *The Times* reflected, there was no divine right to govern badly, however much one might believe in self-government.[83]

The Poor Law Board was clearly the victor in the fracas. Counsel's opinion, taken by the vestry, roundly supported the Board, and in June 1857 the directors abjectly tossed in the sponge. When one of the Board's inspectors attended a meeting of the directors, he took occasion to point out how costly poor relief in the parish had become. In the whole district the average annual cost of a pauper was £6. But in Marylebone in 1853 it had been £8 8s., and in 1856 it had soared to £11 7s. 9d. With only a slight increase in pauperism the cost to the parish had risen 43 percent.[84] It was anybody's guess whether the principal explanation lay in maladministration, in corruption, or in luxurious treatment given to the paupers.

The Poor Law Board was not slow to push its advantage, and in July 1858 it directed the appointment of a Poor Law auditor for Marylebone. There were signs of protest, but again a motion to consider petitioning Parliament to exempt Marylebone was lost.[85] The truth is that one of the weakest areas of local self-government was financial administration, which the Metropolis Local Management Act had left in the hands of the elected members of the vestry, ordinarily men of little special training. Nor was poor-law administration much better, save where the oversight of the central Board was applied and its regulations followed. In Marylebone the directors, who had lost much of their pugnacity, settled down to elect an auditor. There were nine candidates, some of them lawyers of good standing, but the winner was Joshua Gliddon, a vestryman, who conveniently forgot his recent fulminations against nepotism and his strong feelings for local self-government.[86] A shorthand writer with Overend and Gurney, the bill brokers, Gliddon was not ignorant of proper administrative procedures; for him, auditing the work of the directors was a shocking experience. He found chaos in the workhouse storeroom, with, for example, a discrepancy in the bread account that would mean a difference of £1,000 a year, and an inventory that was wholly out of line with the original purchases and the supplies given to inmates. Some 140,000 orders for outdoor relief had been given but no counterfoils filled out. The maladministration, indeed, was so gross that the *Mercury* foresaw the end of the whole system unless it could be brought under control.[87]

Gliddon, in fact, was getting an education in the defects of local self-government. He found the directors committed to a penny-pinching policy, even refusing to allow a request from the storekeeper for a salary increase to be read. Why would they not realize, he asked, that a good storekeeper could mean a difference of £700 to £1,000 a year to the parish? However much one admired local self-government, he continued, there was something bad about a system that threw power into the hands of those unqualified to exercise it.[88] When it was charged that he had failed to audit the directors' accounts, Gliddon replied angrily that the accounts were in such a bad state, with the book in chaos and half a year in arrears, that it was virtually impossible to audit the accounts without first cleaning up the mess. It is true that the system was far too complicated and the accounts were badly kept, but one of the principal troubles was that the bookkeeping was done by two boys, each of whom was paid rather less than a porter. This policy of economy was quite in accordance with "the established principles of parochial expenditures," said the *Mercury* in 1863, "but it is none the less detrimental to the interests of the ratepayers, guardians, and clerks. Economy is the cry dinned week after week into the ears of all; pare down this expense, reduce that allowance, disband that assistant: and by dint of this system low rates are levied, and the payers compliment the vestry, little thinking that they are supporting a state of things as bad as bad can be."[89]

The way was left open for a struggle for power between the vestry and the directors. In the early sixties the specific issue was the auditing of the directors' accounts: was this the exclusive preserve of the Poor Law auditor, or could the parish auditors claim oversight? A public meeting seemed to align the ratepayers with the vestry. But the directors refused to submit their accounts. Counsel to whom the case was submitted thought that parish auditors had no right to check on the work of the Poor Law auditors. This opinion ended the controversy,[90] and also provided belated public recognition of the fact that the directors were no longer, as they had been prior to the Poor Law Amendment Act of 1834, a separate branch of the parish authority, subordinate to the vestry and with accounts requiring the stamp of the parish auditors. The directors were now shown to be responsible not to the vestry but to the Poor Law Board. Such a resolution of the question of power relationships did not, however, put an end to feuds between the directors and the vestry, but henceforth these had to do with specific questions of expense. After all, it was the duty of the vestry to collect the rates requested by the directors—or the rates that the two bodies agreed upon if the vestry managed to moderate the directors' demands.

In 1868 a change in the law enabled the Poor Law Board to replace the vestry-nominated directors with a new board of guardians elected by the ratepayers. These new guardians were therefore considerably more independent of the vestrymen than their predecessors had been, but when they decided in the mid 1870s to build an infirmary for the sick poor there was trouble with the vestry once more. The Metropolitan Poor Act of 1867 had provided for the building of separate hospitals for the poor, and the Local Government Board (the Poor Law Board's successor) was beginning to apply pressure to boards of guardians. The Marylebone guardians had selected a site in North Kensington (Notting Hill) and were contemplating building an infirmary at an estimated cost of £100,000. The vestry resisted, and ratepayers' meetings rallied the public against the "extravagance" of the guardians. The vestry argued earnestly that the infirmary, if it were built, should form a part of the existing workhouse site on Marylebone Road, a site which the Local Government Board thought quite inadequate. The Board refused to give way in spite of eloquent speeches in the vestry (one from Professor Marks) and the pleas of a deputation, and the parish was committed to a new infirmary in Notting Hill.[91] This was opened in 1881, and provided accommodation for 760 inmates; the building, which is still in use, is now known as St. Charles Hospital, Exmoor Street.[92]

Relief policies in Marylebone were always directed at giving some aid to the worthy applicant who was not yet reduced to entering the workhouse. The guardians seemed to incline toward a commonsense policy and away from the hard dogmatism of those who would have forced those on relief into the workhouse. In the seventies and eighties, one leading voice among the guardians was that of Edward Boulnois, a Cambridge man whose family had long been identified with the parish. He was largely influential in recasting the Marylebone system of indoor relief, in reconstructing the workhouse, the largest in London, and in resisting the pressure of those who demanded a tighter system. In 1879 something of a battle took place among the guardians over the question of outdoor relief, with Boulnois and the Reverend Llewellyn Davies as the opposing protagonists. Davies, who had recently come to the parish from East London, brought with him a hankering for the tough policies followed in certain eastern Poor Law unions of parishes, notably Whitechapel, St. George's, and Stepney. Apparently he did not wish to abolish outdoor relief altogether but to curtail it drastically. Davies lost that debate, and he soon resigned the chairmanship of the committee on outdoor relief.[93]

But three years later the issue of outdoor relief arose again, this time under the sponsorship of General H. L. Gardiner of the Charity Organization Society. He was persistent and eloquent, and in 1882 he finally got a vote restricting outdoor relief to thirteen weeks' duration. It was now Boulnois's turn to resign as chairman of the outdoor relief committee, permitting Gardiner to take over; and within a month the guardians began to suspect that the new chairman had pushed in the thin edge of the wedge and would try to abolish all outdoor relief. By the following year (1883), however, they had reconciled themselves to Gardiner's policies, partly because the number of workhouse inmates had declined, contrary to the dire prophecies of his opponents.[94] During the eighties, in fact, the number of poor chargeable to the parish and the number of workhouse inmates were declining. By 1887 the total number chargeable had dropped to below 4,500, with fewer than 1,700 in the workhouse. A census of the 760 female inmates showed a high proportion of servants — 194 of them — in addition to 170 charwomen, 160 laundresses, 120 needlewomen, 30 cooks, 20 dressmakers, and 20 nurses.[95]

In the 1850s and 1860s the directors' school for pauper children at Southall, nine miles west of the metropolis, became a matter of controversy between the directors and the vestry. This was a low period in the record of the directors, and the school, which could accommodate four hundred children, was frequently criticized for maladministration. Two incidents, the vestry thought — the case of fifty girls with sores on their heads from uncleanness, and a case of flogging — had been treated altogether too calmly by the directors.[96] It was clear that the school, built with a good deal of fanfare, had failed to sustain the hopes it had aroused. Apparently the directors, not a notably efficient body, were jealous of both the vestry and the Poor Law Board and would stand firmly on their dignity when questions were raised. Then, too, there were rivalries within the staff and, it was charged, scandalous behavior. No clear line had been drawn between the authority of the master and mistress on the one hand, and the schoolmaster and schoolmistress on the other hand. This question had hardly been settled when a new scandal blew up — a charge of indecent assault by the master. Whether innocent or guilty, he tried to reason, but the directors insisted on holding an inquiry. It seems probable that the charge had little substance and had arisen from the vindictiveness of two female teachers. The Poor Law Board agreed that the charges had not been established, but thought that the master's resignation had better be accepted.[97]

During the 1870s the parish was not shaken by further scandals in the school. A report to the Local Government Board from Inspector E. Carleton Tufnell in 1873 commented favorably on both the administration of the school and the education that it gave the children.[98] But how should the guardians deal with the question of overcrowding, which was clearly a problem by the early 1880s? The school committee came out with a plan for expensive additions, which would have cost more than £20,000. The way to stop this scheme, the parish thought, was to unseat the present guardians, who had come in pledged to economy but had lapsed into the most arrant extravagance. The election of 1885 to the board of guardians, unlike most of its predecessors, was genuinely exciting. The parish was flooded with cards, circulars, and handbills supporting individuals pledged either to economy or to the support of the extravagant Southall School additions. The *Mercury* deplored the ungentlemanly tactics of some of the candidates and their supporters, but rejoiced that at last there were signs of electoral life in parish politics—far better than those elections where there was no contest or where the issue seemed to lie, as it had a number of times, between the teetotalers and the licensed victuallers.[99] The economizers won the election, but the cries of triumph had hardly died when a letter arrived from the Local Government Board calling attention to the crowded condition of the Southall School, now holding about five hundred children. Some of the new "economical" guardians attempted to argue that there was no overcrowding—or, if there was, that the Roman Catholic children could be sent to one of their own institutions. What the new guardians did accomplish, however, was to reduce the size and cost of the new addition to the building. This more modest plan of theirs would, in the absence of the Roman Catholic children, probably prove adequate.[100]

The Marylebone record is a chronicle of neither good nor bad government. Necessarily, in thirty-five years, there were changes in personnel, aspirations, and tone. Yet one cannot miss the immense progress made between 1856 and 1888, especially in the provision of physical amenities necessary for urban living. The accounts of vestry meetings are sometimes boring, even irritating: they continually praise economy as an end of government, and their hosannas to local self-government are really demands for freedom to keep the rates down. Yet over the decades parish autonomy was being gradually reduced. The Poor Law Board (and its successor, the Local Government Board), the School Board, the Metropolitan Asylums Board, not to mention the Metropolitan Police and the MBW, all of these were in fact nibbling away assiduously at the old rights of local self-government. And there were some in Marylebone— the Debenhams, for example—who hailed the change. For although the political establishment in Marylebone was relieved that Ritchie's local government bill did not involve a further attack on the parish position, some of the more clairvoyant of the inhabitants could see that before very long a direct and successful assault would be made on the autonomous parishes.

CHAPTER 13

St. Pancras

by

Francis Sheppard

St. Pancras provides both similarities and contrasts to St. Marylebone. Both these large parishes were bounded on the south by Oxford Street (St. Pancras only in part), and both extended northward toward the wooded heights of Hampstead and Highgate. St. Pancras was, however, considerably longer than Marylebone, its northern extremity embracing Parliament Hill Fields, Ken Wood, and most of the village of Highgate. At the beginning of the eighteenth century both parishes were sparsely populated, and as late as 1776 St. Pancras still contained only some six hundred inhabitants.[1]

But as soon as large-scale building development began, the contrasts became increasingly apparent; they were perhaps most explictly evident in the divergent histories of the local administration of the two parishes. Despite its greater distance from the rest of the built-up area of London, development in Marylebone began considerably earlier than in St. Pancras. Most of the southern part of Marylebone was owned by the Harley-Portland and Portman families, and, principally under the auspices of these two aristocratic dynasties, most of the area between Oxford Street and Marylebone Road had, by about 1800, been laid out in the traditional gridiron pattern of spacious streets and squares. In the field of local government Marylebone's increasingly ineffective old village oligarchy, meeting in open vestry, had been displaced by a select vestry established by act of Parliament in 1768. Here the wealthy residents of the

283

new faubourg were in the ascendant. Within a few years they had established an efficient administrative machine, and as early as 1774 they successfully resisted an attempt to set up a separate statutory commission for the administration of the small wealthy enclave of Stratford Place. This policy was always maintained, and in Marylebone the paving, cleaning, lighting, and watching of the streets remained the exclusive responsibility of the select vestry.* Marylebone's administration was, in fact, and continued to be, strong and highly centralized.[2]

St. Pancras presented the opposite extreme. There the pattern of land ownership was much more fragmented than in Marylebone, and although there were several fairly large estates, only those of the Duke of Bedford and the Foundling Hospital were well managed. Elsewhere building development was in general haphazard and unambitious. St. Pancras, in fact, had none of the fashionable attraction which Regent's Park with its fine approach and the proximity of Mayfair bestowed upon Marylebone. Between 1801 and 1821 the population leaped from 31,000 to 71,000; and the old village open vestry, meeting at a public house in Hampstead Road, proved totally incapable of imposing any authority over the great new township which had so suddenly sprung into existence. Landowners wishing to develop were therefore able to obtain statutory powers for the establishment of paving commissioners for the maintenance of the streets on their estates, and when, after prolonged struggles, a select vestry was finally established in 1819, no less than fourteen such separate commissions, mostly self perpetuating, were already in existence. All of them continued to function until the passing of the Metropolis Local Management Act of 1855, and during this period another three were created, making a total of seventeen separate administrative units. Thus neither the new select vestry nor, after 1832, its elected successor (for St. Pancras was, like Marylebone, one of the parishes where Hobhouse's act was adopted) was ever master in its own house. St. Pancras provided, indeed, the most extreme example of administrative disintegration in the whole of London: even when the paving boards were all swept away in 1855, they bequeathed, through the widespread antagonism which they had inspired, a tradition of virulent radicalism which permeated the affairs of the new vestry for many years, and which indeed still exists today in the St. Pancras vestry's modern successor, the Borough of Camden.

Building development in St. Pancras had begun in the southern part

---

*Excepted, of course, were the Crown Lands forming Regent's Park, where in 1813 the administration of the streets was put under the authority of the Lords of the Treasury and the Commissioners of Woods and Forests and Land Revenues. These streets are still managed independently, by the Crown Estate Paving Commissioners.

of the parish in the latter part of the eighteent century. The estates there were comparatively small, with the notable exception of that of the Duke of Bedford, which was partly situated in the neighboring parish of St. Giles in the Fields. Their often awkward physical configuration prevented the achievement of any coherent overall layout, and despite their convenient proximity to the City and the Inns of Court, access to them from the south was through narrow congested streets. Not even Brunswick Square or Fitzroy Square ever had the fashionable attraction of Cavendish or Portman Square in Marylebone, and the first residents of the half-finished streets often found themselves surrounded by derelict undeveloped land which soon became a favorite scene of disorderly popular festivities. Further north the prospect was hardly more alluring, the King's Cross area being pocked with clay pits from which was dug the brick earth needed for the area's numerous smoking kilns, while at the north end of Gray's Inn Road an enormous hill of ashes had been accumulated for use in the process of brick manufacture.

To the north of the New Road (now Euston Road) the building of the two new hamlets of Somers Town (in the vicinity of St. Pancras Station) and Camden Town had started before 1800, and in the early nineteenth century ribbon development along the roads leading up to the Great North Road at Highgate was proceeding rapidly. By 1841 a third new hamlet further north, Kentish Town, contained some 10,000 inhabitants, and the population of the whole parish had reached 130,000. Only the relatively inaccessible northern heights around Highgate and Ken Wood still remained at least quasi-rural.

Most of the houses built in this period were of the two- or three-story terrace or semidetached variety, and were intended for such relatively impecunious people as Charles Dickens's father, who lived for a while in Bayham Street, Camden Town. The fragmented condition of land ownership again prevented any large coherent layout comparable with that proceeding in Regent's Park or on the Eyre estate at St. John's Wood in Marylebone, and except on the property of the Duke of Bedford and the Crown (where Nash's great stucco terraces on the east side of Regent's Park were within St. Pancras) the landlords took little care for the maintenance of their estates. The social and physical condition of many parts of St. Pancras began, in fact, to decline almost as soon as they were built up, and even in 1810 Nash himself was deploring that "houses of such a mean sort as have been built at Somers Town and are now building on Lord Southampton's ground, should disgrace this apex of the Metropolis."[3]

From the 1830s onward, therefore, St. Pancras provided an easy target for incursions of the greatest instruments of destruction in nineteenth-century London—the railway companies. Carefully avoiding the powerful interest of the Crown in Regent's Park, they burrowed down by tunnel and cut through the northern heights to emerge in Camden Town and descend to their great termini adjacent to Euston Road—Euston itself (1836 onward), King's Cross (1852), and St. Pancras (1868).

The railway companies set a totally ineffaceable imprint upon the social character of large parts of the parish. In hitherto residential districts they stimulated the growth of warehouses, industry, and gasworks (the latter also attracted by the presence of the Regent's Canal); they constantly took more land for sidings and goods yards, and in Camden Town and Kentish Town there were frequent further depredations for the building of branch lines to the City, the docks, and more distant new suburbs. Above all, they created a permanent social barrier between St. Pancras and still well-to-do residential Marylebone.[4] St. Pancras had, in fact, become, and still remains, the poor relation of its more fortunate neighbor to the west.

The effective administration of such a fissionable parish—fissionable both physically and administratively—was to prove for many years beyond the capacity of the vestry, regardless of whether its constitution was open, select, or elected. In its open form the St. Pancras vestry had been wracked with dissension ever since the establishment (by act of Parliament in 1803) of self-perpetuating directors of the poor had left the vestry with very little to do except quarrel with the directors. These "squabbles kept the parish in a state of incessant confusion,"[5] but when the open vestry was finally extinguished by an act of 1819, select vestries were already nearly out of date, and were soon to be the object of violent attack by the London radicals in the later 1820s. In St. Pancras self-elected public bodies were already widely detested, and with good reason; in addition to the directors of the poor, seven of the inefficient district paving boards in existence in 1819 were self-elected, and two more were to be established on the same principle within the next half-dozen years.[6] Nor was this all, for in 1816 an act had established self-perpetuating church trustees, equipped with power to raise a rate for the building of a new parish church and chapel, and in 1821 the trustees had obtained another act to double the amount which they could borrow on the security of the rate.[7] Because many of the select vestrymen were also trustees the new vestry was at once popularly identified with the gross extravagance of the church building program—a fatal association in a parish where Dissenters were strong and exceedingly vociferous.[8] In the later 1820s St. Pancras provided an easy target during the general agitation throughout London against select vestries. Hobhouse's act of 1831 for their regulation was at once adopted, and the short-lived select vestry duly succumbed, its only notable achievement having been the building of a vestry hall in Gordon Street.[9]

Peace was certainly not restored under the new dispensation, however. In this early experiment in municipal representative democracy every ratepayer, man or woman, however low his or her rating assessment, had the right to vote,[10] and in the universal excitement of the climax of the struggle for the parliamentary Reform Bill of 1832, local power passed, in St. Pancras as in Marylebone, to the extreme radicals. In St. Pancras their chief strength lay, to quote a well-informed contemporary, "among the small shopkeepers, the minor rate-payers and the Dissenters," but whereas the "Ultra Reformers" of Marylebone were organized in a single group known as the Barlow Street Committee, those of St. Pancras, true to the fissionable traditions of the parish, formed a number of district public-house clubs. Here "every appearance of order, sobriety and common decency, as well as of common sense and common political honesty" were said to be generally absent, but "constant attendance at and participation in, the smoking and drinking coteries of these pot-house Jacobin clubs" was nevertheless necessary to secure nomination to the democratic lists of candidates for election to the vestry.[11]

For some six or seven years the vestry was dominated by these groups, the two principal leaders being Thomas Murphy, a Roman Catholic demagogue, and William Douglas, whose main object (apart from the usual assertions of pettyfogging economy) was the abolition of church rates. During this period the democratic vestrymen pilloried and persecuted the vicar, clergy, and church trustees unmercifully, quarreled with the Poor Law Commissioners at Somerset House over the application of the Poor Law Amendment Act of 1834 in St. Pancras, and sacked the beadles and even the much respected vestry clerk. Between 1832 and 1838 five parliamentary elections took place in the new parliamentary borough of St. Marylebone, of which St. Pancras formed part, and all of them provided a welcome field of activity for the vestrymen, Murphy himself being an unsuccessful ultraradical candidate on two of these occasions. The only sensible policy pursued during these years seems to have been the attempt to abolish the numerous local boards and consolidate the administration of street paving under the single authority of the vestry; but here, despite four petitions to Parliament, the vestrymen were unsuccessful,[12] as, despite all their sound and fury, they also were in the matter of church rates, the compulsory payment of which did not end until 1841.[13]

By that time the dominance of the extreme radicals in the vestry had been ended by the defection of their Whig supporters at the time of the parliamentary election of 1838.[14] For a while the local affairs of St. Pancras quieted down a little; but they were not likely to stay quiet as long as the vestry remained a large and still substantially radical assembly of some 120 members, holding frequent meetings whose proceedings were well publicized in the press, but having very few routine administrative tasks to perform. The relief of the poor and the management of the paving, lighting, and cleaning of the streets were all outside the vestry's province in St. Pancras, and so there was simply not enough work to occupy the vestrymen. In the highly volatile and frustrated atmosphere of radical politics in London in the 1830s and 1840s it is hardly surprising that the elected representatives of St. Pancras often seem, to modern eyes, to have behaved like petty-minded and obstreperous busybodies.

In the 1840s and early 1850s political dissensions in the parish revolved around two rival groups known as the Blues and the Pinks. The Blues had originally opposed the adoption of Hobhouse's act,[15] but in the 1840s they were "extreme liberals," led by the redoubtable William Douglas. The Pinks were, however, the main antichurch party, and as their organization was better, their district clubs being loosely federated into a Central Parochial Association, they generally held power in the vestry, at any rate after 1848 when the Blues were resoundingly defeated. In 1853 the Blues, backed by the London and North Western Railway Company, with which the Pink vestry was then in dispute over rating assessments, put up a rival list of candidates, but were again defeated despite the help of the company, which "loaded their servants into Pickford's vans" to vote for the Blue candidates.[16]

These factions were based upon personal rivalries and the rivalries of the various public-house associations. Each year one third of the 120 vestrymen retired, and rival lists of candidates for the 40 vacancies were then presented to all the ratepayers of the entire parish, duly assembled in one place. If more than one list was presented (which was not always the case), a vote by ballot could be demanded, but since the parish was not yet divided into wards for electoral purposes, candidates representing minorities — such as moderates or Tories — were effectively excluded.

Whether the Pinks or the Blues won, therefore, made very little difference in practice, for they were all "extreme liberals" or radicals. So the attitudes of the vestry were generally predictable — antichurch and anticentralization. The new vicar, the Reverend Thomas Dale (whose courage in accepting in 1846 the living of the parish which "in the abuse of Church clergymen, perhaps has no equal" can only be admired),[17] was obliged to attend a taproom meeting in order to participate in the election of his own churchwardens;[18] and in 1855 his scheme to build ten new churches was successfully frustrated by the vestry.[19] Endemic squabbling with the Poor Law Commission or Board continued, notably over the vestry's supposed right to dismiss the master of the workhouse, and in 1854 an invitation to send a delegate to a meeting of Toulmin Smith's Anti-Centralisation Union was accepted by the vestry with acclamation.[20]

Centralization within the parish was, however, still supported, and in 1851 Sir Benjamin Hall, one of the local members of Parliament, unsuccessfully sponsored a bill to consolidate the paving boards of St. Pancras.[21] When, as a Government minister four years later, he introduced the bill that became the Metropolis Local Management Act, the vestry was in raptures because the boards were to be cleared out lock, stock, and barrel. The commissioners on the Kentish Town board, who attempted to oppose Sir Benjamin, were sharply told that in Marylebone, where almost all the roads were under the sole control of the vestry, the staff costs for their administration were only £700 per annum, whereas in St. Pancras, where management was divided among seventeen authorities, they were over £4,000;[22] and not even the widespread notoriety suffered by the parish during the parliamentary debates on the bill, when Sir Benjamin ridiculed its existing arrangements,[23] could outweigh the vestrymen's delight that in this field democratic local self-government had triumphed, and that at last they would be the masters in their own parish.

Under the terms of Hall's act membership of the new vestry remained unaltered at 120 — the maximum figure permitted by the act — and as in Marylebone the parish was divided for voting purposes into eight wards. For the first time, therefore, there was an opportunity for the representation of more moderate views than those of the radicals who had hitherto been in the ascendant. In expectation of this, the vicar in July 1855 attempted to test his impression that in the old vestry licensed victuallers and builders had held a disproportionately large number of seats. He found that there were about twenty such vestrymen, and at one of the last meetings before the elections he claimed from the chair that under the existing system nineteen-twentieths of the ratepayers had been virtually disfranchised by the "hole and corner and tap-room system of selecting vestrymen." The only thing that he wanted under the new dispensation was "a fair balance of classes and not a preponderance of any one."[24]

Evidently prompted by these remarks, a new group quickly emerged which was officially known as the St. Pancras Association but was more commonly referred to as Camden Hall — the literary institute where the association held its meetings. Its supporters were chiefly drawn from the professional and well-to-do residents of the four wards of Haverstock Hill, Kentish Town, Camden Town, and Regent's Park. In face of this new and (for the first time) real opposition, the Pinks and the Blues hastily joined forces and deafened the parish with dire warnings about the threatened revival of church rates and clerical influence. Nevertheless, according to the *Observer,* the professed principles of the two parties were "nearly identical," and the ratepayers were puzzled to know what issues were at stake.

At the elections, held in November 1855, a poll was demanded in six of the eight wards. The Camden Hall group was victorious in Haverstock Hill, Camden Town, and Regent's Park, while the Pinks and the Blues, now known as the Ratepayers' Association, won in the Southampton, Tottenham Court Road, and Gray's Inn Road wards. At Kentish Town and Somers Town compromise lists were returned unopposed. Of the 20,000 ratepayers eligible to vote, only 4,325 troubled to do so, and of these fewer than half voted for the Camden Hall candidates. The Camden Hall party was nevertheless regarded as the victor, and although it lost ten seats at the next election, held in April 1857, its members controlled the new vestry until May 1858, when it lost forty-one of the forty-five vacant seats to the Ratepayers' Association.[25]

Shortly after the elections of November 1855 the *Observer* commented that the Camden Hall vestrymen were all respectable and honest, and that some of them were wealthy, well educated, and enjoyed a high position in society. But, it continued, they might not prove well suited to the affairs of a "parochial parliament"; they could not endure the sharp discourteous rebuff or spare the time for frequent meetings, and would soon leave the field to less sensitive men. And so it proved. Under the chairmanship of the vicar they were constantly exposed to anticlerical attacks, the meetings were often rowdy and occasionally interrupted by scuffling, and when they were obliged to increase the rates to provide what they regarded as "a superior and efficient form of government," there were vociferous demonstrations from a large crowd in the public gallery. Within less than thirty months of the first election what had started as "a desire on the part of persons of different status in the parish to come forward and do something under the Metropolitan Local Management Act" had petered out, and Camden Hall was defunct.[26]

In 1858 the Ratepayers' Association won a clear majority of some thirty seats. According to the *Observer,* the Association's attitudes were synonymous with those of the Liberal party, and thereafter the vestrymen within this broad political allegiance never lost control of the vestry. At first the old radical element was strong and the veteran William Douglas, as chairman of the finance committee, inaugurated a campaign of extreme cheeseparing.[27] But with the collapse of Camden Hall after 1858 and the new vicar's decision in 1861 not to attend vestry meetings, popular interest in local elections declined very considerably. Contests were rare, and by 1866 the vestrymen felt that "they would like to elevate their position by getting a superior class of men among them." Lists of candidates were adjusted by compromise in order to avoid a poll, one group saying, "We will submit to such a name in lieu of such a one," and by these methods "one or two ministers, two or three members of the law, and several medical genetlemen" as well as three justices of the peace had by 1866 been admitted. About half of the vestrymen were said to be shopkeepers.[28]

In the 1870s and 1880s rivalry for seats in the vestry seems to have been chiefly between the publicans and the advocates of temperance. In 1888 the vestry contained eleven publicans, fourteen builders, nine retired tradesmen, six bakers, and five furniture dealers, with no fewer than forty-seven different trades and professions being represented. Electoral contests were still rare, and the traditional political affiliations of the parish were demonstrated at the general election of 1885, when all four of the members by whom St. Pancras was to be represented in Parliament were Liberals, one of them being the vestry clerk, T. E. Gibb, described as an "advanced Liberal."[29]

Rowdiness, personal abuse, and bad language still prevailed sometimes in the vestry even in the 1880s,[30] but the general reputation of the St. Pancras vestry had nevertheless evidently improved, for the 1850s and 1860s had been disastrous. Between 1857 and 1862 a series of thefts, misappropriations, and defalcations by the staff of both the directors of the poor and the vestry had been discovered. The clerk to the directors, the relieving officer, and several rate collectors had absconded, the vestry clerk himself, (G. W. F. Cook) had been dismissed in 1857, and soon afterwards the vestry had offered a reward for his arrest.[31] In 1859 the editor of the *Shoreditch Observer*, who was a vestryman of that parish, had remarked that it was scarcely possible that a worse condition could exist in public affairs than in St. Pancras,[32] and in 1867, 1868, 1870, and 1878 there had been more scandals. The vestrymen had frequently been accused of hobnobbing with their officers and of generally being too familiar with them,[33] and it had taken a long time for the vestry and the honest officers (of whom there had always been some, even in the 1850s) to impose proper standards of financial probity. Francis Plaw, who had succeeded Cook as vestry clerk at the low salary of £300, was, it may be conjectured, one of the principal agents in this process, for when he retired in 1869 the vestry, with uncharacteristic generosity, awarded him a pension equivalent to one-third of his salary. His successor, Gibb, had joined the vestry's staff in 1864 as a junior clerk, and remained in office (except while a member of Parliament in 1885–86) until his death in 1894. He was a man of some distinction in municipal affairs, being selected as an alderman of the London County Council in 1889 and subsequently serving as chairman of the London Joint Standing Committee of Magistrates and County Councillors. In 1885, when he was clerk to the directors of the poor, the guardians of the poor, and the assessment committee, as well as being clerk to the vestry, and was earning a total salary of £1,000, he was described as "the guiding influence, the controlling spirit, the governing power" in the vestry, and although this was resented by some members, the vestry was glad to have him back as clerk after he ceased to be a member of Parliament. Without such officers as Gibb the business of such a volatile parish as St. Pancras would, indeed, have come to a complete standstill.[34]

Two of the administrative departments at the Vestry Hall were in no way connected with the financial scandals of the early years. These were those of the Surveyor and the Medical Officer of Health, who between them were responsible for the two most important fields of the vestry's activity. The post of Surveyor was held from 1856 to 1891 by William Booth Scott, who was probably largely responsible for the vestry's good record in road administration. Until 1856 this duty had, of course, been divided among the seventeen paving boards. In addition the Commissioners for the Turnpike Roads North of the Thames managed some of the principal trunk roads, and even the directors of the poor were involved; yet despite this proliferation of authorities there were still several areas of the parish, notably Agar Town and the St. Jude's district around Gray's Inn Road, where no public body had any legal control over the streets.[35] The new vestry was determined to show that it could deal with this extraordinary state of affairs, and throughout the whole of its existence it spent money more freely on roads and street improvements than for any other purpose.

One of the first actions of the vestry was to borrow money to pave the streets of Agar Town, which had hitherto not been made up at all. In 1864, through the abolition of the Turnpike Commissioners, it assumed control of an extra seven and a half miles of main roads, and by 1870 the total number of miles of streets for which it was responsible had risen from forty-six in 1856 to eighty, much of this increase being due of course, to new building development in the northern part of the parish. The old turnpike roads in the parish had been paved with granite on concrete foundations at a cost of £103,000, of which £86,000 had been raised by loans; £256,000 had been spent on repaving the streets taken over, mostly in grossly defective condition, from the old paving boards, or in general repairs; and about another £94,000 had been used by the vestry on behalf of property owners in making the roads and paving the footways in new streets.[36] The number of street lamps had been more than doubled, and the installation of a meter on every twelfth light in 1874—a system invented by Scott himself—brought the vestry a saving of £3,000 per annum on its gas bill.[37] Scott was also largely responsible for the insertion in the London Tramways Act of 1870 of a clause enabling local authorities to purchase all tramways after a period of twenty-one years—a power that was later to be exercised by the London County Council.[38]

The widening and improvement of existing streets was also frequently undertaken by the vestry. It was a constant source of grievance in St. Pancras that the MBW did nothing for the parish in this respect, despite the existence of numerous trunk roads such as Gray's Inn Road and Pancras Road, and indeed the Board's only achievement here was the improvement of the junction of Royal College Street and Kentish Town Road, completed in 1883.[39] So the vestry itself did more, probably, than any other metropolitan local authority. Several of its diversions, widenings, and extensions, were designed to improve east-west communications which the railway companies had destroyed, and sometimes the companies, through Scott's efforts during the incessant parliamentary proceedings, were statutorily compelled to contribute to the costs. The formation of Battle Bridge Road and the diversion of Pancras Road are cases in point, while further north at Gloucester Gate the building of a new and wider bridge across the arm of the canal leading to the Regent's Park Basin put an end to the congestion there.[40]

A large proportion of all this expenditure on paving and street improvement was financed by loans, a total of some £150,000 being borrowed for these purposes between 1856 and 1889, mostly at 3.5 or 3.75 percent interest repayable generally over not more than twenty years. In 1889, however, the vestry's outstanding capital debts for these and all other purposes amounted to only £65,000,[41] and therefore the vestrymen could hardly have been reproached for placing an unfair burden on later generations of ratepayers. They had, indeed, inherited an enormous burden from the old paving boards, and arrangements for the liquidation of it were not completed until 1897. In 1856 the vestry had inherited the seventeen extinct paving boards' debts, which then amounted to £148,000, the ratepayers of each of the former paving districts being alone responsible, under the control of the vestry, for the debts incurred by their former board. By means of additional rates levied by the vestry on each particular district still in debt, the total liability was gradually reduced, but in 1890 it still amounted to over £90,000. In 1879 the vestry had promoted a special act to facilitate repayment, but a legal difficulty had subsequently arisen and it was not until 1897 that all the paving boards' bondholders were paid off by means of a loan of £90,000 from the London County Council, repayable over fifty years at a rate of interest not exceeding 3 percent.[42]

Settlement of the debts of the old paving boards was, of course, a problem confronting all parishes where such boards had existed before 1855, but owing to their unique proliferation this was a problem of peculiar intensity in St. Pancras. Another such problem confronting the vestry was that of the disused burial grounds, and here again, as with the parish roads, the matter was tackled with determination and some success.

In the late eighteenth and early nineteenth centuries half a dozen inner London parishes, finding that their own churchyards were so full that they could no longer be used, had acquired land cheaply in the then outlying parish of St. Pancras for the formation of new burial grounds. By the mid-nineteenth century these, too, had become full, and in the early 1850s all the burial grounds in the parish were closed by Order in Council. In 1852 a burial board, consisting of nine members, was set up by the old vestry, and by 1854 it had opened a cemetery on land which it had acquired at Finchley — the first municipal cemetery to be established under the Metropolis Burials Act. In 1877 the cemetery was enlarged by the purchase of another tract of land adjacent to it. After 1873 the board did not require any assistance out of the parochial rates, to which, indeed, in its later years it was able to contribute many thousands of pounds.[43] Means for the burial of the dead had, in fact, been efficiently provided.

The problem of what to do with the old disused graveyards was, however, much more complicated. As early as 1862 the vestry had attempted unsuccessfully to obtain possession of that of St. Giles in the Fields, which adjoined the churchyard of the old medieval parish church of St. Pancras on the east side of Pancras Road.[44] Shortly afterward these two burial grounds achieved national notoriety through the operations of the Midland Railway Company, which in order to reach its projected terminus (now St. Pancras station) was permitted by statute to build a viaduct (now an embankment) across them and also to make a shallow tunnel under them to connect with the Metropolitan underground railway. The vestry's solicitor was instrumental in inserting a clause in the company's act of 1864 compelling the railway to reinter any human remains disturbed by the tunnel, but the actual removal, during the cholera epidemic of 1866, of an estimated 10,000 corpses and their reburial in newly consecrated adjoining land provoked widespread national disgust.

The vestry accordingly resolved to resume its efforts to acquire the St. Giles's burial ground and lay it and St. Pancras's own churchyard out as a public garden.[45] Owing to legal difficulties this required a special act of Parliament, promoted by the vestry in 1875. Both burial grounds were formally opened to the public in 1877. Twelve years later the Midland Railway acquired a portion of the St. Pancras ground, but the vestry and the London County Council were able to compel the company to pay a large sum toward the extension of the west side of the garden fronting Pancras Road.[46]

After the rumpus of the 1860s with the Midland Railway it became the settled policy of the vestry to acquire all the other disused burial grounds in the parish and convert them into public gardens. This was finally achieved in 1889, after more prolonged legal difficulties. The adjacent burial grounds of St. George's, Bloomsbury, and St. George the Martyr, Holborn, situated to the north of the Foundling Hospital, were opened as public gardens in 1884 and 1889 respectively; that of St. Andrew's, Holborn, in Gray's Inn Road, in 1885; that of St. James's, Westminster, in Hampstead Road, after a struggle with the North Western Railway Company, which acquired part of it, in 1887; and that of St. Martin's-in-the-Fields, in Camden Street, in 1889. Half an acre of ground on the west side of Tottenham Court Road, formerly the burial ground of Whitefield's Tabernacle, was opened as a garden by the London County Council in 1895.[47]

In order to finance the layout of these new gardens the vestry borrowed some £10,000 on mortgage[48]—not a large sum, but one well spent in a parish in which large sections had no open spaces. In addition, in 1888 the vestry contributed £30,000 to the MBW for the purchase of 267 acres at Parliament Hill Fields.[49]

This was, however, one of the very rare occasions when the vestry acted in concert with the MBW, with which St. Pancras's relations were otherwise almost invariably bad. Things had got off to a poor start when Josiah Wilkinson, a member of the Camden Hall group and one of the two representatives chosen by the vestry to represent St. Pancras on the Board, had within a month of his election resigned in order to become a candidate for the salaried post of clerk to the Board. After failing to obtain the post he was duly reelected as a member; but the vestrymen were not unnaturally exasperated, and in 1857 they so long delayed payment of the Board's rate precept on the parish that the Board threatened to collect the money itself.[50] After the victory of the Ratepayers' Association in the parish elections of 1858 the vestry became a constant and vehement critic of both the Board's expenditures and of its centralizing tendencies. The vestry protested at a modest increase in the salary of the

Board's architect, disliked the changes in street names introduced by the Board, and was the only local authority to complain when the Board acquired a site in Spring Gardens for its offices. The St. Pancras vestry regarded itself, indeed, as the leader of the London vestries and district boards in all matters of complaint against the MBW. But the vestries and district boards became increasingly unwilling to support their self-appointed leader, and in 1871 it was said that the announcement at Board meetings of a communication from St. Pancras always raised a laugh among the members.[51] Until about this time the vestry acted on the heroic principle, at least consistent for such a determined supporter of local self-government, that it would not even ask the Board for assistance in the making of local improvements;[52] but such an attitude weakened the force of the vestry's complaints in later years that the Board had done nothing for St. Pancras, one street improvement and the purchase of Parliament Hill Fields being its only important achievements in the parish during the whole course of its existence. Nor, after 1870, were the vestry's relations with the London School Board any better, the rate precepts of this new body rising from £2,300 in 1871 to £30,000 in 1879 — almost as burdensome as the MBW's 1879 precept of £32,000.[53]

The St. Pancras vestry was, indeed, an exceedingly prickly body with which to deal, and nowhere was this more clearly demonstrated than in the field of poor relief. Like Marylebone, St. Pancras was one of a dozen large London parishes where the prior existence of a local act precluded the full application of the Poor Law Amendment Act of 1834. From 1819, when the select vestry had been established, until 1867 the relief of the poor in St. Pancras was managed by forty directors chosen annually by the vestry. But the vestry nevertheless remained the supreme power,[54] and (to quote an inspector reporting to the Poor Law Board in 1856) the execution of all the directors' decisions was constantly "retarded by the necessity of communicating them to the vestry, at whose meetings every proposition is discussed again at the risk of rejection . . . The great obstacle to improvement is the joint control exercised by the two bodies, the Vestry and the Directors."[55] This was bad enough, but after 1834 there were also constant squabbles between the Poor Law Commission (and later the Poor Law Board) on the one hand and the vestry and the directors on the other hand over the extent of the powers of the Commssion (or Board) in St. Pancras. In 1867 a change in the law at last enabled the Poor Law Board to exercise its full powers of control in St. Pancras, and a board of guardians elected by the ratepayers took the place of the old directors; but even then the bickering still continued, the central Board and the local board being the principal protagonists, with the latter often supported by the vestry and the ratepayers.[56]

At first the vestry and the directors had been successful in resisting what they regarded as the vexatious interference of the central Commission or Board in the local affairs of the parish — always a popular war cry in nineteenth-century St. Pancras. In 1836 they successfully asserted in the Court of Queen's Bench that the Poor Law Commission had no power to order the election of a board of guardians in the parish, and in 1852 the vestry by the same means defeated the claim by the Poor Law Board that the master of the workhouse could only be dismissed with the Board's approval. Meanwhile, however, the rapidly increasing population of the parish was causing gross overcrowding in the workhouse (situated on the east side of Pancras Road and St. Pancras Way), and in 1856 the electoral victory of the Camden Hall group, whose members were pledged to cleaning out the Augean stables, plunged local poor relief into the maelstrom of parish party politics. In the same year the Poor Law Board joined in the fray with an order fixing a maximum number of paupers to be accommodated in the workhouse, regulating its management, and directing the appointment of an auditor to inspect its accounts. The vestry, of course, refused to obey, but this time the Board was successful in the resultant action in Queen's Bench over the appointment of an auditor.[57] Thereafter inspectors from the Board began to pay frequent visits to the workhouse to find out what progress had been made in the execution of the new regulations. In general there was very little, but scandals cropped up periodically: the workhouse surgeon was in the habit of sleeping with female inmates and performing abortions as occasion required,[58] a child was "laid out" preparatory for burial while still alive, and in 1865 the Board upheld the complaints of two paupers about their inhuman treatment in the "separation" ward.[59] More serious, perhaps, was the complete failure of the directors and the vestry, despite the constant profession of good intentions, to relieve the intolerable congestion in the workhouse. Originally this was to be done by the removal of the children to an industrial school to be built on a new site, and in 1859 a site at Finchley was actually bought; but the vestry refused to sanction the tenders for building and in 1862 the land was sold. Meanwhile some of the children were boarded out, at great expense, at Forest Gate, Anerley, Hanwell, Plaistow — anywhere that accommodation of some sort could be found for them.[60]

After the election in 1867 of a local board of guardians, closely supervised by the Poor Law Board, a thirty-seven-acre site was quickly acquired at Leavesden near Watford, and an industrial school was opened there in 1870. In the same year an infirmary costing £42,000 was built at Highgate,[61] but a long struggle then began between the local board and the central Board over what should be done with the old workhouse in

Pancras Road. The local guardians wanted to renovate the building or rebuild on the existing site, but the Poor Law Board and its successor, the Local Government Board, wanted a separate workhouse built elsewhere. This question was for some years the principal point of contention in this ever contentious parish; the election of guardians was hotly contested, and public meetings, organized by the Poor Rates Reduction Association, were frequent and always rowdy.[62] The vestry, never otherwise known to be backward in the pursuit of a quarrel, could in this case only play a peripheral and somewhat ambivalent role, sometimes supporting the guardians against the onward march of central control but more often complaining bitterly to anyone who would listen about the increasing cost of expenditure on the poor.[63] In the 1870s and 1880s, in fact, the guardians held the stage in local public affairs, and despite the presence from 1872 onward of one or two women on the board, they fully maintained the vestry's tradition of boorish and disorderly behavior, egged on by crowds of ratepayers who packed the galleries.[64] The entertainment they provided, according to *The North Londoner*, was better than in the theatre, and it was also free; but the more strait-laced editor of the *St. Pancras Guardian* found that the guardians' language was so dreadful and their behavior so inexcusable that he had to eliminate most of his reporter's copy before he felt able to set it up in type.[65]

The principal point at issue, the future of the workhouse, was finally and somewhat surprisingly resolved in favor of the local guardians. As long as overcrowding existed in the workhouse, St. Pancras was deprived of the benefit which it would otherwise have been entitled to receive from the Metropolitan Common Poor Fund (set at some £2,000 in 1880), and in 1878 the guardians therefore decided to negotiate for a new site. But elections ensued and this decision was reversed; abortive plans for rebuilding the old workhouse were drawn up; and meanwhile, of course, the acquisition of a suitable new site was constantly becoming more difficult and expensive. At last in 1882 the Local Government Board agreed to the plan for rebuilding on the existing site, provided that it was first enlarged by the purchase of a strip of extra land fronting Pancras Road. This required an act of Parliament, and the new block that was built there was not opened until 1885. Another five years, spent in disputes with the architect, with the Local Government Board, and within the board of guardians itself, elapsed before even a start was made on the rebuilding of the old workhouse.[66] The various buildings erected on the old site in the 1880s and 1890s still stand, and are now occupied by University College Hospital, St. Pancras Hospital, and the Hospital for Tropical Diseases.

Poor relief in St. Pancras was bedeviled by squabbling between the vestry and the directors, or later the guardians of the poor, and also, after 1834, by dissension between all these parochial authorities on the one hand and the central Commission or Board on the other. In the field of public health the situation was quite different. Here the vestry, having no local rival, was left largely to do as it saw fit, for the use of many of its powers was optional rather than obligatory. But the results were not much more satisfactory than they were in the domain of poor relief.

In 1856 the sanitary condition of the parish was generally fair, judged by the standards of the time. Many of the sewers had been built comparatively recently, the water supplied by the West Middlesex and New River companies was reasonably pure, the average number of inhabitants per house was only 8.9, and the mortality rate of twenty per thousand was below that of London as a whole. But these were diminishing assets, and there was also a darker side to the picture. There were fetid open sewers (notably the Fleet Ditch in Gospel Oak Fields), undrained brickyards, and outworn sewers in the older streets around Gray's Inn Road; and many streets in Agar Town and elsewhere had no sewers at all. Even in 1856 there was already much overcrowding in the southeastern part of the parish, and by 1865 the eviction, through the incursions of the railways, of no fewer than 10,000 parishioners (some 5 percent of the whole population of St. Pancras) was to cause the most acute social problems. It was therefore essential that the vestry should take its responsibilities seriously and be ready to pay the price required for good health.[67]

Unfortunately this did not happen, and the work of all four of the Medical Officers successively employed by the vestry between 1856 and 1900 was gravely inhibited by lack of staff, lack of money, and opposition in the vestry. Dr. Thomas Hillier, a distinguished physician at the Hospital for Sick Children in Great Ormond Street, who held the post from 1856 until his death in 1868, had great difficulty in persuading the vestry to spend money on the renovation or building of new sewers, and in 1862 he stated that "in this respect we are not much better off than when the Metropolis Local Management Act came into operation."[68] In 1858 his own salary was reduced from £400 to £250, and although there were only two inspectors of nuisances one of them was required to act for a while as the coroner's beadle.[69] Prompted by fear after the cholera epidemic of 1866 the vestry did at last begin to build "a great deal more" new sewers, and a third inspector was even appointed — a decision which Dr. Hillier considered, as he tartly informed the vestrymen, "as an indication that you, Gentlemen, are resolved in future, to regard sanitary improvements with more seriousness, and to prosecute them with greater energy than you have ever yet done."[70] Straight speaking of this kind created a great furor in the vestry, of course, and Hillier's successor, Dr. (later Sir) Thomas Stevenson, fared no better. During a severe outbreak of smallpox in 1871, when there were 2,800 cases in the parish, the vestry refused to set up a temporary hospital until it was too late, and in 1875 the vestry's repeated refusals to appoint another sanitary inspector led Dr. Stevenson to send in his resignation, which was only withdrawn when the vestry hastily capitulated.[71]

Some improvements were nevertheless made. Between 1856 and 1870 the vestry built six miles of new sewers; another nine miles were built by private developers under the vestry's supervision; and drains were laid to over seven thousand more houses. According to the vestry the inspectors had dealt with over twenty thousand cases of minor improvements, which included: the filling in of cesspools; the cleansing and repair of houses, the abolition of underground dwellings; the installation of water closets, cisterns, and dustbins; the removal of pigs and dung; and the seizure of unwholesome food. The numerous slaughterhouses, cowhouses, and bakeries had all been inspected periodically, and noxious trades such as tallow melting or the cooking of cats' meat had been abated. Most of these improvements had been made at the cost of the owners, either under notices served by the vestry or, if necessary, after proceedings before a magistrate,[72] but in one respect the vestry itself had creditably undertaken a large and optional expenditure.

This expenditure was made in the provision of public baths and washhouses. The value of such facilities had already been demonstrated in St. Pancras by the Society for Establishing Public Baths and Wash-houses, which by means of voluntary subscriptions had built its own premises near the Hampstead Road as early as 1846.[73] After heated debates the vestry decided in 1866 to build its own baths in another part of the parish, and these were opened in Camden Town in 1868 at a cost of £23,000. In 1878 another set, off Tottenham Court Road, was built at a cost of £35,000. By 1883 the whole establishment was producing a small surplus income,[74] and one of the vestry's last acts before its extinction in 1900 was to start building yet another set, in Prince of Wales Road, Kentish Town. Public health, and still more the expenditure of public money for its promotion, was still something of a newfangled novelty in Victorian London, and it is perhaps significant that in the provision of baths—where St. Pancras had an outstanding record—the vestry was following the successful example provided by a private society.

By the mid 1860s St. Pancras had lost such natural advantages as it had previously possessed. The railway incursions, which had been severe enough in the 1860s, continued in the 1870s for the building of yards and sidings; land values and house rents were mounting; and the overall supply of cheap rented accommodation was constantly diminishing. Pauperism was increasing both absolutely and relatively — by 23 percent between 1855 and 1865, compared with an overall growth of population of only 19 percent — and from about 1870 onward the annual mortality rate in the parish often exceeded that for the whole of London. Both Dr. Hillier and Dr. Stevenson constantly informed the vestry of growing overcrowding,[75] but Dr. Hillier thought in 1864 that it was "impossible at present to prevent" it. He hesitated to use the powers provided by the Nuisance Removal Acts because if he did so, "many families would be turned into the streets from their inability to pay for rooms large enough for them".[76] Nor, thought Dr. Stevenson in 1876, did Torrens's act of 1868 or Cross's act of 1875 provide any help: no insanitary area in St. Pancras was large enough for the application of Cross's while Torrens's was "almost inoperative. The highly penal nature of this latter statute, which, in the event of demolition, gives no compensation to the owner whose property is destroyed, makes Courts of Justice extend every possible leniency to the owner. Moreover the Act does not contemplate any scheme for the reconstruction of the houses demolished, or other provision for the population displaced."[77] So Dr. Stevenson did not apply the act, and meanwhile the average number of inhabitants per house throughout the parish rose steadily from 8.9 to 1851 to 9.5 in 1881, with as many as 11.4 in the Tottenham Court Road district.[78]

When two successive Medical Officers confessed themselves largely helpless to deal with overcrowding, it is hardly surprising that the vestry did little about the problem. But there was one respect in which the vestrymen ignored the repeated recommendations of all four of their successive medical advisers. This was in the implementation of the optional powers contained in section 35 of the Sanitary Act of 1866 for the abatement of overcrowding in houses let in lodgings or occupied by more than one family. Under this clause the local authorities were required to draw up regulations and submit them to the Secretary of State for approval, and when this had been obtained the work of house-to-house inspection and registration could begin. Dr. Hillier had at once urged the vestry to do this, Dr. Stevenson did likewise, his successor (Dr. Shirley F. Murphy) argued the case year after year, and in 1883 even the Local Government Board urged the vestry to act — but all to no avail.[79] The adoption of regulations was frequently discussed in the vestry and strongly supported by the Sanitary Committee, led by its able chairman, Nathan Robinson (a publican), who also supported Dr. Murphy's efforts to use the Torrens acts, primarily for the repair rather than the demolition of houses. Dr. Murphy's evidence, highly critical of the vestry, given in 1884 before the Royal Commission on the Housing of the Working Classes—and in particular his revelation that there were still only four sanitary inspectors for the whole parish (equivalent to one for each 60,000 inhabitants)—led, after much anger in the vestry, to his resignation in the following year.[80] His succesor, Dr. John Sykes, fared no better, however, despite his plea in 1886 that the adoption of regulations was "a course now pursued by nearly all the London Vestries and District Boards."[81] The St. Pancras vestrymen remained obdurate, and it was not until 1890, when the London County Council had been established and endowed with extensive powers in the field of public health, that they at last succumbed; and even then the proposed regulations "were subjected to severe criticism in the Vestry before they were finally adopted."[82]

This was not the end of this discreditable story, however, for in 1897 the LCC publicly criticized the vestry for the inadequate size of its sanitary staff and recommended the appointment of two additional inspectors. The vestry rejected this, whereupon the medical staff of the LCC made a detailed investigation, which revealed that 60,000 persons were living in St. Pancras under conditions of overcrowding and ended by recommending the appointment of no less than seven additional inspectors. Dr. Sykes and the vestry's Health Committee agreed, but the vestry itself would only agree to two appointments, despite the fact that the average number of persons per house in the parish as a whole had risen from 9.5 in 1881 to 10.0 in 1896, with more than 12 per house in the Somers Town and Tottenham Court Road districts. At the LCC's request the Local Government Board then held an inquiry, but the matter was not finally settled until after the creation of the new St. Pancras Borough Council.[83]

There were, to be sure—as was also the case in Shoreditch—many difficulties in applying the regulations for the abatement of overcrowding, but the vestry's complete inertia until 1890 and its half-hearted compliance thereafter allowed large parts of the parish, to quote Dr. Sykes, to become a "dumping ground" for persons displaced from other parishes. Model lodgings for some 3,800 pesons had been provided in St. Pancras by the Improved Industrial Dwellings Company and a number of private agencies, but the minimum rents were too high for the very poor, and the vestry was quite right in insisting, as it began to do in the 1890s, upon the urgent need for more cheap accommodation.[84] It could, of course, have provided such accommodation itself, as the Shoreditch vestry did in partnership with the LCC. But it did not do so, although in 1900 the ratable value per head of population was £7.10 in St. Pancras compared with only £5.97 in Shoreditch. The pettifogging meanness of Victorian radical local politics continued, indeed, to permeate St. Pancras to the end of the nineteenth century, both in the Vestry Hall and among the parishioners at large, for by 1900 the adoption of the Public Libraries Act, which required a poll of all the ratepayers, had still not been achieved (again in marked contrast with Shoreditch), despite three attempts.[85] And not even the enterprise of the St. Pancras vestry in being the first local authority in London to supply its parish with electricity can erase its long-standing deficiencies in dealing with the far more important social problems of housing, sanitation, and the poor.

CHAPTER 14

St. George the Martyr, Southwark

Situated on the south bank a few steps away from the river, the parish of
St. George, Southwark, was ancient in years but small in area and biz-
arre in shape. The bulk of it lay to the west of Newington Causeway, but
a long, narrow spur to the northeast of Tabard Street stretching as far as
Albany Road gave the outline of the parish an irrational character. The
total area was only a little over 280 acres, not the tiniest of the metropolitan parishes but one of the smallest of those that were allowed by the Metropolis Local Management Act to continue handling their own affairs.
By 1851 the population of St. George's had not reached 52,000; its rate
of growth was low—during the succeeding two decades the lowest in
South London.[1] Indeed, as a place of residence St. George's had been
declining almost since Shakespeare's day, and by the mid-century it
housed only a few inhabitants above the social rank of small tradesman.

But St. George's—and, indeed, most of Southwark—was in no way
short of people below the tradesman rank. In the early 1860s (according
to John Binny) the Borough was "chiefly the locality of labouring people
and small shopkeepers—the masses of the people." But off the main
streets, in side lanes and courts, St. George's maintained a flourishing
population of thieves, cheap swindlers, and prostitutes, none of whom
were even among the more select of their class. Binny's investigations
disclosed a state of affairs that was shocking—in fact, almost incredible
—to a man with respectable, middle-class sensibilities. In St. George's

New Town, for example, off Kent Street (now the New Kent Road), he spotted a cluster of men and women between the ages of seventeen and forty, most of whom were convicted thieves. The most disreputable section of the parish was that surrounding the infamous Mint Street, which led out of Borough High Street to Southwark Bridge Road. The reputation of the Mint had not improved since the eighteenth century, when it was known as the hideout of coiners, thieves, and robbers—the headquarters of Jack Sheppard and Jonathan Wild. Indeed, matters had become worse after the opening of New Oxford Street and the wiping out of the worst tenements of St. Giles in the Fields had caused substantial migrations across the river to Southwark, where many paupers had taken up residence in the Mint. It was almost impossible to clean up the Mint area because it was really a network of small lanes and enclosed courts in which every kind of vice could flourish unchecked. When Binny entered a beer shop in Little Surrey Street, Borough Road, he found four men who were all expert burglars; and in Market Street he found every house from basement to attic occupied by prostitutes and thieves. In short, whenever he got off a main street, such as Newington Causeway, and entered the smaller side streets, lanes, and courts, he found crime and viciousness in its myriad forms.[2] The vestry of St. George's, if it had taken its duties seriously, would have had a heavy assignment in trying to govern this small, impoverished parish populated partly by the working class and small tradesmen and partly by criminals.

St. George's was divided into only three wards and had only forty-eight vestrymen. In 1855 the prospect of improvement held out by the Metropolis Local Management Act aroused a good deal of interest, which unfortunately proved to be of short duration. The Ratepayers' Protection Association (established in 1852) at once got down to the business of preparing a list of candidates for the new vestry. But the Association's list was not unchallenged: objections were raised, a partial secession took place, a group called the Independent Ratepayers was created, and an alternative list was formulated. The ratepayers therefore had two lists to choose between, and it looked as if lively days might be in store.[3] But the leaders of the Ratepayers' Protection Association, taking an irenic line, managed to patch up their organization and gained control of the new vestry. Yet throughout its early years the reign of the Association was occasionally challenged and a poll was taken. In 1857, for example, there were polls in all three wards, with the top candidate gaining 331 votes and the lowest 112, though the earlier ward meetings had been exceedingly small.[4] For a number of years the Ratepayers' Protection Association remained the strongest and best organized political group in the parish. Its competitors were highly ephemeral bodies which took their inspiration either from a specific question — usually the rates assessed in the previous year — or from a demagogic resident who saw a chance to build up his own political position.

The vestry was made up almost exclusively of tradesmen, active or retired, with perhaps two or three doctors. Specifically, in 1866 there was one member of independent means, and in 1887–88 there was only one man, a doctor on Newington Causeway, who was clearly above the tradesman class. The vestry met at 6:00 P.M. weekly (fortnightly after 1856), an hour that suited small tradesmen who had to tend to business but would have been highly inconvenient for men of higher social standing.[5] Like other parishes St. George's aspired to a vestry membership drawn from a higher social class and having a more sophisticated attitude, but it recognized such ambitions as hopeless. The parish simply lacked the proper residents.

It was some years before the vestry lapsed into comfortable apathy. In the late 1850s a fight about an able, energetic Medical Officer (Dr. William Rendle) and several quarrels between the vestry and guardians enlivened the local political scene. Even more, demagogues in the vestry disturbed the public tranquility. The most conspicuous of these was Robert Archer, who, in the words of the *South London Journal*, did not appear as a dove of peace with an olive branch, "promoting cordiality among the ratepayers in the disturbed parish of St. George's." Sinbad, the editor continued, had been scarcely more burdened by the Old Man of the Mountain than was the vestry with Archer; it was regrettable that the Metropolis Local Management Act contained no clause by which the vestry could pension off one of their number, so they probably must bear with Archer! It is hard to see what ends Archer had in view other than to make trouble and build up his own position as a parish leader. In the spring of 1858 he was agitating to get a seat on the board of guardians and was throwing out random charges against the board concerning their handling of the upcoming election.[6] In fact, the guardians, who were strongly influenced by the Ratepayers' Protection Association, were a reasonably progressive body that was performing quite creditably.

Archer gathered around him a fairly effective faction that opposed the Ratepayers' Protection Association. In 1858 the Archer faction won the election in one ward and made a good showing in the other two, and in the following year it repeated this performance.[7] One important parish figure, Daniel Birt, a draper, who was later to become the most outstanding leader in the parish, avoided close affilation with either Archer's faction or the Ratepayers' Association. Birt, for example, set himself against Edward Collinson, the leader of the Ratepayers' Association and the parish's member on the MBW, but at the same time he was too shrewd to ally himself with Archer's crowd. Birt's abilities marked him for leadership; yet he was never popular because of his dictatorial tendencies. Though a good orator and a skillful manipulator, he would not admit that others could be as public-spirited as he was. And his lack of sympathy for Collinson's Association inevitably aided the purposes of Archer's group of obstructionists.[8] As for Collinson, he was a native son of the parish who had been active for years on both the vestry and the board of guardians and who probably commanded more respect than any other local leader. Corpulent, heavy, and slow-moving he was not drawn to set orations, but his instincts were all on the humane side.[9] Clearly no love was lost between Birt and Collinson.

During the first three or four years of the new vestry's life, the alignment of factions was largely determined by the activities of the aggressive Medical Officer, Dr. William Rendle (1811–1893). Rendle, who later obtained something of a reputation as author of the standard history of Southwark (and is so described in the *Dictionary of National Biography*), was carrying on a gallant fight against disease, overcrowding, and dangerous nuisances, but he had little help from the parish sewers committee or from its chairman, William Reichenbach, a gas fitter by trade, who persistently blocked and frustrated all efforts at sanitary reform. Unlike some of his colleagues in other parishes, Rendle had a certain literary skill, and his quarterly reports to the vestry were always vivid and trenchant. In one report after another he described the sanitary conditions in the parish. He pointed out, for example, the overcrowding that had been caused by immigration from the country and from Ireland and, indeed, by the influx of paupers from other parishes. St. George's then had 184 persons to the acre as compared with 13 per acre in Camberwell, 30 in all of London, and 104 in Newington. "We are a most melancholy parish, low in level and low in circumstances," he continued. "The lowest and poorest of the human race drop from higher and richer parishes into our courts and alleys, and the liquid filth of higher places finds its way down to us. We receive the refuse as well as the outcomings of more happily situated places."[10]

The Medical Officer was not inclined to speak in whispers or to act other than energetically. In the first quarter of 1858 he observed: "Overcrowding is the normal state in our poorest districts. Small houses of four rooms are usually inhabited by 3 or 4 families, and by 8, 16, or 24 persons . . . [But] I know that we are on the right track. May Pole Alley, a cul-de-sac with its 23 houses and 180 people, was once a nest of infectious diseases. I attended some 10 cases of typhus there . . . With great trouble this coiurt has been cleansed and amended. It is very much more healthy."[11] Rendle continued to pound away at the vestry, sacrificing tact to emphasis. After reading a long list of streets and courts where disease was raging he proclaimed, "It may perhaps be said that all this is in the order of nature, and cannot be prevented. My experience of a quarter of a century among these diseases points quite the other way. Providence does not intend that reservoirs of stinking putrid matter shall stand so close to the poor man's door as to infest him at bed and board . . . Gentlemen, you are the trustees for life and death to a population of well-nigh 30,000 people, who from the force of circumstances are more or less unable to help themselves."[12]

Whether this last attack was directed specifically against the chairman of the sewers committee is not clear. But in any case Reichenbach had asserted epidemics to be matters of divine appointment as mysterious as the potato disease. Contention in the vestry continued, with Rendle generally being supported by the Ratepayers' Protection Association and opposed by what the *South London Journal* termed the antediluvian party led by Reichenbach and backed by Archer and others. When Collinson praised Rendle's reports, the *Journal* ejaculated, "Audacious man! The nitrous combustibles flamed up in a moment, and the reverberations of anti-sanitary wrath reverberated from one end of the hall to another. He who dares commend the Medical Officer's report must look well to himself."[13] It was clear that Rendle would have little freedom to work as long as he was responsible to Reichenbach's sewers committee, which was the bane of the vestry and an incubus on the parish, the *Journal* thought.[14] Besides resisting the Medical Officer and the efforts of the best members of the vestry, the committee disregarded even orders given by the whole vestry and by a police magistrate.

In the fall of 1857 the approach of cholera introduced a sense of urgency, but not enough to stir the committee out of its determined lethargy. Rendle was alarmed, he tried to get the sewers committee to go with him to inspect houses that had been visited by cholera in earlier years. When the committee refused, he went alone and drew up a vigorous report in which he declared that he would not go before the sewers committee again. Eventually it came down to a contest between Rendle and Reichenbach, with the vestry judging between them. The solution, which looked reasonable enough, was to form a new sanitary committee to supervise the work of the Medical Officer, but this committee died within a month, unable to surmount a deadlock in its membership. What was to be done? It was impossible to go back to administration by the sewers committee. Instead, sanitation became the duty of the vestry as a whole. The spleen which had been bottled up in the sewers committee was now poured out in the open vestry, apparently with the intention, fostered by Reichenbach and his friends, of worrying the advocates of sanitation into abandoning the struggle.[15]

One of the reasons for the vestry's opposition to cleaning up the parish may have been that certain of the members owned property which did not meet the minimum sanitary standards. It is not clear how heavily the vestrymen were involved in bad property, but obviously some of them were. Rendle spoke later (1866) of having been asked by one of the principal members of the vestry, an owner of considerable property in the parish "to pass over certain property of his that I found in an extremely bad condition."[16] Since Rendle had worked for seventeen years as a physician under the poor law guardians before becoming Medical Officer, some vestrymen had assumed that his new office would be a sinecure given him as a reward for faithful service to the poor. It looked as though a section of the vestry was determined that it should be no more than that, whether he liked it or not, for "the chairman of the local committee was, as I thought, specially appointed as a positive obstructor of sanitary measures, at all events he acted as such"[17] In the same year (1866) the rector of the parish reported that he had been twitted because so many members of the vestry were interested in bad property, and that he had asked in a vestry meeting for grounds on which he could contradict the charge. One vestryman, a collector of taxes, had flatly denied the charge, but Rendle (then a vestryman), although he remained silent at the meeting, had written to the rector that "there were before him eight persons at least who were owners of poor property, and some of them obstructors."[18] It is little wonder that Rendle felt thwarted and hamstrung when he was faced thus with the opposition of a number of vestrymen who owned property that was bad even by slum standards, and who were strongly supported by a party in the vestry.

The quarrel between the Medical Officer and the vestry continued to shake the "Ancient and celebrated and troublesome parish of St. George the Martyr." At one time the controversy settled on the question of draining cesspools, a procedure opposed by Daniel Birt because such a step would be contrary to providence and would result in contaminating every stream and doing serious injury to agriculture. Next the struggle focused on closing a pump which supplied contaminated water.[19] But finally the argument centered on Rendle's reports, which were hard-hitting documents that did not attempt to spare the vestry rulers. This question was double-barreled: first, whether he should be allowed to read his reports to the vestry (they were long and, to the vestry, unpleasant); and second, whether the vestry should be allowed to edit and cut them before they were printed.

Admittedly, Rendle was a zealot, without the gift of compromise; he would have thought the notion of compromise absurd when people's lives were involved. "I beg to say that I am not prepared to retrogress in sanitary matters in a parish like this, with the highest mortality in London."[20] In fact, the vestry's first attempt at compromise (in August 1858), which would have restricted the opportunities for the Medical Officer to report to the full vestry, brought forth an indignant letter of resignation from Rendle, which he later withdrew under pressure from the vestry.[21] But in December the quarrel broke out again. This time it was about certain admonitory paragraphs in Rendle's quarterly report which had been read before the vestry but did not appear in the printed document. It is not clear whether they had been deleted by the Medical Officer himself or by the vestry authorities, but it was probably the latter. The General Purposes Committee brought in a report that was aimed ostensibly at preventing the Medical Officer from changing his reports after reading them; and after two nights of wild debate, accompanied, no doubt, by maneuvering offstage, the vote went narrowly in favor of the committee's report.[22] Rendle's reply was a second and final resignation, in which he once more reiterated his position. Southwark, he noted, was one of the least healthy places in the metropolis—and largely from preventable causes. As a poor-law physician he had labored for seventeen years in the face of the inadequate powers of the guardians; but now, when the Metropolis Local Management Act had enlarged the powers of vestries, the means which the St. George's local authority had adopted were not only insufficient but at some points quite wrong. And of late, he charged, the efforts of the vestry had begun to fall below even its former cautious level. Thus the parish had emerged in the third quarter of 1858 with a shockingly high death rate—30 in 1,000—higher than that of Bethnal Green, St. Giles, Newington, or Bermondsey. In the end, at the urging of his supporters, some of whom admitted that Rendle had been a little precipitate, the vestry accepted his resignation with "extreme regret"—though other members clearly thought that they were well rid of him.[23]

The vestry, however, had not seen the last of Dr. Rendle. Although he had ceased to hold paid office under the vestry, his zeal for public health had not diminished. He had resigned, in fact, with the intention of being elected to the vestry. On his first attempt he failed—as a result, he charged, of the electioneering activities of a group of bone boilers against whom he had formerly proceeded. But he succeeded in the next election and as a vestryman continued to agitate unceasingly for his favorite causes. Meanwhile the vestry had elected as his successor Henry Bateson, a reasonably able man who had neither Rendle's talent for stirring up the vestry nor his inclination to look for trouble. But at least he had the support of Collinson and the group that had stood by Rendle.[24] The antisanitarians did not offer bitter opposition to Bateson's election; they had goaded Rendle into resigning and that was as far as they were willing to push their luck for the time being. Nevertheless, the battle over censorship continued unabated. A report by the new Medical Officer, which referred critically to the way the vestry was dealing with cesspools, was called into question. And when the General Purposes Committee recommended that this section be suppressed, it seemed doubtful whether anything that reflected unfavorably on the vestry would be permitted to go into print.[25] Rendle's resignation, his final report, an eloquent statement which made a powerful case for more active intervention by the vestry, took three-quarters of an hour to read. It prompted some disagreeable remarks by Archer and a motion to refer the report to the General Purposes Committee "to consider what portion should be printed." Infuriated, Rendle apparently withdrew the report rather than leave it to be mutilated by a committee.[26]

Sanitary affairs in St. George's parish did not take a marked turn for the better until the middle and later 1860s. Progress was constantly obstructed by the vestrymen's self-esteem and their desire to protect their bad property from interference. As Rendle charged, "A parsimonious fear of expenditure is at the root of the evil . . . Low rates rather than low mortality are made the test of public prosperity."[27] In 1861 when the leet jury made a presentment which called attention to the parish's filthy courts, alleys, and lanes, it was denounced in the vestry for not having come to the vestry first. This, it was urged, was interfering with the rights and duties of the vestry.[28]

What seems to have set the parish on the road to gradual reform was the typhus epidemic of the mid-1860s. The fuss in the vestry was set off in the autumn of 1864 by a series of letters from Rendle, who was not then a member. He pointed to the staggering figures for deaths from fever during the first three quarters of 1864, which assured the parish its position as the worst in London. St. George's had 197 deaths per 100,000 of population as compared with 126 in St. Olave's and 124 in Greenwich.[29] The vestry, in reply, made some futile gestures toward an investigation but accomplished nothing of consequence. The drive for sanitation centered now on the demand for a second inspector of nuisances; the first had not been doing his duty properly, and in any case there was more than enough work for two. The motion, of course, failed to pass, and the *South London Press* published a leader under the caption " 'Cheap and Nasty' in Southwark." The following week in another leader the editor suggested that Oxenstierna would have found in the vestry some perfect specimens of the genus homo to whom he would have directed his son, "Go, my son, and see how little wisdom is required to govern the world."[30]

In the summer of 1865 *The Lancet* issued a highly critical report on the St. George's workhouse, which produced a new round of charges and countercharges in the vestry. Bateson attacked the report and lashed out at Rendle, who, he implied, had inspired the writing of the report and whom he clearly regarded as an officious nuisance. Rendle defended the report as accurate on the whole though wrong on some details. For his part he read the vestrymen a long lecture on typhus fever and their lack of action, which at the next meeting drew a reply from one member in an "echoes from Bumbledom" speech.[31] The reform movement drew additional strength in September from a letter published in *The Times* by Dr. Horace Jeaffreson of the London Fever Hospital, who pointed out that although the fever epidemic had been raging for three years, it was not until July 1864 that the first patients were removed from St. George's workhouse to the Fever Hospital. Rendle, whom the writer obviously thought well of, had fought valiantly both as Medical Officer and later as a vestryman, but unfortunately he had been powerless in the hands of the most supine of vestries. Arguing from the number of deaths in the parish that there must have been no fewer than 3,000 cases of typhus, Jeaffreson observed with indignation that there still had been no cleansing and no whitewashing, and that in many cases there was no water tap for a row of several dwellings. St. George's was clearly the worst parish in the metropolis for infection — "a reproach to the Kingdom," in the eyes of the *South London Press*.[32]

On the strength of Jeaffreson's letter, Rendle renewed his demands that the vestry appoint another inspector, but again without success. At the same meeting the vestry was treated to a long report by Bateson, which, when a vestryman moved that it be published and thanks given to the Medical Officer, set off a large-scale brawl. Rendle and Collinson were agreeable to printing the document but not to thanking its author, for Rendle, although admitting that something had been done, thought the work described in the report was sloppy and half-finished.[33] Through it all the vestry was more anxious to clear itself than to get to the root of the trouble. Bateson's report admitted that the epidemic might have been "stayed at the outset" if the parish (the vestry) had done its duty. But the Medical Officer, the *Press* noted, was in a tough spot. He must show first that, as Medical Officer, he had done his duty, and then that the vestrymen had done theirs. Yet, in spite of all the pompous indignation in the vestry, statistics pointed to a mounting incidence of disease.[34]

But victory for the reformers was near. When a motion for another sanitary inspector was once more presented — with Archer interrupting constantly and making such a nuisance of himself that he alienated some of his own allies—it was amended in favor of a committee to look into all the officers and their work. The supporters of the original motion regarded this as simply an attempt to evade the issue. But the committee recommended the appoint of a second inspector, and Archer resigned from the vestry after thirty years of parochial service.[35]

The fact that the local guardians of the poor had, through *The Lancet's* attack on their management of the workhouse, become the first objects of adverse outside comment on the affairs of St. George's was perhaps a little unjust, for, compared with the vestry, the guardians were a reasonably progressive body. Back in 1855 the guardians' establishment at Lewisham for pauper children, which had been in existence for some twenty years, had become overcrowded, and at the instigation of the Poor Law Board the guardians had bought an estate of twenty-eight acres at Mitcham and built a new school there capable of accommodating three or four hundred children. This had of course aroused the fury of the economizers in the vestry, led by the redoubtable Archer, who were not pacified by the guardians' assurance that there would be enough room at Mitcham to accommodate, on a cash basis, pauper children from other parishes. Even the possibility of making a profit out of the guardians' new "farm" did not mollify them, but this acquisition was nevertheless a farsighted action, which gained the support of the editor of the *South London Journal*.[36]

Thus relations between the vestry and the guardians had got off to a bad start, and for a few years endemic petty bickering continued, with the vestry being uncooperative about the guardians' need to enlarge the old workhouse in Mint Street and the guardians refusing to admit the churchwardens to the prize-giving ceremony at the Mitcham school.[37] The fundamental problem confronting the guardians was, however, the utter inadequacy of the parish's financial resources to meet the demands made upon them by the vast number of poor who congregated there. In 1864 one in every sixteen of all the inhabitants was in receipt of relief, and most of the remainder were only a little above actual want; yet over half the houses were rated at twenty pounds per annum or less. Nearly 13,000 poor received casual relief during this year, compared with a mere 200 and 400 respectively in the wealthy parishes of St. George's, Hanover Square, and St. James's, Westminster.[38] Taking the metropolis as a whole, the poor were in fact bearing an overwhelmingly large proportion of the cost of poor relief, while the rich were paying exceedingly little.

The guardians, of course, were continually demanding legislation to equalize the rate burden throughout London,[39] and after the great distress caused by the cold winter of 1860–61, when they were receiving between two and three thousand applications for relief per week, even the vestry began to support the guardians. In 1861 it voted the payment of a subscription of ten pounds to the Metropolitan and County Association for the Equalization of Poor Rates (Archer dissenting); and in 1863, when the case for equalization was beginning to make progress, it resisted the temptation to submit a new scheme of its own to the Government.[40] At last in 1864 the Metropolitan Houseless Poor Act made contributions from a common fund to boards of guardians which provided accommodation for the casual poor.[41]

The Lancet's attack of 1865 upon conditions in the St. George's workhouse in Mint Street was made before this act could be fully applied, and it was followed by other almost equally damaging articles about conditions in other London workhouses.[42] Public attention was suddenly focused upon the whole subject, and in 1867 the much more important Metropolitan Poor Act was passed. This recognized that many unions and parishes could not afford the expense of classifying their poor in separate buildings according to their various needs and therefore established a Metropolitan Asylums Board for the provision of district asylums for the sick and infirm. It also established a common poor fund, to which each union was to contribute according to its ratable value, and from which disbursements to the poorer unions were to be made for many of their principal items of expenditure, including the maintenance of district schools and the relief of the casual poor.[43]

Two years after the passing of the act the Poor Law Board decided to amalgamate the four Southwark parishes of St. Saviour's, Christchurch, St. Mary Newington, and St. George's for poor-law purposes. There was some ill feeling in St. George's parish, but with four separate workhouses in the new union, separate accommodations could now be provided for each category of the poor, and St. George's workhouse was assigned for the use of the able-bodied.[44] Local resistance disappeared when the new union, known as St. Saviour's, began to receive contributions from the new common poor fund. By 1872–73 St. Saviour's Union was receiving over £20,000, or nearly one-fifth of its total expenditure, from this fund, and in these circumstances even the most ardent supporters of local self-government were forced to remain silent.

Moreover, the vestrymen of St. George's had been severely frightened by The Lancet's attacks of 1865, which, although primarily directed at the guardians, had included them as well, as the guardians of the public health. "Unless they [the vestrymen] are perfectly blind and stone-deaf," The Lancet had stated, "they must be conscious of movements and sounds abroad which indicate a stirring of public indignation against parochial incompetency and selfishness such as has never been seen or heard before, and which will surely find open and it may be vindictive expression before long."[45] And, nearer home, the *South London Press* had said: "The St. George's vestry must be told that they cannot cover most shameful neglect by petty and insensate gabble."[46]

Public interest in sanitation had, in fact, been aroused again. In 1866 it was maintained throughout London by the cholera epidemic (which caused thirty-eight deaths in St. George's),[47] and at the parochial level by the indefatigable Rendle, who in this and the following year gave evidence twice before parliamentary committees.[48] The Government woke up sufficiently to pass the great Sanitary Act of 1866, and shortly afterwards even the St. George's vestry roused itself to establish an enlarged sanitary committee. The immediate functions of this committee were to supervise the erection of a mortuary and to prepare regulations for the control of houses let in lodgings or occupied by more than one family,[49] but the committee also began to serve notices on house owners requiring them to provide dustbins and a proper supply of water, and to extinguish nuisances of all kinds. Even Rendle admitted that, with a second inspector of nuisances now available, sanitary matters were improving, although in 1869 he finally resigned from the vestry in protest against its lack of decisive action.[50] By 1871, however, the parish death rate had fallen to 25.0 per thousand—the lowest figure for a decade—and the *South London Journal* reported that the Medical Officer and the sanitary committee were doing their jobs properly, compelling property owners, if necessary by recourse to the courts, to meet the requirements of the law.[51]

This was just as well, for the inquiry of 1870 by the MBW, at the instigation of the House of Commons, into the work (since 1856) of all the vestries presented St. George's with the possibility of another unwelcome dose of bad publicity. In its reply the vestry prevaricated on some points, but it was able to claim that many of the old brick drains connecting the houses with the public sewers had, at the vestry's order, been replaced by glazed earthenware pipes, and that "the general condition of the drainage is very much improved, and may now be considered good." Over £15,000 had been spent on "sewerage works," about 4,000 cesspools had been filled in, and "proper water closets and suitable apparatus" substituted. Cleansing and watering the streets, refuse collection, and general sanitary improvements had cost some £48,000, and paving works another £80,000. A mere £200, however, had been spent on opening up new streets, compared with £55,000 in St. Marylebone; and the total expenditure on sewerage, paving, and "other improvements" amounted to £145,000. This last figure was very close to the £140,000 recorded under the same heading by another poor parish, St. Leonard's Shoreditch; but whereas in Shoreditch no less than 70 percent of the total expenditure had been raised by loans, only 11 percent had been collected in that way in St. George's. The economizers of Southwark had at least been consistent in defending their successors' pockets as well as their own.[52]

The final question presented by the MBW was, "What is the sanitary and general condition of the parish now as compared with before 1856?" The vestry replied, "Greatly improved; more especially as regards the streets and dwellings in the worst localities." And despite all the terrible criticisms leveled at the vestry by *The Lancet* and other sanitarians, there was at least some truth in this claim, for in his annual report of 1870–71 the Medical Officer, Dr. Bateson, stated that since 1856 cesspools, pig keeping, and the use of well water had all been abolished, the roads were cleaner, refuse more efficiently removed, and cowsheds and bakehouses regularly inspected.[53] Things *had* improved; but throughout the whole of London the establishment of even the most rudimentary standards of sanitation had proved a far more formidable task than had been expected, and in St. George's, at least, progress would certainly have been greater if the vestry had shown more determination.

After the alarums and excursions of the late 1860s, and the unwelcome publicity arising from them, the affairs of St. George's lapsed for a decade or more into a period of comparative calm, during which some unobtrusive improvements were made. After repeated complaints about the inefficiency of the contractor responsible for street cleansing and refuse collection the vestry decided in 1877 to buy a yard, keep its own horses and carts, and do the job itself. After 1875 the enforcement of the acts against the adulteration of food became a function of the vestry, the planting of trees in the principal streets began in 1877[54]— there was no public open space anywhere in the parish at that time — and by 1880 a public mortuary had at last been built.[55] The building of much-needed baths and washhouses proved, however, to be beyond the capacity of the vestry. In 1876 the vestrymen decided by an almost unanimous vote to adopt the act of 1846, but after a six-year search for a site the commissioners whom the vestry had appointed under the terms of the act abandoned the project in 1882. The *South London Press* kindly provided them with an epitaph: "To the Baths and Wash-houses Commissioners of St. George's, Southwark, who, after being elected and re-elected for ten [*sic*] years, failed to take advantage of every site which was offered to them, and ended their useless lives unregretted and unesteemed." In 1887 the commissioners were resurrected, but the vestry never did manage to provide any baths in this dirtiest of parishes.[56]

Probably the most important work of the vestry during the 1870s was done by the two inspectors of nuisances, who in 1876–77, for instance, dealt with nearly four thousand items, including the cleansing of some four hundred houses.[57] At last a small but permanent fall in the mortality of the parish became apparent, the death rate declining from an average of 27 per 1,000 in the decades 1851–1860 and 1861–1870 to an average of 25.2 in 1871–1880.[58]

This increasing importance of administrative routine was matched by changes within the vestry establishment. In its early days several of its officers had been involved in financial irregularities, and after the death of the vestry clerk in 1859, his accounts were found to be short. After much debate Daniel Birt, a leading vestryman and also a churchwarden, was appointed to the vacant clerkship even though he was not a solicitor. Three hundred ratepayers presented an unavailing protest, and the *South London Chronicle* referred pointedly to other recent cases of the appointment of vestrymen to paid posts in the vestry's control. So in 1861 the vestry virtuously passed a self-denying resolution whereby no member (or anyone who had been a member within the previous six months) should in future be eligible for a paid office on the parish staff.[59]

Birt remained vestry clerk until his death in 1878. He continued to conduct his business as a draper during the whole of this period, employing assistants (one of whom was his son) at his own expense to do most of the parish business.[60] He ran the vestry much as he pleased, ignoring its orders on occasion, and in 1873 it was said of him that he "had two-thirds of the vestry by the nose." Financial irregularities among the officers did, however, cease, and when the appointment of Birt's successor had to be considered the vestrymen evidently thought that another strong man was required. So they repealed the self-denying ordinance and once again appointed one of their former leaders, Alexander Millar, who had resigned from the vestry immediately after Birt's death. Despite this inauspicious start Millar proved a great success, according to the *South London Press,* which in 1887 said of him that he had such complete mastery over the vestry's work, and over the vestry itself, that he could have done the whole job alone.[61] Much of the improvement that the vestry did achieve may in fact be safely credited to its clerks and its other staff rather than to its members.

The members do, however, seem to have become less petty and irresponsible, and their discussions less unruly, although as late as 1868 there appear to have been no rules of debate.[62] At first they had bitterly complained at the level of expenditure of the MBW,[63] but when the parish began to benefit from the completion of the Board's main drainage scheme and the opening (in 1864, in the adjoining parish of St. Saviour's) of the new Southwark Street, the vestrymen of St. George's abandoned their earlier attitude of automatic hostility. In the 1870s they protested against the cost of the lamps and trees being provided by the Board along the new Embankment,[64] but they were by this time cultivating good relations with the Board over other matters; in St. George's parish, in fact, relations with the Board were never as bad as in Marylebone or St. Pancras. Poor-law matters ceased to interest the vestry very much after the absorption of the St. George's guardians into the larger amalgamated union formed in 1869. The annual vestry elections nearly always passed off quietly — it is said that in one ward in 1870 not even twelve out of twelve thousand electors voted — and current members had no difficulty in getting themselves reelected.[65]

This peaceful state of public indifference was, however, suddenly shattered by the publication in 1883 of *The Bitter Cry of Outcast London*, by Andrew Mearns. Public attention was focused upon the urgent need to provide new dwellings for the poor, and in 1884 a Royal Commission was appointed to examine the housing of the working classes.[66] In the closing years of its existence the vestry was thus working in a new climate of opinion, in which overcrowding was seen to be at the center of the housing problem, and in which sanitary inspection and improvement and the demolition of outworn houses could no longer be regarded as adequate remedies by themselves.

To cure the problem of overcrowding was, however, self-evidently quite beyond the power of the St. George's vestrymen, even if they had been more determined, and it was perhaps for this reason that the publication of *The Bitter Cry,* which included a detailed description of conditions in Collier's Rents, within the parish of St. George's, produced no outraged protests from the vestry. St. George's was one of the inner areas of the metropolis where casually employed laborers congregated in order to be available for any work that might present itself. Andrew Mearns stated in his evidence before the Royal Commission that in and around Mint Street there were "three times the number of labourers there that are employed at any one time." Often these men could only find work for two days a week, and it was this "constant idleness which makes them so poor." With wages of only fivepence an hour their weekly earnings sometimes amounted to only eight or nine shillings, from which a rent of two or three shillings for a single unfurnished room had to be paid. But demolitions necessitated by the building of railways, new streets, or warehouses were constantly reducing the number of houses with rooms these laborers could afford; and rooms in the new dwellings erected by the Peabody Trustees or the Improved Industrial Dwellings Company were beyond their means. They were therefore having to squeeze into ever more overcrowded quarters. Yet, as the stock of such cheap rooms diminished, so even the rents for these were rising in response to the inexorable laws of supply and demand. In the 1880s overcrowding was increasing, and its root cause, according to George Sims, a journalist with extensive local knowledge, was "the glut of the labour market."[67]

Two chief powers were available to the vestry in its attempt to deal with this deep-seated social problem: that of inspection and control conferred by the sanitary and public health acts, and that of repair or demolition of houses unfit for habitation, conferred by the Torrens acts of 1868 and 1879. Both Mearns and Sims stated before the Royal Commission that the work of sanitary inspection had not been done as vigorously in St. George's as it ought to have been, and Mearns asserted that this was because "there are vestrymen who hold property." This statement is reminiscent of similar accusations made some twenty years previously by the very much better informed Dr. Rendle, but because the charge was probably true then, it does not necessarily follow that it was still true in the 1880s. When cross-questioned, Mearns was somewhat unconvincing: he could only produce one specific instance, that of a Mr. Levy, who owned lodging houses and tenements and had formerly been a vestryman; and he admitted that he was not quite sure whether the property was actually owned by this former vestryman himself or by a relative of his — it was, in fact, a relative. By the 1880s, of course, there had been a considerable turnover in the composition of the vestry since Dr. Rendle's day. (And anyone who has ever served as an elected member of a local authority will know how frequently some, at least, of his constituents will be ready to believe the worst of him.) Probably corruption was less responsible for the vestry's sins of omission in this field than were inertia, a misplaced desire for economy, and sheer inefficiency.

But there was also another explanation. As early as 1872 the Medical Officer (Dr. Bateson) had reported to the vestry that although the population of the parish was increasing, demolitions for railways and street improvements were diminishing the number of houses available, and overcrowding was therefore increasing.[68] More vigorous application of the vestry's permissive powers for the abatement of overcrowding by control of houses let out in lodgings or occupied by more than one family would only have exacerbated the situation elsewhere; and the same difficulty also arose over the application of the vestry's powers to compel landlords to make sanitary improvements, for improvements were always followed by demands for increased rent, which many of the tenants could not afford. In the 1870s and 1880s the Medical Officer of St. George's had, indeed, some reason to proceed cautiously in attempting to apply even such sanitary powers as were available to the vestry.

Much the same difficulty was also encountered in the application of the Torrens acts, which required the Medical Officer to report houses unfit for human habitation to the vestry. Notice was then to be served on the owner specifying the work required to be done, or requiring the premises to be demolished. In St. George's a vigorous start was evidently made, and in 1871 Dr. Bateson claimed that the vestry had "done more here than any other Vestry in London."[69] But by 1876 he stated that the Torrens act of 1868 had "all but failed," and claimed that the complaints made by the vestry to the MBW had led to the passing of Cross's act of 1875.[70] This act enabled the Board, upon receipt of an official representation from the local Medical Officer, to clear whole areas of outworn housing and provide new dwellings on the site. In 1875 Dr. Bateson successfully represented three such areas to the Board, and in due course 1,266 inhabitants were displaced for the erection (by the Improved Industrial Dwellings Company and two private contractors), seven years later, of large new blocks accommodating 1,906 persons. The minimum rents were, however, three or four shillings for a single room, or five shillings for two rooms, compared with the rent of two shillings which Dr. Bateson's successor, Dr. Thomas Waterworth, considered necessary in 1884 "to solve the difficulty of overcrowding," and it is unlikely that any of those displaced returned to the accommodation provided in the new dwellings.[71]

After this experience Dr. Bateson made no more representations under Cross's act. More displacements did, however, occur when, at the request of the vestry, the MBW constructed Marshalsea Road through the district of the Mint between 1877 and 1888.[72] Dr. Bateson seems, indeed, to have adopted an attitude of hopelessness which was probably shared by the vestry. As early as 1868 he had stated that he did "not believe suitable houses can be built for the poor which will pay." If old houses were to be pulled down and new ones built, he continued, rents would have to be raised, and this would "render almost nugatory the good done." He was also thoroughly disillusioned with the great blocks of flats erected by the Peabody Trustees or under the aegis of the MBW, for in 1881 he expressed the vain hope that in the Mint Street area, where many old houses had recently been cleared by the Board, "decent houses" would be erected in their place, "but not Industrial dwellings."[73]

The experience of his successor, Dr. Waterworth, provides further illustration of the difficulties confronting the Medical Officer and the vestry. Shortly before the publication of *The Bitter Cry* in 1883 the vestry had been prodded by letters from the Local Government Board requesting it to look into the insanitary condition of the houses in several small areas in the parish. Dr. Waterworth then officially represented four sites to the

MBW, requesting that they be dealt with under Cross's act. But the Board refused to act, and so there was no alternative but to fall back on the Torrens acts, and report a number of houses to the vestry as unfit for human habitation. The futility of action under these acts was, however, being demonstrated at this very time elsewhere in the parish. In this case the Local Government Board's view was that the houses in question were unfit for habitation and should be demolished. Dr. Waterworth did not agree—what was the use of demolition when the inhabitants had nowhere else to go? Notice was, however, served on the landlord under the sanitary acts, requiring him to repair and cleanse the houses, and he was summoned before the local police court. Ultimately he agreed to close the houses until the work was done, and the occupants were evicted. Some time later the houses were still closed, and Dr. Waterworth could only comment that "we want houses in which rooms can be let at two shillings per week."[74]

The final phase of the vestry's existence began in 1889 with the establishment of the London County Council (LCC). The work of the vestry in the 1890s was probably the most creditable—perhaps the only creditable—chapter in its career. In that decade the metropolitan vestries found themselves working in association with a vigorous new body, equipped with its own Medical Officer and with extensive new powers conferred upon it principally by the Housing of the Working Classes Act of 1890 and the Public Health (London) Act of 1891. Decentralization of both employment and population was beginning to make itself felt at about the same time, and for the poor who remained in such inner areas as St. George's, the continuing rise in rents was offset between 1880 and 1895 by a fall in the cost of living.[75]

In May 1889 Dr. Waterworth officially represented several areas to the new Council to be dealt with under Cross's act, but in due course the wider powers of the act of 1890 were used instead. Two schemes eventually emerged, the costs of which were shared by the vestry and the LCC. Some 1,174 inhabitants were displaced, and new accommodation was provided by the Council—after a long interval, for neither scheme was completed before 1897—for 1,098 persons, the minimum rent for a single room being four shillings and sixpence. In 1899 a third rehousing scheme, covering a total area of five acres in which the death rate was 30.5 per 1,000, was commenced at the instigation of Dr. Waterworth's successor.[76]

Much of the vestry's renewed activity in the 1890s seems indeed to have been due to this new Medical Officer, Dr. Frederick Waldo. He reverted to Dr. Rendle's practice of plain speaking, which had been conspicuously absent in the days of Dr. Bateson and Dr. Waterworth, and

in his report, for 1892–93, he told the vestry roundly that "if sanitary reform is coincident with, and a chief cause of effecting a lessened death-
rate, then there is much room yet for improvement in Southwark"; and
he backed up this statement by pointing out that in the decade
1881–1890 the death rate in St. George's had been 25.0 per 1,000, compared with 20.5 for the whole of London. The vestry's bylaws for the
control of houses let in lodgings or occupied by more than one family, he
continued, had "never been enforced" owing to "the insufficiency of the
Inspecting Staff," and he demanded an immediate increase in the establishment to cope with these duties, which the Public Health Act of 1891
had made mandatory instead of permissive as hitherto. To its credit the
vestry immediately appointed a clerk, a mortuary keeper, and an assistant disinfector, and in 1894 the number of sanitary inspectors was doubled to four. By 1895 the vestry had at Dr. Waldo's instigation closed so
many houses as unfit for habitation that the total loss of rate revenue
amounted to £4,000 per annum, and there were still another five hundred to be dealt with. By this time, however, even Dr. Waldo was ad-
vising caution over any further such action, "having regard to the increased overcrowding which would then result." And this caution was
certainly justified, for between 1891 and 1901 the average number of
persons per house in St. George's rose steeply, from 8.6 to 10.4 per
house.[77]

This flurry of activity was matched by the vestry, which in the
mid-1890s was at last drawing up bylaws for the regulation of its own
procedures, building public lavatories, renewing old sewers, providing
shelters for the temporarily homeless, and repaving many of the principal streets, the latter being done by direct labor instead of by expensive
contractors. All this, and the purchase and demolition of many outworn
houses, was costing a great deal of money; but after the passing of the
Equalisation of Rates Act of 1894 the vestry began to receive contributions from the LCC toward its expenditures, and, in 1899–1900, £5,600
was received from this source. In its last days the vestry seems, moreover, to have lost its old fears of spending, or even of borrowing capital,
for whereas in the seventies and eighties the vestry's total repayments of
loans had remained stationary in the region of £2,500 per annum,
repayments doubled in the nineties, and in the last year of its existence
(1900) they amounted to £5,300, with the total loan debt standing at
£34,400. Even so, the St. George's loan charges were among the lowest
incurred by any of the metropolitan vestries.[78]

This more purposeful attitude of the vestry during the final decade of
its existence was, however, probably due more to the greater stringency
of the social legislation of the 1890s, and to the active policies being pur-

sued by the LCC, than to any voluntary change of heart within the vestry itself. Throughout its existence, compulsion had been generally needed to obtain effective and lasting action in St. George's. Matters beyond the vestry's control — endemic poverty and overcrowding, inadequate financial resources, inadequate powers, and an absurdly shaped administrative area, for instance — had all gravely handicapped social progress in the parish, but undoubtedly with more persistent determination the rate of advance could have been less costly in terms of human life. Costly it certainly was, for in the decade 1891–1900 the death rate in St. George's of 24.7 per 1,000 was still higher than that for the whole of London in any decade since the 1840s; and in 1900, the vestry's final year, the parish death rate of 30.1 was exceeded in only one other of the forty-three sanitary districts of London.[79]

CHAPTER 15

St. Leonard, Shoreditch

by

Francis Sheppard

The vestry of the parish of St. Leonard, Shoreditch, provides a useful comparison with that of St. George the Martyr, Southwark. Shoreditch, although a poor parish, was not quite so poor as St. George's, and its vestry was never accused of being stagnant. As at St. George's, much of its most valuable work was done in the closing years of its existence, and in 1899 no less a person than Lord Rosebery actually described it, with good reason, as "one of our model Vestries."[1]

The southern extremity of Shoreditch was immediately contiguous to the City of London. The parish contained some 640 acres and was roughly T-shaped, being about 1.75 miles in length from south to north and about 1.5 miles in breadth at the northern end. Throughout the length of the parish extended the ancient highway which commenced at Bishopsgate and which in Shoreditch was known as Shoreditch High Street and Kingsland Road. By the mid-eighteenth century the whole of the southern extremity, to the north of Finsbury Circus, was already covered with tightly packed courts and alleys, and houses extending back to a considerable depth stood along both sides of the High Street as far as and even beyond the intersection with Hackney Road and Old Street. Here, at the focal point of the parish, stood (and still stands) the handsome church of St. Leonard, which had been rebuilt to the designs of George Dance the elder in 1736–1740.[2] Ribbon development was also proceeding westward along Old Street toward the boundary with St.

Luke's, Clerkenwell, and northward, up Hoxton Street and Kingsland Road, toward Islington and Hackney. In 1801, when the population stood at 34,766, the whole of the area to the south of Old Street had been built over, but to the north most of the rest of the parish was (except, along the principal roads) still undeveloped.

By 1851 the population of the parish had more than trebled, and in 1861 it reached its peak figure of 129,364 inhabitants. By far the greatest part of this increase took place in the northern subdistricts of Hoxton New Town (to the west of New North Road) and of Hoxton Old Town and Haggerston (situated on the west and east side of Kingsland Road respectively). Here row upon row of small terraced cottages, many of them only two stories high, had been erected with virtually no public supervision of building standards, one-third of the whole parish being in 1856 quite unprovided with sewerage.[3] Hardly any of these cottages now survive, almost all of them having been replaced by blocks of Council flats.

The average number of people per house was also increasing throughout the whole parish, rising from 6.60 in 1841 to 8.17 in 1871. In the newer northern districts the number of houses mounted steadily until the catastrophic demolitions, caused by the building of the North London Railway down the length of the parish to its terminus at Broad Street in the 1860s, substantially reduced the supply even there; but in the southern districts around Holywell Street and St. Leonard's Church the total number of houses had already begun to decline in the 1850s. Here in the 1860s it fell by 38 percent, and throughout the whole parish by 9 percent.

The railways were not, however, solely responsible for this decline, for those parts of the parish nearest to the City were being gradually industrialized during the first half of the nineteenth century. By 1861 nearly 7 percent of all printing workers[4] and over 8 percent of all footwear workers[5] throughout the metropolis were employed in Shoreditch, but furniture making provided by far the largest single industry here, the corresponding figures for the parish being over 15 percent. The headquarters of the trade was in Curtain Road, which extended southward from Old Street parallel with Shoreditch High Street, but furniture making also spread out into most of the rest of the parish as well as into Bethnal Green and Stepney. At the beginning of the nineteenth century Curtain Road had still been largely residential, but during the next sixty years many of the furniture-making dealers had been driven out of the City by high rents, and had found a convenient new location in Shoreditch, where between 1812 and 1820 the building of the Regent's Canal across the northern part of the parish to its outlet in the docks had pro vided them with cheap transport for the vast quantities of wood required by the industry. By 1861 many old houses were being used primarily as workshops by cabinetmakers, chairmakers, French polishers, turners, and carvers, and a number of sawmills and warehouses had also been built.[6] A large part of Shoreditch was, in fact, being taken over for industrial purposes, and by 1891 the average number of people per house throughout the parish reached its peak of 8.9. Overcrowding was indeed, as at St. George the Martyr, to be one of the principal problems confronting the vestry.

Before the passing of the Metropolis Local Management Act of 1855 the paving, lighting, and cleansing of the streets of Shoreditch had for many years been in the hands of three separate authorities, exclusive of the turnpike commission, which was responsible for the High Street and Kingsland Road.[7] Poor relief and the administration of the numerous parochial charities were managed by some seventy trustees of the poor, who had been established for these two purposes by a local act of 1813. The trustees were appointed for life, and when vacancies occurred, half of the new appointments were made by the trustees themselves and half by the vestry — an altogether unsatisfactory arrangement evidently much resented throughout the parish.[8] The vestry itself had long since discarded the partly select constitution which had operated in the mid eighteenth century,[9] and its meetings were now open to all ratepayers who chose to attend. This they did, frequently and often in considerable numbers, for printed notices announcing forthcoming meetings were always displayed at the churches and other public places throughout the parish. The meetings were normally held every fortnight in the vestry room at seven o'clock in the evening, but when the room was crowded or the weather was hot they were adjourned to St. Leonard's Church. Special meetings to discuss some specific subject were often held at the request of a dozen ratepayers, and public polls, sometimes spread over two days, were frequently demanded. In 1851, for instance, there were four such occasions, two to fix the poor rate, one to approve various trifling vestry expenditures totaling less than forty pounds, and the other to appoint new trustees of the poor. The number of votes cast at each poll usually ranged between two hundred and more than a thousand, but the vestry did not confine itself to merely parochial matters, either at its meetings or at the polls; and in the closing years of this truly democratic assembly a subject which aroused great interest was whether the Crystal Palace, reerected at faraway Sydenham, should be opened on Sundays or not, with 678 votes being cast in favor and 197 against, and with three parishioners rather perplexingly voting against both propositions.[10]

The Metropolis Local Management Act sternly swept this direct de-

mocracy away and substituted a representative assembly of 120 vestrymen, to be elected by polls (at which all ratepayers were eligible to vote)
to be held in each of the eight wards into which the parish had been divided. In recent years the principal bone of contention in parochial
affairs had been the method of appointment of the trustees of the poor,
and in 1850 the Shoreditch Parochial Reform Association had been
founded for the purpose of having it altered.[11] What happened at the
first elections, held in November 1855, is not clear, for no local
newspaper then existed to record such matters, but by May 1857 the
"Tory or Trustee parties" were clearly on the defensive,[12] and after a
brief comeback in the following year the controversy surrounding the
trustees was finally settled.[13]

This settlement had been engineered by the new vestrymen, the
majority of whom regarded the trustees as a "profligate oligarchy of self-
appointed tyrants."[14] Under the leadership of Enoch Walker, a cabinet-
maker by trade and the founder (in the previous year) of the *Shoreditch
Observer,* they promoted a parliamentary bill in 1858 to abolish the trustees; and despite the vigorous resistance of the trustees, some of whom
were also vestrymen, the bill was passed. The occasion was marked by "a
good hearty ringing of the bells" of St. Leonard's Church and a dinner at
the Crystal Palace.[15] The new act separated the management of poor relief from that of the parochial charities. The former was now made the
responsibility of a board of forty guardians who were to be elected in
each of the eight wards in the manner prescribed by the Poor Law
Amendment Act of 1834, while the parochial charities were to be administered by the vicar, churchwardens, and twelve trustees who were to be
appointed by the Charity Commissioners from a list of forty-eight names
to be submitted by the vestry.[16]

This sensible reform marked an important local extension of the influence of central Government agencies, for the new board of guardians
was specifically subjected to the regulations of the Poor Law Board while
the new charity trustees, in addition to being appointed by the Charity
Commissioners, were also to be subject to their general supervision. The
fact that the reform had been promoted by the vestry indicates that anticentralization was not strong in Shoreditch.

The Metropolis Local Management Act provided that to serve as a
vestryman a candidate must be rated for poor relief at a rental of not less
than forty pounds per annum, but that if the number of such people did
not exceed one-sixth of the total number of assessments in any parish,
then the qualification should be possession of a rental of only twenty-five
pounds per annum. Shoreditch was one of the parishes where the lower
qualification applied,[17] and this was reflected in the social composition of

the vestrymen. In 1859 the largest single occupational group among the members comprised twenty-one men who worked in the furniture and woodworking industry—including, among others, six timber merchants, five cabinetmakers, three chairmakers, and two carvers and gilders—and ten others in associated trades (glass dealer, ironmonger, colorman, and fanlight maker). The next largest groups were twelve publicans, eleven in the clothing industry (bootmaker, tailor, dyer, shirtmaker), nine in the food trades (baker, grocer, corn dealer, cowkeeper), and six in the building industry. There were also five surgeons and a dentist, four esquires, and three pawnbrokers, while the remainder of the vestrymen followed a variety of miscellaneous trades which included auctioneer, tax collector, schoolmaster, gas company official, insurance agent, silversmith, and printer. About twenty-five of the vestrymen were probably men of some substance, for nine of them described themselves as merchants (including the six timber merchants already mentioned), five as wholesalers, and another five as dealers, principally in coal, corn, or tea. At its full strength the vestry evidently provided a fair cross section of the business community of the parish.

Until 1875 the chair at vestry meetings was normally taken by the senior churchwarden or in his absence by his junior colleague,[18] but in the 1880s the vicar, the Reverend Septimus Buss, often presided—an unsuccessful procedure that involved him in party maneuvers and prolonged squabbles with the vestry clerk.[19] The first vestry clerk, W. G. Davis, had previously been clerk to one of the local boards which had been superseded in 1855, and he held the post until his retirement in 1869. As had happened at St. George the Martyr in 1859, his successor was a prominent ex-vestryman, Enoch Walker,[20] who (like his colleague in Southwark) was powerful enough to ignore vestry orders on occasion, and remained in office from 1870 until his death in 1890.[21]

A strong clerk was certainly needed in such a vestry as that of Shoreditch, for there were constant meetings (almost always in the evening), and often they were long and disorderly. In 1859–60, for instance, the full vestry assembled on no less than sixty-eight occasions, sometimes at the special requisition of a few members (the debating tradition being still strong in Shoreditch), while its four main committees—sewers, lighting and paving, finance, and parliamentary—had a total of eighty-seven meetings.[22] The general level of attendance was, of course, poor—in 1860–61 eleven vestrymen did not come at all and almost half attended fewer than ten out of a total of forty-nine vestry meetings; but a sizable number of backwoodsmen could always be brought in to vote on controversial issues (such as in 1870 the grant of a pension to the retiring clerk) and so to hamper the taking of firm, consistent decisions.[23]

The trouble was that there were far too many vestrymen for the efficient conduct of affairs, and because many of them (probably including the most able) virtually dropped out of the meetings, power became concentrated in small party cliques. During the whole life of the vestry there seem to have been two such groups, both of which operated intermittently and with varying fortunes; sometimes they were active, sometimes almost moribund. One was the Shoreditch Parochial Reform Association, the more powerful group, ostensibly radical in attitude, which had been responsible for the abolition of the trustees of the poor in 1858. The other was the Vigilance Committee or Ratepayers' Association, which only enjoyed the ascendancy in the vestry in the early 1870s. Economy seems to have been the sole raison d'être of the latter, the poor rates in Shoreditch being unusually high between 1866 and 1872; but when new rating assessments were applied and the parish began to benefit from the Metropolitan Common Poor Fund,[24] the rate in the pound fell substantially, and in 1874 the Reform Association resumed its customary sway in both the vestry and the board of guardians.[25]

Too much importance should not, however, be attached to these parties. In the 1860s both of them seem to have been almost extinct. Polls were seldom demanded at election time, and when demanded they often attracted only a handful of voters. Although in the 1870s both parties were sufficiently strong to hold annual dinners,[26] the division of the parish into eight wards militated against powerful party organization. Personal relationships or business connections probably exerted a stronger influence than party over the behavior of the vestrymen, which was frequently volatile and unpredictable.

The prevalence of small cliques can provide a fertile field for corruption, but in Shoreditch, unlike Southwark, the vestry was never accused of holding up sanitary work because some of its members were owners of lucrative slums. Some jobbery did, however, exist. In 1857 Enoch Walker's newspaper, the *Shoreditch Observer*, stated that a few vestrymen in "the old party" depended for the daily bread of their families upon what they could make out of their public position.[27] Recorded instances of such practices are, of course, rare, but in 1876 a glaring example — the appointment, by one vote, of a rate collector who was the son of a vestryman — attracted some attention.[28] About the same time the vestry passed a self-denying ordinance prohibiting the employment of anyone who had been a vestryman within three years of the date of the appointment under consideration[29] — a more extreme version of the similar resolution passed in 1861 by the vestry of St. George the Martyr, where the period of severance was only six months. As far as the vestrymen were concerned, more attention seems to have been centered on the payment of a five-shilling expense allowance to members of committees involved in outdoor inspections throughout the parish. In the 1860s some members of the committee concerned with the reassessment of all property in Shoreditch for rating purposes were said to come along to sign the attendance book, go away, and then return to collect their allowance; while of those who remained to do the work, a more virtuous vestryman remarked that he had "followed the committee from public-house to public-house." The payment of an attendance allowance to members for loss of earnings was of course a perfectly reasonable practice which is still followed today, but there were no doubt abuses (as there are occasionally even now), and in 1887 the vestry sensibly reduced the amount to three shillings and sixpence and applied more stringent controls.[30]

In Shoreditch, accusations of jobbery were more commonly made against the officers than against the members, but it must be remembered that one of the functions of a member was and is to ensure honesty among the officers, whereas in those days there was no one to ensure corresponding standards among the vestrymen. In 1857 one of the rate collectors absconded with some £450,[31] and in the early 1860s a prolonged vendetta between Enoch Walker and the surveyor, W. Freebody, over supposed irregularities in paving contracts ended in the dismissal of the surveyor, who quickly popped up again to continue the quarrel as an elected vestryman.[32] His successor as surveyor, W. G. Davis, Jr., was the vestry clerk's son,[33] and between 1877 and 1881 he too found himself in the center of a hurricane of accusations and counteraccusations over irregular paving contracts for Old Street and St. John's Road. He survived, however—incompetent recordkeeping and supervision being evidently the chief explanations—and ultimately the dispute petered out in a successful slander suit brought by an outraged contractor against two disruptive vestrymen.[34]

In 1871 both of the sanitary inspectors were accused of accepting bribes, but the vestrymen belonging to the Ratepayers' Association, who were then in command, defended the inspectors on the flimsy grounds that they had really only accepted "gratuities." Renewed complaints led, however, to the dismissal of both inspectors in 1873. Because of its practical consequences this was perhaps the most serious case of corruption in the history of the vestry.[35]*

The routine financial administration of the parish was carried out by eleven rate collectors and a small office staff, the collectors being paid 2

*This case, incidentally, is a good example of the mutually contradictory criticisms commonly leveled at local authorities. In 1872 the vestry was censured for not dismissing the inspectors; and in 1873, when it did dismiss them, it was widely supposed to have done so only in order to provide jobs for two impoverished vestrymen. See *Hackney Express*, 15 April 1871, 15 November 1873; *Ventilator*, 25 April 1871.

percent (2.5 percent in later years) of what they brought in. The rates were fixed quarterly by the vestry, by far the largest single item being the poor rate, for which the guardians issued precepts to the vestry twice yearly.[36] The vestry also had to raise money to meet the costs of the Metropolitan Police and of the MBW's main drainage scheme, as well as (after 1870) the costs of the London School Board. There was therefore plenty of opportunity for the vestry to discuss the supposedly extravagant policies of these various bodies, but the parish church at least was largely exempt from these debates, for after the local act of 1858 no more church rates were raised, a voluntary payment equivalent to a rate of one penny in the pound being substituted. This system produced some £180 to £275 per annum for such items as the repair of the church and the payment of the salaries of the sexton, beadle, and organist, but although the money was actually raised by the rate collectors, the office of churchwarden became very unpopular in Shoreditch, and until the 1870s there was sometimes difficulty in filling it. The voluntary rate was still being collected in the 1880s.[37]

In the 1860s the vestry was much concerned over the assessments applied to property within the parish. No revision had taken place for twenty years and many anomalies existed. Moreover, the wholesale demolition of old houses to make way for the North London Railway and the erection of large new commercial buildings was rapidly increasing the discrepancies. Shoreditch was also peculiar in its custom of rating property at 44 percent less than the gross estimated rental as compared with some 17 percent less in other parishes, which resulted in the parish having a higher rate in the pound. A special committee was therefore set up to revise the assessments but (despite the inducement of the five-shilling refreshment allowance) there were endless difficulties in getting the vestrymen to attend, and when the committee's revisions were applied in 1867, a time of high poor rates, the vestry hall was invaded by a mob of irate ratepayers.[38] Two years later the Valuation Act of 1869 took the problem out of the Metropolitan vestries' hands and provided for new valuation lists to be prepared on the basis of a system that was uniform throughout the whole of London.[39] This new valuation produced a considerable increase in the total ratable value of the parish, and when it was first applied in 1871,[40] large arrears in the payment of rates accumulated, with three quarterly rates being collected at the same time during one period. But the employment of brokers in 1874 reduced losses from 7 percent in 1872 to 2 percent in 1877, and the recovery of the arrears provided the vestry with a welcome windfall.[41]

The vestry's most endemic financial problems were, however, connected with poor relief, which was by far the largest single item to be

covered by the parish rates. The vestry had to collect the poor rate for
the guardians, but although the local act of 1858 gave the vestry the right
to inspect the guardians' books, it had no responsibility for the disburse-
ment of the money. The guardians' twice-yearly requisitions therefore
provided frequent opportunities for bickering, their demands being
sometimes reduced by a penny or two in the pound,[42] and on one occasion in 1872 the vestry refused for a while to make a rate at all, to which
the guardians retorted by taking out a summons against the refractory
vestrymen — all 120 of them.[43] The trouble was that the vestry tried to
treat the board of guardians as though it was a subordinate body when in
fact it was not only independent but in some respects more important
and more efficient than the vestry. Because the board was chosen by a
different system, based on the distribution of voting papers (ballots)
throughout the parish, the election of guardians evoked greater interest
among the ratepayers than did the hole-and-corner polls for the vestry:
in 1871, for instance, the number of votes cast for the various candidates
in one ward ranged from 241 to 779.[44] Because there were only 40
guardians as compared with 120 vestrymen, they wasted less time in
futile debate, and in 1868 their number was further reduced to 24 by the
Poor Law Board.[45] Their staff — no less than 90 in 1871[46] — and property
were larger than those of the vestry, and in disputes with the vestry they
generally enjoyed the support, backed by powerful statutory sanctions,
of the Poor Law Board and its successor the Local Government Board,
as happened, for instance, in 1872 on the occasion of the vestry's refusal
to make a rate. The fact that in their early days most of the guardians
were also vestrymen (35 out of 40 in 1860) seems only to have added to
the confusion.[47]

As at St. George the Martyr, Southwark, the Shoreditch guardians
were probably more enlightened than their counterparts in the vestry.
They were less rigorous than those in the neighboring parishes of Bethnal Green and Whitechapel in the administration of outdoor relief,[48] and
although they had inherited from the old trustees some fairly new buildings at the workhouse (situated between Kingsland Road and Hoxton
Street)[49] and an industrial school at Brentwood, Essex, built as recently
as 1855,[50] they were already discussing the erection of a new workhouse
in 1862. Building began in the following year,[51] and was still proceeding
when *The Lancet*'s investigators, who had already castigated the guardians at St. George's, came to visit Shoreditch.

The Shoreditch guardians did not emerge from this inspection with as
much credit as did, for instance, those of Islington, but at least they
fared substantially better than had those at St. George's. They were
commended for the drainage, ventilation, and lack of crowding in the

building (which is still used as part of St. Leonard's Hospital), but the nursing, administration of medicines, and diet were all severely criticized. The investigators did, however, make allowance for the temporary problems caused by the rebuilding, and praised the "good intentions," "good-will and openness" of the authorities at the workhouse.[52]

The total cost of this rebuilding amounted to about £60,000, and it was followed between 1869 and 1872 by the enlargement of the Brentwood industrial school and the building of a new infirmary at a total cost of some £28,000 more.[53] The poor rate in Shoreditch in those years was hovering around the high figure of four shillings in the pound, and although the parish was beginning to benefit from the Metropolitan Common Poor Fund, from which £3,600 was received in 1871,[54] to embark on such a large expenditure must have required some courage on the part of the guardians. It was, moreover, in these years of high poor rates that relations with the vestry reached their nadir, the guardians on one occasion in 1874 having written checks for over £7,000 which the vestry refused to honor.[55]

In Shoreditch, economy never quite reached the degree of almost pathological intensity that it did in St. George's. Shoreditch, of course, was not quite so poor, but in 1871 (the year in which the uniform assessments make comparison possible) its ratable value per head of population was only 13.3 percent more than that in St. George's—£3 8s as against £3 per head.[56] But even the vestry, which in its early days assembled in the schoolroom of a Nonconformist chapel in Old Street, had between 1865 and 1867 built itself a handsome new hall (later to be known as Shoreditch Town Hall) at a cost of £30,000.[57] Almost all of this sum had quite rightly been raised by borrowing from an assurance society at 5 percent interest repayable over thirty years. Between 1858 and 1868 the vestry borrowed a total of £98,000 for this and other capital projects, and by 1870 it had repaid £21,633, leaving a balance still outstanding of £76,367.[58] It was this willingness to borrow which more than anything else distinguished the financial arrangements of Shoreditch from those of St. George's, and which made possible the substantial capital works executed in Shoreditch in the sixties, seventies, and nineties.

Most of the other loans incurred by the Shoreditch vestry between 1858 and 1868, amounting to £70,000, were in respect of paving and sewage works,[59] and there can be no doubt that in these early days a vigorous start was made on the sanitary improvement of the parish. Perhaps because of its proximity to the City, where the beneficial effects of Dr. John Simon's reign as Medical Officer of Health from 1848 to 1855 had been widely recognized, Shoreditch never had a "dirty party" in the vestry, and its first Medical Officer, Dr. Robert Barnes, did not become a controversial figure like his counterpart, Dr. Rendle, at St. George the Martyr. Primarily a pioneer in the field of operative gynecology, Dr. Barnes was also interested in the health of seamen, and in 1862 he was commissioned by Dr. Simon to investigate the prevalence of scurvy in the mercantile marine.[60] Barnes, like Simon, advocated expenditure on sanitary works for economic reasons; in almost the first sentence of his first report to the Shoreditch vestry he pointed out that in any parish the establishment of "a well-devised sanitary administration" would also, by diminishing the rates of sickness and mortality, "increase the value of the property, and lessen the burdens upon it."[61]

When he took on his herculean task in the spring of 1856, he at once stated unequivocally that in Shoreditch "the growth of the population has far outstripped the growth of the sanitary provision necessary."[62] Many houses were so badly built, and those in the older southern part of the parish were so densely packed in "courts, rows and nests," without water or ventilation, that they could never be made habitable. In some places, particularly near the Regent's Canal, typhus was endemic, one-third of the entire parish had "no means of getting rid of excreta," and everywhere the water, supplied by the New River and the East London Water companies, was impure and inadequate in quantity. "A large proportion" of the population lived "under conditions which render the preservation of health almost impossible," and the death rate stood at 28 per 1,000.[63]

With the aid of the medical authorities at the workhouse and the local dispensaries, Barnes at once established a system, modeled on that of Dr. Simon in the City, for the notification of disease, and two sanitary inspectors were appointed. Under his direction the inspectors set about issuing notices for the abolition of cesspools, the repair of house drains, the paving of yards, the removal of refuse, the cleansing of houses, and the provision of adequate ventilation. This last requirement he regarded as of even greater importance than the provision of adequate water, for the parish then contained a number of back-to-back houses; but since up to two hundred people often depended for water upon a single standpipe turned on for only half an hour a day, he continually pressed also for the provision of elementary water-storage facilities. In many cases property owners executed works of this kind on the simple recommendation of the inspectors. But if they refused, Barnes first obtained the vestrymen's support by arguing that sanitary improvements were not just "a question between the landlords and tenants," for if the landlord defaulted the rate-payers had to support the sick. And then compulsory orders were often issued, particularly after the members of the sanitary committee had themselves been educated in 1863 by a personal inspection of over two thousand houses.[64]

Between 1858 and 1863 the vestry borrowed £30,000 for sewage and paving works.[65] Applications to connect house drains to the vestry's new sewers were increasing in number, and the incidence of fever was already beginning to decline. The licensing of slaughterhouses, of which there were then about eighty in the parish, accounting for some 65,000 beasts per annum, was made the occasion for the introduction of numerous improvements, and after 1862 the cowkeepers were subjected to similar disciplines. House-to-house visitations urging vaccination against smallpox were organized, a number of trade nuisances (such as the discharge of offensive vapors from a printer's ink factory) were abated, and the ancient churchyards and graveyards were closed to burials. The streets were regularly watered, eight public urinals were erected, and in 1860 Dr. Barnes was even able to persuade the vestry to insist that a new church being built at Haggerston should be provided with water closets for the congregation, for "on Sundays the usual resources for relief are closed."[66]

By 1863, 2,740 cesspools had been filled in, 4,070 water closets erected in place of open privies, 2,200 house drains cleansed and repaired, 689 dustbins had been provided, and the ventilation of 110 houses had been improved by the construction of extra windows. A year later (1864) the death rate, which had been 28 per 1,000 in 1856, had fallen to 23.5;[67] and when the cholera epidemic of 1866 broke out the Shoreditch vestry was one of the most active in the whole of London.[68] Twelve medical visitors were appointed, and during the eleven weeks' duration of the epidemic they attended over 8,000 cases of diarrhea or "choleraic diarrhoea" and 148 cases of cholera, while the sanitary inspectors visited four hundred houses daily. Despite the fact that the attack of 1866 was largely confined to the East End of London, the number of deaths in Shoreditch was only 170, compared with 889 during the epidemic of 1849 — strong presumptive evidence, it was claimed, of the improved sanitary condition of the parish.[69]

This energetic start was not, however, maintained, and the slackening of effort unfortunately coincided with the period when the social and sanitary problems of the parish were greatly intensified by causes quite beyond the vestry's control. As early as 1859 Dr. Barnes had drawn attention to the increasing density of population, but in 1861 he forecast that the demolition of many old outworn houses in the southern part of the parish would be matched by a decline in the total population, and that "compression or crowding" would soon reach its limits. He had, however, underestimated the constant influx of immigrants of procreative age, and had of course not been able to foresee the devastation caused between 1863 and 1865 by the building of the North London Railway down the center of the parish. This resulted in the demolition of some 650 houses and the displacement of some 4,500 people, most of whom, Dr. Barnes pointed out, had simply moved into adjacent accommodation elsewhere in the parish.[70] Almost immediately afterward, in 1867, another 650 houses on the Ecclesiastical Commissioners' estate in Shoreditch and in the neighboring parish of St. Luke, in the vicinity of the future Great Eastern Street, were also demolished when the old leases expired, and although the sites were let to the Improved Industrial Dwellings Company and other agents for the erection of model dwellings, hardly any of the displaced inhabitants were rehoused there, the minimum rent for one room being six shillings and sixpence.[71] Between 1861 and 1871 these and other demolitions for warehouses, workshops, and churches accounted for a reduction of some 1,500 in the total number of houses in Shoreditch; and despite a small decline in the overall population, the number of persons per house rose from 7.58 to 8.17.[72]

The best local comment on the tremendous social problems thus engendered was provided by the vestry's chief sanitary inspector in his report for 1865: "The want of properly constructed suitable dwellings for the working classes still forms one of the great obstacles to sanitary improvement, the work of demolition proceeds rapidly, without any adequate means being taken to provide other [dwellings]; as a matter of course, in houses as in everything else, a short supply increases not only the demand but also the price, the consequent result is overcrowding, people are restricted in house accommodation from inability to pay the rent demanded for what they really require; the evil effects that flow from such a state of things are not confined to those of a sanitary character, but are equally injurious to the social and moral condition of the people."[73]

It was at this critical time in the sanitary affairs of the parish that the Medical Officer, Dr. Barnes, resigned in order to concentrate on his gynecological work. His successor, Dr. Henry Gawen Sutton, who held the post from 1868 until his death in 1891, was a physician for most of this period at the London Hospital and the City of London Hospital for Diseases of the Chest, and was the author of many papers published in the medical journals.[74] His annual reports convey, perhaps with good reason, an impression of growing helplessness in face of the increasingly complex social problems of Shoreditch, and it may not be by chance that he died, aged only fifty-seven, a few months after the publication of a Home Office report criticizing the sanitary condition of certain premises in the parish.

Dr. Sutton may also have been unfortunate in that almost the whole of his term of office coincided with the reign (from 1870 until his death in 1890) of the powerful vestry clerk, Enoch Walker.[75] As a vestryman Walker had been chiefly responsible for both the local act of 1858 and the building of the new vestry hall,[76] and as clerk he seems to have concentrated the wandering attention of the vestry upon the need for street improvements, perhaps to the detriment of more humdrum sanitary work. He was at any rate credited with having played an important part in finally cajoling the MBW into constructing Great Eastern Street and widening Shoreditch High Street (opened in 1876 and 1877 respectively),[77] and he probably had a similar role in the formation of Appold Street (1879) under the joint aegis of the Board and the vestry at a total cost to the latter of some £50,000.[78] There is no evidence that he ever actively interested himself in sanitary matters.

Certainly Dr. Sutton held his post during the most difficult years of the social and sanitary development of the parish. In fact, a careful examination of the criticisms that were leveled at the Shoreditch vestry between 1889 and 1891 may suggest that they were not wholly justified. These criticisms were made in the first place by the Mansion House Council on the Dwellings of the Poor, a body originating from the appeals for funds for the relief of distress which were then frequently made by successive Lord Mayors. In 1889 the Council's inspectors had reported to the vestry 1,948 sanitary defects in Shoreditch, by far the most common items being absence of water supply to water closets. A year later 532 of these defects had not been remedied, the vestry having in many cases dealt with all the houses along certain streets rather than with those few which had been the subject of complaint. The Council then requested the Home Secretary to institute a public inquiry, and this was held at Shoreditch Town Hall in December 1890.[79]

In their report the Home Office inspectors first of all enumerated the favorable points in the vestry's record. They commended the vestry for its activity during the cholera epidemic of 1866, for the provision of a temporary hospital during a severe outbreak of smallpox in 1871, and for the building of a public mortuary in 1875. They found that the food adulteration acts of 1872, 1875, and 1879 and the more recent Notification of Infectious Diseases Act had been well administered; and they described the provision (in 1877, at the instigation of Dr. Sutton and the vestry) of a constant supply of water throughout the parish "worthy of all praise." (They might also have added that Shoreditch was the first parish in London to acquire this indispensable tool of public health, and that the vestry's task in achieving it had been made considerably more difficult by lack of support from the MBW.)[80] Finally they noted two important facts: that the death rate in the parish had fallen in each of the previous four years, from 23.5 per 1,000 in 1886 to 19.1 in 1889; and that the proportion of deaths from typhoid fever during these years had also steadily fallen, whereas for the whole of London it had steadily risen.

This decline in preventable mortality was, however, used by the inspectors as "the strongest possible argument in favour of accelerating and extending the valuable work which has been in progress throughout the parish" during the previous few years. Although they could "speak in terms of praise of the *quality* of the Vestry's sanitary work," they had "nevertheless to record the fact that its insufficiency in *quantity* is very apparent." They therefore recommended that the vestry's sanitary inspectorate (which had recently been increased from two to three posts) should be enlarged by the appointment of a fourth inspector; that houses let in lodgings or in the occupation of more than one family should be regularly inspected; and that the nuisance removal and sanitary acts should be enforced "by necessary magisterial proceedings." They also criticized the vestry for not spending enough money on the scavenging, drainage, and paving of the streets, many of which were in poor condition — an undoubtedly justifiable point since during the previous decade the vestry had spent less than £3,500 per annum on the maintenance of the fifty-one miles of parish streets.

Many other London vestries besides that of Shoreditch were criticized in the eighties and nineties, and more recently by historians, for not employing enough sanitary inspectors, not controlling houses occupied by more than one family, and generally not enforcing their powers under the sanitary acts with sufficient determination. Misplaced and excessive concern for economy, or the self-interest of property-owning vestrymen, may well have provided partial explanations for these failings of the vestries, but in Shoreditch there were also other reasons, and they were not necessarily discreditable.

Shoreditch was one of only seven among all the metropolitan vestries and district boards to make regulations for the abatement of overcrowding in houses let in lodgings or occupied by more than one family.[81] The decision to implement the optional powers contained in section 35 of the Sanitary Act of 1866 was taken, after much debate, in 1867, the opposition of a number of property owners in the vestry having finally been defeated.* Regulations were drawn up and submitted to the Secretary of

*Local newspapers provide almost all the evidence available for the presence of owners of bad property in the Shoreditch vestry, and this evidence was apparently not always correct. The Reverend A. Osborne Jay, writing in 1893, referred to a case where an unnamed newspaper suggested that a Shoreditch vestryman owned some insanitary dwellings which were in fact the property of a West End journalist. See Reverend A. Osborne Jay, *The Social Problem and Its Solution* (London, 1893), p. 267.

State, who amended them before granting his approval,[82] and within a few months over a hundred houses had been placed on the vestry's register.[83] According to Dr. Sutton, "an earnest effort" was made to implement the regulations in the face of opposition from tenants as well as landlords, but the legal enforcement proceedings taken by the vestry proved unsuccessful in the courts. Despite this setback the vestry again instructed Sutton to enforce the regulations, but when he attempted to do so in the case of "some large houses . . . in an exceedingly dirty and otherwise injurious condition," he found that the "apartments" were let at more than six shillings per week and were therefore outside the scope of the regulations.[84] The maximum level of rents for accommodation to which the vestry's regulations applied had evidently not been fixed at an unduly low figure, for in 1895, after more than a decade of rising rents, the maximum rent to which the regulations were applied (with the approval of the Local Government Board) in the neighboring parish of St. Luke was lower than the six shillings established in Shoreditch in 1867; and in any case the Shoreditch regulations had been approved, after careful examination, by the Secretary of State, who, if the level proposed had been unduly low, would presumably have raised it.[85]

The vestrymen may also have doubted whether the more rigorous application of the regulations would in fact have been wholly beneficial for the poorest class of tenants. As early as 1862 the Medical Officer for Clerkenwell had reported that "if the occupation of rooms throughout the district were regulated [under powers contained in the Nuisance Removal Act of 1855], there would not be sufficient accommodation for the inhabitants."[86] Moreover, the Shoreditch vestry had direct evidence, derived from the neighboring district of Hackney, of what happened when the regulations were rigidly enforced. The effect on Hackney itself had been entirely beneficial, but as its Medical Officer, Dr. J. W. Tripe, admitted to the Royal Commission on the Housing of the Working Classes (1884–85), many tenants had had to go elsewhere because they could not afford the rent of uncrowded accommodation in Hackney. Many of the parish's displaced inhabitants had in fact gone, he confessed, to Bethnal Green and Shoreditch. When asked, "To save your having to solve a disagreeable problem [is it] much to be wished that your neighbours may not imitate you?" he could only reply, "That may be so."[87] Hackney's success had indeed been achieved only by shoveling its poorest inhabitants elsewhere, and if the regulations had been equally vigorously applied all over London, many more thousands of people would have been made homeless because they could not have afforded the available accommodation. To attribute the London vestries' failure to abate overcrowding solely to excessive zeal for economy or to the greed of those vestrymen who were themselves owners of poor tenements does not, therefore, provide a complete explanation. The parliamentary legislators who established the vestries with excessively large numbers of members and endowed them with only permissive powers to pursue policies which, if they had been rigorously applied everywhere, might well have produced a social disaster, should also bear a substantial share of the responsibility.*

The parliamentary legislators also deserve a large measure of responsibility for the frustration experienced by the Shoreditch vestry and its Medical Officer in their efforts to improve the sanitary condition of the houses occupied by the poor. Many houses in the parish had been erected before the existence of any public control of building, and they were completely worn out by the latter part of the century. As early as 1859 the vestry began to close houses which the Medical Officer had declared unfit for habitation until sanitary alterations were made.[88] Fifty-five such houses were closed in a single year a decade later. This was not, however, a policy which could reasonably be pursued wholesale when the railway demolitions were already putting tremendous pressure on the remaining accommodation, and many people were being (to quote the sanitary inspector's report of 1868–69) "obliged to get into almost any place, often places totally unfit for so many to reside in"—sometimes even underground. The vestry had therefore sought at first to enforce its inspectors' notices with the utmost stringency, sixty cases of noncompliance being prosecuted in the courts in a single year.[89] But by 1877 Dr. Sutton was reporting: "Year by year the Sanitary Authorities have been more and more convinced that the changes ordered even in Sanitary Notices, have been insufficient and even mischievous, because the alterations lasted but a short time; much money was expended, but the houses soon lapsed into a similar injurious condition. This increasing experience showed that it was wasteful to attempt to improve many of these old defective houses, because their basic materials were disintegrating."[90] Coercion through the courts was therefore largely abandoned, particularly when it was "seen that the owners could ostensibly obey the Magistrate's order without doing the work well." Instead, the vestry began in the early 1880s to show "fair consideration" to landlords, and if that failed, to have the work done itself and charge the cost to the owners.[91]

The vestry's experience in attempting to make use of the Torrens and Cross acts was even less encouraging. Under the Torrens acts a number of houses were closed as unfit, but in 1876–77 when the vestry ordered

---

*Contentious government policies which are left to individual local authorities to implement or not as they see fit seldom make much progress even today, as witness the fluoridation of the water supply and the sale of Council houses.

the demolition of a group of houses in Ann's Place, the owner successfully appealed to the courts, which allowed him to "repair" them instead.
The vestry, however, whose legal costs in this single case amounted to
over £500, remained convinced that the repairs would not last, and in
the following year it stated that the first Torrens act (1868) was "practically a dead letter."[92] Nor did the second Torrens act (1879), by which
an owner under order to repair or demolish his property might require
the vestry to purchase it at arbitration price, find any favor in Shoreditch. After its previous experience of the costly and vexatious appeal
procedure the vestry commented in 1881–82, "This of course is just what
nine out of ten owners would do, and it is also what in nine out of ten
cases the Vestries would not do; the consequence is that the order will
not be made."[93] And in addition to the legal difficulties, the climate of
opinion was not favorable to the pursuit of such policies by a public
body, for even several decades later, in 1923, it was still the opinion
of the Kensington Borough Council that "there are many objections to
the local authority of any area becoming property owners on a large
scale . . ."[94]

After the passing of the first Cross act in 1875 Dr. Sutton had reported
a number of houses off Hackney and Kingsland roads to the MBW, but
the Board refused to deal with them.[95] In 1882 he reported several more
groups of houses, including those in Ann's Place which the vestry had already attempted unsuccessfully to deal with under the Torrens acts; but
to this representation the Board nevertheless replied that the houses
should be dealt with by the vestry under the Torrens acts. To other representations which he made at about this time the Board replied that it
"could not entertain any other schemes in addition to those they already
had in hand." Many of the houses in question were subsequently demolished under sanitary notices from the vestry, the sites being used for
warehouses and other nonresidential purposes, while others were "repaired again and again." These last were again reported by Dr. Sutton
in 1881 and 1890, with a request to designate their site and that of the
adjacent area as an improvement scheme, but the LCC (the successor of
the MBW) requested the vestry to proceed under the Torrens acts, despite Dr. Sutton's protest that "to merely pull down these dwellings under Torrens' Act would be to leave two vacant pieces of ground, both of
which would be too small for proper houses or even cottages to be built
upon."[96]

The problems of the London vestries and their Medical Officers over
how best to implement the powers available to them were, indeed, considerably more complex than was commonly realized by Parliament or
the central Government or such bodies as the Mansion House Council.

In situations such as these a disproportionate amount of blame is generally attributed to the local authorities, and it is helpful to recall the opinion (recently quoted by Professor A. S. Wohl) of the Medical Officer of St. Marylebone in 1883–84 that for the working classes "sanitary improvement is a very car of juggernaut, pretty to look at, but which crushes them. Not a house is rebuilt, not an area cleared, but their possibilities of existence are diminished, their livings made dearer and harder." If the Torrens and Cross acts had been used thoroughly, he continued, "an appalling amount of misery, of overcrowding, and of poverty would have been the result," and "until tenements are built in proportion to those demolished at low rents, it is not humane to press on large schemes."[97]

Yet the Shoreditch vestry was certainly not perfect. In the 1870s and 1880s it was frequently criticized for its pothouse factions, the constant recriminations between different groups of vestrymen, and the general disorderliness of its meetings. According to the *Metropolitan*, the ratepayer "who, explaining why he had heard nothing of a great thunderstorm, said he was at a meeting of the local vestry, [was] commonly understood to have been a Shoreditch resident."[98] In the 1880s both the vestry clerk and the surveyor were past their prime (the latter being dismissed in 1887 because of his "advanced age and infirmity"); and in marked contrast with both the vestry's previous and subsequent records, no more capital loans were incurred during this period. The sanitary inspectorate was not increased until after the unwelcome publicity provided by the Mansion House Council, and no progress was made in the provision of baths and washhouses. In its closing years the old open vestry had adopted the Baths Act of 1846 and provisionally purchased a site; but the reformed vestry had refused to ratify the contract, and although special committees appointed in 1877 and 1887 had twice reported in favor of establishing baths and washhouses, the vestry had on both occasions rejected the idea.[99] Parsimony was evidently still very much in the ascendant.

But in the closing years of its existence the Shoreditch vestry transformed itself into an active, efficient, and enlightened body. The radical revival of the1880s had manifested itself there in 1885 with the election of (Sir) William Randal Cremer as a radical, working-class M.P. for Haggerston, and of Professor James Stuart, a Gladstonian Liberal active in the promotion of popular education, as the member for Hoxton. In the vestry the turnover rate of the members between 1886 and 1896 was double that for the previous ten years, and by 1896 only 20 of the 120 vestrymen had served for more than ten years. In 1896 over 20 of them were prosperous enough to live outside the parish, mostly at Stoke

Newington, Hackney, or Tottenham, qualifying for membership through their business premises. The vestry also included at least one trade union official (of the National Union of Boot and Shoe Clickers). With the appointment in 1891 of a new vestry clerk (H. M. Robinson, a solicitor by profession) and a new Medical Officer, the stage was set for a decade of intensive effort.[100]

Much of this activity was evidently promoted by Robinson, whose new methods of administration included not only the transfer of refuse collection and street scavenging from contractors to the vestry's own labor force but also an improved system of collecting the rates which produced a saving of £2,000 per annum. The influx of new blood to the vestry was also making itself felt, however, for by 1893 an extensive scheme of sewer reconstruction had been adopted, the first public open space in the parish (other than graveyards) had been acquired and opened in Goldsmith Square, and the Baths and Washhouses Act had been adopted once more. Public Libraries Commissioners had also been established; and after John Passmore Edwards, the philanthropist, had paid for the purchase of the old offices of the Independent Gas Company in Kingsland Road, a library was opened there in 1893, and extended in 1896.

Extensive unemployment in the parish prompted the vestry to set up its own labor bureau (public labor exchanges did not, of course, exist then), and the Municipal Technical School for the training of workers in the furniture trade, which the vestry established in 1892–93, was the first institution of its kind in London. The Town Hall was enlarged, and underground lavatories were constructed in the streets. Nor was the more intractable problem of housing neglected; the sanitary inspectorate was again enlarged (twice) to cope with the now obligatory inspection of houses let in lodgings, and the Medical Officer at last prevailed upon the LCC to deal, under part II of the Housing of the Working Classes Act of 1890, with some of the houses in the vicinity of Nile Street originally represented to the MBW in 1883 — a procedure which required the vestry to contribute one-half of the cost.[101]

But the vestry's pièce de résistance was undoubtedly its scheme to provide, on one large site, a library, baths and washhouses, an electricity generating station, and a refuse destructor — with the heat from the furnaces of the destructor being used to provide power for the generators, which would supply the whole parish with electricity. This ingenious and very ambitious project was not only implemented but also proved a great success. The first step, the acquisition of the exclusive right to provide electricity for the parish, was taken in 1891 at the instigation of Robinson, the vestry clerk, who persuaded the vestry to apply to the Board of

Trade for the license required by the electric lighting acts of 1882 and 1888. Shoreditch thus became the second local authority in London to obtain this right (St. Pancras being the first), and in 1894 the vestry acquired a good, centrally placed site in Pitfield Street, recently vacated by the City Iron Works, for £33,500. By 1899 the entire scheme—refuse destructor, generating station, library, and baths and washhouses (the latter heated by exhaust steam from the generators)—had been completed, and in the first nine months of its operation the electricity undertaking made a profit equivalent to a dividend of 5.5 percent.[102]

The Shoreditch vestry's record of capital works during the 1890s was, indeed, a very remarkable achievement by any standard, and of course it all cost a great deal of money, almost all of which was raised by loans. With the progressive industrialization of the parish during the last three decades of the nineteenth century the ratable value per head of population had risen by 75 percent, from £3.4 in 1871 to £5.97 in 1900. This was still well below the average of £8.1 for the whole County of London, but Shoreditch had at any rate gained in relation to St. George the Martyr, Southwark, where during the same period the ratable value per head of population had only risen by 62.6 percent, from £3.0 to £4.88.[103] The difference in resources per head of population in the two parishes had in fact widened from 13.3 percent in 1871 to 22.7 percent in 1900, and Shoreditch, although still among the poor parishes, was no longer among the poorest. Its vestry was also better placed than that of St. George's in having had a tradition of borrowing for capital expenditure during the 1860s and 1870s, followed in the 1880s by a period of stringent economy. By 1890 the vestry's outstanding loan debt, which had been £76,366 in 1870, had fallen to only £49,864, and the prospect for extensive new borrowing was therefore extremely favorable, particularly as the rate of interest paid by the vestry on its new loan debts during the 1890s never exceeded 4 percent. This favorable situation does not, however, diminish in any way the courage, foresight, and determination of the Shoreditch vestry in borrowing some £416,000 between 1891 and 1899,[104] and in raising the rate levy in the pound for parish purposes to two shillings and threepence, equivalent to 8 percent above the average figure for the whole County of London. (The corresponding figure for St. George's was one shilling and elevenpence, equivalent to 8 percent below the County average.[105] By 1900 the total loan debt outstanding in Shoreditch had risen to £408,843, as against £49,864 in 1890, and annual repayments amounted to £24,239—as compared with £5,300 on a loan debt of only £34,400 at St. George's.[106]

This difference between the capital expenditures incurred by the two vestries far exceeded the difference between their respective financial resources, and Shoreditch's example demonstrates what could be achieved, even in a poor parish, if the necessary determination existed in the vestry hall. The vestry's enterprise during the 1890s must have had a favorable general impact upon the quality of life of the majority of the inhabitants of the parish.* The core of Shoreditch's social problems was, of course, bad housing, and it was therefore appropriate that the vestry's final efforts in this field should be celebrated, in the last few weeks of its existence in 1899, by a visit from Lord Rosebery. In partnership with the LCC the vestry had provided new dwellings in the vicinity of Nile Street for the accommodation of four hundred persons, these dwellings being the first to be built in London by any metropolitan vestry or district board. Their construction had involved the displacement of over five hundred people, and the rents, for two- or three-roomed tenements, ranged from six shillings and sixpence to eight shillings and sixpence—far beyond the means of the very poor. The people dispossessed were not, in fact, being rehoused, as Lord Rosebery pointed out when he performed the opening ceremony. But by building the dwellings under its own direction the Shoreditch vestry had nevertheless set a notable example of far-reaching consequence to both its successor, the new Borough Council, and all the other new metropolitan local authorities shortly to be established. "Shoreditch is one of our model Vestries," Lord Rosebery had declared before being taken off to inspect the municipal delights of Pitfield Street—the library, the refuse destructor, the baths and washhouses, and the electricity station; and in 1899 his verdict was, no doubt, well founded.[107]

*The notorious area to the east of Shoreditch High Street known as the Old Nichol—which was graphically described in the 1890s by the local vicar, the Reverend A. Osborne Jay, and by the novelist Arthur Morrison in *A Child of the Jago*—was in the administrative parish of Bethnal Green, not in Shoreditch. Between 1892 and 1900 almost the whole of the Old Nichol was cleared under the aegis of the LCC and blocks of artisans' dwellings were erected on the site, which is now occupied by Arnold Circus and the streets radiating out from it. See LCC, *Housing Question*, pp. 190-213; Arthur Osborne Jay, *Life in Darkest London* (London, 1891), *The Social Problem and Its Solution* (London, 1893), and *A Story of Shoreditch* (London, 1896); and Arthur Morrison, *A Child of the Jago*, ed. P. J. Keating (London, 1969).

Conclusion: Perspectives on Metropolitan Administrative History

by
David Reeder

In a lecture given at the University of Leicester in 1965, David Owen explained that he had been drawn to the study of London's government, not from any addiction to urban or municipal history, but "in a purely empirical fashion." During the course of his work on metropolitan charities, he had come to realize that no one really knew how London had been administered during more than two-thirds of the nineteenth century. He found this disconcerting, and with good reason. Although the achievements of London's present-day institutions were celebrated in print, little had been written about the mid-Victorian predecessors of the London County Council. It was still necessary to rely on older accounts of the Metropolitan Board of Works, for example, even though many of these had been conceived in a spirit of condemnation. Only Percy Edwards, and Sir Gwilym Gibbon and Reginald Bell, of London's earlier municipal historians, had been prepared to give credit to the MBW for laying the foundations, in quite a literal sense, of the civilization that was Victorian London.[1] Gibbon and Bell had gone so far as to suggest that in the record of London's municipal affairs before 1889 there was "a promising field for anyone seeking a good historical subject of interest, and one might say, of entertainment."[2] It is a telling reflection on the development of metropolitan urban history that this challenge has never been properly taken up.

The present volume clearly deals with only some of London's mid-

Victorian administrative responsibilities, not with the administration of the metropolis as a whole. Important areas of policy — the poor law, education, the administration of charities — fell outside the purview of the MBW. David Owen did not consider it realistic to undertake the larger task himself, but he was determined to set straight the most neglected part of the historical record. Except for the authors of two unpublished dissertations, one of them presented after his death, he was the first historian to undertake a thorough investigation of the MBW from a study of its archives.[3] He appreciated, however, that to make any assessment of its work he would need to relate it to the larger problems of government and urban improvement arising from London's development into a complex metropolitan city. The logic of Owen's research carried him into a more ambitious study; he realized that the problems of metropolitan administration could only be understood by looking into the attitudes and policies, the social makeup and political character of the City of London and the metropolitan parishes. The decision to investigate a selection of parish governments was especially important, since without them his account would have been two-dimensional, illuminating the operations of the MBW but not really answering the more important questions about how London government functioned during the transitional years of the nineteenth century.

The history of municipal affairs is as old as the study of urban history. But in recent years there has been a fresh interest in how cities were governed in the past, awakened by our contemporary anxieties about urban problems, and a search has been made for new perspectives on the history of administrative development. The older civic-centered tradition of urban history has given way to a much wider interest in urban growth and development; and the history of local government is being changed by the new approaches of social and political historians.[4] This chapter takes account of recent work, in addition to that contained in the present volume, to show how past interpretations of London's administrative history are being revised. It refers to the special features affecting the government of Victorian London and points to new lines of inquiry into the history of metropolitan reform, the politics and economics of urban improvement, and the growth of urban administrative agencies. Whatever reservations Owen had about the scope of his work, it seems only fitting, and a tribute to his reputation as a scholar and teacher, to indicate how much remains to be done in unraveling the complexities of London government in the nineteenth century.

Although Owen was not deliberately revisionist, he became suspicious of the bad press which the MBW had received. The most obvious reason for this low esteem was that the mid-Victorian administrative agency had become the whipping boy of the municipal reformers. Furthermore, these reformers had been influential in shaping the attitudes of later generations toward Victorian London more generally.[5] The earliest comprehensive accounts of London government served as the standard texts for many years. The most important of these was *Municipal London* (1876), written by J. F. B. Firth, a Liberal M.P. and a leading member of the London Municipal Reform League, founded in 1880 to agitate for a unified and representative government for London. The assumption of London's reformers that municipal institutions and the municipal ethos were necessary to the progress of urban communities was shared by liberal intellectuals, who pioneered the civic-centered tradition of English urban history, based on a study of corporate institutions. For both groups, the provincial city provided the model for urban government: the municipal corporation, reformed in 1835, was regarded as the source of English liberties and as an example of enlightened social progress. London was frequently represented as having lagged behind the provincial cities in municipal activity because it had been excluded from the advantages of the Municipal Reform Act of 1835. As Frederick Whelen observed in 1898, London "is only now developing a municipal constitution which will cope with present necessities and repair its past neglect."[6] For late-Victorian and Edwardian commentators, the founding of the London County Council marked the real beginning of London's municipal life.

From the vantage point of the English provinces, Victorian London seemed out of step politically, not much affected by the radical movements of the century, or, for that matter, by the main thrust of the Industrial Revolution. The provincial radicals thought of London as hostile to radical causes; and the London radicals themselves complained of its apparently supine political and municipal life. There was some truth in these charges. The system of local government established by the Metropolis Local Management Act of 1855 had had a deadening effect. As J. P. D. Dunbabin has put it, "The system was too complex to attract the attention of voters and too anomalous to have the same pretensions to finality as the municipal corporations remodelled in 1835."[7] London's constitutional reformers were frustrated political activists who fretted about the indirect system of election to the MBW. Yet the case for a more democratic system contained an argument which would now be described as invoking a theory of patrician or elite government. This theory reflected the view of John Stuart Mill, the chief intellectual influence on London's constitutional reformers, that representative and free government was morally invigorating, with representative local institutions being the chief instruments of "the public education of the citizens."[8] The reform of metropolitan government was necessary to create a greater sense of public spirit and to bring men of higher caliber, the better educated (and wealthier) citizens, into municipal affairs. Metropolitan reformers (and progressive opinion generally) believed that London was lacking in municipal vitality and its government had become the prey of vested interests and mean minded policies mainly because of the control of house-owners (or investors in house property) and petty shopkeepers over parish affairs.

G. C. Brodrick was almost alone among the radical Liberals in thinking that London government was probably no worse than that of many provincial cities. He also warned that changes in the constitution of London would not necessarily bring changes in its municipal spirit. In the volume of Cobden Club essays which included the famous polemic of J. F. B. Firth on "London Government and How to Reform It," Brodrick wrote:

By virtue of its mere size and population, London is incapable of being governed like an ordinary borough, whatever constitution may be imposed upon it. [London] . . . contains a very small proportion of wealthy and highly educated citizens born and bred within it, attached to it by family ties, and willing to serve it with life-long fidelity. Not merely is the West-End half emptied of inhabitants during eight or nine months of the year, but the great City merchants, and even the wealthier shopkeepers, habitually reside at a distance from their places of business . . . the general want of corporate vitality in the whole metropolitan community . . . [is] the natural consequence of these peculiar conditions rather than defects in the formation of local areas or local governing bodies, which might be cured by legislative measure.[9]

The radical Liberals were deeply impressed, however, by the example of Birmingham, where leading businessmen played a dominant part in extending municipal activity. We know now that there were several reasons for this, among them the influence of Noncomformity in fostering ideals of community service. Birmingham's "West end" suburb of Edgbaston provided a convenient domestic power base for its municipal leaders.[10] But some other provincial cities, with more widely dispersed suburbs, had problems in recruiting the leading inhabitants to municipal service similar to those found in London. From the 1860s onward, Sheffield Liberals were complaining, for example, that the Town Council was not attracting men of property and business. As one of them emphasized in 1867, it was not enough that a man should be responsible in business: "his increased wealth, his wider influence, his deep experience, are public property in part"[11] — a concept which became established in political and academic thinking about local government in England.

A critical attitude toward London's municipal record was set up during the nineteenth century by the tensions between London's different functions as a wealthy industrial and commercial capital city and as a suburban housing area (the largest in the country). The irrigations of commercial capital which sustained London's Victorian housing development were not capable of keeping a larger sense of community alive when it was in danger of being crushed by sheer force of numbers. London was too vast and the consciousness of the crowd too immanent to permit the intimacy of a single community for the whole. There was, instead, the beginning of a fragmentation that has never been reversed. A "progressive" body of opinion in favor of stronger municipal action emerged in London as a a kind of protest against these disintegrative tendencies in metropolitan life. The need for some new initiative which might lead to the creation of a larger sense of community was reinforced by successive disclosures of social investigators on the human condition of the metropolis.[12] Demands for constitutional reform came to be associated with political demands for new social policies; but these demands were only the vociferous manifestations of more general anxieties about London's social problems. In the view of some commentators, the failure to establish a proper government for London had given free reign to a self-seeking, money-making spirit. When Henry Jephson (a former member of the LCC) wrote his classic study, *The Sanitary Evolution of London* in 1907, it was, he said, "the all-powerful, the all-compelling motive and unceasing desire" for "commercial prosperity and success" that provided London's motive power. "That indisputable fact must constantly be borne in mind as one reviews the sanitary and social condition of the people of London."[13]

The first item on any agenda of future historical research must surely be a fresh description of the way in which the concept of "metropolis" was formed. During the course of the century, the "crisis of conscience" to which Donald Olsen has referred in the introduction and which owed much to successive outbreaks of cholera began to turn into something like a crisis of identity. In other words, Victorian London was not merely passing through a series of transitional phases in architectural styles, in economic organization, in demographic adjustment, and in governmental structure; it was also developing a new awareness of itself. By the last quarter of the nineteenth century, the periodical press was carrying innumerable articles and reports on London's pathological condition; many of these were occupied basically with questions about the relationships between the various parts (and the various worlds) of which London was composed. What, indeed, did it mean to be a Londoner?

London did not have a functional identity until the founding of the London County Council in 1888. Until then, the emergence of new functions requiring to be discharged on a larger spatial scale had given birth to new organizational forms, each of them established for a separate purpose, with a separate jurisdiction and a separate rate. In contrast, the provincial cities had been provided with nuclei of effective and unified urban administrations after the reform of the municipal corporations in 1835, although some of the smaller and growing towns remained unincorporated, administered by a parochial or township authority, court leet, board of guardians, or improvement commission. But it was London, a city in the greatest need of reorganization because of the scale and complexity of its metropolitan area, which was the least capable of achieving it. London remained administratively balkanized until almost the very last decade of its Victorian existence.

London's governmental development was evidently affected by special historical factors. Among these was the failure of its own corporate body to embrace the extramural accretions which had been forming outside London proper for two centuries following the Great Fire of 1666. The Corporation of London survived, unreformed, able to defend its privileges, even to defy central Government on occasions: it became a powerful pressure group — the central business district militant — capable of resisting successive bills for the "better government" of the metropolis, illustrating in a most dramatic way the tensions between the metropolis as commercial center and as living environment. Chapter 11 in this volume is the first detailed account of the politics and personalities of the City's Common Council in the Victorian period; and it exposes an inner world of London that has been overlooked or ignored in the hagiographical treatment which the Corporation has tended to receive.

The development of London government was also profoundly influenced by the presence of Westminster. For example, Parliament kept a unique legislative veto over London's transport developments, and over a range of other major issues. The MBW was itself imposed on London from above. But in this case, as in the formation of the Metropolitan Police in 1829 under the direct control of the Home Secretary, it is difficult to see how it could have been otherwise. The matter of a Metropolitan Police was held to be of national — indeed imperial — importance; and the maintenance of civil order in London continued to raise difficult issues of control. The problem of policing metropolitan cities was a source of conflict in other urbanized nations as Wilbur R. Miller has shown in comparing police authority in New York and London.[14] But the issue of the Metropolitan Police might be regarded as a special case. The more general point is that in England,

Parliament had long held fears of a politically ambitious and overly powerful metropolitan city. This was, arguably, the most important factor inhibiting the development of London's civic strength.

Yet both Asa Briggs and David Owen have argued that the parochial attitudes of the suburban vestries posed the essential problem of London government.[15] Here again, London's experience was different from that of other cities. London did not experience what Sidney Webb called the decline of the parish; on the contrary, from the late eighteenth century onward its traditional units of parish government were acquiring new secular functions, although the extent to which they gained control over poor relief, highways, and education varied considerably. Governmental powers continued to be shared with the justices of the peace and such organizations as Turnpike Trusts (abolished in 1857), and with private commissioners for paving and lighting in new residential areas.[16] But the vestries acquired further powers—by means of improvement acts before 1855 and permissive legislation thereafter—and set up committees to undertake new parochial tasks. Even in the more sparsely populated districts, where district boards, formed after 1855, took over the duties of two or more parish vestries, the latter still kept control over rating. In short, the London vestries were strongly entrenched. They were able to keep an eye on developments affecting the metropolitan area, and they defended their separate interests not only through representatives on the MBW but by bringing pressure to bear on London M.P.'s. These parochial involvements reflected the importance of local independence to the Victorians. They were also a consequence of the way London had grown, by the expansion of village centers of economy and population and by the agglomeration of suburbs. The territory of the MBW (an arbitrarily defined area based on the Registrar-General's definition of London) encompassed places which were urban entities and regarded as "cities" in their own right, as well as places still on the building frontier—and even in the outer suburbs, village centers were self-consciously described as "towns." Given the nature of metropolitan growth and the tendency to suburban exclusiveness, the reality of London's community life lay in its constituent parts.

London was a special case in the history of urban politics and administration: the development of its political character and governmental institutions was almost always *sui generis*. Ideas and theories coming out of research on the politics of improvement in English provincial and industrial cities must be treated with caution by students of Victorian London. As Derek Fraser has argued, the major provincial cities had coherent political structures, with an interlocking set of relationships among all the various dimensions of city politics, from national political organization to contests over the control of services and facilities at the most parochial level.[17] London did not fit that picture, at least before the 1870s; but the extent to which its political structure diverged from that of other Victorian cities is still an open question. Even in the provinces, there were many differences between towns and cities in respect of their political setups, and considerable variations in the composition and influence of their urban elites. What actually went on in the provincial cities after 1835 is by no means clear, and in some places at least, the impact of that supposedly epoch-making piece of legislation, the Municipal Corporations Act, was distinctly limited.[18]

The question of who governed the Victorian city, as well as how it was governed, is relevant to any consideration of the role of urbanization in social change: as, for example, the extent to which the rise of the city helped to transform an earlier society, dependent on kinship and patronage, into a society regulated by the new criteria of the cash nexus and bureaucratic direction. It is necessary to be aware of the continuance of aristocratic influence in Victorian cities, and to consider whether aristocratic owners of urban properties, in London and elsewhere, exerted an influence on city affairs beyond that of controlling part of the urban environment.[19] To what extent was the business community itself still kinship-based in Victorian cities? And was the economic power of urban business elites necessarily paralleled by a political control over municipal affairs? On the basis of a study of late-Victorian Cardiff, Martin Daunton has challenged the view that elite rule was the "natural" condition of a Victorian city. It was, he claims, more "natural" for house owners, investors in house property, and retail traders to take over local government, as they were alleged to have done in London.[20] All of them were generally men of slender resources and more directly affected by rate increases than other groups in the community. Then again, there is the question of whether government by the elite was necessarily better or had larger and more visionary aims than that by tradesmen. John Kellett has pointed out that when businessmen became town councillors they were more interested in the efficiency and economy of government than anything else, treating the municipality much like a commercial undertaking. He argues that a practical ad hoc approach to the extension of municipal activity, rather than ideological concerns, brought provincial councils into such new fields as that of municipal trading. According to this argument, the development of municipal trading was an aspect of the entrepreneurial activities of provincial councils: municipal socialism as a political doctrine was born, not in Birmingham in the 1870s, but in London in the 1890s; and even then, A. M. McBriar and other historians have argued, the influence of Fabian socialism on London politics should not be exaggerated.[21] London's experience must be recognized as particularly relevant, nevertheless, in assessing the role of ideology in municipal affairs, and pertinent also to any discussion about the nature of power and control in the Victorian city despite the special features of its governmental history.

What has been done, then, to elucidate the impact of political pressures on government and urban improvement in Victorian London? Much of the research on the political history of London has gone into tracing how the nature of London radicalism changed from its vigorous eighteenth-century manifestations. The most detailed contributions to this theme have been made by historians of London Chartism in studies which also illustrate the relations between the middle- and working-class components of London radicalism.[22] The constitutional reform movement was an aspect of middle-class radicalism. The later phases of this movement have been studied by Francis Nicholson, Jr., in an unpublished dissertation on the politics of metropolitan reform, 1876–1889, and by Ken Young in an article on the background of the founding of the London County Council.[23] Both studies show how national and local pressures combined in generating a political will to change the form of metropolitan government. They give a more detached view of the constitutional reform movement than does the older account of John Lloyd (*London Municipal Government: History of a Great Reform* [1910]) and they extend the work of J. P. D. Dunbabin on the establishment of County Councils in England.[24]

From the 1880s onward, the London constitution and London politics were inextricably mixed, with constitutional issues influenced by the electoral concerns of the Conservative and Liberal-Progressive parties. Ken Young has done the most to analyze the Conservative strategy for London.[25] Other scholars have also demonstrated the interrelations between national and local politics in late-Victorian London. John Stevens has made the only full-scale study of the policies of the Progressive party; and David Rubinstein has highlighted aspects of London's educational politics, describing the affiliations between educational factions and party political aspirations in his study of the London School Board, 1870–1904. Paul Thompson's history of the political struggle for London, 1885–1914, is the most comprehensive account of the relations between the growth of party and the local infrastructure of London's political life.[26] All these studies show how London politics was of national concern by the later nineteenth century.

What then remains to be done? David Owen's work on the politics of London government in the more neglected period before the founding of the London County Council might be extended by further explorations of four main topics.

The first concerns the relationship between constitutional arguments for reforming London government and the attitudes of radical Liberals toward the centralization of governmental powers. Benthamite Liberals were the earliest, most conspicuous supporters of a unitary approach — the "government of the One" in Owen's phrase — but they did not have much influence on the majority of London's middle-class radicals, most of whom remained suspicious of centralized direction and bureaucratic organization until the 1870's. The alternative to a decentralized London (the "Many") was argued by Joshua Toulmin Smith, a London vestryman, who claimed that centralized government would spawn a body of unwanted officials and who defended parish government from the standpoint of a constitutional lawyer's romantic vision of the parish as the source of Anglo-Saxon liberties. Toulmin Smith cannot be dismissed as an eccentric. He not only influenced the London radicals but some northern radicals as well: his pamphlet *Metropolis and Its Municipal Administration* (1852) was intended to show "the essentials of a sound system of municipal government as applicable to all town populations." The argument receiving the strongest support by the 1860s, however, was a compromise between the One and the Many — the idea of a federal London based on a central coordinating body and the incorporation of the parliamentary boroughs. This idea was taken up by the Metropolitan Municipal Reform Association, founded by James Beal, a Westminster estate agent and advocate of "economical" government. Beal sponsored the election of John Stuart Mill as M.P. for Westminster; and Mill himself envisaged a central coordinating body for London rather than a body with supreme power over all local authorities.

The argument for a unified London under the authority of one body did not become uppermost until the founding of a new organization, the London Municipal Reform League. Its spokesman, J. F. B. Firth, was condemned by his critics for being an out-and-out centralizer, as the title of W. J. Devenish's pamphlet indicates — *Municipal Reform Leaguers; Absolute Centralism Knocked into a Cocked Hat: Firth Dissected* (1883). But Firth was not really a centralizer in the Benthamite tradition. His views reflected the wider shift in liberal thought from the old emphasis on the defense of legal freedoms to a new emphasis on "positive freedom" dependent on a concept of community and associated ideals of citizenship. There was support for the Reform Leaguers from political liberals beset with electoral anxieties in a city whose suburban development was beginning to encourage a "flight from liberalism." But the most important factor in hardening radical opinion in favor of a separate unitary government was a growing disillusionment with the attitudes of the City, and resentment over the wealth and privileges of the City Livery Companies. The radical assault on the City, started by the crusaders of the *Westminister Review* when it was edited by W. E. Hickson, a London merchant and friend of Chadwick, was taken over by Charles Buxton, M.P. for Westminster (*Self-Government for London* [1869]) and James Beal, who repeatedly pilloried the "Juggernaut of Guildhall." During the 1880s the position of the City of London was still an important element in the debate about metropolitan reform raging in the periodicals. Strong anti-City, pro-reform articles were carried by the *Edinburgh Review* (J. Roland Phillips, October 1875), the *Fortnightly Review* (J. F. B. Firth, July 1883), the *Contemporary Review* (Edwin Chadwick, June 1884), and the *Westminster Review* (Anon., July 1887). The defense of the City was undertaken in articles in the *Quarterly Review* (George Saintsbury, July 1884), the *Contemporary Review* (Benjamin Scott, February 1882), and the *National Review* (M. E. Harkness, May and September 1883), although the last periodical carried Hobhouse's reply to Scott and his attack on the Livery Companies (December 1886, June 1888). The *Nineteenth Century* also carried articles on London government, some favoring the City (W. M. Torrens, November 1880), others presenting the case for a County Council (Sir W. M. Ackworth, March 1889). The *Fortnightly Review* printed articles linking the case for reform with pleas for action to deal with the problem of London's poor (February 1881, January 1884).

A second topic which might be explored further is the interrelationships among pressure groups formed to assert or resist control over London's government and urban services. It is worth noting, for instance, that Toulmin Smith's arguments for a decentralized London were taken up both by defenders of the ancient customs of the City of London and by representatives of the more ambitious suburban vestries, who formed the Metropolitan Municipalities Association in 1867. Earlier, *Punch* had delighted in satirizing the argument about the dangers of centralization, claiming that it was used as an excuse by parish representatives and other opponents of change to defend vested interests.[27] Yet there were many confusing crosscurrents in the attitudes of London's bourgeoisie toward governmental matters. The London Municipal Reform League drew support, for example, from London's wealthier merchant and professional classes, including City merchants who inhabited such suburban citadels as South Kensington. J. F. B. Firth and other League members were leading figures in the struggle for the control of gas and water in London, partly for social reasons but also because they were expressing, as James Beal had done earlier, the irritations of London householders about intermittent water supplies and the cost of gas lighting. By the 1880s the question of the quantity of water had become mixed up with the question of the quality of water supplied, but as R. A. Lewis pointed out in his account of the public health movement, the mid-century debate over water supply in London centered more on matters of political and economic control than on the effects of unsafe water on public health.[28] The fight for London's water supply — to use the title of T. F. Reddaway's article published in 1950 — has been extensively researched.[29] It is a subject which illustrates particularly well the interplay between radical opinion and London's partisan politics. The battle for the gas supply has not yet received such detailed treatment.

Third, disputes over the supply and control of other urban services can be studied to throw light on the responses of the MBW to pressures for change. For example, F. M. L. Thompson's recent profile of Victorian Hampstead contains an account of the campaign to preserve Hampstead Heath from the builder and shows that on the matter of public parks and open spaces the MBW was rendered impotent by the parochialism of its vestry members.[30] Yet other contests involving the Board enabled it to project a very different image. W. E. Luckin has found, for example, that in the struggle between the MBW and the Thames Conservancy Agency over the question of controlling the pollution of the Thames — a long and protracted struggle — the Board presented itself as a progressive body and regarded the Conservancy Agency as undemocratic and dominated by "upper river" interests.[31] In contrast, the Conservancy — much the older of the two bodies — prided itself, in decidedly eighteenth-century fashion, on its "independence" and immunity from the pressures of municipal democracy. In this case, the MBW seems to have been the more important body in making the control of pollution relatively more efficient by the 1870s. These studies in themselves indicate several directions for further research.

In his work on the vestries, David Owen began to uncover the activities of the many and mostly ephemeral ratepayer associations in London. In addition, he showed that each of his chosen vestries had a political character and a distinctive administrative style. We still, however, do not know precisely how and when the rise of party affected London's municipal life at the vestry level. This suggests a cue to further research on a fourth topic, namely, the changing nature and significance of ratepayer politics. The quarrels among vestry representatives to the MBW cannot be dismissed merely as examples of parochial bickering: they also reflected the tensions that were developing between the inner and outer districts on such matters as the disposal of sewage, riparian

rights, and the cost of poor relief. The administration of London's poor-
law system was complicated by tensions between the wealthier and
poorer suburban parishes, with some of the wealthier parishes contriv-
ing to keep out of regional unions formed after 1837, and with some of
the poorer parishes combining against their wealthier neighbors who
seemed to be bearing relatively less of the burden of London's poor. The
introduction of the Metropolitan Common Poor Fund by the act of 1867
was the first step in the struggle for the equalizing of London's rates.
Other grievances taken up by parochial associations included the compensation paid to property owners when street improvements were projected, the structure as well as the incidence of metropolitan rates, and
the effects of urban leasehold tenures on house owners and
shopkeepers.[32] By the 1880s the political climate in London was favorable to a revision of the whole basis of local taxation. While Sidney
Webb and the Progressives argued that the tax system was the chief obstacle to financing new capital expenditure, Conservative politicians
gave support to local parochial associations and ratepayer defense
leagues. The Conservatives became the chief supporters of the further
decentralization (or "tenification") of the metropolis after the founding of
the London County Council.[33]

The question that arises at this juncture is whether it is possible to relate the nature of parochial agitation to the social composition of vestries, and whether changes in the composition of vestries affected the
tempo and direction of administrative developments. Were the same
factors operating in the suburban districts as in the urban areas selected
by Owen? Since the pioneering analysis of the London suburb by H. J.
Dyos, other London historians have amplified his description of suburban vestry government.[34] Only Janet Roebuck, however, has attempted
a comparative study of the social structure and government of several
London parishes.[35] One of the problems of this kind of analysis is that
after 1855 individual vestries and district boards had less room for
maneuver and were more dependent on the general tone set for London
administration, first by the MBW and later by the LCC. F. M. L.
Thompson has suggested that there may have been a logical and necessary sequence about the order of municipal doings in the London parishes: "The major nuisances and menaces to public health had to be
eliminated first before it was possible to go on to think of providing any
amenities or frills. Although the definition of what was essential for securing public health proved to be elastic, the only major quarrel with
this proposition must concern the timing and speed of the development
from the municipality of drains to the municipality of drains and public
libraries."[36] There are evidently many hazards in trying to relate

changes in the quality and direction of local administration to the changing balance of social forces in a particular district. But this does not
imply that local pressures were unimportant. Thompson's own account
of Hampstead suggests that there was a change in the tempo of municipal affairs after the 1870s which can be associated in part with the
growth of professional groups in the vestry.

The nature of suburban political activity can be further illustrated by
certain parishes in West London.[37] For example, Kensington's professional residents, representing the suburban inhabitants, first challenged
the oligarchy of High Street shopkeepers during the 1850s and 1860s,
but without ever gaining control over the vestry. The contest for power
in Kensington was connected with disputes over the relief of the parish
poor. During the 1860s, with the poor rate rising steeply, members of
the vestry almost came to blows over the proposition to build a new
workhouse. There was a period of retrenchment thereafter, and a hardening of attitudes toward the poor as shown by the vestry's attempts to
evict the inhabitants of a North Kensington slum.[38] At least Kensington,
like Hampstead was an efficiently managed parish, with able vestry
clerks; but in Fulham the maladministration of the rates and the scandals over rate collection were the chief causes of parochial agitation. Fulham illustrates the difficulty of assessing the influence of parochial associations. This was a lively parish with a number of associations, but they
do not seem to have aroused much support for local elections or to have
brought any noticeable change in the social composition of district board
or vestry.[39] Fulham had the reputation of being a heavily rated parish,
mainly because of the expense of draining a low-lying area, and the
burden of an influx of Irish poor. But this did not stop some of the local
builders from supporting the Medical Officer of Health in pressing for
improvements to help sell their housing estates. By contrast, the built-up
parish of Paddington saw new municipal initiatives being taken during
the 1880s by a combination of smaller shopkeepers in conflict with larger
shopkeepers. The smaller shopkeepers placed proportionately higher assessments on the houses of the Bayswater aristocracy — the customers of
the larger shopkeepers — than on their own shops and offices; and they
used the money to provide, among other ventures, new wood-block
street paving and a public bath and washhouse. The leader of the faction, a local auctioneer, became known as "The Lord Beaconsfield of
Paddington".[40] Evidently, the role of suburban interest groups varied in
different places at different times. There is much to be done still by way
of examining their composition and significance if we are to understand
the impact of suburban development on London's government and
administration.

So far this discussion has concentrated on the politics and ideology of municipal policy in Victorian London. It might be claimed that a more important aspect of the administration of the Victorian city was the availability of technical and professional means to implement policy. These are interrelated matters. Public works were one of the great achievements of Roman civil engineering, for example, but with the decline of Roman administration and municipal control, the water supply of Europe reverted to more primitive arrangements. The urban concentrations of the nineteenth century raised quite new and complicated technical and economic questions for both governments and private undertakings; and the development and use of applied science and technology were crucial to the viability of the Victorian city, emancipating it from old restraints and providing new innovations to deal with transportation, atmospheric and water pollution, the removal of sewage, the prevention of food adulteration, and the elaboration of systems of public lighting. New public health legislation stimulated the growth of a branch of civil engineering that had hardly existed at the beginning of the century.[41] Although these are matters of importance to London's administrative history, few of them have attracted research.

Take, for example, the subject of the economics of urban improvement. There has been little published discussion of such matters as the financing of capital outlays, the elaboration of loan procedures, and the reorganization of rating structures. Some attention has been given, however, to the street improvements of the MBW in order to illustrate the nature of urban planning in London, the costs of urban improvement, and the problems of betterment and compensation which arose when public bodies started to purchase land.[42] The construction of new thoroughfares and the widening of streets were not only influenced by the need to relieve traffic congestion; street improvements also offered the Victorians a panacea for dealing with overcrowded and insanitary buildings, and this factor influenced the locations chosen for new streets. In theory, the MBW could have followed the reasoning that the more land acquired for an improvement the better, since its resale would have enabled the Board to recoup some of the betterment value resulting from its investment effort. In practice, the Board engaged in fairly limited recoupment from 1876 onward, and in three out of four cases for which information is available its work was anything but a financial success.[43] The London ad hoc street improvement program was expensive to implement with high rates of compensation being paid to the owners of slum property, and from 1872 onward the MBW had the additional obligation of having to rehouse displaced populations.

The financing of public utilities is one aspect of economics of the urban improvement which has been examined for the country as a whole and in connection with municipal trading in the provincial cities.[44] In the case of London it is still necessary to investigate how private capital was invested in developing an infrastructure of urban services, from transport to bridge building, from improving the burial of the dead to increasing the amenities of the living. Only the economics and technology of London's water supply have been fully documented.[45] Information on the financing of gas supplies has to be culled from the few available business histories of gas undertakings.[46] The economics of London's street transport and underground railways has been fully discussed by T. C. Barker and Michael Robbins;[47] but the existing accounts of London's tramway companies and electricity undertakings have had little to say about finances or operating costs, nor have they discussed the effects of municipal policy on private enterprise. In general, we know relatively little about the sources of capital invested in public works and amenities. There is surely a volume to be written about the importance of London's role in the national and international capital market serving its domestic investment. One example worth citing is that of the Metropolitan Sewage and Reclamation Company, whose London projectors became involved in high finance when they acquired the backing of the International Finance Society, an organization based in Paris. This was the company that secured a contract from the MBW to use London's sewage for farming purposes—a Chadwickian idea much discussed in the 1860s, which proved unprofitable in practice.[48]

For the administrative historian, it is necessary to know not only how knowledge was used by urban governments and private undertakings, but also whether the associated growth of expertise moved with or against the tide of municipal change. There is a need, that is, to describe what T. H. Marshall has called "the assimilation of the professions to the purposes of government." London was itself a force in the development of scientific and medical knowledge, with its wide range of specialized educational institutions. It was also the headquarters of many of the new professional groupings, from the accountants and treasurers to the quantity surveyors, engineers, and architects. The agenda for London research should include a study of the growth and influence of professional opinion and of the bureaucratization of government as new urban problems brought into being this new set of municipal officials. In sanitary engineering, the regulation of buildings, in medical, poor-law and school inspection, London had a special place. The very number of its governmental bodies and authorities gave opportunities for the expansion of official municipal occupations, provided with powers and responsibilities which enabled them, in theory, to exert considerable influence over urban living conditions. Then, to what extent, it may be asked, was the control of speculators and property owners over London's environment modified by the operations of engineers, architects, doctors, inspectors, and, eventually, town planners? What, in the London context, were the relationships between new knowledge and political power, or between knowledge and policy?

The urban dimension of these questions is an important element in the continuing historical debate about the nature of governmental growth and the evolution of the administrative state.[49] This debate began at the central level, but is relevant also to the relations between central and local government and the growth of local governmental responsibilities. The broader conceptual framework of recent governmental history has led to a new emphasis on the dynamics of change, and the history of municipal reform can no longer be considered complete if it neglects such catalysts as the growth of civic consciousness, class expectations, the influence of interest groups, the immediacy of practical problems, and above all, the growth of professional expertise and other factors in what might be called the logic of administrative development. Recently, social historians have recognized the significance of local administrative developments to changes in social policy. So far as the metropolis was concerned, this was a two-way process. In the history of poor-law, education, and housing policy, London was not only a reference point for social policy but a source of new ideas and experiments: on the one hand, metropolitan reformers put pressure on central Government to extend the powers of various metropolitan authorities to act; on the other hand, central Government responded to public opinion and by act and order endeavored to push London into the acceptance of new responsibilities.

How this worked out in the development of policies toward London's poor has been considered in several theses.[50] Work has also been published on the contributions of poor-law inspectors and philanthropic reformers to changes in London's poor-law provision. James O'Neill has emphasized, for example, the significance of philanthropic concern in the making of the Metropolitan Poor Law Amendment Act of 1867. This act, he claims was "the most important individual enactment in the development of the Poor Law Medical Services."[51] The logic of administrative development took over with the setting up of the Metropolitan Asylums Board to superintend the new provisions for the care of London's sick poor. As Gwendoline M. Ayers has shown, this Board eventually expanded its functions to provide a system of public hospitals for all Londoners.[52] Another aspect of poor relief, the administration of London charities, is a subject dealt with most recently by Gareth Stedman Jones, who shows how philanthropic and political reformers influenced the making of new policies toward London's casual laboring population.[53] David Rubinstein anticipated a particular aspect of this theme of "Outcast London" by showing how a new class of officials, the School Attendance Officers, was created to bring the children of the London slums reluctantly to school.[54]

New studies of public health and housing policy have also been concerned with the roles of both philanthropists and metropolitan officials in administrative development and social policy. The setting up of the Office of Metropolitan Buildings between 1844 and 1855 is of interest, for example, as an early attempt to regulate building development by the imposition of new responsibilities on London's district surveyors.[55] In his major study of housing and social policy, Anthony Wohl not only demonstrates how London government responded to new housing legislation, but brings out the way in which metropolitan Medical Officers of Health worked toward creating a machinery of sanitary regulation.[56] The place of doctors in the early public health movement and their growing concern with urban pathology have been treated in general studies, complemented by profiles of the work of individual Medical Officers, notably Royston Lambert's account of John Simon's work for the City of London.[57] A point to notice is that even the antiquated government of the City did not preclude the appointment of enterprising officials. Anthony Wohl has gone further in emphasizing how the specialized education of Medical Officers of Health in Victorian London, and their growing competence in preventative medicine, "gave local government in the second half of the nineteenth century an authority and expertise hitherto lacking, and they [the Medical Officers] supplied a lead in the agitation for and administration of legislation which laymen were bound to follow."[58]

Ironically, the broad concerns of the Medical Officers resulted from confusion over the reasons for the spread of infectious diseases. As W. E. Luckin has pointed out, the confused state of contemporary medical and professional opinion about the cause and remedy for water pollution could serve as a protection to vested interest: for example, in the 1860s, only an "elite within an elite" of medical authorities was "willing to subscribe to the view that the cholera had been spread via unsafe water, distributed by the East London Water Company."[59] Another aspect of the importance of the metropolitan water supply was the emergence of a philanthropic movement to supply drinking fountains. In a recent article on the supply of free water in Victorian London, Harold Malchow has illustrated the way in which philanthropic and amenity groups came to occupy a middle ground between government and public opinion, keeping up pressure on local authority while mobilizing voluntary resources to provide urban amenities.[60] This was also a theme in the work of the "Five Per Cent" housing associations, which recognized that the free market could not cope with the housing needs of Londoners, but at the same time believed that the state should not intervene to provide assistance except in supporting the work of respectable voluntary societies.[61] It was largely the failure of London to solve its housing problems, Anthony Wohl has argued, that eventually forced the conclusion that public intervention in housing "ought to be at the expense of the central taxpayer."[62] It was in London that the Victorian solutions had been developed furthest, and had failed most conspicuously.

What difference did the founding of the London County Council make to London's social and civic life before the turn of the century? The LCC was heralded as marking a new era in municipal policy, and extravagant claims were made about the radical character of the first Council. But there was much leeway to be made up in comparison with the municipal enterprise of the provincial cities. The municipalizing of London's services continued to be hampered by the expense of buying out the water companies (at a cost of £50 million), and the Council was beset with the problems that had inhibited the work of the MBW, particularly those arising from the power of the larger vestries to obstruct new schemes. In other ways too, political hopes for radically new policies had to be modified. On a range of matters — such as the taxation of ground rents, new housing schemes, the regulation of London transport — the Council had to contend with difficult technical and legal issues, while the very complexity of municipal affairs in London meant that it became involved in much routine administration. Hence the claim that the political rhetoric of the "rads, cads and fads" of the first Council was toned down as members grappled with the realities of governing London.[63]

But at the same time the LCC acquired some eminent and forceful personalities; and it had large resources and perhaps a more determined sense of purpose than the MBW. It embarked on some major schemes of redevelopment, such as the Boundary Street Estate;[64] and it caught up with and surpassed provincial cities in the provision of scientific and technical education. As chairman of the London Technical Education Board, Sidney Webb set out to create a "capacity-catching machine" for London's working-class populations and to strengthen the industrial and commercial resources of the city; but in establishing the Technical Education Board as the de facto authority for London education, Webb and his colleagues contributed to the downfall in 1904 of the London School

Board, which had always received much support from the Liberal and Socialist members of the Progressive party.[65] Furthermore, the Council's new social and environmental policies soon fell prey to other difficulties and uncertainties. The vigor of the 1890s and early 1900s was relatively shortlived, and by the first decade of the new century London government was tending to stagnate again.

Perhaps too much had been expected from a change in the character of London government. It is doubtful, for example, whether the founding of the LCC really succeeded in stimulating a greater interest in politics and civic life on the part of the great mass of Londoners. When François Béderida attempted to test this claim by investigating Council elections, the results were inconclusive: he found that there was considerable variation in London's electoral geography, with some places having a smaller turnout and others a larger turnout than in provincial city elections.[66] Other, more impressionistic evidence suggests that even after the creation of the Metropolitan Boroughs in 1899–1900, deliberate attempts had to be made to foster civic feeling among Londoners.[67]

Yet the new Council undoubtedly created considerable interest among civic reformers in other urbanized countries as a type of solution to the problem of metropolitan government; and it fired the imagination of some American civic reformers especially. The Americans held assumptions, common to those of English liberals, about the importance of securing a quality of urban leadership in a representative democracy, and, from that point of view, they were impressed by the LCC, even when they were critical of its policies and of the political doctrine of municipal socialism.[68] The more radical of Australian civic reformers also thought highly of the LCC, but in that country conservative municipal administrators associated the Council with an interventionist style of politics and were disturbed by Fabian boasting about the London program. The political anxieties of Australian administrators over the way the Labour party was gaining ground in the cities in the later nineteenth century inclined them to turn away from the idea of a representative council and to favor the idea of a Metropolitan Board of Works; and this formula was actually adopted to solve the problem of governing the sprawling suburban area of Melbourne. The Town Clerk of Melbourne's municipal council—the most influential of the Australian supporters of an MBW—believed that such a solution would give the city a corporate organization less susceptible to political pressure and more amenable to administrative direction.[69] The demand for some form of metropolitan government had come to a head in Melbourne in the 1880s due mainly, as in London earlier, to a crisis in the sanitary condition of the city, which had acquired the title "Marvellous Smellbourne." There were special political factors in Australia which encouraged the various autonomous suburbs of Greater Melbourne to accept (though not without conflict) the scheme for an MBW that would take charge of water supply and sewage and would draw representatives from the municipalities according to their financial resources. In 1891, two years after the demise of the MBW in London, the Melbourne MBW was established. It survives still, despite mounting criticism. In Australia the only real triumph for the County Council model occurred in Brisbane in 1924.

David Owen's study of the London MBW has more than parochial interest. London set a precedent followed by other cities, in the USA as well as Australia, faced with similar problems of developing area-wide services, especially sanitation. The crisis of government in early Victorian London was a consequence of strains put on an old sewage disposal system by the multiplication of housing and feeding units, and the lack of effective machinery for the enforcement of building regulations. The MBW was set up to replace earlier and more centralized Benthamite attempts at metropolitan organizations, such as the Metropolitan Commission of Sewers and the Office of Metropolitan Buildings. Its subsequent history can be regarded as a prime example of ad hoc development in response to the pressures of metropolitan growth.

Looking at London through Owen's account, we can understand more fully the administrative significance of the MBW. In Owen's view there were two related problems which weakened its position as an administrative body. The first was that it changed, almost unintentionally, from being a sewer-building agency into something approaching a supervisory intelligence for London. It began to assume the position of a first-tier authority while retaining the constitutional weakness of a delegated body with delegated powers. The second problem was its anomalous position in relation to central Government. With its two big jobs of sewers and embankment building virtually completed, the Board looked for other things to do and found them, but it had thereafter to engage continually in difficult and protracted negotiations with Parliament in order to achieve its purposes.

Owen did not think the Board entirely blameless, however, for the delay in obtaining new powers and for other examples of ineffectiveness. As he explained to his Leicester audience, the growing complexity of metropolitan life, and also the failure of the Board to create effective machinery, explain the "nemesis of its history." This was more important in his view than the "odor of corruption" which surrounded its demise. With such an organization, there were bound to be gossip and charges of jobbery, although from Owen's American perspective these must have seemed less than hair-raising, and by his own account they came down to one or two incidents in which the Board appeared to have been quite innocent. Charges were commonly laid against London vestrymen, especially over the disposal of contracts, and some of these were trumped up by parochial associations. The charges against the MBW may have been of that kind. Certainly Owen thought that the final scandal had little to do with the liquidation of the Board, except that political capital might be made of it. "One gets the feeling," he remarked at Leicester, "that in its latter days the situation in London had gone beyond the resources of the Board—that it had found things too complicated and that London had finally reached the point where it had to secure a form of government better adjusted to its growing needs." The experience of thirty-three years of the MBW had advanced the case for more comprehensive and democratic procedures in the conduct of London's government.

But the debate about the most appropriate form of metropolitan government was not settled with the founding of the LCC. From the turn of the century there was a new political and academic interest in the idea of a Greater London authority, as represented in William A. Robson's classic statement *The Government and Misgovernment of London* (1939). This kind of debate has arisen in all the urbanized nations of the Western world. In the view of modern political scientists this is because the problem of metropolitan government is a reflection of the essential dualism of metropolitan life, wherever the metropolis is to be found. As Ken Young has said, we may regard that dualism, from the governmental aspect, as "a tension between the need for area-wide administration of common services and the forces making for identity — maintaining suburban separatism."[70] From the early twentieth century, and even before that in some metropolitan cities, the expansion of metropolis has raised not only the question of how to provide for area-wide services, but also the problem of containment and of extending government over the burgeoning new suburbs. From the latter point of view, the founding of the Greater London Council is best understood as an attempt to achieve the political integration of the metropolis.[71] In Europe, however, problems of growth and size seem to have affected the administration of capital cities much more than provincial metropolitan centers. Indeed, the difficulties experienced by European capitals in developing effective controls and environmental policies in the nineteenth and twentieth centuries have been such as to suggest that status as a capital city was of itself the most important factor creating special problems of government and restricting the authorities' power to take remedial action.[72]

The history of London government and administration in the nineteenth century is a subject then of wide ranging significance. From London's Victorian experience we can learn how the distinctive problem of governing a metropolis, that was also a capital city, actually began. We can learn too about the organizational challenges and problems of policy which confronted a metropolitan center seeking to achieve control over its own physical and social development. As this brief review shows, the evolution of forms and agencies of public policy in London has been studied extensively, but in a piecemeal manner and in scattered and unpublished writing. The fresh description of London government in this volume is not only the most substantial account of the administration of the Victorian metropolis to have been published in recent years, but it shows how absorbing and far-reaching this kind of history can be. Owen's account of London government and administration is a demonstration, in effect, of how Victorian society wrestled with the opportunities and difficulties of a new kind of urban civilization and of a type of urbanity which has come to dominate the urban ethos of our own times.[73]

Notes

INTRODUCTION

I wish to thank the John Simon Guggenheim Memorial Foundation for a fellowship which permitted me to write this chapter during the year 1979-80.

1. G. W. Steevens, *Glimpses of Three Nations* (Edinburgh, 1901), p. 74.
2. [J. C. Robertson and T. Byerley], *London* (London, 1823), III, 355.
3. "Marquis de Vermont," in Marquis de Vermont and Sir Charles Darnley, Bart. [pseuds.], *London and Paris, or Comparative Sketches* (London, 1823), pp. 227-228.
4. Sir John Summerson, *Georgian London* (Harmondsworth, 1962), p. 181.
5. John Nash and J[ohn] White, *Some Account of the Proposed Improvements of the Western Part of London,* 2nd ed. (London, 1815), app. p. xxxvii.
6. Summerson, *Georgian London,* pp. 189-190.
7. Sir William Hillary, *Suggestions for the Improvement and Embellishment of the Metropolis* (London, 1825), pp. 22-24.
8. Priscilla Metcalf, *Victorian London* (London, 1972), p. 29.
9. John Ruskin, *Seven Lamps of Architecture* (London, [1907]), pp. 188-189.
10. [Samuel] *Leigh's New Picture of London* (London, 1818), pp. 33-34.
11. J[ohn] Britton, *The Original Picture of London, Enlarged and Improved,* 26th ed. (London, [1826]), p. 22.
12. Ibid., pp. 22-23.
13. C. W. Chalklin, *The Provincial Towns of Georgian England* (London, 1974), pp. 140-146.
14. For the immediate impact of the collapse of 1825 on ground rents, see James Noble, *The Professional Practice of Architects* (London, 1836), pp. 99-105;

Hermione Hobhouse, *Thomas Cubitt, Master Builder* (London, 1971), pp. 172–184. For the low cost of suburban building land in the 1920s and 1930s, see Alan A. Jackson, *Semi-Detached London* (London, 1973), pp. 92, 225, 253, 275, 301, 303, 317.

15. *The Builder,* 3 June 1871, p. 421.

2. THE CREATION OF THE METROPOLITAN BOARD OF WORKS

1. Royston Lambert, *Sir John Simon (1816–1904) and English Social Administration* (London, 1963), pp. 222–223.

2. *Hansard's Parliamentary Debates* (hereafter, *Hansard*), 3rd ser., *137*, c. 715–716 (16 March 1855).

3. *The Times,* 14 August 1855.

4. Henry Labouchere, first Baron Taunton (1798–1869), Liberal M.P. for Taunton, 1830; President, Board of Trade, 1839–1841, 1847–1852; Secretary of State for the Colonies, 1855–1858. (*Dictionary of National Biography*)

5. An Act for the Better Local Management of the Metropolis, 1855.

6. *Hansard,* 3rd ser., *137*, c. 699ff (16 March 1855).

7. *The Times,* 7 November 1854.

8. For a detailed account of the confusion caused by the overlapping responsibilities of the paving boards, see Hall's speech on the second reading of the bill, *Hansard,* 3rd ser., *137*, c. 703–707 (16 March 1855).

9. *Observer,* 15 October 1854.

10. *The Times,* 1 December 1859.

11. Maxwell Frazer, "Sir Benjamin Hall and the Administration of London," *Transactions Cymmrodorion,* 1 (1963), 75.

12. Henry Fitzroy (1807–1859), Liberal M.P. for Lewes, 1837–1859; Under Secretary of State, Home Department, 1852–1855; First Commissioner of Works, 1859 (*Dod's Parliamentary Companion* [London, 1859] [hereafter, *Dod's*]).

13. Viscount Ebrington (1783–1861), Whig M.P. for Tavistock, 1820–1830, and for Devonshire North, 1832–1841; Parliamentary Secretary to the Poor Law Board, 1847–1851 (*Dod's*).

14. *Hansard,* 3rd ser., *138*, c. 569 (14 May 1855).

15. Ibid., *137*, c. 722–724, 726 (16 March 1855); *Observer,* 29 April 1855.

16. *Observer,* 24 June 1855.

17. *Hansard,* 3rd ser., *139*, c. 409–413 (3 July 1855).

18. This was the act introduced by John Cam Hobhouse (1786–1869), later Lord Broughton, in 1831 (1 and 2 Will. iv, *cap.* 20). It applied only to vestries "where two-thirds of the ratepayers were in favour of adopting it" and established vestries elected by all ratepayers, voting by ballot. One-third of the vestry retired each year; thus, the act required annual elections. See E. L. Woodward, *The Age of Reform, 1815–1870* (Oxford, 1938, 1949), p. 441.

19. The *Observer* reported that there were only six petitions with 211 signatures against the bill — and those were focused on the details rather than the principles of the bill. See *Observer,* 29 April, 24 June 1855.

20. These were St. Marylebone, St. Pancras, Islington, St. George's, Hanover Square, Shoreditch, and Lambeth.

21. An Act to Amend the Laws Relating to the Construction of Buildings in the Metropolis and Its Neighbourhood, 1855.

22. See S. E. Finer, "The Transmission of Benthamite Ideas, 1820–50," and Alan Ryan, "Utilitarianism and Bureaucracy: The Views of J. S. Mill," in Gillian Sutherland, ed., *Studies in the Growth of Nineteenth Century Government* (London, 1972), pp. 11–62.

23. Henry Lowman Taylor (1808–1883), elected to the Common Council in 1843; chairman of the Markets Improvement Committee and responsible (among others) for the opening of the new meat and provision markets in Smithfield in 1867 and 1873; appointed in 1849 to the Metropolitan Commission of Sewers; member of the MBW until his death in 1883. *Metropolitan,* 20 March 1880, p. 189. According to the *Elector* (4 July 1857), he suffered from enormous "self-appreciation."

24. Lambert, *Sir John Simon,* pp. 195, 203. Simon was Medical Officer of the City from 1848 to 1855.

25. *Elector,* 11 July 1857.

26. John Leslie (1794–1879), member of the St. George's, Hanover Square, vestry for forty years; described as "an inventor" (*Metropolitan,* 24 February 1877, p. 121), he was notorious for his "angular" personality. As the *Elector* described him (27 June 1857), "His forte was to startle with apparently random hits." His powers of "heroic attack" were "enormous." He had "smashed out of being several Commissions for the improvement of London," and his "strongly marked individualism" put him frequently in the minority.

27. For an account of the havoc wrought by Leslie's "captious opposition" on the Metropolitan Sanitary Commission, see S. E. Finer, *The Life and Times of Sir Edwin Chadwick* (London, 1952), pp. 356–370, 372–380.

28. *Elector,* 13 June 1857.

29. According to the *South London News* (24 October 1857), Thwaites had a "distinguished role" in the fight against gas monopolies. The Surrey Gas Consumers Company reduced the cost of gas from six shillings per 1,000 units to three shillings and sixpence per 1,000 units. *Observer,* 23 December 1855.

30. John Thwaites, *A Sketch of the History and Prospects of the Metropolitan Drainage Question* (London, 1855).

31. *Marylebone Mercury,* 13 August 1870.

32. Greater London Record Office (L), MBW Minutes, 23 September 1870.

33. Sir John Shelley (1808–1867); Liberal M.P. for Westminster, 1852–1865; supported the extension of the franchise and political reform (*Dod's*).

34. GLRO (L), MBW Minutes, 19 December 1855; *Observer,* 23 December 1855; *The Times,* 24 December 1855.

35. The *Observer* (27 April 1856), reviewing one meeting, described how, after five hours spent in an interminable debate on the "Royal Surrey Zoological Gardens" the MBW had not covered half its agenda.

36. *Elector,* 25 July 1857.

37. *Observer,* 4 May 1856.

38. Ibid., 9 November 1856.

39. The *Observer* (20 April 1856), criticizing the Board's affection for closed committees, commented acidly that the House of Commons did not find it necessary to exclude the public.

40. Woolrych's election was criticized in the *Observer* (13 January 1856) on the grounds that he was too representative of the City's interests. He felt rather confined in the role of the neutral official, for as the *Elector* observed (29 June 1857), "His warm, semi-Italian blood is not at home in mere silent routine."

41. GLRO (L), MBW Minutes, 23 December 1859.

42. Ibid., 18 November, 9 December 1859.

43. Ibid., 5 March 1861. William Wyke Smith was solicitor to the Metropolitan Commission of Sewers and, from 1861 to 1878, legal adviser to the MBW. A "zealous public servant, his most conspicuous quality was caution" (*Metropolitan,* 27 July 1878, p. 478).

44. Frederick Marrable was then thirty-eight. A pupil of the architect Edward Blore, he had been in the profession since the age of sixteen. GLRO (L), MBW Minutes, 1 February 1856. His manner of conducting business attracted some spiteful criticism. The *Elector* (27 June 1857) observed that "if it is business to gallop through reports as he does, squeezing every word to death almost in a half-closed mouth, so that nobody scarcely knows what he says, except for a few determined men that go close to him and regularly move and second the reception of his reports . . . we know not what the Board's business can be."

45. GLRO (L), MBW Minutes, 15 February 1861.

46. *The Builder,* 20 November 1886, pp. 724–725.

47. *Elector,* 5 August 1857.

48. GLRO (L), MBW Minutes, 25 January 1856. *Observer,* 20 January 1856; *The Builder,* (21 March 1891), p. 235. J. W. Bazalgette (1819–1891) remained chief engineer to the MBW until 1889. He was elected President of the Institution of Civil Engineers in 1884 (*DNB*).

49. *Observer,* 2 March 1856.

50. The *Observer* (6 January 1856) was particularly suspicious of Bazalgette's City connections.

51. *Observer,* 24 February 1856.

52. GLRO (L), MBW 692.

53. GLRO (L), MBW 212, 5 January 1856.

54. *Observer,* 11 October 1857.

55. *Observer,* 26 September 1858; *Marylebone Mercury,* 2, 16 April, 7 May 1859.

56. GLRO (L), MBW Minutes, 8 August, 27 September 1861.

57. GLRO (L), MBW 707, 2 February 1863.

58. *Second Report of the Select Committee on Metropolis Local Taxation,* 1861, viii (372), Mins. Evid., John Thwaites, Q. 3370.

59. Ibid., Major William Lyon, Q. 2583. Lyon was disgruntled with the Board and all its concerns.

3. THE PROBLEM OF MAIN DRAINAGE

1. Joseph Bramah (1748–1814), b. Yorkshire, the son of a farmer; took out his first patent for a water closet in 1778; his design has remained basically unchanged since then; also invented an "unpickable" lock and a hydraulic press (*DNB*).

2. An Act for the Better Regulation of the Metropolitan Districts and the Provision of Drainage Thereof, 1844.

3. This was accomplished through the implementation of the emergency provisions of the "cholera bill"—the Nuisances Removal and Diseases Prevention Act of 1846. See W. M. Frazer, *A History of English Public Health* (London, 1950), pp. 46, 63.

4. *The Builder,* 3 July 1858, p. 449.

5. Ibid., 2 February 1856, p. 65.

6. See S. E. Finer, *The Life and Times of Sir Edwin Chadwick* (London, 1952), pp. 223–224.

7. GLRO (L), MBW Minutes, 8 February 1856.

8. GLRO (L), MBW 215, Bazalgette's Report on Drainage South of the Thames, 3 April 1856.

9. GLRO (L), MBW 217, Bazalgette's Report on Drainage North of the Thames, 22 May 1856.

10. GLRO (L), MBW Minutes, 25 April 1856.

11. Ibid., 14 May, 11 June 1856.

12. Ibid., 3, 15 July 1856.

13. GLRO (L), MBW 221, Bazalgette's Report on Metropolitan Drainage, 25 September 1856.

14. GLRO (L), MBW Minutes, 15 October 1856.

15. *Observer,* 26 October 1856.

16. GLRO (L), MBW Minutes, 9 December 1856.

17. *The Builder,* 18 October 1856, p. 565–567, complained that it was "overwhelmed" with correspondence in which the Board was blamed "in no unmeasured terms for waste of time with regard to this most important question."

18. *Illustrated London News,* 13 December 1856, p. 605.

19. *Elector,* 5 August 1857.

20. Ibid., 12 August 1857.

21. *Report presented to the Metropolitan Board of Works by Messers Bidder, Hawksley and Bazalgette, 6 April 1858,* 1857–58, xlviii (419), 145.

22. *City Press,* 19 June 1858.

23. *Observer,* 21 June 1858.

24. *Correspondence respecting the State of the Thames,* 1857 (Second Session), xli, p. iv.

25. *Hansard,* 3rd ser., *151,* c. 150 (11 June 1858).

26. *The Times,* 21 July 1858. *The Times* had, a few weeks earlier (1 July 1858), complained that "Parliament would give [the Government] any powers they might have the courage and honesty to ask for . . . They are now doing nothing but throwing a few boatloads of lime into the river, in the vain hope of sweetening the classic shores of Lambeth and Millbank."

27. GLRO (L), MBW Minutes, 26 May 1858.

28. *Hansard,* 3rd ser., *151,* c. 1515–16 (15 July 1858).

29. Ibid., c. 1937.

30. Ibid., c. 2075.

31. *The Builder,* 24 July 1858, p. 494. The *Illustrated London News,* 10 February 1859, p. 173, observed: "After ten years of rival schemes, rival estimates, and rival formulae, Parliamentary committees, blue-books and counter-reports; after warm debates between successive Commissioners of Sewers, followed by those of the MBW, the First Commissioner of Her Majesty's Works and Parliament itself, the plan is finally settled, and the mighty work begun."

32. GLRO (L), MBW Minutes, 11 August, 15 October 1858.

33. *The Builder,* (14 May 1859), p. 322, pointed out that the highest tender was £117,570 more than the lowest.

34. GLRO (L), MBW Minutes, 17 December 1858.

35. *The Builder,* 13 August 1859, p. 529.

36. GLRO (L), MBW Minutes, 29 June, 27 December 1860.

37. Ibid., 24 September, 2 November 1860. GLRO (L), MBW 675. Special Committee of the MBW.

38. GLRO (L), MBW Minutes, June–July 1860.

39. Ibid., 6 January 1860.

40. Ibid., 27 July, 10 August 1860. For a brief account of the routes and dimensions of the various sewers, see *Annual Report of the MBW for 1858–59,* xxxi (178), 2–10.

41. *The Times,* 7 November 1859.

42. Ibid., 1 December 1859.

43. GLRO (L), MBW Minutes, 4 January 1861 (Engineer's Report for December 1860).

44. Ibid., 6 July 1861 (Engineer's Annual Report).

45. *Observer,* 14 April 1861; *City Press,* 14 September 1861.

46. *Marylebone Mercury,* 12 October 1861.

47. *Observer,* 6 July 1862. There were also a few unexpected discoveries. Among the archeological finds were fossil remains of a Roman sarcophagus, three Roman coffins, and miscellaneous pottery. GLRO (L), MBW Minutes. 1 April 1864.

48. GLRO (L), MBW Minutes, 4 October 1861.

49. *Report of the Select Committee on Metropolitan Sewage,* 1864, xiv (487), Mins. Evid., J. Bazalgette, Q. 5121–22 (hereafter, *Report of the Select Committee on Metropolitan Sewage,* 1864).

50. *The Builder,* 25 January 1862, pp. 536ff.

51. GLRO (L), MBW Minutes, 4 October 1861.

52. Ibid., 5 June 1863. Some of the reasons offered for the rise in the cost of materials (which were 30 percent higher in 1862 than in 1858) were the strike of London artisans, the "unusually wet" summer of 1860, and the unprecedented demand for bricks.

53. GLRO (L), MBW 707, Bazalgette's Report on the Drainage System, 27 February 1863.

54. GLRO (L), MBW Minutes, 15 May 1863.

55. Ibid., 7 April 1865.

56. Ibid., 12 and 26 May 1865.

57. The *City Press,* 20 May 1865, reported the strong opposition of the Court of Sewers to this gratuity.

58. *The Builder,* 26 September 1868, p. 719.

59. GLRO (L), MBW Minutes, 7 May 1869.

60. *Marylebone Mercury,* 2 February, 9 March 1861.

61. GLRO (L), MBW Minutes, 27 May 1864.

62. *Annual Report of the MBW, 1863–64,* 1864, 1 (67), 13–14.

63. *First Report of the Select Committee on the best means of utilizing the sewage of cities and towns of England,* 1862, xiv (160), 321.

64. *Report of the Select Committee on Metropolitan Sewage,* 1864, Mins. Evid., Q. 10–13, 99–271.

65. Ibid.

66. *The Builder,* 9 July 1864, p. 503.

67. *Report of the Select Committee on Metropolitan Sewage,* 1864, p. v.

68. Finer, *Chadwick,* p. 397.

69. GLRO (L), MBW Minutes, 15 November 1864.

70. *The Times,* 15 November 1864, 2 March 1865. *City Press,* 19 November 1864.

71. GLRO (L), Correspondence between Liebig and the Lord Mayor of London, 21 February 1865, reprinted in MBW Minutes, 17 March 1865.

72. *Special Report of the Select Committee on Metropolitan Sewage and Essex Reclamation Bill,* 1865, viii (171), Mins. Evid., John Thwaites, Q. 233ff.

73. Ibid., p. iii, Mins. Evid., Augustus Voelcker, Q. 817, 820.

74. GLRO (L), MBW Minutes, 12 June 1868.

75. Ibid., 1 July, 28 September, 11 and 18 November 1870.

76. Ibid., 17 November 1865; *Annual Report of the MBW, 1865–66,* 1867, lviii (34), 15, 16.

77. The Native Guano Company offered to supply members of the Board with sample bags of the company's guano, so that they could make their own tests of its manurial quality. The MBW voted solemnly: "The members of the Board are not desirous of availing themselves of the Company's offer." GLRO (L), MBW Minutes, 17, 31 May 1872.

78. Ibid., 31 January 1873; *Annual Report of the MBW for 1873,* 1874, lvii (153), 15–16.

79. *The Times,* 18 August 1873.

80. GLRO (L), MBW Minutes, 19 May 1865.

81. *Hansard,* 3rd ser., *190,* c. 1220 (9 March 1868); GLRO (L), MBW Minutes, 3 January, 13 and 20 March, 29 May 1868.

82. GLRO (L), MBW Minutes, 14 May, 17 December 1869; *Annual Report of the MBW 1869–70,* 1871, lvii (24), 15–17.

83. *Annual Report of the MBW for 1872,* 1873, lvi (146), 439.

84. J. T. Coppock and Hugh C. Prince, *Greater London* (London, 1964), p. 34.

85. *The Builder,* 26 April 1876, p. 380; *Select Committee on Thames River (Prevention of Floods) Bill,* 1877, xvii (280), Mins. Evid., J. Bazalgette, Q. 45 (hereafter, *Select Committee on Thames River Bill,* 1877).

86. *The Builder,* 20 January 1877, pp. 49–50.

87. *Select Committee on Thames River Bill,* 1877, Q. 75–77.

88. Ibid., Mins. Evid., Charles Mills Roche, Q. 2296.

89. The Thames River (Prevention of Floods) Bill received its second reading on 23 June 1879. Lords amendments were taken on 25 July 1879, but the bill was lost in the pressure of business at the end of the session.

90. *Select Committee on Prevention of Floods, 1878–79,* xiii (178), Mins. Evid., Q. 561.

91. Ibid., Q. 69.

92. Ibid., Q. 679.

93. Ibid., Q. 2127.

94. This was a private act to amend the Metropolis Local Management Act, 1855, insofar as it related to the protection of the metropolis from flooding.

95. GLRO (L), MBW Minutes, 16 May 1879.

96. *Saturday Review,* 28 June 1879, p. 795.

97. *Select Committee on Thames River Bill,* 1877, Q. 364.

98. *Echo,* 27 August 1878.

99. *City Press,* 24 July 1878.

100. *The Builder,* 12 July 1879, p. 784.

101. *Annual Report of the MBW for 1879,* 1880, lxii (212) (Session 2), no. 415, pp. 17–19; and for *1888,* 1889, lxvi (326), 14 (hereafter, *Annual Report of the MBW*

for 1888). GLRO (L), MBW Minutes, 1 August 1879.

102. *The Times,* 12, 18 December 1877; *Annual Report of the MBW for 1877,* 1878, 1xv (213), 15–16.

103. *The Times,* 19 September 1878; *Saturday Review,* 20 October 1878, p. 423.

104. *Saturday Review,* 5 October 1878, p. 424.

105. *The Builder,* 7 December 1878, p. 1275.

106. *The Times,* 23 November 1878.

107. GLRO (L), the Thames Navigation Act, 1870, in Arbitration: The Thames Conservators and the MBW: Minutes of Proceeding, Report and Determination (1879–80). There was no disagreement on the existence of shoals, or that they were of fairly recent origin.

108. *The Times,* 19, 20 August 1881.

109. GLRO (L), MBW Minutes, 4 November 1881.

110. Ibid., 7, 14 July 1882.

111. It was "commonly reported [that] a cricket match was played . . . on the bed of the stream within a mile or two of Richmond." *Morning Post,* 30 September 1885.

112. *First Report of the Royal Commission on Sewage in the Thames,* 1884, xli (C. 3842), lxii–lxiii; *Second Report,* 1884–85, xxxi (C. 4253), Mins. Evid., Q. 19, 364.

113. GLRO (L), MBW Minutes, 15 June 1884.

114. Ibid., 25 July 1884.

115. *The Times,* 12 December 1884.

116. GLRO (L), MBW Minutes, 27 March 1885; *Daily News,* 3 September 1885.

117. *Annual Report of the MBW for 1888,* p. 20.

118. *Pall Mall Gazette,* 7 January 1886.

119. *The Times,* 30 November 1885.

120. *The Builder,* 9 October 1886, pp. 509–510.

4. THE EMBANKMENT

1. *First Report of the Commission on Improving the Metropolis,* 1844, xv (15), 3.

2. Ibid., pp. 40–42.

3. *Select Committee on the best means for providing for the increasing traffic of the Metropolis by the Embankment of the Thames,* 1860, xx (494), Mins. Evid., Q. 316 (hereafter, *Select Committee on the Embankment,* 1860).

4. GLRO (L), MBW 1444, 20 January 1857.

5. *Select Committee on the Embankment,* 1860, p. 321.

6. Ibid., Min. Evid., Q. 61, 93, 281, 74ff. The coal and wine dues were an immemorial—and anachronistic—income of the City which the Corporation treated like any other revenue. They were usually applied to improvements in the City. These controversial charges had figured for at least two centuries in London history and had been the instrument, for example, of the rebuilding of St. Paul's and other churches after the Great Fire.

7. *Report of the Royal Commission on Plans for Embanking the River Thames with in the Metropolis,* 1861, xxxi (2782), 267.

8. Ibid., p. iii.

9. As Bazalgette noted in his evidence, below Blackfriars the wharves were more essential, and thus the wharfingers were more stubborn. Ibid., Mins. Evid., Q. 1068.

10. Ibid., Q. 1099.

11. Ibid., Q. 1896–1923.

12. Ibid., Q. 629.

13. Ibid., Mins. Evid., pp. v, vii.

14. *City Press,* 7 September 1861.

15. GLRO (L), MBW Minutes, 26 July 1861.

16. Ibid., 20 September 1861; *Sixth Annual Report of the MBW for 1861–62,* 1862, xlvii (11), 5–6.

17. This was the Thames Embankment (North Side) Bill.

18. *Hansard,* 3rd ser., *165,* c. 1819ff (18 March 1862).

19. Ibid., *166,* c. 698–701 (7 April 1862).

20. *The Times,* 20 March 1862.

21. *Select Committee on the Thames Embankment Bill,* 1862, xv (344), Mins. Evid., Q. 595, 607 (hereafter, *Select Committee on the Thames Embankment Bill,* 1862).

22. On the Office of Woods and Forests, see Sir Harold Emmerson, *The Ministry of Works* (London, 1956).

23. *Select Committee on the Thames Embankment Bill,* 1862, apps. 1 and 2.

24. Ibid., Mins. Evid., Q. 3855.

25. Edward Horsman (1807–1876), Whig M.P. for Stroud (1853–1876) and Liskeard (1869–1876); with Lowe, formed the "Cave of Adullam" (*DNB*). He was one of the Crown lessees threatened by the Whitehall Embankment.

26. *Select Committee on the Thames Embankment,* 1862, Mins. Evid., Q. 2857–61.

27. *The Times,* 2 July 1862.

28. *Hansard,* 3rd ser., *167,* c. 1396 (3 July 1862).

29. *The Times,* 5 July 1862.

30. The bill had its second reading on 8 April 1861. *Hansard,* 3rd ser., *162,* c. 293.

31. GLRO (L), MBW Minutes, 18 February, 29 May, 26 June 1863.

32. *The Times,* 6 October 1863.

33. GLRO (L), MBW 708. Printed copy of specifications circulated to contractors, 22 July 1863.

34. Ibid., MBW 706. Report by the engineer on riverside property, 6 November 1862.

35. *The Builder,* 9 May 1863, p. 327.

36. Ibid., 7 May 1864, p. 326.

37. *The Times* (30 May 1862) urged the reconciliation of public and private interests, arguing that "our grand public quay along the Thames . . . will do more to beautify and improve the Metropolis than any work since the erection of the White Tower."

38. This was not a problem anticipated by the Conservators, who found the clause "quite unobjectionable." GLRO (L), MBW 1117, 4 May 1863.

39. GLRO (L), MBW Minutes, 14 November 1862.

40. GLRO (L), MBW 706. Report by the engineer on riverside property, 6 November 1862.

41. Ibid., MBW 1117, 21 December 1863.

42. Ibid., MBW 708, 18 January 1864.

43. Ibid., MBW 1118, 2 March 1864.

44. Ibid., 15 and 22 March, 28 July 1864.

45. Ibid., 28 July 1864.

46. There were several cases of personal hardship caused by the interference of the Embankment which the Board refused to consider liable for compensation.

A steamboat operator—"an honest, industrious and respectable man"—was denied compensation for the loss of his livelihood on the grounds that he had no actual *legal* rights and that compensation would create a dangerous precedent. GLRO (L), MBW 1120, 30 May 1865.

47. Ibid., MBW 1121, 17 January 1866.

48. *Metropolitan,* 4 May 1872, pp. 200–201.

49. GLRO (L), MBW Minutes, 30 December 1864.

50. GLRO (L), MBW 708, 16 October 1863.

51. Ibid., 3, 24 November 1863.

52. Ibid., 19 October 1863.

53. *The Builder,* 8 October 1864, pp. 739, 773.

54. GLRO (L), MBW 1121, 23 January 1864.

55. GLRO (L), MBW Minutes, 2, 9 December 1864.

56. GLRO (L), MBW 1119, 1 February 1865.

57. Ibid., 21 February, 8 March 1865.

58. GLRO (L), MBW Minutes, 6 October 1865.

59. GLRO (L), MBW 1117, 13 April 1863.

60. GLRO (L), MBW Minutes, 8 July, 9 December 1864.

61. GLRO (L), MBW 1119, 7 November 1864.

62. GLRO (L), MBW Minutes, January–June 1865.

63. Ibid., 5 January 1866.

64. Ibid., 13 July, and 26, 28 September 1866.

65. Ibid., 21 February 1868.

66. The scale of the operation is illustrated by the fact that 600 men were employed, and that 700,000 bricks, 18,000 bushels of Portland cement, and 11,500 cubic feet of granite were consumed within a month. Ibid., 5 October 1866.

67. *Annual Report of the MBW for 1867–68,* 1868–69, li (23), 16 (hereafter, *Annual Report of the MBW for 1867–68*).

68. T. C. Barker and Michael Robbins, *A History of London Transport* (London, 1963), I, 153.

69. John (later Sir John) Hawkshaw (1811–1891), railway engineer, was appointed arbitrator in the dispute.

70. *Annual Report of the MBW for 1867–68,* pp. 19–20.

71. GLRO (L), MBW Minutes, 28 October, and 7, 14 November 1862.

72. Ibid., 14, 21 July 1865.

73. *Annual Report of the MBW for 1869–70,* 1871, lvii (24), p. 1 (hereafter, *Annual Report of the MBW for 1869–70*).

74. GLRO (L), MBW Minutes, 7 August 1863.

75. *Annual Report of the MBW for 1869–70,* pp. 20–21.

76. *City Press,* 4 April, 2 May 1863.

77. Select Committee on Thames Embankment (North Side) Bill, 1863, xxvi (C. 6096), Mins. Evid., Q. 1326.

78. *Hansard,* 3rd ser., *170,* c. 1702–05 (14 May 1863).

79. *Ibid.,* c. 1705–08.

80. *Ibid.,* c. 1713–14.

81. *City Press,* 30 May 1863.

82. Mr. Deputy Harrison, one of the charter members of the Board.

83. *Select Committee on the Thames Embankment,* 1871, xii (411), Mins. Evid., Q. 61, 1499–1500 (hereafter, *Select Committee on the Thames Embankment, 1871*).

84. *Annual Report of the MBW for 1869-70,* p. 21.
85. *The Times,* 26 August 1870.
86. GLRO (L), MBW Minutes, 11 December 1868.
87. Ibid., 5, 12 November, and 3 December 1869.
88. Ibid., 15 July 1870.
89. *City Press,* 16 July 1870.
90. *The Times,* 13 July 1870.
91. *Annual Report of the MBW for 1869-70,* p. 21.
92. *The Times,* 14 April 1871.
93. *Hansard,* 3rd ser., *202,* c. 1760-63, 1768-74 (8 July 1870).
94. *The Times,* 11 July 1870, 14 April 1871.
95. *The Builder,* 6 May 1871, p. 353; *The Times,* 11 May 1871.
96. *Hansard,* 3rd ser., *207,* c. 196 (16 June 1871).
97. Ibid., *209,* c. 865 (22 February 1872).
98. *Select Committee on the Thames Embankment,* 1871, Q. 541, 788.
99. *Hansard,* 3rd ser., *209,* c. 865 (22 February 1872).
100. GLRO (L), Correspondence reproduced in MBW Minutes, 1 March 1872.
101. *Hansard,* 3rd ser., *212,* c. 1579-80 (22 July 1872).
102. *The Times,* 12 March 1872.
103. The Thames Embankment (Land) Bill was introduced on 8 March 1872 by the Chancellor of the Exchequer (*Hansard,* 3rd ser., *209,* c. 1742), and was committed to a Select Committee under the chairmanship of Sir Percy Herbert on 13 May. The bill was lost, however, in the pressure of business at the end of the session. *Hansard,* 3rd ser., *212,* c. 1579 (22 July 1872).
104. GLRO (L), MBW Minutes, 21 February 1873.
105. *Hansard,* 3rd ser., *210,* c. 1808 (25 April 1872).
106. Ibid., *214,* c. 1026-29 (27 February 1873).
107. *Metropolitan,* 5 April 1873, p. 217; *The Times,* 3 August 1874.
108. GLRO (L), MBW Minutes, 10 July 1874.
109. Ibid., 31 March, 6, 21 April, and 6 May 1871.
110. Sir James McGarel-Hogg confirmed, in reply to a question on Thames flooding by Mr. Watney, that the bill had been lost. *Hansard,* 3rd ser., *235,* c. 191 (25 June 1877).
111. GLRO (L), MBW Minutes, 1 February 1878.
112. Ibid., 1 October 1880.

5. THOROUGHFARES AND BUILDINGS

1. *Select Committee on Metropolitan Communications,* 1854-55, x (415), iii-iv.
2. Ibid.
3. The list is reprinted in the *Annual Report of the MBW for 1858-59,* 1859 (Session 2), xxvi, no. 178, pp. 6-7.
4. The net cost of Southwark Street was estimated, for example, at about £173,000. GLRO (L), MBW 1444, 5 April 1856.
5. *Annual Report of the MBW for 1859-60,* 1860, xl (556), 6.
6. *Annual Report of the MBW for 1860-61,* 1862 (ii), xlvii (391), 7.
7. *Annual Report of the MBW for 1888,* 1889, lxvii (326), 27 (hereafter, *Annual Report of MBW for 1888*).

8. The London Bridge Approaches Fund [arose] in the seventeenth century as an Orphans Fund for those injured in the calamities of the age, and it was maintained by a duty of eightpence on coal and a penny on wine. It came to an end by act of Parliament in 1861 and was absorbed into the Thames Embankment and Metropolis Improvement Fund, from which the embankments were financed. During the two years before its appropriation, the yield from the London Bridge Approaches Fund was a little over £160,000 annually. *Select Committee on the Metropolitan Toll Bridges Bill,* 1865, vii (380) Mins. Evid., Q. 1167–69.

9. GLRO (L), MBW Minutes, 16 April, 15 October 1858.

10. *Annual Report of the MBW for 1888,* pp. 26–29.

11. This was the Piccadilly and Park Lane New Road Bill, 1865.

12. See the *Report of the Select Committee on the Piccadilly and Park Lane New Road Bill,* 1865, viii (260), 647.

13. *Special Report of the Select Committee on Piccadilly and Park Lane,* 1867–68, viii (293), 689.

14. GLRO (L), MBW Minutes, 5 March 1869.

15. Ibid., 24 September 1869, 18 and 25 November 1870.

16. *First Report of the Commissioners on the Most Effectual Means of Improving the Metropolis,* 1844, xv (15), 1. There were seven reports, concluding with 1851, xxix (1356), 287.

17. *The Builder,* 1 and 8 December 1866, pp. 877–878.

18. *Report of the Select Committee on the MBW (Shoreditch) Improvement Bill,* 1871, xl (142), 281.

19. Ibid., Mins. Evid., Q. 993.

20. Ibid., Q. 468ff.

21. *Report of the Select Committee on Metropolitan Taxation,* 1866, xiii (186), Q. 614.

22. GLRO (L), MBW Minutes, 17 May 1867.

23. Ibid., 15 December 1871.

24. *The Times,* 26 January 1872.

25. There was, however, some reason to charge Haywood with opposition to any scheme which would draw traffic away from the congested streets of the City. Apparently he was bothered by the fact that the Board's plan would conflict with a mid-London scheme which had strong City backing. GLRO (L), MBW Minutes, 9 August 1872.

26. *Hansard,* 3rd ser., *210,* c. 965 (9 April 1872).

27. See chapter 8.

28. *The Times,* 7 November 1876.

29. GLRO (L), MBW Minutes, 3, 24 November 1876.

30. *Hansard,* 3rd ser., *236,* c. 212–217 (31 July 1877).

31. *Ibid.,* c. 451–454 (6 August 1877).

32. *Daily Chronicle,* 3 May 1879.

33. H. J. Dyos, "Railways and Housing in Victorian London," *Journal of Transportation History,* 2 (1955–56), 14.

34. Peter Hall, "The Development of Communications," in J. T. Coppock and Hugh C. Prince, eds., *Greater London* (London, 1964), p. 62.

35. An Act to Provide Better Dwellings for Artisans and Labourers, July 1868.

36. *The Globe,* 23 May 1874; *Pall Mall Gazette,* 9 May 1874.

37. Whereas the Torrens Act empowered local authorities to demolish in-

dividual unsanitary houses, the Cross Act of 1875 applied to whole areas in which houses "are so structurally defective as to be incapable of repair and so ill placed with reference to each other as to require to bring them up to a proper sanitary standard nothing short of demolition and reconstruction." Frederick Berry, *Housing: The Great British Failure* (London, 1974), pp. 27–28.

38. *Annual Report of the MBW for 1877*, 1878, lxv (213), 23–28.

39. *Annual Report of the MBW for 1876*, 1877, lxxi (225), 51; for plans see the *Select Committee on Artisans and Labourers (Dwelling Acts) 1881*, 1881, vii (358), app. 26 (hereafter, *Select Committee on Artisans and Labourers, 1881*).

40. GLRO (L), MBW Minutes, 27 October 1876.

41. *Select Committee on Artisans and Labourers, 1881*, Mins. Evid., Q. 5188.

42. GLRO (L), MBW Minutes, 10 August 1877.

43. Ibid., 4 July 1879.

44. By 1883, *The Times* reported, the sale of land had proceeded with "a slowness puzzling to those who note how rapidly the poor are removed when great money-getting projects are on foot. It is indeed a 'killing slowness.' " *The Times*, 20 November 1883.

45. Indeed, the *Daily News* sparked off an ill-tempered exchange with the *Daily Telegraph* and *The Times* when it accused the MBW of contributing to the death of Elizabeth Mason, who had died from "lack of fresh air." Her family had been evicted in the wake of MBW "improvements" in Red Lion Square and the family of six had been housed in one room. The coroner held the MBW responsible for rehousing as well as eviction, an interpretation of its powers which was challenged in the *Daily Telegraph* (19 August 1878) and *The Times* (21 August 1878).

46. *Daily News*, 9 June 1879.

47. In reply to a letter from the Home Office expressing "regret" at the delay in implementing the provisions of the Artisans Dwelling Act, the Works and General Purposes Committee of the MBW denied any responsibility for delay, pointing instead to all its problems. GLRO (L), MBW Minutes, 17 January 1879. The MBW was also criticized in the *Saturday Review* of 22 February 1879 for neglecting its duties imposed by the act.

48. *Metropolitan*, 5 July 1879, p. 428, described the act as an admirable device for defeating the ends which it had been designed to accomplish, in that thirty-one requests had been received and fifteen "schemes" for site clearance had gone ahead, but not a yard of land had been sold for working-class dwellings.

49. See C. J. Stewart, *The Housing Question in London, 1855–1870* (London, 1901). The total came to a little over £100,000. See also J. N. Tarn, "The Peabody Donation Fund: The Role of a Housing Society in the Nineteenth Century," *Victorian Studies*, 10 (September 1966), 7–38.

50. *The Builder*, 12 July 1879, p. 786; GLRO (L), MBW Minutes, 4 July 1879.

51. GLRO (L), MBW Minutes, 18 July 1879.

52. *The Builder*, 9 August 1879, p. 896.

53. *Select Committee on Artisans and Labourers, 1881*.

54. GLRO (L), MBW Minutes, 25 June 1880.

55. Some idea of the congestion which the act was intended to relieve was given in the description of Bedfordbury, where some of the houses in enclosed courts contained as many as thirty-three people in six rooms. In a three-acre site the population was 2,163 in 1871. GLRO (L), MBW Minutes, 5 November 1875.

56. Ibid., 2 January 1880; *The Times,* 3 January 1880.

57. GLRO (L), MBW Minutes, 1, 15, 22 October 1880.

58. Ibid., 3 March 1882.

59. Ibid., 6, 16 March 1883.

60. *Hansard,* 3rd ser., *285,* c. 827–838 (7 March 1884).

61. See the *Annual Report of the MBW for 1888,* p. 30.

62. Coppock and Prince, *Greater London,* p. 57.

63. *Daily News,* 14 December 1885.

64. *The Builder,* 19 February 1887, p. 276; *The Times,* 12 December 1885.

65. The *Observer,* 14 December 1856, commented on the confusion caused by the repeated use of common names. It was calculated that 571 streets had but 17 names among them—including 62 named George, 55 named Charles, 45 named John, 44 named King, and 38 named Queen.

66. *The Builder,* 13 December 1862, p. 891.

67. *Select Committee on the Metropolitan Buildings and Management Bill,* 1874, x (285), 333, Mins. Evid.

68. Ibid., Q. 2520, 2523, 2617.

69. See, for example, the Sanitary Registration of Building Act, 1886, and the Public Buildings (Doors) Act, 1883.

70. *Select Committee on the Metropolitan Fire Brigade,* 1877, xiv (342), Q. 2655ff.

71. *Hansard,* 3rd ser., *268,* c. 788–793 (17 April 1882).

72. For further details of Shaw's career, see chapter 6.

73. *Punch,* 5 August 1882, p. 38.

74. *Daily Chronicle,* 15 October 1883; see also *The Echo,* 11 March 1886.

75. *Annual Report of the MBW for 1888,* pp. 98–101.

76. GLRO (L), MBW Minutes, 1 August, 17 October 1884.

77. Ibid., 16 October, 11 December 1885.

78. *Daily Telegraph,* 11 March 1886; *The Times,* 11 March 1886.

79. *Royal Commission on the Metropolitan Board of Works,* 1888, lvi (C. 5560), Mins. Evid., Q. 4383.

80. *Financial News,* 12 December 1887; see also the *St. James's Gazette,* 12 March 1886.

81. *Select Committee on Metropolitan Bridges,* 1854, xiv (370).

82. Ibid., Mins. Evid., Q. 341.

83. *Ibid.,* Q. 814.

84. *City Press,* 18 July 1857; GLRO (L), MBW Minutes, 30 October 1857.

85. GLRO (L), MBW Minutes, 10 March 1865.

86. *Metropolitan,* 24 August 1878, p. 541.

87. *Select Committee on Toll Bridges (River Thames),* 1876, xiv (244), Q. 427 (hereafter, *Select Committee on Toll Bridges (River Thames),* 1876).

88. Ibid., Mins. Evid., Q. 266.

89. *Hansard,* 3rd ser., *199,* c. 708–712 (22 February 1870), and c. 1633–34 (10 March 1870).

90. *Select Committee on Toll Bridges (River Thames),* 1876, Mins. Evid., Q. 432.

91. *Metropolitan,* 12 October 1878, p. 603.

92. GLRO (L), MBW Minutes, 6 December 1871.

93. Ibid., 25 April 1873; *Select Committee on Toll Bridges (River Thames),* 1876, Mins. Evid., Q. 28.

94. *Metropolitan,* 18 December 1875, p. 812.

95. *Select Committee on Toll Bridges (River Thames),* 1876, Mins. Evid., Q. 974ff; ibid., 1877, XIV (156), Mins. Evid., Q. 56.

96. *Standard,* 7 October 1878; *Daily Telegraph,* 5 October 1878.

97. *Daily Chronicle,* 7 October 1878.

98. *Annual Report of the MBW for 1888,* p. 33.

99. *Annual Report of the MBW for 1888,* p. 33; GLRO (L), MBW Minutes, 21 July 1880.

100. GLRO (L), MBW Minutes, 22 March 1878.

101. Ibid., 25 October 1878.

102. *The Times,* 22 July 1879.

103. Ibid., 16 July 1883; *Daily News,* 20 July 1883; *Daily Chronicle,* 17 July 1883.

104. *City Press,* 21 July 1883, 23 February 1884.

105. *Hansard,* 3rd ser., *295,* c. 266-267 (6 March 1885).

106. Ibid., 267-270.

107. *The Times,* 16 March 1889.

6. THE MISCELLANEOUS DUTIES OF A MUNICIPAL GOVERNMENT

1. J. A. Nicholay (d. 1873), furrier to the Queen and Royal Family; member of the MBW for St. Marylebone, 1856-1873 (Frederick Boase, *Modern English Biography* [London, 1965] [hereafter, *Boase*]).

2. For a description of the "Great Fire of Tooley Street," see G. V. Blackstone, *A History of the British Fire Service* (London, 1957), pp. 160-161.

3. Ibid., p. 117.

4. *Report of the Select Committee on Fires in the Metropolis,* 1862, ix (221) (hereafter, *Select Committee on Fires in the Metropolis,* 1862).

5. Ibid., p. vii, Mins. Evid., Q. 106.

6. *The Hornet* (23 October 1878) said of Captain Shaw, "when seen in his fireman's tunic, his helmet and his jackboots, [he] looks every inch a soldier. He also looks every inch a sailor. In reality, he is both a soldier and a sailor. He is also a scholar and a man of letters."

7. *Select Committee on Fires in the Metropolis,* 1862, Mins. Evid., Q. 649.

8. Sir Richard Mayne (1796-1868), barrister; chief commissioner of the Metropolitan Police, 1850-1866 (*DNB*).

9. GLRO (L), MBW Minutes, 31 March 1865.

10. *Marylebone Mercury,* 19 December 1863, and 21 May, 18 June 1864.

11. GLRO (L), MBW 708, 26 April 1864.

12. In October 1871, for example, he applied unsuccessfully to the Board for six weeks' leave to investigate the "late calamitous fire" in Chicago. In February 1875, however, he was invited by the Khedive of Egypt to organize a fire brigade in Cairo. He was then granted the six weeks' leave. GLRO (L), MBW Minutes, 27 October 1871, 15 January 1875.

13. By January 1870 (five years later) there were 378 firemen, 50 fire engine stations, 2 river stations, 25 land steam engines, and 85 manual engines. GLRO (L), MBW Minutes, 7 January 1870.

14. *Annual Report of the MBW for 1888,* 1889, lxvi (326), 46-48 (hereafter, *Annual Report of the MBW for 1888*).

15. For this purpose four districts were created to cover London. Only one parish (Islington) refused to comply. GLRO (L), MBW Minutes, 24 November 1865.

16. *Annual Report of the MBW for 1888,* p. 51.

17. GLRO (L), MBW Minutes, 21 June 1867.

18. *Select Committee on the Metropolitan Fire Brigade,* 1876, xl (371), Mins. Evid., Robert Freeman, Q. 4371 (hereafter, *Select Committee on the Metropolitan Fire Brigade,* 1876).

19. Sailors had special qualifications as prospective firemen. They were accustomed to discipline and to climbing, and had "acquired the knack of keeping a steady footing." The course of training cost £100 per man. *The Globe,* 15 July 1878.

20. *Select Committee on the Metropolitan Fire Brigade,* 1876, Mins. Evid., Capt. Shaw, Q. 918, 931. See also ibid., *Appendix Nine: Memorial of the Officers and Men of the Metropolitan Fire Brigade praying the Board to adopt a scale of pensions for the Brigade,* 28 February 1874.

21. Ibid., Select Committee Report.

22. *Hansard,* 3rd ser., *228,* c. 352–361 (21 March 1876). See also *Select Committee on the Metropolitan Fire Brigade,* 1876, Appendix Nine.

23. *Select Committee on the Metropolitan Fire Brigade,* 1876, Mins. Evid., Q. 3422, 3425.

24. Ibid., Q. 6308.

25. Ibid., Q. 6464.

26. *The Globe,* 31 July, 17 October 1874.

27. Ibid., 4 May 1874.

28. *Report of the Select Committee on the Metropolitan Fire Brigade,* 1877, xiv (342), xi–xii (hereafter, *Select Committe on the Metropolitan Fire Brigade,* 1877).

29. Ibid., Q. 94, pp. xii–xiv.

30. *Select Committee on the Metropolitan Fire Brigade,* 1876, Mins. Evid., Capt. W. E. Harris, Q. 8031.

31. Ibid.

32. GLRO (L), MBW Minutes, 14 December 1877.

33. *The Select Committee on the Metropolitan Fire Brigade,* 1876 (para. 26), reported that "in the course of ten years the proportion of . . . 'serious fires' . . . has been reduced, having fallen from 24% of the whole in 1865, to 11% in 1875, and having, in 1872, been as low as 8%."

34. *The Times,* 24 May 1879; GLRO (L), MBW Minutes, 20 April 1883.

35. GLRO (L), MBW Minutes, 9 February 1883.

36. Ibid., 4 May 1883.

37. The *Daily News,* 17 May 1886, applauded the management and efficiency of the Fire Brigade, but feared that were it not for the damp climate and the fire-resisting brick of London, the service would be "fatally overmatched." The *Daily News* called for the laying down of high-pressure mains with hydrants under the control of the police—a job, it was felt, for a municipal government.

38. *Annual Report of the MBW for 1888,* p. 52.

39. Ibid., p. 53.

40. *Select Committee on East London Water Bills,* 1867, ix (399), 1.

41. The Committee seems to have been formed in reaction to the outbreak of cholera in the autumn of 1866, which had prompted a deputation from the East End vestries to the MBW, urging it to use its influence to prevent the East London waterworks from supplying water from the River Lee until the river had been protected from sewage. GLRO (L), MBW Minutes, 13 July 1866. Report of Capt. Tyler to the Board of Trade, 1867. The vestries in general seemed to want a constant supply, but they were inclined to resist the MBW's taking over

of the water companies. GLRO (L), MBW Minutes, 4 February 1870.

42. A. S. Ayrton (1816–1886), Liberal member for Tower Hamlets; 1857–1874, First Commissioner of Works 1869–1873 (*DNB*). On his stormy relationship with Joseph Hooker over the management of Kew Gardens, see R. MacLeod, "The Ayrton Incident: A Commentary on the Relations of Science and Government in England, 1870–1873," in Arnold Thackray and Everett Mendelsohn, eds., *Science and Values* (New York, 1974), pp. 45–78.

43. *Report of the Royal Commission on Water Supply*, 1868–1869, xxxiii (C. 4169), para. 249.

44. *Hansard*, 3rd ser., *206*, c. 1222–31 (23 May 1871).

45. GLRO (L), Minutes of Proceedings of the Board of Trade Commissioners on a Constant Water Supply, 1873.

46. *Hansard*, 3rd ser., *206*, c. 1323 (26 May 1871).

47. *Annual Report of the MBW for 1888*, p. 67.

48. *Select Committee on the Metropolitan Fire Brigade*, 1876, Mins. Evid., Q. 168.

49. For a while, Shaw was able to encourage turncocks by paying two shillings and sixpence to the first two who arrived at the fire. The system of water-pipes and plugs was so complicated that the assistance of the turncocks was essential. GLRO (L), MBW Minutes, 9 March 1866.

50. *Select Committee on the Metropolitan Fire Brigade*, 1876, p. xxi. There was a good deal of argument about when or whether hydrants would make superfluous the use of fire engines. Certainly not for some time, the Committee agreed.

51. The East London and Kent water companies.

52. *Annual Report of the MBW for 1888*, p. 69.

53. S. E. Finer, *Life and Times of Sir Edwin Chadwick* (London, 1952), pp. 403–412, 423–425.

54. Cf. *Select Committee on the Metropolitan Fire Brigade*, 1877, p. xxii.

55. *The Times*, 8 December 1877.

56. *Hansard*, 3rd ser., *238*, c. 1231 (12 March 1878).

57. *Journal of Gas Lighting*, 29 October 1879.

58. GLRO (L), MBW Minutes, 16 May 1879.

59. This was the Metropolitan Board of Works (Water Expenses) Bill, *Hansard*, 3rd ser., *248*, c. 123–132 (10 July 1879).

60. Ibid., c. 130 (10 July 1879).

61. Ibid., *249*, c. 917ff (13 August 1879).

62. *Report from the Select Committee on London Water Supply*, 1880, x (Session 2), (329), iv.

63. Ibid.

64. *The Times*, 3, 12 January 1882.

65. The Metropolitan Board of Works (Further Powers) Bill, *Hansard*, 3rd ser., *285*, c. 33–51 (27 February 1884).

66. *Annual Report of the MBW for 1888*, p. 66.

67. *The Times*, 25 December 1885, 12 January 1886.

68. *Select Committee on Gas (Metropolis) Bill*, 1860, xxi (493), Mins. Evid., Dr. John Challice, Q. 1ff, 58, 68.

69. The Metropolis Gas Act, 1860.

70. *City Press*, 16 November 1861, 22 October 1864.

71. Ibid., 9 December 1865.

72. *Hansard*, 3rd ser., *181*, c. 1610 (6 March 1866).

73. *Report from the Select Committee on London (City) Corporation Gas (etc.) Bills,* 1866, xii, (270), v.

74. *Annual Report of the MBW for 1888,* pp. 53–58.

75. *Special Report from the Select Committee on the Metropolitan Gas Bill,* 1867, xii (520), 1.

76. GLRO (L), MBW Minutes, 16 April 1869.

77. Ibid., 30 April 1869.

78. Ibid., 7 May 1869.

79. George John Shaw-Lefevre (Baron Eversley), 1831–1928. Liberal M.P. for Reading, 1863–1885; for Central Bradford, 1886–1895; instrumental in forming Commons Preservation Society, and chairman, 1866–1928; First Commissioner of Works, 1880–1883, 1892–1894; Postmaster General, 1883; very active member of the LCC; created Baron, 1906 (*DNB*).

80. GLRO (L), MBW Minutes, 11 November 1870.

81. *Weekly Times,* 9 August 1874.

82. GLRO (L), MBW Minutes, 26 June 1874.

83. Ibid., 6 November 1874.

84. *Daily News,* 12 November 1874.

85. *Hansard,* 3rd ser., *224,* c. 611–625 (13 May 1875). *Report of the Select Committee on Metropolitan Gas Companies Bill,* 1875, xii (281), 1.

86. GLRO (L), MBW Minutes, 6 August 1875.

87. *The Builder,* 11 August 1877, pp. 799–800.

88. George Shaw Lefevre, *English Commons and Forests* (London, 1894), p. 314.

89. GLRO (L), MBW Minutes, 16 April 1869; see also *North Londoner,* 20 March 1869. A. H. Layard, describing the deputation introduced by Lord Enfield and Mr. Torrens, said he had rarely received "a larger or more influential deputation . . ."

90. GLRO (L), MBW Minutes, 20 January 1869; *Marylebone Mercury,* 20 January 1872.

91. *Report from the Select Committee on the Metropolitan Board of Works. (Leicester Square Improvement) Bill,* 1871, xl (142), Mins. Evid., Q. 389.

92. *Marylebone Mercury,* 7 March 1863.

93. *Observer,* 22 March 1857.

94. GLRO (L), MBW 1444, 5 January 1857.

95. *Annual Report of the MBW for 1871,* lvii (436), 21–22.

96. Ibid.

97. *Second Report from the Select Committee on Open Spaces (Metropolis),* 1865, viii (390), Mins. Evid., Q. 4321 (hereafter, *Select Committee on Open Spaces,* 1865).

98. The *Metropolitan,* 24 January 1874, p. 28, applauded this "munificent, appropriate and timely gift."

99. *Select Committee on Open Spaces,* 1865, p. 259.

100. Ibid., Mins. Evid., Q. 4296–99.

101. The Statute of Merton (20 Henry III, *cap.* 4, 1235) was the first enclosure act. It allowed the lords of the manors to enclose or approve parts of the waste lands of their manors, "provided it should appear on complaint of the free tenants that there was enough common left to satisfy their rights." See Shaw-Lefevre, *English Commons,* pp. 11–12.

102. *Annual Report of the MBW for 1888,* p. 38; GLRO (L), MBW Minutes, 3 April 1868, 20 February 1874.

103. Shaw-Lefevre, *English Commons,* p. 314.

104. The Manor of Hampstead had been granted by Henry VIII to Sir Thomas North. In 1743 it became the property of the Maryon family. Sir Thomas Maryon Wilson was Lord of the Manor until 1868. Ibid., pp. 48–52.

105. GLRO (L), MBW Minutes, 1 February 1867.

106. Ibid., 21 October 1870.

107. Shaw-Lefevre, *English Commons,* p. 53.

108. Ibid., p. 55.

109. GLRO (L), MBW Minutes, 17 July 1885.

110. Ibid., 12 November 1886; Shaw-Lefevre, *English Commons,* p. 57.

111. GLRO (L), MBW Minutes, 14 October 1887.

112. *The Times,* 3 November 1887.

113. Shaw-Lefevre, *English Commons,* pp. 134–135.

114. GLRO (L), MBW Minutes, 9 February 1872.

115. *The Times,* 15 April 1872.

116. *Morning Post,* 5 July 1878; *The Echo* and *The Globe,* 4 July 1878; *Spectator,* 27 July 1878, p. 949.

117. *The Times,* 5 May 1882; *The Echo,* 19 October 1883.

118. GLRO (L), MBW Minutes, April–July 1883, and 15 February, 4 July 1884; *Hansard,* 3rd ser., *278,* c. 891–892 (23 April 1883), and *280,* c. 213–215 (11 June 1883).

119. *Marylebone Mercury,* 30 December 1865.

120. *Annual Report of the MBW for 1888,* p. 79.

121. Ibid.

122. Ibid., p. 82.

7. THE ROUTINE OF ADMINISTRATION

1. *Second Report from the Select Committee on Metropolitan Taxation,* 1861, viii (372), Mins. Evid., John Thwaites, Q. 3370 (hereafter, *Second Report from the Select Committee on Metropolitan Taxation,* 1861).

2. *Observer,* 14 February 1875.

3. William Newton (d. 1876), radical engineer, one-time President of the Labour Representation League (*Metropolitan,* 11 March 1876, p. 173); a member of the MBW for Mile End Old Town, 1862–1876 (*Boase*). General William John Codrington (1804–1884), Commander-in-Chief at Sebastopol, 1855–56; M.P. for Greenwich, 1857; Governor of Gibraltar, 1859–1865 (*DNB*). As for Alfred Lawrence, nothing is known of him other than the fact that he was the brother of two London Aldermen (*Observer,* 14 February 1875).

4. *Elector,* 25 July 1857.

5. *The Hornet,* 5, 19 October 1870.

6. Ibid., 24 August 1870.

7. Sir James MacNaghten McGarel-Hogg (1823–1890), First Baron Magheramorne; Conservative M.P. for Bath, 1865–1868, for Truro, 1871–1885, and for Hornsey, 1885–1887; chairman, MBW, 1870–1879 (*DNB*).

8. GLRO (L), MBW Minutes, 7 October 1870.

9. *Evening News,* 24 June 1887.

10. *Observer,* 8 November 1856.

11. *Second Report from the Select Committee on Metropolitan Taxation,* 1861, Mins. Evid., John Thwaites, Q. 1944–45.

12. *Interim Report of the Royal Commission on the MBW,* 1888, lvi (C. 5560-I), Mins. Evid., J. E. Wakefield, Q. 39.

13. *Annual Report of the MBW for 1867-68,* 1868-69, li (23), 51.

14. *Annual Report of the MBW for 1888,* 1889, lxvi (326), 103 (hereafter, *Annual Report of the MBW for 1888*).

15. This return was unofficial and was not issued by the Home Office. How the office received the information is not clear. Thwaites was furious that it had been published, but he did not challenge the accuracy of the return.

16. *Return of the Present Permanent and Temporary Staff of the MBW, 1867-68,* lviii (17), 221-240.

17. *Annual Report of the MBW for 1880,* 1881, lxxix (240), 123.

18. Ibid.

19. *Second Report from the Select Committee on Metropolitan Taxation,* 1861, Q. 2224. *Observer,* 26 September 1858.

20. *Second Report from the Select Committee on Metropolitan Taxation,* 1861, Q. 2234.

21. *Observer,* 18 March 1860.

22. *Second Report from the Select Committee on Metropolitan Taxation,* 1861, Q. 2213, 2215.

23. See chapter 3 at note 35.

24. *Observer,* 14 November 1858.

25. GLRO (L), MBW Minutes, 14 October 1859.

26. Ibid., 4 March 1859.

27. Ibid., 10 June 1859.

28. GLRO (L), *MBW 706,* 16 December 1862.

29. *First Report of the Select Committee on Metropolitan Local Government,* 1866, xiii (186), Mins. Evid., John Thwaites, Q. 614 (hereafter, *Select Committee on Metropolitan Local Government,* 1866).

30. Thus the poor relief rate varied from three shillings and threepence per pound of rate property in Bermondsey to one shilling and sevenpence per pound in the City, and sixpence per pound in St. George's, Hanover Square. *Select Committee on Metropolitan Local Government,* 1866, app. 1, p. 269.

31. *Observer,* 20 May 1865.

32. *Select Committee on Metropolitan Local Government,* 1866, Q. 547.

33. GLRO (L), MBW Minutes, 16 November 1866.

34. Ibid., 12 May 1865.

35. *Annual Report of the MBW for 1888,* 1889, p. 85.

36. *The Hornet,* 3 June 1868.

37. *Hansard,* 3rd ser., *190,* c. 1025-27 (21 February 1868).

38. *The Times,* 21 December 1868.

39. *Hansard,* 3rd ser., *198,* 326-332 (20 July 1869).

40. See Asa Briggs, *Victorian Cities* (London, 1963), p. 334.

41. *Annual Report of the MBW for 1888,* 1889, p. 86.

42. Ibid., p. 142.

43. GLRO (L), MBW Minutes, 1 December 1871.

44. *Annual Report of the MBW for 1888,* 1889, p. 85.

45. GLRO (L), MBW Minutes, 17 July 1874.

46. *Annual Report of the MBW for 1888,* 1889, pp. 90-92.

47. GLRO (L), MBW Minutes, 26 February, 25 June 1875.

48. *Hansard,* 3rd ser., *318,* c. 1668-72 (8 August 1887).

49. Ibid., *263*, c. 1226–28, 1723ff (18 July 1881).

50. GLRO (L), MBW 681, Minutes of Special Committee (1876).

51. *Annual Report of the MBW for 1888,* 1889, p. 94.

52. *Metropolitan,* 12 December 1883, p. 802.

8. THE ODOR OF CORRUPTION

1. *The Times,* 1 December 1859.

2. Ibid., 3 March 1862.

3. Ibid., 10 April 1862.

4. James Beal (1829–1891), auctioneer and estate agent; Hon. Secretary of the Municipal Reform Association, 1870–91; member of the LCC for Fulham, 1889–1891; "prominent politician in Westminster from 1852 to death" *(Boase).*

5. GLRO (L), MBW 510, 22 November, 20 December 1864.

6. GLRO (L), MBW 711, 7 January 1865.

7. The petition was laid on 15 June 1865; it was described in the Journal of the House of Commons as having been withdrawn "without any reason being entered." *Journal of the House of Commons,* cxx, 372.

8. Frederick Doulton, pottery manufacturer, member of the MBW from its formation until 1872; Liberal M.P. for Lambeth, 1862–1868 *(Dod's)*; Sir William Jackson, (1805–1876), Liberal M.P. for Newcastle, 1847–1865, and Derbyshire, 1865–1868 *(Dod's)*. Meaburn Staniland (b. 1809), Liberal M.P. for Boston, 1859–1865, 1866–67 *(Dod's)*.

9. *Interim Report of the Royal Commission on the Metropolitan Board of Works,* 1888, lvi (C. 5560), 1; Mins. Evid. (C. 5560–61), 36; Q. 12,802–05, 12, 844 (hereafter, *Interim Report,* 1888).

10. GLRO (L), MBW Minutes, 1 January, 9 April 1869.

11. GRLO (L), 26 July 1878.

12. *The Echo,* 22, 30 July 1878.

13. GLRO (L), MBW Minutes, 26 July 1878.

14. *Clerkenwell Press,* 20 November, 6 December 1878.

15. Ibid., 19 March 1879.

16. Ibid., 26 April 1879.

17. Ibid., 4 June 1879.

18. *Hansard,* 3rd ser., *225,* c. 1931–32, 1936–38, and 1940–41 (23 July 1875).

19. Ibid., *279,* c. 1622–24 (4 June 1883).

20. GLRO (L), MBW 680, 23 July 1875.

21. GRLO (L), MBW 683, 10 October 1883.

22. See *Financial News,* 23, 30 July, 6 August, 13 September 1887.

23. *Standard, The Times, Daily News,* and *The Globe,* 19 November 1886.

24. *The Echo,* 8 December 1886.

25. Quoted in G. V. Blackstone, *A History of the British Fire Service* (London, 1957), p. 216.

26. The best secondary account of the Pavilion scandal appears in *The Parish of St. James, Westminster,* pt. II, Survey of London, vol. XXXI, ed. F. H. W. Sheppard (London, 1963), pp. 71–74.

27. *Interim Report,* 1888, pp. 6–7.

28. Ibid., Q. 3978.

29. *Financial News,* 23 November 1886.

30. *Interim Report,* 1888, p. 10.

31. The vestries were Paddington and Wandsworth, together with the Tooting District Board Ratepayers' Association, and the newspapers were *The Times,* 1 October 1885, and the *Pall Mall Gazette,* 1 October and 15 November 1885.

32. GLRO (L), MBW Minutes, 15 July 1887.

33. Ibid.

34. *Pall Mall Gazette,* 16 July 1887.

35. *Lloyds,* 17 July 1887.

36. GLRO (L), MBW Minutes, 22, 29 July 1887.

37. Keevil's allegations were published in the *Pall Mall Gazette,* 20 July 1887.

38. Mark Judge (b. 1846), an Associate of the Royal Institute of British Architects, was an "ardent municipal reformer" who was elected to the MBW in 1888 but was identified as a critic of the MBW from 1885 onward. (*Metropolitan,* 1 December 1888, pp. 760–761.) He appeared as a witness on 16 August 1887 (GLRO [L], MBW 684).

39. *Daily News,* 6 October 1887.

40. *Standard,* 8 October 1887.

41. *The Times,* 10 October 1887.

42. *Financial News,* "The Metropolitan Board of Works," (1888) p. 39.

43. *Financial News,* 11 November 1887.

44. *Lloyds,* 24 July 1887.

45. T. G. Fardell (b. 1833), barrister; on the MBW for Paddington from 1884 onward (*Dod's LCC* [London, 1889]).

46. *The Times,* 11 October 1887.

47. *St. James Gazette,* 19 November 1887; *Pall Mall Gazette,* 19 November 1887.

48. *Dod's LCC,* 1889.

49. *Hansard,* 3rd ser., *322,* c. 664–677 (16 February 1888).

50. Ibid., c. 679–685. Robert Grant Webster was a barrister and Middlesex magistrate (*Metropolitan,* 20 June 1885, p. 404).

51. *Hansard,* 3rd ser., *322,* c. 687 (16 February 1888).

52. *South London Journal,* 30 June 1888.

53. *Pall Mall Gazette,* 19 November 1888.

54. Ibid., 23 March 1888.

55. *Financial News,* 25 October 1887.

56. *Financial News,* "The Metropolitan Board of Works," (1888) p. 7.

57. See, for example, *Interim Report,* 1888, Mins. Evid., J. E. Saunders, Q. 1644–47.

58. *Pall Mall Gazette,* 6 July 1888.

59. *Interim Report,* 1888, Mins. Evid., John Fleuret, Q. 6393.

60. See chapter 2, note 44.

61. *Interim Report,* 1888, Mins. Evid., Edward Ryde, Q. 5604ff.

62. Ibid., pp. 12–13.

63. Ibid.

64. Ibid., p. 15.

65. Ibid., p. 17.

66. *The Builder,* 17 December 1887, p. 833.

67. *The Times,* 14 January 1888.

68. *Interim Report,* 1888, Mins. Evid., Q. 11, 184.

69. Ibid., Mins. Evid., G. B. Richardson, Q. 11, 258–260.

70. Ibid., Mins. Evid., Lord Magheramorne, Q. 10, 575.

71. Ibid., p. 20.

72. Ibid., Mins. Evid., R. E. Villiers, Q. 5229.

73. *Financial News,* 11 November 1887.

74. The presidents were John Whichcord, G. E. Street, and Alfred Waterhouse, who were inaugurated in 1879, 1881, and 1883 respectively. *RIBA Transactions* for session 1879, pp. 1–15; *RIBA Journal* for session 1881-82, pp. 55–68, and 1889, pp. 17–29.

75. *Interim Report,* 1888, p. 25.

76. Ibid., pp. 30–31.

77. Ibid., pp. 24–25.

78. Ibid., pp. 22–24.

79. Ibid., Mins. Evid., Frederick Gordon, Q. 9111ff.

80. Barrington Kaye, *The Development of the Architectural Profession in Britain* (London, 1960).

81. *Interim Report,* 1888, Mins. Evid., F. H. Fowler, Q. 3640.

82. Ibid., Q. 11, 322ff.

83. Ibid., Q. 12, 187.

84. Ibid., Q. 11, 102ff.

85. Ibid., Q. 12, 568.

86. Ibid.,Mins. Evid., John Jones, Q. 12, 468-12, 471.

87. Ibid., p. 39.

88. GLRO (L), MBW Minutes, 30 November, 7 December 1888; *Interim Report,* Mins. Evid., Q. 11, 434ff.

89. *Interim Report,* 1888, Mins. Evid., Q. 13, 257.

9. THE TWILIGHT OF THE METROPOLITAN BOARD OF WORKS

1. Hall's comment in the tribute to Sir William Fraser, *Sessional Proceedings of the Social Science Association* (1877-78), 128.

2. *The Times,* 14 August 1855.

3. *Hansard,* 3rd ser., *191,* c. 1862 (15 May 1868).

4. *The Times,* 19 June 1868.

5. Ibid., 7 November 1854.

6. Ibid., 1 December 1859.

7. Ibid., 23 March 1882.

8. J. S. Mill, *Representative Government* (London, 1861), p. 275.

9. *Second Report from the Select Committee on Local Taxation,* 1861, viii (372), Mins. Evid., Q. 2492ff.

10. W. McCullagh Torrens, "The Government of London," *Nineteenth Century,* 8 (1880), 766.

11. *Select Committee on Metropolitan Local Government,* 1866, xiii (186),171.

12. *Second Report from the Select Committee on Metropolitan Local Government,* 1867, xxi (268), v-vi.

13. W. McCullagh Torrens, "The Government of London," *Nineteenth Century,* 8 (1880), 766–786.

14. Joshua Toulmin Smith, *Local Government and Centralisation* (London, 1851), *The Metropolis and its Municipal Administration* (London, 1852), *The Parish, Its Obligations and Powers* (London, 1854), and *The People and the Parish* (London, 1853).

15. Tom Taylor, *Transactions of the National Social Science Association*, (1857), 475.

16. *Shoreditch Observer*, 24 April 1869.

17. *Hansard*, 3rd ser., *239*, c. 679 (5 April 1878).

18. *Third Report of the Select Committee on Local Taxation*, 1861, viii (476), xii.

19. Thomas Hughes, "The Anarchy of London," *Macmillan's Magazine*, 21 (1869–70), 275; *City Press*, 24 January 1882.

20. Mill, *Representative Government*, ch. 15, pp. 266–287.

21. *Hansard*, 3rd ser., *181*, c. 1140 (20 February 1866).

22. Ibid., *191*, c. 1862 (5 May 1868).

23. Mill, *Representative Government*, pp. 266–287.

24. Ibid., p. 273.

25. *The Times*, 19 June 1868.

26. *Hansard*, 3rd ser., *196*, c. 1939ff (16 June 1869).

27. GLRO (L), MBW Minutes, 27 May 1870.

28. *Metropolitan*, 24 May 1873, p. 328.

29. *Hansard*, 3rd ser., *229*, c. 1784ff (13 June 1876).

30. Ibid., *239*, c. 675ff (5 April 1878).

31. Ibid., c. 705.

32. Ibid., c. 841.

33. James Edward Thorold Rogers (1823–1890), clergyman and professor of political economy at Oxford, 1862–1868; Liberal M.P. successively for Southwark and Bermondsey, 1880–1886 (*Dod's*). Thomas Bayley Potter (1817–1898), a "radical reformer," M.P. for Rochdale, 1865–1895 (*Dod's*). Sir Walter Henry James (1846–1923), Liberal M.P. for Gateshead, 1874–1893 (*Dod's*). Henry Robert Brand (1841–1906), Liberal M.P. for Hertfordshire, 1868–1874, and for Stroud, 1880–1886; became second Viscount Hampden (*Dod's*).

34. *Marylebone Mercury*, 10 June 1880.

35. Arthur Hobhouse, *Some Reasons for a Single Government for London*, Municipal Reform Pamphlet no. 11 (London: London Municipal Reform League, 1884).

36. Arthur Hobhouse, "The Government of London," *Contemporary Review*, 41 (1882), 404–416.

37. *Daily Telegraph*, 9 June 1883.

38. *Daily Chronicle*, 9 January 1884.

39. *Hansard*, 3rd ser., *287*, c. 54–69 (18 April 1884).

40. Ibid.

41. *The Times*, 11 April 1884; William A. Robson, *The Government and Misgovernment of London* (London, 1939), pp. 74–75.

42. GLRO (L), MBW Minutes, 2 May 1884.

43. *Metropolitan*, 14 June 1884, p. 384.

44. *Hansard*, 3rd ser., *289*, c. 1926 (3 July 1884).

45. Ibid., c. 1927.

46. Ibid.

47. Rt. Hon. Charles Thomson Ritchie (1838–1906), President, Local Government Board, 1886–1892; President of the Board of Trade, 1895–1900; Home Secretary, 1900–1902; Chancellor of the Exchequer, 1902–03; Conservative M.P., Tower Hamlets, 1874–1885, St. George's in the East, Tower Hamlets, 1885–1892, Croydon, 1895–1905; elected Alderman of the LCC, 1894 (*DNB*).

48. *Hansard*, 3rd ser., *290*, c. 532 (8 July 1884).

49. Ibid., c. 573.

50. Ibid., c. 556.
51. Ibid., c. 567–571.
52. Ibid., *289,* c. 1843–59 (3 July 1884).
53. *City Press,* 1 August 1885.
54. Ibid., 10 October 1885.
55. LCC Bill, 1884, *Hansard,* 3rd ser., *289,* c. 1924 (3 July 1884).
56. *Report from the Select Committee on London Corporation (Charges of Malversation),* 1887, x (161), 13.
57. Ibid., p. iv.
58. *City Press,* 25 May 1887.
59. *Hansard,* 3rd ser., *323,* c. 1663 (19 March 1888).
60. Ibid., *324,* c. 1748 (19 April 1888).
61. *City Press,* 21 July 1888.
62. Ibid., 3 October 1888.
63. *Metropolitan,* 7 July 1888, pp. 424–425.
64. Serjeant Pulling, "The Need and Practicability of Systematic Local Government for London," *Sessional Proceedings of the Social Science Association,* (1877–78), 116–117.
65. *Pall Mall Gazette,* 2 June 1888.
66. *The Times,* 30 October 1888.
67. *City Press,* 10 January 1889.
68. *The Times,* 17 December 1888.
69. *The Builder,* 16 March 1889, p. 198.
70. *The Times,* 20 March 1889.
71. G. L. Gomme, *London, 1837–1897* (London, 1898), p. 38; Sir Gwilym Gibbon and R. W. Bell, *History of the London County Council, 1889–1939* (London, 1939), p. 53.
72. *The Times,* 2 February 1889.
73. Ibid., 20 March 1889.

10. A BIRD'S-EYE VIEW OF VESTRYDOM

1. *Second Report from the Select Committee on Metropolitan Local Government,* 1866, xiii (452), Mins. Evid., T. Beggs, Q. 2534.
2. Ibid., W. F. Jebb, Q. 4468–79, and C. Lahee, Q. 4904.
3. Beginning with twenty-four for the 1,000–2,000 householders bracket.
4. See Sidney and Beatrice Webb, *English Local Government from the Revolution to the Municipal Corporations Act: The Parish and the County* (London, 1906), pp. 36, 49, 107.
5. *South London Advertiser,* 1 September 1855.
6. *Second Report from the Select Committee on Metropolitan Local Government,* 1866, xiii (452), Mins. Evid., D. E. Cameron, Q. 5632.
7. *Metropolitan,* 2 November 1856.
8. *Second Report from the Select Committee on Metropolitan Local Government,* 1866, xiii (452), Mins. Evid., J. Beal, Q. 2099.
9. *Marylebone Mercury,* 27 January 1866.
10. *Second Report from the Select Committee on Metropolitan Local Government,* 1866, xiii (452), Mins. Evid., C. Lahee, Q. 4914; H. Chester, Q. 4763ff, and J. Dangerfield, Q. 3014.
11. J. F. B. Firth, *Municipal London; or, London Government As It Is, and London*

under a Municipal Council (London, 1876), p. 302.

12. *Second Report from the Select Committee on Metropolitan Local Government,* 1866, xiii (452), Mins. Evid., W. Newton, Q. 5428.

13. J. F. B. Firth, *Reform of Local Government and of City Guilds* (London, 1888), p. 45.

14. *Metropolitan,* 19 May 1877.

15. Ibid., 17 May 1873.

16. Ibid., 2 June 1883.

17. *First Report from the Select Committee on Metropolitan Local Government,* 1866, xiii (186), Mins. Evid., Sir J. Thwaites, Q. 614.

18. *Metropolitan,* 19 July 1872.

19. Firth, *Municipal London,* p. 312.

20. *Second Report from the Select Committee on Metropolitan Local Government,* 1866, xiii (452), Mins. Evid., C. Lahee, Q. 4889.

21. Ibid., H. Bidgood, Q. 5291–99, and J. Beal, Q. 1782.

22. Ibid., J. Beal, Q. 2091.

23. Ibid., R. Freeman, Q. 3438.

24. Ibid., J. Dangerfield, Q. 2928–30.

25. Ibid., J. Fuller, Q. 6064–65.

26. Ibid., W. Clark, Q. 4139.

27. Ibid., W. Newton, Q. 5444.

28. Ibid., W. Clark, Q. 4244, and J. Fuller, Q. 6064.

29. Ibid., J. Beal, Q. 1856, and W. Newton, Q. 5448.

30. *Metropolitan,* 17 August 1872.

31. *East London Observer,* 10 October 1857.

32. *Second Report from the Select Committee on Metropolitan Local Government,* 1866, xiii (452), Mins. Evid., R. Gladding, Q. 3141–59.

33. *South London Press,* 12 April 1884.

34. *Metropolitan,* 19 April 1879.

35. *Royal Commission on the Housing of the Working Classes,* 1884–85, xxx (4402), Mins. Evid., T. Jennings, Q. 2947–69, and R. Paget, Q. 17,659.

36. Ibid., Lord W. Compton, Q. 724.

37. *Replies from Vestries and District Boards relative to Sanitary and Street Improvements,* 1872, xlix (298), 1–63.

38. Ibid.

39. Firth, *Municipal London,* p. 330.

40. *Royal Commission on the Housing of the Working Classes,* 1884–85, xxx (4402), 9.

41. Ibid., H. Owen, Q. 263–266.

42. Firth, *Municipal London,* p. 312.

43. Ibid., p. 338.

11. THE CITY

1. William Ferneley Allen, *The Corporation of London* (London, 1858), p. 80.

2. *Second Report of the Commissioners appointed to inquire into the Municipal Corporations in England and Wales (London and Southwark, City Companies),* 1837, xxv (239).

3. J. F. B. Firth, *Municipal London; or, London Government As It Is, and London under a Municipal Council* (London, 1876), p. 187.

4. Percy J. Edwards, *History of London Street Improvements, 1855-1897* (London, 1898), pp. 15-16: Firth, *Municipal London,* pp. 184-186.

5. *The Hornet,* 23 March 1870.

6. Firth, *Municipal London,* p. 206.

7. Ibid., p. 207.

8. Ibid., p. 109.

9. *Report and Evidence of Royal Commission on State of the Corporation of the City of London* (hereafter, *Royal Commission on State of City Corporation*) 1854, xxvi (1772), Mins. Evid., F. Bennoch. Q. 1158.

10. Ibid., Q. 1155-57.

11. Ibid., J. Cattley, Q. 1322-26.

12. Ibid., J. Acland, Q. 146.

13. Ibid., Q. 168.

14. Ibid., Q. 417.

15. Ibid., J. I. Travers, Q. 216, 220.

16. Ibid., T. Hankey junior, Q. 1695.

17. Ibid., W. Cotton, Q. 1783-85, 1797-98.

18. Ibid., Samuel Morley, Q. 2139-43.

19. *Second Report of the Commissioners appointed to inquire into the Municipal Corporations in England and Wales (London and Southwark, City Companies),* 1837, xxvi (239), 8.

20. *Royal Commission on State of City Corporation,* 1854, xxvi (1772), Mins. Evid., T. Dakin, Q. 7374-83.

21. Ibid., C. Pearson, Q. 8478.

22. *Number of Electors in each Ward of the City of London, and Number of Aldermen and Common Councilmen Elected by Each Ward, and Their Occupations,* 1865, xliv (483), 555.

23. Firth, *Municipal London,* pp. 111-113.

24. *Royal Commission on State of City Corporation,* 1854, xxvi (1772), Mins. Evid., Lord Mayor, Q. 7154, and T. Dakin, Q. 7380.

25. Firth, *Municipal London,* pp. 110-111.

26. *Royal Commission on State of City Corporation,* 1854, xxvi (1772), Mins. Evid., Sir John Key, Q. 5840-50.

27. *Third Report of Select Committee on Metropolitan Local Government,* 1867, xii (301), Mins. Evid., J. Jones, Q. 2278.

28. Royston Lambert, *Sir John Simon, 1816-1904, and English Social Administration* (London, 1963), chs. 4-9.

29. Ibid., p. 132.

30. Ibid., p. 208.

31. "The Corporation of London and Municipal Reform," *Westminster Review,* 39 (1843), 496-571, and addenda, 572-586.

32. Sir Gilbert F. Lewis, ed., *Letters of Sir George Cornewall Lewis* (London, 1870), p. 274.

33. *Royal Commission on State of City Corporation,* 1854, xxvi (1772), Mins. Evid., Serjeant Merewether, Q. 4723-40.

34. Ibid., W. E. Hickson, Q. 2698-70.

35. Ibid., B. Scott, Q. 4497, and E. Tyrrell, Q. 5388-5412.

36. Ibid., E. Tyrrell, Q. 5441.

37. Ibid., Serjeant Merewether, Q. 4679-5360, and C. Pearson, Q. 5516-5697, 6932-37, 8460-96.

38. Ibid., Statement by the Corporation, pp. 371–385.

39. Ibid., pp. xxvi, xxvii–xxxviii.

40. *Third Report of Select Committee on Metropolitan Local Government,* 1867, xii (301), Mins. Evid., B. Scott, Q. 1177.

41. *Observer,* 2 March 1856.

42. *City Press,* 25 June 1859.

43. Ibid., 17 May 1862.

44. Ibid., 28 February 1863.

45. *Report from Select Committee on Thames Embankment (North Side) Bill,* 1863, xii (219), Mins. Evid., B. Scott, Q. 1326.

46. *City Press,* 4 April 1863.

47. Ibid., 16, 23, 30 May 1863.

48. Ibid., 30 May 1863.

49. Ibid., 20 June 1863.

50. Ibid., 4 July 1863.

51. Ibid., 25 July 1863.

52. Ibid., 4 June 1864.

53. Ibid., 2 July 1864.

54. Ibid., 23 July 1864.

55. Ibid., 30 September 1865.

56. Ibid., 14 November 1865.

57. Ibid., 6 February 1864.

58. *Royal Commission on State of City Corporation,* 1854, xxvi (1772), Mins. Evid., W. Haywood, Q. 5951.

59. *City Press,* 30 January, 13 February 1864.

60. Ibid., 11 February 1865.

61. *The Times,* 4 January 1898.

62. *City Press,* 4 April 1863.

63. *Punch,* 21 January 1882, p. 28.

64. *Report of Select Committee on Metropolitan Communications,* 1854–55, x (415), Mins. Evid., T. H. Hall, Q. 533–535.

65. Firth, *Municipal London,* pp. 205–206; Charles Welch, *Modern History of the City of London* (London, 1896), p. 262.

66. *Report of Select Committee on Metropolitan Communications,* 1854–55, x (415), Mins. Evid., C. Pearson, Q. 1375.

67. *City Press,* 11 June, 22 October 1864.

68. Ibid., 14 October, 14 November 1865.

69. Ibid., 17 March, 8 December 1866.

70. Ibid., 21 June, 5 July 1873.

71. Ibid., 17 June 1876.

72. Ibid., 1 July 1876.

73. Ibid., 28 October 1876.

74. Ibid., 25 November 1865.

75. Ibid., 28 November 1868.

76. *The Hornet,* 12, 26 April 1871; Welch, *City of London,* pp. 273, 309, 349–350.

77. *City Press,* 28 December 1872; Welch, *City of London,* pp. 271, 290.

78. *City Press,* 30 July, and 10, 14, 17 September 1881.

79. Ibid., 2, 12 November 1881, and 1, 8, 18 October 1884.

80. Lord Eversley (formerly George Shaw-Lefevre), *Commons, Forests and Footpaths* rev. ed. (London, 1910), pp. 73, 81, 84, 86.

81. Ibid., pp. 91–93.

82. GLRO (L), MBW Minutes, 17 June, 14 October 1864.

83. Ibid., 22 July, 5 August 1870.

84. Ibid., 9 February 1872.

85. *City Press*, 6 July 1878; Eversley, *Commons, Forests and Footpaths,* pp. 104, 109.

86. *Report of Select Committee on Metropolitan Communications,* 1854–55, x (415), Mins. Evid., W. Tite, Q. 55–56, 74.

87. Ibid., F. Bennoch, Q. 270.

88. *City Press,* 29 January 1859.

89. Ibid., 7 July 1866.

90. *The Hornet,* 27 September 1871.

91. Firth, *Municipal London,* p. 194.

92. *City Press,* 22 June 1878.

93. Ibid., 10 January 1883.

94. Firth, *Municipal London,* pp. 204–206.

95. *City Press,* 16 March 1867.

96. Ibid., 23 March 1867.

97. Ibid., 27 April 1867.

98. *The Hornet,* 8 April 1868.

99. *City Press,* 13 June 1863.

100. *Third Report of Select Committee on Metropolitan Local Government,* 1867, xii (301), Mins. Evid., W. Corrie, Q. 678, 2012.

101. *City Press,* 23 April 1864.

102. Ibid., 5 January 1867.

103. Ibid., 18 May 1867.

104. Ibid., 22 February 1868; Firth, *Municipal London,* p. 575.

105. *City Press,* 21 March 1868.

106. Ibid., 28 March 1868.

107. Ibid., 4 April 1868.

108. *The Hornet,* 6 April, 18 May 1870.

109. *City Press,* 21 May 1870.

110. Ibid., 3 April, 1 May 1880.

111. *Hansard,* 3rd. ser., *268,* c. 2020–22 (2 May 1882).

112. *City Press,* 3 January, 24 February 1883.

113. Ibid., 20 January, 16, 19 April, 3 May 1884; Wilfrid Blunt, *Cockerell* (London, 1964), pp. 27–28.

114. William A. Robson, *The Government and Misgovernment of London* (London, 1948), pp. 73–76.

115. *Report from the Select Committee on London Corporation (Charges of Malversation),* 1887, x (161), ii, iii.

116. *Hansard,* 3rd. ser., *311,* c. 895–915 (1 March 1887).

117. *Report from the Select Committee on London Corporation (Charges of Malversation),* 1887, x (161), iii, viii–x.

118. Ibid., p. xi, and evid. of G. P. Goldney, Q. 1255–57.

119. Ibid., evid. of J. F. B. Firth, Q. 167ff, and of G. P. Goldney, Q. 1178ff.

120. Ibid., pp. iv, xiii–xiv.

121. *City Press,* 25 May 1887; Robson, *Government and Misgovernment,* p. 78.

122. *City Press,* 11 February 1888.

123. 12 June, 12 July 1884.

124. Ibid., 26 July 1884, 7 January 1885.

125. Ibid., 26 November 1886.
126. Ibid., 4 January 1888.
127. Ibid., 21 March 1888.

12. ST. MARYLEBONE

1. J. F. B. Firth, *Municipal London; or, London Government As It Is, and London under a Municipal Council* (London, 1876), pp. 323–324.
2. Hugh C. Prince, "North-west London, 1864–1914," in J. T. Coppock and Hugh C. Prince, eds., *Greater London* (London, 1964), p. 121.
3. Michael Sadleir, *Forlorn Sunset* (London, 1947), pp. 173–175.
4. *Marylebone Mercury,* 22 August 1857.
5. Sadleir, *Forlorn Sunset,* p. 175.
6. F. H. W. Sheppard, *Local Government in St. Marylebone, 1688–1835* (London, 1958), p. 297.
7. James Williamson Brooke, *The Democrats of Marylebone* (London, 1839), gives a disillusioning and apparently accurate account of the early years of the new vestry.
8. *Observer,* 11 January, 11 April 1852.
9. Ibid., 20 February, 7 March 1852.
10. Ibid., 17 May 1852.
11. Ibid., 12 June 1853, 29 April 1855.
12. Ibid., 13 May 1855.
13. Ibid., 13, 20 May 1855.
14. Ibid., 19 March 1854.
15. Ibid., 6 May 1855.
16. *Metropolitan,* 19 June 1886.
17. *Observer,* 18 November 1855.
18. Ibid., 17 May 1857.
19. Ibid., 18 November 1855.
20. St. Marylebone Vestry Proceedings, 1856.
21. *Elector,* 26 August 1857.
22. *Marylebone Mercury,* 14 November 1857.
23. *Observer,* 14, 22 November 1858.
24. *Marylebone Mercury,* 22 March 1862.
25. Ibid., 10 May 1862.
26. Ibid., 17 May 1862.
27. Ibid., 20 October 1866.
28. Ibid., 22 February 1873, 10 February 1876.
29. Ibid., 1 April 1876, 15 December 1877.
30. Ibid., 25 June 1859.
31. Ibid., 18 June 1859, 29 May, 10 July 1880.
32. Ibid., 31 May 1879, 22 May 1880.
33. Ibid., 21 May 1881.
34. Ibid., 16 April 1859.
35. *Observer,* 17 October 1858, 17 June, 4 November 1860, 10 August 1862.
36. Ibid., 24 March 1861.
37. *Marylebone Mercury,* 21 May 1859.
38. *Observer,* 10, 17 February 1861.

39. Ibid., 20 December 1863.
40. *Marylebone Mercury,* 28 November 1863.
41. Ibid., 12 March 1864.
42. Ibid., 11 March 1865.
43. Ibid., 27 May, 3 June 1865.
44. Ibid., 6 October, 8 December 1866.
45. Ibid., 4 April–30 May 1868; *Observer,* 5–19 May 1868.
46. *Marylebone Mercury,* 20–27 November 1880.
47. *Observer,* 9 December 1855, 17 February 1856.
48. Vestry Proceedings, 8–22 March 1856.
49. *Marylebone Mercury,* 15 December 1862.
50. Ibid., 24 September, 8, 15, 29 October 1864.
51. *Supplement to the 35th Annual Report of the Registrar-General,* 1875, xviii (1155), cxc–cxci.
52. *Marylebone Mercury,* 27 September 1873.
53. Ibid., 20 January 1877.
54. Ibid., 12 November 1881.
55. Ibid., 4 June 1887.
56. *Replies from Vestries and District Boards relative to Sanitary and Street Improvements,* 1872, xlix (298), 5–8.
57. Henry Jephson, *The Sanitary Evolution of London* (London, 1907), p. 105.
58. *Replies from Vestries and District Boards relative to Sanitary and Street Improvements,* 1872, xlix (298), 5–8.
59. *Marylebone Mercury,* 9 December 1876.
60. Ibid., 11 February, 5 May 1888.
61. Ibid., 13 February 1864.
62. Ibid., 9 November 1861.
63. Ibid., 18 January, 8 February 1862.
64. Ibid., 30 March, 6 April, 15, 22 June, 6 July 1867.
65. Ibid., 8 February 1879, 30 January 1880.
66. Ibid., 22 October 1881.
67. Ibid., 10 February 1883.
68. Ibid., 2 February 1884.
69. Ibid., 29 March 1884, 7 November 1885.
70. Ibid., 9 April 1887.
71. Ibid., 27 November 1869, 18 March, 8 July 1871, 2 February 1878.
72. Ibid., 26 February 1876, 29 October 1881.
73. Ibid., 31 May 1884.
74. Ibid., 14 June 1884.
75. *Metropolitan,* 26 April 1873, 9 October 1880.
76. *Observer,* 31 August 1856.
77. Ibid., 26, 28 September 1856.
78. *Observer,* September–November 1856.
79. Vestry Proceedings, 25 April 1857; *Observer,* 20 April 1857.
80. *Correspondence between the Poor Law Board and St. Marylebone, etc.,* 1857 (i), xiii (119), 1–86.
81. *Observer,* 24 May 1857.
82. Ibid., 31 May 1857.
83. *The Times,* 22 May 1857.
84. *Observer,* 14, 21 June, 19 July 1857.

85. Ibid., 18 July 1858.

86. Ibid., 19 September 1858.

87. *Marylebone Mercury,* 1, 8 January 1859.

88. Ibid., 25 January 1864.

89. Ibid., 23 July 1863.

90. *Observer,* 24 March, 2 June 1861.

91. *Marylebone Mercury,* 1, 15 July, 7, 14 October, and 4, 11 November 1876.

92. *Northern Kensington, Survey of London,* xxxvii (London, 1973), 330.

93. *Marylebone Mercury,* 20 December 1879; *Metropolitan,* 2 August 1884.

94. *Marylebone Mercury,* 10, 24 June, 22 July 1882, and 6 January, 13 October 1883.

95. Ibid., 4 February 1888.

96. *Observer,* 5, 19 January, 17 July 1862.

97. *Marylebone Mercury,* 18 November 1865–13 January 1866.

98. Ibid., 28 June 1873; *Second Annual Report of the Local Government Board,* 1873, xxix (748), 83.

99. *Marylebone Mercury,* 14, 28 March, 11, 18 April 1885.

100. Ibid., 4 July, 28 November 1885.

13. ST. PANCRAS

1. F. H. W. Sheppard, *Local Government in St. Marylebone, 1688–1835* (London, 1958), p. 9.

2. Ibid., pp. 158–160.

3. Quoted by Hugh C. Prince in J. T. Coppock and Hugh C. Prince (eds.) *Greater London* (London, 1964), pp. 95, 97.

4. Ibid., pp. 80–141.

5. James Williamson Brooke, *The Democrats of Marylebone* (London, 1839), pp. 20–21.

6. *St. Pancras Vestry. Report of the Chairman of the St. Pancras Vestry Finance Committee on Old Paving Commissioners' Mortgage Debts,* 14 May 1897, pp. 8–9 (copy in GLC History Library, County Hall, London, bound with *Abstract of Cash Received etc. by Vestry of Saint Pancras,* 1896–97).

7. *St. Pancras,* pt. IV, in *Survey of London,* vol. xxiv (London, 1952), p. 7.

8. Brooke, *Democrats of Marylebone,* pp. 21–3, 27.

9. Walter E. Brown, *The St. Pancras Book of Dates* (London, 1908), pp. 17–18.

10. Sheppard, *Local Government,* p. 296.

11. Brooke, *Democrats of Marylebone,* pp. 27, 29, 59, 121.

12. Ibid.

13. *Return of Names of Church Trustees of St. Pancras,* 1852–3, lxxviii (530), p. 237.

14. Brooke, *Democrats of Marylebone,* p. 113.

15. *Second Report from Select Committee on Poor Relief,* 1861, ix (323), Mins. Evid., Streeten, Q. 7215.

16. *Observer,* 1, 14 March 1852, 13, 28 February, 28 March, 10 April, 8 May 1853, 28 May 1854, 7 October 1860.

17. *Marylebone Mercury,* 2 April 1859.

18. *Observer,* 29 July 1855.

19. Brown, *Book of Dates,* p. 25.

20. *Observer,* 25 March, 30 May, 7, 14 June 1852, 17 April 1853, 22 January 1854.

21. *Hansard,* 3rd ser., *137,* c. 712 (16 March 1855).

22. *Observer,* 10 December 1854, 1 April 1855.

23. *Hansard,* 3rd ser., *137,* c. 709–711 (16 March 1855).

24. *Observer,* 7, 15, 29 July, 5 August 1855.

25. Ibid., 30 September, 7, 14 October, 18, 25 November 1855, 12 April 1857, 30 May 1858.

26. Ibid., 25 November, 9 December 1855, 3 February, 29 June 1856, 31 May 1857; *Metropolitan,* 28 June, 5 July 1856; *Second Report from Select Committee on Metropolitan Local Government,* 1866, xiii (452), Mins. Evid., D. E. Cameron, Q. 5632.

27. *Observer,* 30 May 1858, 2 January 1860; *Marylebone Mercury,* 28 May 1859.

28. *Second Report from Select Committee on Metropolitan Local Government,* 1866, xiii (452), Mins. Evid., J. Salter, Q. 3568, 3576, 3622, and D. E. Cameron, Q. 5633.

29. *St. Pancras Guardian,* 25 May 1878, 5 August 1882, 4 October 1884, 20 October 1888; *McCalmont's Parliamentary Poll Book: British Election Results, 1832–1918* (London, 1972).

30. *St. Pancras Guardian,* 5 August 1882, 4 October 1884.

31. *Observer,* 27 September, 11, 31 October, 7 November 1857, 14, 28 November 1858, 15 May, 18 September 1860, 25 May, 15 June 1862; *St. Pancras Times,* 30 October, 6, 20 November 1858.

32. *Shoreditch Observer,* 6 November 1859.

33. *Marylebone Mercury,* 28 June, 18 October 1862, 19 October 1867, 1 February 1868, 9 July 1870, 1 June 1878.

34. *Abstract of Cash Received and Expended by the Vestry of Saint Pancras,* 1859–60, p. 10, 1863–64, p. 12, and 1869–70, p. 17 (copies of these and the other *Abstracts of Cash* cited are in the GLC History Library, County Hall); *St. Pancras Guardian,* 7 February 1885; Frederick Boase, *Modern English Biography* (London, 1965).

35. William Booth Scott, *St. Pancras, 1890: Report on Condition Anterior to 1856* . . . (London, c. 1891), pp. 12–16 (copy in GLC History Library, County Hall).

36. *Replies from Vestries and District Boards relative to Sanitary and Street Improvements,* 1872, xlix (298), 9–12.

37. *Metropolitan,* 29 August 1874; *St. Pancras Guardian,* 11 March 1876.

38. Brown, *Book of Dates,* p. 39.

39. Percy J. Edwards, *History of London Street Improvements, 1855–1897* (London, 1898), p. 65.

40. Scott, *St. Pancras, 1890,* pp. 21–26, 120–153.

41. *Abstract of Cash,* 1888–89, p. 145.

42. *Report of the Chairman of the St. Pancras Vestry Finance Committee on Old Paving Commissioners' Mortgage Debts,* 14 May 1897.

43. Walter E. Brown, *A Short History of St. Pancras Cemeteries* (London, 1896), pp. 28, 29, 33, 37.

44. Ibid., pp. 15–16.

45. *The Times,* 7, 30 June, 3, 4, July, 21 November, 8 December 1866; *Illustrated London News,* 7 July 1866; Scott, *St. Pancras, 1890,* pp. 40–41.

46. Brown, *St. Pancras Cemeteries,* pp. 16–17.

47. Ibid., pp. 17–24.

48. *St. Pancras Vestry Annual Accounts and Reports,* 1895–96, pp. 161–173 (copy

in GLC History Library, County Hall).

49. Brown, *Book of Dates*, p. 51.

50. *Observer*, 16 December 1855, 20 January, 3 February 1856, 31 January 1858.

51. Ibid., 27 January, 24 February 1861, 4 January, 7 June 1863; *Marylebone Mercury*, 25 February 1865, 23 March 1867; *St. Pancras Times*, 17 July 1858; *North Londoner*, 21 October 1871.

52. *North Londoner*, 9 March 1872; *St. Pancras Guardian*, 5 August 1876.

53. *Marylebone Mercury*, 10, 26 October 1872; *St. Pancras Guardian*, 20 March 1875; *St. Pancras Vestry: Abstracts of Accounts*.

54. Walter E. Brown, *The St. Pancras Poor* (London, 1905), p. 18.

55. *Correspondence . . . between the Poor Law Board and the Local Authorities of St. Marylebone and St. Pancras . . . 1857* (i), xiii (119), 87, 185.

56. Brown, *St. Pancras Poor*, p. 26; *Twentieth Annual Report of the Poor Law Board*, 1867–68, xxxiii (4039), 15.

57. Brown, *St. Pancras Poor*, pp. 19, 21, 24–25.

58. *Observer*, 22 March, 14 November, 12 December 1858.

59. *The Times*, 19 July 1865, 22 March 1866.

60. Brown, *St. Pancras Poor*, pp. 40–41.

61. Ibid., pp. 33–34, 41.

62. *Marylebone Mercury*, 13, 27 March, 3 April, 11 December 1869, 2, 16 April 1881.

63. Ibid., 25 March 1871, 6 July 1872.

64. Ibid., 18 December 1869, 14 April 1877; *South London Journal*, 17 August 1872.

65. *North Londoner*, 31 August 1872; *St. Pancras Guardian*, 19 August 1876.

66. Brown, *St. Pancras Poor*, pp. 27–32.

67. *First Annual Report of M.O.H. of St. Pancras*, 1856, pp. 1–24; *Tenth Report of M.O.H.*, 1865, pp. 1–4; *Sixteenth Report of M.O.H.*, 1871, p. 2 (copies of these and other M.O.H. Reports cited are in GLC History Library, County Hall).

68. *Seventh Report of M.O.H.*, 1862, p. 6.

69. *Marylebone Mercury*, 17 April 1858; *Third Report of M.O.H.*, 1858, pp. 1–18.

70. *Eleventh Report of M.O.H.*, 1866, p. 19.

71. *Sixteenth Report of M.O.H.*, 1871, pp. 4, 5; *Twentieth Report of M.O.H.*, 1875, p. 3; *Marylebone Mercury*, 20, 27 January 1866; *St. Pancras Guardian*, 18 December 1875.

72. *Replies from Vestries and District Boards relative to Sanitary and Street Improvements* 1872, xlix (298), 9–12.

73. *First Report of M.O.H.*, 1856, p. 10; *The Builder*, 4 October 1845, p. 470, 5 September 1846, p. 421.

74. *St. Pancras Vestry. Report of the Commissioners for Public Baths and Wash-houses*, 1882–83 (copy in GLC History Library, County Hall).

75. *Sixth Annual Report of M.O.H.*, 1861, p. 2; *Ninth Annual Report*, 1864, p. 3; *Tenth Annual Report*, 1865, pp. 2–3.

76. *Ninth Annual Report of M.O.H.*, 1864, p. 3.

77. *Twenty-First Annual Report of M.O.H.*, 1876, p. 6.

78. *Twenty-Sixth Annual Report of M.O.H.*, 1881, p. 3.

79. *Eleventh Annual Report of M.O.H.*, 1866, p. 19: *Nineteenth Annual Report*, 1874, p. 8: *Twenty-Fifth Annual Report*, 1880, p.18: *Twenty-Seventh Annual Report*, 1882, p. 29: *Twenty-Eighth Annual Report*, 1883, p. 22.

80. *St. Pancras Vestry. Reports of the Chairman of the Sanitary Committee,* 1884, 1885, 1887 (copy in GLC History Library, County Hall); *Royal Commission on the Housing of the Working Classes,* 1884–85, xxx (4402), Mins. Evid., Dr. Murphy, Q. 1572–1892.

81. *Thirty-First Annual Report of M.O.H.,* 1886, p. 28.

82. *St. Pancras Vestry. Report of the Chairman of the Sanitary Committee,* 1890 (copy in GLC History Library, County Hall).

83. *St. Pancras Vestry. Report of a Special Committee, adopted by the Vestry,* 10 May 1899 (copy in GLC History Library, County Hall); *LCC Minutes,* 1 November 1898, pp. 1244–45, 25 July 1899, pp. 1139–41, 13 March 1900, p. 388, 23 July 1901, p. 1071.

84. *St. Pancras Vestry. Report of a Special Committee, adopted by the Vestry,* 10 May 1899; *Thirty-First Annual Report of M.O.H.,* 1886, p. 27.

85. Brown, *Book of Dates,* pp. 58, 61, 66.

14. ST. GEORGE THE MARTYR

1. R. Price-Williams, "The Population of London, 1801–81," *Journal of the Statistical Society,* 48 (1885), 351–440.

2. John Binny, "Thieves and Swindlers," in Henry Mayhew, *London Labour and the London Poor: Those That Will Not Work* (London, 1862), pp. 330–334.

3. *South London News,* 3 November 1855.

4. *South London Journal,* 2 June 1857.

5. *Second Report from the Committee on Metropolitan Local Government,* 1866, xiii (452), Mins. Evid., D. Birt, Q. 5022–26, 5037–39; *South London News,* 2 August 1856.

6. *South London Journal,* 23, 30 March 1858.

7. Ibid., 30 March, 18 May, 1 June 1858, 21, 28 May 1859.

8. Ibid., 13 April 1858; *South London News,* 29 June 1857.

9. *South London Journal,* 7 April 1857; *South London News,* 16 May 1857.

10. *South London (Local) Journal,* 3 June 1856, 10 November 1857; Henry Jephson, *The Sanitary Evolution of London* (London, 1907), pp. 143–144 (quotation).

11. Jephson, *Sanitary Evolution,* p. 147.

12. Ibid., p. 149.

13. *South London Journal,* 4 August, 8 September, 10 November 1857.

14. Ibid., 10 November 1857.

15. Ibid., 10, 30 November, 29 December 1857.

16. *Second Report from the Committee on Metropolitan Local Government,* 1866, xiii (452), Mins. Evid., W. Rendle, Q. 6904.

17. Ibid., Q. 6900, 6904.

18. Ibid., Q. 6908.

19. *South London Journal,* 31 August, 21 September 1858.

20. Ibid., 21 September, 14 December 1858.

21. Ibid., 31 August 1858.

22. Ibid., 14, 28 December 1858.

23. Ibid., 5, 19 February 1859.

24. Ibid, 26 March 1859.

25. Ibid., 27 August 1859.

26. *South London Chronicle,* 12 May 1860.

27. *South London Journal,* 10 September 1859.

28. Ibid., 7 December 1861.

29. Ibid., 5 November 1864.

30. Ibid., 17 December 1864; *South London Press,* 4, 11 February 1865.

31. *South London Press,* 29 July, 12, 16 August 1865.

32. Ibid., 9 September 1865, *The Times,* 7 Sept. 1865.

33. *South London Press,* 30 September 1865.

34. Ibid., 7 October 1865.

35. Ibid., 21 October, 11, 18 November 1865.

36. *South London Journal,* 6 October 1857, 14 January 1860.

37. Ibid., 24 August 1858, 26 November 1859.

38. Ibid., 30 January, 27 February 1864.

39. Ibid., 15 June 1858, 26 February 1859, 5 January 1861.

40. Ibid., 24 August 1861, 17 January 1863.

41. 27 and 28 Vict., *cap.* 116; Thomas Mackay, *A History of the English Poor Law,* vol. III (London, 1899).

42. *The Lancet,* 15 July 1865, pp. 73–74, 23 December 1865, p. 711.

43. 30 Vict., *cap.* 6; Mackay, *English Poor Law,* III, 491–492.

44. *South London Press,* 4 September 1869, 30 March 1872.

45. *The Lancet,* 2 September 1865, p. 267.

46. *South London Press,* 2 September 1865.

47. *Eleventh Annual Report of the Vestry of St. George the Martyr, Southwark,* 1867, p. 15 (the GLC History Library, County Hall, contains this and the other cited vestry reports).

48. *Second Report from the Committee on Metropolitan Local Government,* 1866, xiii (452), Mins. Evid., W. Rendle, Q. 6899–6982; *Third Report from the Committee on Metropolitan Local Government,* 1867, xii (301), Mins. Evid., W. Rendle, Q. 1220–90.

49. *Eleventh Annual Report of the Vestry,* 1867, p. 3.

50. *South London Press,* 7 July 1866, 21 September 1867, 3 April 1869.

51. *South London Journal,* 28 January 1871.

52. *Replies from Vestries and District Boards relative to Sanitary and Street Improvements,* 1872, xlix (298), 27.

53. *Fifteenth Annual Report of the Vestry,* 1871, pp. 11–12.

54. *South London Press,* 21 January 1865, 10 February, 22 September 1877, 14 February 1880.

55. *Twenty-Fourth Annual Report of the Vestry,* 1880, p. 15.

56. *South London Press,* 8 January 1876, 11 February 1882, 19 March 1887.

57. *Twenty-First Annual Report of the Vestry,* 1877, pp. 26–27.

58. *Thirty-Eighth Annual Report of the Vestry,* 1894, p. 24.

59. *South London News,* 7 November, 13, 27 December 1856, 30 May 1857; *South London Chronicle,* 3, 10 December 1859, 14 January 1860; *South London Journal,* 9 June 1860, 13 July 1861.

60. *South London Press,* 25 May, 1 June 1878.

61. Ibid., 10 May, 5 July 1873, 23 June, 9 July 1878, 7 May 1887.

62. Ibid., 20 June 1868, 17 February 1876.

63. *South London Journal,* 8 January 1859; *South London Chronicle,* 18 February 1860.

64. *South London Press,* 22 June 1872, 8 May 1875.

65. Ibid., 14 May 1870, 15 May 1875, 13 May 1876.

66. Anthony S. Wohl, ed., *The Bitter Cry of Outcast London* (Leicester, 1970).

67. *Royal Commission on the Housing of the Working Classes, 1884–85,* xxx (4402), Mins. Evid., Andrew Mearns and George Sims, Q. 5344–5793.

68. *Sixteenth Annual Report of the Vestry,* 1872, p. 10.

69. *Fifteenth Annual Report of the Vestry,* 1871, p. 12.

70. *Twentieth Annual Report of the Vestry,* 1876, p. 10.

71. *Twenty-Eighth Annual Report of the Vestry,* 1884, p. 14; London County Council, *The Housing Question in London, 1855–1900* (London, 1900), pp. 123–126, 299.

72. Percy J. Edwards, *History of London Street Improvements, 1855–1897* (London, 1898), p. 73.

73. *Twelfth Annual Report of the Vestry,* 1868, p. 42; *Twenty-Fifth Annual Report,* 1881, p. 11.

74. *Twenty-Eighth Annual Report of the Vestry,* 1884, p. 14.

75. Gareth Stedman Jones, *Outcast London: A Study of Relationships between the Classes in Victorian Society* (Oxford, 1971), pp. 322, 326.

76. LCC, *Housing Question,* pp. 226–228, 243–247.

77. *Thirty-Seventh Annual Report of the Vestry,* 1893, pp. 14–15, 28; *Fortieth Annual Report,* 1896, pp. 12–13.

78. *Thirty-Eighth Annual Report of the Vestry,* 1894, pp. 8–13: London County Council, *London Statistics,* XI (London, 1902), 138–144.

79. LCC, *London Statistics,* XII (London, 1903), 86.

15. ST. LEONARD, SHOREDITCH

1. *Borough of Shoreditch, 1899–1900. Municipal Reports and Accounts,* XLIV, 39 (copy in GLC History Library, County Hall).

2. *St. Leonard, Shoreditch,* in *Survey of London,* vol. VIII (London, 1922), pp. 99–100, plate 1.

3. GLRO (L), MBW 234, second quarterly report of Shoreditch M.O.H., 30 September 1856.

4. P. G. Hall, *The Industries of London since 1861* (London, 1962), p. 99.

5. P. G. Hall, "The East London Footwear Industry," *East London Papers,* 5, (1962), 7.

6. Hall, *Industries,* pp. 71–93.

7. *Replies from Vestries and District Boards relative to Sanitary and Street Improvements,* 1872, xlix (298), 15.

8. *Shoreditch Observer,* 27 February 1858.

9. Sidney and Beatrice Webb, *English Local Government: The Parish and the County* (London, 1906), p. 228.

10. St. Leonard, Shoreditch Vestry Minutes, 1849–1853 (Hackney Public Library, Pitfield Street).

11. *Shoreditch Advertiser,* 5 June, 26 July 1862.

12. *Shoreditch Observer,* 9 May 1857.

13. Ibid., 24 April 1858.

14. Ibid., 3 April 1858.

15. Ibid., 7 August, 11 September 1858.

16. 21 and 22 Vict., *cap.* 132, local.

17. *Hackney Express,* 24 May 1884.

18. Ibid., 14 April 1875; *Ventilator,* 16 April 1875.

19. *Hackney Express,* 5 November 1881, 12 June 1886, 28 January 1888.

20. Ibid., 5 March 1870.

21. Ibid., 26 May 1888; *Thirty-Fifth Annual Report of the Vestry of St. Leonard, Shoreditch,* 1891, p. 10 (the GLC History Library, County Hall, contains this and the other vestry annual reports that are cited).

22. *Fourth Annual Report of the Vestry,* 1860, p. 31.

23. *Shoreditch Observer,* 11 May 1861; *Hackney Express,* 10 September 1870.

24. *Hackney Express,* 21 January 1871.

25. Ibid., 24 January 1874.

26. Ibid., 5 December 1877, 12 January 1878.

27. *Shoreditch Observer,* 2 May 1857.

28. *Hackney Express,* 24 June 1876.

29. Ibid., 20 May 1876.

30. Ibid., 19 December 1885, 25 December 1886, 29 January 1887; *Shoreditch Observer,* 30 June 1860.

31. *Shoreditch Observer,* 24 January 1857.

32. Ibid., 18 August 1860, 28 September, 2 November, 14, 28 December 1861, 4 January, 1, 8, 22 February, 8 March, 19 April, 3, 24 May 1862, 21 May, 13 August 1864.

33. Ibid., 5 July 1862.

34. *Hackney Express,* 15 September 1877, 11 September 1880, 7 May 1881; Report of Vestry Committee Appointed 7 September 1880 on the Surveyor's Department (Hackney Public Library, Pitfield Street).

35. *Hackney Express,* 15 April 1871; *Ventilator,* 25 April 1871, 12 December 1873.

36. *Hackney Express,* 20 January 1872.

37. Ibid., 6 June 1874, 27 April 1878, 30 June 1883; *Shoreditch Observer,* 3 July 1858, 16, 30 April, 13 August 1859, 10 April, 29 September 1860, 20 March, 7 September 1861, 28 July 1866.

38. *Shoreditch Observer,* 23 October 1858, 30 June, 28 July 1860, 13 June 1863, 14 January, 21 October 1865, 16 November 1867.

39. 32 and 33 Vict., *cap.* 67.

40. *Fifteenth Annual Report of the Vestry,* 1871, p. 6.

41. *Hackney Express,* 5 July 1873, 12 December 1874, 9 October 1875, 6 October 1877.

42. *Shoreditch Observer,* 7 January, 8 April 1865.

43. *Hackney Express,* 13, 20, 27 January 1872.

44. Ibid., 19 August 1871.

45. *Shoreditch Observer,* 28 December 1867, 18 January 1868.

46. *Hackney Express,* 19 August 1871.

47. *Shoreditch Observer,* 1 September 1860.

48. Ibid., 21 August 1858, 22 March 1862; *Hackney Express,* 9 October 1869, 12 August 1882.

49. *The Builder,* 5 August 1848, p. 382.

50. *Hackney Express,* 6 July 1874.

51. *Shoreditch Observer,* 11 October 1862, 28 February 1863.

52. *The Lancet,* 29 July 1865, pp. 131–133.

53. *Hackney Express,* 17 December 1870; *The Builder,* 18 May 1872, p. 382.

54. *Hackney Express,* 21 January 1871.

55. Ibid., 24 January 1874.

56. Figures calculated by dividing the total ratable values by the population figures contained in the census of 1871.

57. *Shoreditch Observer,* 29 July 1865, 7 December 1867.

58. *Fourteenth Annual Report of the Vestry,* 1870, pp. 12–13.

59. Ibid.

60. Royston Lambert, *Sir John Simon (1816–1904) and English Social Administration* (London, 1963), p. 342; *DNB.*

61. GLRO (L), MBW 234, preliminary report of Dr. Robert Barnes, 10 April 1856.

62. Ibid.

63. GLRO (L), MBW 234, quarterly reports of M.O.H., 1856–57.

64. Ibid.; *Eighth Annual Report of the Vestry.* 1864, pp. 20–23.

65. *Fifteenth Annual Report of the Vestry,* 1871, pp. 26–27.

66. *Fourth Annual Report of the Vestry,* 1860, pp. 24–25; see also generally, GLRO (L), MBW 234, quarterly reports of M.O.H., 1856–57, and *Third Annual Report* to *Eighth Annual Report of the Vestry,* 1859–1864.

67. *Seventh Annual Report of the Vestry,* 1863, p. 27: *Eighth Annual Report,* 1864, pp. 11, 18.

68. *Report of a Public Inquiry into the Sanitary Condition of Certain Premises in Shoreditch,* 1890–91, lxviii (143), 8.

69. *Eleventh Annual Report of the Vestry,* 1867, pp. 23–30.

70. *Third Annual Report of the Vestry,* 1859, p. 10; *Fifth Annual Report,* 1861, p. 11; *Eighth Annual Report,* 1864, p. 12; *Ninth Annual Report,* 1865, p. 22.

71. *Royal Commission on the Housing of the Working Classes,* 1884–85, xxx (4402), Mins. Evid., Rev. J. W. Horsley, Q. 2266–68, and Ralph Clutton, Q. 6410–22.

72. R. Price-Williams, "The Population of London, 1801–81," *Journal of the Statistical Society,* 48 (1885), 418–419.

73. *Ninth Annual Report of the Vestry,* 1865, p. 34.

74. Frederick Boase, *Modern English Biography* (London, 1965), under Sutton.

75. *Hackney Express,* 5 March 1870.

76. Ibid., 28 January 1888.

77. Ibid., 19 November 1870, 28 January 1888.

78. *Twenty-Third Annual Report of the Vestry,* 1879, p. 8; Percy J. Edwards, *History of London Street Improvements, 1855–1897* (London, 1898), p. 109.

79. For this and the following paragraphs in the text see, except where otherwise stated, *Report of a Public Inquiry into the Sanitary Condition of Certain Premises in Shoreditch,* 1890–91, lxviii (143), pp. 643–653.

80. *Thirty-Fifth Annual Report of the Vestry,* 1891, p. 119.

81. Henry Jephson, *The Sanitary Evolution of London* (London, 1907), p. 267.

82. *Shoreditch Observer,* 21 September 1867.

83. *Thirteenth Annual Report of the Vestry,* 1869, pp. 21–22.

84. *Twenty-Ninth Annual Report of the Vestry,* 1885, p. 85.

85. London County Council, *The Housing Question in London, 1855–1900* (London, 1900), p. 82; Gareth Stedman Jones, *Outcast London* (Oxford, 1971), p. 325.

86. Quoted in Anthony S. Wohl, "The Housing of the Working Classes in London, 1815–1914," in *The History of Working-Class Housing: A Symposium,* ed. Stanley D. Chapman (Newton Abbot, 1971), pp. 20, 45.

87. *Royal Commission on the Housing of the Working Classes,* 1884–85, xxx (4402),

Mins. Evid., Dr. J. W. Tripe, Q. 9555–64.

88. *Third Annual Report of the Vestry*, 1859, p. 14.

89. *Thirteenth Annual Report of the Vestry*, 1869, p. 20.

90. *Twenty-First Annual Report of the Vestry*, 1877, p. 38.

91. *Twenty-Ninth Annual Report of the Vestry*, 1885, p. 83.

92. *Twenty-First Annual Report of the Vestry*, 1877, p. 39: *Twenty-Second Annual Report*, 1878, pp. 39–42: *Twenty-Third Annual Report*, p. 9: *Twenty-Eighth Annual Report*, 1884, pp. 75–76.

93. *Twenty-Sixth Annual Report*, 1882, p. 16.

94. *Kensington M.O.H. Report*, 1923.

95. *Thirty-Fifth Annual Report of the Shoreditch Vestry*, 1891, p. 120.

96. Ibid., pp. 120–121; *Thirty-Fourth Annual Report*, 1890, pp. 80–81.

97. Wohl, "The Housing of the Working Classes," p. 20.

98. *Hackney Express*, 1870–1888, esp. 13 August 1881 (quotation).

99. *Thirty-Second Annual Report of the Vestry*, 1888, pp. 12–14.

100. *Thirty-Sixth Annual Report of the Vestry*, 1892, pp. 3, 17, 20; and generally *Twenty-Ninth Annual Report* to *Thirty-Ninth Annual Report*, 1885–1895, and *Borough of Shoreditch, 1895–96. Municipal Reports and Accounts*, vol. XL.

101. *Thirty-Sixth Annual Report of the Vestry*, 1892, p. 2; *Thirty-Seventh Annual Report*, 1893, pp. 3–4; LCC, *Housing Question*, pp. 249–250.

102. *Thirty-Sixth Annual Report of the Vestry*, 1892, pp. 12–17; *Thirty-Ninth Annual Report*, 1895, p. 2; *Borough of Shoreditch, 1897–98. Municipal Reports and Accounts*, XLII, 1–4; *1898–99*, XLIII, 1–3.

103. Figures calculated by dividing the total ratable values contained in London County Council, *London Statistics*, XI (London, 1900–01), 139, by the population figures contained in the census of 1901.

104. The individual items, in round figures, were as follows:

Street improvements and paving	£63,300
Sewers	43,700
Street lighting	2,800
Underground lavatories	10,500
Scavenging depot	5,700
Open spaces	2,500
Town Hall additions	10,500
Nile Street housing scheme (land and buildings)	46,900
Libraries	17,000
Baths and wash-houses	69,500
Refuse destructor (land and plant)	22,500
Electricity works (land and plant)	121,300

See *Borough of Shoreditch, 1899–1900. Municipal Reports and Accounts*, XLIV, 359–361.

105. LCC, *London Statistics*, XI, 340–341.

106. *Borough of Shoreditch, 1899–1900. Municipal Reports and Accounts*, XLIV, 362–361.

107. *Borough of Shoreditch, 1899–1900. Municipal Reports and Accounts*, XLIV, 39–40.

CONCLUSION

1. Percy J. Edwards, *History of London Street Improvements, 1855–1897* (London, 1898); I. G. Gibbon and R. W. Bell, *History of the London County Council, 1889–1939* (London, 1939).

2. Gibbon and Bell, *London County Council,* p. xix.

3. Dorothy M. Corlett, "The Metropolitan Board of Works, 1855–1889" (Ph.D. diss., University of Illinois, 1943); D. S. Elliott, "The Metropolitan Board of Works, 1855–1889" (M.Phil. thesis, University of Nottingham, 1972).

4. There is a bibliographical survey in H. J. Dyos, "Agenda for Urban Historians," in H. J. Dyos, ed., *The Study of Urban History* (London, 1968), pp. 1–46.

5. Donald Olsen, *The Growth of Victorian London* (London, 1976), pp. 17–18.

6. Frederick Whelen, *The Government of London* (London, 1898), p. 4. See also G. L. Gomme, *London, 1837–1897* (London, 1898), p. 38.

7. J. P. D. Dunbabin, "British Local Government Reform: The Nineteenth Century and After," *English Historical Review,* 365, no. 92 (1977), 785.

8. John Stuart Mill, *Considerations on Representative Government* (London, 1861), p. 268.

9. Quoted in J. W. Probyn, ed., *Local Government and Taxation in the United Kingdom* (London, 1882), pp. 81–82.

10. Asa Briggs, "Birmingham: The Making of a Civic Gospel," in Asa Briggs, *Victorian Cities* (London, 1963), pp. 187–243; E. P. Hennock, *Fit and Proper Persons: Ideal and Reality in Nineteenth Century Urban Government* (London, 1973).

11. J. D. Gledstone, *Public Opinion and Public Spirit in Sheffield* (Sheffield, 1867), cited in Dennis Smith "Social Conflict and Urban Education," in D. A. Reeder, ed., *Urban Education in the Nineteenth Century* (London, 1977), pp. 112–113.

12. H. J. Dyos and D. A. Reeder, "Slums and Suburbs," in H. J. Dyos and Michael Wolff, eds., *The Victorian City: Images and Realities,* I (London and Boston, 1973), 539–560. See also A. D. King's edition of George Godwin, *Town Swamps and Social Bridges, 1851* (Leicester, 1971), and Anthony Wohl's edition of *The Bitter Cry of Outcast London, 1883* (Leicester, 1970).

13. Henry Jephson, *The Sanitary Evolution of London* (London, 1907), pp. 7–8.

14. *Cops and Bobbies: Police Authority in New York and London, 1830–1870* (Chicago, 1977). For the London police, see T. F. Reddaway, "London in the Nineteenth Century: The Origins of the Metropolitan Police," *The Nineteenth Century,* 147 (1950), 104–118; B. E. Lewis, "The Home Office, the Metropolitan Police, and the Problem of Civil Disorder, 1886–1892" (M. Phil. thesis, University of Leeds, 1972); and John Wilkes, *London Police in the Nineteenth Century* (Cambridge, 1977).

15. Asa Briggs, "London: The World City," in Briggs, *Victorian Cities,* pp. 323–372.

16. George Rudé, *Hanoverian London, 1714–1808* (London, 1971), ch. 7; F. H. W. Sheppard, *Local Government in St. Marylebone, 1688–1835: A Study of the Vestry and the Turnpike Trust* (London, 1958).

17. Derek Fraser, *Urban Politics in Victorian England* (Leicester, 1976).

18. David Cannadine, "Victorian Cities: How Different," *Social History,* 4, no. 1 (1977), 457–482; G. A. B. Finlayson, "The Politics of Municipal Reform, 1835," *English Historical Review,* 81 (1966), 673–692; E. P. Hennock, "Finance and Politics in Urban Local Government in England, 1835–1900," *Historical Jour-*

nal, 6, no. 2 (1963), 212–225, and *Fit and Proper Persons;* Peter Searby, "Progress and the Parish Pump: Local Government in Coventry, 1820–1860," *Birmingham Archaeological Proceedings and Transactions,* 88 (1976); D. Smith, "Social Conflict," pp. 95–114.

19. David Cannadine, "From Feudal Lords to Figureheads," *Urban History Yearbook, 1978* ((Leicester, 1978), pp. 23–35.

20. M. J. Daunton, *Coal Metropolis: Cardiff, 1870–1914* (Leicester, 1977). For a different point of view, see Hennock, *Fit and Proper Persons*; and H. E. Meller, *Leisure and the Changing City, 1870–1914* (London, 1976).

21. J. R. Kellett, "Municipal Socialism, Enterprise, and Trading in the Victorian City," *Urban History Yearbook, 1978,* pp. 36–45. See also A. M. McBriar, *Fabian Socialism and English Politics, 1884–1918* (Cambridge, 1972).

22. For example, D. J. Rowe, "The Failure of London Chartism," *The Historical Journal,* 9 (1968), 472–487; and I. J. Prothero, "Chartism in London," *Past and Present,* 44 (1969), 76–105. There is a description of London's politics and government in Francis Sheppard, *London, 1808–1870: The Infernal Wen* (London, 1971).

23. Francis Nicholson, Jr., "The Politics of English Metropolitan Reform, 1876–1889" (Ph.D. thesis, University of Toronto, 1972); and Ken Young, "The Politics of London Government, 1880–1889," *Public Administration,* 51 (Spring 1973), 91–108.

24. J. P. D. Dunbabin, "The Politics of the Establishment of County Councils," and "Expectations of the New County Councils," *Historical Journal,* 6, no. 2 (1963), 226–252, and 8, no. 3 (1965), 353–379.

25. Ken Young, "The Conservative Strategy for London, 1855–1875," *The London Journal,* 1, no. 1 (1975), 56–81, and *Local Politics and the Rise of Party: The London Municipal Society and the Conservative Intervention in Local Elections, 1894–1963* (Leicester, 1975).

26. John Stevens, "The London County Council under the Progressives, 1889–1907" (M.A. thesis, University of Sussex, 1966); David Rubinstein, "Socialisation and the London School Board, 1870–1904: Aims, Methods, and Public Opinion," in Philip McCann, ed., *Popular Education and Socialisation in the Nineteenth Century* (London, 1977), pp. 231–264; Paul Thompson, *Socialists, Liberals, and Labour: The Struggle for London, 1885–1914* (London, 1967).

27. "Our Mean Metropolis," *Punch,* 27 (1854), 158.

28. R. A. Lewis, *Edwin Chadwick and the Public Health Movement, 1832–1854* (London, 1952).

29. T. F. Reddaway's article is in *The Nineteenth Century,* 148 (1950), 118–130. See also A. K. Mukhophadhay, "The Politics of London Water," *The London Journal,* 1, no. 2 (1975), 207–224; and Pedro Schwartz, "John Stuart Mill and Laissez-Faire: London Water," *Economica* 33 (February 1966), 71–83.

30. F. M. L. Thompson, *Hampstead: Building a Borough 1650–1964* (London, 1974), pp. 75–209.

31. This information was provided by W. E. Luckin from an unpublished article on the politics of pollution in Victorian London.

32. For these grievances, see D. A. Reeder, "The Politics of Urban Leaseholds in Late-Victorian England," *International Review of Social History,* 6 (1961), 1–18.

33. "Tenification" was a term used by Progressives to refer to Conservative plans to divide London into separate municipalities: see Young, "Conservative Strategy," p. 64, n. 33.

34. H. J. Dyos, *Victorian Suburb: A Study of the Growth of Camberwell* (Leicester, 1961). For other descriptions of parish government, see the references in *Local History in London: Research and Publications* (London, 1975).

35. Janet Roebuck, "Local Government and Some Aspects of Social Change in the Parishes of Lambeth, Battersea, and Wandsworth, 1838–1888" (Ph.D. thesis, University of London, 1968). Published as *Urban Development in Nineteenth-Century London* (London, 1979).

36. Thompson, *Hampstead,* pp. 399–400.

37. For a fuller discussion of this subject, see D. A. Reeder, "Capital Investment in the Western Suburbs of Victorian London" (Ph.D. thesis, University of Leicester, 1965).

38. This has been studied by Patricia Malcolmson, "The Potteries of Kensington: A Study in Slum Development in Victorian London" (M.Phil. thesis, University of Leicester, 1970).

39. C. A. Maclaren, "Local Government, 1855–1964," in P. D. Whitting, ed., *A History of Fulham* (London, 1970), pp. 114–129. Thirty-seven out of sixty-seven members of the District Board represented trade interests prior to 1870, and sixteen out of thirty-seven members after 1870.

40. There is a description of this war of the shopkeepers in Richard Lambert's biography of William Whiteley, *The Universal Provider* (London, 1938).

41. Norman F. Smith, "Nineteenth Century Civil Engineering," *History of Science,* 13 (1975), 104–113.

42. Ralph Turvey, *The Economics of Real Property* (London, 1957); and H. J. Dyos, "Urban Transformation: A Note on the Objects of Street Improvement in Regency and Early Victorian London," *International Review of Social History,* 2 (1957),259–265. For a comparative view, see Anthony Sutcliffe, *The Autumn of Central Paris: The Defeat of Town Planning, 1850–1970* (London, 1970).

43. Turvey, *Real Property,* pp. 102–122.

44. W. M. Stern, "Water Supply in Britain: The Development of a Public Service," *Royal Sanitary Institute Journal,* 74 (1954), 998–1004; and Malcolm Falkus, "The Development of Municipal Trading in the Nineteenth Century," *Business History Review,* 19 (1977), 134–161.

45. LCC, *London Water Supply* (London, 1905); H. W. Dickinson, *The Water Supply of Greater London* (London, 1954); R. W. Morris, "Geographical and Historical Aspects of the Public Water Supply of London, 1852–1902" (Ph.D. thesis, University of London, 1941).

46. For example, Stirling Everard, *History of the Gas, Light, and Coke Company, 1812–1849* (London, 1949).

47. T. C. Barker and Michael Robbins, *A History of London Transport,* vol. I (London, 1963).

48. The details of this financial story are in Philip Cottrell, "Investment Banking in England, 1856–1882: Case Study of the International Finance Society" (Ph.D. thesis, University of Hull, 1974).

49. A select list of more recent contributions would include: Valerie Cromwell, "Interpretations of Nineteenth Century Administration," *Victorian Studies,* 9, no. 3 (1966), 245–255; Jennifer Hart, "Nineteenth Century Social Reform: A Tory Interpretation," *Past and Present,* 31 (1965), 73–86; Gillian Sutherland, ed., *Studies in the Growth of Nineteenth Century Government* (London, 1972), and *Policy Making in Elementary Education, 1870–1885* (London, 1973), and "Recent Trends in Administrative History," *Victorian Studies,* 13, no. 4 (1970),

408–411; R. S. Lambert, "Central and Local Relations in Mid-Victorian England: The Local Government Act Office," *Victorian Studies*, 6, no. 2 (1962), 121–150; Roy M. MacLeod, "The Alkali Acts Administration," *Victorian Studies*, 9, no. 3 (1966), 85–112, and *Treasury Control and Social Administration: a Study of Establishment Government at the Local Government Board, 1871–1905* (London, 1968). The most important stimulus to local studies was E. C. Midwinter's *Social Administration in Lancashire: Poor Law, Public Health, and Police* (Manchester, 1969).

50. For example, A. M. Froshaug, "Poor Law Administration in a Number of London Parishes, 1750–1850" (M.A. thesis, University of Nottingham, 1969). Other local studies of London and the provinces are cited in Derek Fraser, ed., *The New Poor Law in the Nineteenth Century* (London, 1976).

51. James O'Neill, "Finding a Policy for the Sick Poor," *Victorian Studies*, 7, no. 3 (1964), 265–284.

52. Gwendoline M. Ayers, *England's First State Hospitals and the Metropolitan Asylums Board, 1867–1930* (London, 1971).

53. Gareth Stedman Jones, *Outcast London: A Study of Relationships between the Classes in Victorian Society* (Oxford, 1971).

54. David Rubinstein, *School Attendance in London, 1870–1904: A Social History* (Hull, 1969).

55. A. G. Ruffhead, "The Office of Metropolitan Buildings, 1844–1855" (M.Phil. thesis, University of Leicester, 1973).

56. Anthony Wohl, *The Eternal Slum: Housing and Social Policy in Victorian London* (London, 1977).

57. Royston Lambert, *Sir John Simon (1816–1904) and English Social Administration* (London, 1963).

58. Anthony Wohl, "Unfit for Human Habitation," in Dyos and Wolff, *Victorian City*, II, 603.

59. W. E. Luckin, "The Final Catastrophe — Cholera in London, 1866," *Medical History*, 21, no. 1 (1977), 32–42. See also Luckin's bibliographical survey, "Death and Survival in the City: Approaches to the History of Disease," *Urban History Yearbook, 1980* (Leicester, 1980), pp. 53–62.

60. Harold Malchow, "Free Water: The Public Drinking Fountain Movement in Victorian London," *The London Journal*, 4, no. 2 (1978), 181–201.

61. J. S. Tarn, *Five Per Cent Philanthropy: An Account of Housing in Urban Areas, 1840–1914* (Cambridge, 1973).

62. Wohl, *Eternal Slum*, p. 339.

63. Kellett, "Municipal Socialism," p. 40.

64. J. V. Steffel, "The Boundary Street Estate: An Example of Urban Redevelopment by the London County Council, 1889–1914," *Town Planning Review*, 47, no. 2 (1976), 161–173.

65. E. J. T. Brennan, ed., *Education for National Efficiency: The Contribution of Sidney and Beatrice Webb* (London, 1975). Several theses and dissertations have been written on London's educational development in this period. For a general survey, see J. S. Maclure, *One Hundred Years of London Education, 1870–1970* (London, 1970).

66. According to a report of François Béderida's lecture to the Urban History Group conference, in *Urban History Yearbook, 1974* (Leicester, 1974), pp. 11–12.

67. See, for example, W. Pett Ridge, "Faults of Londoners," *Nineteenth Century*, 66 (1909), 303–309.

68. National Civic Federation, *Municipal and Private Ownership of Public Utilities*

(New York, 1907); Hugo R. Meyer, *Municipal Ownership in Great Britain* (London, 1906).

69. David Dunstan, Department of History, University of Melbourne, has kindly provided information on colonial responses to the MBW and LCC arising from his own research on Melbourne and the Melbourne — London links: "The Life and Times of the Board of Works," *The Australian Municipal Journal,* May 1978. See also Bernard Barrett, *The Inner Suburbs* (Melbourne, 1971).

70. Ken Young, " 'Metropology' Revisited: On the Political Integration of Metropolitan Areas," in *Essays on the Study of Urban Politics,* ed. Ken Young (London, 1975), p. 135.

71. For the background to the formation of the Greater London Council, see Gerald Rhodes and G. R. Ruck, *The Government of Greater London* (London, 1970); and Frank Smallwood, *Greater London: The Politics of Metropolitan Reform* (New York, 1965). See also Ken Young and John Kramer, *Strategy and Conflict in Metropolitan Housing: Suburbia versus the Greater London Council, 1965–1975* (London, 1978).

72. See Anthony Sutcliffe, "Environmental Control and Planning in European Capitals, 1850–1914: London, Paris, and Berlin," in Ingrid Hammarstrom and Thomas Hall, eds., *Growth and Transformation of the Modern City* (Stockholm, 1979), pp. 71–88.

73. H. J. Dyos and Michael Wolff, "The Way We Live Now," in *Victorian City,* pp. 893–907; and D. E. C. Eversley, "Searching for London's Lost Soul," *The London Journal,* 1, no. 1 (1975), 103–107.

Bibliography

This bibliography not only lists materials used by David Owen but is intended to provide a guide to the study of London government and administration in the nineteenth century.

The main primary sources for the history of London government are the 25,000 or more volumes of the records of the predecessors of the London County Council, as listed by Ida Darlington, *Guide to the Records of the London Record Office*, pt. I (London: LCC, 1963). Students should also refer to her commentaries, "The Registrar of Metropolitan Buildings and His Records" and "The London Commissioners of Sewers and Their Records," *Journal of the Society of Archivists,* 1 (1955) and 2 (1962). Another useful guide is Ralph Hyde's catalogue, *The Printed Maps of Victorian London, 1851–1900* (Folkestone: William Dawson, 1975), based on the archival resources of the City and County of London. This catalogue lists numerous maps of London's municipal areas. In addition to the central records, each of the London borough libraries holds a collection of archives, including minute books of vestries and vestry committees. These local archives, a considerable but underused resource for London history, contain much incidental information on housing, medical, and social conditions in the London parishes. The annual reports of Medical Officers of Health are especially informative.

For this volume, David Owen sampled local archives and went through all sixty volumes of the minute books of the MBW. He also read the annual reports of the Board and looked more selectively at some of the other series of accounts and papers, to gain a better understanding of the official record. Yet he found the minute books disappointingly reticent about the goings-on behind the scenes: they told him little, as he admitted later, about the pressures and attitudes which affected decisionmaking. That is why it is so necessary for students of London government to consult newspapers, periodicals, and the parliamentary papers, all of which throw light on national and local opinion about the mechanics and nature of London administration. The extent to which David Owen made use of such sources is a significant feature of this book. In particular, the coverage given to London's municipal affairs in national and London newspapers seems to have been almost a revelation to him: the color and detail of their reports opened up the possibility of studying the politics of London's mid-Victorian government.

This bibliography (which does not include the papers of the MBW) lists only those newspapers and periodicals that David Owen himself consulted; but the section on Parliamentary papers includes most of the papers that are concerned with London government and urban services in the nineteenth century. The very number of these papers is testimony to the importance of London's affairs to Parliament. The bibliography divides them into two main groups: General Finance and Administration, and Specific Topics. The Specific Topics include Bridges, Communications, and Improvements; Fire Brigades; Gas Lighting; The Thames: Main Drainage and Pollution; The Thames Embankment; and The Metropolitan Water Supply. The last subgroup under Specific Topics, headed Other Topics, is a very selective listing of the more important papers relating to the Metropolitan Police, Housing, Poor Relief, and Open Spaces. This list of parliamentary papers does not include, however, the series containing the annual reports of the MBW. The conventions used for citations of parliamentary papers are those of the General Index to the Irish University Press series.

The list of published writings (books, pamphlets, and articles), 1800–1914, sets out to provide a comprehensive guide to contemporary literature — descriptive, critical, and polemical. While the descriptive writings listed here are only a selection, there is a fuller listing of contributions to the politics and constitutional problems of London government. This part of the bibliography is divided into sections for ease of reference, as follows:

London General and Descriptive
London Government and Administration: General
London Government and Administration: Specific Topics
   (Buildings and Street Improvements; Gas, Water, and Electricity; Housing
   and Sanitation; Open Spaces; Police; Schooling and Education)
Municipal Reform: City Corporation and City Companies
Metropolitan Government Reform (to 1879, 1880–1890, 1891–1900, and
   1900–1914)
London Politics and Elections

In this section publishers are listed where such information is provided in catalogues and finding lists. Otherwise the place of publication only is given. The remainder of the bibliography, covering *secondary sources* since 1914, includes texts which David Owen consulted. It also includes a selection of writings about the twentieth-century problems of metropolitan government in London. But the main purpose of this part of the bibliography is to guide students to writings on the history of local government, administration, and social policy, both with regard to London and (more selectively) for the country as a whole. For London, this listing is supplemented by a section of biographical and autobiographical writings. Books and pamphlets listed in this bibliography are held by one of the following libraries: British Library, London Library, Members' Library County

Hall, and Guildhall Library. Finally, a list of theses and dissertations on London government and administration is provided. It was abstracted from the fuller compilation of P. L. Garside, "The Development of London: a classified list of theses presented to the Universities of Great Britain and Ireland, and the CNAA, 1908–1977" (*Guildhall Studies in London History*, 3, no. 3 [1978]). The list has been updated and supplemented by dissertations presented to American universities.

PARLIAMENTARY PAPERS, 1830–1900

General Finance and Administration

Select Committee Reports and Royal Commissions

Report of the Select Committee on Select Vestries, 1830, iv (215, 25), 425, 469.

Report of the Royal Commission on Municipal Corporation, Second Report, London and Southwark, 1837, xxv [239], 133.

Report of the Select Committee on Coal Duties (Metropolis), 1852–53, xxii (916), 125.

Report of the Royal Commission on Corporation of the City of London with information respecting its constitution, order and government, 1854, xxvi [1772], 1.

Report of the Select Committee on Metropolitan Taxation, 1861, viii (211), 1; *Second Report,* 1861, viii (372), 135; *Third Report,* viii (476), 381.

Report of the Select Committee on Metropolitan Government; First Report, 1861, viii (211), 1; *Second Report,* viii (372), 135; *Third Report,* viii (476), 381.

Report of the Select Committee on Metropolitan Taxation, 1866, xiii (186), 171; *Second Report,* xiii (186), 317.

Report of the Select Committee on Metropolitan Government; First Report, 1866, xiii (452), 171; *Second Report,* xiii (452), 317.

Report of the Select Committee on Improvement Rates Bill (City of London), 1867, xii (135), 431; *Second Report,* xii (268), 435; *Third Report,* xii (301), 443.

Report of the Select Committee on Metropolitan Buildings and Management Bill, 1874, x (285), 333.

Report of the Select Committee on Metropolis Local Management Acts Amendment Bill, 1875, xii (194), 569.

Report of the Select Committee on the Metropolis Management and Building Acts Amendment Bill, 1878, xvi (98), 487.

Report of the Select Committee on the London Corporation (Charges of Malversation), 1887, x (161), 13.

Report of the Royal Commission on the Working of the MBW, Interim Report, 1888, lvi [c. 5560], 1; *Final Report,* 1889, xxxix [c. 5705], 319.

Report of the Select Committee on Coal Duties Abolition Bill, 1889, ix (228), 473.

Reports of the Commission on the Amalgamation of the City and County of London, 1894, xvii and xviii [c. 7493].

Accounts and Papers

Sums annually paid as Duty on Coals brought into the City of London since 1831, 1852–53, xcix (236), 65.

Number of inhabited houses in each of the parishes within the Registrar-General's Metropolitan District, and of rateable value . . . , 1854–55, liii (190), 51.

Number of parishes in schedules (A) and (B) of Acts 18 and 19 Vict. cap. 120; names and

*numbers of wards into which each parish has been divided; number of parochial represen-
tatives; number of ratepayers entitled to vote at parochial election in 1855*, 1857, xli
(3333), 229, 235.

*Return of annual amount of salary paid to each vestry clerk of Metropolitan parishes under the
Metropolis Local Management Act*, 1857 (Sess. 2), xli (345), 273.

*Return from the MBW of replies received from Vestries and District Boards of Metropolis
asking for information of works of sanitary and street improvements since the passing of
Metropolis Local Management Act, 1855*, 1857, xlix (298), 585.

*Number of ratepayers in each of twenty-three parishes in Schedule (A) of the Metropolis Local
Management Board of Works. Similar returns from parishes united into districts under
Schedule (B) of Act*, 1862, xlvii (240), 239.

*Sum placed to credit of Thames Embankment and Metropolis Improvement Fund on passing
of Coal and Wine Duties Act*, 1863, 1 (317), 161.

*Return of rateable value of property and of population of each Parish comprised in Metropolis
Local Management Act; number of officers employed and salaries paid*, 1864, 1 (379), 47.

Total quantities of coal brought by sea, rail or canal within limits of coal duty radius, 1867,
lviii (212), 437.

*Return by the MBW of the number of sites, set apart under the Metropolitan Street Improve-
ment Act, 1872*, 1877, lxxi.

Returns showing staff, etc. of the Metropolitan Board of Works, 1867–68, lviii (17), 221.

*Sum contributed by MBW to improvements within City of London specifying proportion to-
wards estimated gross total cost of improvements since date of Metropolitan Local Management Act, 1855, to end of 1874*, 1875, lxiv (113), 791.

*Return of salaries, fees, or other emoluments received by officers of Boards, during year ended
25 March 1889*, 1890–91, lxix (14), 29.

Specific Topics

Bridges, Communications, and Improvements

Report of the Select Committee on Blackfriars Bridge, 1836, xx (418), 65.

Report of the Select Committee on Waterloo and Southwark Bridges, 1836, xx (517), 1.

Reports of the Select Committee on Metropolitan Improvements; First Report, 1837–38, xvi
(418), 1; *Second Report*, 1837–38, xvi (661), 9.

Report of the Select Committee on Metropolitan Improvements, 1839, xiii (136), 459.

Reports of the Select Committee on Metropolitan Improvements; First Report, 1840, xii
(410), 1; *Second Report*, 1840, xii (485), 117.

Report of the Select Committee on the Embankment of the Thames, 1840, xii (554), 271.

Report of the Select Committee on Metropolitan Improvements, 1841, ix (398), 601.

Report of the Royal Commission on Metropolitan Improvements, 1844, xv [15], 1; 1845,
xvii [348, 619, 627]; 1846, xxiv [682]; 1847, xvi [861].

Report of the Royal Commission on Metropolitan Termini, 1846, xvii [719, 750–I, II], 91.

Report of the Select Committee on Condition etc. of Metropolitan Toll Bridges, 1854, xiv
(370), 1.

Report of the Select Committee on Metropolitan Communications, 1854–55, x (415), 1.

Proceedings of the Select Committee on Metropolitan Buildings Bill, 1854–55, vii (349),
469.

Report of the Select Committee on Chelsea Bridge Bill, 1857, ix (250), 27.

*Special Report of the Select Committee on Metropolitan Toll Bridges Bill and Chelsea Bridge
Toll Abolition Bill*, 1865, vii (380), 119.

Report of the Select Committee on the Piccadilly and Park Lane New Road Bill, 1865, viii (260), 647.

Report of the Select Committee on Metropolitan Board of Works (Leicester Square Improvement) Bills in case of Metropolitan Board of Works (Shoreditch Improvement) Bill, 1871, xl (142), 281.

Report of the Select Committee on Freeing of Remaining Toll-paying Bridges over the Thames, 1876, xiv (244), 435.

Report of the Select Committee on Toll Bridge (River Thames) Bill, 1876, xiv (328), 555.

Return of expenditure by Corporation of London out of Bridge Estate for erection of London Bridge; maintenance during present century; purchase (and maintenance) of Southwark Bridge; erection of Blackfriars Bridge; maintenance since charged on Bridge Estates, 1876, lxiii (143), 511.

Return by Metropolitan Board of Works of number, etc. of sites set apart under the Metropolitan Street Improvement Act, 1872, for dwellings, 1877, lxxi (146), 695.

Report of the Select Committee on the Metropolis Toll Bridges Bill, 1877, xiv (156), 1.

Report of the Select Committee on Metropolitan Board of Works (Thames Crossings) Bill, 1884, xiv (299), 1.

Report of the Select Committee on Corporation of London Tower Bridge Bill, 1884–85, viii (228), 47.

Report of the Select Committee on Town Improvements (Betterment), 1894, xv (92), 235.

Fire Brigades

Report of the Select Committee on Metropolitan Fire Brigades, 1844, xiv (347).

Report of the Select Committee on Fires in the Metropolis, 1862, ix (221), 1.

Report on the Constitution, Efficiency, Emoluments and Finance of the Metropolitan Fire Brigade, and into the most Efficient Means of providing security from loss of life and property by fire in the Metropolis, 1876, xl (371), 53.

Similar Report, 1877, xiv (342), 37.

Correspondence between the Metropolitan Board of Works and the Home Office on the Origin of Fires in London during the last four years, 1886, lvii (116), 325.

Gas Lighting

Report of the Select Committee as to existing arrangements for Metropolis Supply, 1857–58, xi (393), 665.

Report of the Select Committee as to existing arrangements for Metropolis Supply, 1859 (Sess. 1), iii (224), 507.

Select Committee, Minutes of Evidence, on Sale of Gas Act Amendment Bills, 1860, xxi (462), 429.

Report of the Select Committee on Metropolis Gas Bill, 1860, xxi (493), 29.

Report of the Select Committee on London (City Corporation Gas, etc.) Bills, 1866, xii (270), 63.

Special Report of the Select Committee on the Metropolis Gas Bill, 1867, xii (520), 1.

Report of the Select Committee on the Metropolis Gas Companies Bill, 1875, xii (281), 1.

Report of the Select Committee on the Metropolis Gas (Surrey Side) Bill, 1876, xi (384), 1.

The Thames: Main Drainage and Pollution

Report of the Select Committee on Metropolis Sewers, 1834, xv (584), 197.

Report of the Select Committee on the Embankment of the Thames, 1840, xii (554), 271.

Report of the Select Committee on Metropolis Sewage Manure, 1846, x (474), 535.
Minutes of Evidence of Select Committee on Greater London Drainage Bill (1853), 1852–53, xxvi (629), 387.
Reports of the Metropolitan Sewers Commissioners, 1854, lxi (84), 389.
Reports of the Board of Health on the Drainage of Metropolis, 1854, lxi [180], 113.
Report (on Metropolitan Sewage and Drainage) presented to Board of Works by Messrs Hawkesley, Bidder and Bazalgette (with plans), 1857–58, xlviii (419), 145.
Report to First Commissioner of Works by Commander Burstal on State of River from Putney to Rotherhithe, 1857 (Sess. 1), xiii (17), 165.
Report of Mr. Gurney to First Commissioner of Works on the State of the Thames in the Neighbourhood of Houses of Parliament, 1857–58, xlviii (21), 423.
Report of the Select Committee on the best means of providing for increasing traffic of Metropolis by Embankment of Thames, 1860, xx (494), 321.
Report of the Select Committee on the best means of utilising sewage of cities and towns of England, with view to reduction of local taxation and benefit of agriculture, 1862, xiv (160), 321.
Report of the Select Committee on the Thames Embankment Bill, 1863, xii (344), 413.
Report of the Select Committee on plans for dealing with sewage of Metropolis and other large towns, with view to its utilisation to agricultural purposes, 1864, xiv (487), 1.
Report of Dr. Letheby and Bazalgette on inspection of manure and chemical works in neighbourhood of Northern and Southern outfalls of main drainage, 1865, xlvii (332), 39.
Special Report of the Select Committee on Metropolitan Sewage and Essex Reclamation Bill, 1865, viii (171), 29.
First Report of the Royal Commission on the best means of preventing Pollution of Thames, vols. I and II, 1866, xxxiii [3634], 1.
Report of the Royal Commission upon Inquiry as to Pollution of Thames at Barking, 1870, xl [c. 7], 545.
Special Report on Local Government Provisional Orders (No. 3) Bill (relating to Drainage of Lower Thames Valley), 1884, xiii (272), 71.
Report of the Select Committee on Lower Thames Valley Main Sewerage Bill, 1884–85, x (217), 5.
First Report of the Royal Commission on the effects of discharge into Thames, 1884, xli [c. 3842], 1; *Second Report*, 1884–85, xxxi [c. 4253], 341.

The Thames Embankment

Report of the Select Committee on the Embankment of the River Thames, 1860, xx (494).
Report of the Royal Commission on Plans for Embanking River Thames within Metropolis, 1861, xxxi [2872], 267.
Correspondence relating to works under Thames Embankment Bill, 1862, xlvii (369), 507.
Report on Plans for Embanking Surrey Side of Thames within Metropolis, 1862, xxviii [3043], 61; 1863, xxvi [3093].
Report of the Royal Commission for making communication between Embankment at Blackfriars Bridge and Mansion House, and also between Embankment at Westminster Bridge and Embankment at Millbank, 1863, xxvi [3093], 431.
Report on Thames Embankment (South Side), Bill, 1863, xii (367), 547.
Correspondence with Conservators of River Thames with regard to filling in Embankment with gravel dredged from River, 1865, xlvii (209), 13.
Report of the Select Committee on whether land reclaimed from Thames between Whitehall

Place and Whitehall Gardens should be appropriated to advantage of inhabitants of the Metropolis, 1871, xii (411), 375.

Correspondence with Mr. Charles Gore on Land on Thames Embankment, 1872, xxxvi (609).

Minutes of the Evidence of Select Committee on Thames Embankment (Land) Bill, 1872, xii (287), 73.

Report from the Select Committee appointed on Thames Conservancy Acts, and to inquire and report what amendments are required to deal with injuries by floods, 1877, xvii (367), 1.

Report from the Select Committee on Thames River (Prevention of Floods) Bill, 1877, xvii (280), 301.

Report of the Select Committee on Thames River (Prevention of Floods) Bill, 1878–79, xiii (178), 515.

Reports of the Select Committee on Metropolitan Board of Works (Thames Crossings) Bill, 1884, xiv (255), 1.

The Metropolitan Water Supply

Report of the Select Committee (House of Lords) on Metropolis Water Supply, 1852, xxi [H. of L. 253].

Report of the Select Committee on Metropolis Water Supply, 1852, xii (395), 1.

Reports of the Board of Health on Metropolis Water Supply, 1852, lii [2137], 251; 1857, xiii [2203], 49.

Special Report on Waterworks Bill, 1865, xii (401), 445.

Report of Select Committee on East London Water Bills and on operation of Metropolis Water Act, 1852, 1867, ix (399), 1.

Report by Capt. Tyler to Board of Trade on Quantity and Quality of Water supplied by East London Waterworks Co., 1867, lviii (339), 441.

Report of the Royal Commission on means of obtaining additional supplies of good water for the Metropolis and other large towns, 1868–69, xxxiii [c. 4169], 1.

Special Report of the Select Committee on Metropolis Water (No. 2) Bill, 1871, xi (381), 1.

Reports by Mr. William Pole on Constant Service System in 1870 and 1871, 1872, xlix (101), 725.

Minutes of proceedings taken before Commissioners appointed by the Board of Trade under the Metropolis Water Act, 1871, 1873, xxxviii (679), 1.

Report of the Select Committee on London Water Supply, 1880, x (329), 111.

Report from the Select Committee of the House of Lords on Water Companies (Regulation of Powers) Bill, 1884–85, xii (197), 385.

Report of the Royal Commission on the Water Supply of the Metropolis, 1893–94, xl [c. 7172], 1.

Report of the Royal Commission on Water Supply within the limits of the Metropolitan Water Companies; First Report, 1899, xli [c. 9122], 491.

Other Topics

Metropolitan Police

Reports of the Select Committee on Metropolitan Police, 1833, xiii (675), 401; 1834, xvi (600), 1.

Metropolitan Housing

Report of the Select Committee on Artisans' and Labourers' Dwellings Improvement Acts and Metropolis Streets Improvements Act; First Report, 1881, vii (358), 395; *Second Report,* 1882, vii (235), 249.

Report of the Royal Commission on the Housing of the Working Classes, 1884–85, xxx, xxxi [c. 4402–I and II].

Return of Buildings erected in the Metropolis and City of London (Artisans' and Labourers' Dwellings Act), 1886, lvii.

Metropolitan Poor Relief

Reports of the Select Committee on Poor Relief, Second Report, 1861, x (323).

Metropolitan Open Spaces

Report of the Select Committee on Open Spaces (Metropolis), 1865, viii (390), 259.

Return of Commons and Open Spaces (Metropolis), 1866, xlvii (461), 757.

NEWSPAPERS AND PERIODICALS, 1850–1900
(cited or used by David Owen)

General

The Builder
Contemporary Review
Daily Chronicle
Daily News
Daily Telegraph
The Echo
Edinburgh Review
Elector
Evening News
Financial News
Fortnightly Review
Gas Lighting
The Globe
Hansard
Illustrated London News
The Lancet
Lloyds
London and Westminster Review
Morning Post
National Review
Nineteenth Century
Observer
Pall Mall Gazette
Punch
Quarterly Review
St. James Gazette
Saturday Review

Spectator
Standard
The Times
Weekly Times
Westminster Review

London City and District Newspapers (dates refer to the years covered by David Owen's notes)

City Press, 1857–1888
Clerkenwell Press, 1878
East London Observer, 1857
Hackney Express, 1869–1888
The Hornet, 1868–1872
Marylebone Mercury, 1857–1888
Metropolitan, 1856–1857, 1872–1886
North Londoner, 1871–1872
St. Pancras Guardian, 1874–1888
St. Pancras Times, 1858
Shoreditch Advertiser, 1862
Shoreditch Observer, 1857–1869
South London Advertiser, 1855
South London Chronicle, 1859–1860
South London Journal, 1856–1871
South London News, 1855–1857
South London Press, 1865–1887
Ventilator, 1871–1875

BOOKS, PAMPHLETS, AND ARTICLES, 1800–1914

London, General and Descriptive

Besant, Sir Walter. *East London.* London: Chatto and Windus, 1901.
———— *London in the Nineteenth Century.* London: Adam & Charles Black, 1909.
———— *South London.* London: Chatto and Windus, 1899.
———— and Gerald Mittoni. *The Fascination of London.* 2 vols. London: Adam & Charles Black, 1902.
Booth, Charles. *Life and Labour of the People in London.* 9 vols. London and New York: Macmillan, 1895.
Bosanquet, C. B. P. *London: Some Account of Its Growth, Charitable Agencies, and Wants.* London: Hatchard and Co., 1868.
Britton, J[ohn.] *The Original Picture of London, Enlarged and Improved,* 26th ed. London, 1826.
Brooke, James Williamson. *The Democrats of Marylebone.* London: W. J. Cleaver, 1839.
Brown, Walter E. *The St. Pancras Book of Dates.* London: St. Pancras, 1908.
———— *The St. Pancras Poor.* London: St. Pancras, 1905.
Cotton, W. J. R. "The City of London: Its Population and Position," *Contemporary Review,* 41 (January 1882), 72–87.
[Dodd, George.] "The Growth of the Map of London," *Edinburgh Review,* 104 (1856), 51–73.

Elmes, James. *London and Its environs in the Nineteenth Century, Illustrated by a Series of Views from Original Drawings, etc.* London, 1831.

[Fonblanque, Albany de] "Social Progress in London," *Temple Bar,* 50 (1877), 392.

Gilbert, William. *The City.* London: Daldy, Isbisler and Co., 1877.

Gomme, Sir G. Laurence. *London.* London: Williams and Norgate, 1914.

———— *London in the Reign of Victoria, 1837–1897.* London: Blackie and Son, 1898.

———— *The Making of London.* Oxford: Clarendon Press, 1912.

Hillary, Sir William. *Suggestions for the Improvement and Embellishment of the Metropolis.* London, 1825.

Hogg, John. *London As It Is: Being a Series of Observations on the Health, Habits, and Amusements of the People.* London, 1837.

"How London Grows," *Chambers' Edinburgh Journal,* 23 April 1853, pp. 257–260.

Jay, Rev. Arthur Osborne. *Life in Darkest London.* London, 1891.

———— *The Social Problem and Its Solution.* London, 1893.

———— *A Story of Shoreditch.* London, 1896.

Kelly, Sir Fitzroy. *The City of London.* London, 1884.

Leigh [Samuel]. *Leigh's New Picture of London.* London, 1818.

Loftie, W. J. *A History of London.* 2 vols. London: Edward Stanford, 1883–1884.

———— *London City: Its History, Streets, Traffic, Buildings, People.* London: Leadenhall Press, 1891.

Low, Sydney J. "The Rise of the Suburbs: A Lesson of the Census," *Contemporary Review,* 60 (October 1891), 545–558.

Mayhew, Augustus. *Paved with Gold, or the Romance and Reality of the London Streets.* London: Downey, 1899.

Mayhew, Henry. *London Labour and the London Poor.* 4 vols. London: Griffen Bohn, 1861–1862.

Moore, H. C. *Omnibuses and Cabs: Their Origins and History.* London: Chapman Hall, 1902.

Nash, John, and J[ohn] White. *Some Account of the Proposed Improvements of the Western Part of London,* 2nd ed. London, 1815.

Pasquet, D. "Le Developpement de Londres," *Annales de Géographie,* 8 (1899).

———— *Londres et les Ouvriers de Londres.* Paris, 1913.

Price-Williams, H. "The Population of London, 1801–1881," *Journal of the Statistical Society,* 48 (1885), 349–432.

Reddie, James. "England's Future Bulwarks," *Cornhill Magazine,* 2 (October 1860), 493–500.

Ritchie, J. E. *Here and There in London.* London; Tweedie, 1859.

[Robertson, J. C., and T. Byerley.] *London.* 3 vols. London, 1823.

Sala, G. A. "The Great Invasion," in *Looking at Life, or Thoughts and Things.* London, 1860.

Salmon, James, ed. *Ten Years Growth of the City of London: Report, Local Government and Taxation Committee of the Corporation with the Results of the Day Census, 1891.* London: Corporation of London, 1891.

Smith, G. Barnett. "The Growth of London," *Cornhill,* 39 (January 1879), 41–60.

Steevens, G. W. *Glimpses of Three Nations.* London and Edinburgh: William Blackwood, 1902.

Tyler, F. E. "The Transformation of London," *Home Counties Magazine,* 7 (1905), 105–256.

Vermont, Marquis de, and Sir Charles Darnley [pseuds.] *London and Paris, or Comparative Sketches.* London, 1823.

Wheatley, Henry Benjamin. *The Story of London.* London: J. M. Dent and Co., 1904.

White, James. "London and Rome," *Blackwoods,* 42 (August 1837), 159–169.

Yates, Edmund. *The Business of Pleasure.* London, 1865.

London Government and Administration: General

Arnold, Arthur. *Social Politics.* Ch. 5, "The Government of London"; Ch. 6, "The City." London, 1878.

Ashley, Percy W. L. *Local and Central Government: A Comparative Study of England, France, Russia, and the United States.* London: John Murray, 1906.

────── "The London Government Act of 1899," *Municipal Affairs,* 4 (September 1900), 481.

[Baumann, A. A.] "London County Council," *Universal Review,* 7 (1894), 493–518.

[Beachcroft, R. M., and H. P. Harris.] "Work and Policy of the LCC," *The National Review,* 24 (February 1895), 828–846.

Beaven, Alfred B. *The Aldermen of the City of London, Henry III–1912.* 2 vols. London: Corporation of London, 1908–1913.

Birch, Walder de Gray [An Antiquary], ed. *The Historical Charters and Constitutional Documents of the City of London.* London: Whiting & Co., 1884.

Burns, John, and R. E. Prothero. "London County Council: i. Towards a Commune (Burns); ii. Towards Common Sense (Prothero)," *Nineteenth Century,* 31 (March 1892), 496–524.

Carpenter, William. *The Corporation of London, As It Is, and As It Should Be, with an Appendix of the Officers of the Corporation, and the Members of the Council.* London: W. Strange, 1847.

Chalmers, M. D. *Local Government:* London: MacMillan and Co., 1883.

Clarke, Henry. *London Government: The Local Government Act, 1888, in Its Application to London,* 3rd ed. London: Simpkins, Marshall & Co., 1888.

Collinridge, W. H. and L. *Sixty Years' Work of the Corporation of the City of London.* London: Corporation of London, 1897.

"Councillors and Contractors," *Spectator,* 4 May 1895, pp. 306–307.

Dexter, J. T. *The Government of London.* London: Edward Stanford, 1875.

Dickens, Charles. "The Metropolitan Vestry," *Household Words,* 5 (1852), 549–552.

Dickinson, W. H. "London County Council," *Municipal Journal,* 12 (19 October 1900), 813–883.

Dod's Handbook to the London County Council. London: George Bell & Sons, 1889.

"The Doings of the Metropolitan Board of Works," *Westminster Review,* 130 (1888), 568–580.

Dolman, Frederick. *Municipal Policy and Finance: The Case for the Defence.* London, 1906.

Donald, Sir Robert. *Six Years' Service for the People: Being a Brief Account of the Work of the London County Council.* London, 1895.

Dover, Ralph. *Metropolitan Board of Works.* London, 1856.

[Dyson, W. F.] "London County Council, Department of Works," *Saturday Review,* 83 (1897), 34, 57.

Fardell, T. G., and Charles Harrison. "The London County Council: i. The Impeachment (Fardell); ii. The Defence (Harrison)," *New Review*, 6 (1892), 257-272.

Firth, J. F. B. *The Constitution, Proceedings and Work of the London Council.* London: Knight and Co., 1888.

_____ *Municipal London: Or London Government As It Is and London under a Municipal Council.* London: Longmans, Green and Co., 1876.

_____ Edgar R. Simpson. *London Government under the Local Government Act, 1888.* London: Knight and Co., 1888.

Fletcher, Joseph. "The Metropolis: Its Boundaries, Extent, and Division for Local Government," *The Journal of the Statistical Society,* parts I and II, April and June 1844, pp. 69-85, 103-143.

[Fox, G. L.] "London County Council and Its Work," *Yale Review* (New Haven), 4 (1896), 80.

Gomme, Sir G. Laurence. *The Governance of London.* London: T. Fisher Unwin, 1907.

_____ *The L.C.C.: Its Duties and Powers according to the Local Government Act of 1888.* London, 1888.

Guyot, Yves. *L'Organisation Municipal de Paris et de Londres: Present et Avenir.* Paris: C. Marpen et E. Flammanan, 1883.

Harris, Percy A. *London and Its Government.* London: J. M. Dent and Sons, 1913.

[Harrison, Frederic.] "Lord Roseberry and the London County Council," *Nineteenth Century,* 27 (June 1890), 1026-39.

_____ "The Transformation of London," in *The Meaning of History,* pp. 412-436. New York: Macmillan, 1894.

[Hobhouse, Lord.] "London County Council and Its Assailants," *Contemporary Review,* 61 (March 1892), 404-416.

Hopkins, Albert Bassett. *The Boroughs of the Metropolis: A Handbook to Local Administration in London under the London Government Act, 1899.* London: Bemrose, 1900.

Hunt, John. *London Local Government.* 2 vols. London: Stevens & Sons, 1897.

"The Inefficiency of Municipal Administration," *Spectator,* 22 November 1890, pp. 724-725.

Isaacs, Sir Henry A. *Memories of My Mayoralty.* [London, 1890].

Judge, Mark H. *The Working of the Metropolitan Board of Works.* London: Trubner & Co., 1888.

London County Council. *Annual Reports of the Proceedings of the Council, 31 March 1890 to 31 March 1910.* London: LCC, 1910.

_____ *A Review of the First Year's Work, in a Series of Addresses by the Earl of Roseberry, Chairman of the Council, in April and May, 1890.* London: LCC, 1890.

_____ *London County Council and Poor-Law Administration.* London: LCC, [1908].

"The London County Council," *Spectator,* 29 December 1888, pp. 1845-46.

London Reform Union. *The Truth about the Works Dept. of the L.C.C.,* 2nd ed. Progressive Pamphlets, no. 21. London: London Reform Union, 1898.

Londoner, A. [pseud.] *The London Government Bill: Some Observations.* London: Sir Joseph Causton and Sons, 1883.

Macgill, G. H. *The London Poor and the Inequality of the Rates Raised for Their Relief.* London, 1858.

Mackay, Charles. *The Local Government of the Metropolis.* London, 1884.

Marks, Harry, and W. R. Lawson. *The Metropolitan Board of Works: A Brief Ac-*

count of the Disclosures Which Have Led to the Appointment of a Royal Commission to Investigate the Charges Brought against It. Reprint from the *Financial News.* London: Argus Printing Co., 1888.

[Martin, J.] "London County Council and Reform," *Forum,* 31 (1901), 318.

[Meath, Earl of.] "Works for the London County Council," *Nineteenth Century,* 25 (April 1889), 505–512.

Metropolitan Board of Works. *Pocket Book and Diary.* London, 1855–1888.

———— *Reports, 1865/66–1888.* London: MBW, 1889.

Metropolitan Board of Works Inquiry Committee. *First Report, Adopted at St. James's Hall, on December 21, 1888.* London, 1889.

"Metropolitan Board of Works," *Leisure Hour,* 32 (1883), 368.

The Metropolitan Year-Book. London, 1889.

Meyer, Hugo R. *Municipal Ownership in Great Britain.* London: Macmillan, 1906.

National Civic Federation. *Municipal and Private Ownership of Public Utilities.* 3 vols. New York: National Civic Federation, 1907.

New London: Her Parliament and Its Works. London: *Daily Chronicle,* 1895.

Newton, William. *Statement, at the Mile-End Vestry, in Relation to the Charges in Mr. Beal's Pamphlet against the Metropolitan Board of Works.* N.p., n.d.

Norton, George. *Commentaries on the History, Constitution and Chartered Franchises of the City of London,* 3rd ed. London: Longmans, 1869.

Orridge, B. Broyden. "The Corporation of London and Their Records," *Macmillans Magazine,* 20 (October 1869), 562–567.

———— *Some Account of the Citizens of London and Their Rulers, from 1060 to 1867.* London: William Tegg, 1867.

Pascoe, Charles E. "How London Is Governed," parts 1-V, *Appleton's Journal of Literature, Science and Art,* 12, 19, 26 July, 2, 23, August 1873.

Pell, Albert. *Reminiscences,* ed. with intro. by T. Makay. London: John Murray, 1908.

Phillips, William. *Sixty Years of Citizen Work and Play: Realities, Trivialities, Reminiscences and Letters,* with intro. by W. H. Dickinson. London: Alexander and Shepheard, [1910].

Powell, J. Enoch. *Municipal Trading: Report of a Conference.* London: London Municipal Society, 1902.

Price, John Edward. *A Descriptive Account of the Guildhall of the City of London: Its History and Associations.* London: Blades, East and Blades, 1886.

Probyn, J. W., ed. *Local Government and Taxation in the United Kingdom. A Series of Essays Published under the Sanction of the Cobden Club.* London: Cassen, Petter, Galpin & Co., 1882.

[Pulling, Alexander.] *The Laws, Customs, Usages and Regulations of the City and Port of London, with a Summary of the Commissioners' Report on the Corporation of London and the Municipal Government of the Metropolis,* 2nd ed. London: William Henry Bond, [1854].

Radford, G. H. *The Story of the London County Council.* London, [c. 1901].

Richardson, R. W. C. *Thirty-two Years of Local Self Government.* London, 1888.

Robinson, Daniel. "The Local Government of the Metropolis and Other Populous Places," *Blackwoods,* 36 (January 1831), 82–104.

Saunders, William. *History of the First London County Council.* London: National Press Agency, 1892.

Scott, William Booth. *St. Pancras, 1890: Report on Conditions Anterior to 1856, Works Executed, Improvements Effected since 1856, with Observations of a Comparative Nature.* London: Vestry of St. Pancras, 1890.

Seager, J. Renwick. *The Government of London under the London Government Act, 1899.* London: P. S. King & Son, 1899.

[Shaw, A.] "The Government of London," *Century* (New York), 19 (1891), 132.

_____ "The Government of London," *Review of Reviews* (New York), 10 (1892), 282.

Shaw, Albert. *Municipal Government in Great Britain.* New York: Macmillan, 1901.

Smith, J. Toulmin. *The Metropolis and Its Municipal Administration: Showing the Essentials of a Sound System of Municipal Self-Government.* London: Trelawny Saunders, 1852.

_____ *The Parish: Its Obligations and Powers.* London, 1854.

[Strachey, St. Loe.] "The Government of London: Municipal Administration," *Edinburgh Review,* 175 (1892), 500–517.

St. Pancras. *Medical Office of Health Reports,* 1856–1886. London: St. Pancras.

St. Pancras Vestry. *Report to Commission for Public Baths and Washhouses,* 1882–83.

_____ *Reports to the Chairman of the Sanitary Committee,* 1884, 1885, 1887.

_____ *Report of Chief Surveyor on Conditions anterior to 1856, Works Executed, Improvements Effected since 1856,* 1890.

_____ *Report to Special Committee Adopted by the Vestry,* 10 May 1899.

St. Pancras Vestry Finance Committee. *Report,* 1897.

The Times. The Story of the L. C. C. London, 1907.

Torrens, W. M. *The Government of London.* London: Kegan, Paul, Trench & Co., 1884.

[Tyler, G. R.] "Municipal Problems of London," *North American Review,* 159 (1894), 448.

[Webb, Sidney.] "The London County Council and Its Work," *Contemporary Review,* 67 (January 1895), 130–152.

Welch, Charles. *Modern History of the City of London: A Record of Municipal and Social Progress from 1760 to the Present Day.* London: Blades East & Blades, 1896.

Wemyss, Earl of, et al. *The Dangers of Municipal Trading.* London: Liberty and Property Defence League, 1899.

Whale, George. *Greater London and Its Government. A Manual and Yearbook.* London: T. Fisher Unwin, 1888.

Whelen, Frederick. *The Government of London.* London: Grant Richards, 1898.

Wilkins, Harold. *The New County of London, Showing the Practical Working of the Local Government Act, 1888, As Applied to the Metropolis.* London, 1888.

Wood, T. M. *Under Moderate Rule. First Year of Municipal Reform.* London, 1898.

[Wood, T. M.] "Attack on the London County Council," *Contemporary Review,* 73 (February 1898), 202–218.

London Government and Administration: Specific Topics

Buildings and Street Improvements

Bremner, C. S. "London Buildings," *Fortnightly Review,* 72 (August 1899), 291–316.

Edwards, Percy J. *History of London Street Improvements, 1855–1897.* London: P. S. King, 1898.

Elmes, James, and Thomas H. Shepherd. *Metropolitan Improvements, or London in the Nineteenth Century.* London: [Jones], 1827.

Fletcher, Banister. *Metropolitan Building Acts.* London: Batsford, 1882.

Harrison, Frederic. "London Improvements," *New Review,* 7 (October 1892), 414–421.

Hickson, W. E., and W. H. Leeds. "Metropolitan Improvements," *Westminster Review,* 36 (October 1841), 404–435.

"Metropolitan Buildings Act," *Penny Magazine,* 13 (1844), 479.

"Mud," *All the Year Round,* 11 February 1865.

"A Quarter of a Century of London Street Improvement," *The Builder,* 24 (1886), 887–888, 898–899.

Shaw-Lefevre, George. "London Street Improvements," *Contemporary Review,* 75 (February 1899), 203–217.

"Streets of London and the County Council," *Spectator,* 85 (1900), 740.

Williams, Robert. *More Light and Air for Londoners: the Effect of the New Streets and Buildings Bill on the Health of the People.* London: L. Reeve, 1894.

Gas, Water, and Electricity

Ashley, Percy."The Water, Gas and Electric Light Supply of London," *Annals of the American Academy of Political and Social Science,* 27 (January 1906), 20–36.

Chubb, Harry. "The Gas Supply of London," *Journal of the Statistical Society,* 39 (1876), 350–380.

"The City Lighting Muddle," *Municipal Journal,* 2 June 1899, p. 665.

Colburn, Zerah. *The Gas Works of London.* New York: Van Nostrand, 1868.

Dobbs, Archibald E. "The London Water Companies," *Contemporary Review,* 61 (January 1892), 26–38.

Firth, J. F. B. *The Gas Supply of London.* London: Edward Stanford, 1874.

Kent, W. G. *The Water Wastes of London.* London: E. and F. N. Spon, 1892.

Keppel, W. C. "Houselighting by Electricity," *Nineteenth Century,* 14 (July 1883), 31–52.

Kingsley, Charles. "The Water Supply of London," *North British Review,* 15 (May 1851), 228–253.

Liberty, W. J. "The Gas Supply of London," *Journal of Gas Lighting,* 75 (20 March 1900), 756.

Lloyd, John. *The London Water Companies versus the London People.* [London, 1886].

London County Council. *London Water Supply.* LCC Publication no. 882. London, 1905.

"The L.C.C. and the Increased Price of Gas in London," *Journal of Gas Lighting,* 76 (24 July 1900), 230, and 76 (23 October 1900), 1028.

London Reform Union. *The London Water Supply Question.* London Reform Union Pamphlet no. 77. London, [1896].

[Lubbock, J.] "London and the Water Companies," *Nineteenth Century,* 37 (April 1895), 657–664.

———— "The London Water Supply," *Nineteenth Century,* 31 (February 1892), 224–232.

Mathews, William. *Hydraulia: The Water Works of London.* London, 1835.

Nash, Vaughan. "The East London Water Company," *Contemporary Review,* 74 (October 1898), 474–479.

Preece, Arthur H. "The Electricity Supply of London," *American Gas Light Journal,* 68 (2 May 1898), 702.

Richards, A. G., and F. W. Pember. *The Metropolitan Water Act, 1902.* London: Butterworth & Co., 1903.

Richards, H. C., W. H. C. Payne, and J. P. H. Soper. *London Water Supply, Being a Compendium of the History, Law and Transactions Relating to the Metropolitan*

Companies from the Earliest Times to the Present Day, 2nd ed. London: P. S. King & Son, 1899.

Shadwell, Arthur. *The London Water Supply.* London: Longmans & Co., 1899.

Watherston, Edward J. *The Water Supply of the Metropolis: Addresses to the Delegates from the Vestries and District Boards of the Metropolis, March 27, 1879, and April 24, 1879.* London: J. Davy and Sons, [1879].

Williams, R. Price, and W. Shelford. *London Water Supply.* London: Waterlow and Sons, 1877.

Wright, John. *The Water Question.* London, 1828.

Housing and Sanitation, Including Drainage

Arnold-Forster, H. O. "The Dwellings of the Poor, no. iii: The Existing Law," *Nineteenth Century,* 14 (December 1883), 940–951.

Bazalgette, Joseph. *On the Main Drainage of London.* London, 1865.

Beames, Thomas. *The Rookeries of London: Past, Present and Prospective,* 2nd ed. London: Thomas Bosworth, 1852.

Booth, Charles. *Improved Means of Locomotion as a First Step towards the Cure of the Housing Difficulties of London.* London: Macmillan, 1901.

Brand, H. R. "The Dwellings of the Poor in London," *Fortnightly Review,* 35 (February 1881), 218–228.

Brown, Walter E. *A Short History of St. Pancras Cemeteries.* London: St. Pancras, 1896.

City of London. *The City of London Sewers Act, 1848 . . . 1851 and . . . 1897.* London: Corporation of London, 1899.

Coutts, Baroness Burdett, et. al. *Manual of the Law Affecting the Housing and Sanitary Condition of Londoners.* London: Kegan Paul, Tench & Co., 1884.

Cox, Harold. "Rehousing the Poor of London," *Westminster Review,* 134 (December 1890), 611–623.

Cross, Sir Richard. "Homes of the Poor in London," *Nineteenth Century,* 12 (August 1882), 231–242.

Fabian Society. *The House Famine and How to Relieve it.* London: Fabian Society, 1900.

Gavin, Hector. *The Habitations of the Industrial Classes: Their Influence on the Physical and on the Social and Moral Conditions of These Classes.* London: Society for Improving the Condition of the Labouring Classes, 1851.

———— *Sanitary Ramblings: Being Sketches and Illustrations of Bethnal Green.* London, 1848.

———— *The Unhealthiness of London and the Necessity for Remedial Measures.* London, 1847.

Godwin, George. *Town Swamps and Social Bridges.* London: Routledge, Warnes & Routledge, 1859

Greenwood, James. *The Seven Curses of London.* London: S. Rivers, 1869.

Greg, Percy. "Homes of the London Workmen," *Macmillans Magazine,* 6 (May 1862), 63–70.

[Harris, H. P.] "The London Housing Problem," *The National Review,* 34 (February 1900), 923–931.

[Hickson, W. E.] "The Corporation of London and Sanitary Improvement," *Westminster Review,* 49 (July 1848), 421–440.

Hill, Octavia. "The Housing of the London Poor," *Macmillans Magazine,* 30 (June 1874), 131–138.

Hole, James. *The Homes of the Working Classes with Suggestions for Their Improvement.* London: Longmans, Green, 1866.

Hoole, Elijah. "The Housing of the London Poor, no. iii," *Contemporary Review,* 45 (February 1884), 238–240.

Jephson, Henry. *The Sanitary Evolution of London.* London: T. Fisher Unwin, 1907.

Jones, Charles S. "The LCC's Housing Policy," *Fortnightly Review,* 68 (December 1900), 967–981.

Knowles, C. M. *The Housing Problem in London.* London: London Reform Union, 1889.

London County Council. *Housing of the Working Classes in London.* London: LCC, 1913.

———— *The London Housing Question, 1855–1900.* London: LCC, 1900.

"The LCC's Housing Policy," *Municipal Journal,* 9 (14 December 1900), 981, and 9 (21 December 1900), 100.

Marshall, Alfred. "The Housing of the London Poor, no. i," *Contemporary Review,* 45 (February 1884), 224–231.

Metropolitan Sanitary Association. *Public Agency or Trading [Companies]: Memoirs of Sanitary Reform.* London, 1851.

Mulhall, M. G. "The Housing of the London Poor. Ways and Means, no. ii," *Contemporary Review,* 45 (February 1884), 231–237.

Philips, William. *The Packing of the Poor.* London: London Municipal Reform League, [1883].

Porritt, Edward. "Housing of the Poor and Working Classes in London," *Political Science Quarterly,* 10 (1895), 22.

Rendle, William. *London Vestries and Their Sanitary Work.* London, 1865.

Rowe, Leo S. "London County Council and the Slum Problem," *The Citizen,* 2 (1896), 268.

[Shaw, Benjamin.] "Sanitary Reform in London," *Quarterly Review,* 118 (1865), 254–280.

Simon, John. *Reports Relating to the Sanitary Condition of the City of London.* London, 1854.

Simon, Sir J[ohn]. *English Sanitary Institutions, Reviewed in Their Course of Development, and in Some of Their Political and Social Relations,* 2nd ed. London: Smith, Elder, 1897.

Smith, Alfred. "Rehousing of the Poor in London," *Municipal Journal,* 7 (2 June 1898), 350.

Stewart, C. J. *The Housing Question in London, 1855–1900.* London: LCC, 1900.

Sykes, J. F. J. "The Results of the State, Municipal and Organised Private Action on the Housing of the Working Classes in London . . .," *Journal of the Royal Statistical Society,* 64 (1901), 189–253.

Thwaites, John. *A Sketch of the History and Prospects of the Metropolitan Drainage Question.* London, 1855.

Waterlow, David. "Municipal Housing in London," *Municipal Journal,* 8 (19 January 1899), 71.

Webb, Sidney. *The House Famine.* London, 1900.

Williams, R. *The Face of the Poor, or the Crowding of London's Labourers.* London, 1897.

Open Spaces

London County Council. *Return of Parks, Open Spaces.* London: LCC, 1892–93.
Meath, Earl of. "County Council and Open Spaces in London," *New Review,* 7 (December 1892), 701–707.
Shaw-Lefevre, George (Lord Eversley). *English Commons and Forests.* London, 1894.

Police

Evans, Howard. "The London County Council and the Police," *Contemporary Review,* 55 (March 1889), 445–461.
Fletcher, Joseph. "Statistical Account of the Police of the Metropolis," *The Journal of the Statistical Society,* 13 (March 1850), 221–261.
"The Metropolitan Police and What Is Paid for Them," *Chambers Journal,* 27 (July 1864), 423–426.
"The Metropolitan Police System," *Westminster Review,* 45 (January 1874), 31–56.
Murray, Grenville. "The French and English Police System," *Cornhill Magazine,* 44 (October 1881), 421–435.
"Principles of Police and Their Application to the Metropolis," *Frasers' Magazine,* 16 (August 1837), 169–178.
Smiles, Samuel. "The Police of London," *Quarterly Review,* 129 (July 1870), 87–129.
Stuart, James. "The Metropolitan Police," *Contemporary Review,* 55 (April 1889), 622–636.
Ward, John. "Police of the Metropolis," *Edinburgh Review,* 66 (January 1838), 358–395.
Warren, C. "Police of London," *Murray's Magazine,* November 1888.

Schooling and Education

Collins, Sir William. *The Educational Work of the LCC.* London: National Liberal Club, 1905.
MacNamara, T. J. "Three Years' Progressivism at the London School Board," *Fortnightly Review,* 74 (1900), 790–802.
Philpott, Hugh B. *London at School: The Story of the London School Board, 1860–1904.* London: T. Fisher Unwin, 1904.
[Robbins, Alfred F.] *Nemesis. Abuses of School Board Expenditure: The Ratepayers' Burning Question.* [London], 1885.
Smith, Llewellyn H. "The Teaching of London: A Scheme for Technical Instruction," *Contemporary Review,* 61 (May 1892), 741–753.
Spalding, Thomas, and T. S. A. Canney. *The Work of the London School Board.* London: P. S. King and Son, 1900.
Webb, S[idney]. *London Education.* London: Longmans and Co., 1914.

Municipal Reform: City Corporation and City Companies

Allen, William Ferneley. *The Corporation of London: Its Rights and Privileges.* London, 1858.

Anti-Coal Tax Committee. *Bogus Agitation in the City: How Public Opinion Is Formed.* London: Anti-Coal Tax Committee, 1887.

Beal, James. *Address to Members of the Metropolitan Vestries and Others, 4 November 1867.* London: Metropolitan Municipalities Association, 1867.

Blakesley, G. H. *The London Companies Commission: A Comment on the Majority Report.* London: Kegan Paul, Tench & Co., 1885.

Breitel, Vivian. *The City of London: An Anachronism, 1835–1854.* London, 1854.

Carpenter, William. *The Corporation of London, As It Is, and As It Should Be.* London: W. Strange, 1847.

Citizen, A. [pseud.] *The Necessity of Reforming the Corporation of London Demonstrated by a Plain Statement of Facts, to Which Is Added an Account of the Income of the Corporation for 1841 . . .* London, 1843.

City of London Corporation. *Proceedings in the Bills for the Regulation of the Corporation of London.* London: City of London Corporation, 1858.

"The Corporation of London Killed by Its Friends," and "The Corporation of London: A Dawn of Hope," *Illustrated London News,* 24 (1854), 127, 258–259.

"The Decline and Fall of the London Corporation," *Frazer's Magazine,* 44 (January–June 1854), 3–18, 198–209, 318–329, 453–462, 561–571, 687–697.

Dilke, Charles Wentworth. *City of Guilds Reform.* London, 1886.

Firth, J. F. B. *The Coal and Wine Dues: The History of the London Coal Tax and Arguments for and against Its Renewal.* London Municipal Reform League, Pamphlet no. 20. London: Anti-Coal Tax Committee, 1886.

————— *Reform of London Government and of City Guilds.* London: Swan Sonnenschein, Laurey and Co., 1888.

[Flanagan, J. Wailfe.] *The City Companies and Their Property: A Plea for Fair Play.* London: Hamilton, Adams, and Co., 1886.

[Franks, R. H.] *Report to the Committee in Aid of Corporate Reform, November 8, 1833: Containing a Statement of Some of the Evils and Abuses Existing in the Corporation and in the Municipal Trading Companies of the City of London.* London: The Corporate Commission, 1833.

Gilbert, William. *The City: An Inquiry into the Corporation, Its Livery Companies, and the Administration of Their Charities and Endowments.* London: Daldy, Isbisten & Co., 1877.

"Gilt and Gingerbread, or Tom Fool's Day in the City," *Fraser's Magazine,* 50 (December 1854), 618–628.

Grey, Sir George. *Speech . . . on the Bill for the Better Regulation of the Corporation of London, April 1, 1856.* London, 1856.

"Grip." *The Monster Municipality, or Gog and Magog Reformed: A Dream.* London: Sampson Law, Marston, Searle & Rivington, 1882.

Harkness, M. E. "The Municipality of London," *The National Review,* pts. I and II, 1 (May and September 1883), 395–407, 96–105.

[Hickson, W. E.] "The Apologists of City Administration," *Westminster Review,* 41 (June 1844), 553–579.

————— "London Government—Corporate and Municipal Reform," *Westminster Review,* 39 (May 1843), 495–586.

Hobhouse, Sir Arthur. "The City Companies," *Contemporary Review,* 47 (January 1885), 1–24.

————— "Municipal Government of London," *Contemporary Review,* 41 (March 1882), 404–428.

The Livery Companies. *The Livery Companies: The Royal Commission of Inquiry.* Reprinted from *The Citizen,* 28 August 1880. London, 1880.

London Municipal Reform League. *City Livery Companies: £700,000 a Year Waiting to be Claimed by the London People.* [London, 1886.]

London Municipal Reform League. *City Tactics: The City Corporation and the London Bill.* N.p., n.d.

———— *How the City Expend Public Money.* N.p., n.d.

———— *How the City Interferes with Public Meetings.* N.p., n.d.

"Lord Mayor's Day, an Heroical Ode, after Dryden by Jim Dried'Un," *Bentley's Miscellany,* 5 (January 1839), 109–112.

[Nelson, T. James.] *The City of London: "Strike, but Hear."* London: Blades, East and Blades, 1884.

Norton, George. *An Address to the Citizens of London on the Impending Corporation Bill.* Printed by order of the Committee of the Court of Aldermen. [London, 1856.]

Phillips, William. *Municipal Reformers v. the City Fathers.* [London, 1883.]

Pulling, Alexander. *The City of London Corporation Inquiry.* London, 1854.

———— *Observations on the Disputes at Present Arising in the Corporation of the City of London, and on the Powers of Internal Reform Possessed by the Citizens in Common Council.* London, 1847.

"The Renovation of the London Corporation, 1850," *Eclectic Review,* 90 (1850), 129.

Reynolds, John [pseud.]. "Corporation Reform," *The National Review,* 8 (December 1886), 559–564.

Scott, Benjamin. "Municipal Government of London," *Contemporary Review,* 41 (February 1882), 308–324.

———— *The Municipal Government of London.* London: Effingham Wilson, 1884.

———— *Statistical Vindication of the City of London,* 3rd ed. London, 1877.

S[ebastian], L. B. *The City Livery Comnpanies and Their Property.* London: Rivingtons, 1885.

Smith, J. Toulmin. *What Is the Corporation of London? And Who are the Freemen?* London: Effingham Wilson, 1850.

To the Rt. Hon. the Lord Mayor, Aldermen, and Commons of the City of London - by Arnicus. London: Metropolitan Municipalities Association, 1870.

[Walter, Major James.] *The Royal Commission: The London City Livery Companies' Vindication.* London: Gilbert and Rivington, 1885.

Webster, Robert G. "The Metropolitan Coal and Wine Dues," *The National Review,* 9 (March 1887), 125–132.

[Williams, Hurme.] A Citizen. *Six Letters on Corporation Reform.* Reprinted from *The Morning Advertiser.* London, 1882.

Woolacott, J. E. *The Curse of Turtledom: An Exposé of the Methods and Extravagant Expenditure of the Livery Companies.* Reprinted from *The Financial Times.* London, Effingham Wilson & Co., 1894.

Metropolitan Government Reform

To 1879

Buxton, Charles. *Self-Government for London: The Leading Ideas on Which a Constitution for London Should Be Based. A letter to the Right Hon. H. A. Bruce, M.P. (Secretary of State for Home Affairs).* London: Metropolitan Municipal Association, 1869.

[Conder, F. R.] "The Government of London," *Frazer's Magazine*, 93 (June 1876), 769–776.

Firth, J. F. B. *Municipal London, or, London As It Is, and London under a Municipal Council*. London: Longmans, Green & Co., 1876.

Fraser, Sir William. *London Self-Governed*. London: Francis Harvey, 1866.

Gog and Magog [pseud.]. *Ye Comick Historie of Ye Citie of London*. London, 1878.

"The Government of London," *Westminster Review*, 105 (January 1876), 93–123.

[Hickson, W. E. "The Government of London," *Westminster Review*, 41 (1844), 553–579 and 43 (1845), 193–228.

—————— "Municipal Reform As Required for the Metropolis," *The London and Westminster Review*, 25 (April 1836), 71–103.

[Horton, George.] A Londoner [pseud.]. *The Municipal Government of the Metropolis*. London: Robert Hardwicke, 1865.

Hughes, Thomas. "The Anarchy of London," *Macmillans Magazine*, 21 (January 1870), 273–278.

"The Local Government of the Metropolis," *Westminster Review*, 25 (April 1836), 71–103.

"Local Self-Government and Centralisation," *Eclectic Review*, 94 (1851), 354.

"London Government: Municipal Reform," *Gentleman's Magazine*, n.s., 14 (1875), 31.

Metropolitan Municipalities Association. *First Annual Report* through *Ninth Annual Report*. London: Metropolitan Municipalities Association, 1867–1875.

—————— *Opinions on Schemes to Improve the Government of London, 1870*. London: Metropolitan Municipalities Association, 1870.

Mill, John Stuart. *Considerations on Representative Government*, London: Longmans, Green and Co., 1876.

Newall, W. H. "London Local Government," *Contemporary Review*, 22 (1873), 73–86.

Newton, William. *The Government of London. Speech . . . at the Metropolitan Board of Works on the Municipal Government of the Metropolis, April 22, 1870*. London: Coningham Brothers, 1870.

[Phillips, J. Roland.] "The Government of London," *Edinburgh Review*, 142 (October 1875), 549–558.

Pulling, Serjeant. "The Need and Practicability of Systematic Local Government for London," *Sessional Proceedings of the Social Science Association* (1877–78), 116–117.

Shuttleworth, Sir Ughtred J. Kay. *Reform of London Government: Speech . . . in the House of Commons, 5 April 1878*. London Municipal Reform League Pamphlet no. 2. London, 1881.

Smith, Joshua Toulmin. *Centralisation or Representation? A Letter to the Metropolitan Sanitary Commissioners . . .* 2nd ed. London, 1848.

—————— *Local Self-Government and Centralisation*. London, 1851.

—————— *The Metropolis and Its Municipal Administration, Showing the Essentials of a Sound System of Municipal Self-Government As Applicable to All Town Populations*. London: Trewlawney Saunders, 1852.

—————— *The People and the Parish*. London, 1853.

1880–1890

[Acworth, W. M.] "County Council for London," *Nineteenth Century*, 25 (March 1889), 418–430.

[Baumann, A. A.] "The London Clauses of the Local Government Bill, 1888," *National Review*, 11 (June 1888), 539–552.

Buxton, Sydney C. *A Handbook to the Political Questions of the Day*, 3rd ed. London: John Murray, 1881.

Chadwick, Edwin. "London Centralised," *Contemporary Review*, 45 (June 1884), 794–810.

———— *On the Evils of Disunity in Central and Local Administration Especially with Relation to the Metropolis and Also the New Centralisation for the People*. London: Longmans, Green and Co., 1885.

Clark, J. W. *Concerning London Government, and the Proposed "Clean Sweep" of Local Institutions*. London: National Press Agency, 1884.

"County Council for London," *Saturday Review*, 69 (1890), 340.

Devenish, W. J. *Municipal Reform Leaguers. Absolute Centralisation Knocked into a Cocked Hat: Firth Dissected*. London: Judd & Co., 1883.

[Ellis, Sir J. W.] "The Bill for London Government, 1884," *The National Review*, 3 (1884), 488.

[Emmett, J. T.] "County Council for London," *Quarterly Review*, 170 (January 1890), 226–256.

Firth, J. F. B. *Justice to the People of London: Reform of London Government: Speech . . . on the Second Reading of "The London Government Bill" . . . 3 July 1884*. [London: London Municipal Reform League, 1884.]

———— *London Government and How to Reform It*. London: London Municipal Reform League, 1882.

———— *London Government Reform*. Municipal Reform Pamphlet no. 10. London: London Municipal Reform League, 1884.

———— *A Practical Scheme for London Municipal Reform, Being an Epitome of "The Municipality of London Bill" . . . 1880. London: London Municipal Reform League, 1881*.

———— *Speech . . . on the Debate upon the Second Reading of the Local Government (England and Wales) Bill*. London: Cornelius Buck & Son, 1888.

———— *Synopsis of the London Government Bill*. London: London Municipal Reform League, 1884.

[Firth, J. F. B.] "The Fate of the London Government Bill," *Fortnightly Review*, 40 (July 1883), 97–110.

Fortescue, Earl. "'Imperium in Imperio': The Bill for Local Government, 1888, As Applied to London," *Nineteenth Century*, 24 (October 1888), 481–486.

Gibb, T. Ecclesten. *London Government: A Report on the Bill for the Better Government of London . . . Introduced to the House of Commons by the Home Secretary, Session 1884*. [London, 1884.]

"Government of London," *Saturday Review*, 53 (1882), 35.

"The Government of London," *Westminster Review*, 127 (January 1887), 151–170.

"H.A.P." *The Truth about the London Government Bill*. London, 1882.

Hare, Thomas. *London Municipal Reform: A Reprint, with Additions of Several Papers Thereon*. Political Tract Society. London: E. J. Kibblewhite, 1882.

Hart, E. *Local Government As It Is and As It Ought to Be*. London: Smith and Elder, [1885].

[Hobhouse, Henry.] "London Government and the Local Government Bill, 1888," *Contemporary Review*, 53 (June 1888), 773–786.

Hobhouse, Lord Arthur. *Some Reasons for a Single Government for London*. Municipal Reform Pamphlets no. 11. London: London Municipal Reform League, 1884.

Johns, Philip. *London Municipal Reform: Is a Single Central Municipality to Be Preferred to Ten Municipalities? If Not, Why?* Reprinted from *Lambeth Post,* 16 February 1884. London: Lile and Fawcett, 1884.

Leighton, Stanley. "The Municipalities on Trial," *The National Review,* 9 (May 1887), 418–426.

Lloyd, John. *Lord Randolph Churchill and London.* [London: London Municipal Reform League, 1887.]

London Government Bill: Resolutions against the Bill. London, 1884.

———— *Public Opinion on the London Government Bill: Being Extracts from the Principal Newspapers in London and the Provinces, and from the Speeches of Public Men.* [London, 1884.]

"London Municipal Reform Bill, 1883," *Saturday Review,* 55 and 56 (1883), 169, 391, 294.

"London Municipal Reform Bill, 1883," *Spectator,* 56 (1883), 206.

London Municipal Reform League. *London Municipal Reform: Conference of Members of Parliament and Other Influential Friends, Held at the Cannon St. Hotel, on Friday, the Fifth August, 1881 . . . the Right Hon. J. Stansfield in the Chair.* London: London Municipal Reform League, 1881.

———— *The London Municipal Reform League and Mr. John Lloyd.* (London: Unwin Brothers, 1889.]

———— *The Reform of London Government, and the Advantages of One Municipality.* Municipal Reform Pamphlet no. 5. London: London Municipal Reform League, 1882.

———— *Why Should London Wait?* [London, 1883.]

Londoner, A. [pseud.]. *The London Government Bill: Some Observations on Its Scope and Probable Working.* London: Sir Joseph Causton and Sons, 1883.

McArthur, Sir William. *Alderman Sir W. McArthur, M.P., on the London Government Bill.* London, 1884.

Metropolitan Local Government Defence Association. *London Government Bill: A Lesson for Ratepayers.* London, 1884.

"The New London Government, 1882," *Spectator,* 55 (1882), 110.

[Pennell, E. R.] "The Government of London," *Nation,* 48 (1889), 135.

P[erry], H[arold] A. *The Truth about the London Government Bill.* London: E. J. Stoneham, [1884].

Phillips, William. *"Home Rule" for London: An Appeal and a Warning.* [London, 1888.]

Ratepayer, A. [pseud.]. *The Future Local Government of London.* [London, 1884.]

Rearden, D. J. *The Local and Imperial Municipal Corporations Metropolis (England) Bill . . .* London, [1882].

Round, J. H. *The Commune of London.* London, 1889.

[Saintsbury, George.] "Government of London," *Quarterly Review,* 158 (July 1884), 1–39.

[Scott, B.] "Municipal Government of London," *Contemporary Review,* 41 (February 1882), 308–324.

Selway, W. Robbins. *Speech . . . at the Metropolitan Board of Works on the London Government Bill, Friday, Second May, 1884.* London: Judd & Co., [1884].

Torrens, W. M. "The Government of London," *Nineteenth Century,* 8 (November 1880), 766–786.

Whitehead, James. *Letter . . . on the London Government Bill.* [London, 1884.]

1891-1900

"The Bill for London Government," *Saturday Review,* 87 (1899), 260.

"A Many-Headed Aedile," *Spectator,* 69 (1892), 760-761.

[Burns, John.] "The Government of London: Let London Live," *Nineteenth Century,* 31 (April 1892), 673-685.

Civis [pseud.]. *The "L.C.C." and the City, with a Few Words on the Home Secretary's "More Excellent Way."* London: Eden Fisher & Co., 1895.

[Collins, W. J.] "The Bill for London Government," *Contemporary Review,* 75 (April 1899), 515-521.

Dickinson, W. H. *London's Past and Future: A Retrospect of the Various Attempts to Give Municipal Government to the Metropolis and the Prospects of the Dangers of Separate Metropolitan Municipalities.* London: "Eighty Club," 1899.

————— *Unification of London.* London, [1894].

Emmett, J. T. *The Basis of Municipal Reform.* London: Simpkin and Marshall, 1895.

[Gomme, G. L.] "The Future of London Government," *Contemporary Review,* 66 (November 1894), 746-760.

Harrison, Charles. "The Unification of London," *Fortnightly Review,* 59 (June 1893), 836-845.

Harrison, Frederic. "The Amalgamation of London," *Contemporary Review,* 66 (November 1894), 737-745.

————— "The Amalgamation of London," *Saturday Review,* 78 (1894), 375-400.

Hobhouse, Lord. *London Government: Speech . . . at the Dinner on Monday, 29 February 1892.* London: The "Eighty Club," 1893.

Knott, G. H. "The Unification of London," *American Law Review,* 29 (1895), 395.

London Municipal Society. *The Government of London,* pt. III, *Facts & Arguments.* London: Edward Arnold, 1895.

————— *The County Council and the Vestries: Two Partners in London Government.* London Government. London: London Reform Union, 1896.

————— *How to Reform the Government of London.* London: London Reform Union, 1898.

————— *"Tenification" and What It Means.* London: London Reform Union, 1895.

[Lubbock, Sir John.] "A Few Words on the Government of London," *Fortnightly Review,* 57 (February 1892), 158-172.

[Lubbock, Sir J., et al.] "The Government of London," *The National Review,* 24 (February 1895), 530.

"The Problem of London," *Chamber's Journal,* 11 (March 1899), 223-230.

[Whitmore, C. A.] "Government of London," *Quarterly Review,* 189 (April 1899), 492-518.

1900-1914

Benn, J. Williams. *Exploited London, 1832-1912.* London, 1912.

————— *Our London and What We Make of It.* London, 1906.

Collins, Sir William. *The Reform of London Government.* London, 1909.

Debate on the Reform of London Government at the National Liberal Club, December Third, 1906. N.p., n.d.

Fisher, W. Hayes. *The Progress of Municipal Reform.* London, 1912.

Hemphill, Fitzroy. *A Debate on the Reform of London Government.* London: Reform Club, 1906.

Jephson, Henry. *The Making of Modern London: Progress and Reaction.* London: 1910.

Lloyd, John. *London Municipal Government: History of a Great Reform, 1880–1888.* London: P. S. King & Son, 1910.

London Liberal Federation. *Reform of London Government: Report by a Special Committee of the London Liberal Federation.* London: London Liberal Federation, 1912.

London Municipal Society. *Municipal Reform Leaflets.* London: London Municipal Society, 1906.

_____ *The Progress of Municipal Reform.* London: London Municipal Society, 1907.

London Reform Union. *Annual Reports, 1892–1918.* London: London Reform Union, 1918.

_____ *Greater London: How It Should Be Governed.* London: London Reform Union, 1914.

_____ *London Today and Tomorrow.* London: London Reform Union, 1908.

_____ *Proposals for the Reform of London Government, 1908.* N.p., n.d.

Peel, W. R. W. *A Year of Municipal Reform.* London, 1908.

Ridge, W. Pett. "Faults of the Londoner," *Nineteenth Century,* 66 (1909), 303–309.

Sanders, William. *Municipalisation by Provinces.* London, 1905.

Spender, Harold E. *The Future of London Government.* London, Liberal Publications Dept., 1909.

Towler, W. G. *Problems of London Government.* London, London Municipal Society, 1912.

Tyler, P. E. "The Transformation of London," *Home Counties Magazine,* 7 (1905), 105–113, 187–198, 247–255.

London Politics and Elections, 1880–1914

Chamberlain, Joseph. *The Radical Platform: Speeches by the Rt. Hon. Joseph Chamberlain.* Edinburgh: Morrison and Gibb, 1885.

Churchill, W. Spencer. *Lord Randolph Churchill.* London: Macmillan & Co., 1907.

"Conservatism of London," *Spectator,* 59 (1886), 902.

Diggle, Joseph R. "London Progressives v. London Education," *The National Review,* 24 (November 1894), 307–315.

Doom of the County Council of London. London: *Daily Chronicle,* 1892.

Fabian Society. *Facts for Londoners.* London: Fabian Society, 1889.

_____ *The London Education Act, 1903: How to Make the Best of It.* Fabian Tract 117. London: Fabian Society, 1904.

Farrer, T. H. "Sir William Harcourt's Budget," *Contemporary Review,* 66 (August 1894), 153–164.

Gilbert, J. D. *The Two-and-a-Half Years' Record of the Moderate Party on the London County Council.* London, 1909.

Harrison, Frederic. "Sir John Lubbock and the London County Council," *New Review,* 5 (November 1891), 395–403.

Hobhouse, Arthur. "Local Taxation of Rents in London," *Contemporary Review,* 54 (July 1888), 140–156.

_____ "The London County Council and Its Assailants," *Contemporary Review,* 61 (March 1892), 332–349.

Hobhouse, Lord. *The Dead Hand: Addresses on the Subject of Endowments and Settlements of Property.* London: Chatto & Windus, 1880.

Hobhouse, L. T., and J. L. Hammond. *Lord Hobhouse: A Memoir.* London: Edward Arnold, 1905.

Jones, H. C. *Questions for Candidates: Metropolitan Borough Councils, June 1900.* Fabian Tract 102. London: Fabian Society, 1900.

Lawson, H. L. W. "The County Council Election," *Fortnightly Review,* 69 (8 February 1898), 197–209.

_____ "The Fifth London County Council," *Fortnightly Review,* 75 (1901), 623–631.

[Lee, Sidney.] "London County Council," *Quarterly Review,* 177 (January 1898), 259–275.

LCC. *General Elections of County Councillors.* London: LCC, 1907.

_____ *London County Council Election.* London: LCC, 1901.

"London County Council Election, 1892," *Saturday Review,* 73 (1892), 296.

"London Government in 1893: New London Programme," *Spectator,* 71 (1893), 168.

"London Opinion in Politics," *Spectator,* 55 (1883), 554.

London Reform Union. *L.C.C. Election, 1895. The Elector's Guide: What the L.C.C. Has Done for the People of London.* London: London Reform Union, 1895.

_____ *The London County Council of 1895.* London: London Reform Union, 1898.

_____ *L.C.C. Election, 1898.* Progressive Leaflets nos. 2–11, 13–22, 25, 26, 30–34. London: London Reform Union, 1898.

Moss, Frank. *How the Liberals May Win London.* London, 1886.

Pall Mall Gazette. House of Commons, 1889, and London County Council, 1889: The Popular Guide. London: *Pall Mall Gazette* Office, 1889.

_____ *House of Commons, 1889, and London County Council: "Memos" about Members and 100 Portraits.* London: *Pall Mall Gazette* Office, 1889.

_____ *The Popular Guide to the Second London County Council with Full Particulars of the Polls, "Memos" about Members and 120 Portraits.* London: *Pall Mall Gazette* Office, 1892.

Progressive Election Committee. *Progressive Pamphlets.* London: Progressive Election Committee, 1909.

The Radical Programme, [with] *Preface by J. Chamberlain.* London, 1885.

Smalley, George. *The Life of Sir Sidney H. Waterlow, Bart.: London Apprentice, Lord Mayor, Captain of Industry, and Philanthropist.* London: Edward Arnold, 1909.

Smith, Sir Henry. *From Constable to Commissioner: The Story of Sixty Years, Most of Them Misspent.* London, 1910.

The Star. Six Years of Progress. London, 1895.

Three Years' Good Work for the People. London, 1892.

Stead, W. T. *The L.C.C. Election, 1892: The Elector's Guide.* London, 1892.

[Stuart, James.] "The London Progressives," *Contemporary Review,* 61 (April 1892), 521–532.

The Times. Municipal Socialism. London: *The Times,* 1902.

Torrens, W. McCullagh. *Twenty Years in Parliament.* London: Richard Bentley and Son, 1893.

Webb, Sidney. "The Cause of Municipal Socialism in the United Kingdom," *Labour Annual*, 1894.

———— *The London Programme*. London: Fabian Society, 1891.

Whelen, Frederick. *The Citizen and the Council: Issues of the Contest*. London, 1898.

Whitmore, C. A. "Conservatives and the London County Council," *The National Review*, 21 (April 1893), 175-186.

———— "The Elections for the London County Council," *The National Review*, 12 (February 1889), 781-786.

———— "The Progressive [Party] in Recent Elections," *The National Review*, 25 (April 1895), 239-246.

Wood, T. McKinnon. *The Attack on the London County Council*. London, 1898.

———— *The Progressive Policy: Past and Present*. London: London Publications Dept., 1904.

———— *Under Moderate Rule*. London: Liberal Publications Dept., 1908.

Secondary Sources: Books and Articles since 1914

History of London: Growth and Development

Barker, T. C. "Passenger Transport in Nineteenth Century London," *Journal of Transport History*, 6 (1963-4) 166-174.

———— and Michael Robbins. *A History of London Transport*, vol. I, *The Nineteenth Century*. London: George Allen & Unwin, 1963.

Bédarida, François. "L'histoire sociale de Londres au XIXe siècle," *Annales*, 5 (September-October 1960), 949-962.

Briggs, Asa. "London: The World City," in Asa Briggs, ed., *Victorian Cities*. London: Odhams 1963; new ed., London: Harmondsworth, 1968.

Broodbank, J. G. *History of the Port of London*. London: O'Connor, 1921.

Cooney, E. W. "The Origins of the Victorian Master Builders," *Economic History Review*, 2nd ser., 8 (1955), 167-176.

Coppock, J. T., and H. G. Prince. *Greater London*. London: Faber, 1964.

Dyos, H. J. "Railways and Housing in Victorian London," *Journal of Transport History*, 2 (1955), 11-21, 90-100; and "Some Social Costs of Railway Building in London," ibid., 3 (1957-58), 23-30.

———— "The Speculative Builders and Developers of Victorian London," *Victorian Studies*, 11 (Supplement, Summer 1968), 641-690.

———— "Urban Transformation: The Objects of Street Improvements in Regency and Early Victorian London," *International Review of Social History*, 2 (1957), pt. 2, 259-265.

———— *Victorian Suburb: A Study of the Growth of Camberwell*. Leicester: Leicester University Press, 1961.

———— and D. A. Reeder. "Slums and Suburbs," in H. J. Dyos and Michael Wolff, eds., *The Victorian City: Images and Realities*, vol. I. London and Boston: Routledge and Kegan Paul, 1973.

Eversley, D. E. C. "Searching for London's Lost Soul," *The London Journal*, 1, no. 1 (1975), 103-117.

Foley, D. L. *Controlling London's Growth*. Berkeley, Calif.: University of California Press, 1963.

Garside, P. L. "The Development of London: A Classified List of Theses, 1908-1977," *Guildhall Studies in London History*, 3, no. 3 (October 1978), 175-194.

Greater London Council. *London Statistics, New Series.* London: Greater London Council, 1968.

Haig, R. M. "Towards an Understanding of the Metropolis," *Quarterly Journal of Economics,* 40 (1926), 179ff, 402ff.

Hall, Peter G. *The Industries of London since 1861.* London: Hutchinson, 1962.

Harrison, Michael. *London by Gaslight, 1861-1911.* London: P. Davies, 1963.

Hobhouse, Hermione. *Thomas Cubitt, Master Builder.* London: Macmillan, 1971.

Jackson, Alan. *Semi-Detached London.* London: George Allen and Unwin, 1973.

Johnson, James H. "The Suburban Expansion of London, 1918-1939," in J. T. Coppock and H. G. Prince, eds., *Greater London.* London: Faber, 1964.

Metcalf, Priscilla. *Victorian London.* London: Cassell, 1972.

Olsen, Donald J. *The Growth of Victorian London.* London: Batsford, 1976.

_____ *Town Planning in London in the Eighteenth and Nineteenth Centuries.* New Haven and London: Yale University Press, 1964.

Rasmussen, S. E. *London: The Unique City,* new and rev. ed. London: Cape, 1948.

Reddaway, T. F. "London in the Nineteenth Century," *Nineteenth Century and After,* 145 (June 1949), 363-374.

Reeder, D. A. "Keeping up with London's Past: Local History in the Metropolis," in *Urban History Yearbook, 1977.* Leicester: Leicester University Press, 1977.

_____ "A Theatre of Suburbs. Some Patterns of Development in West London, 1801-1911," in H. J. Dyos, ed., *The Study of Urban History.* London: Edward Arnold, 1968.

Rudé, George. *Hanoverian London.* London: Secker and Warburg, 1971.

Sadleir, Michael. *Forlorn Sunset.* London: Constable, 1947.

Sekon, G. A. [pseud.] *Locomotion in Victorian London.* London: Oxford University Press, 1938.

Shannon, Herbert Austin. "Migration and the Growth of London," *Economic History Review,* 5 (1935), 79-86.

Sheppard, Frank. *London, 1808-1870: The Infernal Wen.* London: Secker and Warburg, 1971.

Spate, O. H. K. "The Growth of London, 1600-1800," in H. C. Darby, ed., *Historical Geography of England.* Cambridge: Cambridge University Press, 1935.

Summerson, Sir John. *Georgian London.* London: Harmondsworth, 1962.

Survey of London, vol. VIII, *St. Leonard Shoreditch.* London: LCC, 1922.

_____ vol. XXIV, *St. Pancras,* pt. IV. London: GLC, 1952.

_____ vol. XXXI, *The Parish of St. James Westminster,* pt. II. London: GLC, 1963.

_____ vol. XXXVII, *Northern Kensington.* London: GLC, 1973.

Thompson, E. J. "The Growth of Greater London," *Greater London Research,* September 1969.

Thompson, F. M. L. *Hampstead Building a Borough, 1650-1964.* London: Routledge and Kegan Paul, 1974.

Thornhill, James Frederick Patrick. *Greater London: A Social Geography.* London: Christophers, 1935.

Westergaard, John. "The Structure of Greater London," in *London: Aspects of Change.* London: MacGibbon and Kee, 1964.

Whetham, E. H. "The London Milk Trade, 1860-1900," *English History Review,* 17 (1964), 369-380.

Metropolitan Government Reform since 1914

Barber, Brian. *Labour in London: A Study in Municipal Achievement.* London: George Routledge & Sons, 1946.

Bennett, Sir John. *Gog and Magog.* London, 1920

Davies, A. E. *The Story of the London County Council.* London: The Labour Publishing Co., 1925.

London Council of Social Service. A Royal Commission on the Housing of the Poor and the Regional Planning of London. London: Council of Social Service, 1926.

London Municipal Society. *The Greater London Scheme.* London: London Municipal Society, 1924.

_____ *The Problem of Greater London.* London: London Municipal Society, 1921.

Mais, S. P. B. *Fifty Years of the L.C.C. Cambridge:* Cambridge University Press, 1939.

Morrison, Herbert. *How Greater London Is Governed.* Rev. ed. London: People's Universities Press, 1949.

Rhodes, Gerald. *The New Government of London: The Struggle for Reform.* London: Allen and Unwin, 1970.

_____ *The New Government of London: The First Five Years.* London: Allen and Unwin, 1972.

Roberts, Henry. "From L.C.C. to G.L.C.," *London Society Journal,* 370 (May 1965), 14–24.

Robson, W. A. *The Government and Misgovernment of London.* London: George Allen and Unwin, 1939; 2nd ed., 1948.

_____ *The Greater London Boroughs.* Greater London Papers 3. London: London School of Economics, 1961.

Smallwood, Frank. *Greater London: The Politics of Metropolitan Reform.* Indianapolis: Bobbs-Merrill Co., 1965.

Towler, W. G. *The Dual System of London Government.* London: London Municipal Society, 1933.

Young, Ken, and John Kramer. *Strategy and Conflict in Metropolitan Housing: Suburbia versus the Greater London Council, 1965–1975.* London: Heinemann, 1978.

Biography and Autobiography

Boase, Frederick. *Modern English Biography.* 6 vols. Truro: Netherton and Worth, 1892–1921; new ed., London: Cass, 1965.

British Biographical Company. *Leading Men of London: A Collection of Biographical Sketches.* London: British Biographical Co.

Burgess, Joseph. *John Burns: The Rise and Progress of a Right Honourable.* Glasgow: The Reformers' Bookstall Ltd., 1911.

Cecil, Lady Gwendoline. *Life of Robert, Marquis of Salisbury.* 4 vols. London: Hodder and Stoughton, 1931–32.

Chamberlain, Joseph. *Mr. Chamberlain's Speeches,* ed. Charles W. Boyd. 2 vols. London: Constable & Co., 1914.

Clarke, Sir Edward. *The Story of My Life.* London: John Murray, 1918.

Clarke, Percy. *Serving His Generation: Being Short Notes of the Public Life of Henry Clarke, J.P.* London, 1915.

Cole, Margaret. *Servant of the County.* London: Dennis Dobson, 1951.

Douglas, E. A. A., Viscount Chilston. *Chief Whip: The Political Life and Times of Aretas Akers Douglas.* London: Routledge and Kegan Paul, 1961.

Dugdale, Blanche. *Arthur James Balfour.* 2 vols. London: Hutchinson and Co., 1936.

Duschinsky, M. P. *The Political Thought of Lord Salisbury, 1854–1868.* London: Constable, 1967.

Finer, S. E. *The Life and Times of Sir Edwin Chadwick.* London: Methuen, 1952.

Gardiner, A. G. *John Benn and the Progressive Movement.* London: Ernest Benn, 1925.

Garvin, J. L. *The Life of Joseph Chamberlain.* 4 vols. London: Macmillan and Co., 1932–1951.

Hamilton, Lord George. *Parliamentary Reminiscences and Reflections, 1868–1906.* 2 vols. London: John Murray, 1917–1922.

Haward, Sir Harry. *The London County Council from Within: Forty Years' Official Recollections.* London: Chapman & Hall, 1932.

Jacks, Lawrence Pearsall. *Life and Letters of Stopford Brooke.* 2 vols. New York: Charles Scribner's Sons, 1917.

James, Robert Rhodes. *Rosebery: A Biography.* London: Weidenfeld and Nicholson, 1963.

Jenkins, Roy. *Sir Charles Dilke: A Victorian Tragedy.* London: Collins, 1958.

Jones, G. W. and Bernard Donoughue. *Herbert Morrison: Portrait of a Politician.* London: Donoughue, Weidenfeld and Nicholson, 1973.

Kent, W. R. G. *John Burns: Labour's Lost Leader.* London: Williams and Norgate, 1950.

———— *London Worthies.* London: Heath Cranston, 1939; rev. ed., Phoenix House, 1949.

———— *My Lord Mayor.* London: Herbert Jenkins, 1947.

Lambert, Royston. *Sir John Simon (1816–1904) and English Social Administration.* London: MacGibbon & Kee, 1963.

Lewis, R. A. *Edwin Chadwick and the Public Health Movement, 1832–54.* London: Longmans, Green and Co., 1952.

Magnus, Philip. *Gladstone: A Biography.* London: John Murray, 1954.

Morrison, Lord of Lambeth. *An Autobiography.* London: Odhams, 1960.

Ramm, Agatha. *The Political Correspondence of Mr. Gladstone and Lord Granville, 1876–1886.* 2 vols. Oxford: Clarendon Press, 1962.

Sayer, T. Lewes. *Gog and Magog and I: Some Recollections of Forty-Nine Years at Guildhall.* London: Sampson Law, Marston & Co., 1931.

Simey, T. S. *Charles Booth, Social Scientist.* London: Oxford University Press, 1960.

Soutter, F. W. *Recollections of a Labour Pioneer,* 2nd ed. London: T. F. Unwin, 1924.

Tucker, A. V. "W. H. Mallock and Later Victorian Conservatism," *University of Toronto Quarterly,* January 1962.

Walker-Smith, Derek, and Edward Clarke. *Life of Sir Edward Clarke.* London: Thornton Butterworth, 1939.

Webb, Beatrice. *My Apprenticeship.* London: Longmans, Green & Co., 1929.

———— *Our Partnership.* London: Longmans, Green & Co., 1948.

Wraxall, Sir N. W. *Historical Memoirs.* London: Hutchinson & Co., 1923.

Young, Kenneth. *Arthur James Balfour.* London: G. Bell and Son, 1963.

History of London's Government, Administration, and Social Policy

Atkins, F. Merton. *London Tramways.* London, 1951.

Ayers, Gwendoline M. *England's First State Hospitals and the Metropolitan Asylums Board, 1867–1930.* London: Wellcome Institute, 1971.

Bell, Walter G. "The Birth of the London Rate-payer," *History,* 12 (1927–28), 117–129.

Birch, Raymond W. "London Bus Organisation in the Nineteenth Century," *Omnibus Magazine,* 7 (1939), 44–59.

Bosanquet, Helen. *Social Work in London, 1869–1912: A History of the Charity Organisation Society.* London: John Murray, 1914.

Brennan, E. J. T., ed. *Education for National Efficiency: The Contribution of Sydney and Beatrice Webb.* London: Athlone Press, 1975.

Browne, D. G. *The Rise of Scotland Yard: A History of the Metropolitan Police.* London: Harrop and Co., 1956.

Buchan, Stevenson. "The Water Supply of the County of London from Underground Sources," *Memoirs of the Geological Survey of Great Britain.* London: HMSO, 1939.

Chevalier, W. S. "Fifty Years of Progress," *Journal of the British Waterworks Association,* 35 (1953), 98–107.

City of London Corporation. *The Corporation of London: Its Origin, Constitution, Powers, and Duties.* London: Corporation of London, 1949.

Coleman, Reginald, and W. Allen Daley. "The Development of Hospital Services with Particular Reference to the Municipal Hospital System of London," *Proceedings of the Royal Society of Medicine,* 35 (1941–42), 741–752.

Darlington, Ida. *Guide to the Records of the London County Record Office,* pt. 1, *Records of the Predecessors of the L. C. C., except the Board of Guardians.* London: LCC, 1963.

–––––– "The London Commissioners of Sewers and Their Records," *Journal of the Society of Archivists,* 2 (April 1962), 196–215.

–––––– "The Metropolitan Buildings Office," *The Builder,* 191 (12 October 1956), 628–632.

Davies, Ernest. "The London Passenger Transport Board," in W. A. Robson, ed., *Public Enterprise.* London: New Fabian Research Bureau, 1937.

Dawe, Donovan. *The City of London: A Select Book List.* London: Guildhall Library, 1973.

Dickinson, H. W. *Water Supply of Greater London.* London: Newcomen Society, 1954.

Everard, Stirling. *The History of the Gas Light and Coke Company, 1812–1949.* London: E. Benn, 1949.

Fox, P. W. "The Early Fabians: Economists and Reformers," *Canadian Journal of Economic and Political Science,* 17 (1951).

Fraser, Maxwell. "Sir Benjamin Hall and the Administration of London," *Transactions, Cymmrodorian,* 1 (1963), 70–81.

Gibbon, I. G., and R. W. Bell. *History of the London County Council, 1889–1939.* London: Macmillan, 1939.

Heath, G. D. *The Formation of the Local Boards of Twickenham, Teddington, Hampton and Hampton Wick.* Twickenham: Local History Society, 1967.

Holloway, Sally. *London's Noble Fire Brigades.* London: Cassell, 1973.

Jackson, W. E. *Achievement: A Short History of the L. C. C.* London: Longmans, 1965.

Jones, Gareth Stedman. *Outcast London: A Study of Relationships between the Classes in Victorian Society.* Oxford: Oxford University Press, 1971.

Jones, P. E. *The Corporation of London: Its Origins, Constitution, Powers and Duties.* London: Geoffrey Cumberlege, 1950.

—— and Raymond Smith. *A Guide to the Records of the Corporation of London Records Office and the Guildhall Library Muniment Room.* London: Guildhall Library, 1951.

Kahl, William F. *The Development of London Livery Companies.* Boston: Baker Library, 1960.

King, A. D., ed. *Town Swamps and Social Bridges by George Godwin.* The Victorian Library. Leicester: Leicester University Press, 1971.

Knowles, C. C., and P. H. Pitt. *The History of Building Regulations in London, 1189-1972.* London: Architectural Press, 1972.

Lambert, R. S. *The Universal Provider: A Study of William Whiteley.* London: G. G. Harrop and Co., 1938.

Levin, Jennifer. *The Constitutional Implications of the London Charter Controversy in the City of London.* London: Athlone Press, 1965.

London County Council. *Centenary of London's Main Drainage, 1855-1955.* London: LCC, 1955.

—— *Main Drainage of London.* London: LCC, 1930.

London Municipal Society [J. Enoch Powell]. *The London Municipal Society, 1894-1954.* London: London Municipal Society, 1954.

The London Parochial Charities, Trustees of. *A History of the City Parochial Foundation, 1891-1951.* London: Parochial Charities Trustees, 1951.

Luckin, W. E. "The Final Castastrophe: Cholera in London, 1866," *Medical History,* 21, no. 1 (1977), 32-42.

McBriar, Alan. "Sidney Webb and the London County Council," in Margaret Cole, ed., *The Webbs and Their Work.* London: Frederick Muller, 1949.

MacLaren, C. A. "Local Government, 1855-1962," in P. D. Whitting, ed., *A History of Fulham.* Fulham: Fulham Historical Society, 1970.

Maclure, J. S. *One Hundred Years of London Education, 1810-1970.* London: Allen and Lane, 1970.

Malchow, Harold. "Free Water: The Public Drinking Fountain Movement in Victorian London," *The London Journal,* 4, no. 2 (1978), 181-201.

Metropolitan Water Board. *London's Water Supply, 1903-1953.* London: MWB, 1955.

Middlesex County Council. *The County Council of Middlesex.* History of Local Government since 1889. London: MCC, 1965.

Miller, Wilbur R. *Cops and Bobbies: Police Authority in New York and London, 1830-1870.* Chicago: Chicago University Press, 1977.

Mukhopadhyay, A. K. "The Politics of London Water," *The London Journal,* 1, no. 2 (1975), 207-224.

Neate, A. R. *The St. Marylebone Workhouse and Institution, 1730-1965.* London: St. Marylebone Society, 1967.

O'Neill, J. E. "Finding a Policy for the Sick Poor," *Victorian Studies,* 7, no. 3 (1964), 265-284.

Pike, A. R. "The Metropolitan Police," *London Society Journal,* 394 (1972), 2-14.

Powell, Sir Allan. *The Metropolitan Asylums Board and Its Work, 1867-1930.* London: Metropolitan Asylums Board, 1930.

Prothero, I. J. "Chartism in London," *Past and Present,* 44 (1969), 76-105.

Pruitt, R. Bruce. "More Smoke Than Fire: Corruption at the Metropolitan Board of Works, 1855–1889," *History*, 242, 16 January 1967.

Reddaway, T. F. "London in the Nineteenth Century: The Fight for a Water Supply," *Nineteenth Century*, 147 (August 1950), 110–130.

_____ "The Origins of the Metropolitan Police," *Nineteenth Century*, 141 (February 1950), 104–118.

Rhodes, Gerald, and G. R. Ruck. *The Government of Greater London*. London: Allen and Unwin, 1970.

Robson, W. A. *The Government and Misgovernment of London*. London: Allen and Unwin, 1939.

Roebuck, Janet. *Urban Development in Nineteenth Century London, Lambeth, Battersea and Wandsworth, 1838–1888*. London and Chichester: Phillimore, 1979.

Rowe, D. J. "The Failure of London Chartism," *The Historical Journal*, 9 (1968), 472–487.

Rubinstein, David. *School Attendance in London, 1860–1914: A Social History*. Hull: University of Hull, 1969.

_____ "Socialisation and the London School Board, 1870–1914: Aims, Methods and Public Opinion," in Philip McCann, ed., *Popular Education and Socialisation in the Nineteenth Century*. London: Methuen, 1977.

Schwartz, Pedro. "John Stuart Mill and Laissez-faire: London Water," *Economica*, 33 (February 1966), 71–83.

Sheppard, Francis. *Local Government in St. Marylebone, 1688–1835: A Study of the Vestry and the Turnpike Trust*. London: Athlone Press, 1958.

Sheppard, Frank. "London before the L.C.C.: The Work of the Vestries," *History Today*, 3 (March 1953), 174–180.

_____ (ed.) *The Parish of St. James Westminster*. pt. II, Survey of London, xxxi, London, 1963.

Smallwood, Frank. *Greater London: The Politics of Metropolitan Reform*. New York: Bobbs-Merrill, 1965.

Steffel, R. V. "The Boundary Street Estate: An Example of Urban Redevelopment by the London County Council, 1889–1914," *Town Planning Review*, 47, no. 2 (1976), 161–173.

_____ "The Slum Question: The London County Council and Decent Dwellings for the Working Classes, 1880–1914," *Albion*, 5, no. 4 (1973), 314–325.

Sutcliffe, Anthony. "Environmental Control and Planning in European Capitals 1850–1914: London, Paris and Berlin," in Hammarström, Ingrid and Thomas Hall, eds., *Growth and Transformation of the Modern City*. Stockholm: Swedish Council for Building Research, 1979.

Thompson, Paul. *Socialists, Liberals and Labour: The Struggle for London, 1885–1914*. London: Routledge & Kegan Paul, 1967.

Unwin, George. *The Gilds and Companies of London*, 4th ed. London: Frank Cass and Co., 1963.

Wilkes, J. *London Police in the Nineteenth Century*. Cambridge: Cambridge University Press, 1977.

Wohl, Anthony S. *The Eternal Slum: Housing and Social Policy in Victorian London*. London: Edward Arnold, 1977.

_____ "The Housing of the Working Classes in London, 1815–1914," in S. D. Chapman, ed., *The History of Working Class Housing*. Newton Abbot: David and Charles, 1971.

_____ "Unfit for Human Habitation," in H. J. Dyos and Michael Wolff, eds.,

The Victorian City: Images and Realities, vol. II. London and Boston: Routledge and Kegan Paul, 1973.

_____ ed. *The Bitter Cry of Outcast London.* The Victorian Library. Leicester: Leicester University Press, 1971.

Wyman, A. L. "Poor Law Medicine and the Development of Fulham Hospital," in P. D. Whitting, ed., *A History of Fulham.* Fulham: Local History Society, 1970.

Young, Ken. "The Conservative Strategy for London, 1855–1975," *The London Journal,* 1 (1975), 56–81.

_____ *Local Politics and the Rise of Party: The London Municipal Society and the Conservative Intervention in Local Elections, 1894–1963.* Leicester: Leicester University Press, 1975.

_____ "The Politics of London Government, 1880–1899," *Public Administration,* 51 (Spring 1973), 91–108.

_____ and John Kramer. *Strategy and Conflict in Metropolitan Housing: Suburbia versus the Greater London Council, 1965–75.* London: Heinemann, 1978.

History of Government and Administration, and other General Works

Alban, Sir F. J. *The Future Relationship of Central and Local Government.* London: C. Knight and Co., 1934.

Ashworth, William. *The Genesis of Modern British Town Planning.* London: Routledge, 1954.

Balfour-Browne, J. H. *State and Municipal Trading and Where It Leads.* London: Longmans, 1910.

Berry, Frederick *Housing: The Great British Failure.* London: C. Knight, 1974.

Blackstone, G. V. *A History of the British Fire Service.* London: Routledge and Kegan Paul, 1957.

Block, Geoffrey. *Party Politics in Local Government.* London: Conservative Political Centre, 1962.

Briggs, Asa. *History of Birmingham,* vol. II, *Borough and City, 1865–1938.* London: Oxford University Press, 1952.

Brooks, Robert C. *A Bibliography of Municipal Problems and City Conditions.* New York: Arno Press and *New York Times,* 1970.

Bulpitt, J. G. *Party Politics in English Local Government.* London: Longmans, 1967.

Cannadine, David. "From Feudal Lords to Figureheads," in H. J. Dyos, ed., *Urban History Yearbook, 1978.* Leicester: Leicester University Press, 1978.

_____ "Victorian Cities: How Different," *Social History,* 4, no. 1 (1977), 457–482.

Chalkin, C. N. *The Provincial Towns of Georgian England.* London: Edward Arnold, 1974.

Checkland, S. G. "The Urban Historian and the Political Will," in D. A. Reeder, ed., *Urban History Yearbook, 1980.* Leicester: Leicester University Press, 1980.

Clarke, John Joseph. *A History of Local Government of the United Kingdom.* London: Herbert Jenkins, 1955.

Clarke, P. F. "The Progressive Movement in England," *Transactions of the Royal Historical Society,* 5th ser., 24 (1974), 159–181.

Critchley, T. A. *The History of the Police in England and Wales, 980–1966.* London: Constable, 1967.

Cromwell, Valerie. "Interpretations of Nineteenth Century Administration," *Victorian Studies,* 9, no. 3 (1966), 245-255.

Cullingworth, J. B. *Housing and Local Government in England and Wales.* London: Allen and Unwin, 1966.

Daunton, M. J. *Coal Metropolis: Cardiff, 1870–1914.* Leicester: Leicester University Press, 1977.

Dunbabin, J. P. D. "British Local Government Reform: The Nineteenth Century and After," *English Historical Review,* 92, no. 365 (October 1977), 777–805.

———— "Expectations of the New County Councils and Their Realization," *Historical Journal,* 8, no. 3 (1965), 353–379.

———— "The Politics of the Establishment of County Councils," *Historical Journal,* 6, no. 2 (1963), 226–252.

Dyos, H. J. "Agenda for Urban Historians," in H. J. Dyos, ed., *The Study of Urban History.* London: Edward Arnold, 1968.

Emmerson, Sir Harold. *The Ministry of Works.* London: Allen and Unwin, 1956.

Falkus, Malcolm. "The Development of Municipal Trading in the Nineteenth Century," *Business History Review,* 19 (1977), 134–161.

Finer, Herman. *Municipal Trading: A Study in Public Administration.* London: Allen and Unwin, 1941.

Finer, S. E. "The Transmission of Benthamite Ideas, 1820–1850," in Gillian Sutherland, ed., *Studies in the Growth of Nineteenth Century Government.* London: Routledge and Kegan Paul, 1970.

Finlayson, G. B. A. M. "The Municipal Corporations Commission and Report, 1833–35," *Bulletin of the Institute of Historical Research,* 36, no. 93 (May 1963), 36–52.

———— "The Politics of Municipal Reform, 1835," *English Historical Review,* 81, no. 321 (October 1966), 673–692.

Fraser, Derek. *Urban Politics in Victorian England.* Leicester: Leicester University Press, 1976.

———— ed. *The New Poor Law in the Nineteenth Century.* London: Macmillan, 1976.

Frazer, W. M. *A History of English Public Health.* London: Baillière, Tindall and Cox, 1950.

Griffith, E. S. *The Modern Development of City Government in the United Kingdom and the United States.* 2 vols. London: Oxford University Press, 1927.

Gross, Charles. *A Bibliography of British Municipal History, Including Gilds and Parliamentary Representation.* Leicester: Leicester University Press, 1966.

Hart, Jennifer M. "The County and Borough Police Act, 1856," *Public Administration,* 34 (1956), 405–417.

———— "Nineteenth Century Social Reform: A Tory Interpretation of History," *Past and Present,* 31 (1965), 73–86.

———— "Reform of the Borough Police, 1835–56," *English Historical Review,* 70, no. 276 (July 1955), 411–427.

Hennock, E. P. "Finance and Politics in Urban Local Government in England, 1835–1900," *Historical Journal,* 6, no. 2 (1963), 212–225.

———— *Fit and Proper Persons: Ideal and Reality in Nineteenth Century Urban Government.* London: Edward Arnold, 1973.

Jennings, William Ivor, and Harold J. Laski. *A Century of Municipal Progress.* London: G. Allen and Unwin, 1936.

Kaye, Barrington. *The Development of an Architectural Profession in England.* London:

Allen and Unwin, 1960.

Keith-Lucas, Bryan. *The English Local Government Franchise*. Oxford: Oxford University Press, 1952.

Kellett, J. R. "Municipal Socialism, Enterprise and Trading in the Victorian City," in *Urban History Yearbook 1978*. Leicester: Leicester University Press, 1978.

Lambert, Royston. "Central and Local Relations in Mid-Victorian England," *Victorian Studies*, 6 (1962–63), 121–150.

———. *Sir John Simon (1816–1904) and English Social Administration*. London: MacGibbon & Kee, 1963.

Laski, Harold J., Ivor W. Jennings, and William Robson, eds. *A Century of Municipal Progress, 1835–1935*. London: George Allen & Unwin, 1935.

Lee, J. M. *Social Leaders and Public Persons*. Oxford: Clarendon Press, 1963.

Lipman, V. D. *Local Government Areas, 1834–1945*. Oxford: Basil Blackwell, 1949.

Luckin, W. E. "Death and Survival in the City: Approaches to the History of Disease," in *Urban History Yearbook, 1980*. Leicester: Leicester University Press, 1980.

Maas, Arthur, ed. *Area and Power: A Theory of Local Government*. Glencoe, Ill.: The Free Press, 1959.

McBriar, A. M. *Fabian Socialism and English Politics, 1884–1918*. Cambridge: Cambridge University Press, 1972.

MacKenzie, W. J. M. *Theories of Local Government*. Greater London Papers, no. 2. N.p.: London School of Economics and Political Science, 1961.

MacLeod, Roy "The Alkali Acts Administration, 1863–84: The Emergence of a Civil Scientist," *Victorian Studies*, 9 (1965), 85–112.

———. *Treasury Control and Social Administration: A Study of Establishment Government and the Local Government Board, 1871–1905*. London: Bell, 1968.

Marshall, J. D., ed. *The History of Lancashire County Council, 1889–1974*. Martin Robertson, 1977.

Meller, H. E. *Leisure and the Changing City, 1870–1914*. London: Routledge and Kegan Paul, 1976.

Midwinter, Eric. *Social Administration in Lancashire: Poor Law, Public Health and Police*. Manchester: Manchester University Press, 1969.

Moylan, Prudence Ann. *The Form and Reform of County Government: Kent, 1889–1914*. Leicester: Leicester University Press, 1978.

National Civic Federation. *Municipal and Private Ownership of Public Utilities*. New York, 1907.

Redford, Arthur, and I. S. Russell. *History of Local Government in Manchester*. 3 vols. London: Longmans and Co., 1939–40.

Redlich, Joseph, and Francis W. Hurst. *The History of Local Government in England*. ed. Bryan Keith-Lucas. London: Macmillan, 1970.

———. *Local Government in England*. Vol. I (of 2). London: Macmillan & Co., 1903.

Reeder, D. A. "The Politics of Urban Leaseholds in Late-Victorian England," *International Review of Social History*, 6 (1961), 1-18.

Roberts, David. *Victorian Origins of the British Welfare State*. New Haven: Yale University Press, 1960.

Robins, F. W. *The Story of Water Supply*. London: Oxford University Press, 1949.

Robson, W. A. *The Development of Local Government*. London: Allen & Unwin, 1931.

———— *Local Government in Crisis,* 2nd ed., rev. London: Allen & Unwin, 1968.

———— and D. E. Regan. *Great Cities of the World: Their Government, Politics and Planning.* 2 vols. London: Allen & Unwin, 1973.

Rose, Barry, ed. *The Councillor's Job.* London: L. C. Knight, 1971.

Ryan, Alan. "Utilitarianism and Bureaucracy: The Views of J. S. Mill," in G. Sutherland, ed., *Studies in the Growth of Nineteenth Century Government.* London: Routledge and Kegan Paul, 1970.

Schwartz, Pedro. *The New Political Economy of J. S. Mill.* London: Weidenfeld, 1972.

Searby, Peter. "Progress ad the Parish Pump: Local Government in Coventry, 1820–1860," *Birmingham Archaeological Society Proceedings and Transactions,* 88 (1976).

Self, P. J. O. *Cities in Flood.* London: Faber and Faber, 1961.

Smellie, K. G. *A History of Local Government.* London: George Allen and Unwin, 1946.

Smith, Dennis. "Social Conflict and Urban Education," D. A. Reeder, ed. *Urban Education in the Nineteenth Century.* London: Taylor and Francis, 1977.

Stern, W. M. "Water Supply in Britain: The Development of a Public Service," *Royal Sanitary Institute Journal,* 74 (1954), 998–1004.

Sutherland, Gillian. *Policy-making in Elementary Education, 1870–1895.* Oxford: Oxford University Press, 1973.

———— "Recent Trends in Administrative History," *Victorian Studies,* 13, no. 4 (1970), 408–411.

———— ed. *Studies in the Growth of Nineteenth Century Government.* London: Routledge and Kegan Paul, 1970.

Tarn, J. S. *Five Per Cent Philanthropy: An Account of Housing in Urban Areas, 1840–1914.* Cambridge: Cambridge University Press, 1973.

———— "The Peabody Donation Fund: The Role of a Housing Society in the Nineteenth Century," *Victorian Studies,* 10 (September 1966), 7–38.

Turvey, Ralph. *The Economics of Real Property.* London: Allen and Unwin, 1957.

Webb, Sidney and Beatrice. *English Local Government from the Revolution to the Municipal Corporations Act.* 5 vols. London: Longmans, Green and Co., 1906–1922; new ed., Oxford: Oxford University Press, 1963.

Whalen, Hugh. "Ideology, Democracy and the Foundations of Local Self-Government," *Canadian Journal of Economics and Political Science,* 26, no. 3 (1960).

White, Brian D. *A History of the Corporation of Liverpool, 1835–1914.* Liverpool: Liverpool University Press, 1951.

Woodward, E. L. *The Age of Reform, 1815–1870.* Oxford: Clarendon Press, 1938, 1946.

Young, Ken. " 'Metropology' Revisited: On the Political Integration of Metropolitan Areas," in Ken Young, ed., *Essays on the Study of Urban Politics.* London: Macmillan & Co., 1975.

Theses and Dissertations

Andrews, D. H. B. " Elementary Education in Lewisham at the Time of the School Board for London, 1870–1903." M.A., University of London, 1965.

Andrews, P. H. "Post-Elementary Education in the Area of the London Technical Education Board, 1893–1904." M.A., University of London, 1959.

_____ "The Organisation, Development and Administration of Public Education in the Area of the L.C.C., 1903-1922." Ph.D., University of London, 1964.

Baer, Marc Bradley. "The Politics of London, 1852-1868: Parties, Voters and Representation." Ph.D., University of Northern Illinois, 1978.

Bennett, T. A. "A Study of London Radicalism: The Democratic Association, 1837-1841." M.A., University of Sussex, 1968.

Binford, H. C. "Residential Displacement by Railway Construction in North Lambeth, 1859-61 (mainly Charing Cross Railway)." M.Phil., University of Sussex, 1967.

Chatterton, D. A. "Gas Supply of London to 1847." M.Sc., University of London, 1964.

Clark, E. A. G. "The Ragged School Union and the Education of the London Poor in the Nineteenth Century." M.A., University of London, 1967.

Corlett, Dorothy Maxine. "The Metropolitan Board of Works, 1855-1889." Ph.D., University of Illinois, 1943.

Dowell, J. S. "The Walthamstow School Board, 1880-1903." M.Phil., University of Reading, 1972.

Dyos, H. J. "The Suburban Development of Greater London, South of the Thames, 1836-1914." Ph.D., University of London, 1952.

Elliott, D. S. "The Metropolitan Board of Works, 1855-99." M.Phil., University of Nottingham, 1972.

Froshaug, A. M. "Poor Law Administration in a Number of London Parishes, 1750-1850." M.A., University of Nottingham, 1969.

Hogarth, A. H. "The Present Position of the Housing Problem in and around London." D.M., University of Oxford, 1908.

Lawrence, G. "Fifty Years of Vestry Government, 1800-1850." Diss. in Kensington Library, 1960.

Lewis, B. E. "The Home Office, the Metropolitan Police and the Problem of Civil Disorder, 1886-1892." M.Phil., University of Leeds, 1975.

Malcolmson, Patricia E. "The Potteries of Kensington: A Study of Slum Development in Victorian London." M.Phil., University of Leicester, 1970.

Mellor, J. P. "The Policy of the School Board for London in Relation to Education in and above Standard V." M.A., University of London, 1955.

Morley, R. "The Development in London of Elementary Education of a Higher Type, 1900-1910." M.A., University of London, 1961.

Morris, Reginald William. "Geographical and Historical Aspects of the Public Water Supply of London, 1852-1902." Ph.D., University of London, 1941.

Mukhopadhyay, A. K. "The Politics of London Water Supply, 1871-1971." Ph.D., University of London, 1972.

Pinkus, Rosa Lynn Brothman. "The Conceptual Development of Metropolitan London, 1800-1855." Ph.D., State University of New York, 1975.

Reeder, D. A. " Capital Investment in the Western Suburbs of Victorian London." Ph.D., University of Leicester, 1965.

Rees, M. "The Economic and Social Development of Extra-Metropolitan Middlesex during the Nineteenth Century (1800-1914)." M.Sc.Econ., University of London, 1955.

Roebuck, Janet. "Local Government and Some Aspects of Social Change in the Parishes of Lambeth, Battersea and Wandsworth, 1838-1888." Ph.D., University of London, 1968.

Rowe, D. J. "London Radicalism, 1829–1841, with Special Reference to the Relationship of its Middle Class and Working Class Components." M.A., University of Southampton, 1965.

Ruffhead, A. G. "The Office of Metropolitan Buildings, London, 1840–1855." M.Phil., University of London, 1973.

Schwartz, Pedro. "John Stuart Mill and Laissez-Faire: London Water." Ph.D., University of London, 1964.

Smith, Phillip Thurmond. "The London Metropolitan Police and Public Order and Security, 1850–1868." Ph.D., University of Columbia (Pennsylvania), 1978.

Soar, J. R. "The Historical Development of Technical and Vocational Education in West Ham since 1850." M.A., University of London, 1966.

Somper, S. "The London School Board and the Development of Evening Education, 1870–1893." M.A.., University of London, 1953.

Sopenoff, Ronald Charles. "The Police of London: The Early History of the Metropolitan Police, 1829–1856." Ph.D., Temple University (Pennsylvania), 1978.

Statham, J. "The Location and Development of London's Leather Manufacturing Industry since the Early Nineteenth Century." M.A.., University of London, 1965.

Stevens, John. "The London County Council under the Progressives, 1889–1907."M.A., University of Sussex, 1966.

Tuson, R. C. "Historical Development and Planning Problems of an Inner London Suburb." M.Phil., University of London, 1968.

Wohl, A. S. "The Housing of the Artisans and Labourers in Nineteenth Century London, 1815–1914." Ph.D., Brown University, 1966.

Woodhead, J. R. "The Rulers of London: The Composition of the Courts of Aldermen and Common Council of the City of London." M.A., University of London, 1961.

Young, K. C. "The London Municipal Society, 1894–1963: A Study in Conservatism and Local Government." Ph.D., University of London, 1974.

Zoond, Vera. "Housing Legislation in England, 1851–1867, with Special Reference to London." M.A., University of London, 1931.

Index